ADVENTURES OF SUPERMAN

VOLUME
THREE

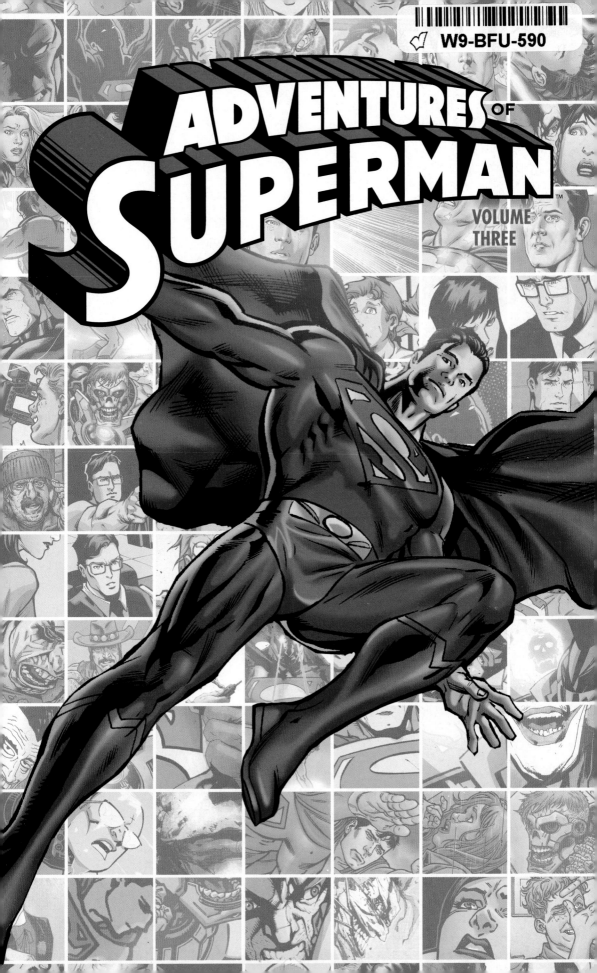

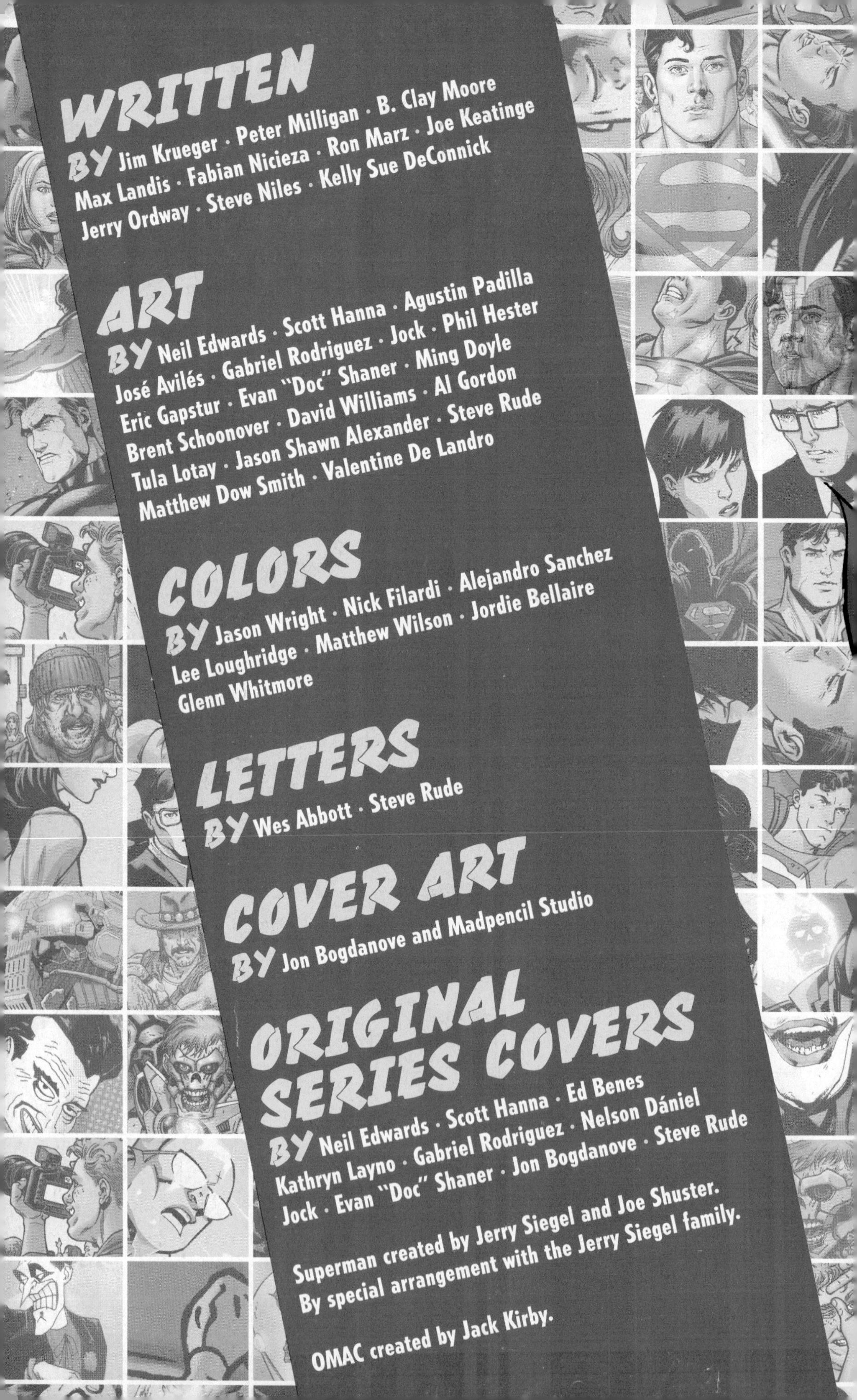

WRITTEN BY
Jim Krueger · Peter Milligan · B. Clay Moore · Max Landis · Fabian Nicieza · Ron Marz · Joe Keatinge · Jerry Ordway · Steve Niles · Kelly Sue DeConnick

ART BY
Neil Edwards · Scott Hanna · Agustin Padilla · José Avilés · Gabriel Rodriguez · Jock · Phil Hester · Eric Gapstur · Evan "Doc" Shaner · Ming Doyle · Brent Schoonover · David Williams · Al Gordon · Tula Lotay · Jason Shawn Alexander · Steve Rude · Matthew Dow Smith · Valentine De Landro

COLORS BY
Jason Wright · Nick Filardi · Alejandro Sanchez · Lee Loughridge · Matthew Wilson · Jordie Bellaire · Glenn Whitmore

LETTERS BY
Wes Abbott · Steve Rude

COVER ART BY
Jon Bogdanove and Madpencil Studio

ORIGINAL SERIES COVERS BY
Neil Edwards · Scott Hanna · Ed Benes · Kathryn Layno · Gabriel Rodriguez · Nelson Dániel · Jock · Evan "Doc" Shaner · Jon Bogdanove · Steve Rude

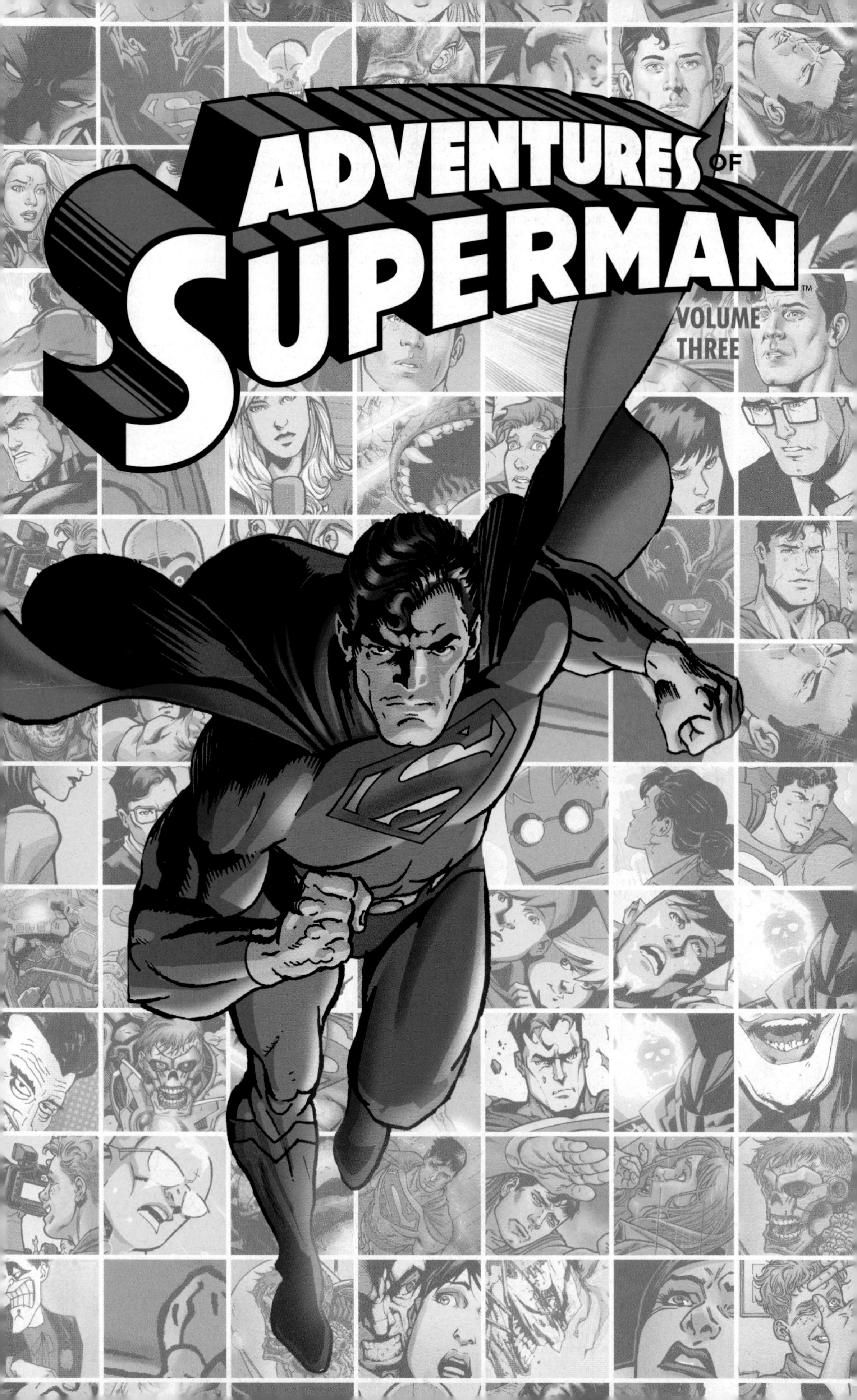
ADVENTURES OF
SUPERMAN™
VOLUME THREE

ALEX ANTONE EDITOR – ORIGINAL SERIES SCOTT NYBAKKEN EDITOR
ROBBIN BROSTERMAN DESIGN DIRECTOR – BOOKS DAMIAN RYLAND PUBLICATION DESIGN

HANK KANALZ SENIOR VP – VERTIGO & INTEGRATED PUBLISHING

DIANE NELSON PRESIDENT DAN DIDIO AND JIM LEE CO-PUBLISHERS GEOFF JOHNS CHIEF CREATIVE OFFICER
AMIT DESAI SENIOR VP – MARKETING & FRANCHISE MANAGEMENT AMY GENKINS SENIOR VP – BUSINESS & LEGAL AFFAIRS
NAIRI GARDINER SENIOR VP – FINANCE JEFF BOISON VP – PUBLISHING PLANNING MARK CHIARELLO VP – ART DIRECTION & DESIGN
JOHN CUNNINGHAM VP – MARKETING TERRI CUNNINGHAM VP – EDITORIAL ADMINISTRATION
LARRY GANEM VP – TALENT RELATIONS & SERVICES ALISON GILL SENIOR VP – MANUFACTURING & OPERATIONS
JAY KOGAN VP – BUSINESS & LEGAL AFFAIRS, PUBLISHING JACK MAHAN VP – BUSINESS AFFAIRS, TALENT
NICK NAPOLITANO VP – MANUFACTURING ADMINISTRATION SUE POHJA VP – BOOK SALES
FRED RUIZ VP – MANUFACTURING OPERATIONS COURTNEY SIMMONS SENIOR VP – PUBLICITY BOB WAYNE SENIOR VP – SALES

ADVENTURES OF SUPERMAN VOL. 3

DC COMICS
1700 BROADWAY, NEW YORK, NY 10019
A WARNER BROS. ENTERTAINMENT COMPANY.
PRINTED BY RR DONNELLEY, SALEM, VA, USA. 2/20/15. FIRST PRINTING.
ISBN: 978-1-4012-5330-1

LIBRARY OF CONGRESS CATALOGING-IN-PUBLICATION DATA

LANDIS, MAX, 1985- AUTHOR.
  ADVENTURES OF SUPERMAN VOLUME 3 / MAX LANDIS, WRITER ; JOCK, ARTIST.
    PAGES CM
  ISBN 978-1-4012-5330-1 (PAPERBACK)
  1. GRAPHIC NOVELS. I. JOCK, 1972- ILLUSTRATOR. II. TITLE.

PN6728.S9L36 2015
741.5'973—DC23

2014046032

SUSTAINABLE
FORESTRY
INITIATIVE

Certified Chain of Custody
20% Certified Forest Content,
80% Certified Sourcing
www.sfiprogram.org
SFI-01042
APPLIES TO TEXT STOCK ONLY

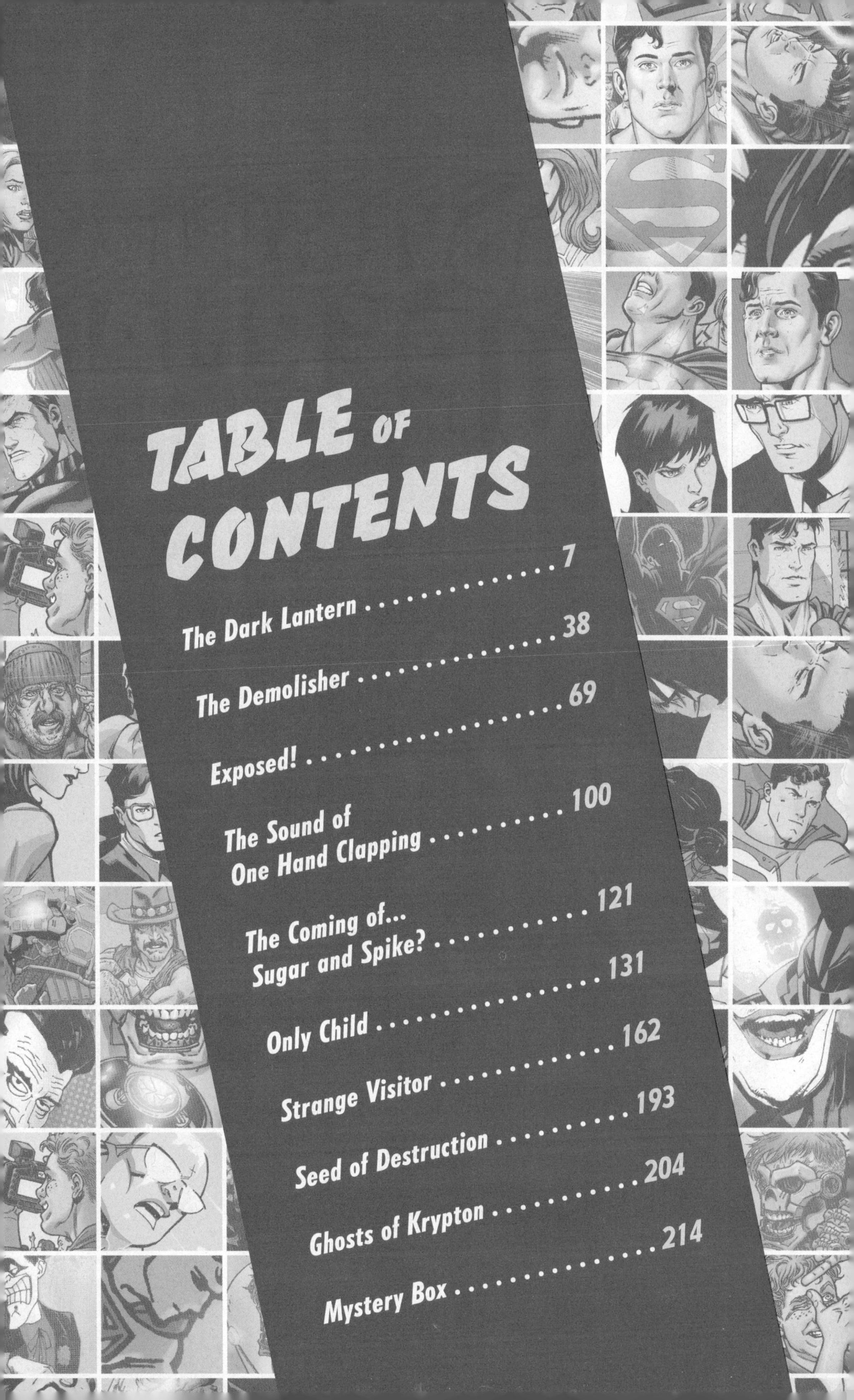

TABLE of CONTENTS

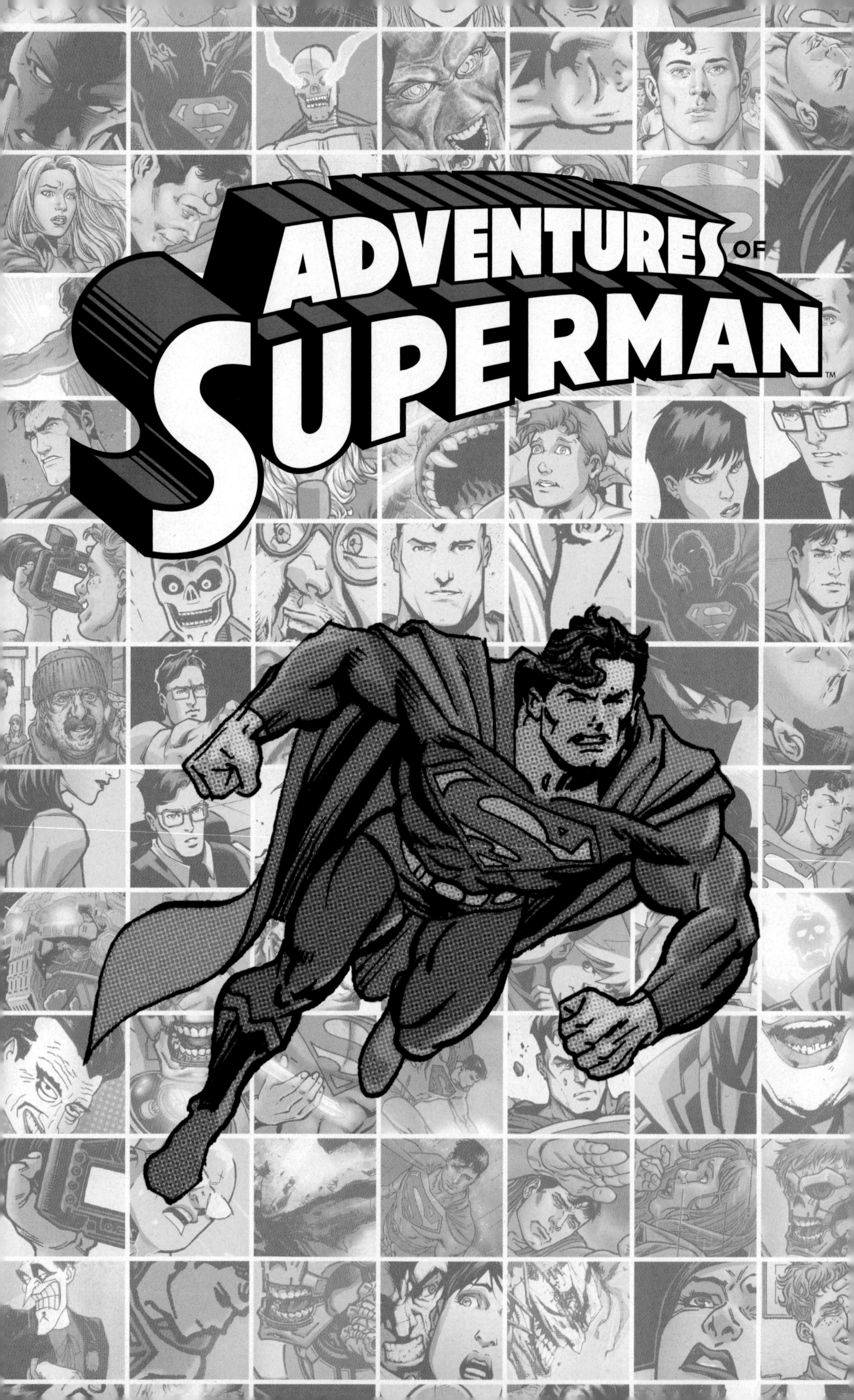
ADVENTURES OF
SUPERMAN™

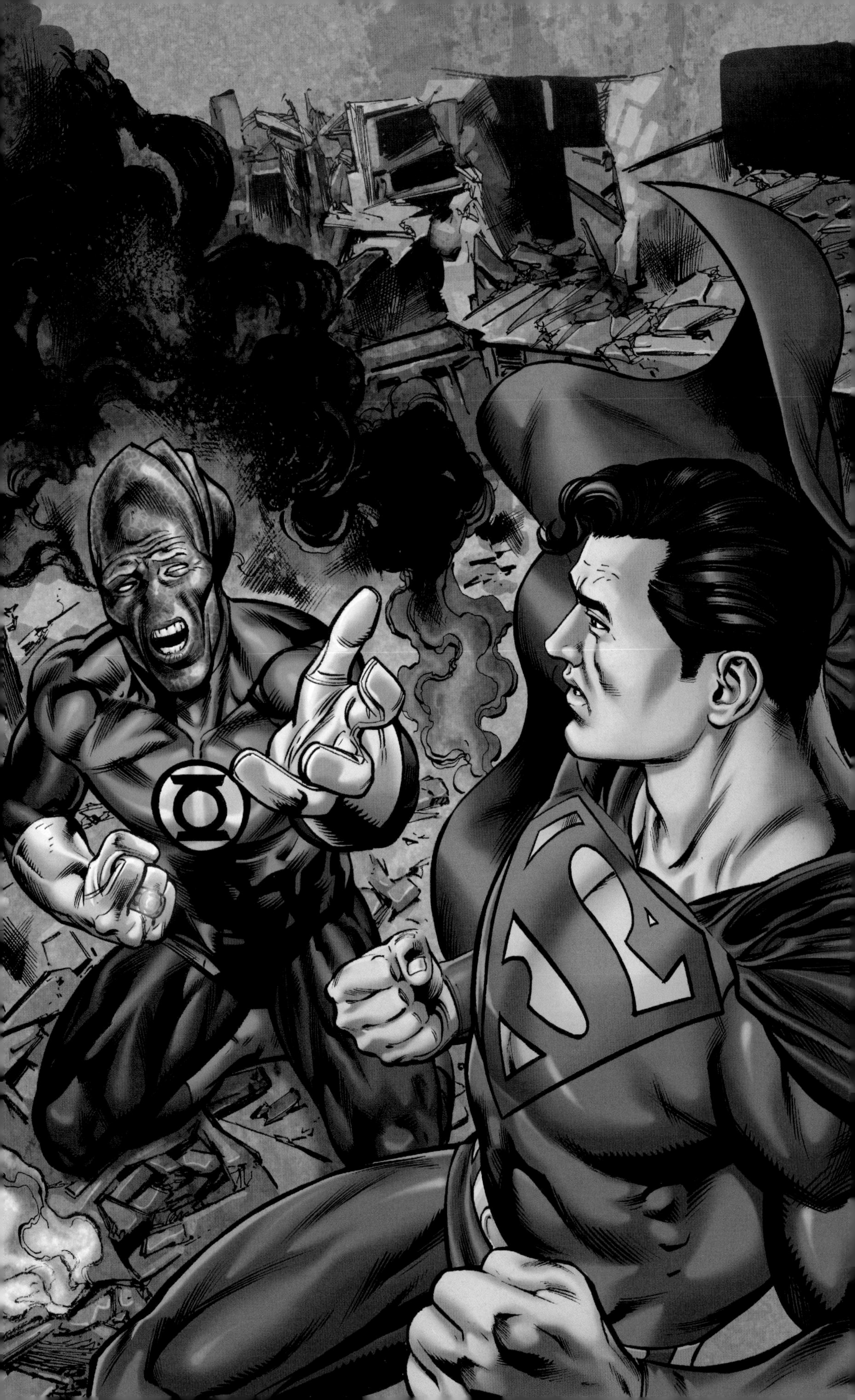

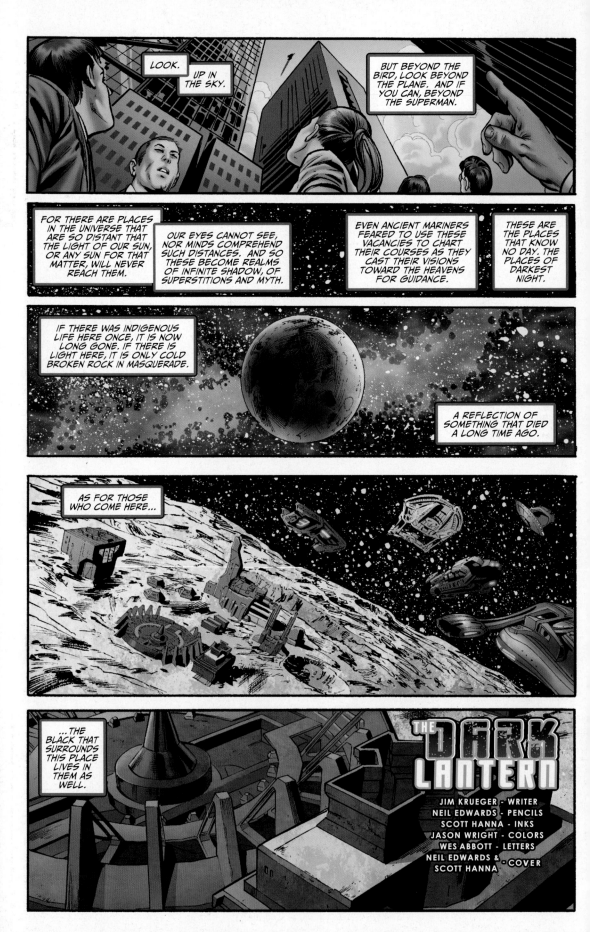

LOOK.

UP IN THE SKY.

BUT BEYOND THE BIRD, LOOK BEYOND THE PLANE. AND IF YOU CAN, BEYOND THE SUPERMAN.

FOR THERE ARE PLACES IN THE UNIVERSE THAT ARE SO DISTANT THAT THE LIGHT OF OUR SUN, OR ANY SUN FOR THAT MATTER, WILL NEVER REACH THEM.

OUR EYES CANNOT SEE, NOR MINDS COMPREHEND SUCH DISTANCES. AND SO THESE BECOME REALMS OF INFINITE SHADOW, OF SUPERSTITIONS AND MYTH.

EVEN ANCIENT MARINERS FEARED TO USE THESE VACANCIES TO CHART THEIR COURSES AS THEY CAST THEIR VISIONS TOWARD THE HEAVENS FOR GUIDANCE.

THESE ARE THE PLACES THAT KNOW NO DAY. THE PLACES OF DARKEST NIGHT.

IF THERE WAS INDIGENOUS LIFE HERE ONCE, IT IS NOW LONG GONE. IF THERE IS LIGHT HERE, IT IS ONLY COLD BROKEN ROCK IN MASQUERADE.

A REFLECTION OF SOMETHING THAT DIED A LONG TIME AGO.

AS FOR THOSE WHO COME HERE...

...THE BLACK THAT SURROUNDS THIS PLACE LIVES IN THEM AS WELL.

THE DARK LANTERN

JIM KRUEGER - WRITER
NEIL EDWARDS - PENCILS
SCOTT HANNA - INKS
JASON WRIGHT - COLORS
WES ABBOTT - LETTERS
NEIL EDWARDS &
SCOTT HANNA - COVER

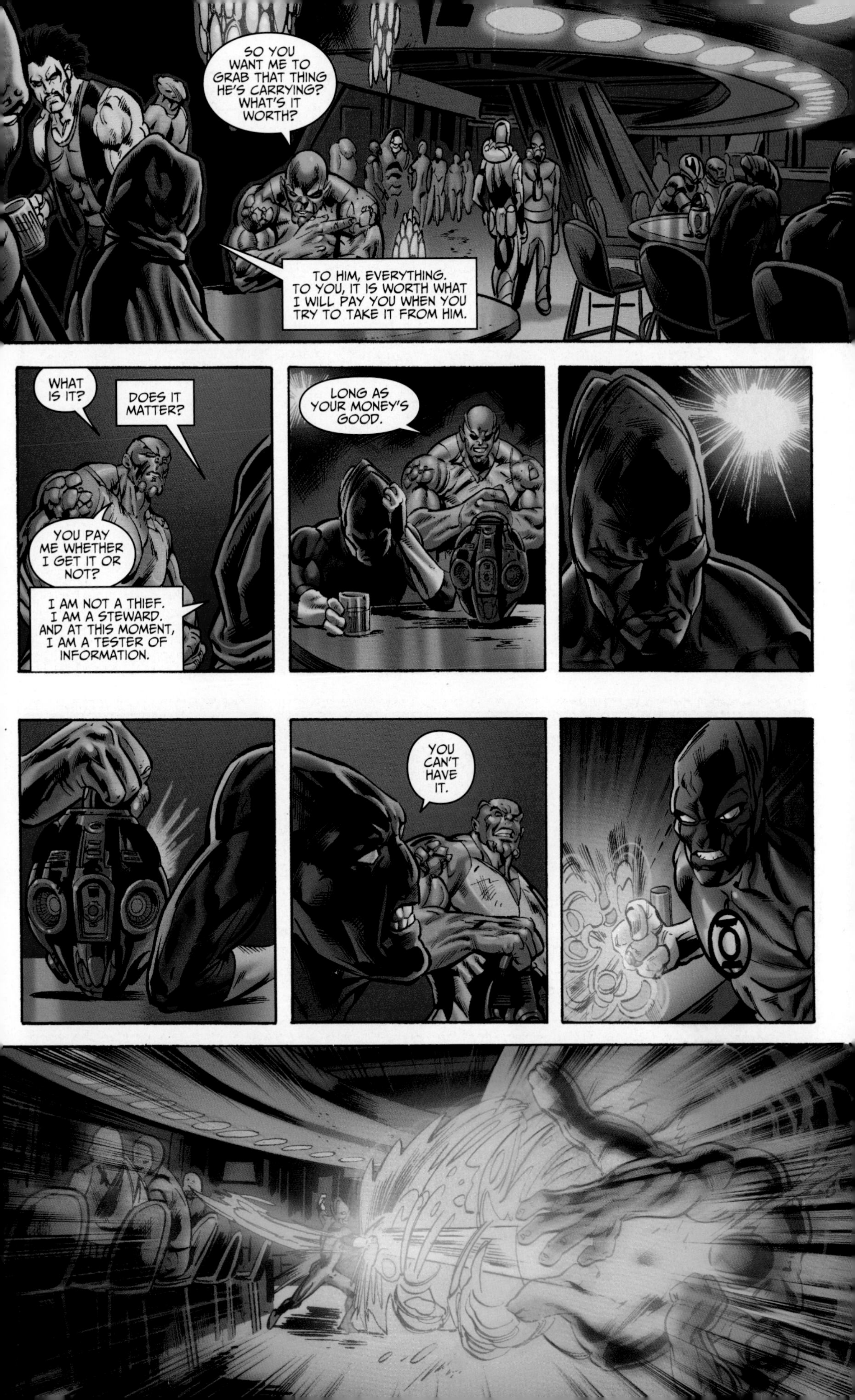
SO YOU WANT ME TO GRAB THAT THING HE'S CARRYING? WHAT'S IT WORTH?
TO HIM, EVERYTHING. TO YOU, IT IS WORTH WHAT I WILL PAY YOU WHEN YOU TRY TO TAKE IT FROM HIM.
WHAT IS IT?
DOES IT MATTER?
YOU PAY ME WHETHER I GET IT OR NOT?
I AM NOT A THIEF. I AM A STEWARD. AND AT THIS MOMENT, I AM A TESTER OF INFORMATION.
LONG AS YOUR MONEY'S GOOD.
YOU CAN'T HAVE IT.

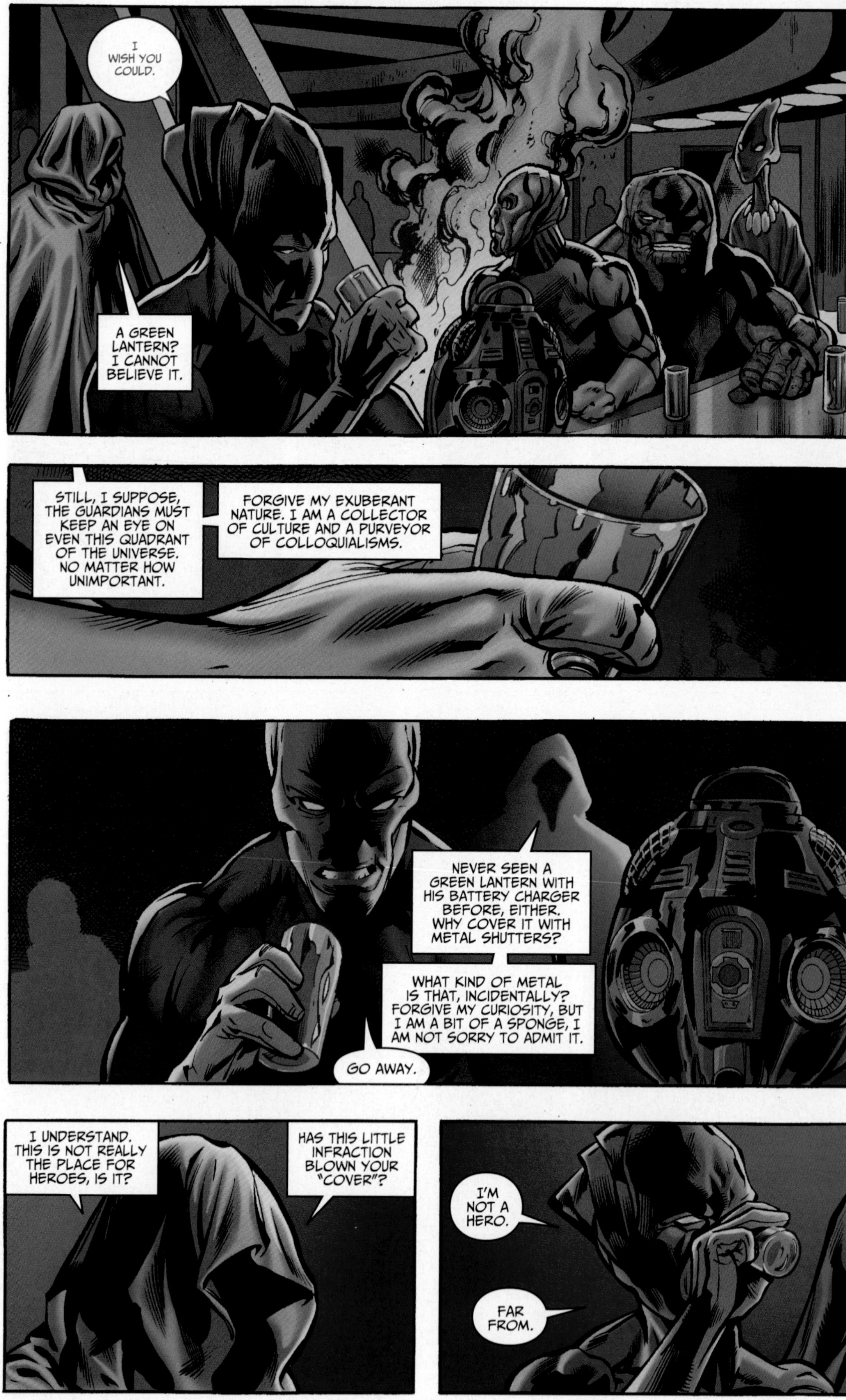
I WISH YOU COULD.
A GREEN LANTERN? I CANNOT BELIEVE IT.
STILL, I SUPPOSE, THE GUARDIANS MUST KEEP AN EYE ON EVEN THIS QUADRANT OF THE UNIVERSE. NO MATTER HOW UNIMPORTANT.
FORGIVE MY EXUBERANT NATURE. I AM A COLLECTOR OF CULTURE AND A PURVEYOR OF COLLOQUIALISMS.
NEVER SEEN A GREEN LANTERN WITH HIS BATTERY CHARGER BEFORE, EITHER. WHY COVER IT WITH METAL SHUTTERS?
WHAT KIND OF METAL IS THAT, INCIDENTALLY? FORGIVE MY CURIOSITY, BUT I AM A BIT OF A SPONGE, I AM NOT SORRY TO ADMIT IT.
GO AWAY.
I UNDERSTAND. THIS IS NOT REALLY THE PLACE FOR HEROES, IS IT?
HAS THIS LITTLE INFRACTION BLOWN YOUR "COVER"?
I'M NOT A HERO.
FAR FROM.

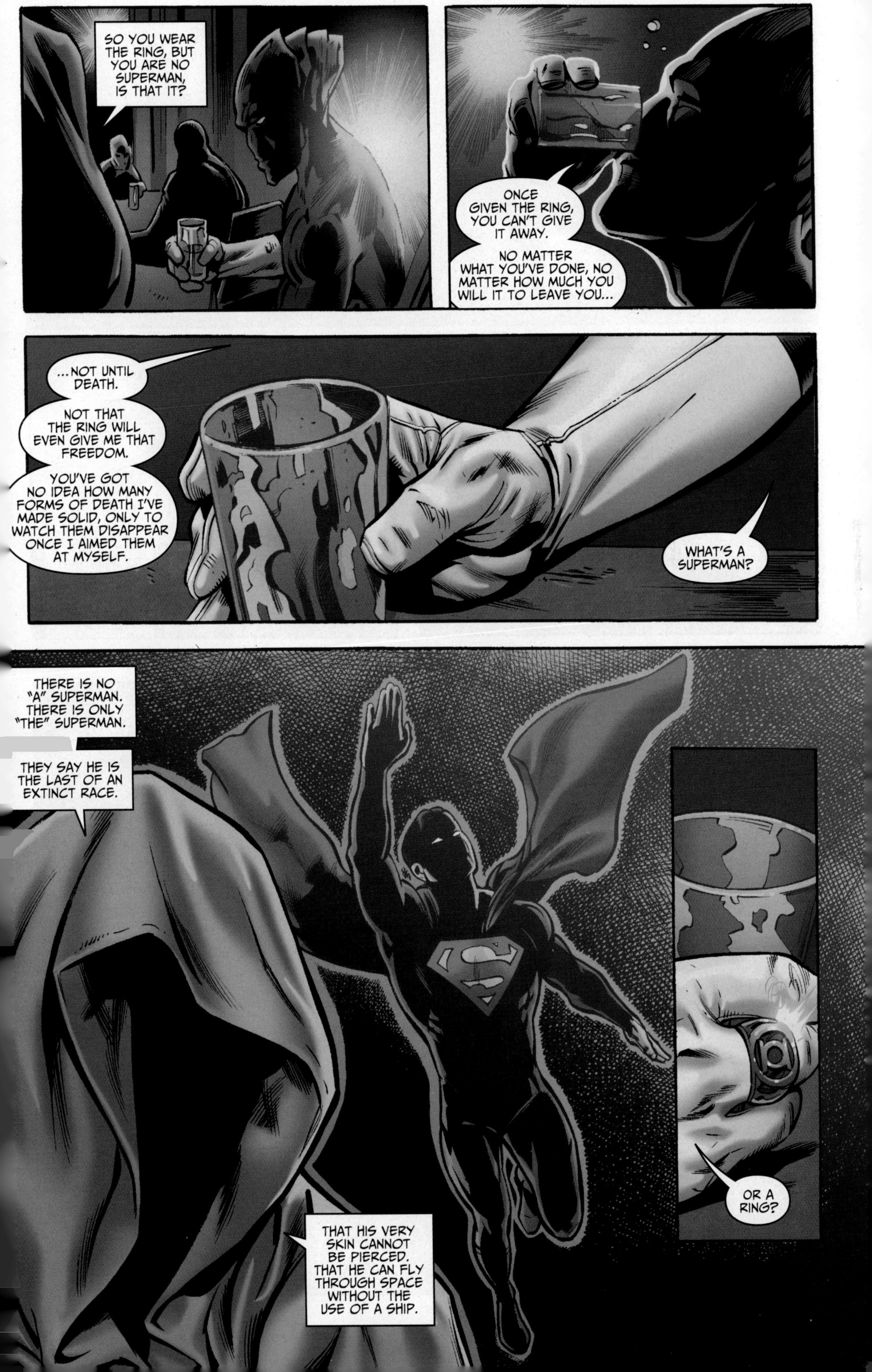
SO YOU WEAR THE RING, BUT YOU ARE NO SUPERMAN, IS THAT IT?
ONCE GIVEN THE RING, YOU CAN'T GIVE IT AWAY.
NO MATTER WHAT YOU'VE DONE, NO MATTER HOW MUCH YOU WILL IT TO LEAVE YOU...
...NOT UNTIL DEATH.
NOT THAT THE RING WILL EVEN GIVE ME THAT FREEDOM.
YOU'VE GOT NO IDEA HOW MANY FORMS OF DEATH I'VE MADE SOLID, ONLY TO WATCH THEM DISAPPEAR ONCE I AIMED THEM AT MYSELF.
WHAT'S A SUPERMAN?
THERE IS NO "A" SUPERMAN. THERE IS ONLY "THE" SUPERMAN.
THEY SAY HE IS THE LAST OF AN EXTINCT RACE.
OR A RING?
THAT HIS VERY SKIN CANNOT BE PIERCED. THAT HE CAN FLY THROUGH SPACE WITHOUT THE USE OF A SHIP.

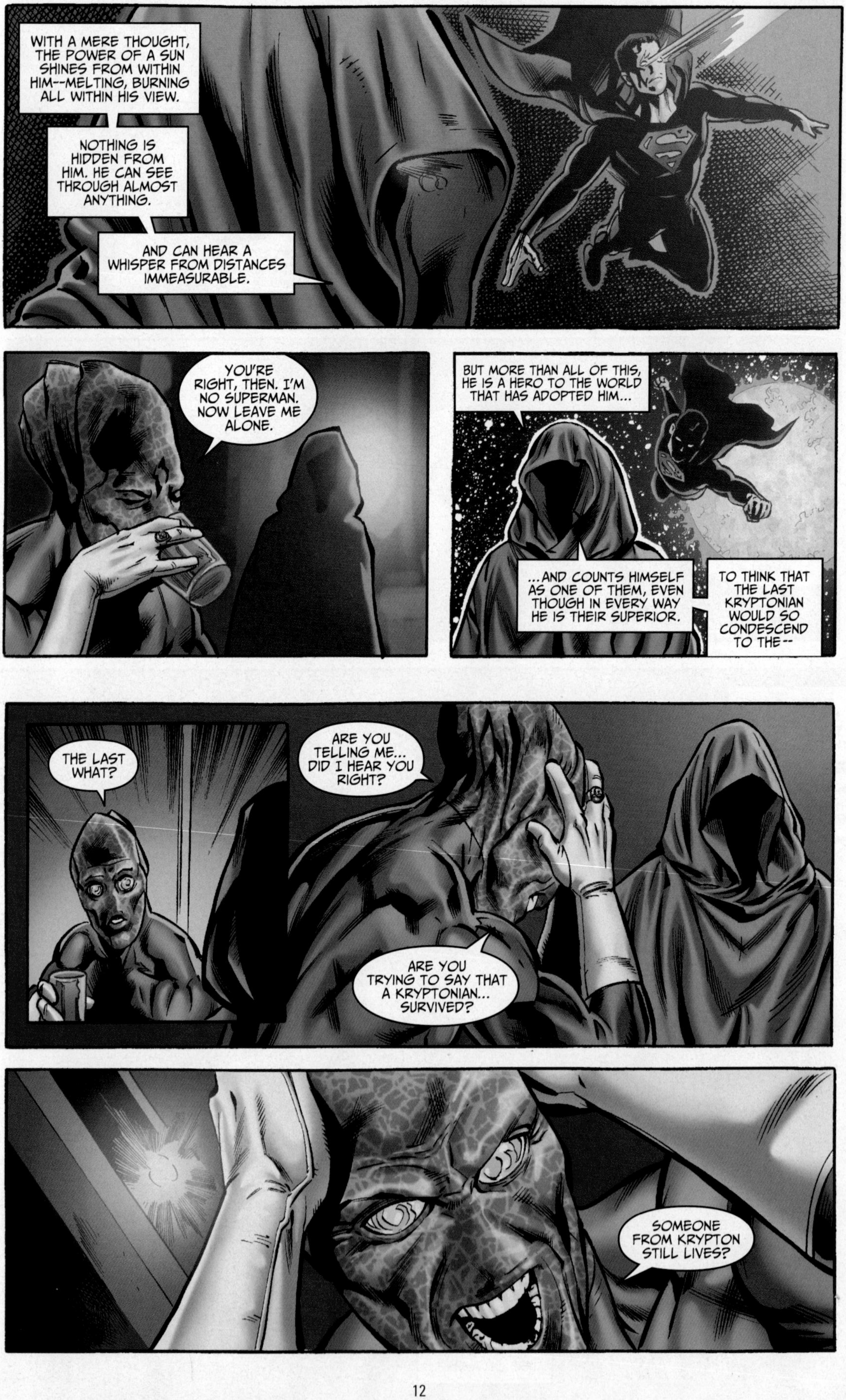
WITH A MERE THOUGHT, THE POWER OF A SUN SHINES FROM WITHIN HIM--MELTING, BURNING ALL WITHIN HIS VIEW.
NOTHING IS HIDDEN FROM HIM. HE CAN SEE THROUGH ALMOST ANYTHING.
AND CAN HEAR A WHISPER FROM DISTANCES IMMEASURABLE.
YOU'RE RIGHT, THEN. I'M NO SUPERMAN. NOW LEAVE ME ALONE.
BUT MORE THAN ALL OF THIS, HE IS A HERO TO THE WORLD THAT HAS ADOPTED HIM...
...AND COUNTS HIMSELF AS ONE OF THEM, EVEN THOUGH IN EVERY WAY HE IS THEIR SUPERIOR.
TO THINK THAT THE LAST KRYPTONIAN WOULD SO CONDESCEND TO THE--
THE LAST WHAT?
ARE YOU TELLING ME... DID I HEAR YOU RIGHT?
ARE YOU TRYING TO SAY THAT A KRYPTONIAN... SURVIVED?
SOMEONE FROM KRYPTON STILL LIVES?

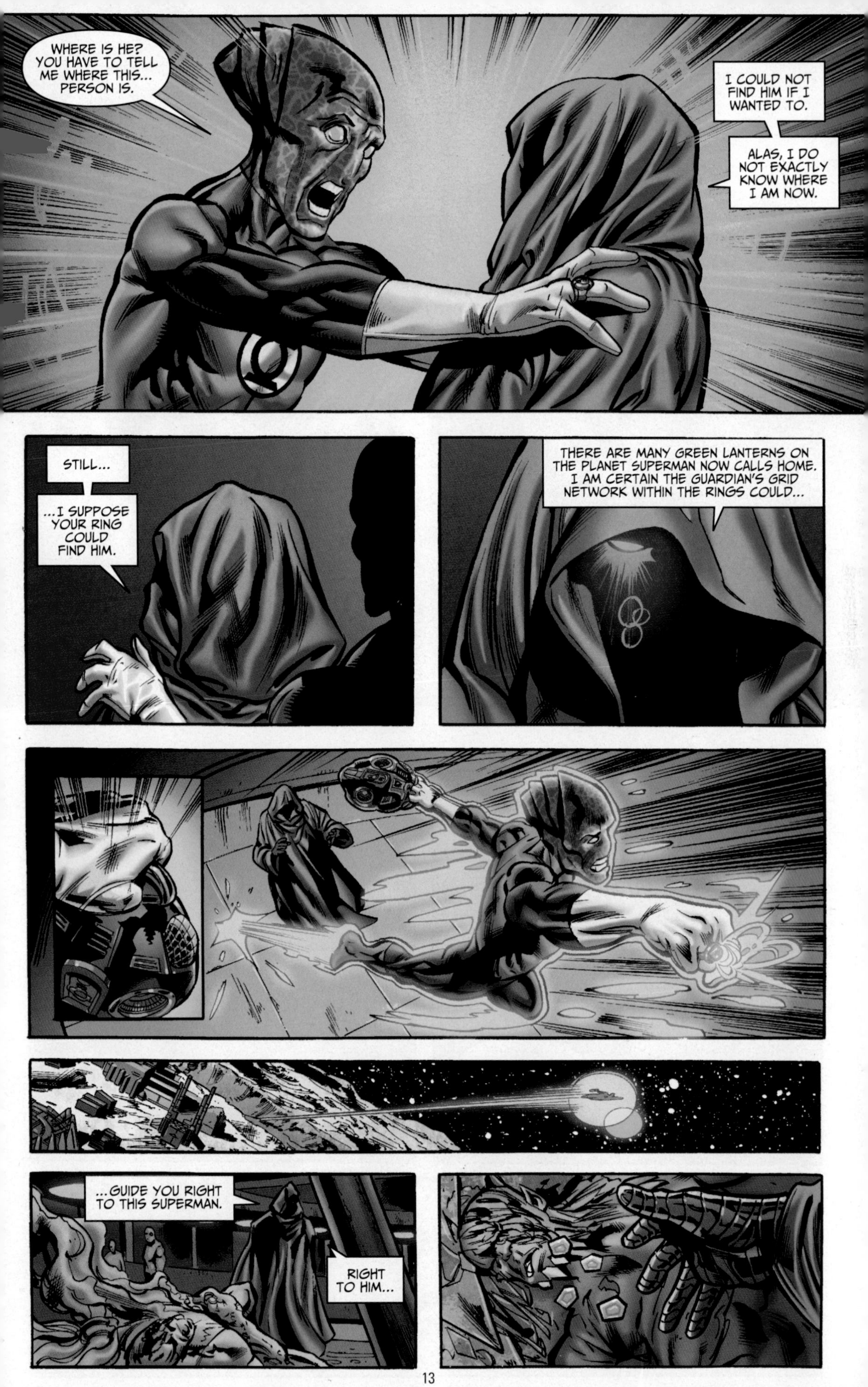

WHERE IS HE? YOU HAVE TO TELL ME WHERE THIS... PERSON IS.
I COULD NOT FIND HIM IF I WANTED TO.
ALAS, I DO NOT EXACTLY KNOW WHERE I AM NOW.
STILL...
...I SUPPOSE YOUR RING COULD FIND HIM.
THERE ARE MANY GREEN LANTERNS ON THE PLANET SUPERMAN NOW CALLS HOME. I AM CERTAIN THE GUARDIAN'S GRID NETWORK WITHIN THE RINGS COULD...
...GUIDE YOU RIGHT TO THIS SUPERMAN.
RIGHT TO HIM...

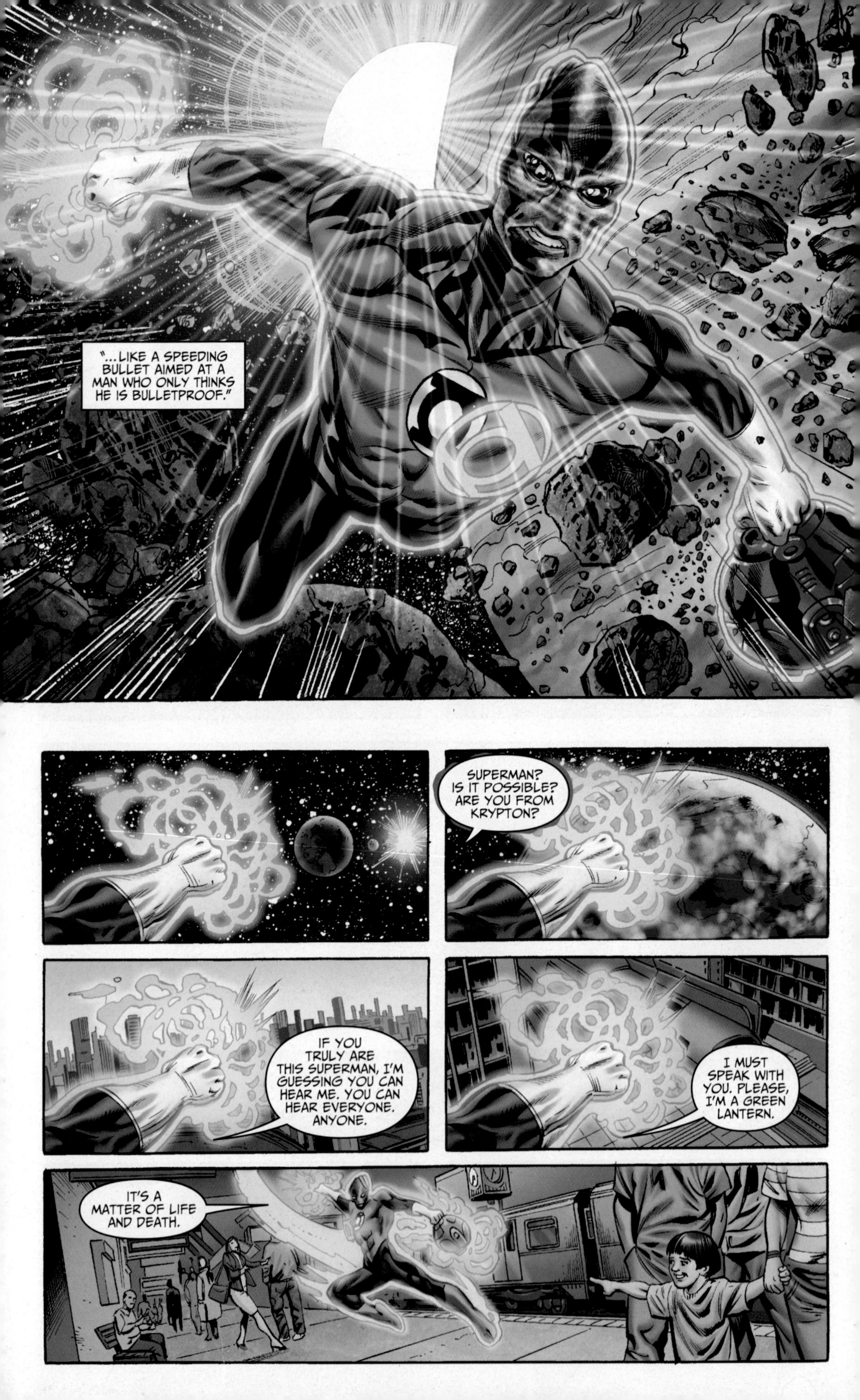
"...LIKE A SPEEDING BULLET AIMED AT A MAN WHO ONLY THINKS HE IS BULLETPROOF."
SUPERMAN? IS IT POSSIBLE? ARE YOU FROM KRYPTON?
IF YOU TRULY ARE THIS SUPERMAN, I'M GUESSING YOU CAN HEAR ME. YOU CAN HEAR EVERYONE. ANYONE.
I MUST SPEAK WITH YOU. PLEASE, I'M A GREEN LANTERN.
IT'S A MATTER OF LIFE AND DEATH.

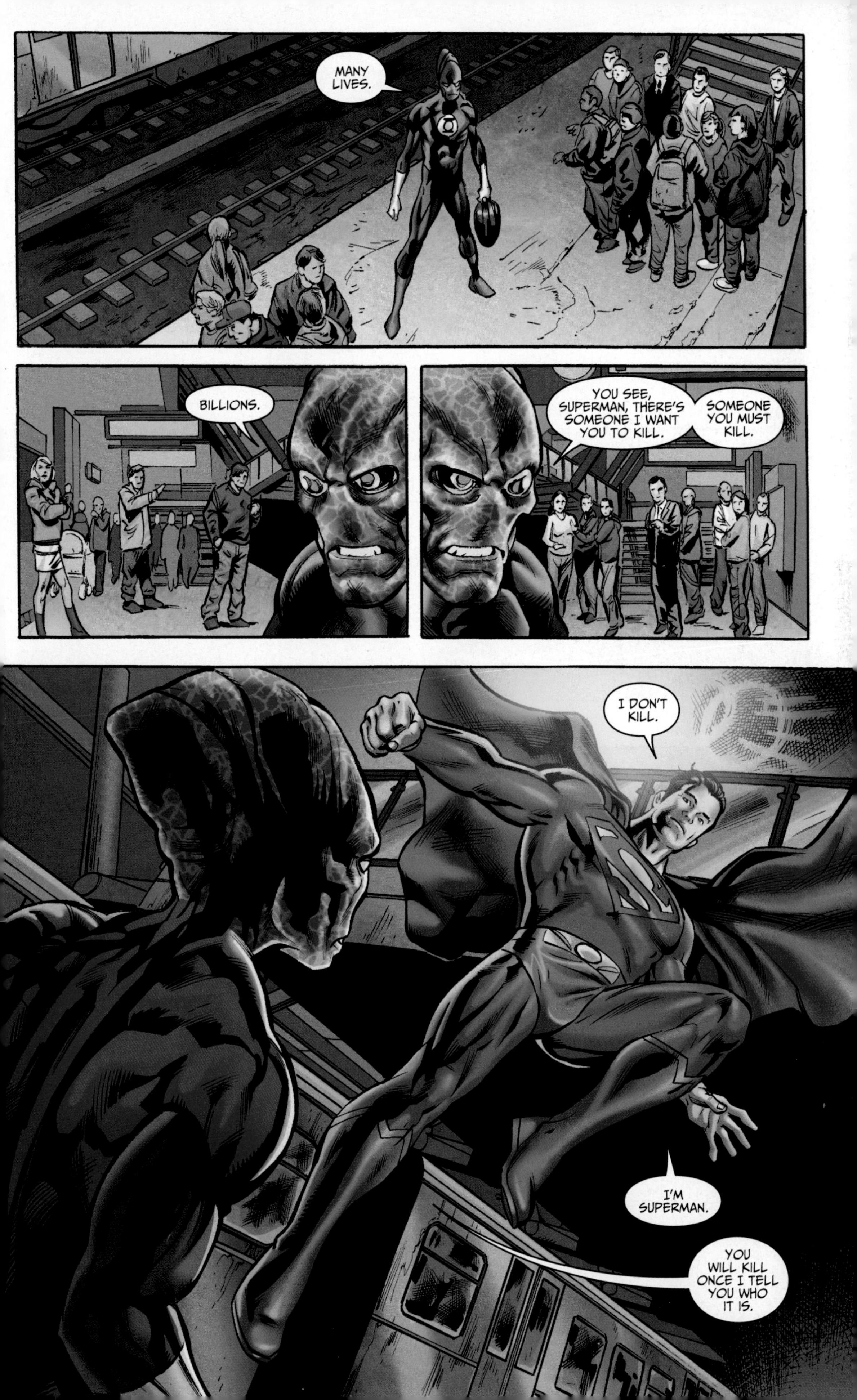
MANY LIVES.
BILLIONS.
YOU SEE, SUPERMAN, THERE'S SOMEONE I WANT YOU TO KILL.
SOMEONE YOU MUST KILL.
I DON'T KILL.
I'M SUPERMAN.
YOU WILL KILL ONCE I TELL YOU WHO IT IS.

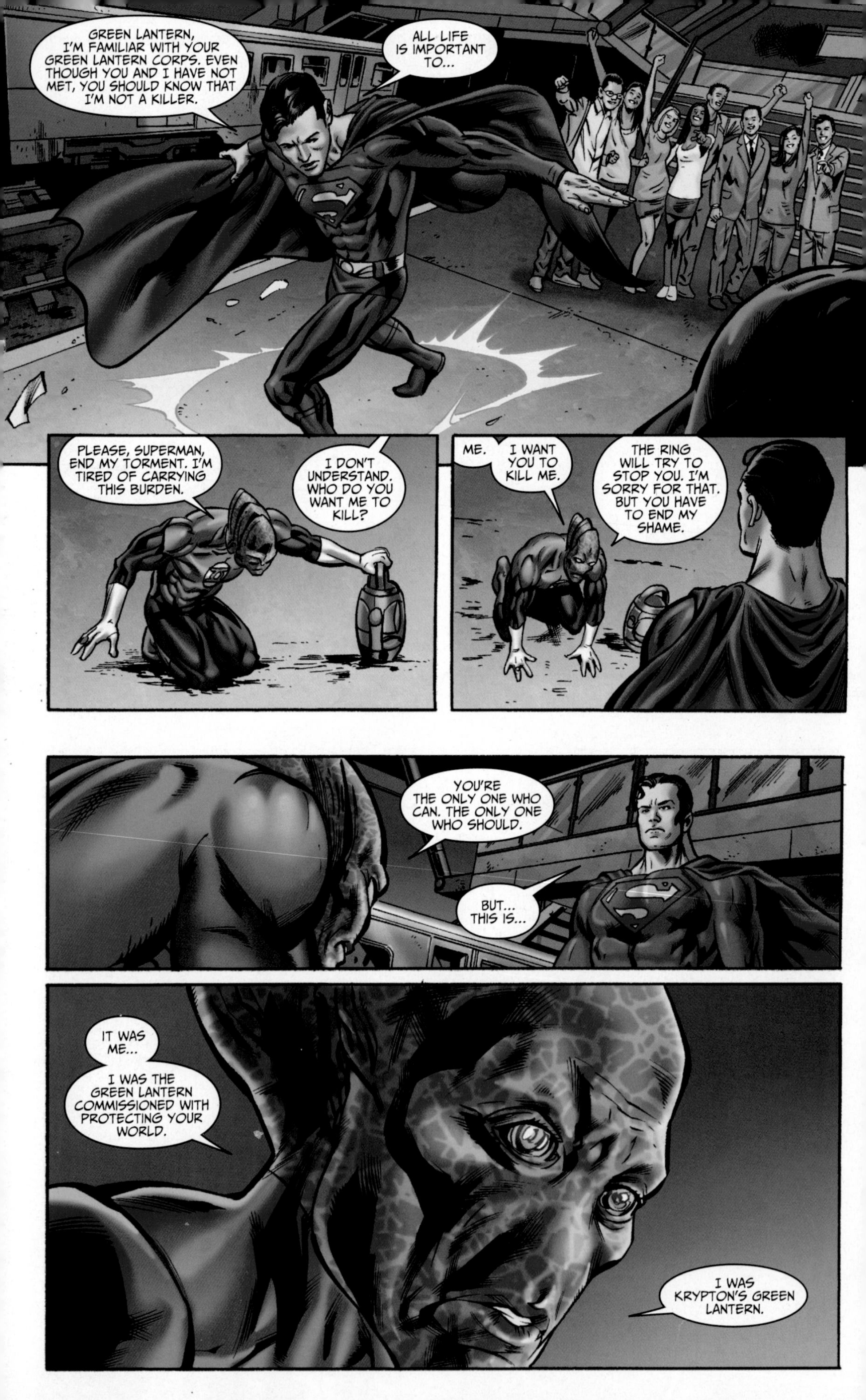
GREEN LANTERN, I'M FAMILIAR WITH YOUR GREEN LANTERN CORPS. EVEN THOUGH YOU AND I HAVE NOT MET, YOU SHOULD KNOW THAT I'M NOT A KILLER.
ALL LIFE IS IMPORTANT TO...
PLEASE, SUPERMAN, END MY TORMENT. I'M TIRED OF CARRYING THIS BURDEN.
I DON'T UNDERSTAND. WHO DO YOU WANT ME TO KILL?
ME.
I WANT YOU TO KILL ME.
THE RING WILL TRY TO STOP YOU. I'M SORRY FOR THAT. BUT YOU HAVE TO END MY SHAME.
YOU'RE THE ONLY ONE WHO CAN. THE ONLY ONE WHO SHOULD.
BUT... THIS IS...
IT WAS ME...
I WAS THE GREEN LANTERN COMMISSIONED WITH PROTECTING YOUR WORLD.
I WAS KRYPTON'S GREEN LANTERN.

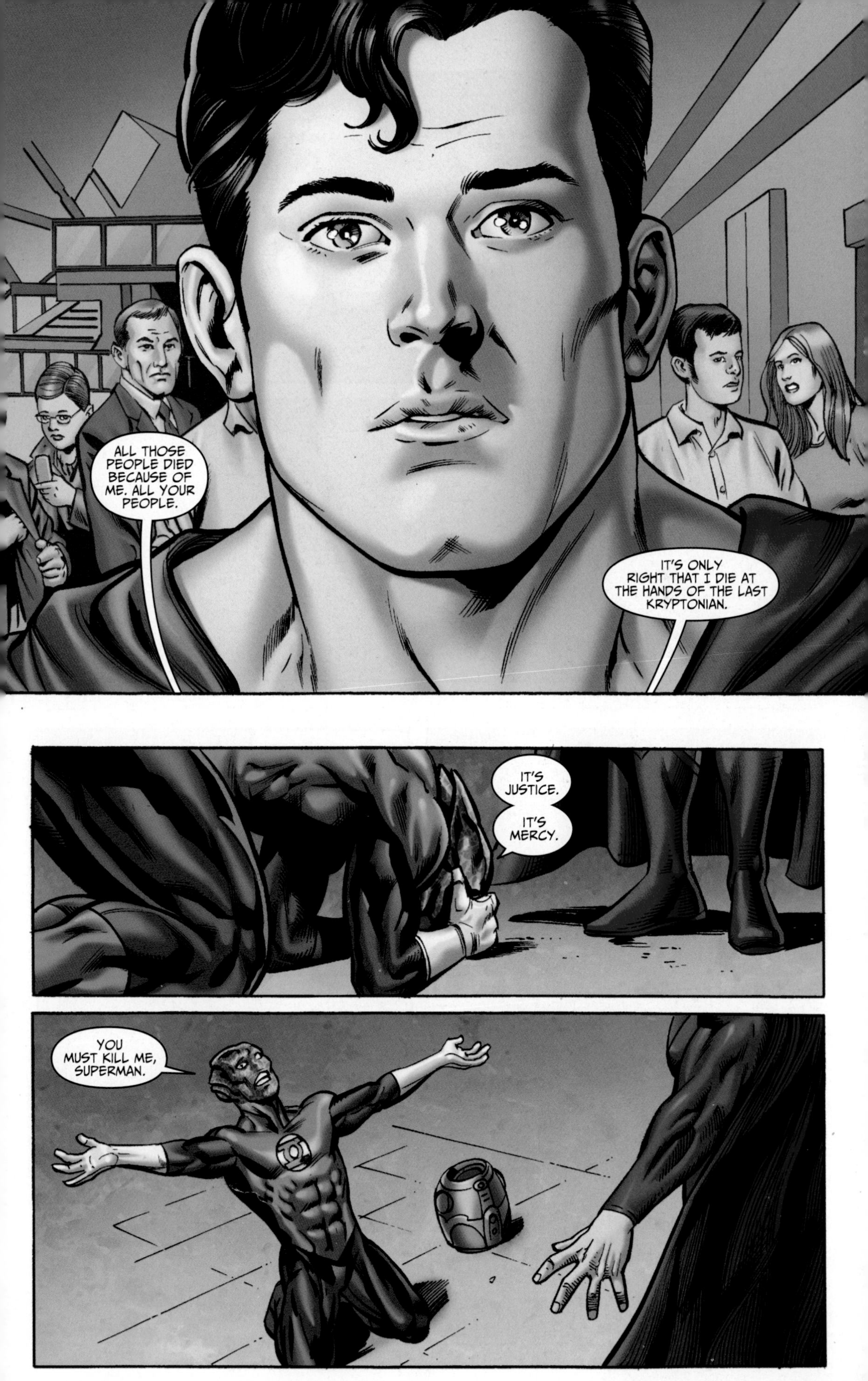
ALL THOSE PEOPLE DIED BECAUSE OF ME. ALL YOUR PEOPLE.
IT'S ONLY RIGHT THAT I DIE AT THE HANDS OF THE LAST KRYPTONIAN.
IT'S JUSTICE.
IT'S MERCY.
YOU MUST KILL ME, SUPERMAN.

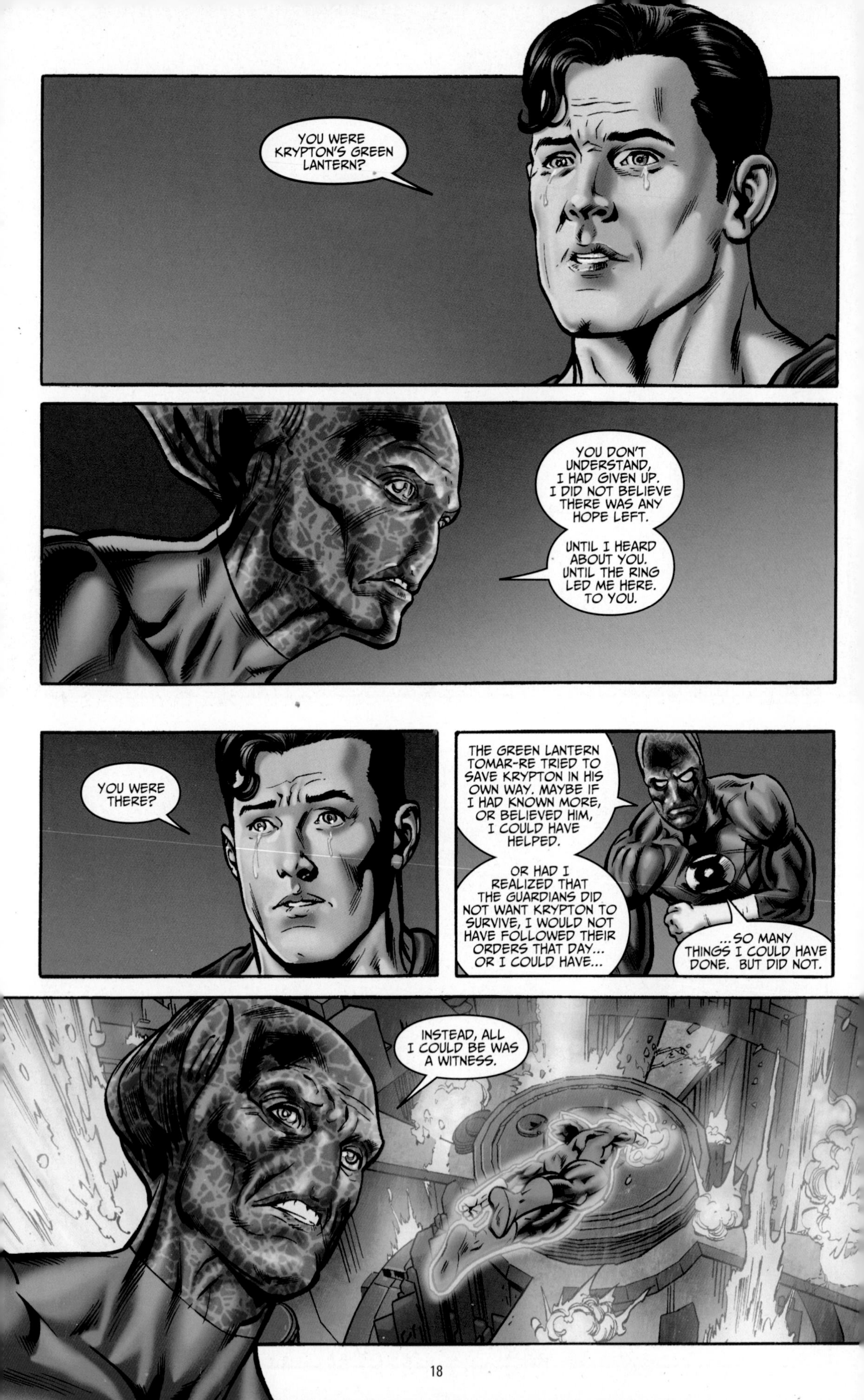
YOU WERE KRYPTON'S GREEN LANTERN?
YOU DON'T UNDERSTAND, I HAD GIVEN UP. I DID NOT BELIEVE THERE WAS ANY HOPE LEFT.
UNTIL I HEARD ABOUT YOU. UNTIL THE RING LED ME HERE. TO YOU.
YOU WERE THERE?
THE GREEN LANTERN TOMAR-RE TRIED TO SAVE KRYPTON IN HIS OWN WAY. MAYBE IF I HAD KNOWN MORE, OR BELIEVED HIM, I COULD HAVE HELPED.
OR HAD I REALIZED THAT THE GUARDIANS DID NOT WANT KRYPTON TO SURVIVE, I WOULD NOT HAVE FOLLOWED THEIR ORDERS THAT DAY... OR I COULD HAVE...
...SO MANY THINGS I COULD HAVE DONE. BUT DID NOT.
INSTEAD, ALL I COULD BE WAS A WITNESS.

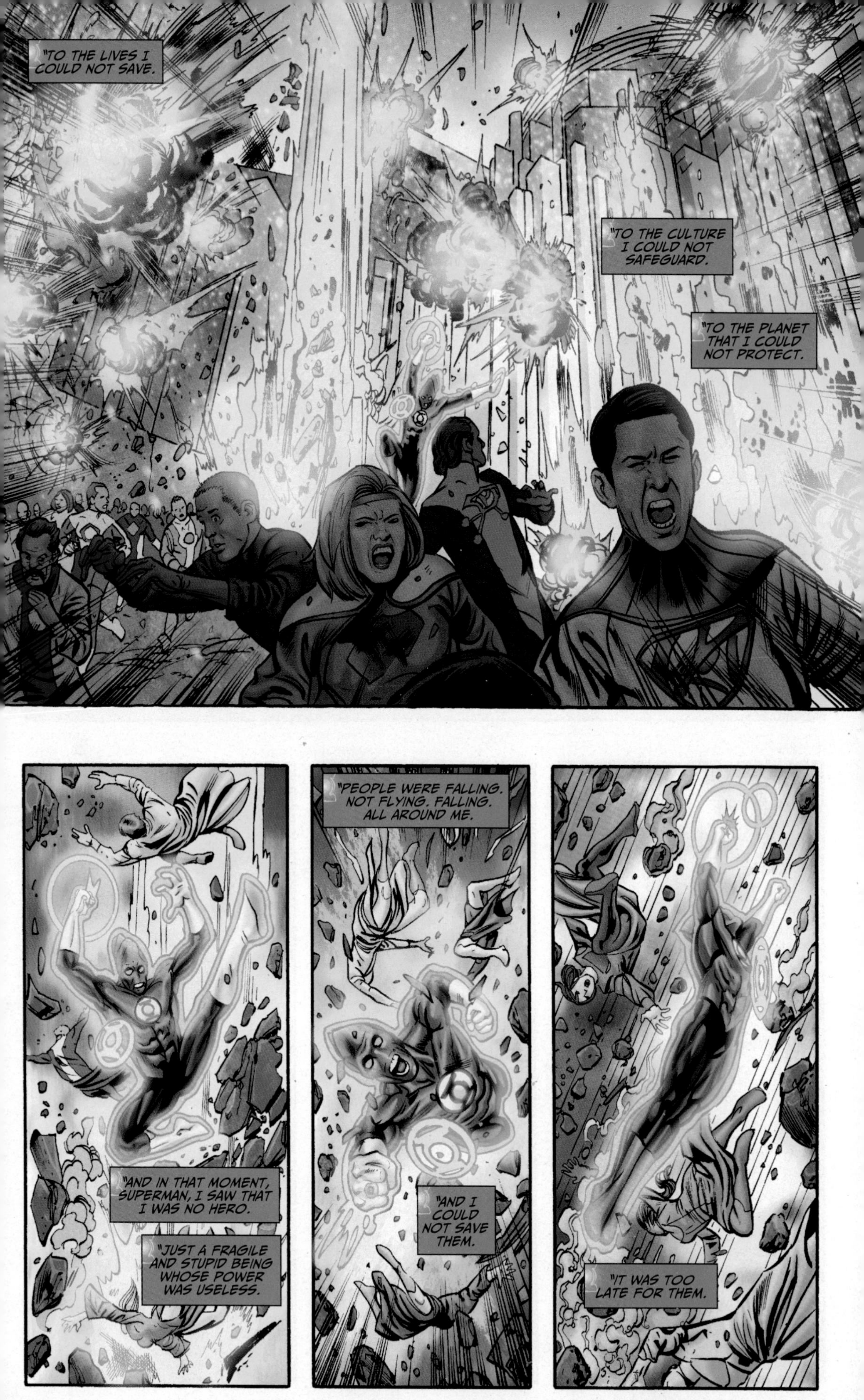
"TO THE LIVES I COULD NOT SAVE.
"TO THE CULTURE I COULD NOT SAFEGUARD.
"TO THE PLANET THAT I COULD NOT PROTECT.
"AND IN THAT MOMENT, SUPERMAN, I SAW THAT I WAS NO HERO.
"JUST A FRAGILE AND STUPID BEING WHOSE POWER WAS USELESS.
"PEOPLE WERE FALLING. NOT FLYING. FALLING. ALL AROUND ME.
"AND I COULD NOT SAVE THEM.
"IT WAS TOO LATE FOR THEM.

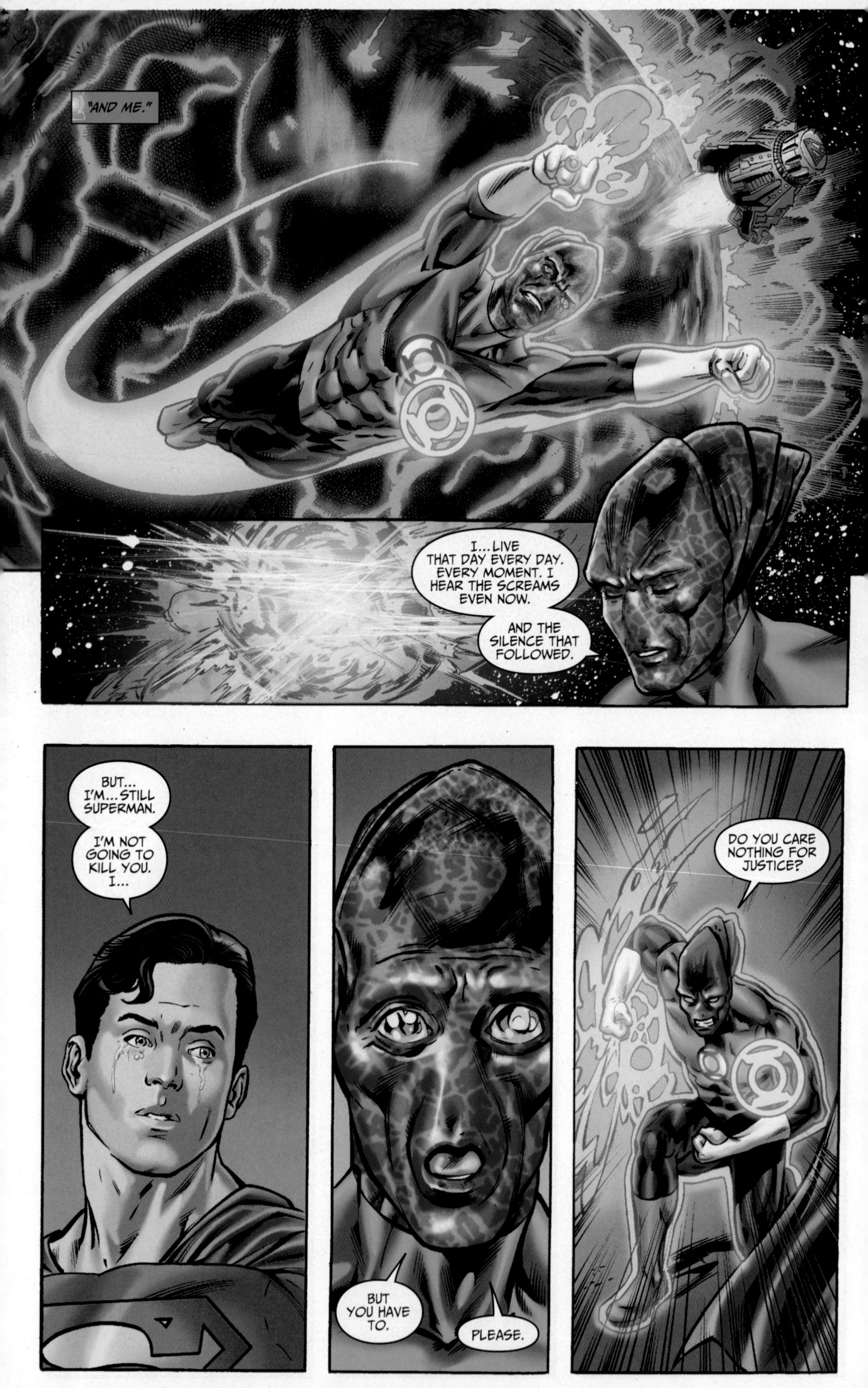
"AND ME."
I...LIVE THAT DAY EVERY DAY. EVERY MOMENT. I HEAR THE SCREAMS EVEN NOW.
AND THE SILENCE THAT FOLLOWED.
BUT... I'M...STILL SUPERMAN.
I'M NOT GOING TO KILL YOU. I...
BUT YOU HAVE TO.
PLEASE.
DO YOU CARE NOTHING FOR JUSTICE?

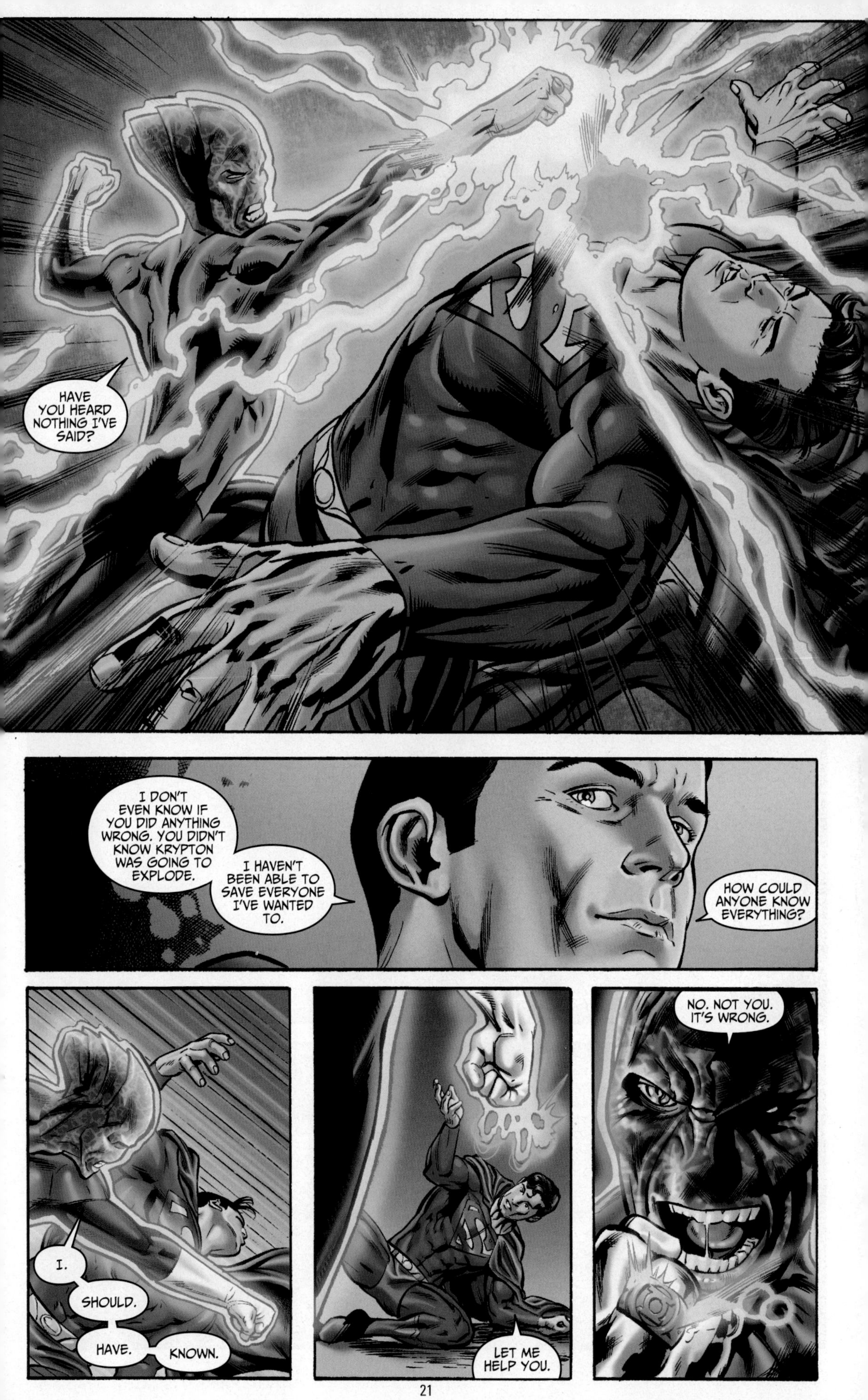

HAVE YOU HEARD NOTHING I'VE SAID?
I DON'T EVEN KNOW IF YOU DID ANYTHING WRONG. YOU DIDN'T KNOW KRYPTON WAS GOING TO EXPLODE.
I HAVEN'T BEEN ABLE TO SAVE EVERYONE I'VE WANTED TO.
HOW COULD ANYONE KNOW EVERYTHING?
I.
SHOULD.
HAVE.
KNOWN.
LET ME HELP YOU.
NO. NOT YOU. IT'S WRONG.

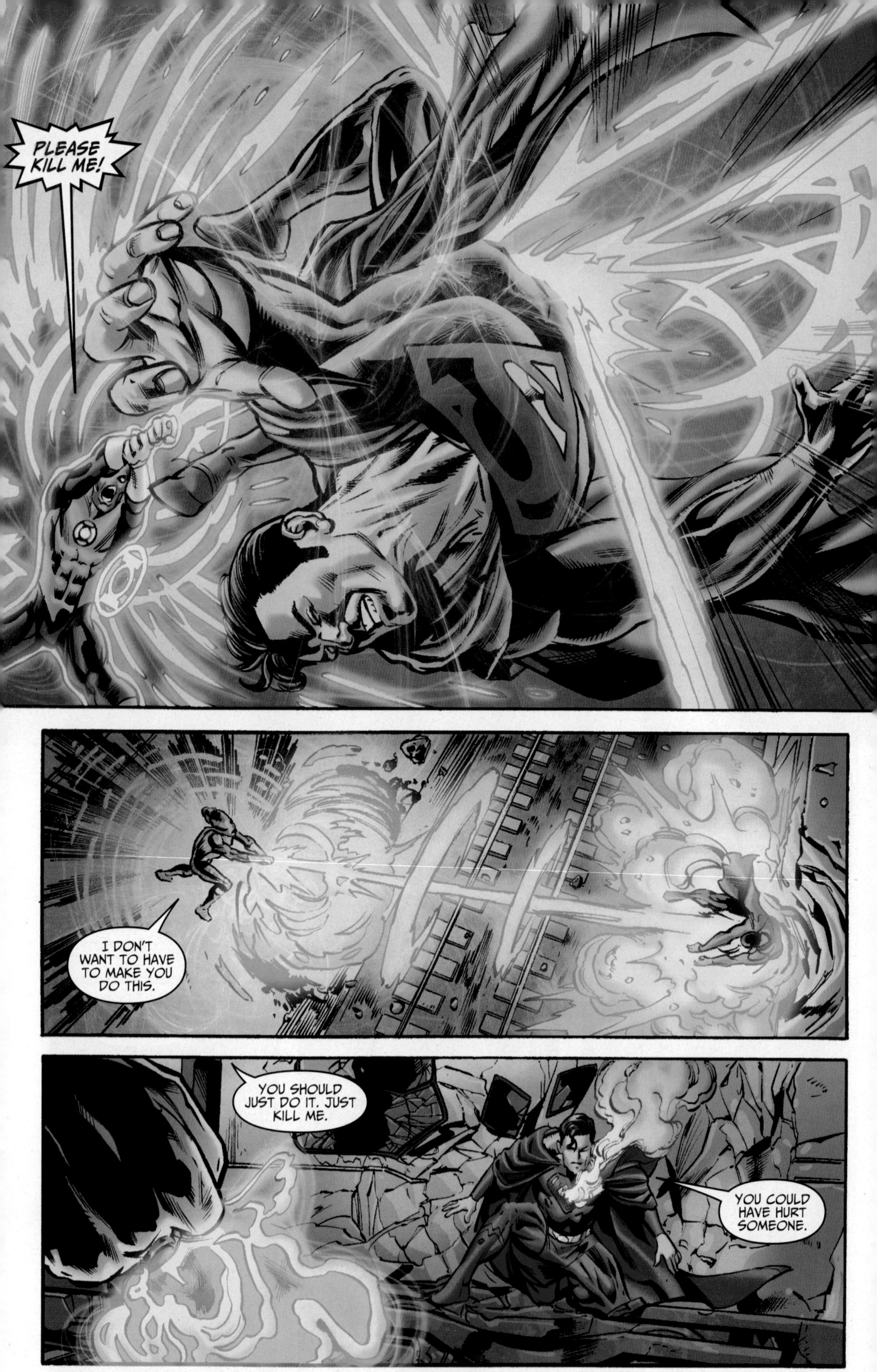
PLEASE KILL ME!
I DON'T WANT TO HAVE TO MAKE YOU DO THIS.
YOU SHOULD JUST DO IT. JUST KILL ME.
YOU COULD HAVE HURT SOMEONE.

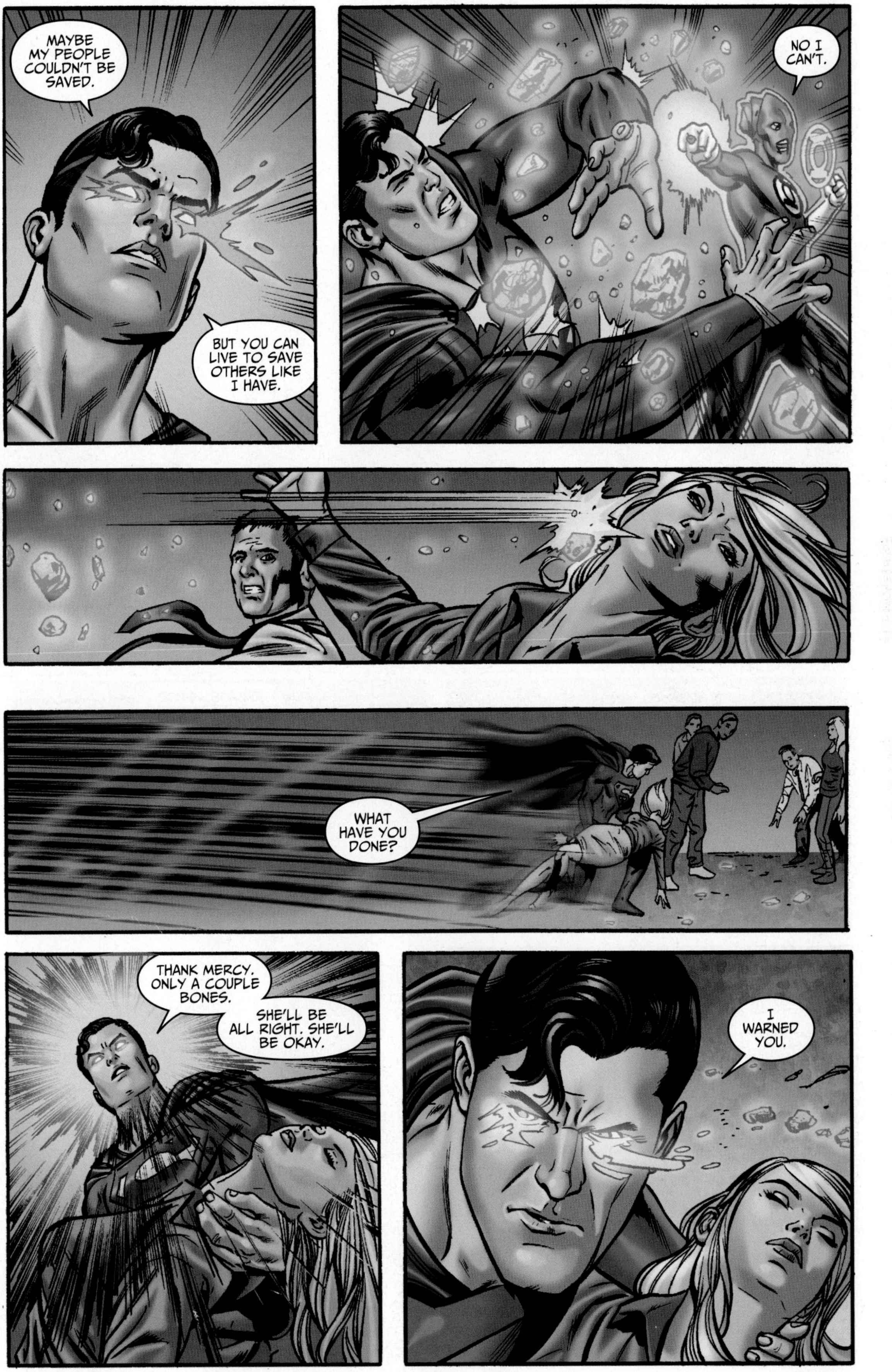
MAYBE MY PEOPLE COULDN'T BE SAVED.
BUT YOU CAN LIVE TO SAVE OTHERS LIKE I HAVE.
NO I CAN'T.
WHAT HAVE YOU DONE?
THANK MERCY. ONLY A COUPLE BONES.
SHE'LL BE ALL RIGHT. SHE'LL BE OKAY.
I WARNED YOU.

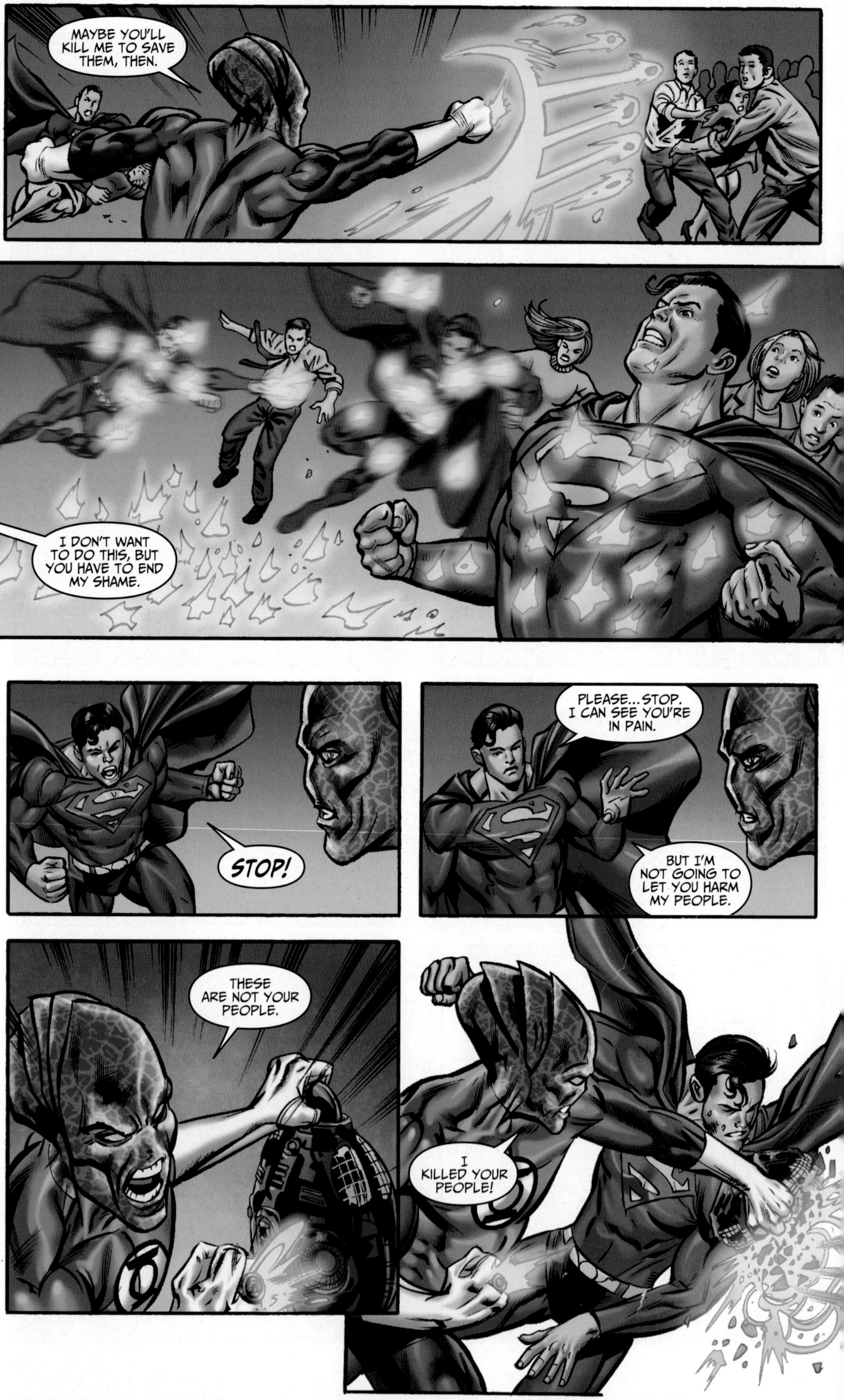

MAYBE YOU'LL KILL ME TO SAVE THEM, THEN.
I DON'T WANT TO DO THIS, BUT YOU HAVE TO END MY SHAME.
STOP!
PLEASE... STOP. I CAN SEE YOU'RE IN PAIN.
BUT I'M NOT GOING TO LET YOU HARM MY PEOPLE.
THESE ARE NOT YOUR PEOPLE.
I KILLED YOUR PEOPLE!

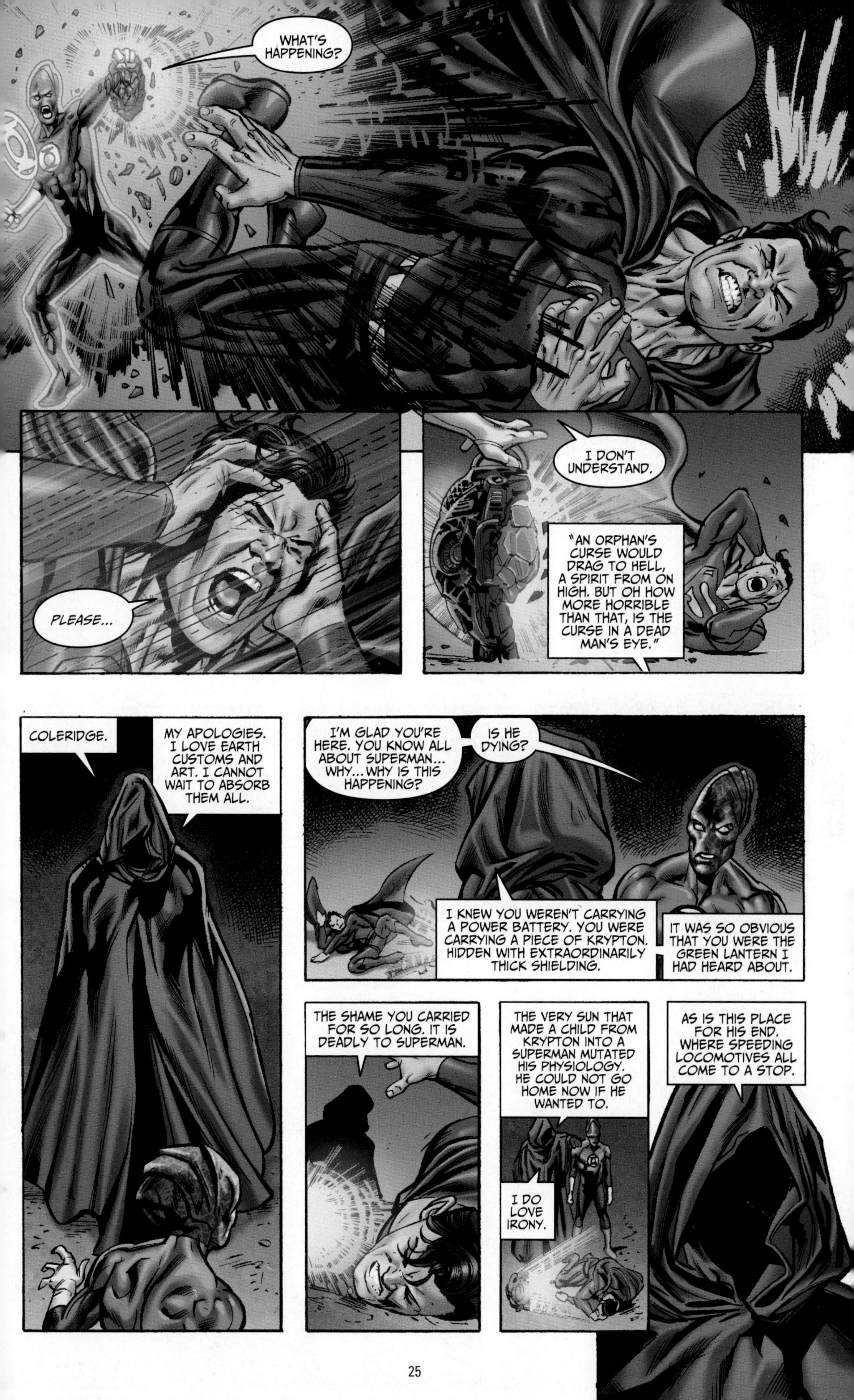
WHAT'S HAPPENING?
PLEASE...
I DON'T UNDERSTAND.
"AN ORPHAN'S CURSE WOULD DRAG TO HELL, A SPIRIT FROM ON HIGH. BUT OH HOW MORE HORRIBLE THAN THAT, IS THE CURSE IN A DEAD MAN'S EYE."
COLERIDGE.
MY APOLOGIES. I LOVE EARTH CUSTOMS AND ART. I CANNOT WAIT TO ABSORB THEM ALL.
I'M GLAD YOU'RE HERE. YOU KNOW ALL ABOUT SUPERMAN... WHY...WHY IS THIS HAPPENING?
IS HE DYING?
I KNEW YOU WEREN'T CARRYING A POWER BATTERY. YOU WERE CARRYING A PIECE OF KRYPTON. HIDDEN WITH EXTRAORDINARILY THICK SHIELDING.
IT WAS SO OBVIOUS THAT YOU WERE THE GREEN LANTERN I HAD HEARD ABOUT.
THE SHAME YOU CARRIED FOR SO LONG. IT IS DEADLY TO SUPERMAN.
THE VERY SUN THAT MADE A CHILD FROM KRYPTON INTO A SUPERMAN MUTATED HIS PHYSIOLOGY. HE COULD NOT GO HOME NOW IF HE WANTED TO.
I DO LOVE IRONY.
AS IS THIS PLACE FOR HIS END. WHERE SPEEDING LOCOMOTIVES ALL COME TO A STOP.

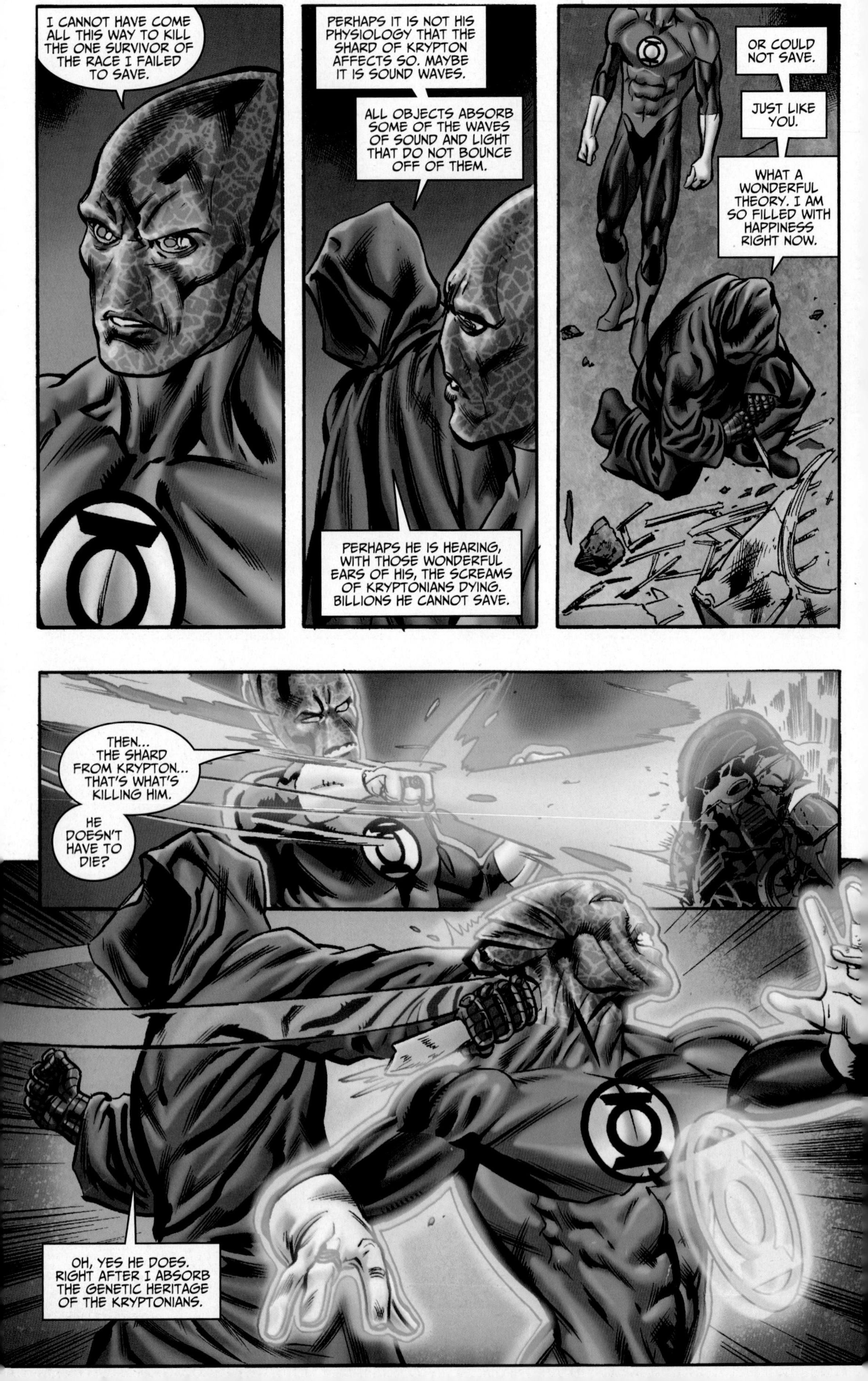
I CANNOT HAVE COME ALL THIS WAY TO KILL THE ONE SURVIVOR OF THE RACE I FAILED TO SAVE.
PERHAPS IT IS NOT HIS PHYSIOLOGY THAT THE SHARD OF KRYPTON AFFECTS SO. MAYBE IT IS SOUND WAVES.
ALL OBJECTS ABSORB SOME OF THE WAVES OF SOUND AND LIGHT THAT DO NOT BOUNCE OFF OF THEM.
PERHAPS HE IS HEARING, WITH THOSE WONDERFUL EARS OF HIS, THE SCREAMS OF KRYPTONIANS DYING. BILLIONS HE CANNOT SAVE.
OR COULD NOT SAVE.
JUST LIKE YOU.
WHAT A WONDERFUL THEORY. I AM SO FILLED WITH HAPPINESS RIGHT NOW.
THEN... THE SHARD FROM KRYPTON... THAT'S WHAT'S KILLING HIM.
HE DOESN'T HAVE TO DIE?
OH, YES HE DOES. RIGHT AFTER I ABSORB THE GENETIC HERITAGE OF THE KRYPTONIANS.

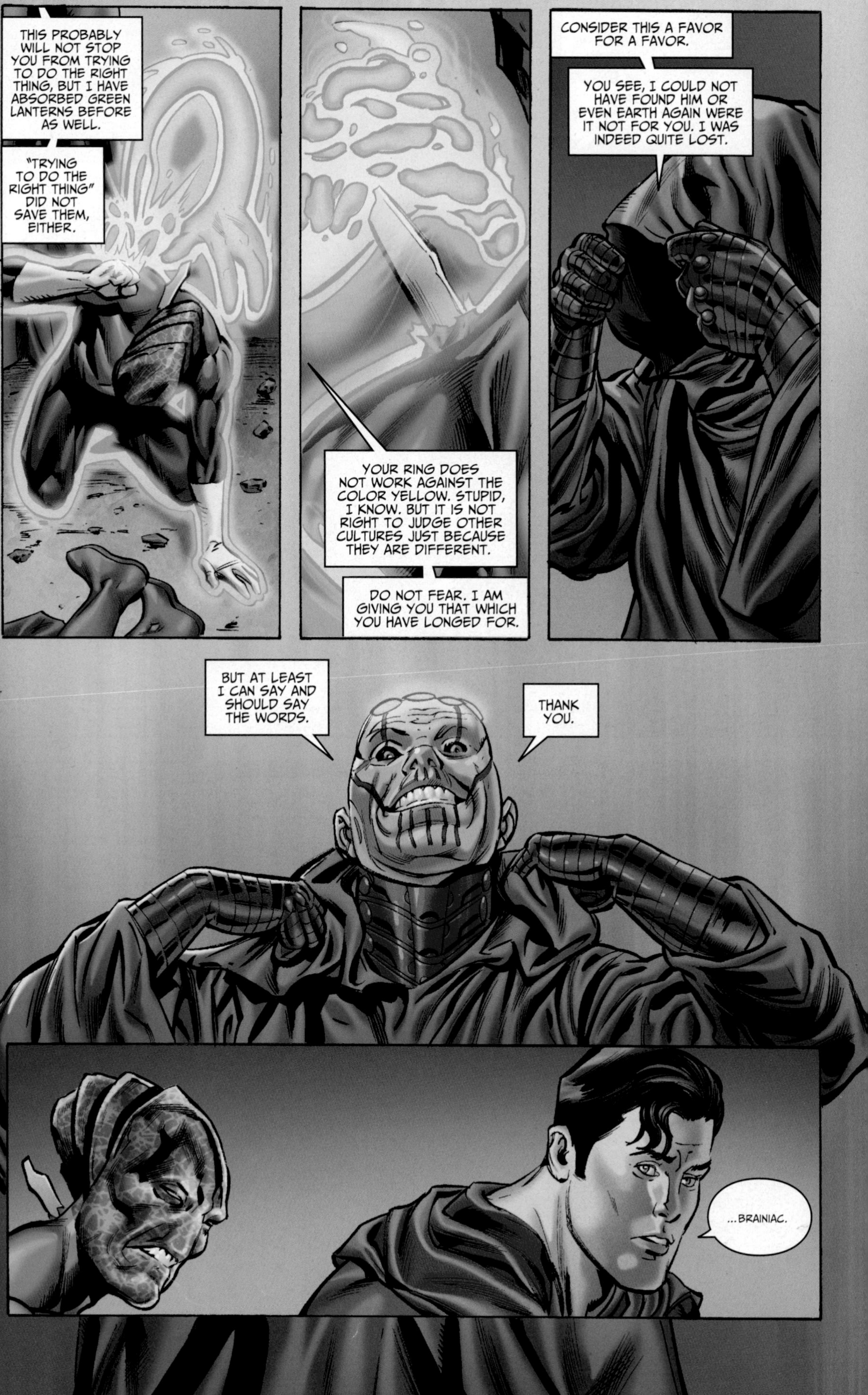
THIS PROBABLY WILL NOT STOP YOU FROM TRYING TO DO THE RIGHT THING, BUT I HAVE ABSORBED GREEN LANTERNS BEFORE AS WELL.
"TRYING TO DO THE RIGHT THING" DID NOT SAVE THEM, EITHER.
YOUR RING DOES NOT WORK AGAINST THE COLOR YELLOW. STUPID, I KNOW. BUT IT IS NOT RIGHT TO JUDGE OTHER CULTURES JUST BECAUSE THEY ARE DIFFERENT.
DO NOT FEAR. I AM GIVING YOU THAT WHICH YOU HAVE LONGED FOR.
CONSIDER THIS A FAVOR FOR A FAVOR.
YOU SEE, I COULD NOT HAVE FOUND HIM OR EVEN EARTH AGAIN WERE IT NOT FOR YOU. I WAS INDEED QUITE LOST.
BUT AT LEAST I CAN SAY AND SHOULD SAY THE WORDS.
THANK YOU.
...BRAINIAC.

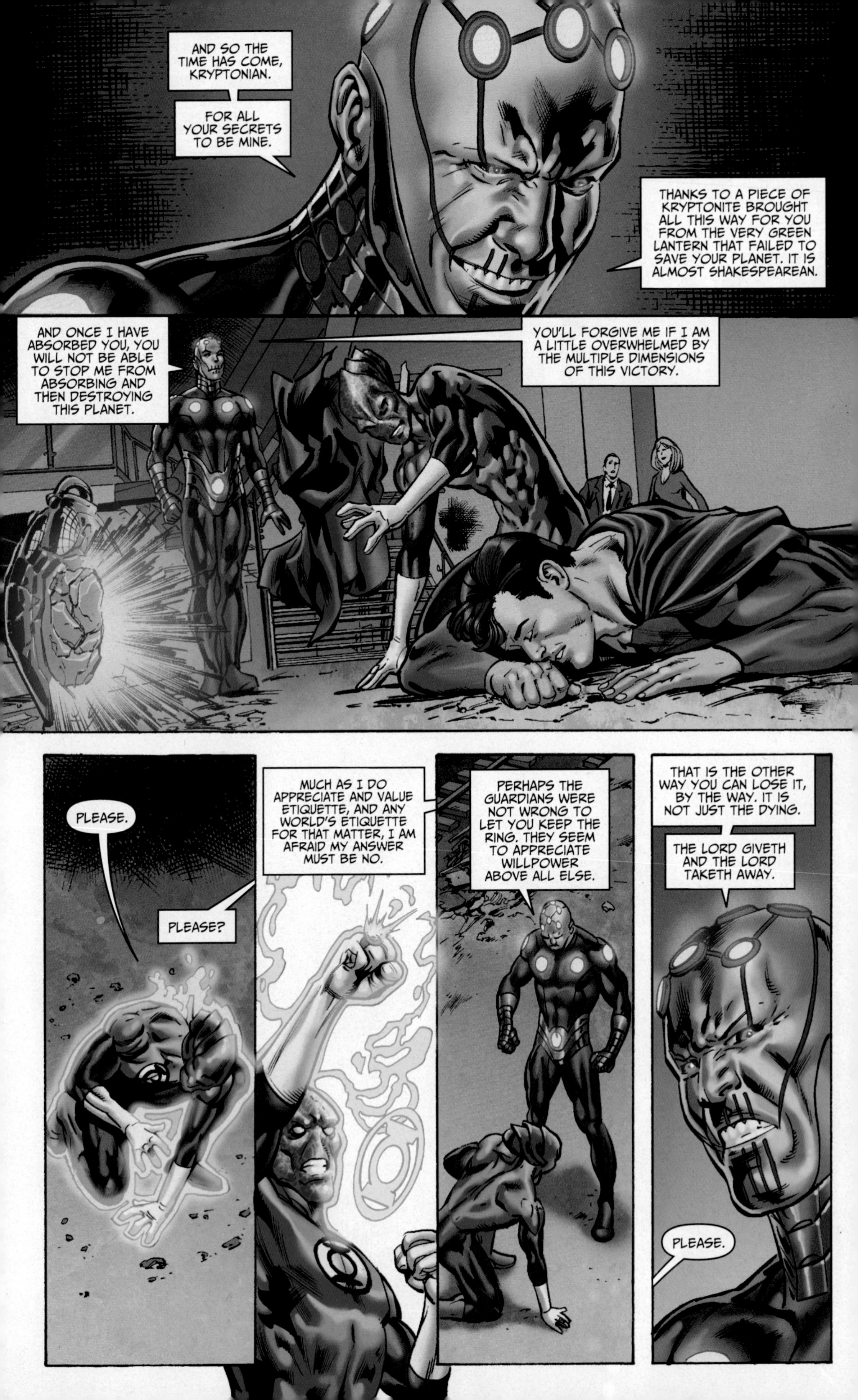

AND SO THE TIME HAS COME, KRYPTONIAN.
FOR ALL YOUR SECRETS TO BE MINE.
THANKS TO A PIECE OF KRYPTONITE BROUGHT ALL THIS WAY FOR YOU FROM THE VERY GREEN LANTERN THAT FAILED TO SAVE YOUR PLANET. IT IS ALMOST SHAKESPEAREAN.
AND ONCE I HAVE ABSORBED YOU, YOU WILL NOT BE ABLE TO STOP ME FROM ABSORBING AND THEN DESTROYING THIS PLANET.
YOU'LL FORGIVE ME IF I AM A LITTLE OVERWHELMED BY THE MULTIPLE DIMENSIONS OF THIS VICTORY.
PLEASE.
PLEASE?
MUCH AS I DO APPRECIATE AND VALUE ETIQUETTE, AND ANY WORLD'S ETIQUETTE FOR THAT MATTER, I AM AFRAID MY ANSWER MUST BE NO.
PERHAPS THE GUARDIANS WERE NOT WRONG TO LET YOU KEEP THE RING. THEY SEEM TO APPRECIATE WILLPOWER ABOVE ALL ELSE.
THAT IS THE OTHER WAY YOU CAN LOSE IT, BY THE WAY. IT IS NOT JUST THE DYING.
THE LORD GIVETH AND THE LORD TAKETH AWAY.
PLEASE.

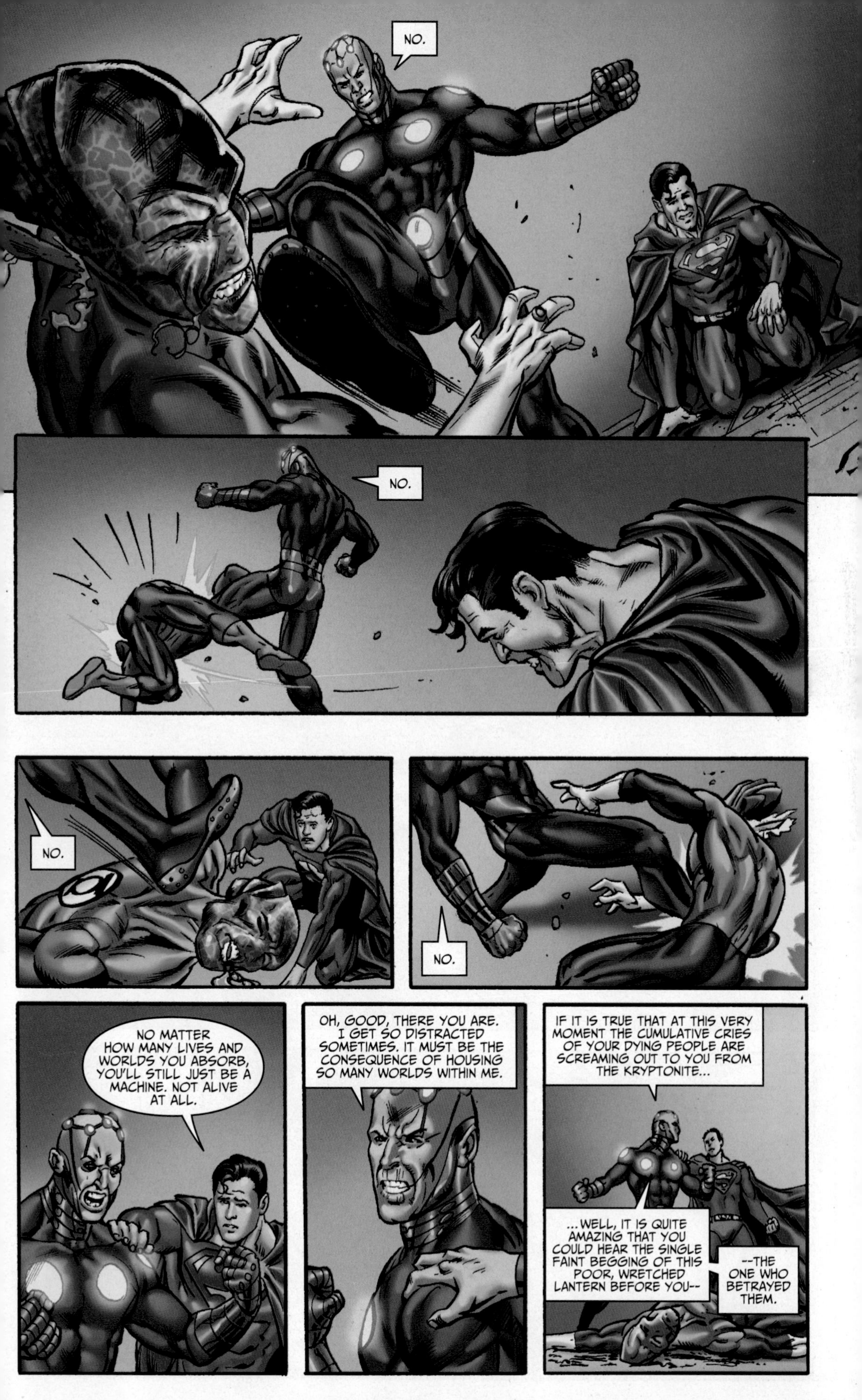
NO.
NO.
NO.
NO.
NO MATTER HOW MANY LIVES AND WORLDS YOU ABSORB, YOU'LL STILL JUST BE A MACHINE. NOT ALIVE AT ALL.
OH, GOOD, THERE YOU ARE. I GET SO DISTRACTED SOMETIMES. IT MUST BE THE CONSEQUENCE OF HOUSING SO MANY WORLDS WITHIN ME.
IF IT IS TRUE THAT AT THIS VERY MOMENT THE CUMULATIVE CRIES OF YOUR DYING PEOPLE ARE SCREAMING OUT TO YOU FROM THE KRYPTONITE...
...WELL, IT IS QUITE AMAZING THAT YOU COULD HEAR THE SINGLE FAINT BEGGING OF THIS POOR, WRETCHED LANTERN BEFORE YOU--
--THE ONE WHO BETRAYED THEM.

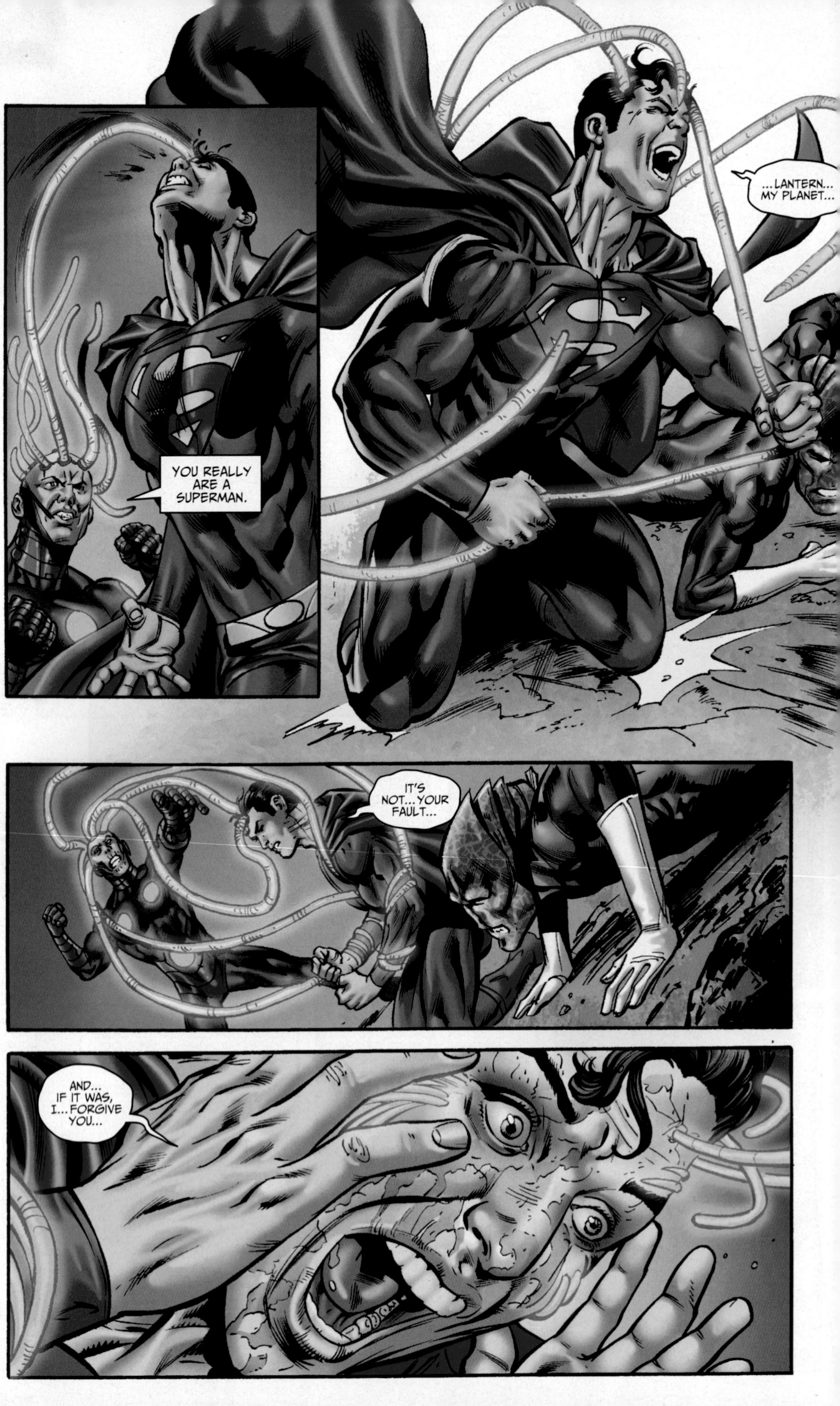
YOU REALLY ARE A SUPERMAN.
...LANTERN... MY PLANET...
IT'S NOT...YOUR FAULT...
AND... IF IT WAS, I...FORGIVE YOU...

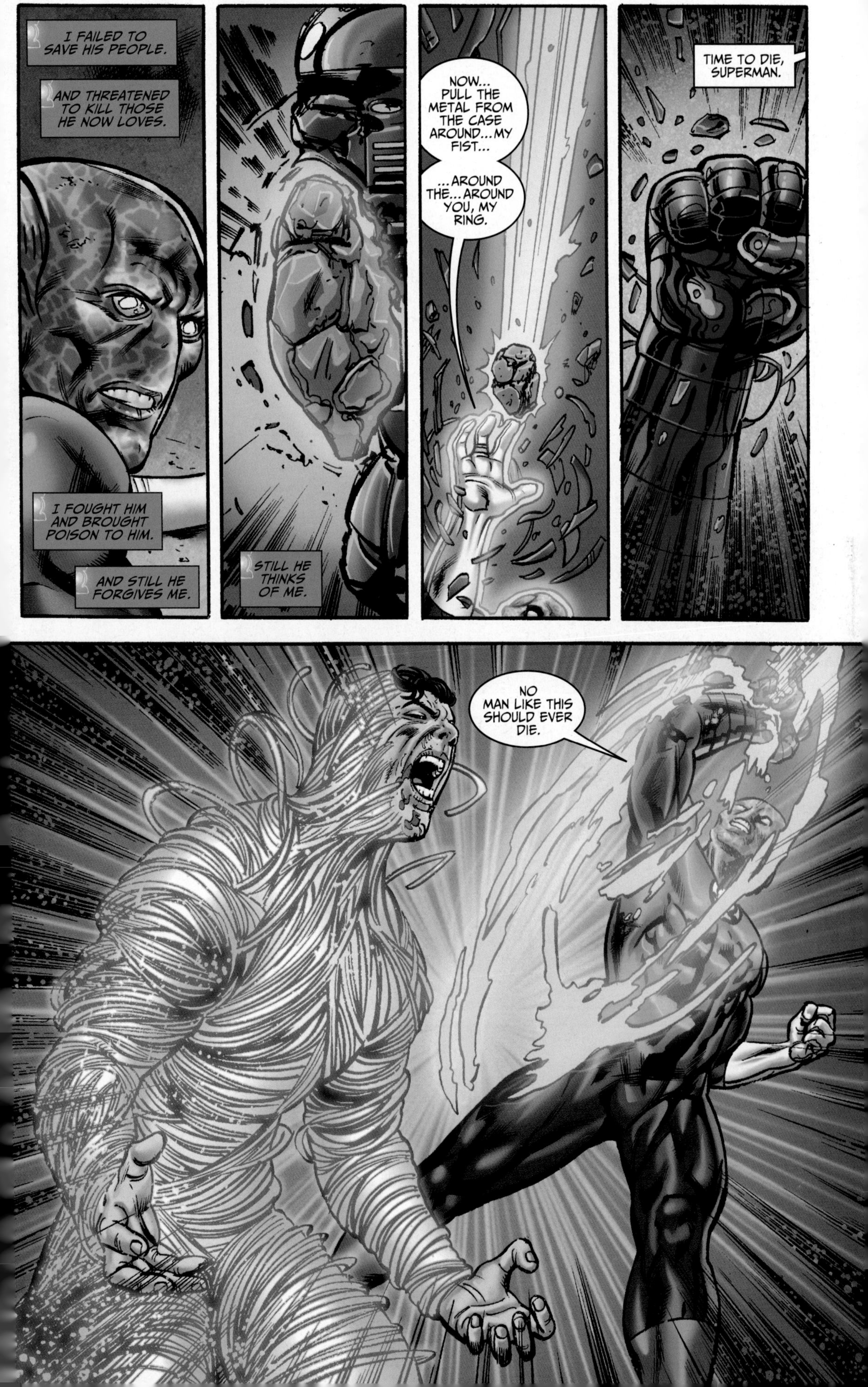
I FAILED TO SAVE HIS PEOPLE.
AND THREATENED TO KILL THOSE HE NOW LOVES.
I FOUGHT HIM AND BROUGHT POISON TO HIM.
AND STILL HE FORGIVES ME.
STILL HE THINKS OF ME.
NOW... PULL THE METAL FROM THE CASE AROUND... MY FIST...
...AROUND THE... AROUND YOU, MY RING.
TIME TO DIE, SUPERMAN.
NO MAN LIKE THIS SHOULD EVER DIE.

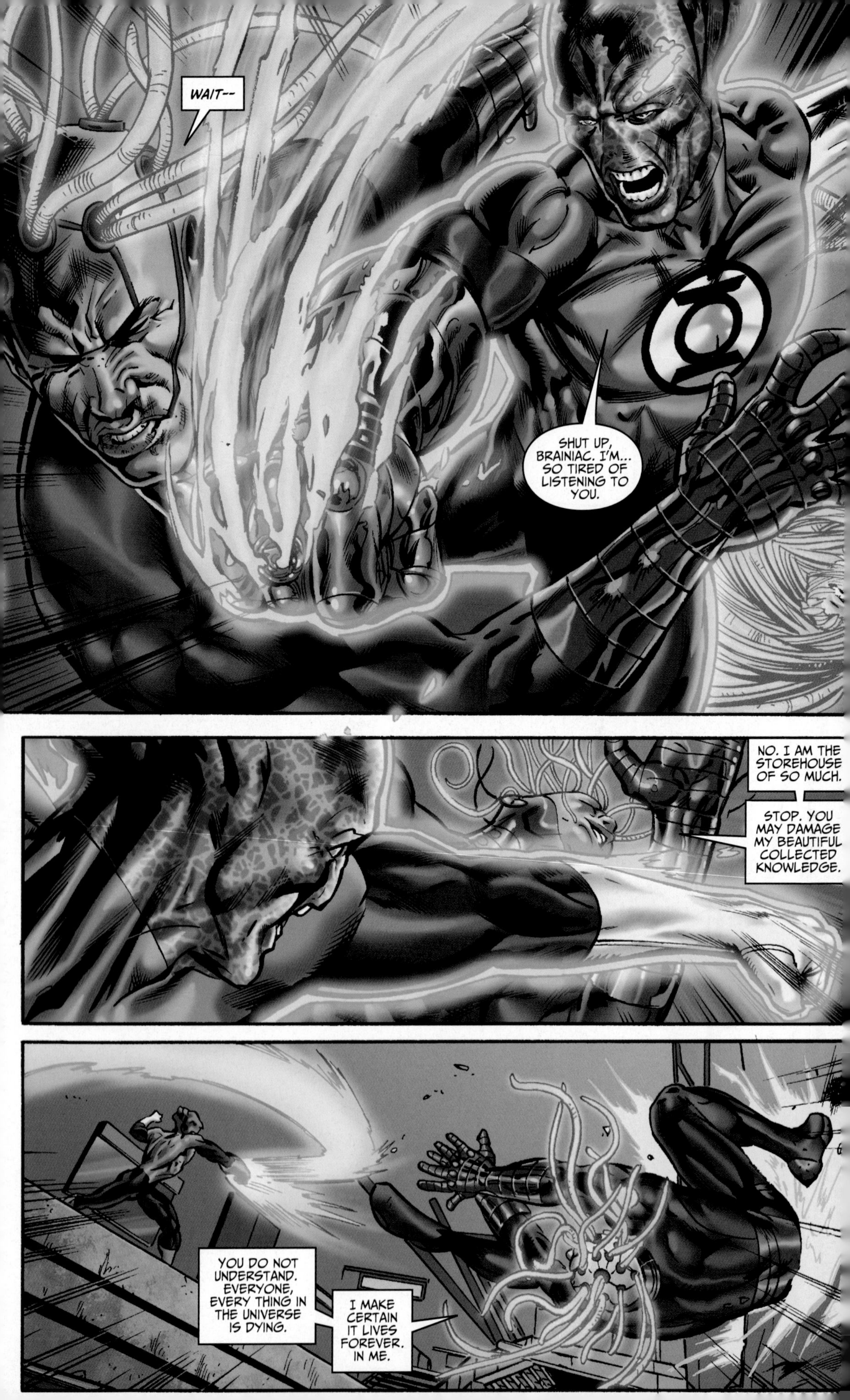
WAIT--
SHUT UP, BRAINIAC. I'M... SO TIRED OF LISTENING TO YOU.
NO. I AM THE STOREHOUSE OF SO MUCH.
STOP. YOU MAY DAMAGE MY BEAUTIFUL COLLECTED KNOWLEDGE.
YOU DO NOT UNDERSTAND. EVERYONE, EVERY THING IN THE UNIVERSE IS DYING.
I MAKE CERTAIN IT LIVES FOREVER. IN ME.

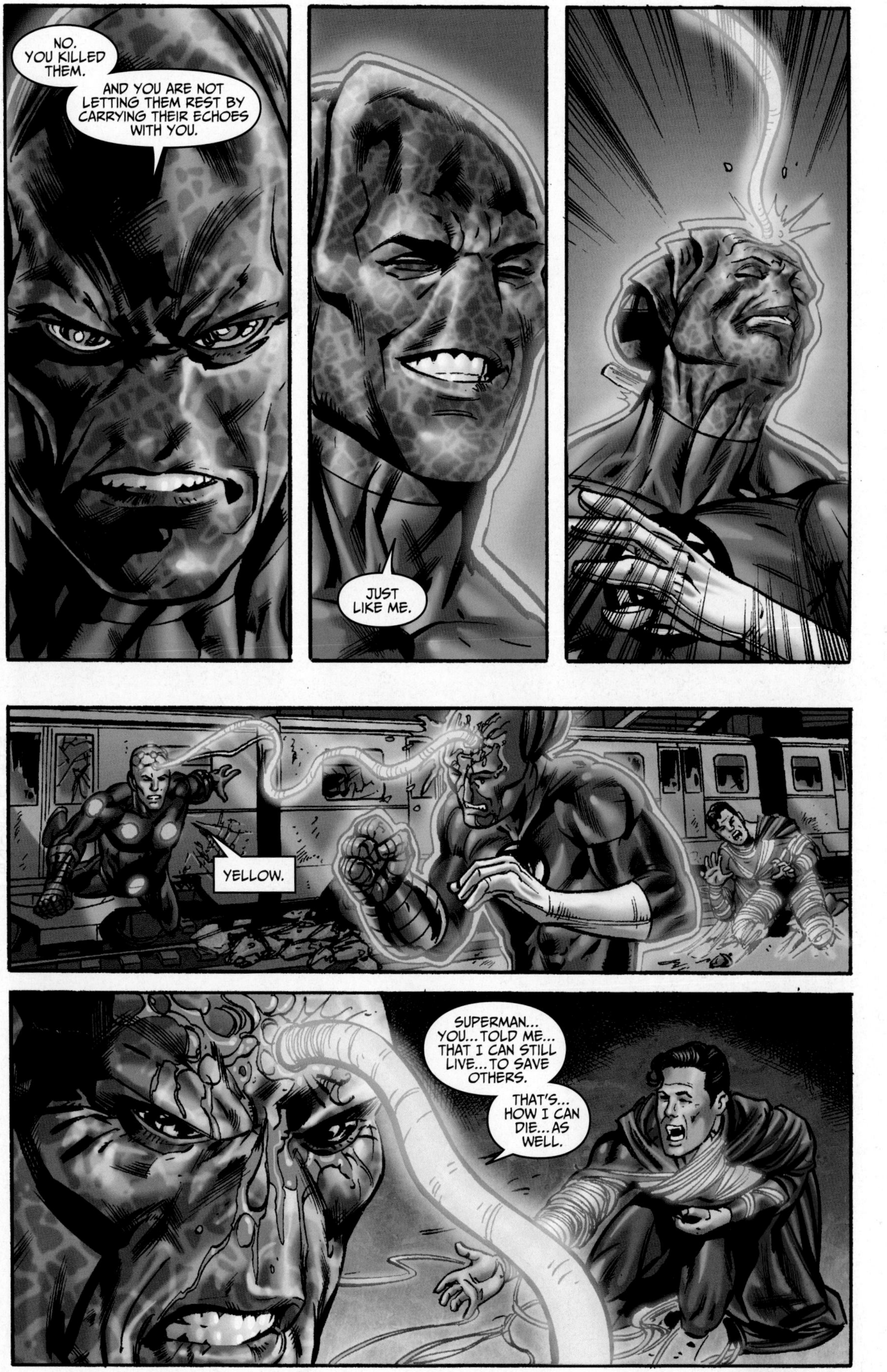
NO. YOU KILLED THEM.
AND YOU ARE NOT LETTING THEM REST BY CARRYING THEIR ECHOES WITH YOU.
JUST LIKE ME.
YELLOW.
SUPERMAN... YOU...TOLD ME... THAT I CAN STILL LIVE...TO SAVE OTHERS.
THAT'S... HOW I CAN DIE...AS WELL.

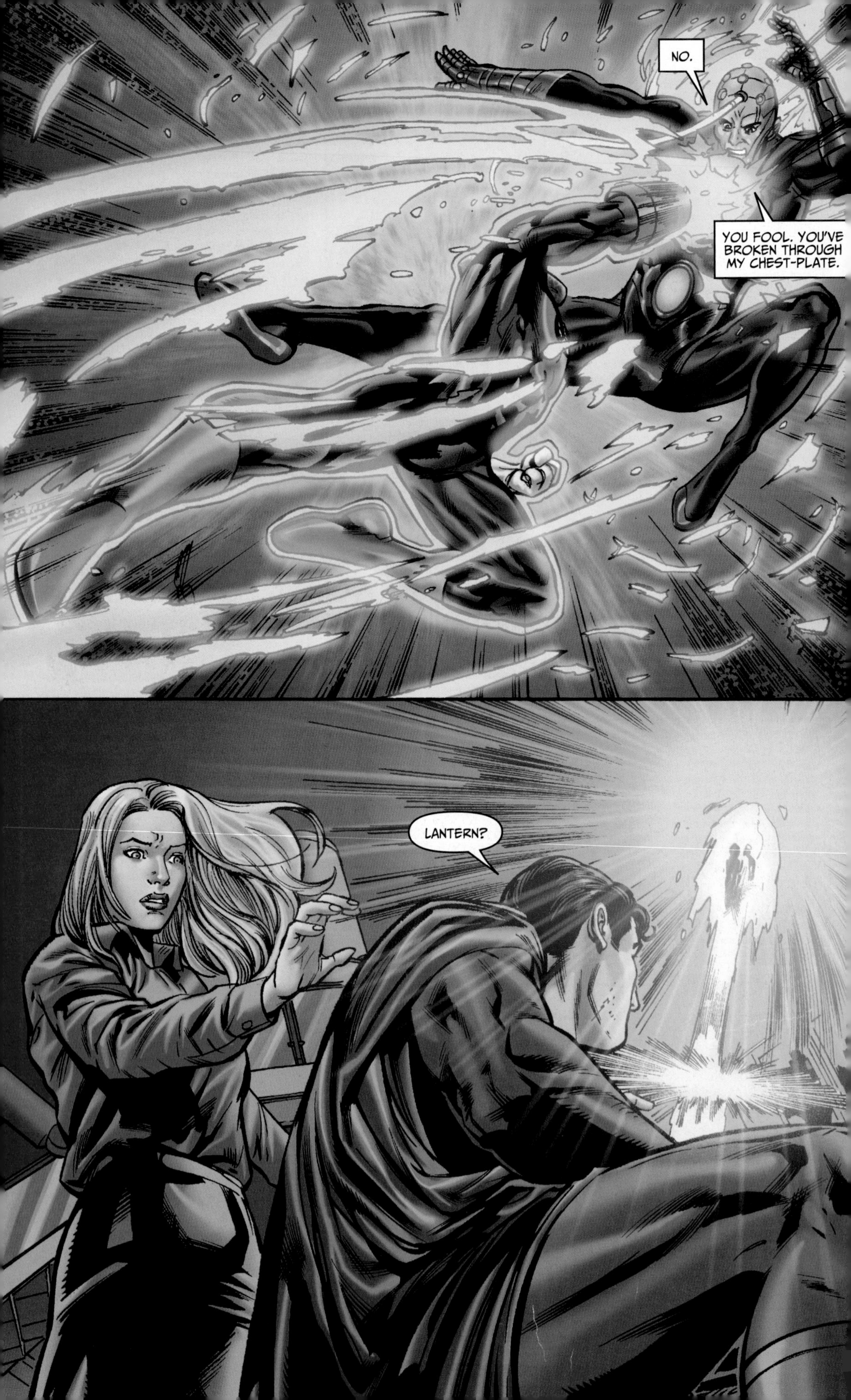
NO.
YOU FOOL. YOU'VE BROKEN THROUGH MY CHEST-PLATE.
LANTERN?

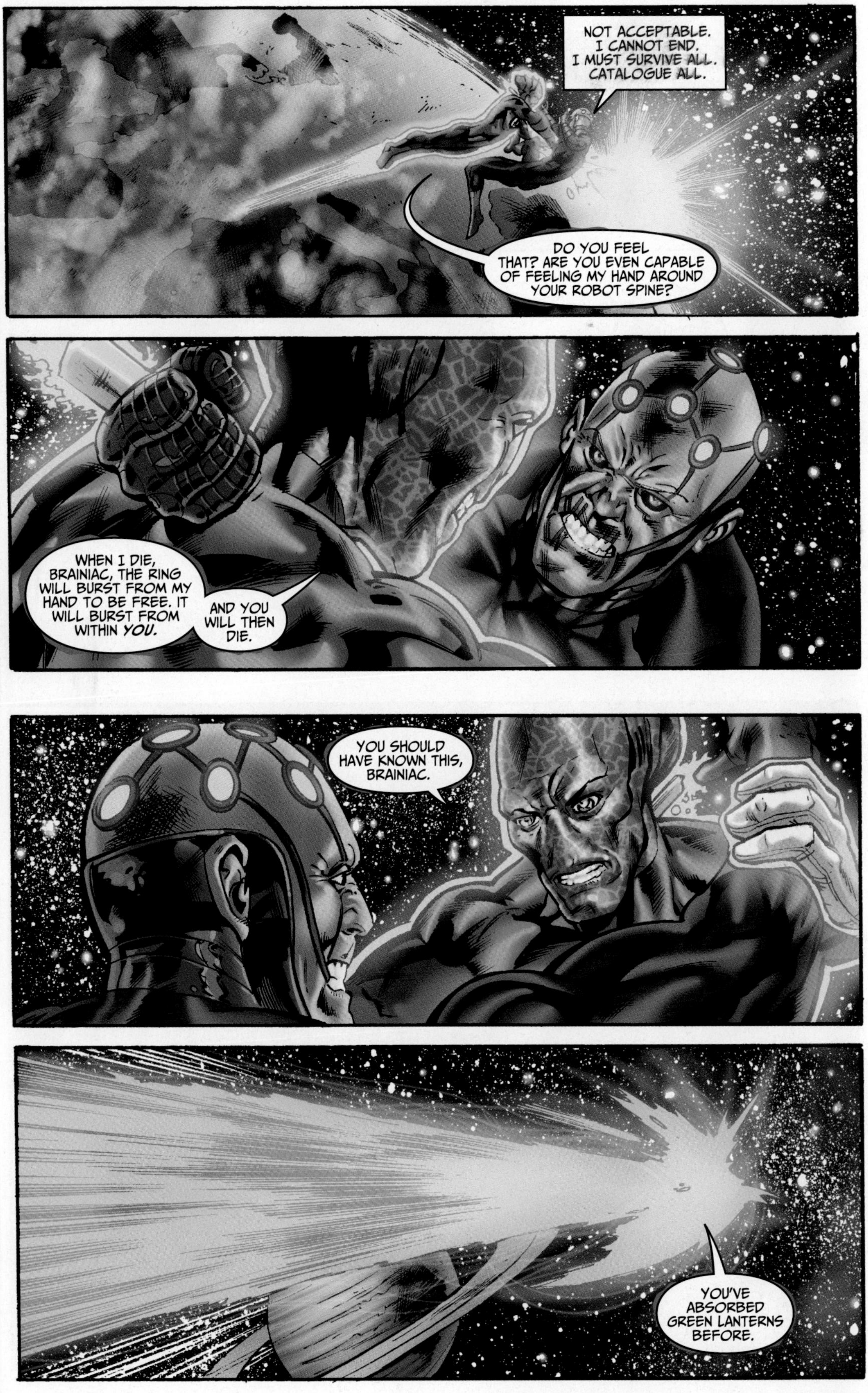
NOT ACCEPTABLE. I CANNOT END. I MUST SURVIVE ALL. CATALOGUE ALL.
DO YOU FEEL THAT? ARE YOU EVEN CAPABLE OF FEELING MY HAND AROUND YOUR ROBOT SPINE?
WHEN I DIE, BRAINIAC, THE RING WILL BURST FROM MY HAND TO BE FREE. IT WILL BURST FROM WITHIN *YOU.*
AND YOU WILL THEN DIE.
YOU SHOULD HAVE KNOWN THIS, BRAINIAC.
YOU'VE ABSORBED GREEN LANTERNS BEFORE.

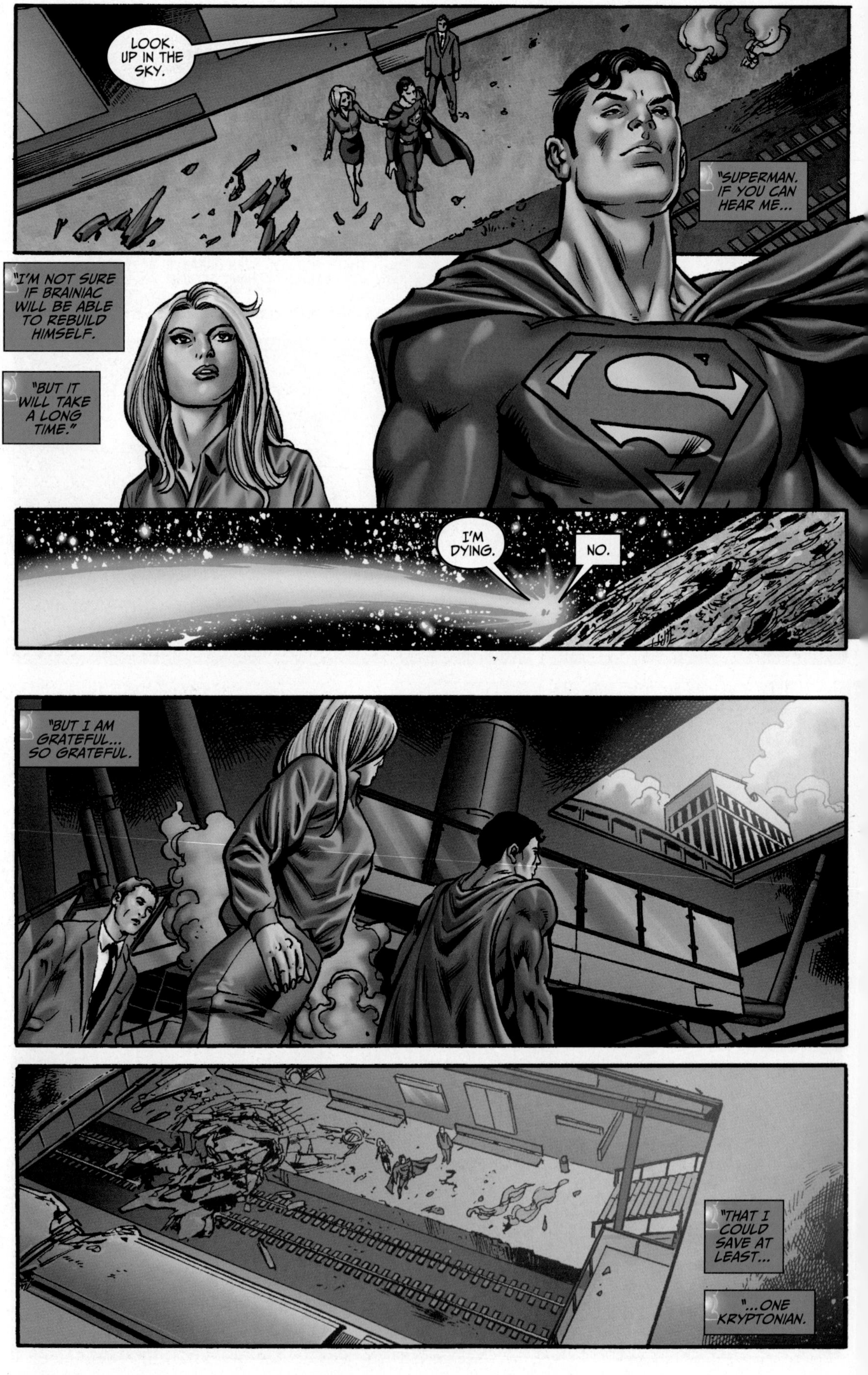
LOOK. UP IN THE SKY.
"SUPERMAN. IF YOU CAN HEAR ME...
"I'M NOT SURE IF BRAINIAC WILL BE ABLE TO REBUILD HIMSELF.
"BUT IT WILL TAKE A LONG TIME."
I'M DYING.
NO.
"BUT I AM GRATEFUL... SO GRATEFUL.
"THAT I COULD SAVE AT LEAST...
"...ONE KRYPTONIAN.

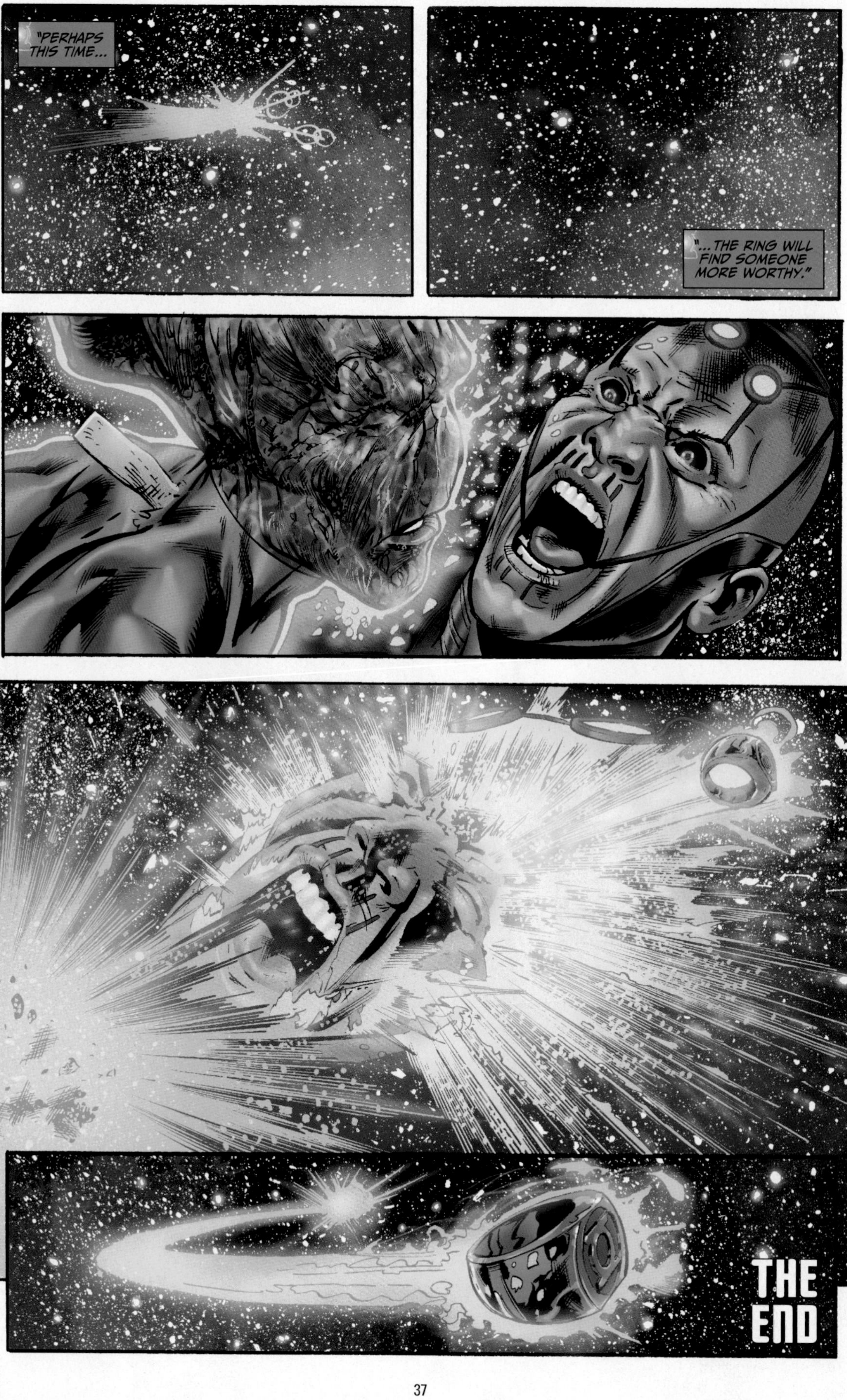
"PERHAPS THIS TIME...
"...THE RING WILL FIND SOMEONE MORE WORTHY."
THE END

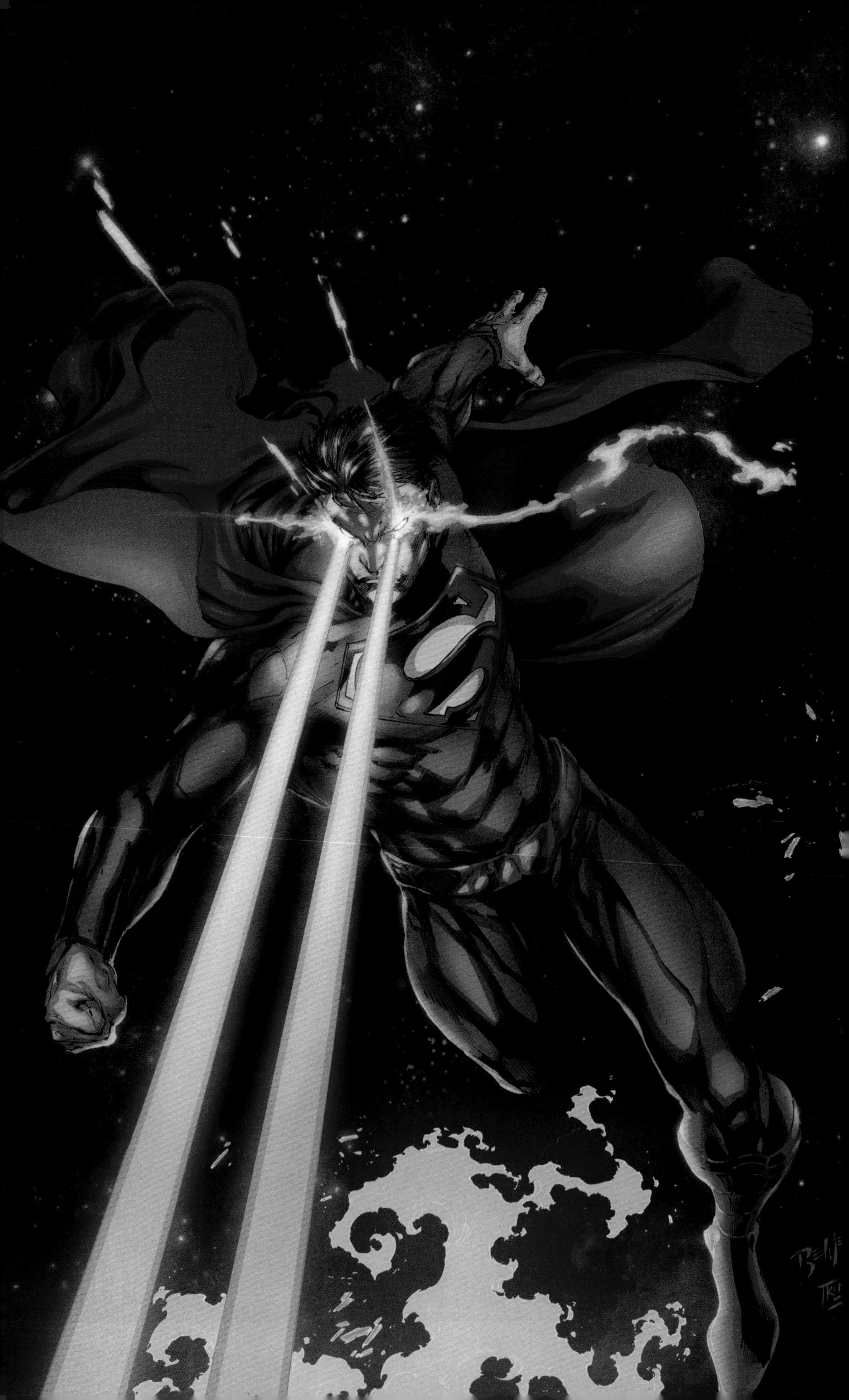

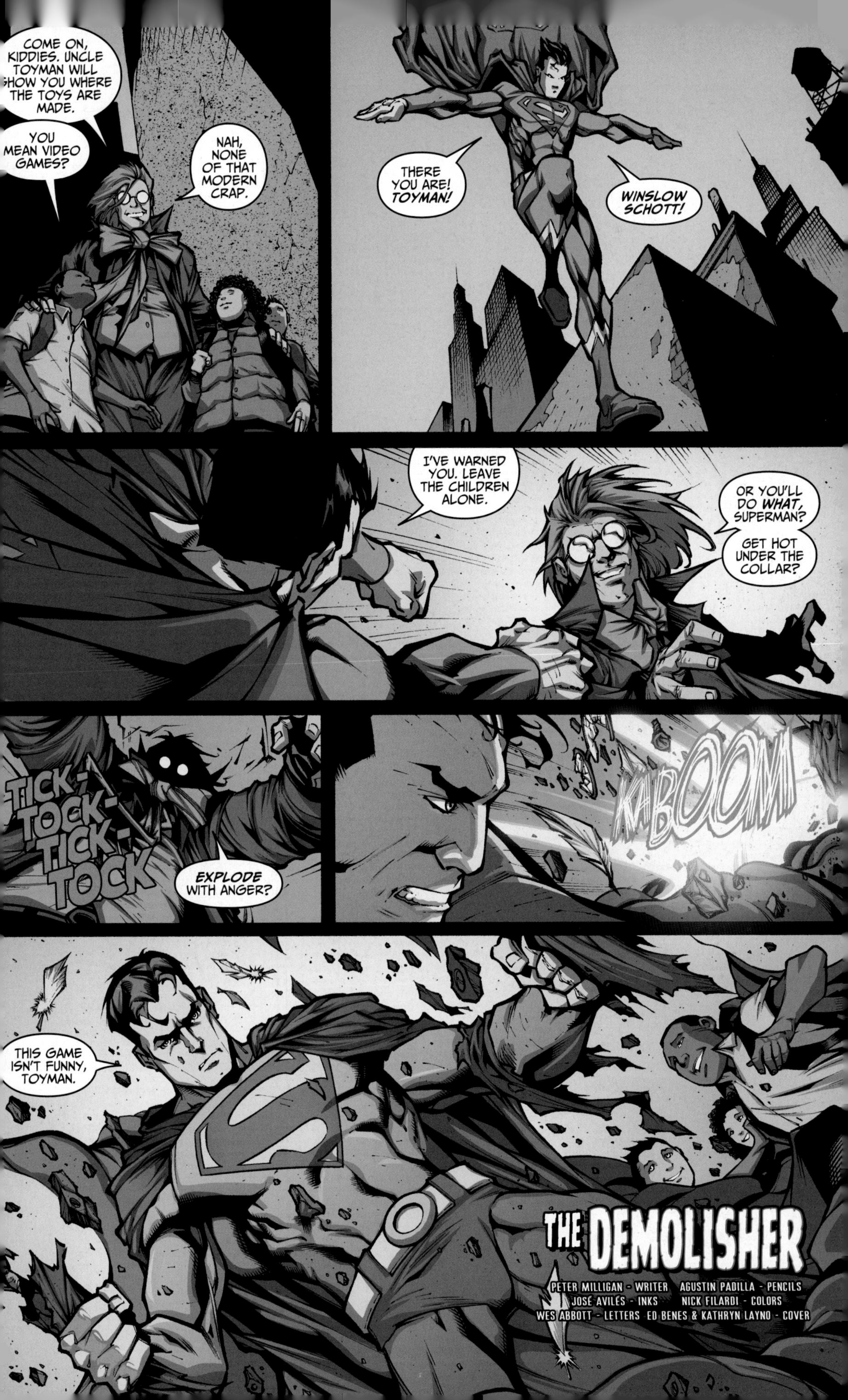

COME ON, KIDDIES. UNCLE TOYMAN WILL SHOW YOU WHERE THE TOYS ARE MADE.
YOU MEAN VIDEO GAMES?
NAH, NONE OF THAT MODERN CRAP.
THERE YOU ARE! TOYMAN!
WINSLOW SCHOTT!
I'VE WARNED YOU. LEAVE THE CHILDREN ALONE.
OR YOU'LL DO WHAT, SUPERMAN?
GET HOT UNDER THE COLLAR?
TICK-TOCK-TICK-TOCK
EXPLODE WITH ANGER?
KABOOM
THIS GAME ISN'T FUNNY, TOYMAN.
THE DEMOLISHER
PETER MILLIGAN - WRITER AGUSTIN PADILLA - PENCILS
JOSÉ AVILÉS - INKS NICK FILARDI - COLORS
WES ABBOTT - LETTERS ED BENES & KATHRYN LAYNO - COVER

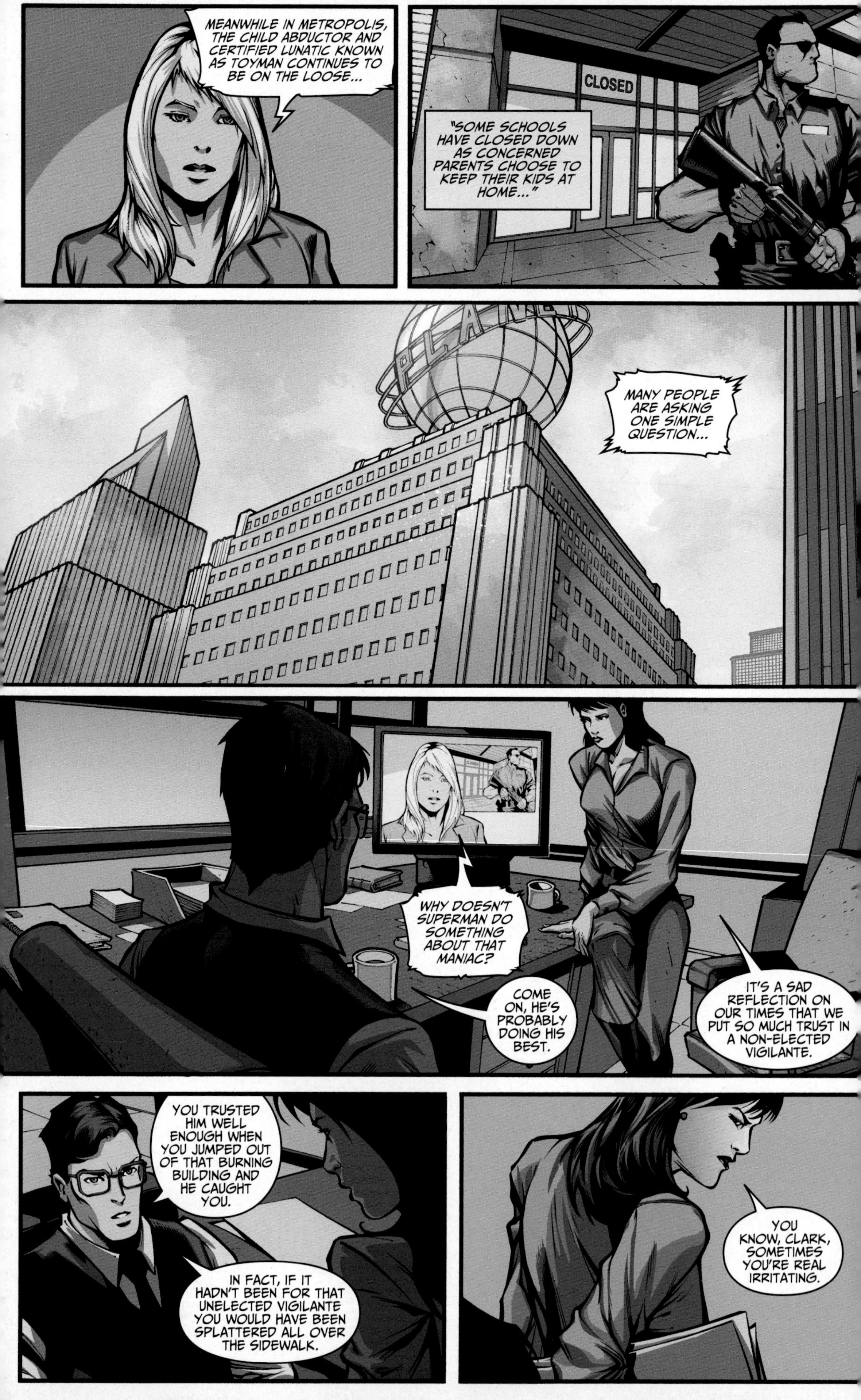
MEANWHILE IN METROPOLIS, THE CHILD ABDUCTOR AND CERTIFIED LUNATIC KNOWN AS TOYMAN CONTINUES TO BE ON THE LOOSE...
CLOSED
"SOME SCHOOLS HAVE CLOSED DOWN AS CONCERNED PARENTS CHOOSE TO KEEP THEIR KIDS AT HOME..."
MANY PEOPLE ARE ASKING ONE SIMPLE QUESTION...
WHY DOESN'T SUPERMAN DO SOMETHING ABOUT THAT MANIAC?
COME ON, HE'S PROBABLY DOING HIS BEST.
IT'S A SAD REFLECTION ON OUR TIMES THAT WE PUT SO MUCH TRUST IN A NON-ELECTED VIGILANTE.
YOU TRUSTED HIM WELL ENOUGH WHEN YOU JUMPED OUT OF THAT BURNING BUILDING AND HE CAUGHT YOU.
IN FACT, IF IT HADN'T BEEN FOR THAT UNELECTED VIGILANTE YOU WOULD HAVE BEEN SPLATTERED ALL OVER THE SIDEWALK.
YOU KNOW, CLARK, SOMETIMES YOU'RE REAL IRRITATING.

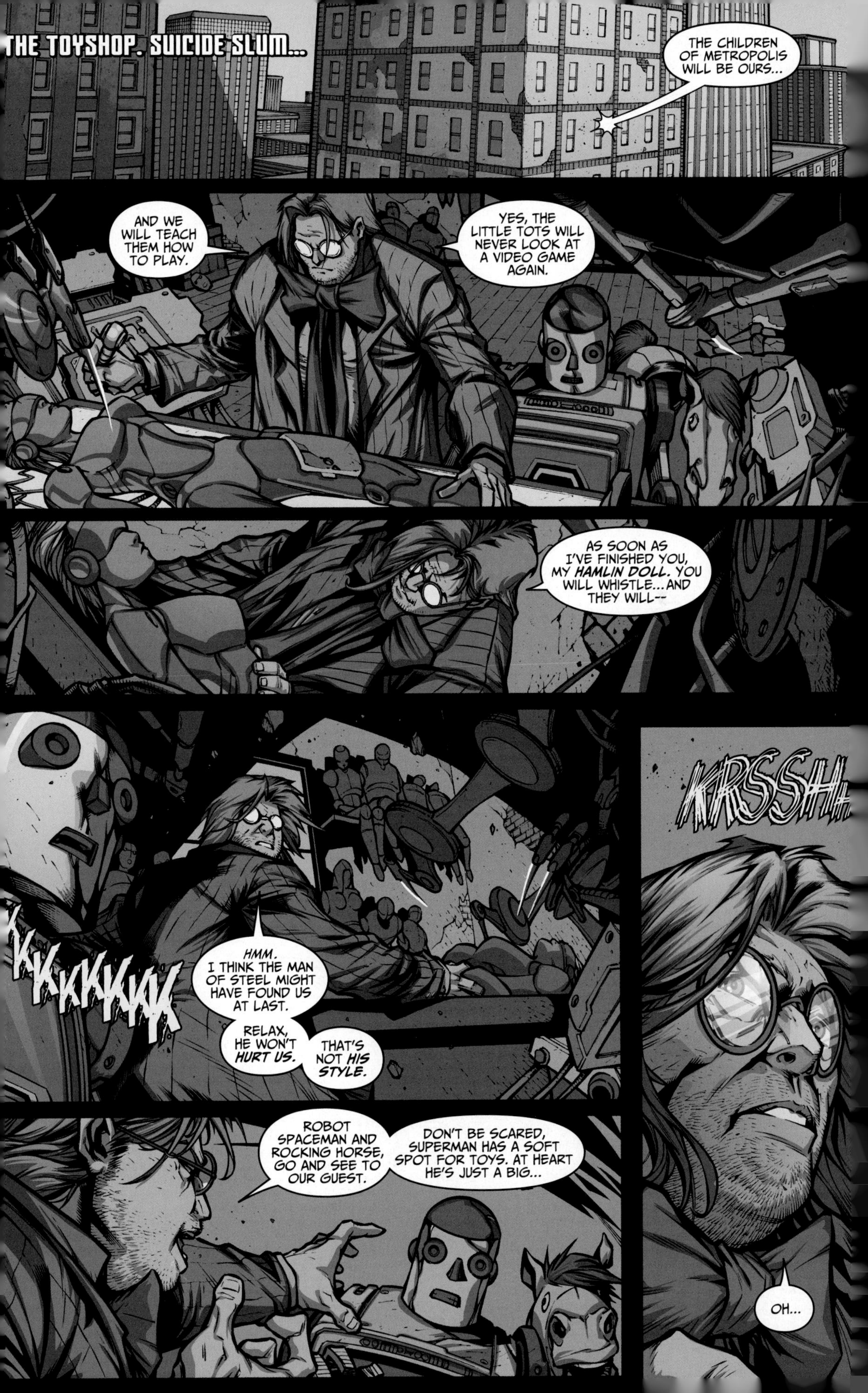
THE TOYSHOP. SUICIDE SLUM...
THE CHILDREN OF METROPOLIS WILL BE OURS...
AND WE WILL TEACH THEM HOW TO PLAY.
YES, THE LITTLE TOTS WILL NEVER LOOK AT A VIDEO GAME AGAIN.
AS SOON AS I'VE FINISHED YOU, MY HAMLIN DOLL. YOU WILL WHISTLE...AND THEY WILL--
KKKKKKK
HMM. I THINK THE MAN OF STEEL MIGHT HAVE FOUND US AT LAST.
RELAX, HE WON'T HURT US.
THAT'S NOT HIS STYLE.
KRSSH
ROBOT SPACEMAN AND ROCKING HORSE, GO AND SEE TO OUR GUEST.
DON'T BE SCARED, SUPERMAN HAS A SOFT SPOT FOR TOYS. AT HEART HE'S JUST A BIG...
OH...

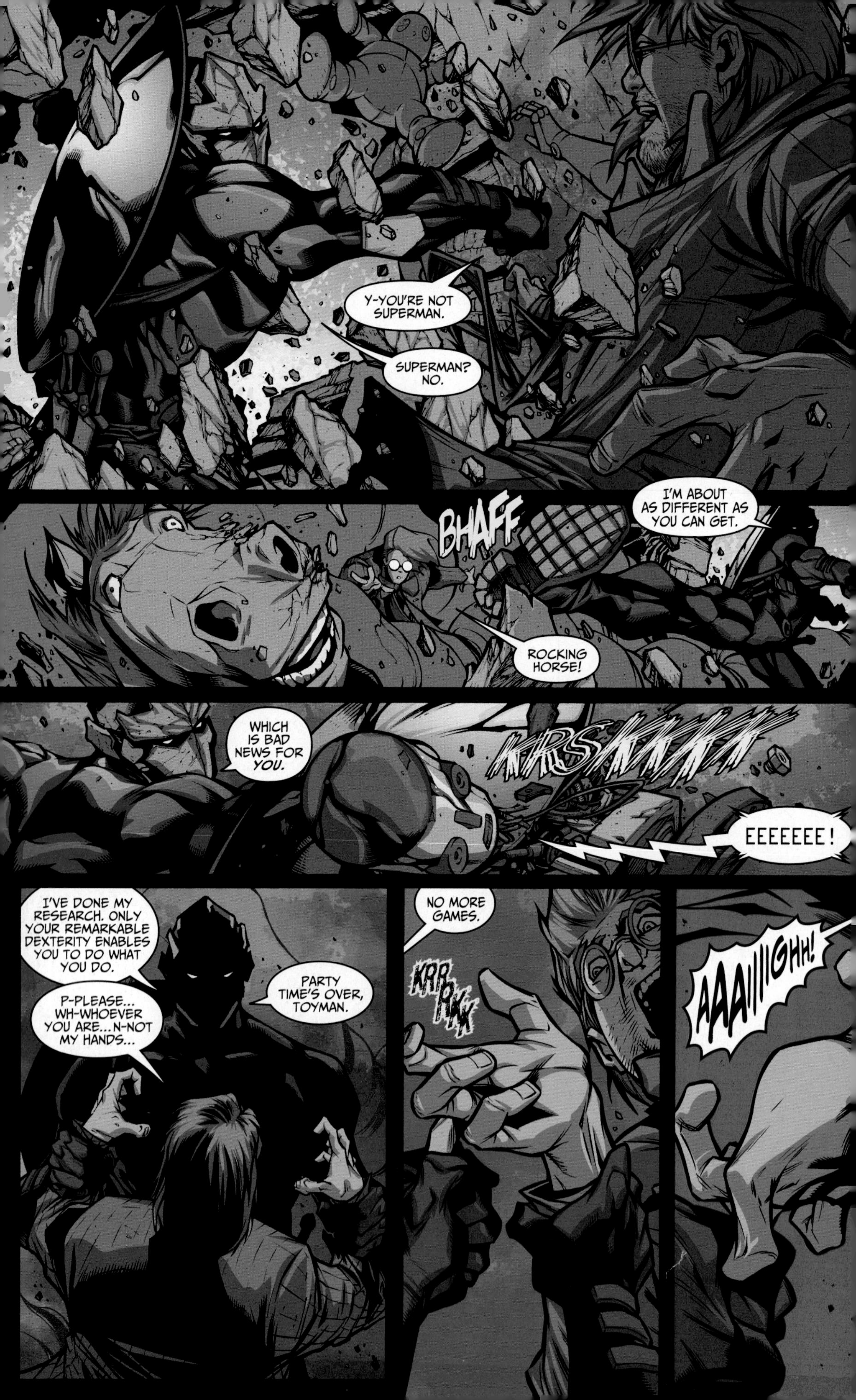
Y-YOU'RE NOT SUPERMAN.
SUPERMAN? NO.
I'M ABOUT AS DIFFERENT AS YOU CAN GET.
BHAFF
ROCKING HORSE!
WHICH IS BAD NEWS FOR YOU.
KRSKKKK
EEEEEEE!
I'VE DONE MY RESEARCH. ONLY YOUR REMARKABLE DEXTERITY ENABLES YOU TO DO WHAT YOU DO.
P-PLEASE... WH-WHOEVER YOU ARE...N-NOT MY HANDS...
PARTY TIME'S OVER, TOYMAN.
NO MORE GAMES.
KRRRKK
AAAIIIIGHH!

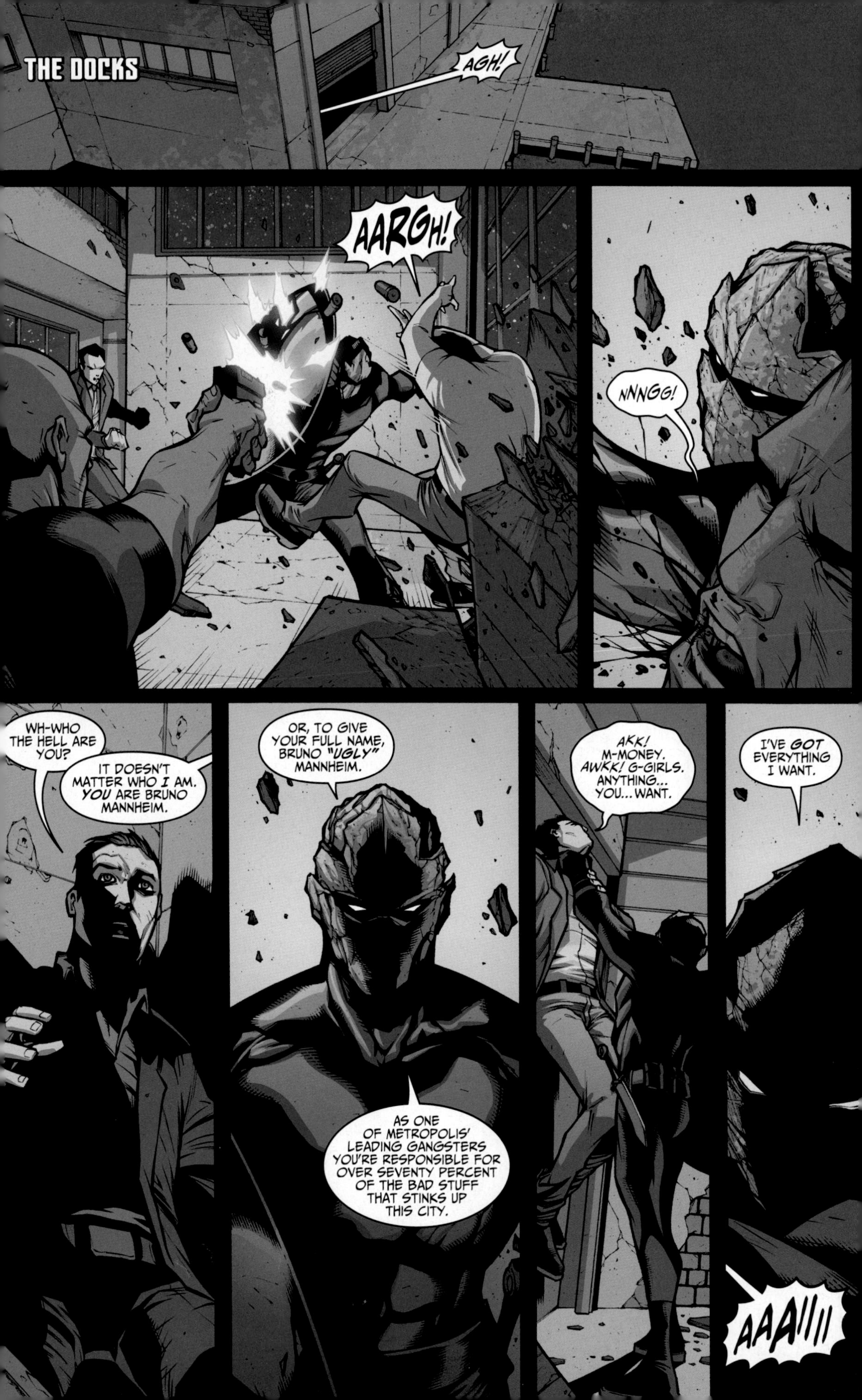
THE DOCKS
AGH!
AARGH!
NNNGG!
WH-WHO THE HELL ARE YOU?
IT DOESN'T MATTER WHO I AM. YOU ARE BRUNO MANNHEIM.
OR, TO GIVE YOUR FULL NAME, BRUNO "UGLY" MANNHEIM.
AS ONE OF METROPOLIS' LEADING GANGSTERS YOU'RE RESPONSIBLE FOR OVER SEVENTY PERCENT OF THE BAD STUFF THAT STINKS UP THIS CITY.
AKK! M-MONEY. AWKK! G-GIRLS. ANYTHING... YOU... WANT.
I'VE GOT EVERYTHING I WANT.
AAA!!!!!

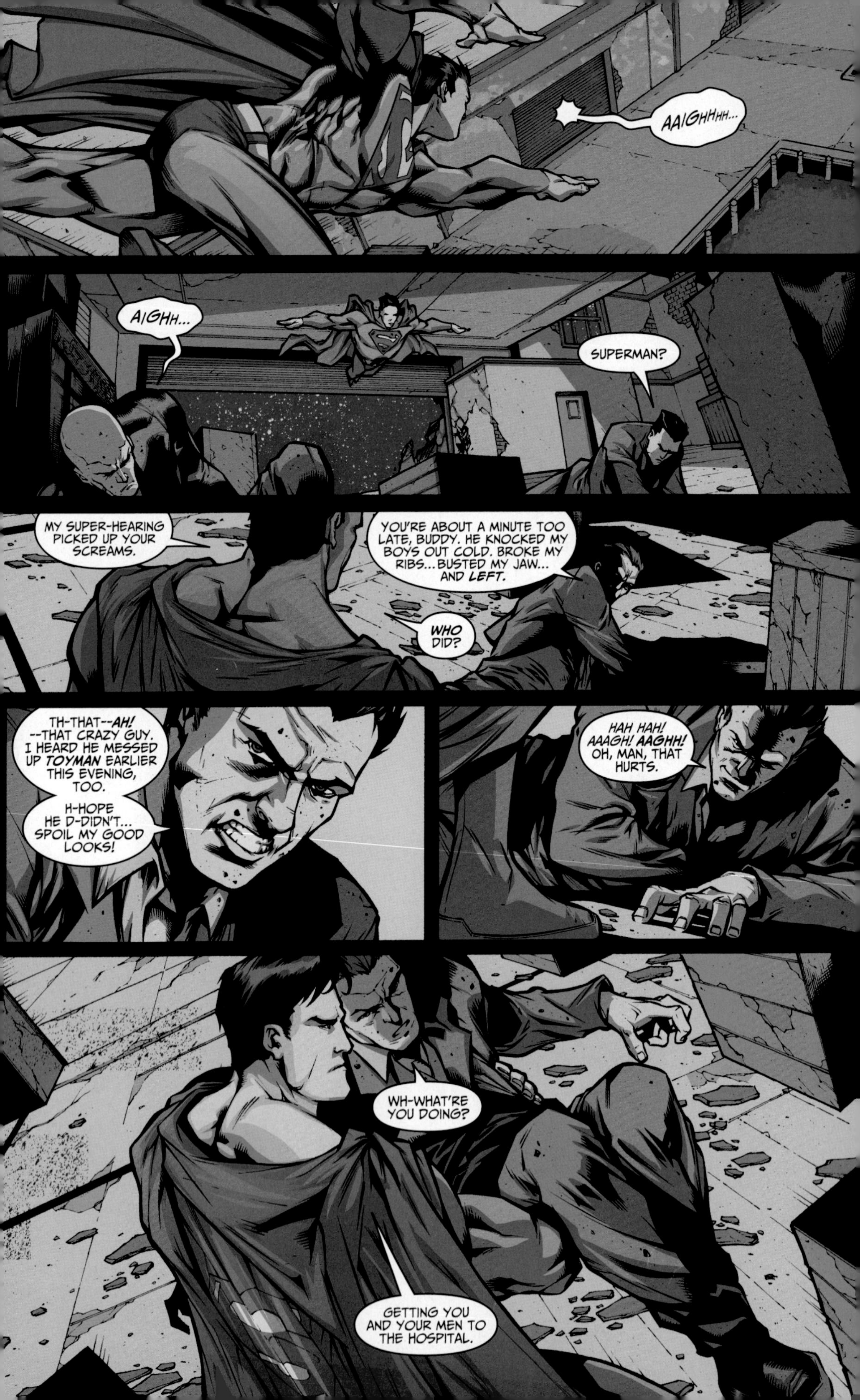
AAIGHHHH...
AIGHH...
SUPERMAN?
MY SUPER-HEARING PICKED UP YOUR SCREAMS.
YOU'RE ABOUT A MINUTE TOO LATE, BUDDY. HE KNOCKED MY BOYS OUT COLD. BROKE MY RIBS...BUSTED MY JAW... AND LEFT.
WHO DID?
TH-THAT--AH! --THAT CRAZY GUY. I HEARD HE MESSED UP TOYMAN EARLIER THIS EVENING, TOO.
H-HOPE HE D-DIDN'T... SPOIL MY GOOD LOOKS!
HAH HAH! AAAGH! AAGHH! OH, MAN, THAT HURTS.
WH-WHAT'RE YOU DOING?
GETTING YOU AND YOUR MEN TO THE HOSPITAL.

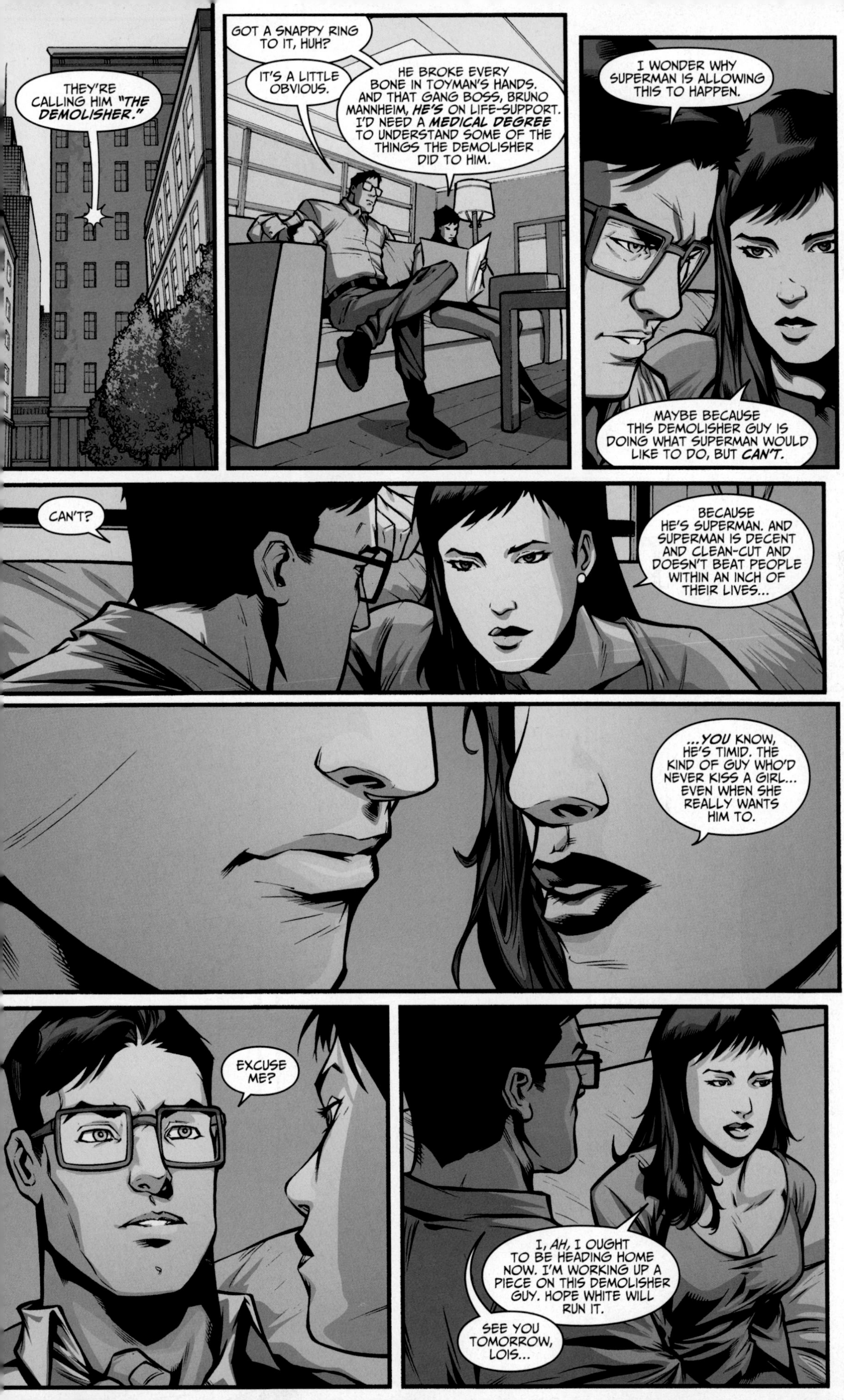
THEY'RE CALLING HIM "THE DEMOLISHER."
GOT A SNAPPY RING TO IT, HUH?
IT'S A LITTLE OBVIOUS.
HE BROKE EVERY BONE IN TOYMAN'S HANDS. AND THAT GANG BOSS, BRUNO MANNHEIM, HE'S ON LIFE-SUPPORT. I'D NEED A MEDICAL DEGREE TO UNDERSTAND SOME OF THE THINGS THE DEMOLISHER DID TO HIM.
I WONDER WHY SUPERMAN IS ALLOWING THIS TO HAPPEN.
MAYBE BECAUSE THIS DEMOLISHER GUY IS DOING WHAT SUPERMAN WOULD LIKE TO DO, BUT CAN'T.
CAN'T?
BECAUSE HE'S SUPERMAN. AND SUPERMAN IS DECENT AND CLEAN-CUT AND DOESN'T BEAT PEOPLE WITHIN AN INCH OF THEIR LIVES...
...YOU KNOW, HE'S TIMID. THE KIND OF GUY WHO'D NEVER KISS A GIRL... EVEN WHEN SHE REALLY WANTS HIM TO.
EXCUSE ME?
I, AH, I OUGHT TO BE HEADING HOME NOW. I'M WORKING UP A PIECE ON THIS DEMOLISHER GUY. HOPE WHITE WILL RUN IT.
SEE YOU TOMORROW, LOIS...

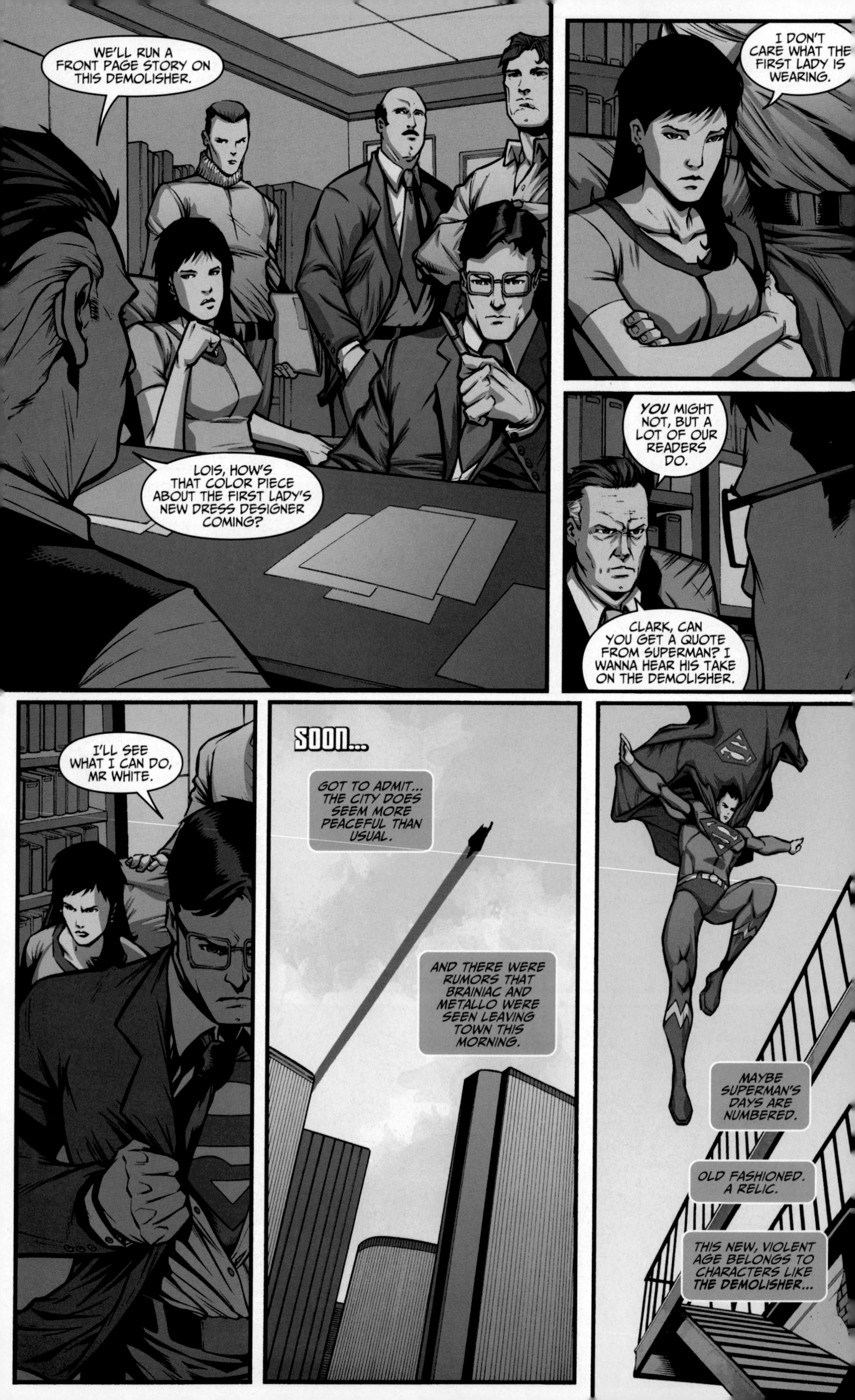
WE'LL RUN A FRONT PAGE STORY ON THIS DEMOLISHER.
LOIS, HOW'S THAT COLOR PIECE ABOUT THE FIRST LADY'S NEW DRESS DESIGNER COMING?
I DON'T CARE WHAT THE FIRST LADY IS WEARING.
YOU MIGHT NOT, BUT A LOT OF OUR READERS DO.
CLARK, CAN YOU GET A QUOTE FROM SUPERMAN? I WANNA HEAR HIS TAKE ON THE DEMOLISHER.
I'LL SEE WHAT I CAN DO, MR WHITE.
SOON...
GOT TO ADMIT... THE CITY DOES SEEM MORE PEACEFUL THAN USUAL.
AND THERE WERE RUMORS THAT BRAINIAC AND METALLO WERE SEEN LEAVING TOWN THIS MORNING.
MAYBE SUPERMAN'S DAYS ARE NUMBERED.
OLD FASHIONED. A RELIC.
THIS NEW, VIOLENT AGE BELONGS TO CHARACTERS LIKE THE DEMOLISHER...

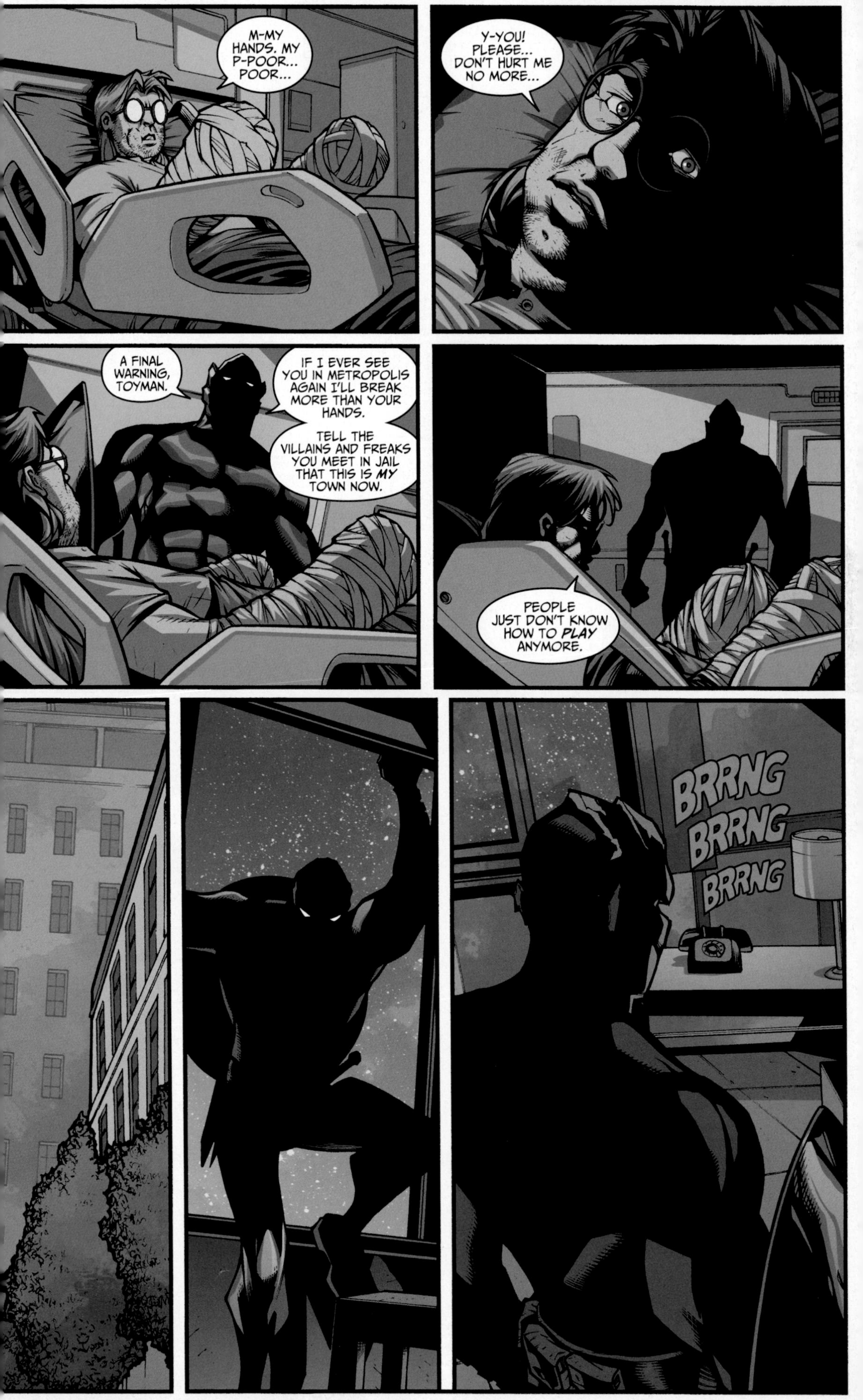
M-MY HANDS. MY P-POOR... POOR...
Y-YOU! PLEASE... DON'T HURT ME NO MORE...
A FINAL WARNING, TOYMAN.
IF I EVER SEE YOU IN METROPOLIS AGAIN I'LL BREAK MORE THAN YOUR HANDS.
TELL THE VILLAINS AND FREAKS YOU MEET IN JAIL THAT THIS IS MY TOWN NOW.
PEOPLE JUST DON'T KNOW HOW TO PLAY ANYMORE.
BRRNG
BRRNG
BRRNG

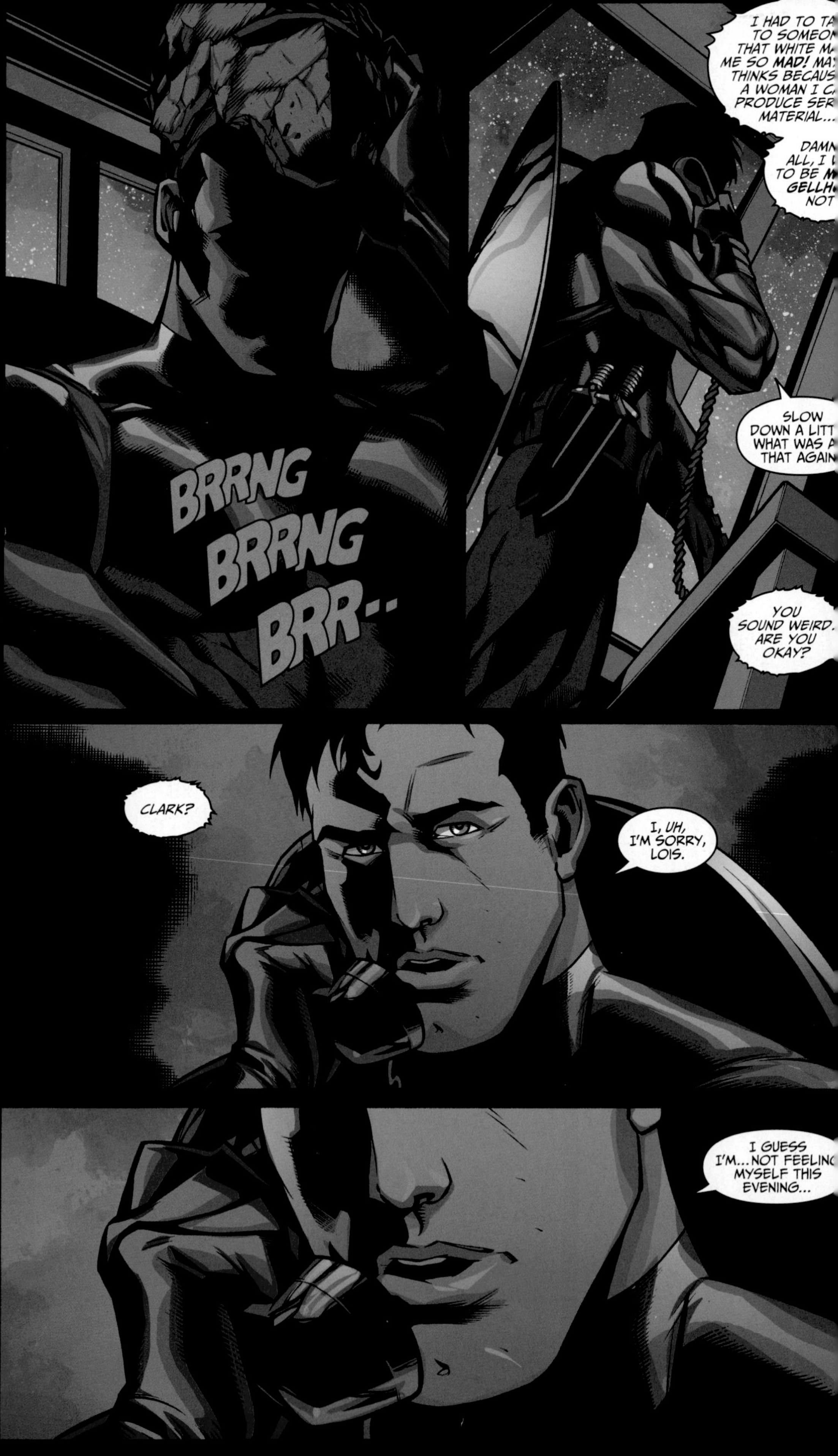
I HAD TO TA TO SOMEON THAT WHITE MA ME SO MAD! MA THINKS BECAUS A WOMAN I CA PRODUCE SER MATERIAL...
DAMN ALL, I TO BE M GELLH NOT
BRRNG BRRNG BRR...
SLOW DOWN A LITT WHAT WAS THAT AGAIN
YOU SOUND WEIRD. ARE YOU OKAY?
CLARK?
I, UH, I'M SORRY, LOIS.
I GUESS I'M...NOT FEELIN MYSELF THIS EVENING...

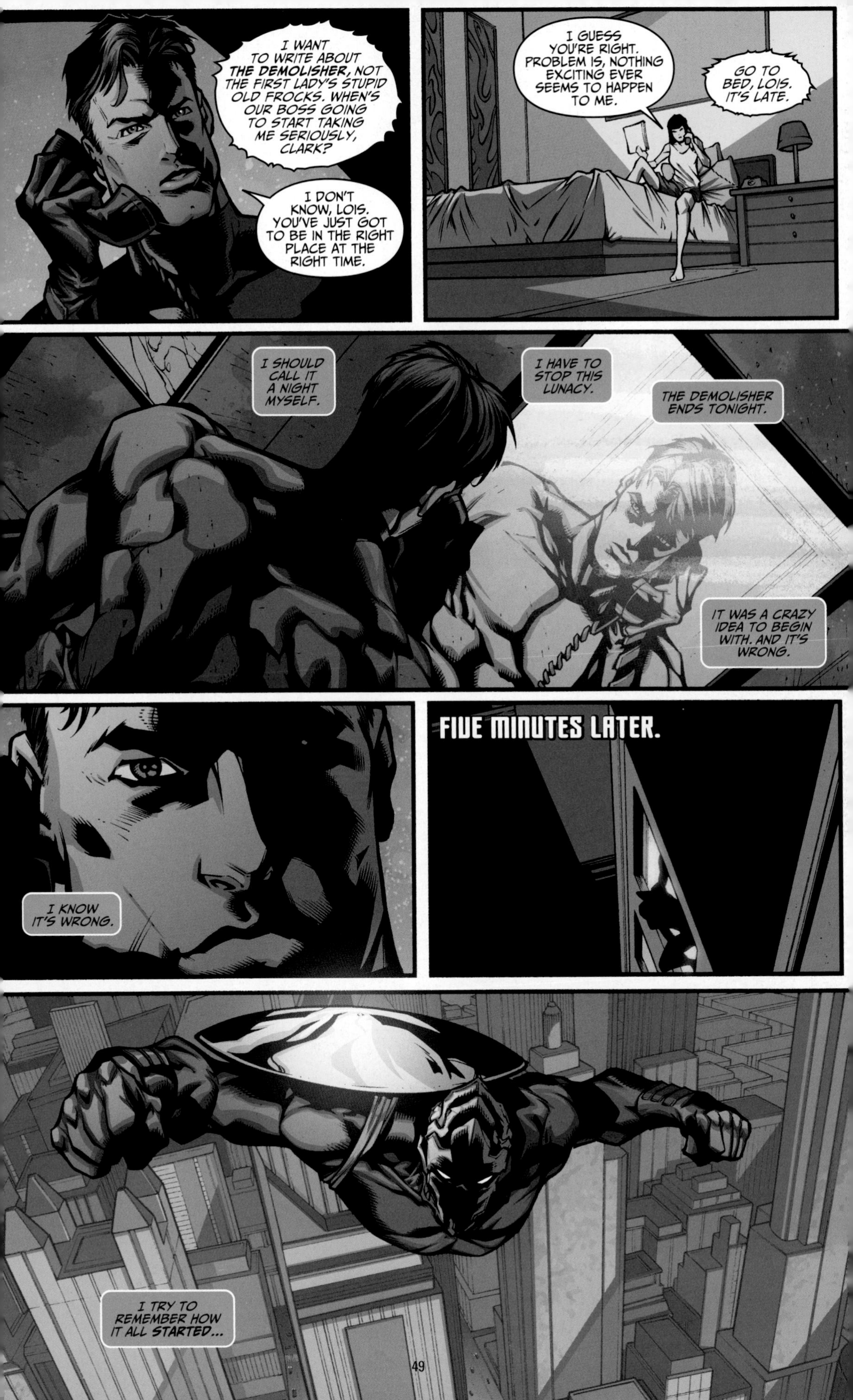
I WANT TO WRITE ABOUT THE DEMOLISHER, NOT THE FIRST LADY'S STUPID OLD FROCKS. WHEN'S OUR BOSS GOING TO START TAKING ME SERIOUSLY, CLARK?
I DON'T KNOW, LOIS. YOU'VE JUST GOT TO BE IN THE RIGHT PLACE AT THE RIGHT TIME.
I GUESS YOU'RE RIGHT. PROBLEM IS, NOTHING EXCITING EVER SEEMS TO HAPPEN TO ME.
GO TO BED, LOIS. IT'S LATE.
I SHOULD CALL IT A NIGHT MYSELF.
I HAVE TO STOP THIS LUNACY.
THE DEMOLISHER ENDS TONIGHT.
IT WAS A CRAZY IDEA TO BEGIN WITH. AND IT'S WRONG.
I KNOW IT'S WRONG.
FIVE MINUTES LATER.
I TRY TO REMEMBER HOW IT ALL STARTED...

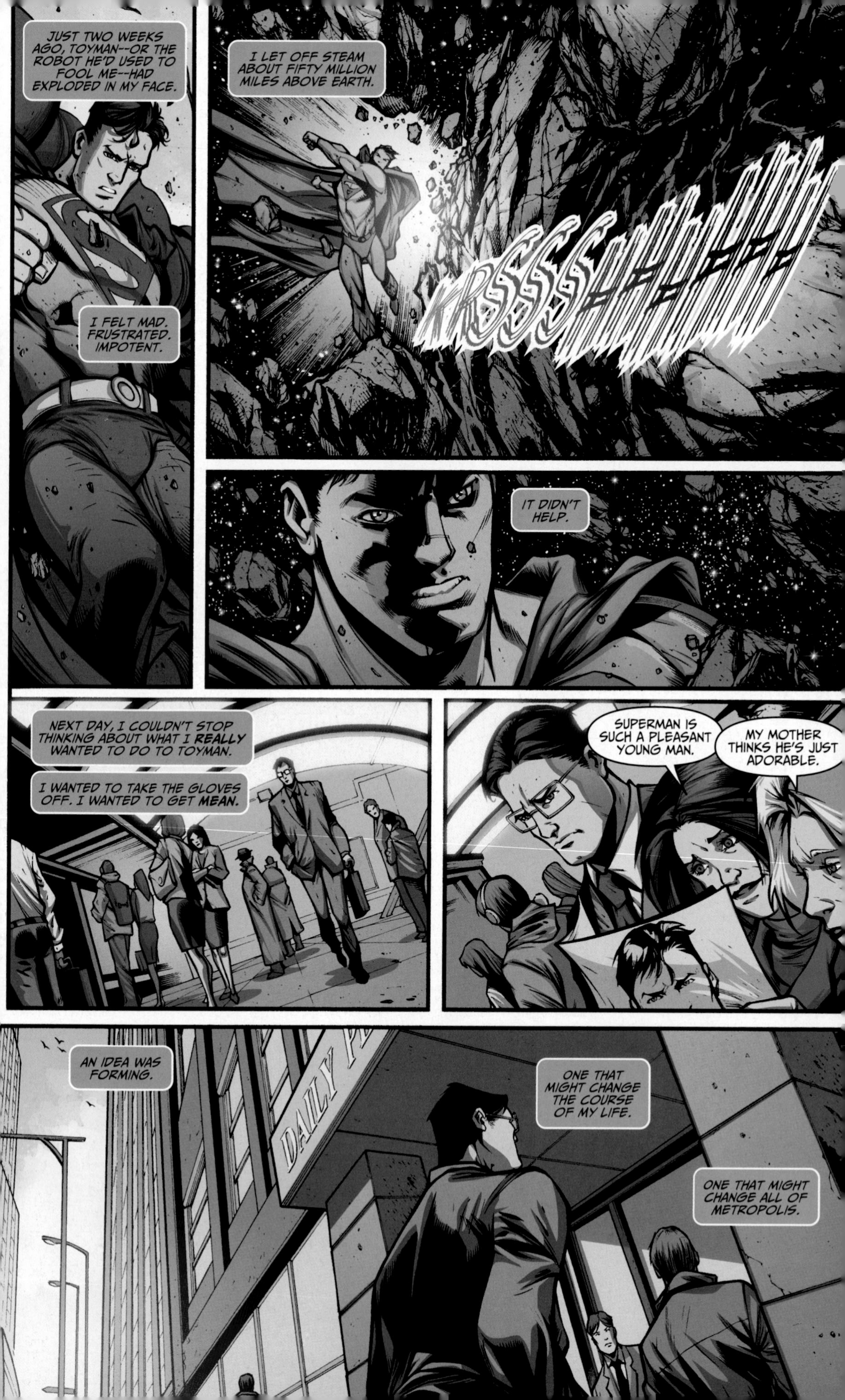
JUST TWO WEEKS AGO, TOYMAN--OR THE ROBOT HE'D USED TO FOOL ME--HAD EXPLODED IN MY FACE.
I FELT MAD. FRUSTRATED. IMPOTENT.
I LET OFF STEAM ABOUT FIFTY MILLION MILES ABOVE EARTH.
KRSSSSHHHHH-H-H
IT DIDN'T HELP.
NEXT DAY, I COULDN'T STOP THINKING ABOUT WHAT I **REALLY** WANTED TO DO TO TOYMAN.
I WANTED TO TAKE THE GLOVES OFF. I WANTED TO GET **MEAN**.
SUPERMAN IS SUCH A PLEASANT YOUNG MAN.
MY MOTHER THINKS HE'S JUST ADORABLE.
AN IDEA WAS FORMING.
ONE THAT MIGHT CHANGE THE COURSE OF MY LIFE.
ONE THAT MIGHT CHANGE ALL OF METROPOLIS.

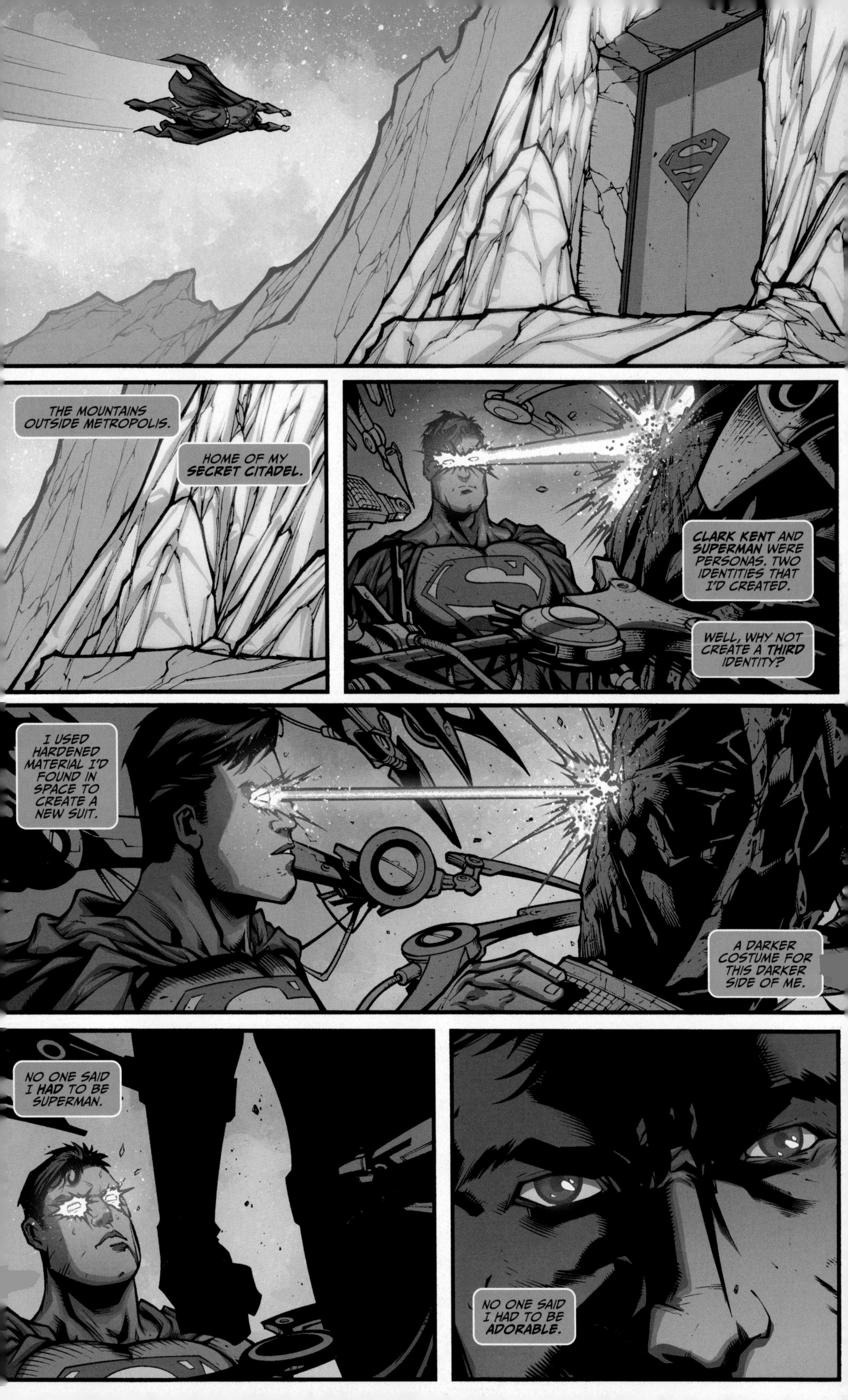
THE MOUNTAINS OUTSIDE METROPOLIS.
HOME OF MY SECRET CITADEL.
CLARK KENT AND SUPERMAN WERE PERSONAS. TWO IDENTITIES THAT I'D CREATED.
WELL, WHY NOT CREATE A THIRD IDENTITY?
I USED HARDENED MATERIAL I'D FOUND IN SPACE TO CREATE A NEW SUIT.
A DARKER COSTUME FOR THIS DARKER SIDE OF ME.
NO ONE SAID I HAD TO BE SUPERMAN.
NO ONE SAID I HAD TO BE ADORABLE.

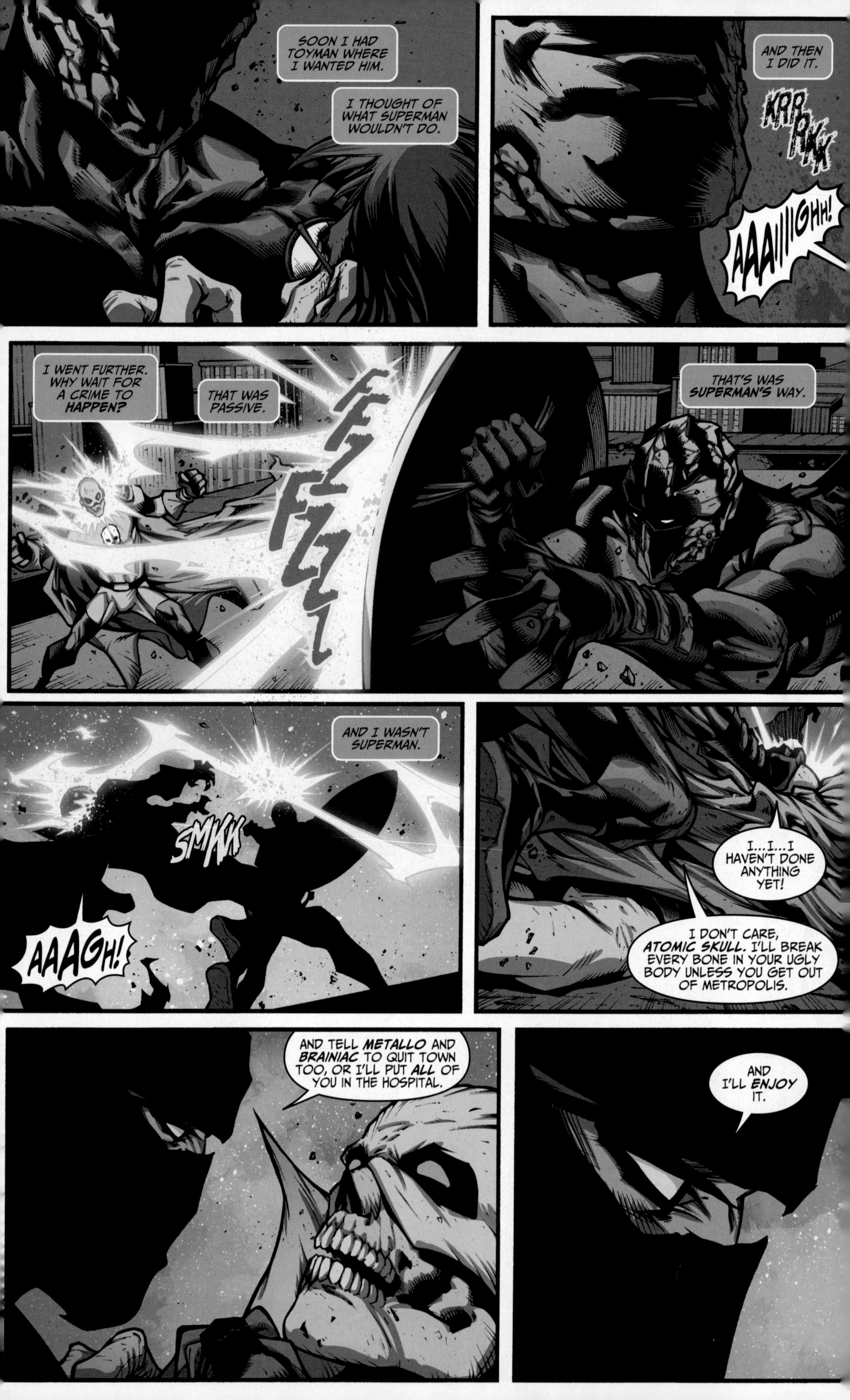
SOON I HAD TOYMAN WHERE I WANTED HIM.
I THOUGHT OF WHAT SUPERMAN WOULDN'T DO.
AND THEN I DID IT.
KRRRKK
AAAIIIIGHH!
I WENT FURTHER. WHY WAIT FOR A CRIME TO HAPPEN?
THAT WAS PASSIVE.
FFZZFZZZ
THAT'S WAS SUPERMAN'S WAY.
AND I WASN'T SUPERMAN.
SMKK
AAAGH!
I...I...I HAVEN'T DONE ANYTHING YET!
I DON'T CARE, ATOMIC SKULL. I'LL BREAK EVERY BONE IN YOUR UGLY BODY UNLESS YOU GET OUT OF METROPOLIS.
AND TELL METALLO AND BRAINIAC TO QUIT TOWN TOO, OR I'LL PUT ALL OF YOU IN THE HOSPITAL.
AND I'LL ENJOY IT.

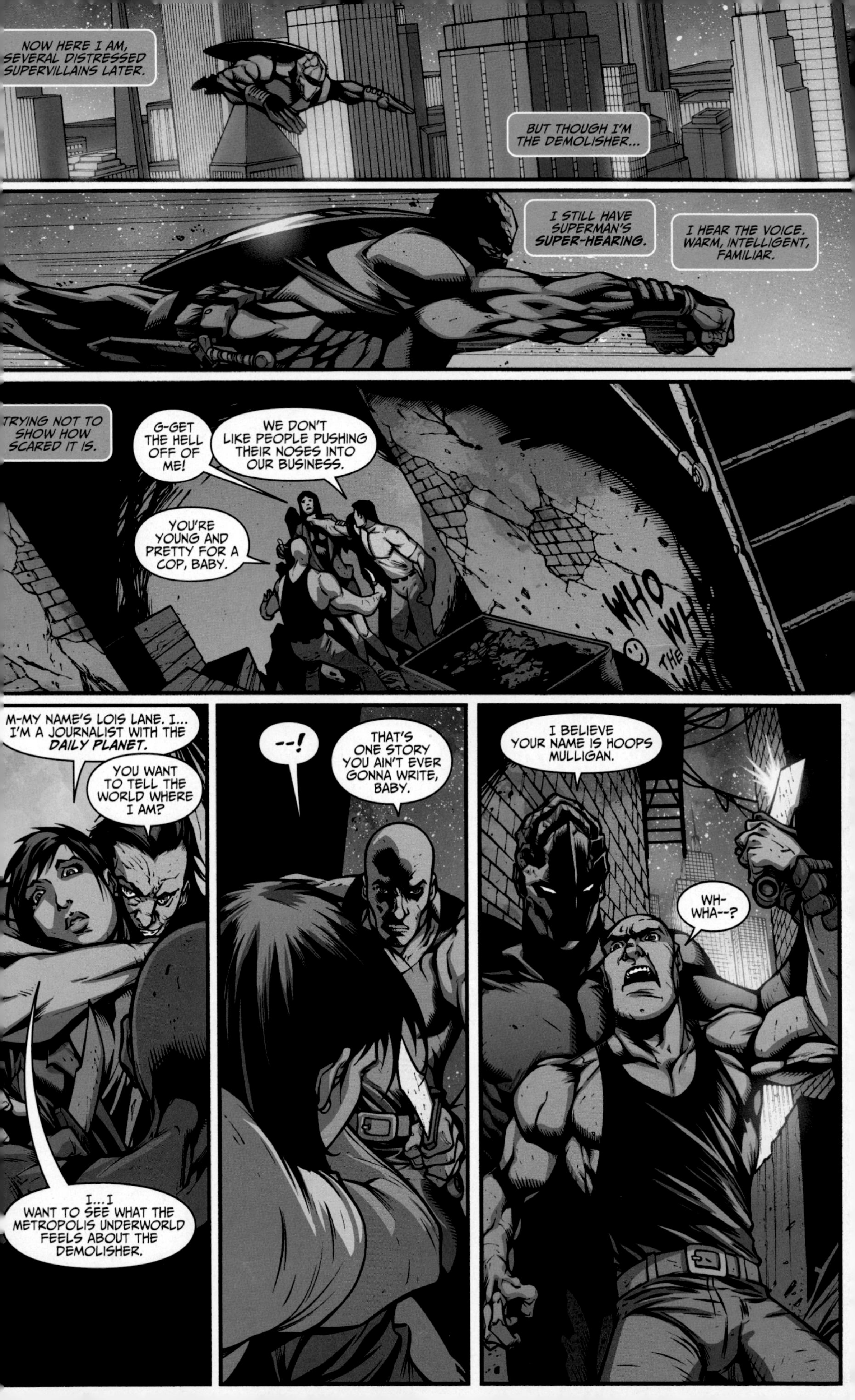
NOW HERE I AM, SEVERAL DISTRESSED SUPERVILLAINS LATER.
BUT THOUGH I'M THE DEMOLISHER...
I STILL HAVE SUPERMAN'S SUPER-HEARING.
I HEAR THE VOICE. WARM, INTELLIGENT, FAMILIAR.
TRYING NOT TO SHOW HOW SCARED IT IS.
G-GET THE HELL OFF OF ME!
WE DON'T LIKE PEOPLE PUSHING THEIR NOSES INTO OUR BUSINESS.
YOU'RE YOUNG AND PRETTY FOR A COP, BABY.
WHO
M-MY NAME'S LOIS LANE. I... I'M A JOURNALIST WITH THE DAILY PLANET.
YOU WANT TO TELL THE WORLD WHERE I AM?
I...I WANT TO SEE WHAT THE METROPOLIS UNDERWORLD FEELS ABOUT THE DEMOLISHER.
--!
THAT'S ONE STORY YOU AIN'T EVER GONNA WRITE, BABY.
I BELIEVE YOUR NAME IS HOOPS MULLIGAN.
WH- WHA--?

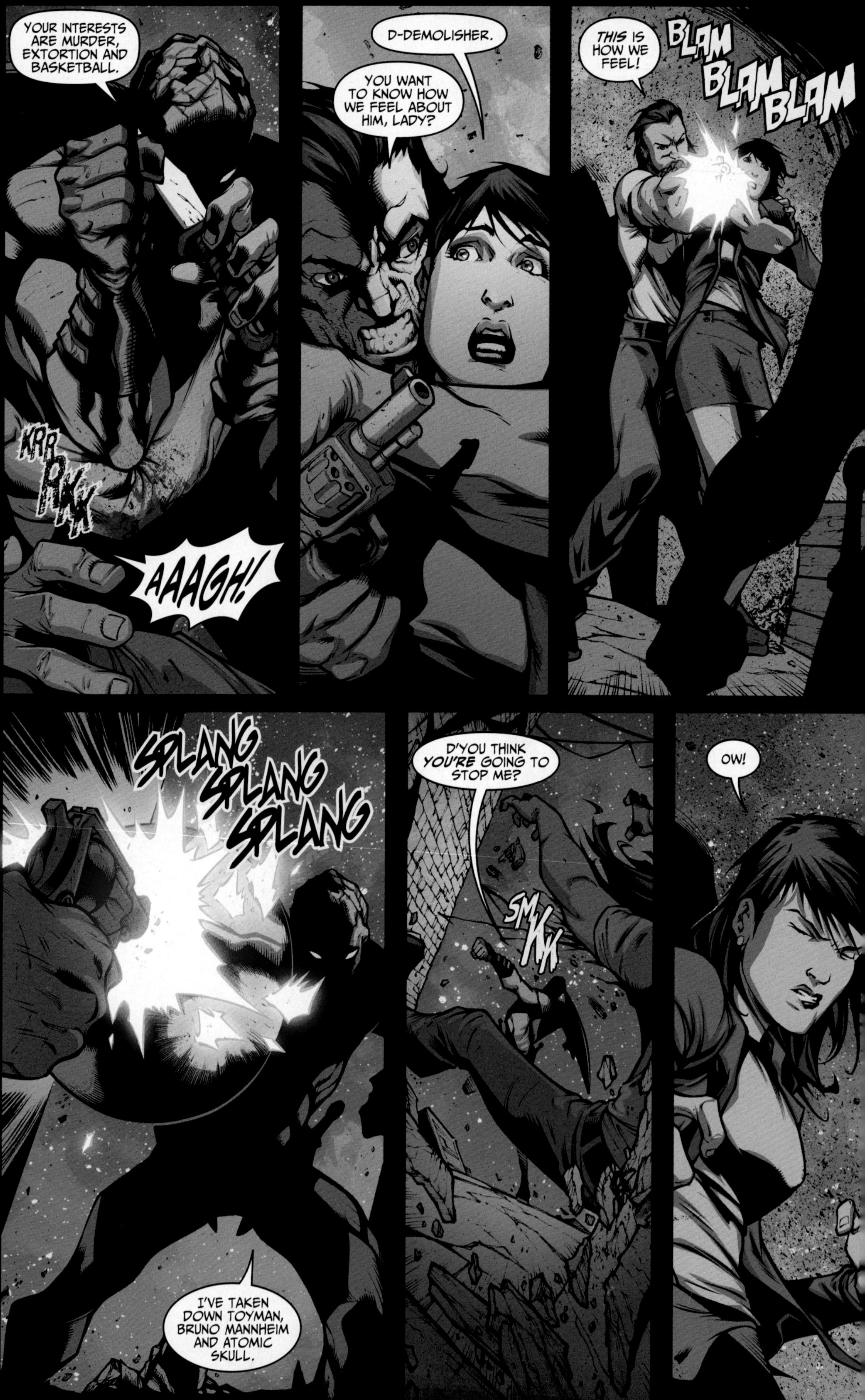
YOUR INTERESTS ARE MURDER, EXTORTION AND BASKETBALL.
KRRRKK
AAAGH!
D-DEMOLISHER.
YOU WANT TO KNOW HOW WE FEEL ABOUT HIM, LADY?
THIS IS HOW WE FEEL!
BLAM BLAM BLAM
SPLANG SPLANG SPLANG
I'VE TAKEN DOWN TOYMAN, BRUNO MANNHEIM AND ATOMIC SKULL.
D'YOU THINK YOU'RE GOING TO STOP ME?
SMKK
OW!

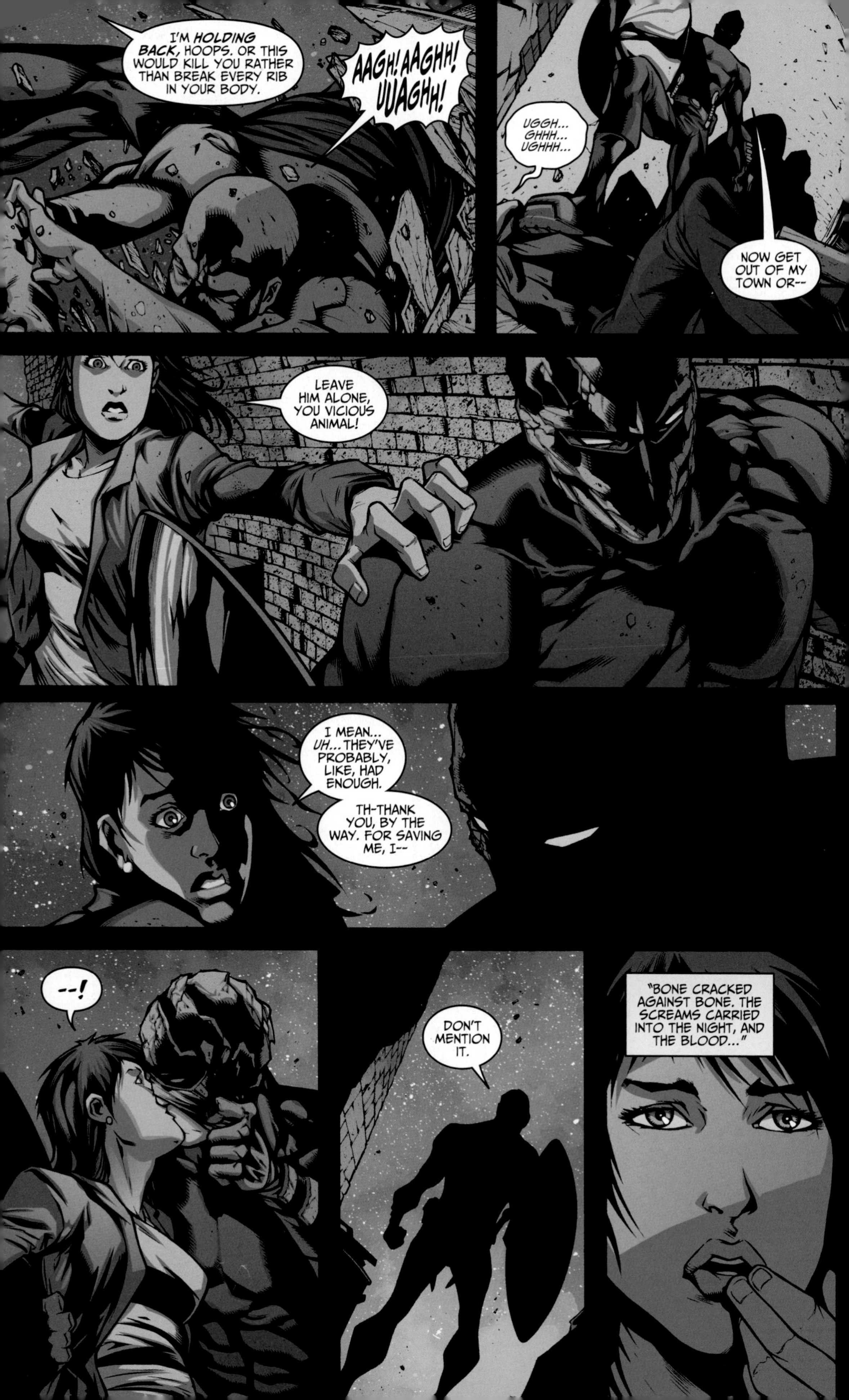
I'M **HOLDING BACK**, HOOPS. OR THIS WOULD KILL YOU RATHER THAN BREAK EVERY RIB IN YOUR BODY.
AAGH! AAGHH! UUAGHH!
UGGH... GHHH... UGHHH...
NOW GET OUT OF MY TOWN OR--
LEAVE HIM ALONE, YOU VICIOUS ANIMAL!
I MEAN... *UH*... THEY'VE PROBABLY, LIKE, HAD ENOUGH.
TH-THANK YOU, BY THE WAY. FOR SAVING ME, I--
--!
DON'T MENTION IT.
"BONE CRACKED AGAINST BONE. THE SCREAMS CARRIED INTO THE NIGHT, AND THE BLOOD..."

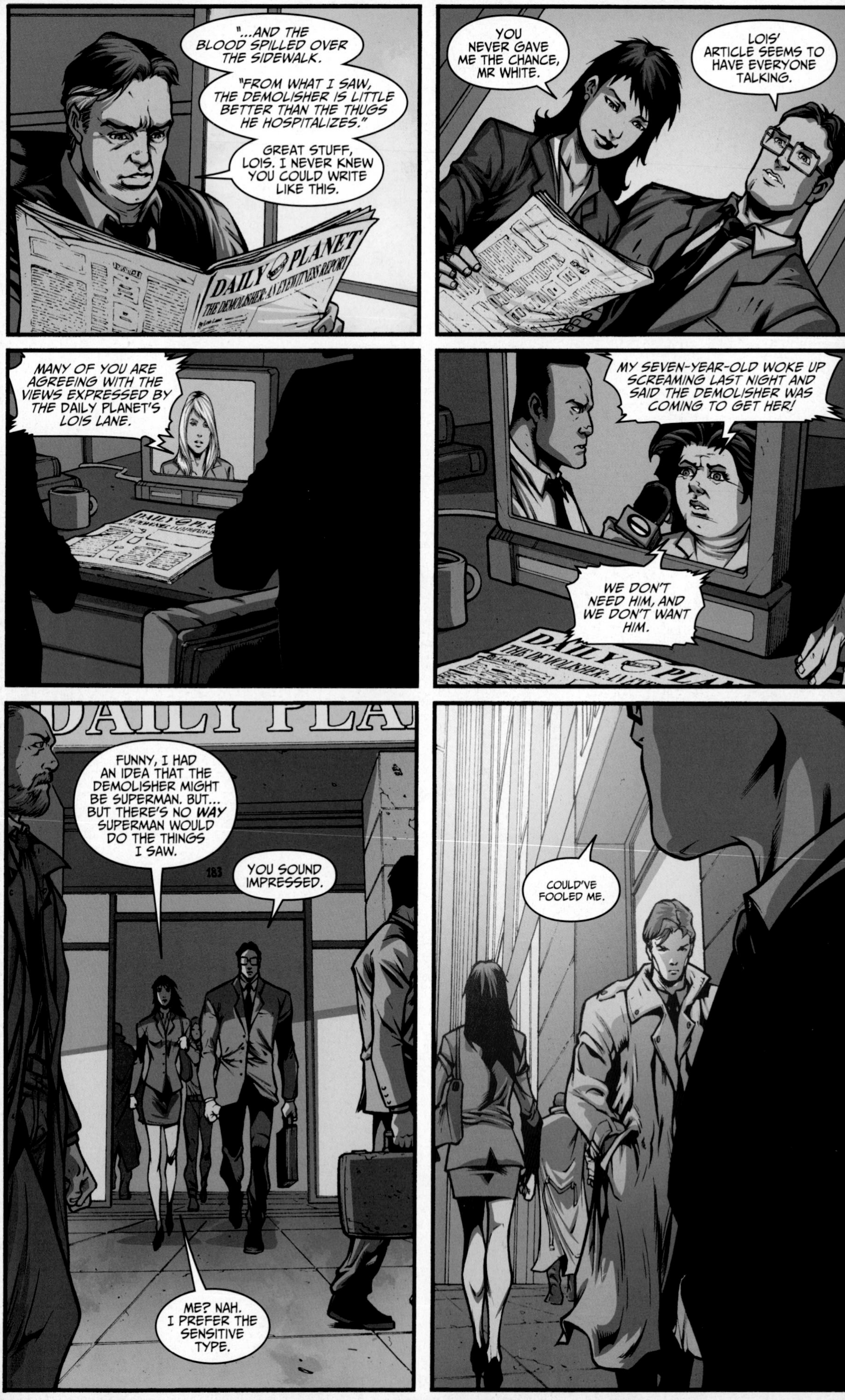
"...AND THE BLOOD SPILLED OVER THE SIDEWALK.
"FROM WHAT I SAW, THE DEMOLISHER IS LITTLE BETTER THAN THE THUGS HE HOSPITALIZES."
GREAT STUFF, LOIS. I NEVER KNEW YOU COULD WRITE LIKE THIS.
DAILY PLANET
THE DEMOLISHER: AN EYEWITNESS REPORT
YOU NEVER GAVE ME THE CHANCE, MR WHITE.
LOIS' ARTICLE SEEMS TO HAVE EVERYONE TALKING.
MANY OF YOU ARE AGREEING WITH THE VIEWS EXPRESSED BY THE DAILY PLANET'S LOIS LANE.
MY SEVEN-YEAR-OLD WOKE UP SCREAMING LAST NIGHT AND SAID THE DEMOLISHER WAS COMING TO GET HER!
WE DON'T NEED HIM, AND WE DON'T WANT HIM.
FUNNY, I HAD AN IDEA THAT THE DEMOLISHER MIGHT BE SUPERMAN. BUT... BUT THERE'S NO WAY SUPERMAN WOULD DO THE THINGS I SAW.
YOU SOUND IMPRESSED.
ME? NAH. I PREFER THE SENSITIVE TYPE.
COULD'VE FOOLED ME.

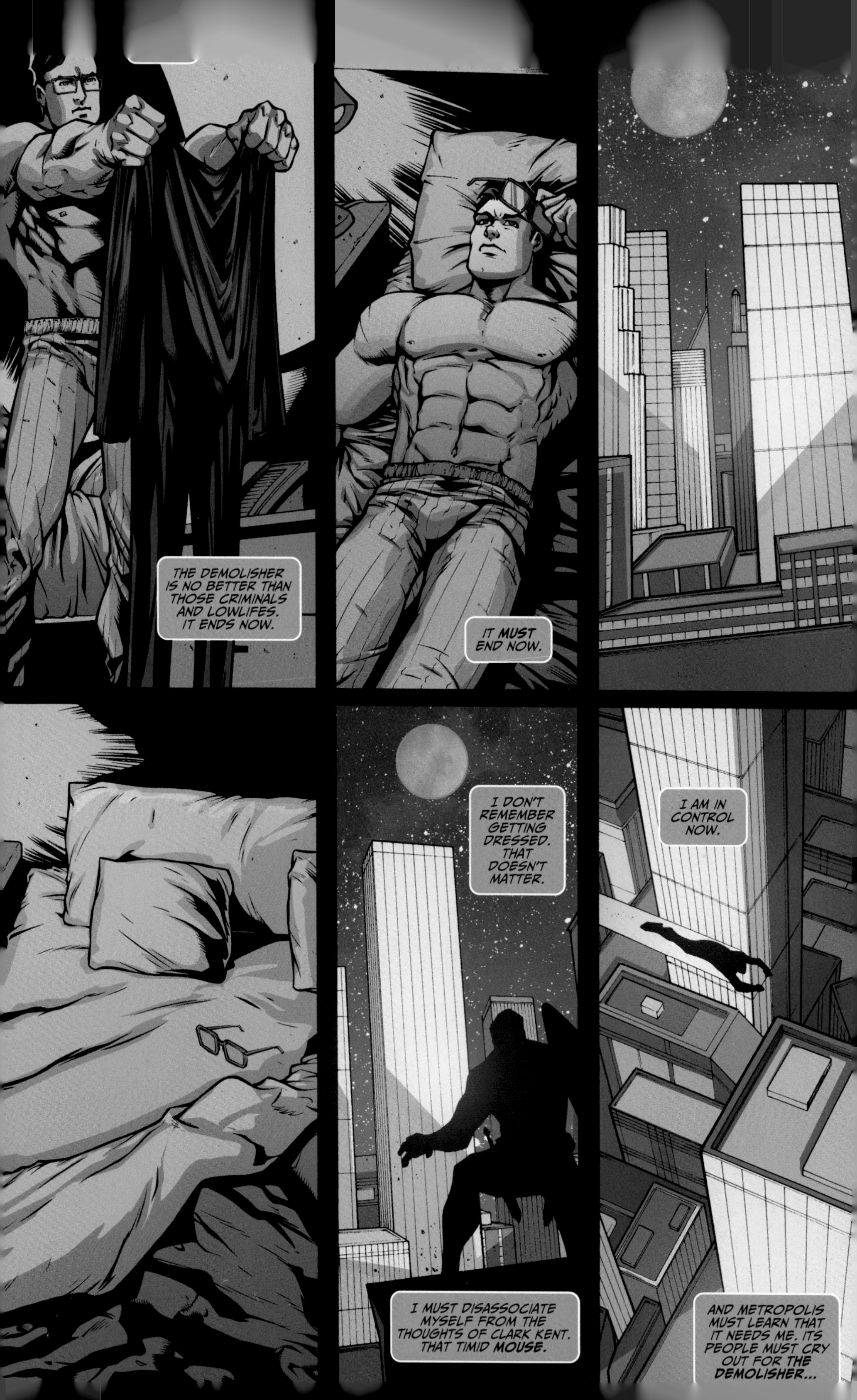
THE DEMOLISHER IS NO BETTER THAN THOSE CRIMINALS AND LOWLIFES. IT ENDS NOW.
IT MUST END NOW.
I DON'T REMEMBER GETTING DRESSED. THAT DOESN'T MATTER.
I MUST DISASSOCIATE MYSELF FROM THE THOUGHTS OF CLARK KENT. THAT TIMID MOUSE.
I AM IN CONTROL NOW.
AND METROPOLIS MUST LEARN THAT IT NEEDS ME. ITS PEOPLE MUST CRY OUT FOR THE DEMOLISHER...

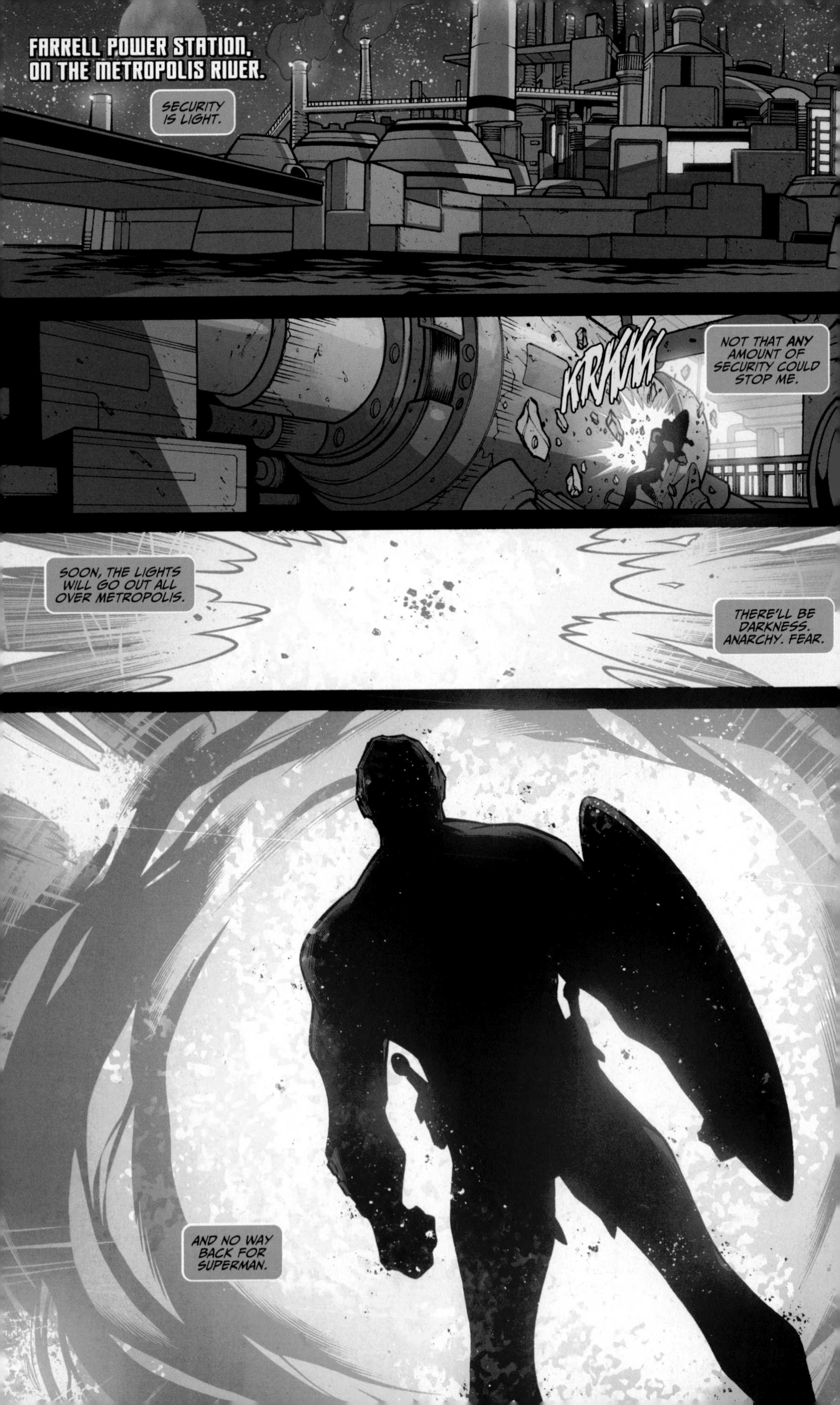
FARRELL POWER STATION. ON THE METROPOLIS RIVER.
SECURITY IS LIGHT.
KRKKK
NOT THAT ANY AMOUNT OF SECURITY COULD STOP ME.
SOON, THE LIGHTS WILL GO OUT ALL OVER METROPOLIS.
THERE'LL BE DARKNESS. ANARCHY. FEAR.
AND NO WAY BACK FOR SUPERMAN.

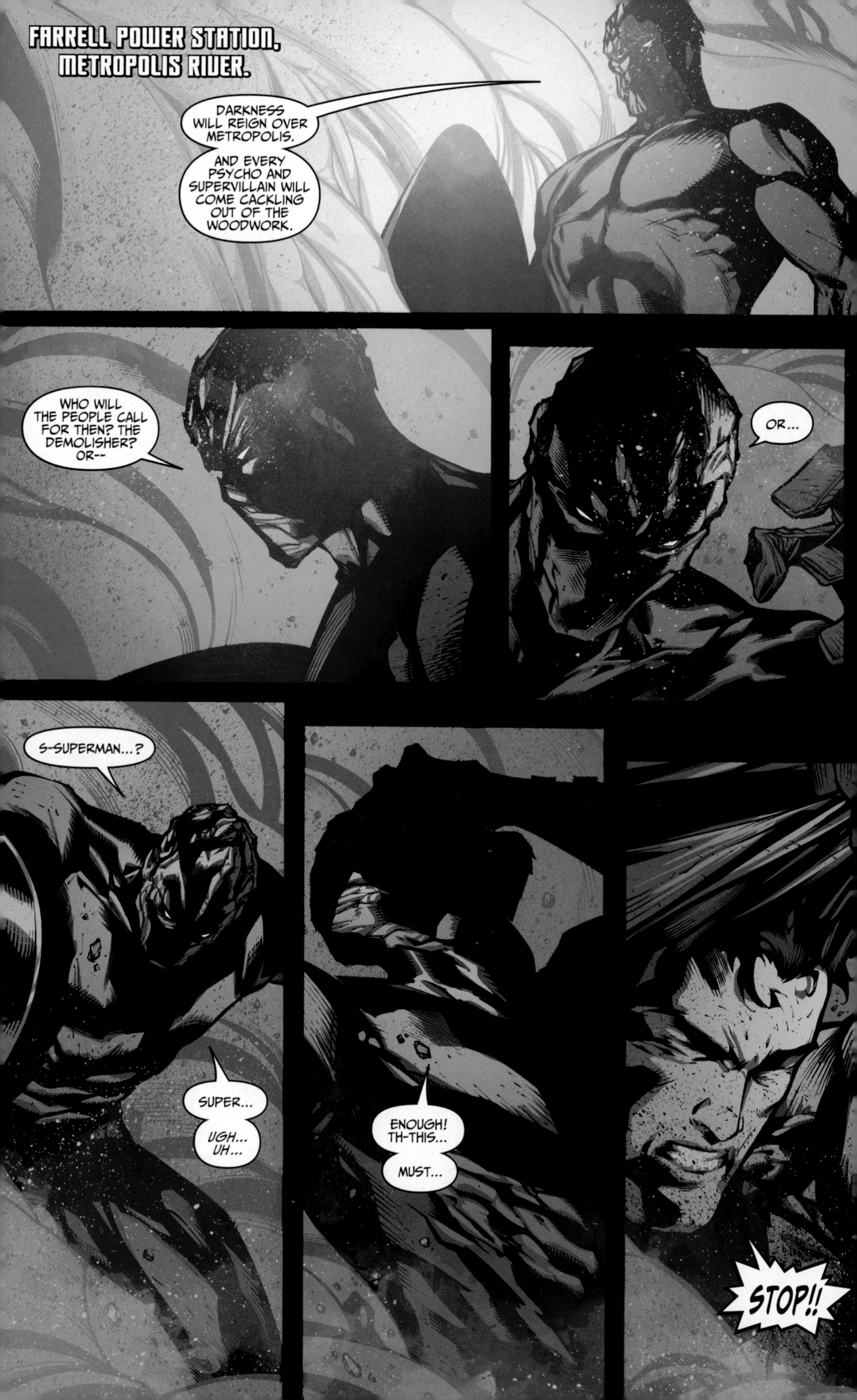
FARRELL POWER STATION, METROPOLIS RIVER.
DARKNESS WILL REIGN OVER METROPOLIS.
AND EVERY PSYCHO AND SUPERVILLAIN WILL COME CACKLING OUT OF THE WOODWORK.
WHO WILL THE PEOPLE CALL FOR THEN? THE DEMOLISHER? OR--
OR...
S-SUPERMAN...?
SUPER...
UGH... UH...
ENOUGH! TH-THIS...
MUST...
STOP!!

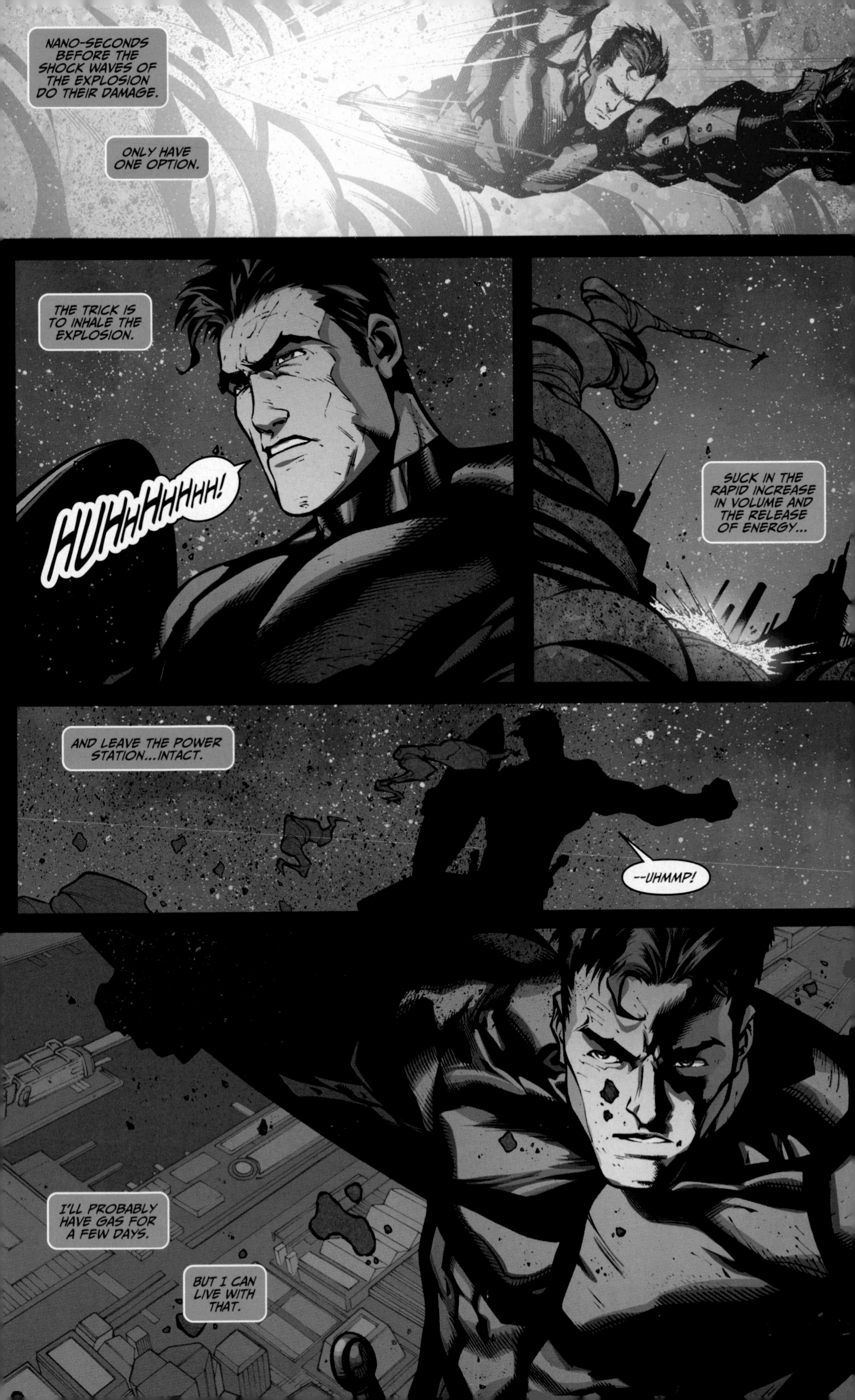
NANO-SECONDS BEFORE THE SHOCK WAVES OF THE EXPLOSION DO THEIR DAMAGE.
ONLY HAVE ONE OPTION.
THE TRICK IS TO INHALE THE EXPLOSION.
HUHHHHHHH!
SUCK IN THE RAPID INCREASE IN VOLUME AND THE RELEASE OF ENERGY...
AND LEAVE THE POWER STATION...INTACT.
--UHMMP!
I'LL PROBABLY HAVE GAS FOR A FEW DAYS.
BUT I CAN LIVE WITH THAT.

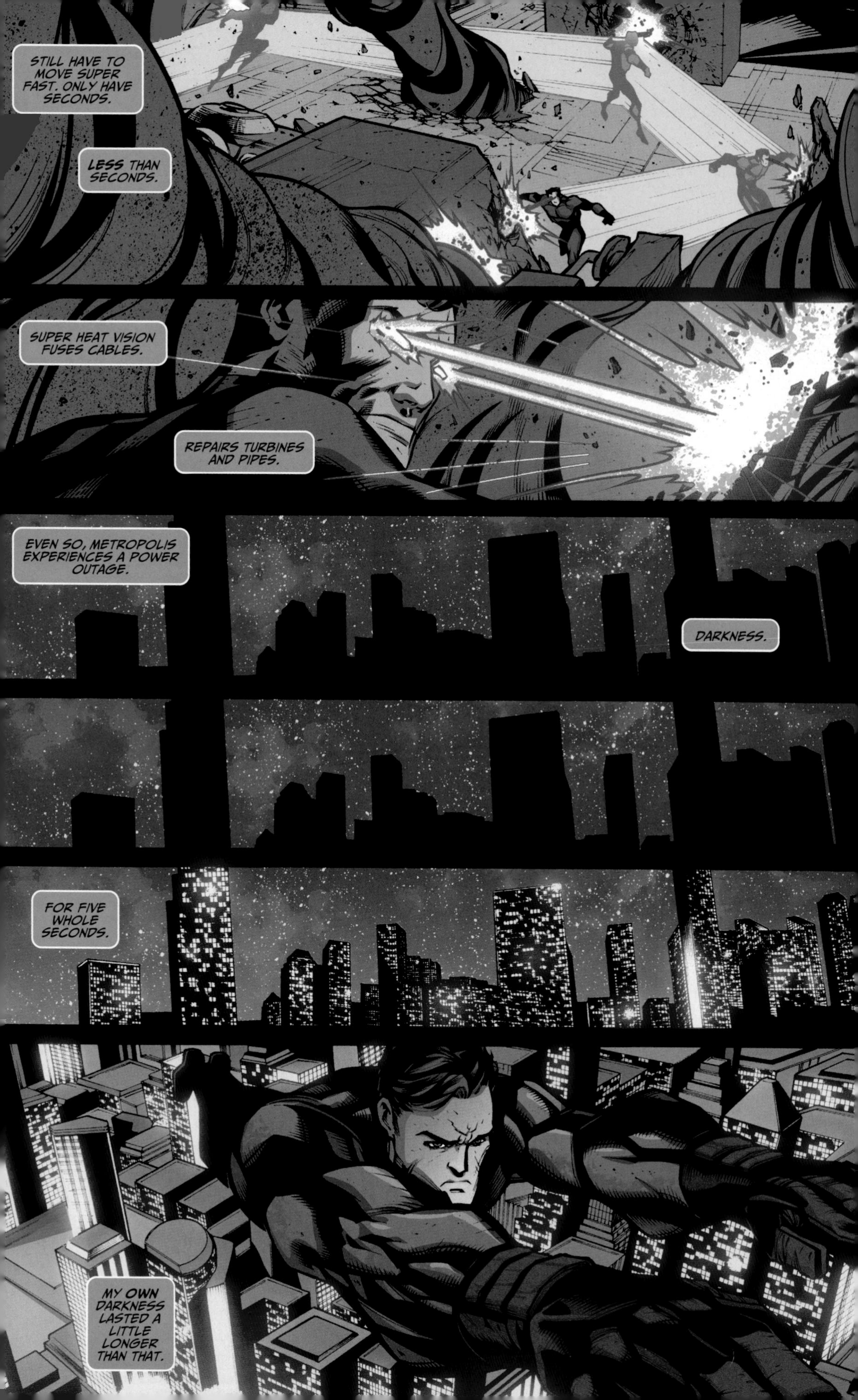
STILL HAVE TO MOVE SUPER FAST. ONLY HAVE SECONDS.
LESS THAN SECONDS.
SUPER HEAT VISION FUSES CABLES.
REPAIRS TURBINES AND PIPES.
EVEN SO, METROPOLIS EXPERIENCES A POWER OUTAGE.
DARKNESS.
FOR FIVE WHOLE SECONDS.
MY OWN DARKNESS LASTED A LITTLE LONGER THAN THAT.

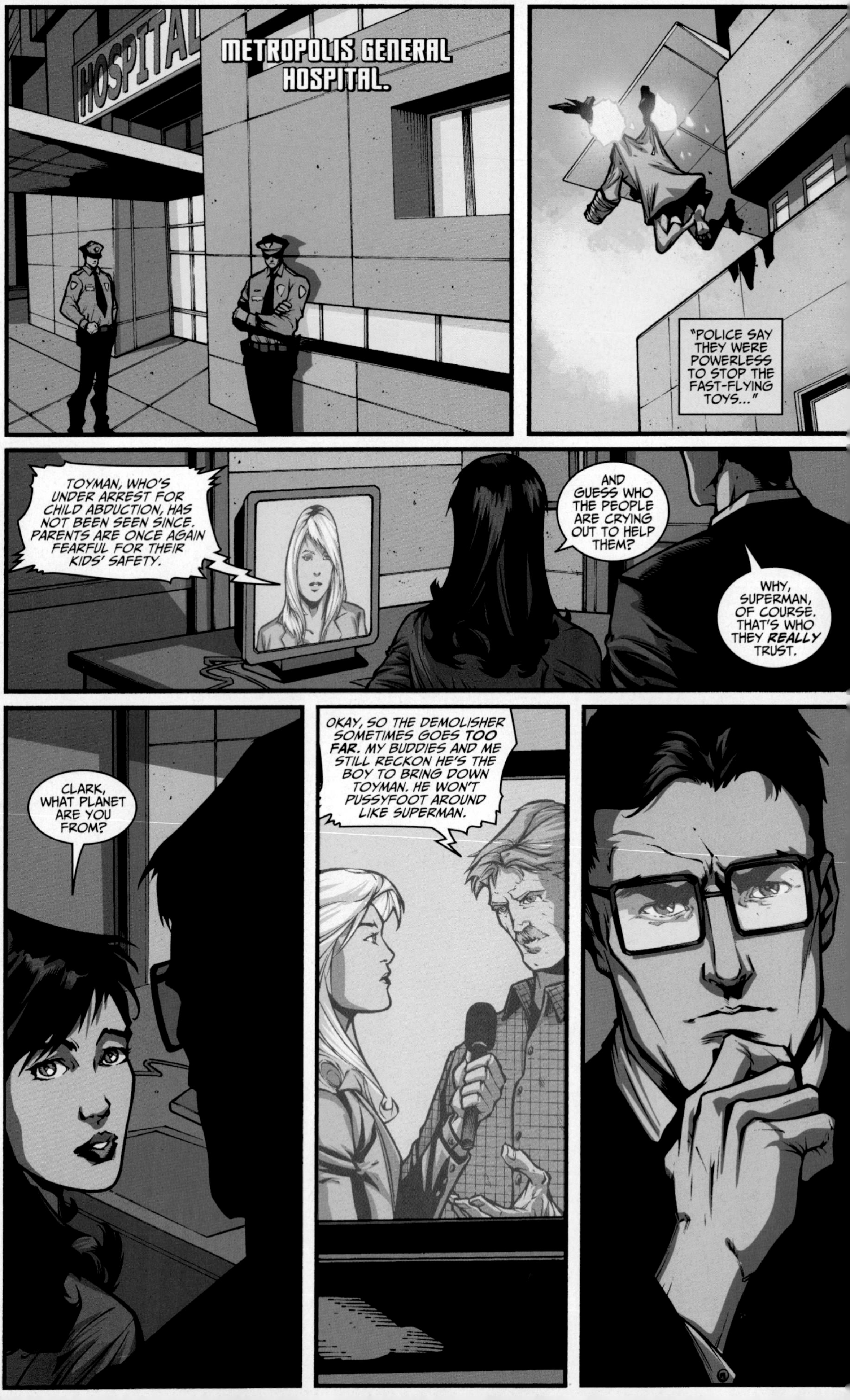
HOSPITAL
METROPOLIS GENERAL HOSPITAL.
"POLICE SAY THEY WERE POWERLESS TO STOP THE FAST-FLYING TOYS..."
TOYMAN, WHO'S UNDER ARREST FOR CHILD ABDUCTION, HAS NOT BEEN SEEN SINCE. PARENTS ARE ONCE AGAIN FEARFUL FOR THEIR KIDS' SAFETY.
AND GUESS WHO THE PEOPLE ARE CRYING OUT TO HELP THEM?
WHY, SUPERMAN, OF COURSE. THAT'S WHO THEY REALLY TRUST.
CLARK, WHAT PLANET ARE YOU FROM?
OKAY, SO THE DEMOLISHER SOMETIMES GOES TOO FAR. MY BUDDIES AND ME STILL RECKON HE'S THE BOY TO BRING DOWN TOYMAN. HE WON'T PUSSYFOOT AROUND LIKE SUPERMAN.

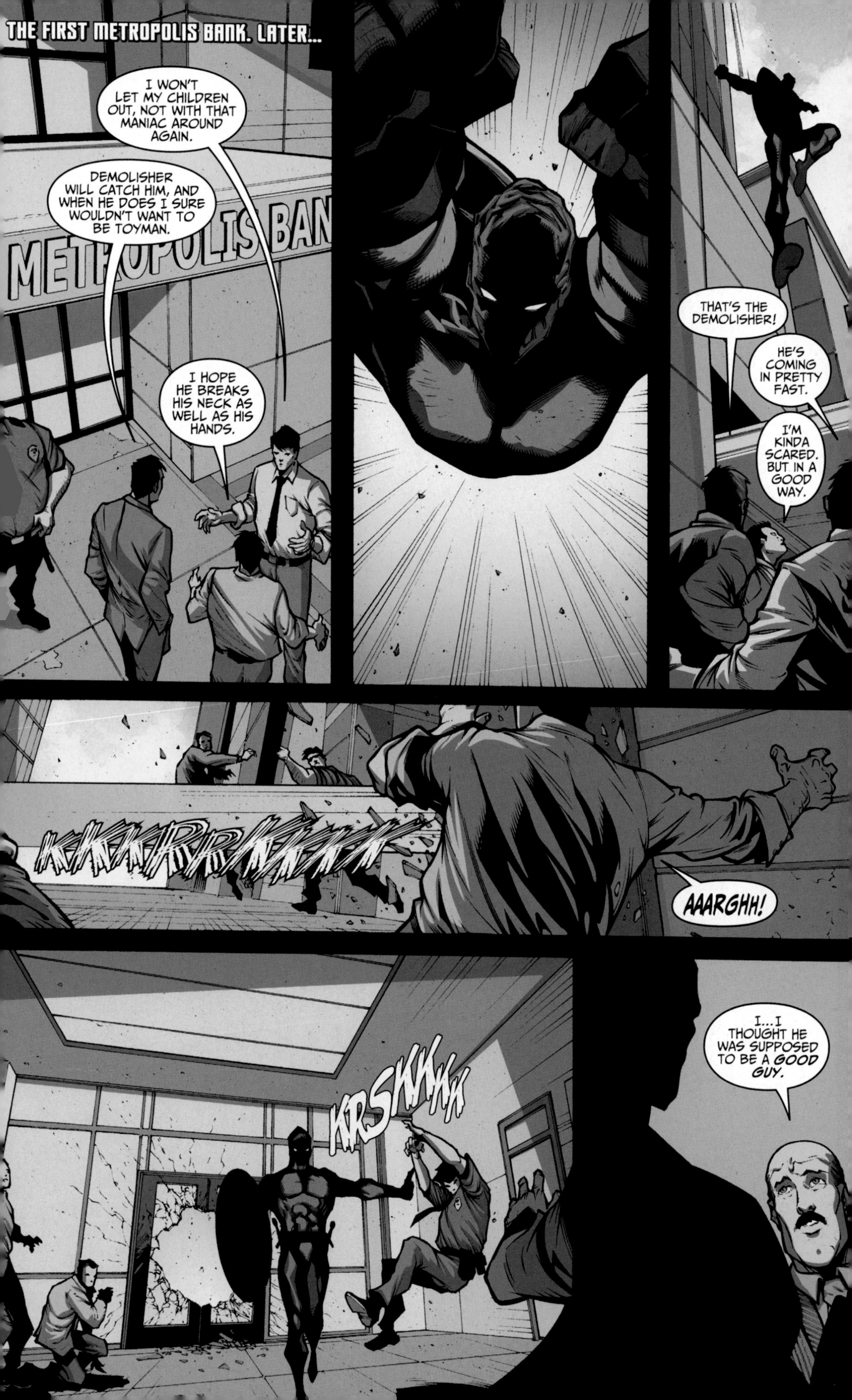
THE FIRST METROPOLIS BANK. LATER...
I WON'T LET MY CHILDREN OUT, NOT WITH THAT MANIAC AROUND AGAIN.
DEMOLISHER WILL CATCH HIM, AND WHEN HE DOES I SURE WOULDN'T WANT TO BE TOYMAN.
METROPOLIS BAN
I HOPE HE BREAKS HIS NECK AS WELL AS HIS HANDS.
THAT'S THE DEMOLISHER!
HE'S COMING IN PRETTY FAST.
I'M KINDA SCARED. BUT IN A GOOD WAY.
KKKRRKKKKK
AAARGHH!
KRSKKKK
I...I THOUGHT HE WAS SUPPOSED TO BE A *GOOD GUY*.

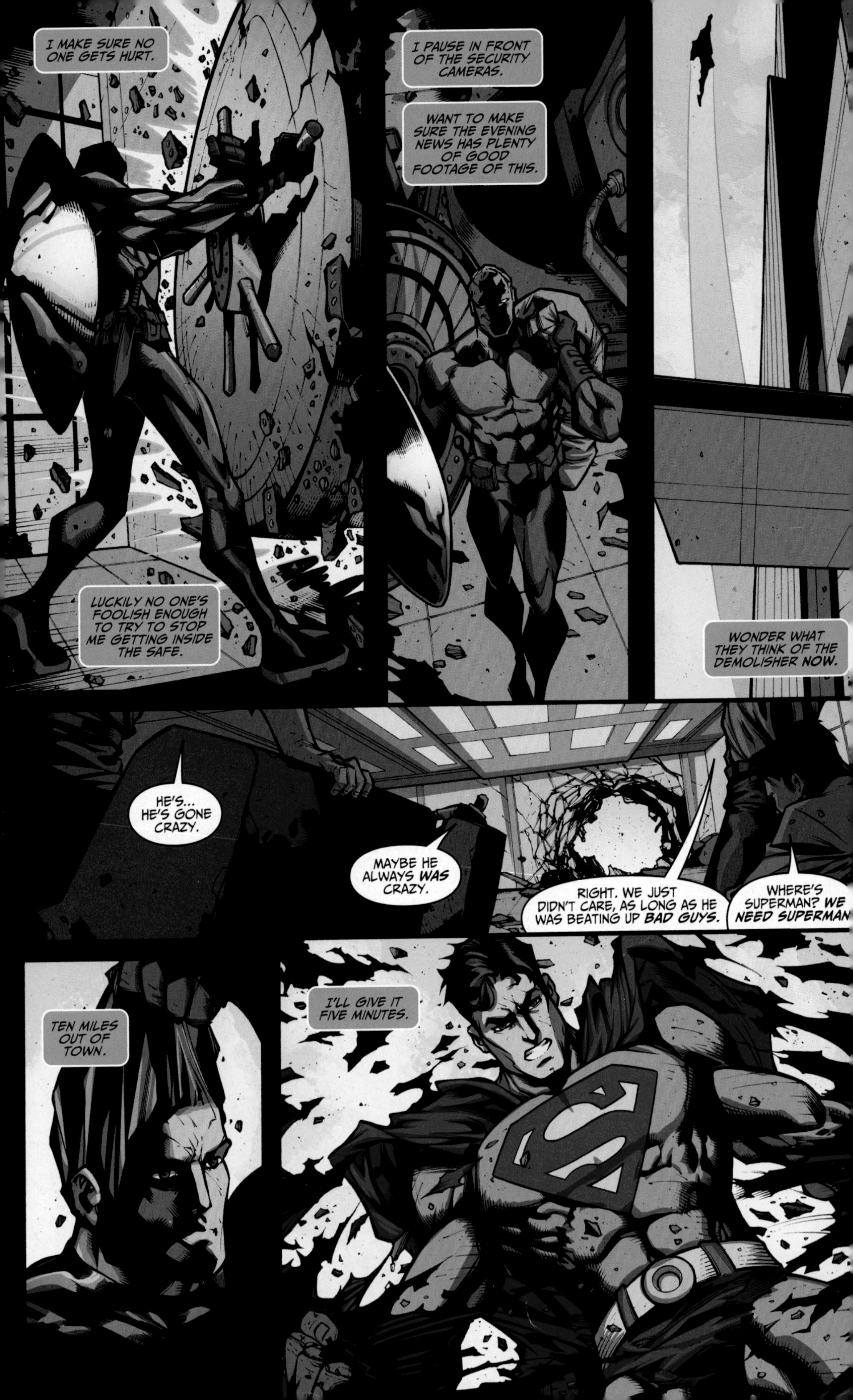
I MAKE SURE NO ONE GETS HURT.
LUCKILY NO ONE'S FOOLISH ENOUGH TO TRY TO STOP ME GETTING INSIDE THE SAFE.
I PAUSE IN FRONT OF THE SECURITY CAMERAS.
WANT TO MAKE SURE THE EVENING NEWS HAS PLENTY OF GOOD FOOTAGE OF THIS.
WONDER WHAT THEY THINK OF THE DEMOLISHER NOW.
HE'S... HE'S GONE CRAZY.
MAYBE HE ALWAYS WAS CRAZY.
RIGHT. WE JUST DIDN'T CARE, AS LONG AS HE WAS BEATING UP BAD GUYS.
WHERE'S SUPERMAN? WE NEED SUPERMAN
TEN MILES OUT OF TOWN.
I'LL GIVE IT FIVE MINUTES.

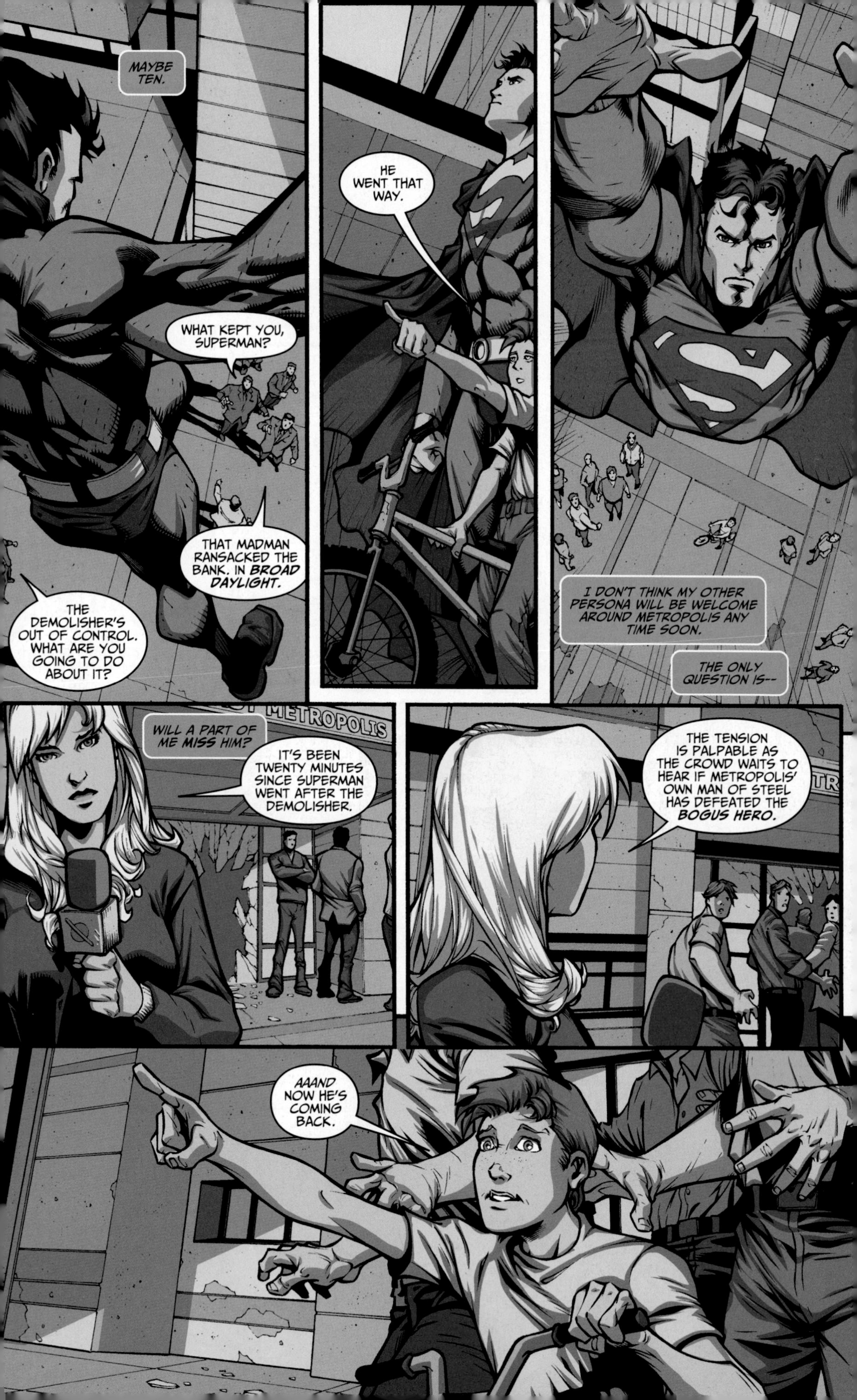
MAYBE TEN.
WHAT KEPT YOU, SUPERMAN?
THAT MADMAN RANSACKED THE BANK. IN BROAD DAYLIGHT.
THE DEMOLISHER'S OUT OF CONTROL. WHAT ARE YOU GOING TO DO ABOUT IT?
HE WENT THAT WAY.
I DON'T THINK MY OTHER PERSONA WILL BE WELCOME AROUND METROPOLIS ANY TIME SOON.
THE ONLY QUESTION IS--
METROPOLIS
WILL A PART OF ME MISS HIM?
IT'S BEEN TWENTY MINUTES SINCE SUPERMAN WENT AFTER THE DEMOLISHER.
THE TENSION IS PALPABLE AS THE CROWD WAITS TO HEAR IF METROPOLIS' OWN MAN OF STEEL HAS DEFEATED THE BOGUS HERO.
AAAND NOW HE'S COMING BACK.

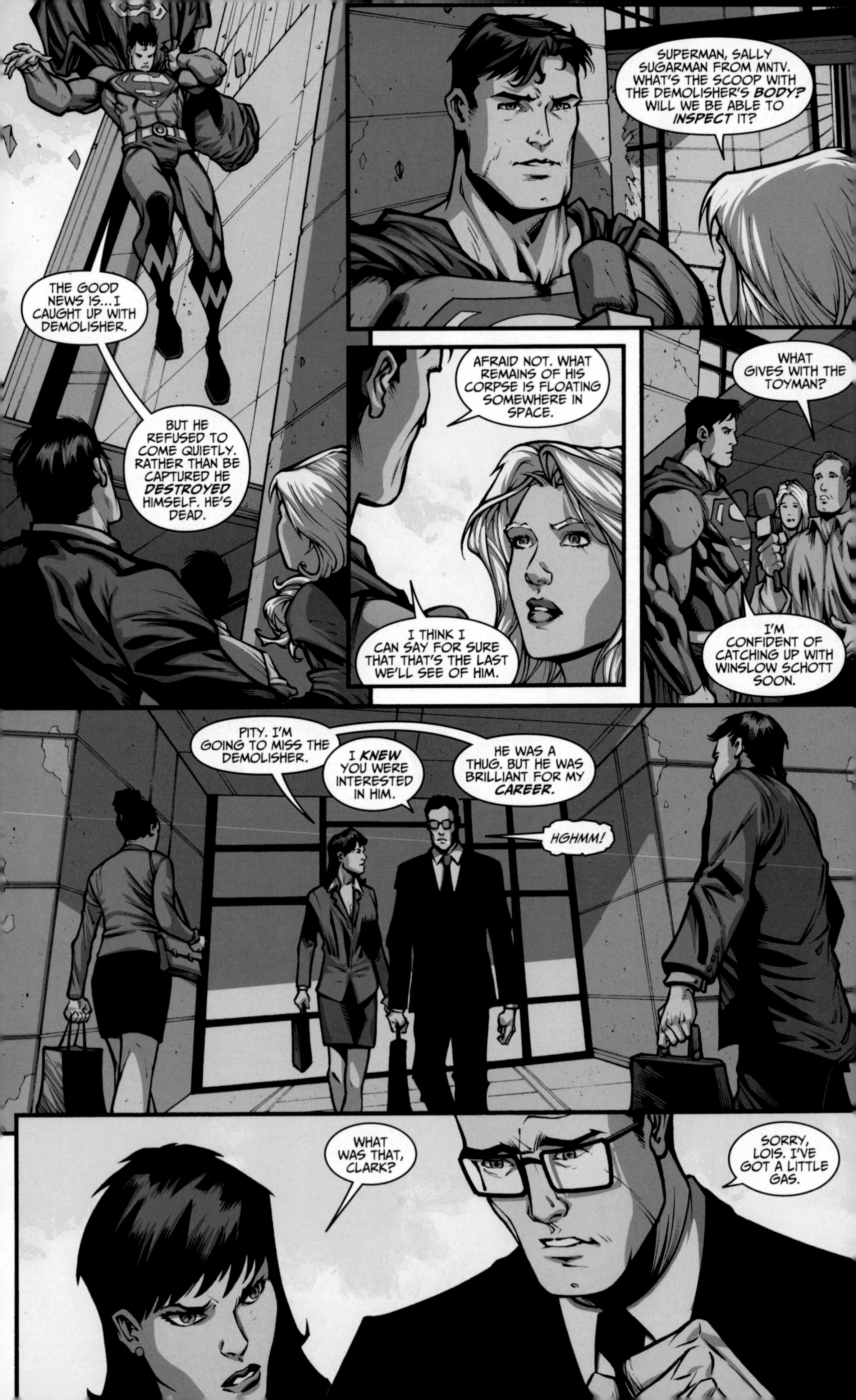
THE GOOD NEWS IS...I CAUGHT UP WITH DEMOLISHER.
BUT HE REFUSED TO COME QUIETLY. RATHER THAN BE CAPTURED HE DESTROYED HIMSELF. HE'S DEAD.
SUPERMAN, SALLY SUGARMAN FROM MNTV. WHAT'S THE SCOOP WITH THE DEMOLISHER'S BODY? WILL WE BE ABLE TO INSPECT IT?
AFRAID NOT. WHAT REMAINS OF HIS CORPSE IS FLOATING SOMEWHERE IN SPACE.
I THINK I CAN SAY FOR SURE THAT THAT'S THE LAST WE'LL SEE OF HIM.
WHAT GIVES WITH THE TOYMAN?
I'M CONFIDENT OF CATCHING UP WITH WINSLOW SCHOTT SOON.
PITY. I'M GOING TO MISS THE DEMOLISHER.
I KNEW YOU WERE INTERESTED IN HIM.
HE WAS A THUG. BUT HE WAS BRILLIANT FOR MY CAREER.
HGHMM!
WHAT WAS THAT, CLARK?
SORRY, LOIS. I'VE GOT A LITTLE GAS.

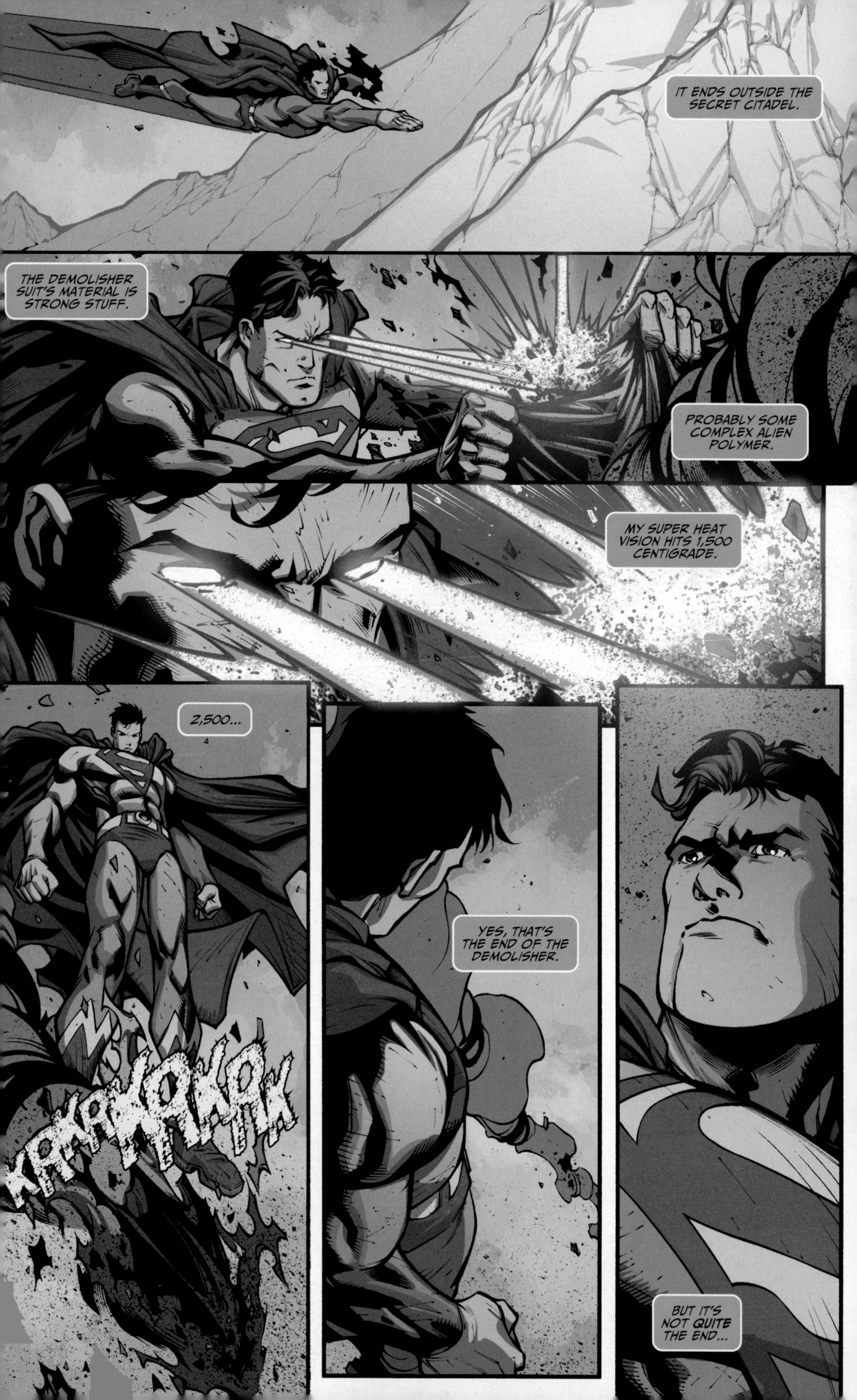
IT ENDS OUTSIDE THE SECRET CITADEL.
THE DEMOLISHER SUIT'S MATERIAL IS STRONG STUFF.
PROBABLY SOME COMPLEX ALIEN POLYMER.
MY SUPER HEAT VISION HITS 1,500 CENTIGRADE.
2,500...
KRAKAKAKAKAKAKK
YES, THAT'S THE END OF THE DEMOLISHER.
BUT IT'S NOT QUITE THE END...

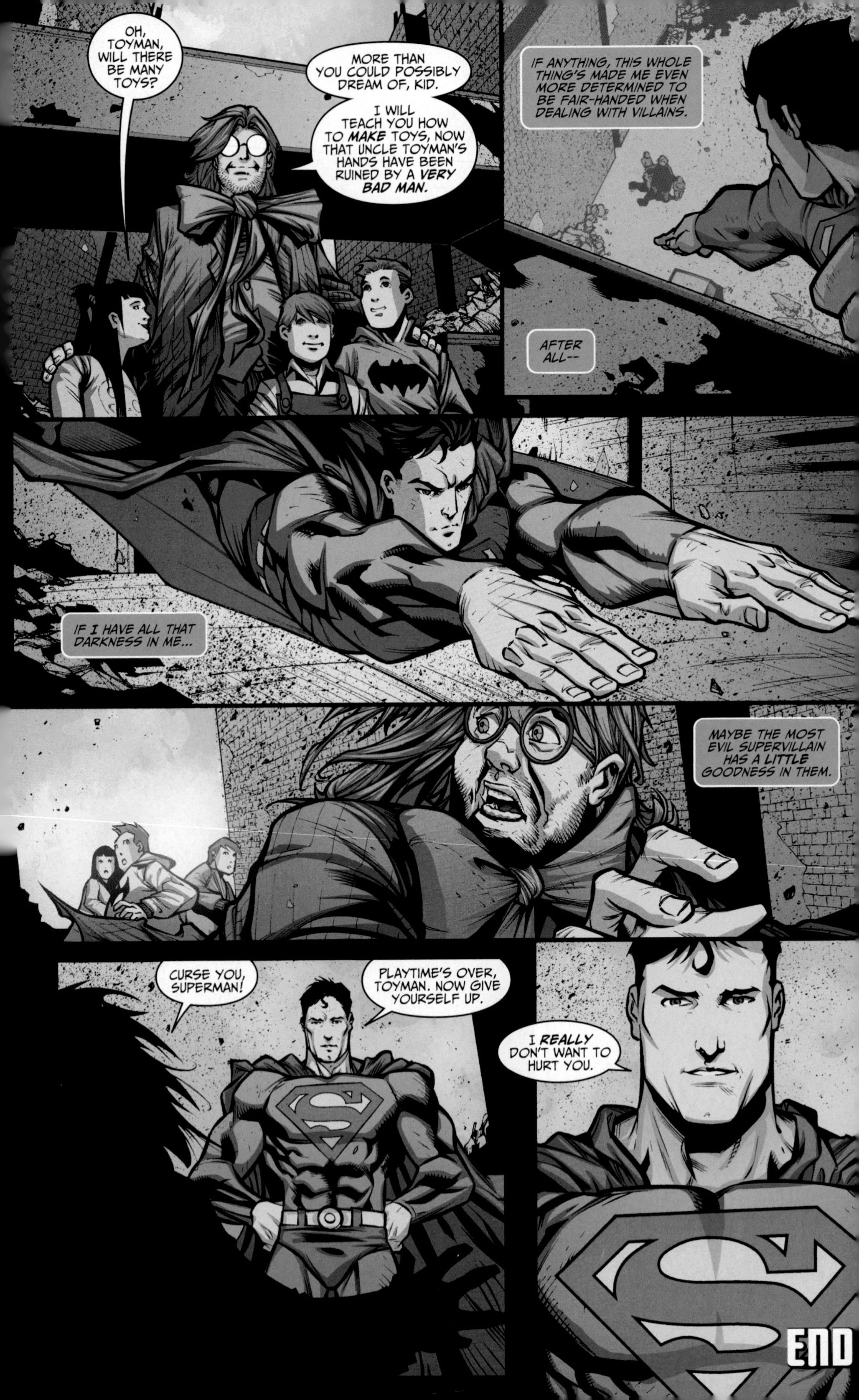
OH, TOYMAN, WILL THERE BE MANY TOYS?
MORE THAN YOU COULD POSSIBLY DREAM OF, KID.
I WILL TEACH YOU HOW TO MAKE TOYS, NOW THAT UNCLE TOYMAN'S HANDS HAVE BEEN RUINED BY A VERY BAD MAN.
IF ANYTHING, THIS WHOLE THING'S MADE ME EVEN MORE DETERMINED TO BE FAIR-HANDED WHEN DEALING WITH VILLAINS.
AFTER ALL--
IF I HAVE ALL THAT DARKNESS IN ME...
MAYBE THE MOST EVIL SUPERVILLAIN HAS A LITTLE GOODNESS IN THEM.
CURSE YOU, SUPERMAN!
PLAYTIME'S OVER, TOYMAN. NOW GIVE YOURSELF UP.
I REALLY DON'T WANT TO HURT YOU.
END

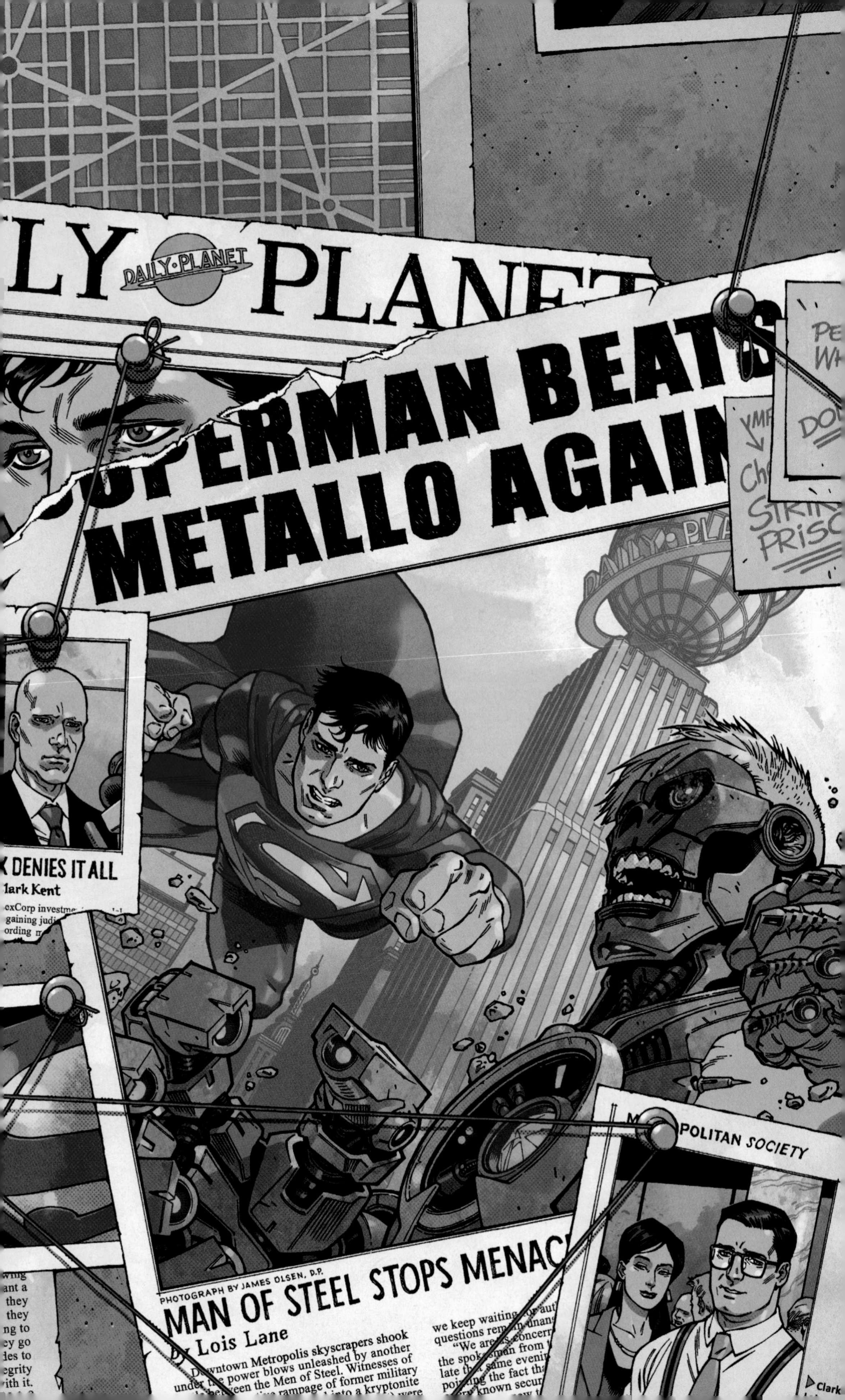

LY
DAILY PLANET
PLANET
ERMAN BEAT
METALLO AGAI
K DENIES IT ALL
lark Kent
PHOTOGRAPH BY JAMES OLSEN, D.P.
MAN OF STEEL STOPS MENAC
Lois Lane
Downtown Metropolis skyscrapers shook
power blows unleashed by another
the Men of Steel. Witnesses of
rampage of former military
a kryptonite
we keep waiting
questions rem
"We are
the spoke
late th same evenin
the fact tha
known secur
POLITAN SOCIETY
Clark

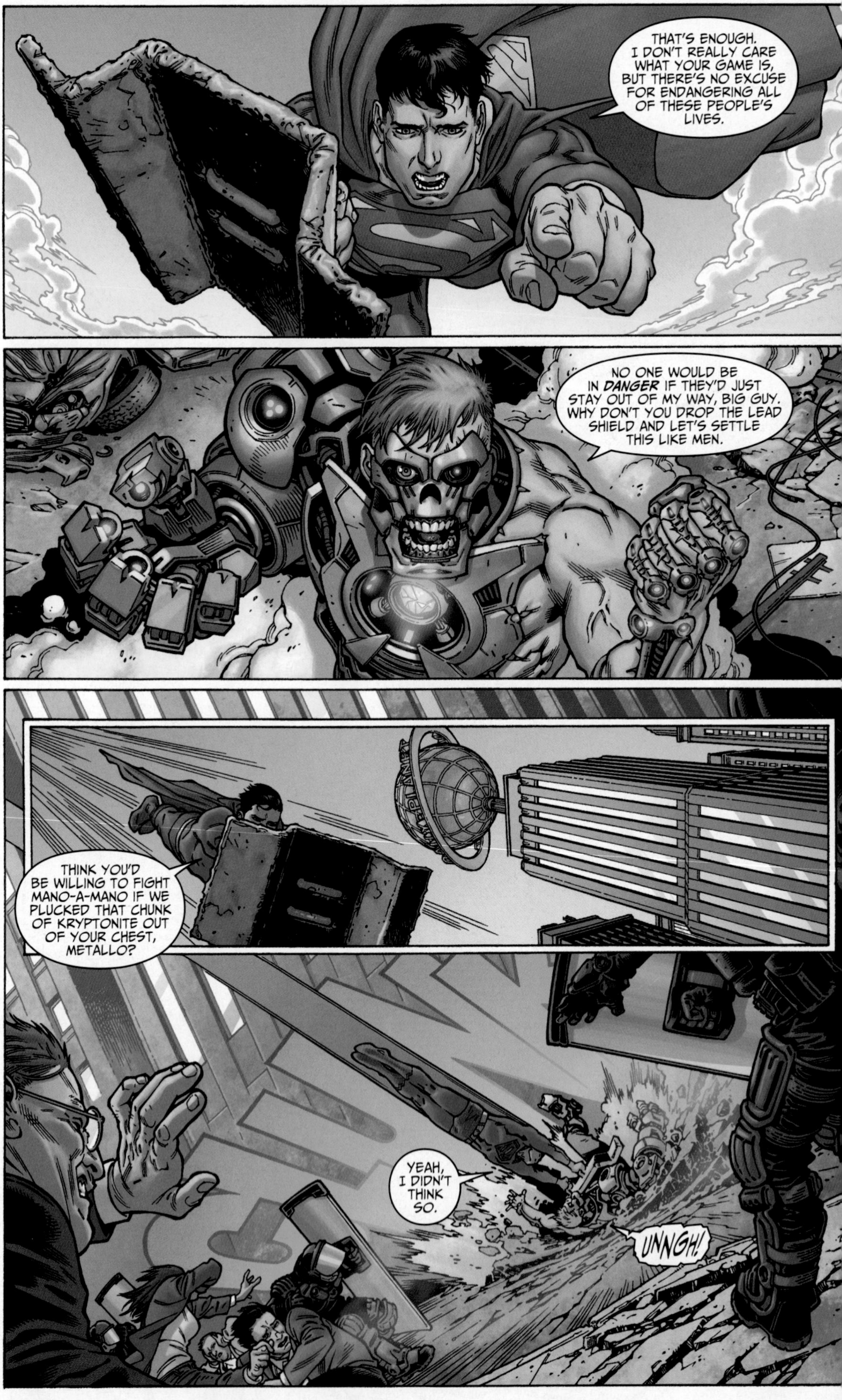
THAT'S ENOUGH. I DON'T REALLY CARE WHAT YOUR GAME IS, BUT THERE'S NO EXCUSE FOR ENDANGERING ALL OF THESE PEOPLE'S LIVES.
NO ONE WOULD BE IN DANGER IF THEY'D JUST STAY OUT OF MY WAY, BIG GUY. WHY DON'T YOU DROP THE LEAD SHIELD AND LET'S SETTLE THIS LIKE MEN.
THINK YOU'D BE WILLING TO FIGHT MANO-A-MANO IF WE PLUCKED THAT CHUNK OF KRYPTONITE OUT OF YOUR CHEST, METALLO?
YEAH, I DIDN'T THINK SO.
UNNGH!

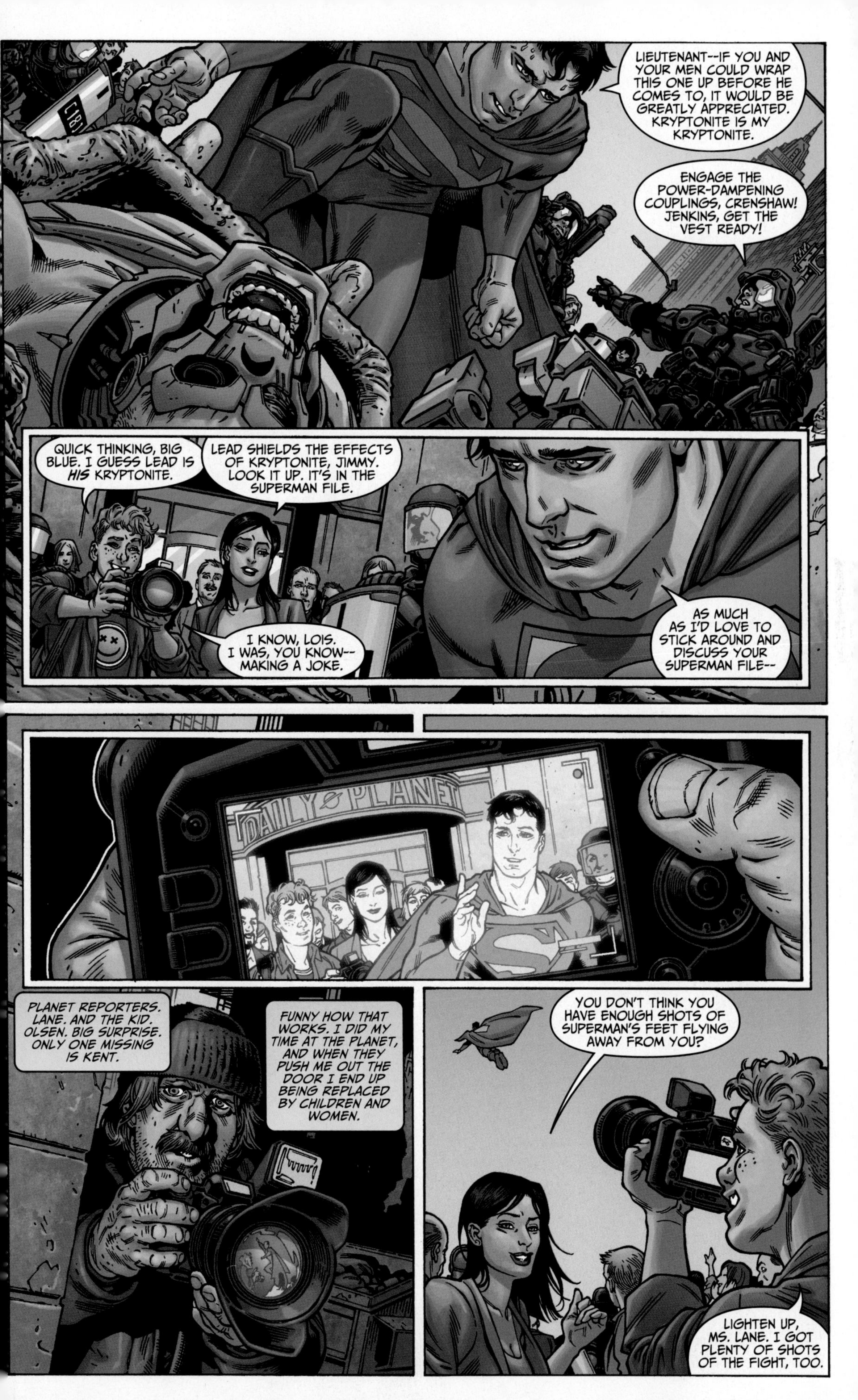
LIEUTENANT--IF YOU AND YOUR MEN COULD WRAP THIS ONE UP BEFORE HE COMES TO, IT WOULD BE GREATLY APPRECIATED. KRYPTONITE IS MY KRYPTONITE.
ENGAGE THE POWER-DAMPENING COUPLINGS, CRENSHAW! JENKINS, GET THE VEST READY!
QUICK THINKING, BIG BLUE. I GUESS LEAD IS *HIS* KRYPTONITE.
LEAD SHIELDS THE EFFECTS OF KRYPTONITE, JIMMY. LOOK IT UP. IT'S IN THE SUPERMAN FILE.
I KNOW, LOIS. I WAS, YOU KNOW--MAKING A JOKE.
AS MUCH AS I'D LOVE TO STICK AROUND AND DISCUSS YOUR SUPERMAN FILE--
DAILY PLANET
PLANET REPORTERS. LANE. AND THE KID. OLSEN. BIG SURPRISE. ONLY ONE MISSING IS KENT.
FUNNY HOW THAT WORKS. I DID MY TIME AT THE PLANET, AND WHEN THEY PUSH ME OUT THE DOOR I END UP BEING REPLACED BY CHILDREN AND WOMEN.
YOU DON'T THINK YOU HAVE ENOUGH SHOTS OF SUPERMAN'S FEET FLYING AWAY FROM YOU?
LIGHTEN UP, MS. LANE. I GOT PLENTY OF SHOTS OF THE FIGHT, TOO.

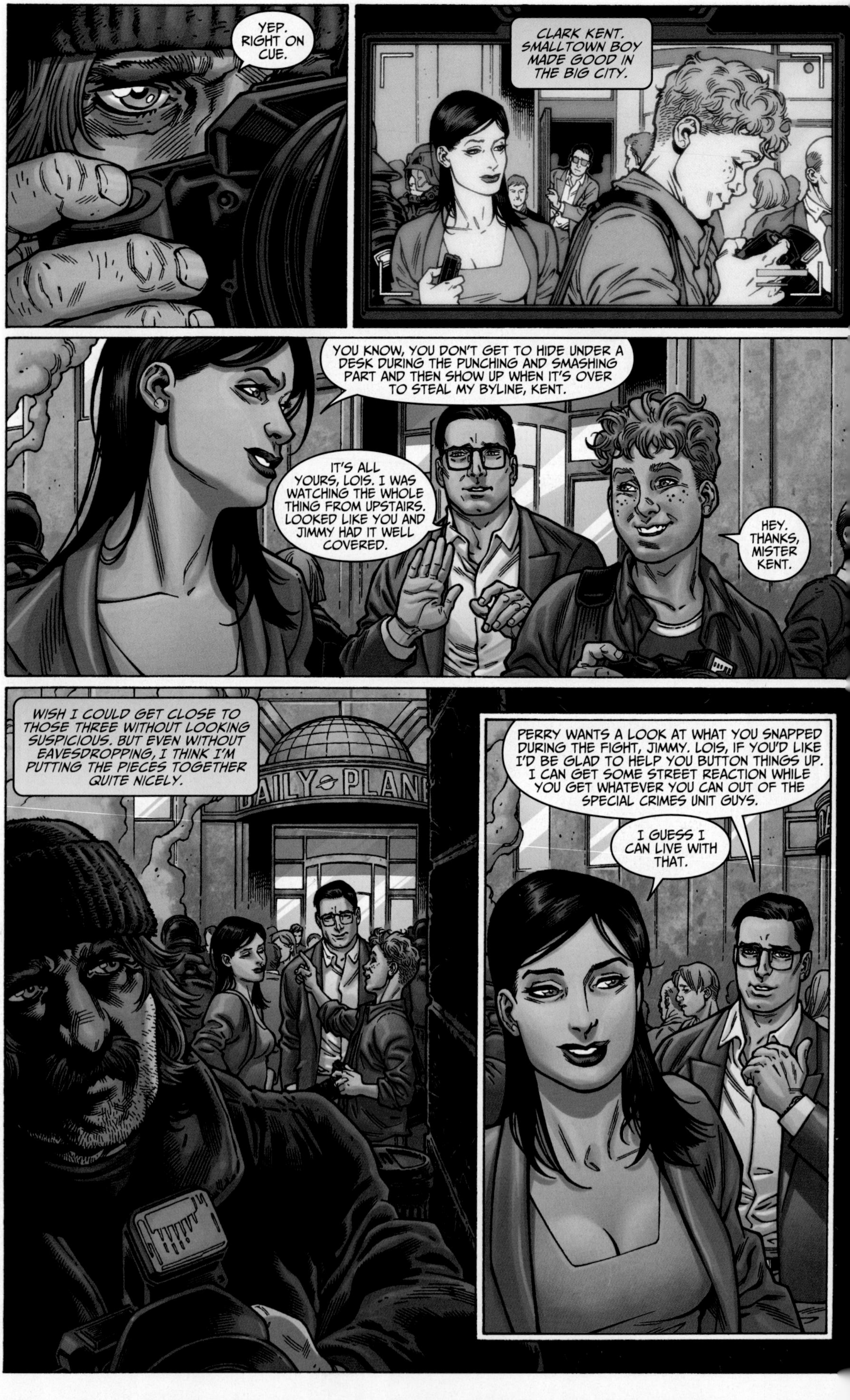
YEP. RIGHT ON CUE.
CLARK KENT. SMALLTOWN BOY MADE GOOD IN THE BIG CITY.
YOU KNOW, YOU DON'T GET TO HIDE UNDER A DESK DURING THE PUNCHING AND SMASHING PART AND THEN SHOW UP WHEN IT'S OVER TO STEAL MY BYLINE, KENT.
IT'S ALL YOURS, LOIS. I WAS WATCHING THE WHOLE THING FROM UPSTAIRS. LOOKED LIKE YOU AND JIMMY HAD IT WELL COVERED.
HEY. THANKS, MISTER KENT.
WISH I COULD GET CLOSE TO THOSE THREE WITHOUT LOOKING SUSPICIOUS. BUT EVEN WITHOUT EAVESDROPPING, I THINK I'M PUTTING THE PIECES TOGETHER QUITE NICELY.
DAILY PLAN
PERRY WANTS A LOOK AT WHAT YOU SNAPPED DURING THE FIGHT, JIMMY. LOIS, IF YOU'D LIKE I'D BE GLAD TO HELP YOU BUTTON THINGS UP. I CAN GET SOME STREET REACTION WHILE YOU GET WHATEVER YOU CAN OUT OF THE SPECIAL CRIMES UNIT GUYS.
I GUESS I CAN LIVE WITH THAT.

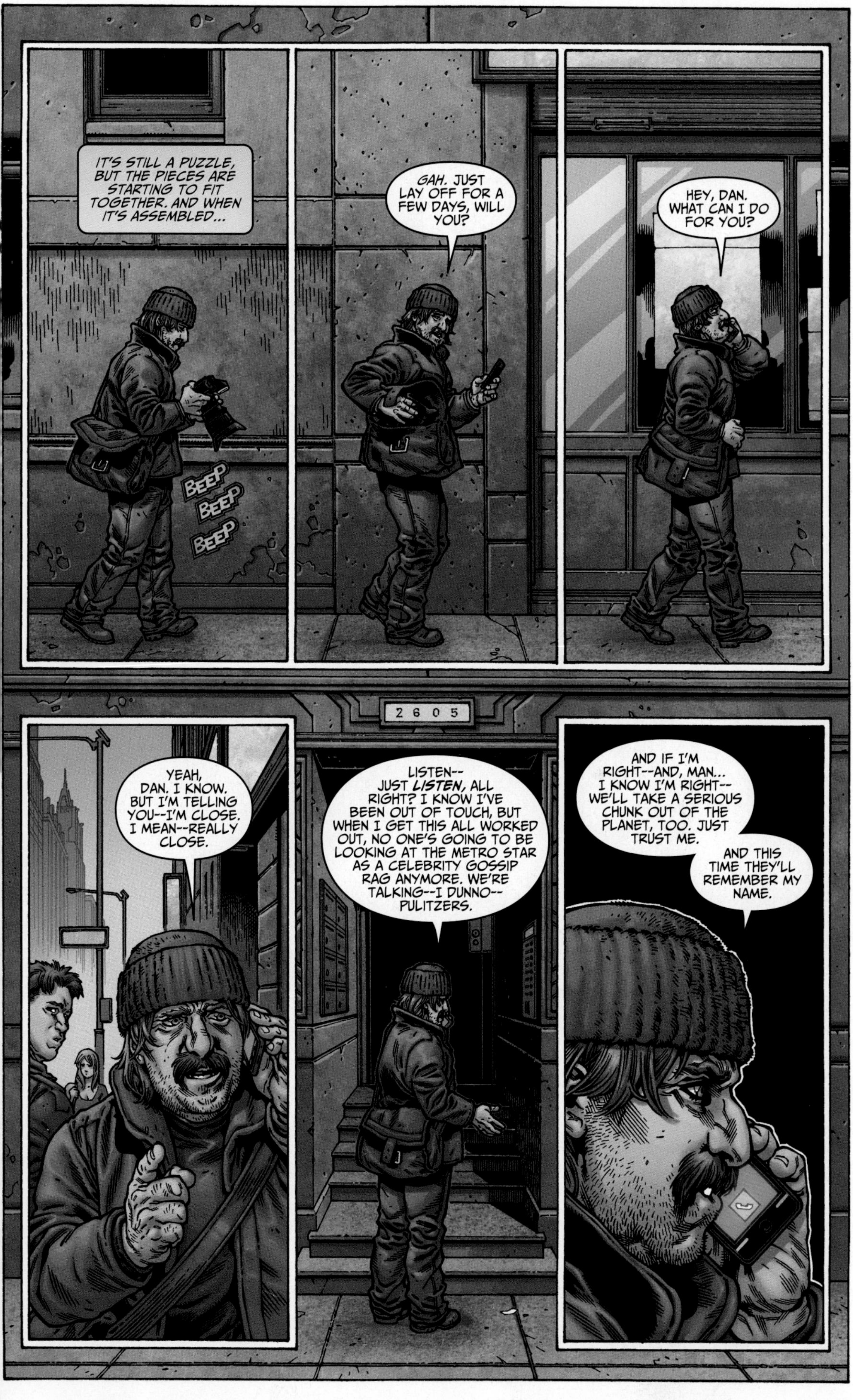
IT'S STILL A PUZZLE, BUT THE PIECES ARE STARTING TO FIT TOGETHER. AND WHEN IT'S ASSEMBLED...
BEEP
BEEP
BEEP
GAH. JUST LAY OFF FOR A FEW DAYS, WILL YOU?
HEY, DAN. WHAT CAN I DO FOR YOU?
2605
YEAH, DAN. I KNOW. BUT I'M TELLING YOU--I'M CLOSE. I MEAN--REALLY CLOSE.
LISTEN-- JUST LISTEN, ALL RIGHT? I KNOW I'VE BEEN OUT OF TOUCH, BUT WHEN I GET THIS ALL WORKED OUT, NO ONE'S GOING TO BE LOOKING AT THE METRO STAR AS A CELEBRITY GOSSIP RAG ANYMORE. WE'RE TALKING--I DUNNO-- PULITZERS.
AND IF I'M RIGHT--AND, MAN... I KNOW I'M RIGHT-- WE'LL TAKE A SERIOUS CHUNK OUT OF THE PLANET, TOO. JUST TRUST ME.
AND THIS TIME THEY'LL REMEMBER MY NAME.

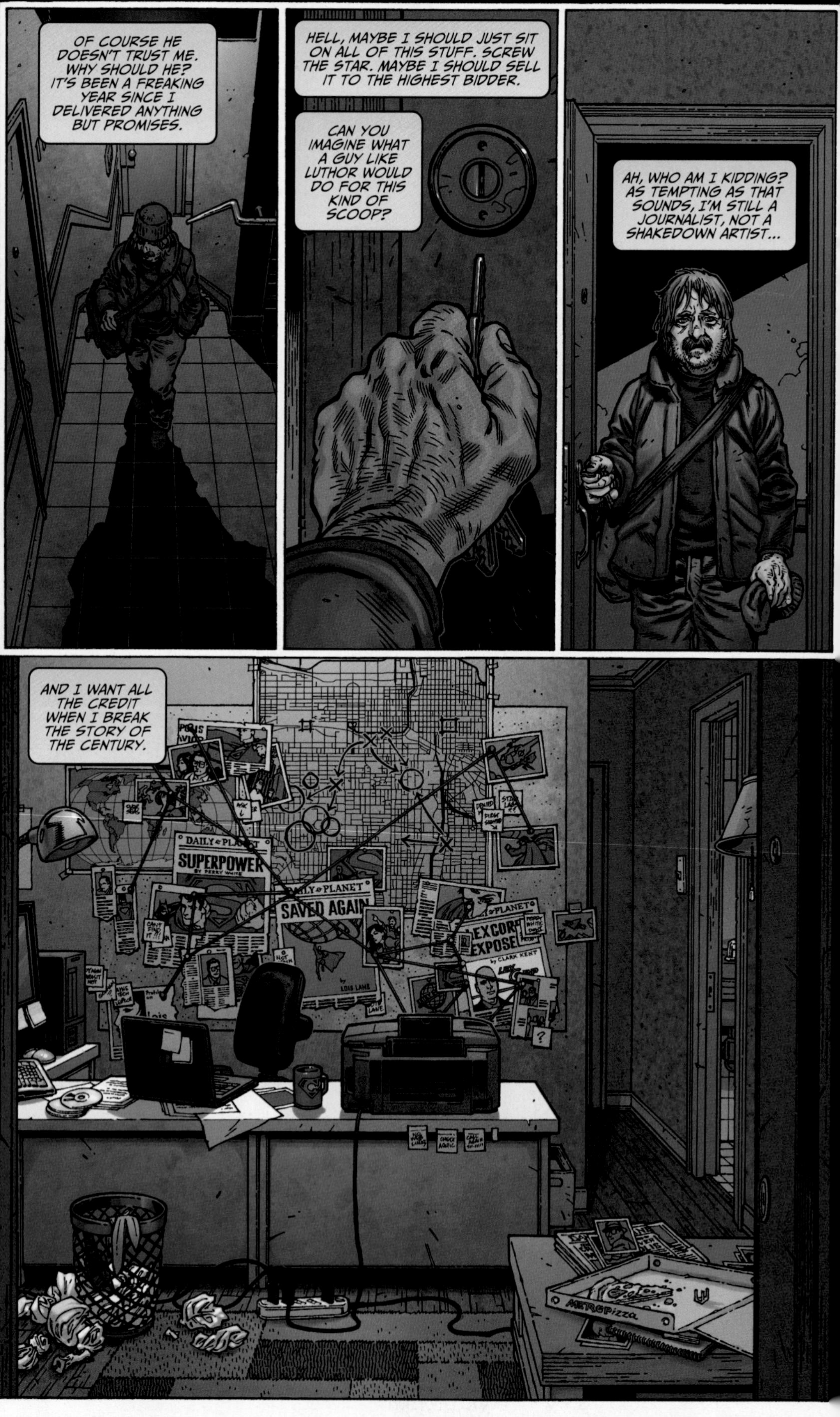
OF COURSE HE DOESN'T TRUST ME. WHY SHOULD HE? IT'S BEEN A FREAKING YEAR SINCE I DELIVERED ANYTHING BUT PROMISES.
HELL, MAYBE I SHOULD JUST SIT ON ALL OF THIS STUFF. SCREW THE STAR. MAYBE I SHOULD SELL IT TO THE HIGHEST BIDDER.
CAN YOU IMAGINE WHAT A GUY LIKE LUTHOR WOULD DO FOR THIS KIND OF SCOOP?
AH, WHO AM I KIDDING? AS TEMPTING AS THAT SOUNDS, I'M STILL A JOURNALIST, NOT A SHAKEDOWN ARTIST...
AND I WANT ALL THE CREDIT WHEN I BREAK THE STORY OF THE CENTURY.
DAILY PLANET
SUPERPOWER
BY PERRY WHITE
DAILY PLANET
SAVED AGAIN
LOIS LANE
PLANET
LEXCORP EXPOSE
by CLARK KENT
METRO Pizza

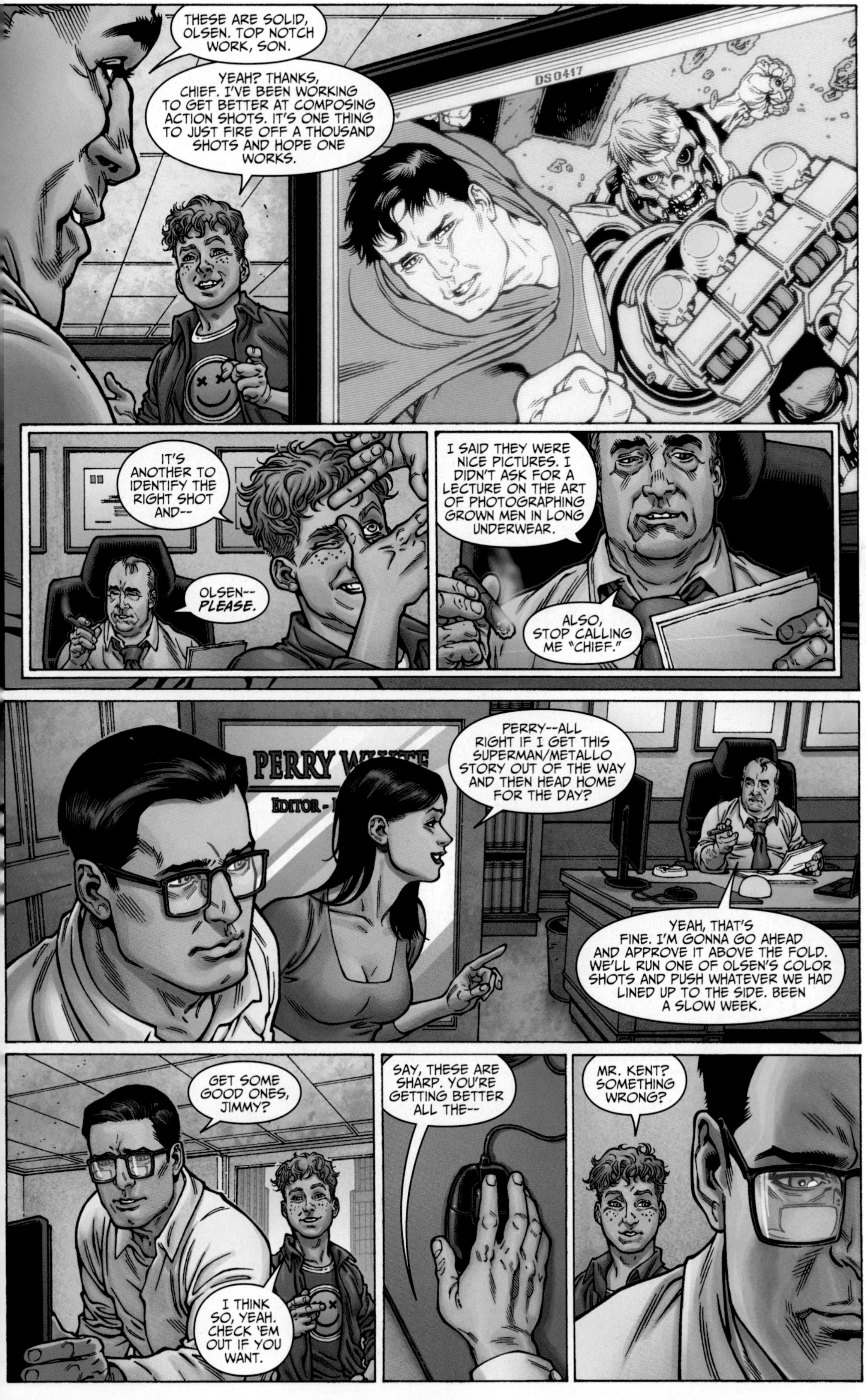
THESE ARE SOLID, OLSEN. TOP NOTCH WORK, SON.
YEAH? THANKS, CHIEF. I'VE BEEN WORKING TO GET BETTER AT COMPOSING ACTION SHOTS. IT'S ONE THING TO JUST FIRE OFF A THOUSAND SHOTS AND HOPE ONE WORKS.
DS0417
IT'S ANOTHER TO IDENTIFY THE RIGHT SHOT AND--
OLSEN-- PLEASE.
I SAID THEY WERE NICE PICTURES. I DIDN'T ASK FOR A LECTURE ON THE ART OF PHOTOGRAPHING GROWN MEN IN LONG UNDERWEAR.
ALSO, STOP CALLING ME "CHIEF."
PERRY WH
EDITOR -
PERRY--ALL RIGHT IF I GET THIS SUPERMAN/METALLO STORY OUT OF THE WAY AND THEN HEAD HOME FOR THE DAY?
YEAH, THAT'S FINE. I'M GONNA GO AHEAD AND APPROVE IT ABOVE THE FOLD. WE'LL RUN ONE OF OLSEN'S COLOR SHOTS AND PUSH WHATEVER WE HAD LINED UP TO THE SIDE. BEEN A SLOW WEEK.
GET SOME GOOD ONES, JIMMY?
I THINK SO, YEAH. CHECK 'EM OUT IF YOU WANT.
SAY, THESE ARE SHARP. YOU'RE GETTING BETTER ALL THE--
MR. KENT? SOMETHING WRONG?

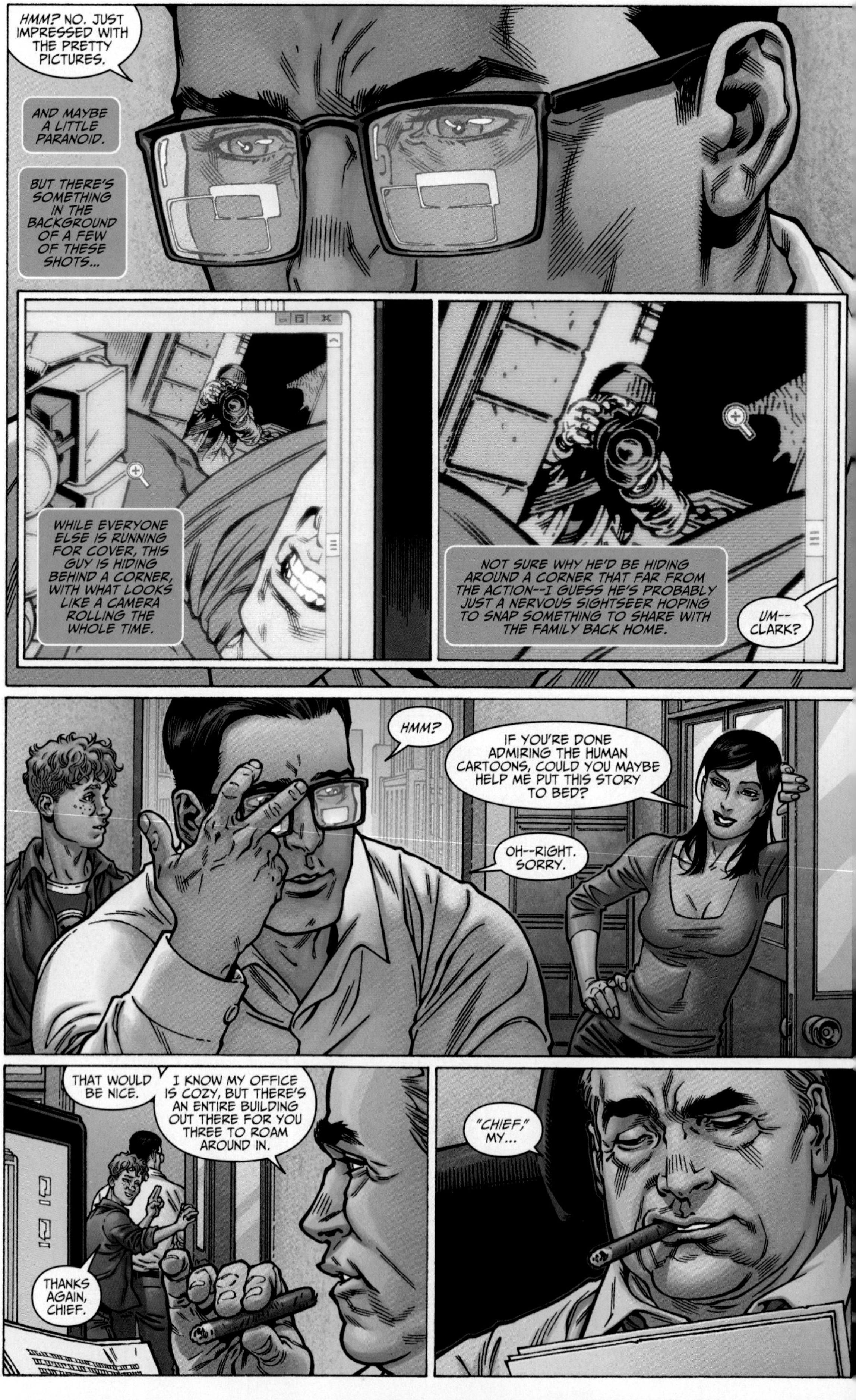
HMM? NO. JUST IMPRESSED WITH THE PRETTY PICTURES.
AND MAYBE A LITTLE PARANOID.
BUT THERE'S SOMETHING IN THE BACKGROUND OF A FEW OF THESE SHOTS...
WHILE EVERYONE ELSE IS RUNNING FOR COVER, THIS GUY IS HIDING BEHIND A CORNER, WITH WHAT LOOKS LIKE A CAMERA ROLLING THE WHOLE TIME.
NOT SURE WHY HE'D BE HIDING AROUND A CORNER THAT FAR FROM THE ACTION--I GUESS HE'S PROBABLY JUST A NERVOUS SIGHTSEER HOPING TO SNAP SOMETHING TO SHARE WITH THE FAMILY BACK HOME.
UM--CLARK?
HMM?
IF YOU'RE DONE ADMIRING THE HUMAN CARTOONS, COULD YOU MAYBE HELP ME PUT THIS STORY TO BED?
OH--RIGHT. SORRY.
THAT WOULD BE NICE.
I KNOW MY OFFICE IS COZY, BUT THERE'S AN ENTIRE BUILDING OUT THERE FOR YOU THREE TO ROAM AROUND IN.
THANKS AGAIN, CHIEF.
"CHIEF," MY...

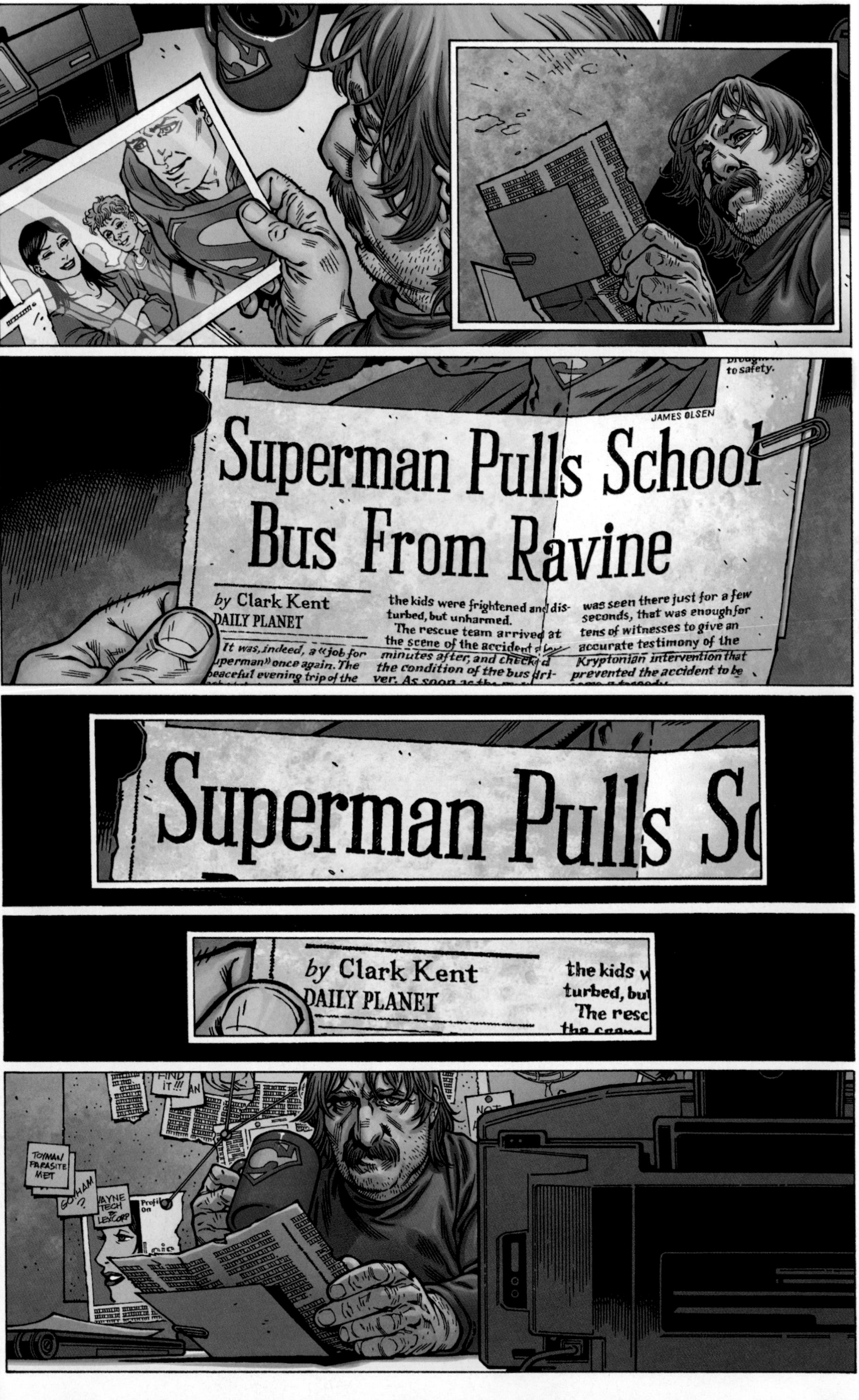

to safety.
JAMES OLSEN
Superman Pulls School Bus From Ravine
by Clark Kent
DAILY PLANET
It was, indeed, a «job for
uperman» once again. The
peaceful evening trip of the
the kids were frightened and dis-
turbed, but unharmed.
The rescue team arrived at
the scene of the accident
minutes after, and checked
the condition of the bus dri-
was seen there just for a few
seconds, that was enough for
tens of witnesses to give an
accurate testimony of the
Kryptonian intervention that
prevented the accident to be
Superman Pulls
by Clark Kent
DAILY PLANET
FIND IT!!!
TOYMAN
PARASITE
MET
GOTHAM
?
WAYNE
TECH
&
LEXCORP

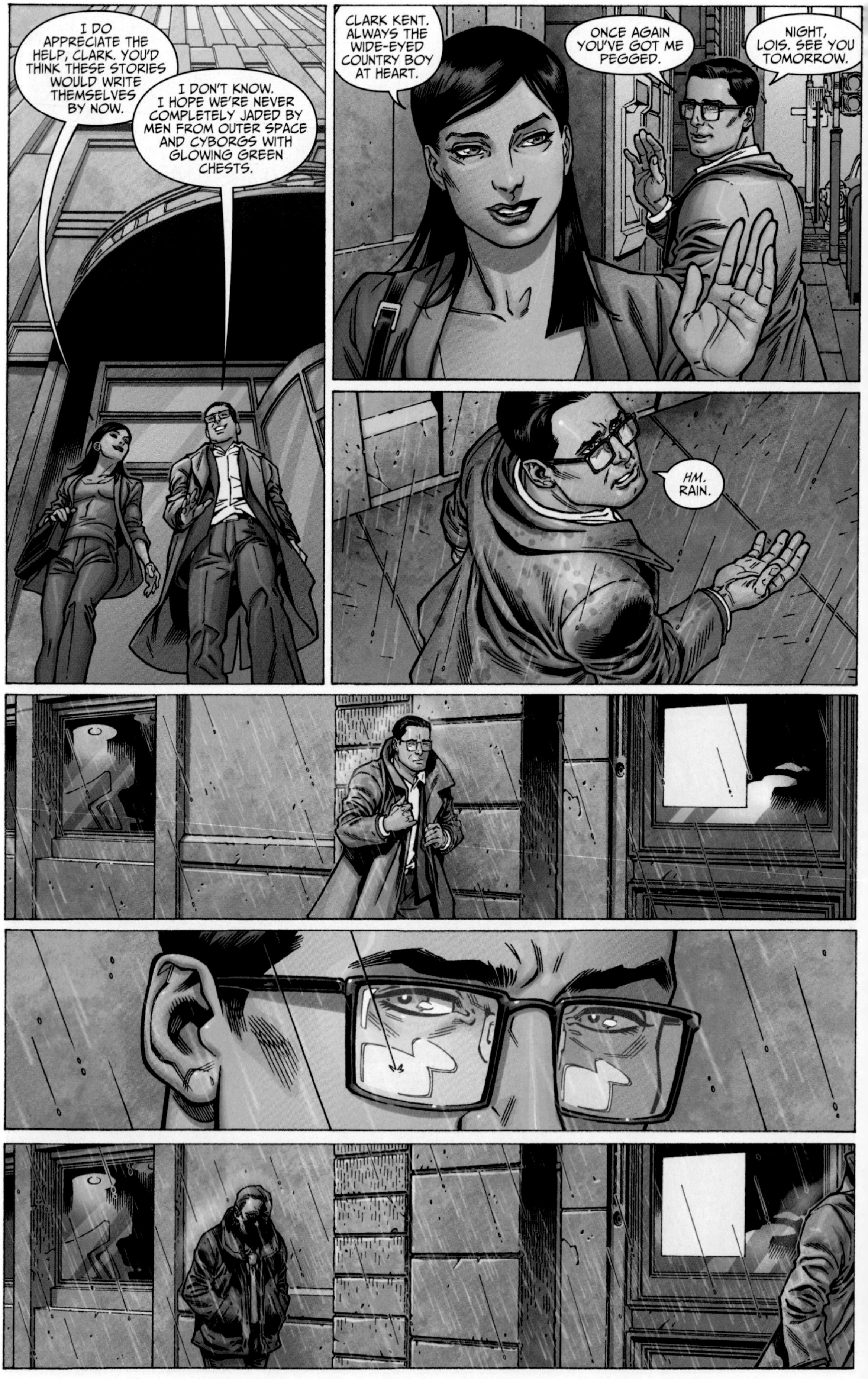
I DO APPRECIATE THE HELP, CLARK. YOU'D THINK THESE STORIES WOULD WRITE THEMSELVES BY NOW.
I DON'T KNOW. I HOPE WE'RE NEVER COMPLETELY JADED BY MEN FROM OUTER SPACE AND CYBORGS WITH GLOWING GREEN CHESTS.
CLARK KENT. ALWAYS THE WIDE-EYED COUNTRY BOY AT HEART.
ONCE AGAIN YOU'VE GOT ME PEGGED.
NIGHT, LOIS. SEE YOU TOMORROW.
HM. RAIN.

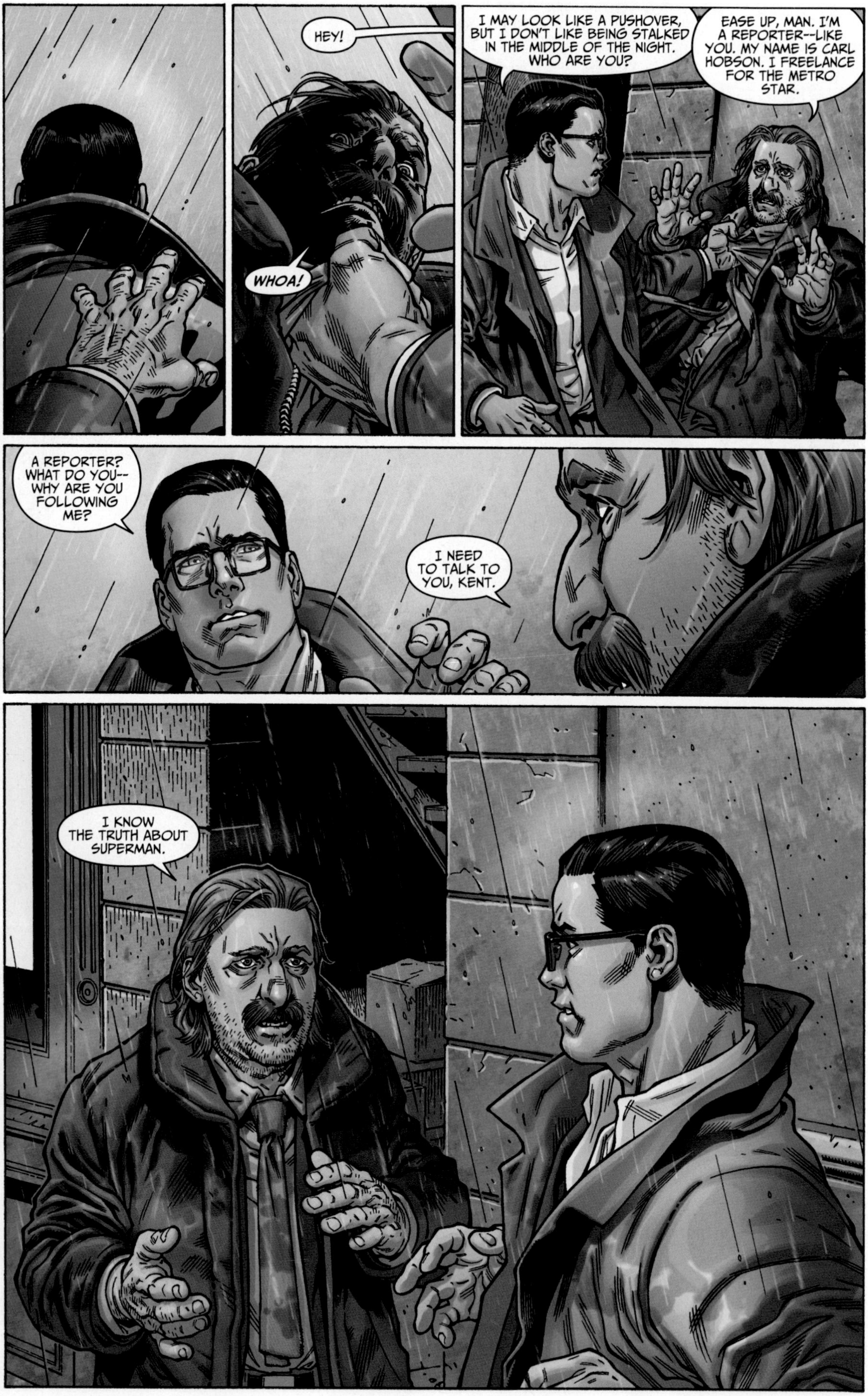
HEY!
WHOA!
I MAY LOOK LIKE A PUSHOVER, BUT I DON'T LIKE BEING STALKED IN THE MIDDLE OF THE NIGHT. WHO ARE YOU?
EASE UP, MAN. I'M A REPORTER--LIKE YOU. MY NAME IS CARL HOBSON. I FREELANCE FOR THE METRO STAR.
A REPORTER? WHAT DO YOU-- WHY ARE YOU FOLLOWING ME?
I NEED TO TALK TO YOU, KENT.
I KNOW THE TRUTH ABOUT SUPERMAN.

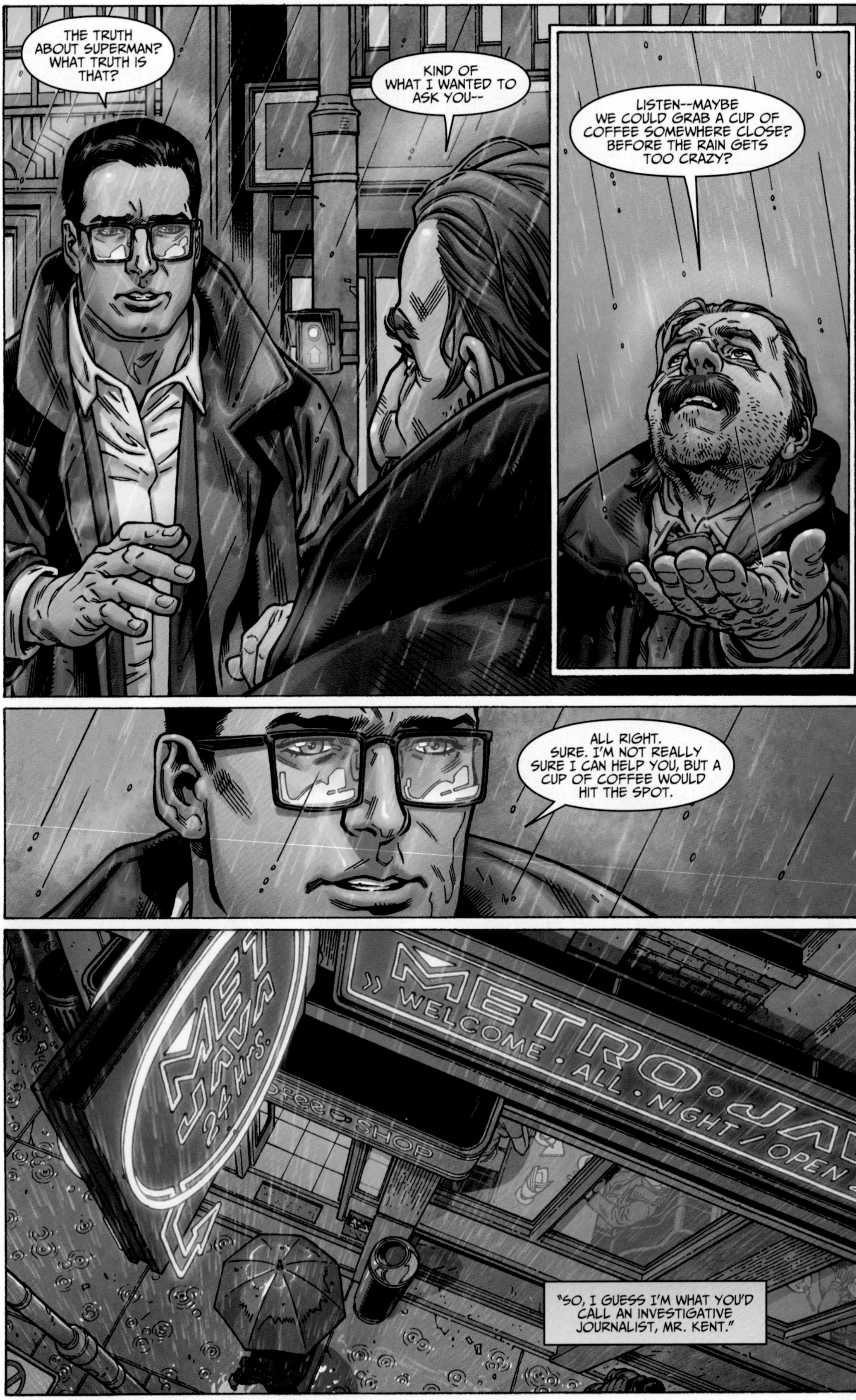
THE TRUTH ABOUT SUPERMAN? WHAT TRUTH IS THAT?
KIND OF WHAT I WANTED TO ASK YOU--
LISTEN--MAYBE WE COULD GRAB A CUP OF COFFEE SOMEWHERE CLOSE? BEFORE THE RAIN GETS TOO CRAZY?
ALL RIGHT. SURE. I'M NOT REALLY SURE I CAN HELP YOU, BUT A CUP OF COFFEE WOULD HIT THE SPOT.
METRO • WELCOME • ALL • NIGHT / OPEN 2
"SO, I GUESS I'M WHAT YOU'D CALL AN INVESTIGATIVE JOURNALIST, MR. KENT."

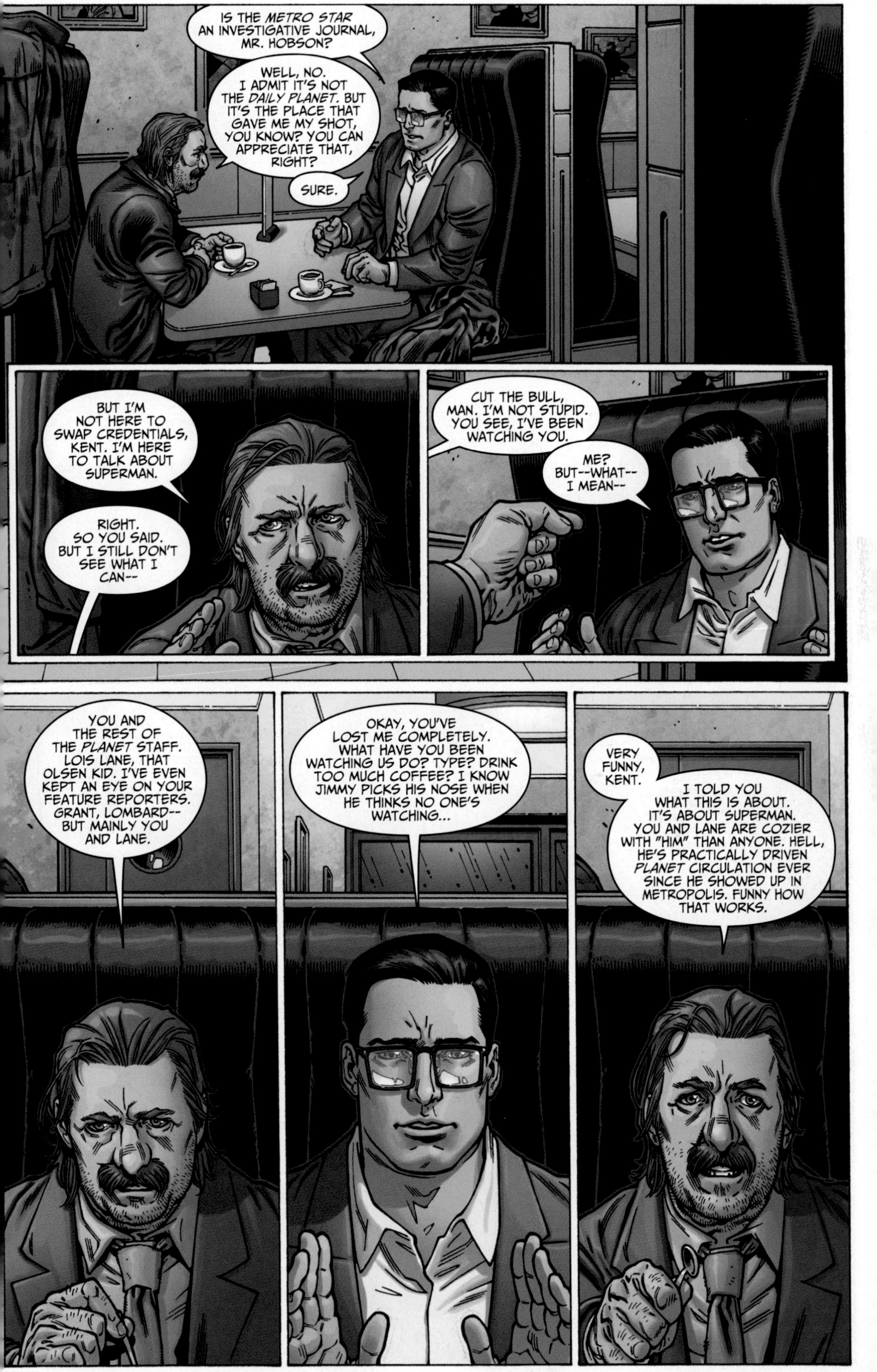
IS THE *METRO STAR* AN INVESTIGATIVE JOURNAL, MR. HOBSON?
WELL, NO. I ADMIT IT'S NOT THE *DAILY PLANET*. BUT IT'S THE PLACE THAT GAVE ME MY SHOT, YOU KNOW? YOU CAN APPRECIATE THAT, RIGHT?
SURE.
BUT I'M NOT HERE TO SWAP CREDENTIALS, KENT. I'M HERE TO TALK ABOUT SUPERMAN.
RIGHT. SO YOU SAID. BUT I STILL DON'T SEE WHAT I CAN--
CUT THE BULL, MAN. I'M NOT STUPID. YOU SEE, I'VE BEEN WATCHING YOU.
ME? BUT--WHAT--I MEAN--
YOU AND THE REST OF THE *PLANET* STAFF. LOIS LANE, THAT OLSEN KID. I'VE EVEN KEPT AN EYE ON YOUR FEATURE REPORTERS. GRANT, LOMBARD--BUT MAINLY YOU AND LANE.
OKAY, YOU'VE LOST ME COMPLETELY. WHAT HAVE YOU BEEN WATCHING US DO? TYPE? DRINK TOO MUCH COFFEE? I KNOW JIMMY PICKS HIS NOSE WHEN HE THINKS NO ONE'S WATCHING...
VERY FUNNY, KENT.
I TOLD YOU WHAT THIS IS ABOUT. IT'S ABOUT SUPERMAN. YOU AND LANE ARE COZIER WITH "HIM" THAN ANYONE. HELL, HE'S PRACTICALLY DRIVEN *PLANET* CIRCULATION EVER SINCE HE SHOWED UP IN METROPOLIS. FUNNY HOW THAT WORKS.

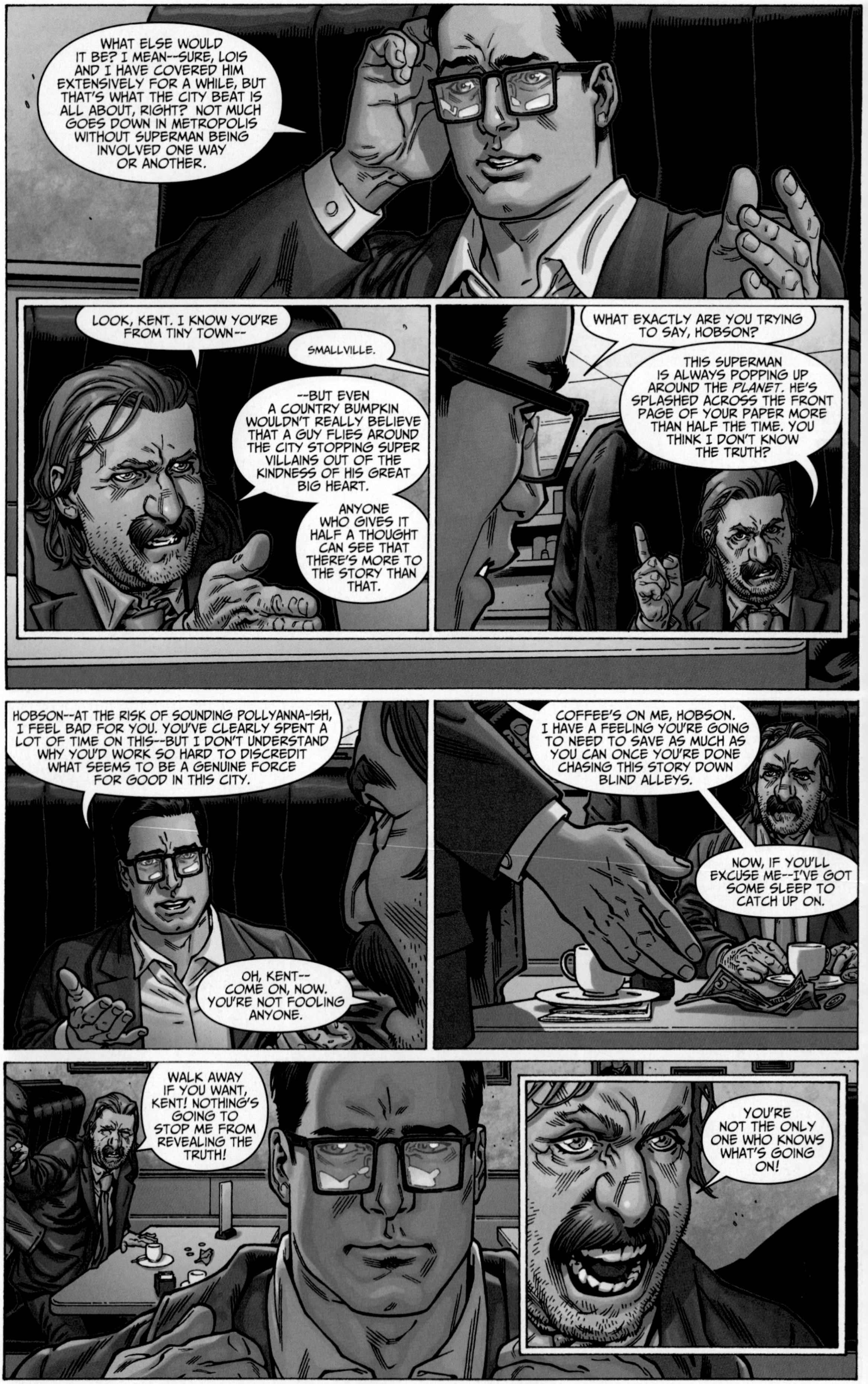
WHAT ELSE WOULD IT BE? I MEAN--SURE, LOIS AND I HAVE COVERED HIM EXTENSIVELY FOR A WHILE, BUT THAT'S WHAT THE CITY BEAT IS ALL ABOUT, RIGHT? NOT MUCH GOES DOWN IN METROPOLIS WITHOUT SUPERMAN BEING INVOLVED ONE WAY OR ANOTHER.
LOOK, KENT. I KNOW YOU'RE FROM TINY TOWN--
SMALLVILLE.
--BUT EVEN A COUNTRY BUMPKIN WOULDN'T REALLY BELIEVE THAT A GUY FLIES AROUND THE CITY STOPPING SUPER VILLAINS OUT OF THE KINDNESS OF HIS GREAT BIG HEART.
ANYONE WHO GIVES IT HALF A THOUGHT CAN SEE THAT THERE'S MORE TO THE STORY THAN THAT.
WHAT EXACTLY ARE YOU TRYING TO SAY, HOBSON?
THIS SUPERMAN IS ALWAYS POPPING UP AROUND THE *PLANET*. HE'S SPLASHED ACROSS THE FRONT PAGE OF YOUR PAPER MORE THAN HALF THE TIME. YOU THINK I DON'T KNOW THE TRUTH?
HOBSON--AT THE RISK OF SOUNDING POLLYANNA-ISH, I FEEL BAD FOR YOU. YOU'VE CLEARLY SPENT A LOT OF TIME ON THIS--BUT I DON'T UNDERSTAND WHY YOU'D WORK SO HARD TO DISCREDIT WHAT SEEMS TO BE A GENUINE FORCE FOR GOOD IN THIS CITY.
OH, KENT-- COME ON, NOW. YOU'RE NOT FOOLING ANYONE.
COFFEE'S ON ME, HOBSON. I HAVE A FEELING YOU'RE GOING TO NEED TO SAVE AS MUCH AS YOU CAN ONCE YOU'RE DONE CHASING THIS STORY DOWN BLIND ALLEYS.
NOW, IF YOU'LL EXCUSE ME--I'VE GOT SOME SLEEP TO CATCH UP ON.
WALK AWAY IF YOU WANT, KENT! NOTHING'S GOING TO STOP ME FROM REVEALING THE TRUTH!
YOU'RE NOT THE ONLY ONE WHO KNOWS WHAT'S GOING ON!

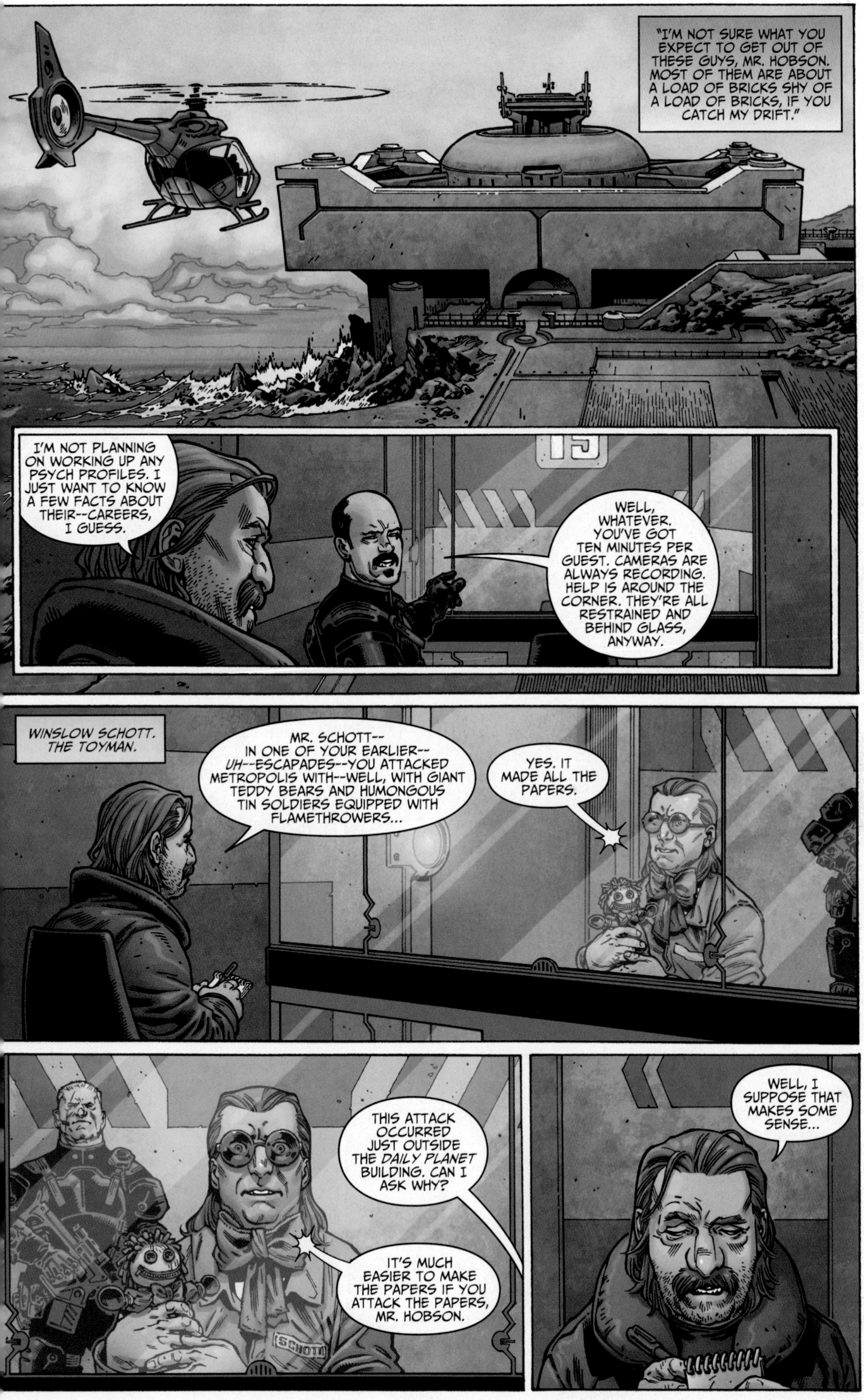
"I'M NOT SURE WHAT YOU EXPECT TO GET OUT OF THESE GUYS, MR. HOBSON. MOST OF THEM ARE ABOUT A LOAD OF BRICKS SHY OF A LOAD OF BRICKS, IF YOU CATCH MY DRIFT."
I'M NOT PLANNING ON WORKING UP ANY PSYCH PROFILES. I JUST WANT TO KNOW A FEW FACTS ABOUT THEIR--CAREERS, I GUESS.
WELL, WHATEVER. YOU'VE GOT TEN MINUTES PER GUEST. CAMERAS ARE ALWAYS RECORDING. HELP IS AROUND THE CORNER. THEY'RE ALL RESTRAINED AND BEHIND GLASS, ANYWAY.
WINSLOW SCHOTT. THE TOYMAN.
MR. SCHOTT-- IN ONE OF YOUR EARLIER-- UH--ESCAPADES--YOU ATTACKED METROPOLIS WITH--WELL, WITH GIANT TEDDY BEARS AND HUMONGOUS TIN SOLDIERS EQUIPPED WITH FLAMETHROWERS...
YES. IT MADE ALL THE PAPERS.
THIS ATTACK OCCURRED JUST OUTSIDE THE DAILY PLANET BUILDING. CAN I ASK WHY?
IT'S MUCH EASIER TO MAKE THE PAPERS IF YOU ATTACK THE PAPERS, MR. HOBSON.
WELL, I SUPPOSE THAT MAKES SOME SENSE...
SCHOTT

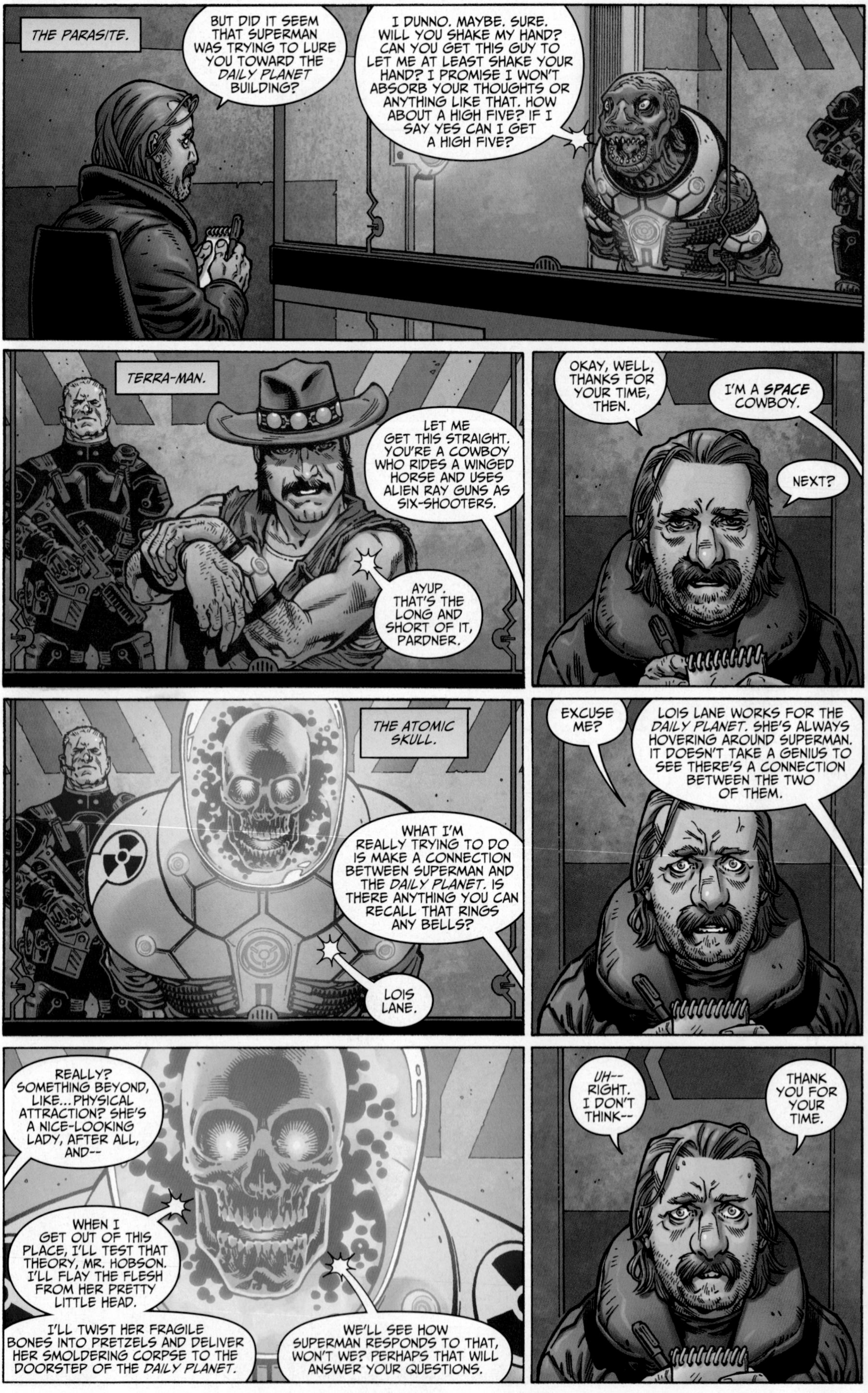
THE PARASITE.
BUT DID IT SEEM THAT SUPERMAN WAS TRYING TO LURE YOU TOWARD THE DAILY PLANET BUILDING?
I DUNNO. MAYBE. SURE. WILL YOU SHAKE MY HAND? CAN YOU GET THIS GUY TO LET ME AT LEAST SHAKE YOUR HAND? I PROMISE I WON'T ABSORB YOUR THOUGHTS OR ANYTHING LIKE THAT. HOW ABOUT A HIGH FIVE? IF I SAY YES CAN I GET A HIGH FIVE?
TERRA-MAN.
LET ME GET THIS STRAIGHT. YOU'RE A COWBOY WHO RIDES A WINGED HORSE AND USES ALIEN RAY GUNS AS SIX-SHOOTERS.
AYUP. THAT'S THE LONG AND SHORT OF IT, PARDNER.
OKAY, WELL, THANKS FOR YOUR TIME, THEN.
I'M A SPACE COWBOY.
NEXT?
THE ATOMIC SKULL.
WHAT I'M REALLY TRYING TO DO IS MAKE A CONNECTION BETWEEN SUPERMAN AND THE DAILY PLANET. IS THERE ANYTHING YOU CAN RECALL THAT RINGS ANY BELLS?
LOIS LANE.
EXCUSE ME?
LOIS LANE WORKS FOR THE DAILY PLANET. SHE'S ALWAYS HOVERING AROUND SUPERMAN. IT DOESN'T TAKE A GENIUS TO SEE THERE'S A CONNECTION BETWEEN THE TWO OF THEM.
REALLY? SOMETHING BEYOND, LIKE...PHYSICAL ATTRACTION? SHE'S A NICE-LOOKING LADY, AFTER ALL, AND--
WHEN I GET OUT OF THIS PLACE, I'LL TEST THAT THEORY, MR. HOBSON. I'LL FLAY THE FLESH FROM HER PRETTY LITTLE HEAD.
I'LL TWIST HER FRAGILE BONES INTO PRETZELS AND DELIVER HER SMOLDERING CORPSE TO THE DOORSTEP OF THE DAILY PLANET.
WE'LL SEE HOW SUPERMAN RESPONDS TO THAT, WON'T WE? PERHAPS THAT WILL ANSWER YOUR QUESTIONS.
UH--RIGHT. I DON'T THINK--
THANK YOU FOR YOUR TIME.

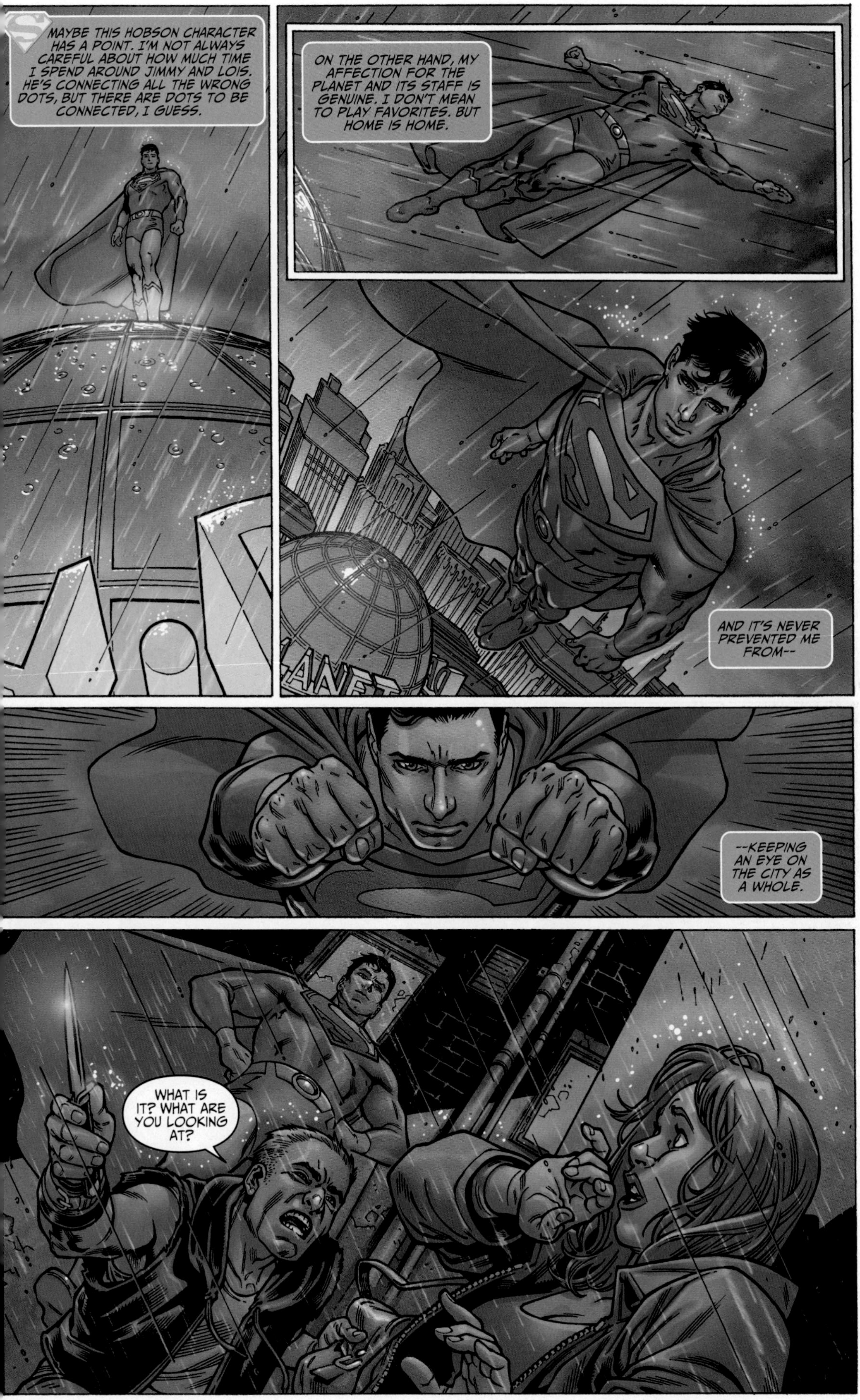
MAYBE THIS HOBSON CHARACTER HAS A POINT. I'M NOT ALWAYS CAREFUL ABOUT HOW MUCH TIME I SPEND AROUND JIMMY AND LOIS. HE'S CONNECTING ALL THE WRONG DOTS, BUT THERE ARE DOTS TO BE CONNECTED, I GUESS.
ON THE OTHER HAND, MY AFFECTION FOR THE PLANET AND ITS STAFF IS GENUINE. I DON'T MEAN TO PLAY FAVORITES. BUT HOME IS HOME.
AND IT'S NEVER PREVENTED ME FROM--
--KEEPING AN EYE ON THE CITY AS A WHOLE.
WHAT IS IT? WHAT ARE YOU LOOKING AT?

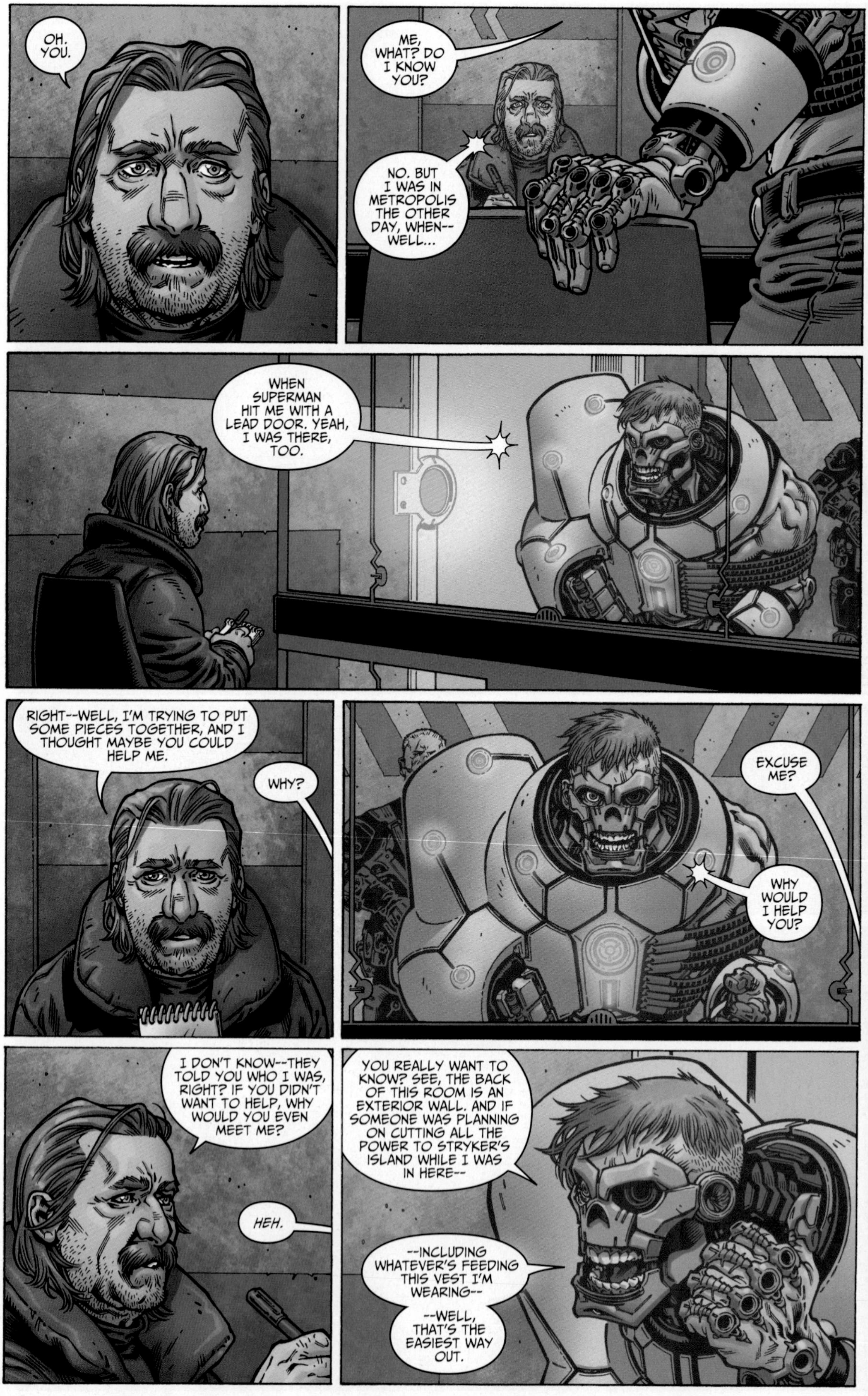
OH. YOU.
ME, WHAT? DO I KNOW YOU?
NO. BUT I WAS IN METROPOLIS THE OTHER DAY, WHEN-- WELL...
WHEN SUPERMAN HIT ME WITH A LEAD DOOR. YEAH, I WAS THERE, TOO.
RIGHT--WELL, I'M TRYING TO PUT SOME PIECES TOGETHER, AND I THOUGHT MAYBE YOU COULD HELP ME.
WHY?
EXCUSE ME?
WHY WOULD I HELP YOU?
I DON'T KNOW--THEY TOLD YOU WHO I WAS, RIGHT? IF YOU DIDN'T WANT TO HELP, WHY WOULD YOU EVEN MEET ME?
HEH.
YOU REALLY WANT TO KNOW? SEE, THE BACK OF THIS ROOM IS AN EXTERIOR WALL. AND IF SOMEONE WAS PLANNING ON CUTTING ALL THE POWER TO STRYKER'S ISLAND WHILE I WAS IN HERE--
--INCLUDING WHATEVER'S FEEDING THIS VEST I'M WEARING--
--WELL, THAT'S THE EASIEST WAY OUT.

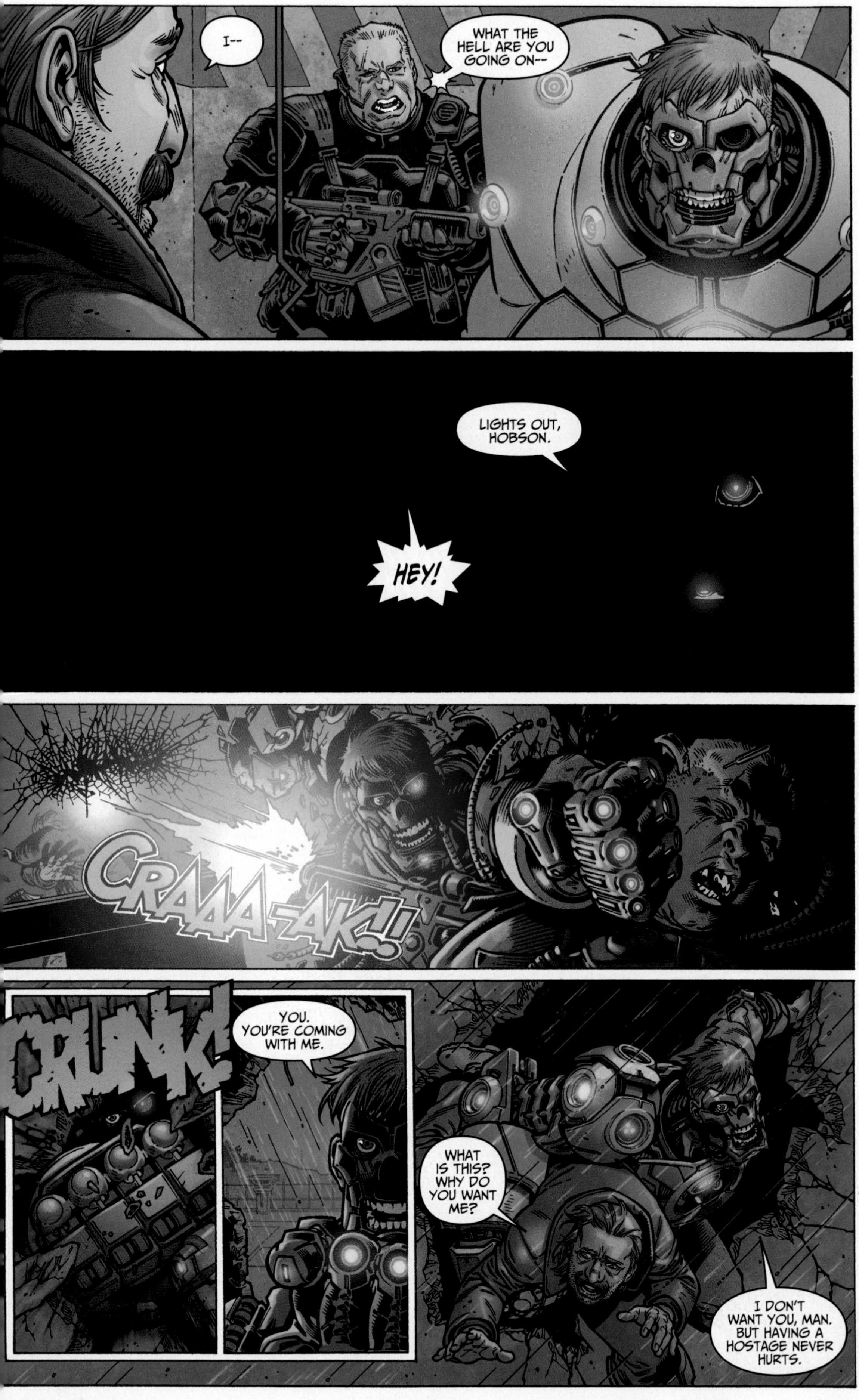
I--
WHAT THE HELL ARE YOU GOING ON--
LIGHTS OUT, HOBSON.
HEY!
CRAAAZAK!!
CRUNK!
YOU. YOU'RE COMING WITH ME.
WHAT IS THIS? WHY DO YOU WANT ME?
I DON'T WANT YOU, MAN. BUT HAVING A HOSTAGE NEVER HURTS.

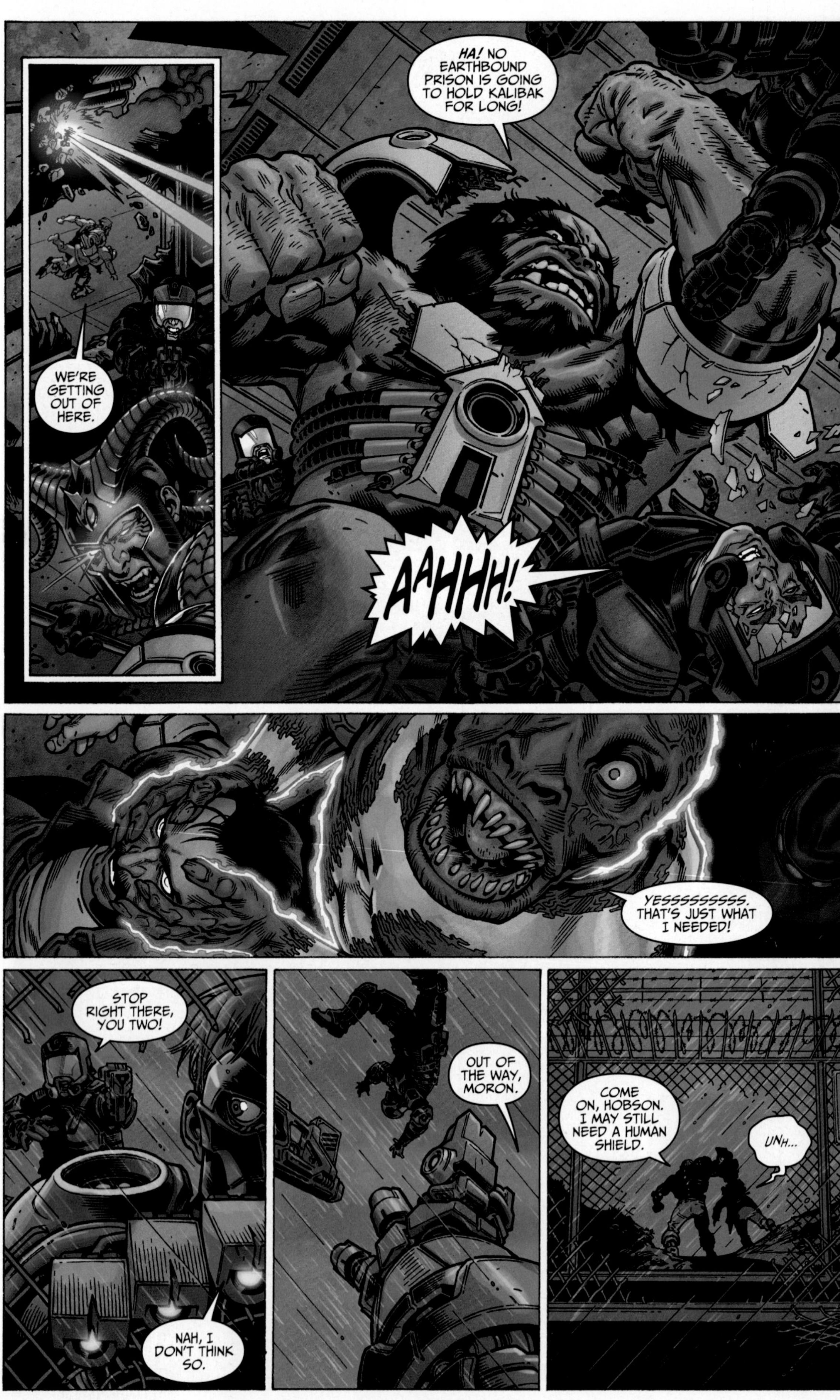
HA! NO EARTHBOUND PRISON IS GOING TO HOLD KALIBAK FOR LONG!
WE'RE GETTING OUT OF HERE.
AAHHH!
YESSSSSSSSS. THAT'S JUST WHAT I NEEDED!
STOP RIGHT THERE, YOU TWO!
NAH, I DON'T THINK SO.
OUT OF THE WAY, MORON.
COME ON, HOBSON. I MAY STILL NEED A HUMAN SHIELD.
UNH...

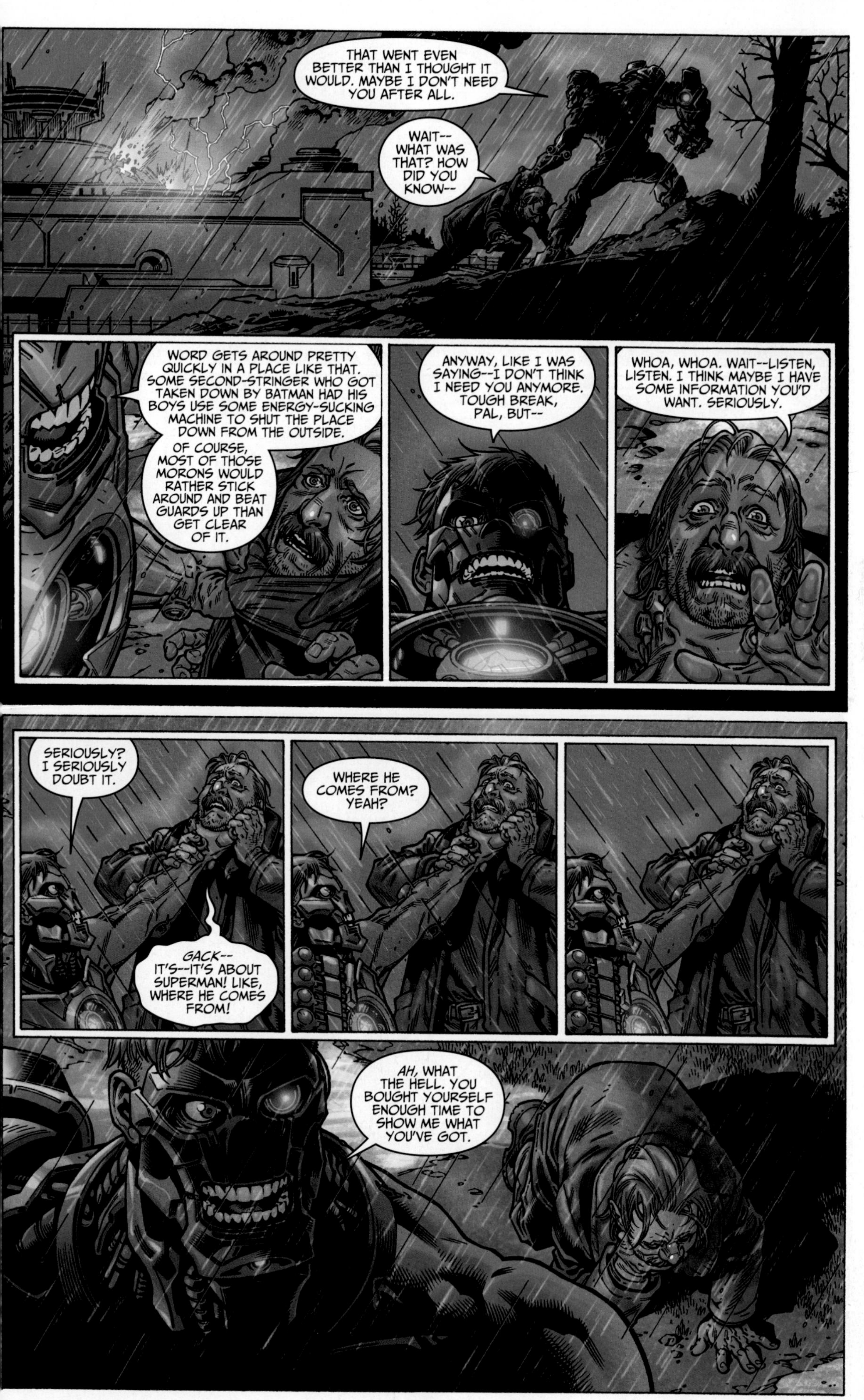
THAT WENT EVEN BETTER THAN I THOUGHT IT WOULD. MAYBE I DON'T NEED YOU AFTER ALL.
WAIT-- WHAT WAS THAT? HOW DID YOU KNOW--
WORD GETS AROUND PRETTY QUICKLY IN A PLACE LIKE THAT. SOME SECOND-STRINGER WHO GOT TAKEN DOWN BY BATMAN HAD HIS BOYS USE SOME ENERGY-SUCKING MACHINE TO SHUT THE PLACE DOWN FROM THE OUTSIDE.
OF COURSE, MOST OF THOSE MORONS WOULD RATHER STICK AROUND AND BEAT GUARDS UP THAN GET CLEAR OF IT.
ANYWAY, LIKE I WAS SAYING--I DON'T THINK I NEED YOU ANYMORE. TOUGH BREAK, PAL, BUT--
WHOA, WHOA. WAIT--LISTEN, LISTEN. I THINK MAYBE I HAVE SOME INFORMATION YOU'D WANT. SERIOUSLY.
SERIOUSLY? I SERIOUSLY DOUBT IT.
GACK-- IT'S--IT'S ABOUT SUPERMAN! LIKE, WHERE HE COMES FROM!
WHERE HE COMES FROM? YEAH?
AH, WHAT THE HELL. YOU BOUGHT YOURSELF ENOUGH TIME TO SHOW ME WHAT YOU'VE GOT.

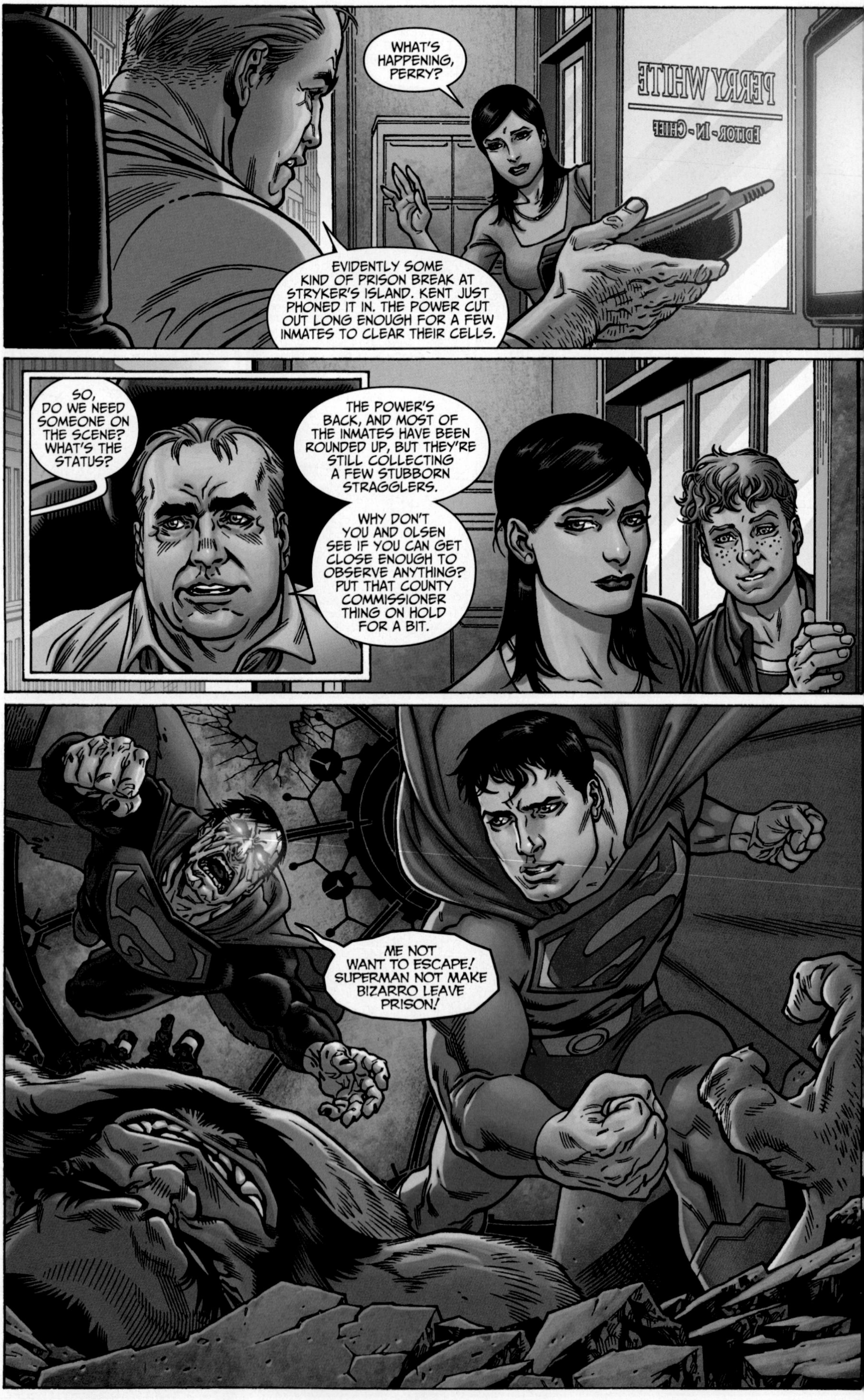

WHAT'S HAPPENING, PERRY?
PERRY WHITE
EDITOR - IN - CHIEF
EVIDENTLY SOME KIND OF PRISON BREAK AT STRYKER'S ISLAND. KENT JUST PHONED IT IN. THE POWER CUT OUT LONG ENOUGH FOR A FEW INMATES TO CLEAR THEIR CELLS.
SO, DO WE NEED SOMEONE ON THE SCENE? WHAT'S THE STATUS?
THE POWER'S BACK, AND MOST OF THE INMATES HAVE BEEN ROUNDED UP, BUT THEY'RE STILL COLLECTING A FEW STUBBORN STRAGGLERS.
WHY DON'T YOU AND OLSEN SEE IF YOU CAN GET CLOSE ENOUGH TO OBSERVE ANYTHING? PUT THAT COUNTY COMMISSIONER THING ON HOLD FOR A BIT.
ME NOT WANT TO ESCAPE! SUPERMAN NOT MAKE BIZARRO LEAVE PRISON!

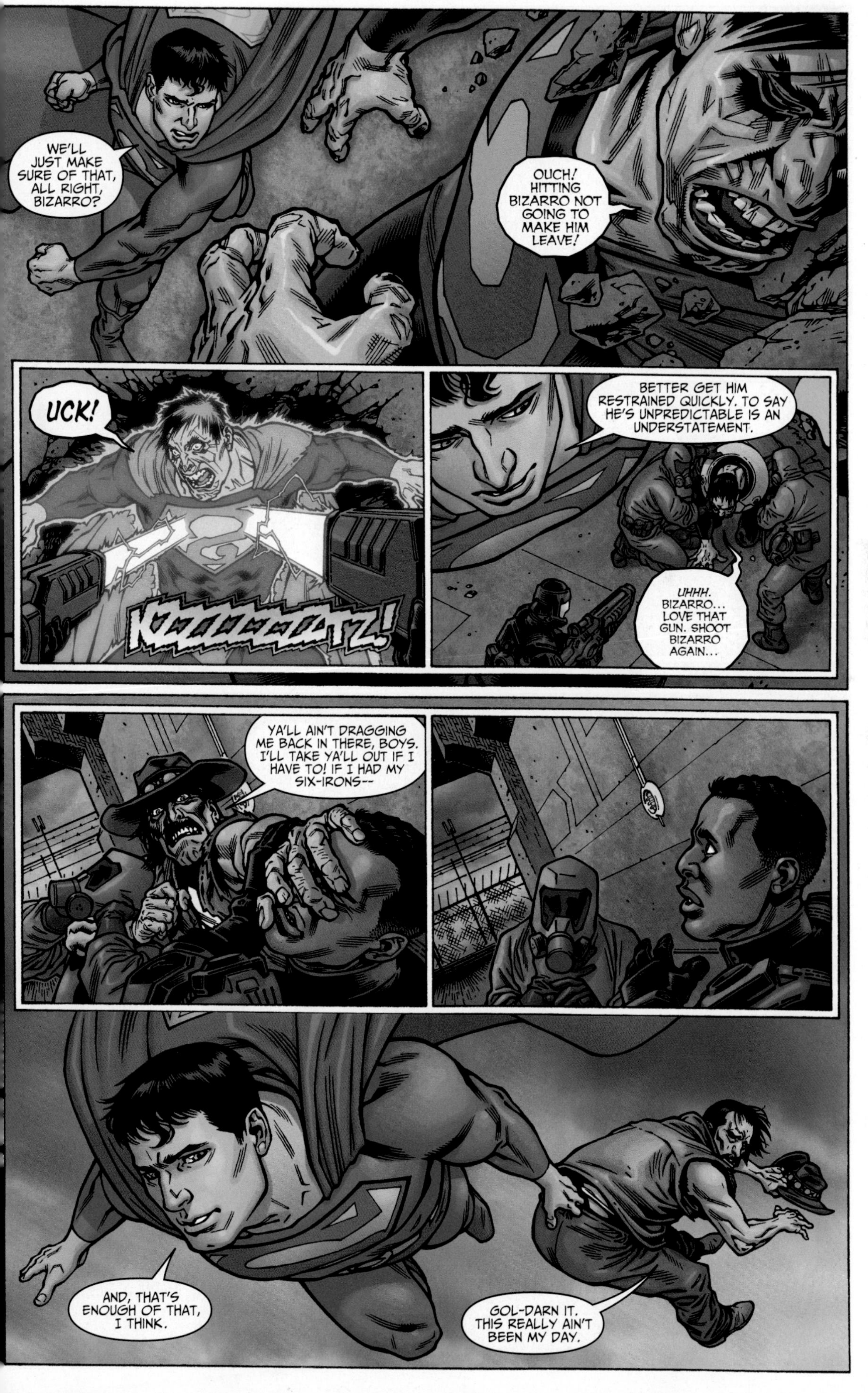
WE'LL JUST MAKE SURE OF THAT, ALL RIGHT, BIZARRO?
OUCH! HITTING BIZARRO NOT GOING TO MAKE HIM LEAVE!
UCK!
KZZZZZZZZTZ!
BETTER GET HIM RESTRAINED QUICKLY. TO SAY HE'S UNPREDICTABLE IS AN UNDERSTATEMENT.
UHHH. BIZARRO... LOVE THAT GUN. SHOOT BIZARRO AGAIN...
YA'LL AIN'T DRAGGING ME BACK IN THERE, BOYS. I'LL TAKE YA'LL OUT IF I HAVE TO! IF I HAD MY SIX-IRONS--
AND, THAT'S ENOUGH OF THAT, I THINK.
GOL-DARN IT. THIS REALLY AIN'T BEEN MY DAY.

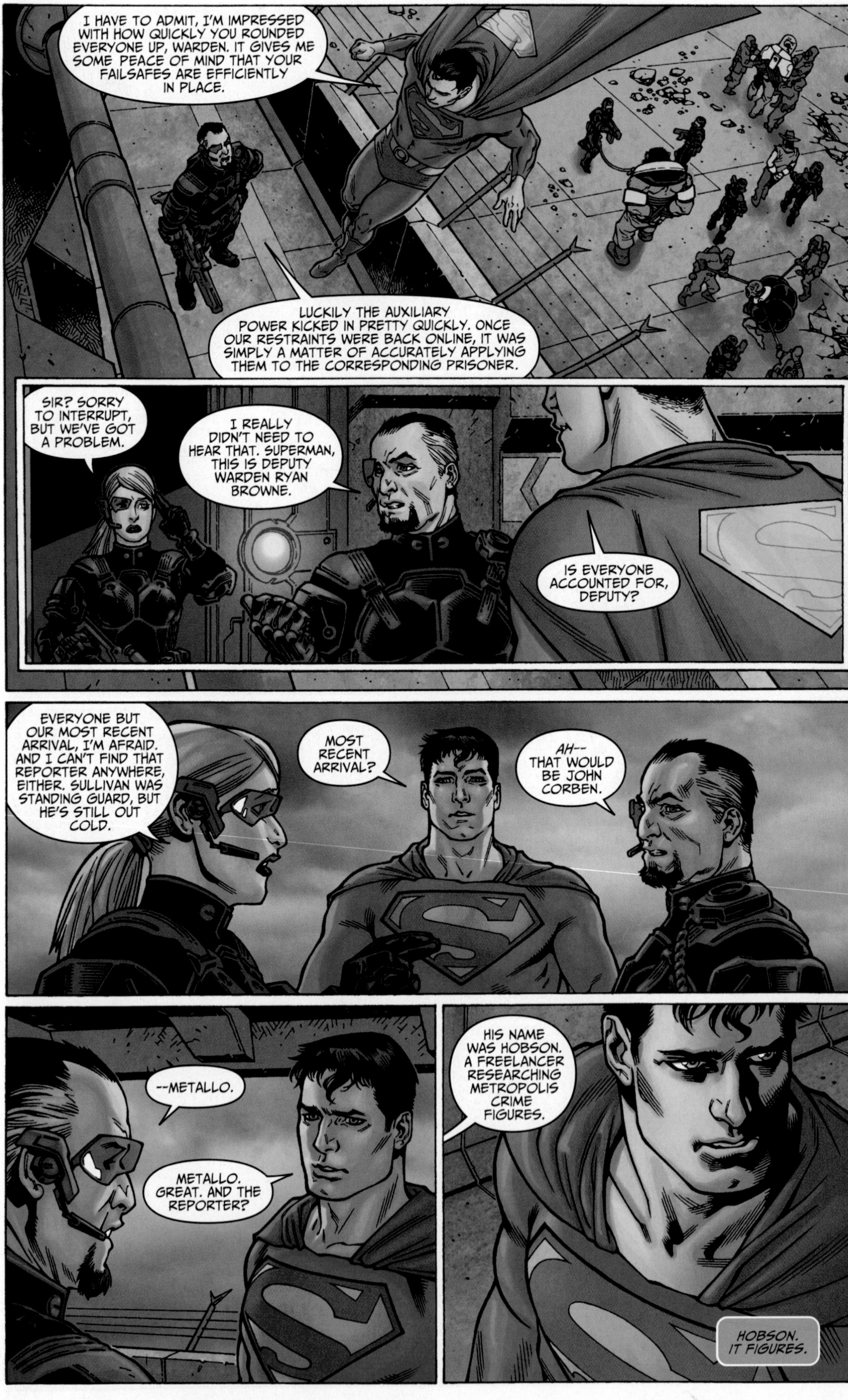
I HAVE TO ADMIT, I'M IMPRESSED WITH HOW QUICKLY YOU ROUNDED EVERYONE UP, WARDEN. IT GIVES ME SOME PEACE OF MIND THAT YOUR FAILSAFES ARE EFFICIENTLY IN PLACE.
LUCKILY THE AUXILIARY POWER KICKED IN PRETTY QUICKLY. ONCE OUR RESTRAINTS WERE BACK ONLINE, IT WAS SIMPLY A MATTER OF ACCURATELY APPLYING THEM TO THE CORRESPONDING PRISONER.
SIR? SORRY TO INTERRUPT, BUT WE'VE GOT A PROBLEM.
I REALLY DIDN'T NEED TO HEAR THAT. SUPERMAN, THIS IS DEPUTY WARDEN RYAN BROWNE.
IS EVERYONE ACCOUNTED FOR, DEPUTY?
EVERYONE BUT OUR MOST RECENT ARRIVAL, I'M AFRAID. AND I CAN'T FIND THAT REPORTER ANYWHERE, EITHER. SULLIVAN WAS STANDING GUARD, BUT HE'S STILL OUT COLD.
MOST RECENT ARRIVAL?
AH-- THAT WOULD BE JOHN CORBEN.
--METALLO.
METALLO. GREAT. AND THE REPORTER?
HIS NAME WAS HOBSON. A FREELANCER RESEARCHING METROPOLIS CRIME FIGURES.
HOBSON. IT FIGURES.

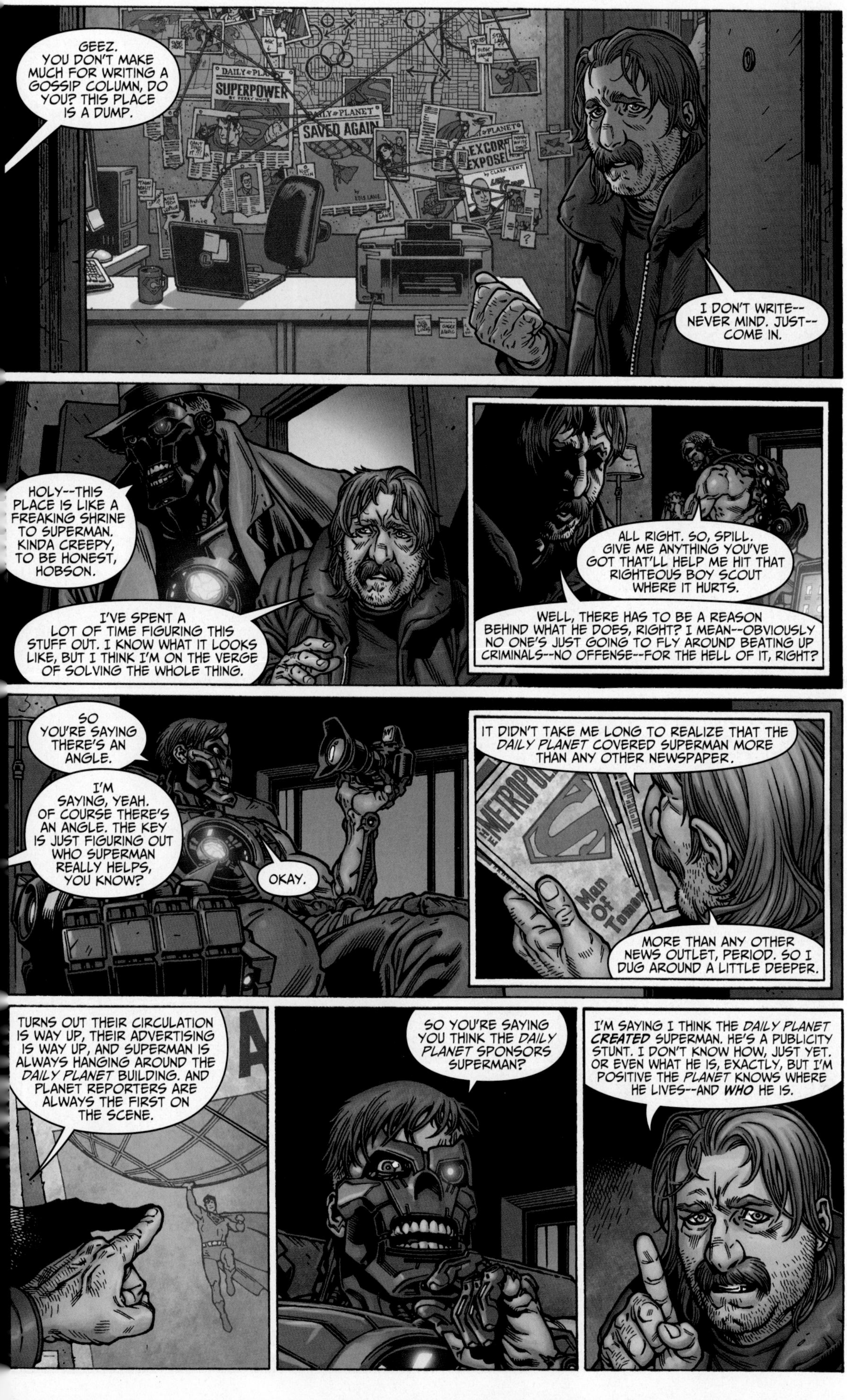
GEEZ. YOU DON'T MAKE MUCH FOR WRITING A GOSSIP COLUMN, DO YOU? THIS PLACE IS A DUMP.
DAILY PLANET
SUPERPOWER
SAVED AGAIN
EXCORP EXPOSE
I DON'T WRITE-- NEVER MIND. JUST-- COME IN.
HOLY--THIS PLACE IS LIKE A FREAKING SHRINE TO SUPERMAN. KINDA CREEPY, TO BE HONEST, HOBSON.
I'VE SPENT A LOT OF TIME FIGURING THIS STUFF OUT. I KNOW WHAT IT LOOKS LIKE, BUT I THINK I'M ON THE VERGE OF SOLVING THE WHOLE THING.
ALL RIGHT. SO, SPILL. GIVE ME ANYTHING YOU'VE GOT THAT'LL HELP ME HIT THAT RIGHTEOUS BOY SCOUT WHERE IT HURTS.
WELL, THERE HAS TO BE A REASON BEHIND WHAT HE DOES, RIGHT? I MEAN--OBVIOUSLY NO ONE'S JUST GOING TO FLY AROUND BEATING UP CRIMINALS--NO OFFENSE--FOR THE HELL OF IT, RIGHT?
SO YOU'RE SAYING THERE'S AN ANGLE.
I'M SAYING, YEAH. OF COURSE THERE'S AN ANGLE. THE KEY IS JUST FIGURING OUT WHO SUPERMAN REALLY HELPS, YOU KNOW?
OKAY.
IT DIDN'T TAKE ME LONG TO REALIZE THAT THE *DAILY PLANET* COVERED SUPERMAN MORE THAN ANY OTHER NEWSPAPER.
METROPOL
Man Of Tomor
MORE THAN ANY OTHER NEWS OUTLET, PERIOD. SO I DUG AROUND A LITTLE DEEPER.
TURNS OUT THEIR CIRCULATION IS WAY UP, THEIR ADVERTISING IS WAY UP, AND SUPERMAN IS ALWAYS HANGING AROUND THE *DAILY PLANET* BUILDING. AND PLANET REPORTERS ARE ALWAYS THE FIRST ON THE SCENE.
SO YOU'RE SAYING YOU THINK THE *DAILY PLANET* SPONSORS SUPERMAN?
I'M SAYING I THINK THE *DAILY PLANET* ***CREATED*** SUPERMAN. HE'S A PUBLICITY STUNT. I DON'T KNOW HOW, JUST YET. OR EVEN WHAT HE IS, EXACTLY, BUT I'M POSITIVE THE *PLANET* KNOWS WHERE HE LIVES--AND ***WHO*** HE IS.

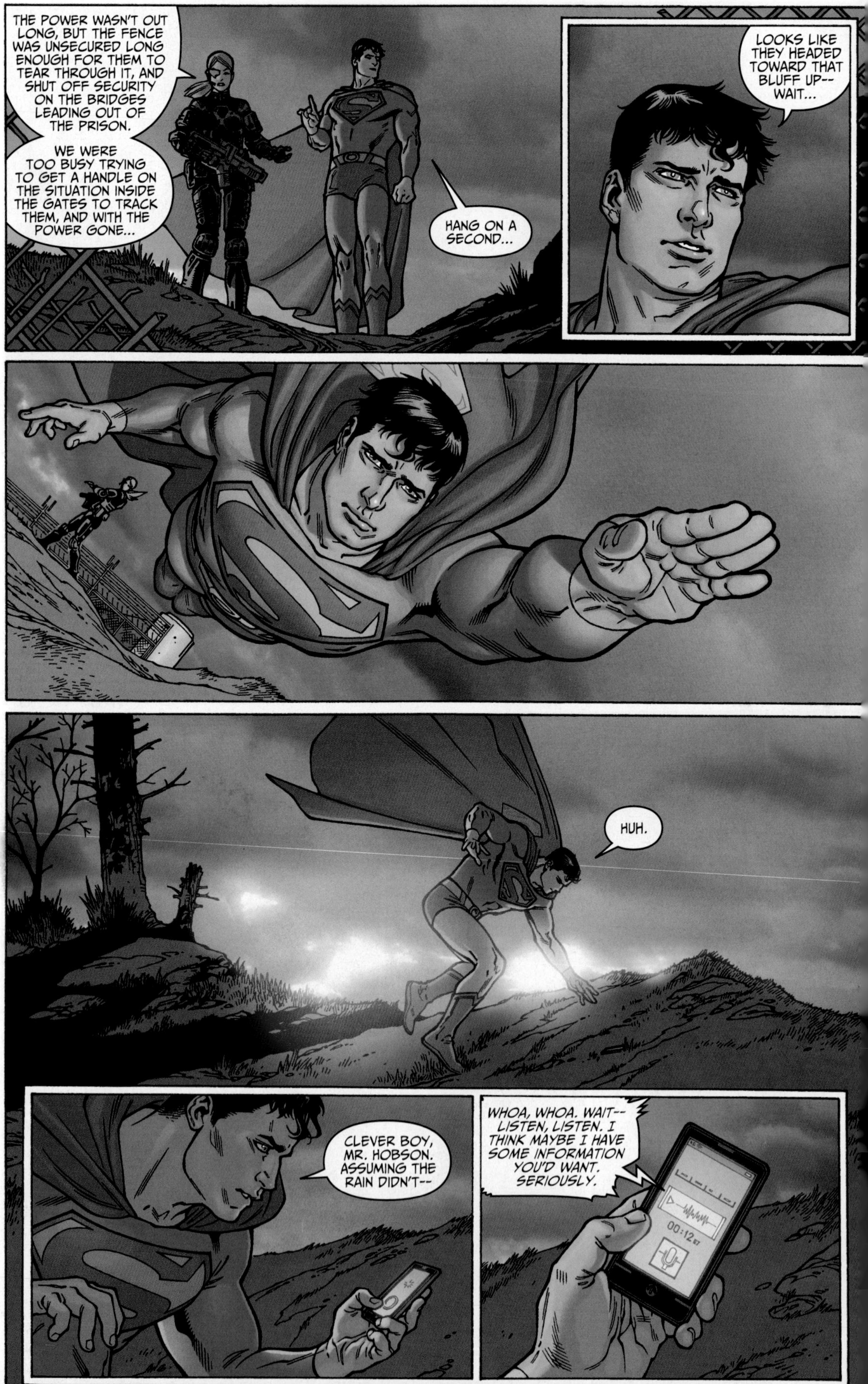
THE POWER WASN'T OUT LONG, BUT THE FENCE WAS UNSECURED LONG ENOUGH FOR THEM TO TEAR THROUGH IT, AND SHUT OFF SECURITY ON THE BRIDGES LEADING OUT OF THE PRISON.
WE WERE TOO BUSY TRYING TO GET A HANDLE ON THE SITUATION INSIDE THE GATES TO TRACK THEM, AND WITH THE POWER GONE...
HANG ON A SECOND...
LOOKS LIKE THEY HEADED TOWARD THAT BLUFF UP-- WAIT...
HUH.
CLEVER BOY, MR. HOBSON. ASSUMING THE RAIN DIDN'T--
WHOA, WHOA. WAIT-- LISTEN, LISTEN. I THINK MAYBE I HAVE SOME INFORMATION YOU'D WANT. SERIOUSLY.
00:12

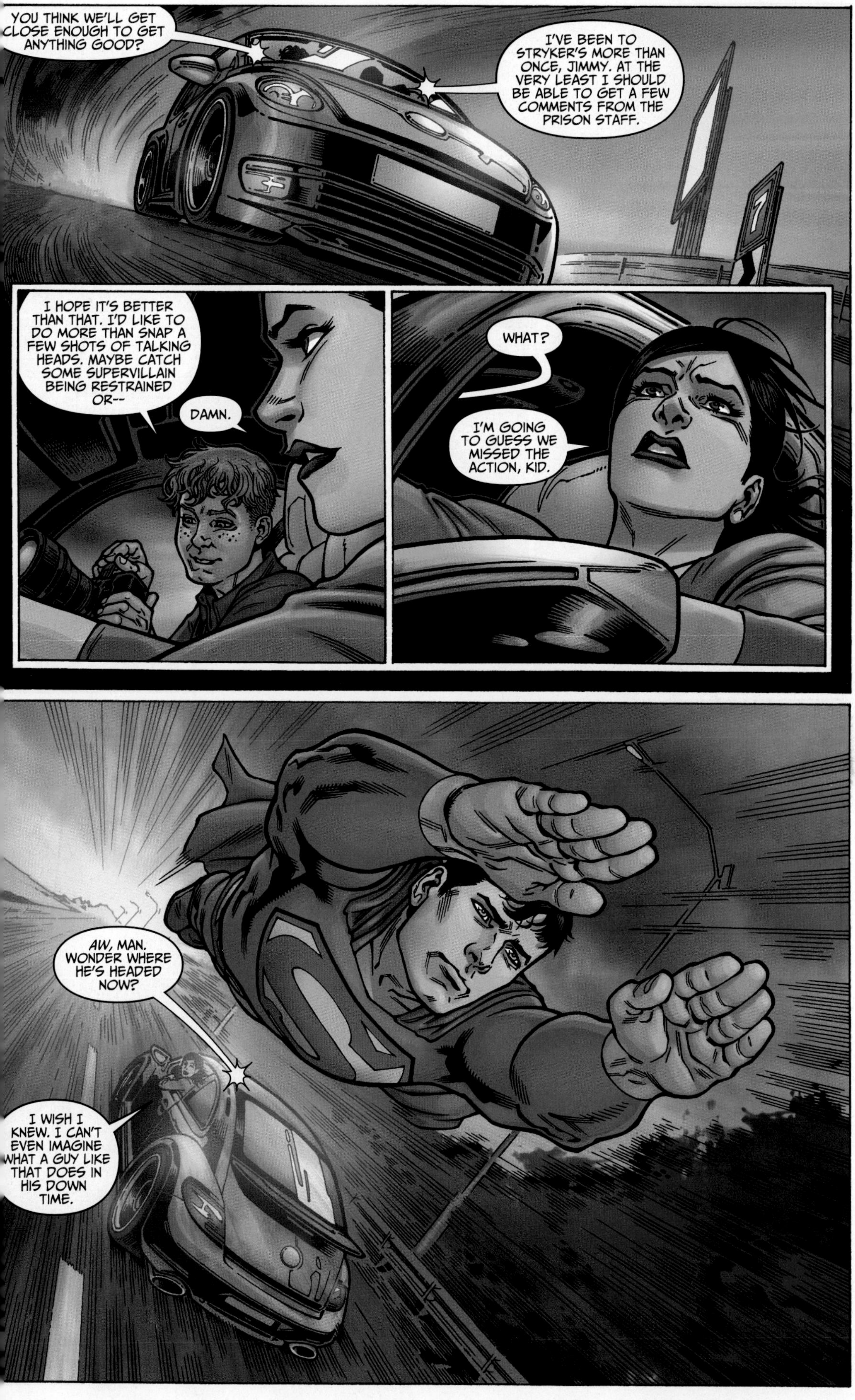
YOU THINK WE'LL GET CLOSE ENOUGH TO GET ANYTHING GOOD?
I'VE BEEN TO STRYKER'S MORE THAN ONCE, JIMMY. AT THE VERY LEAST I SHOULD BE ABLE TO GET A FEW COMMENTS FROM THE PRISON STAFF.
I HOPE IT'S BETTER THAN THAT. I'D LIKE TO DO MORE THAN SNAP A FEW SHOTS OF TALKING HEADS. MAYBE CATCH SOME SUPERVILLAIN BEING RESTRAINED OR--
DAMN.
WHAT?
I'M GOING TO GUESS WE MISSED THE ACTION, KID.
AW, MAN. WONDER WHERE HE'S HEADED NOW?
I WISH I KNEW. I CAN'T EVEN IMAGINE WHAT A GUY LIKE THAT DOES IN HIS DOWN TIME.

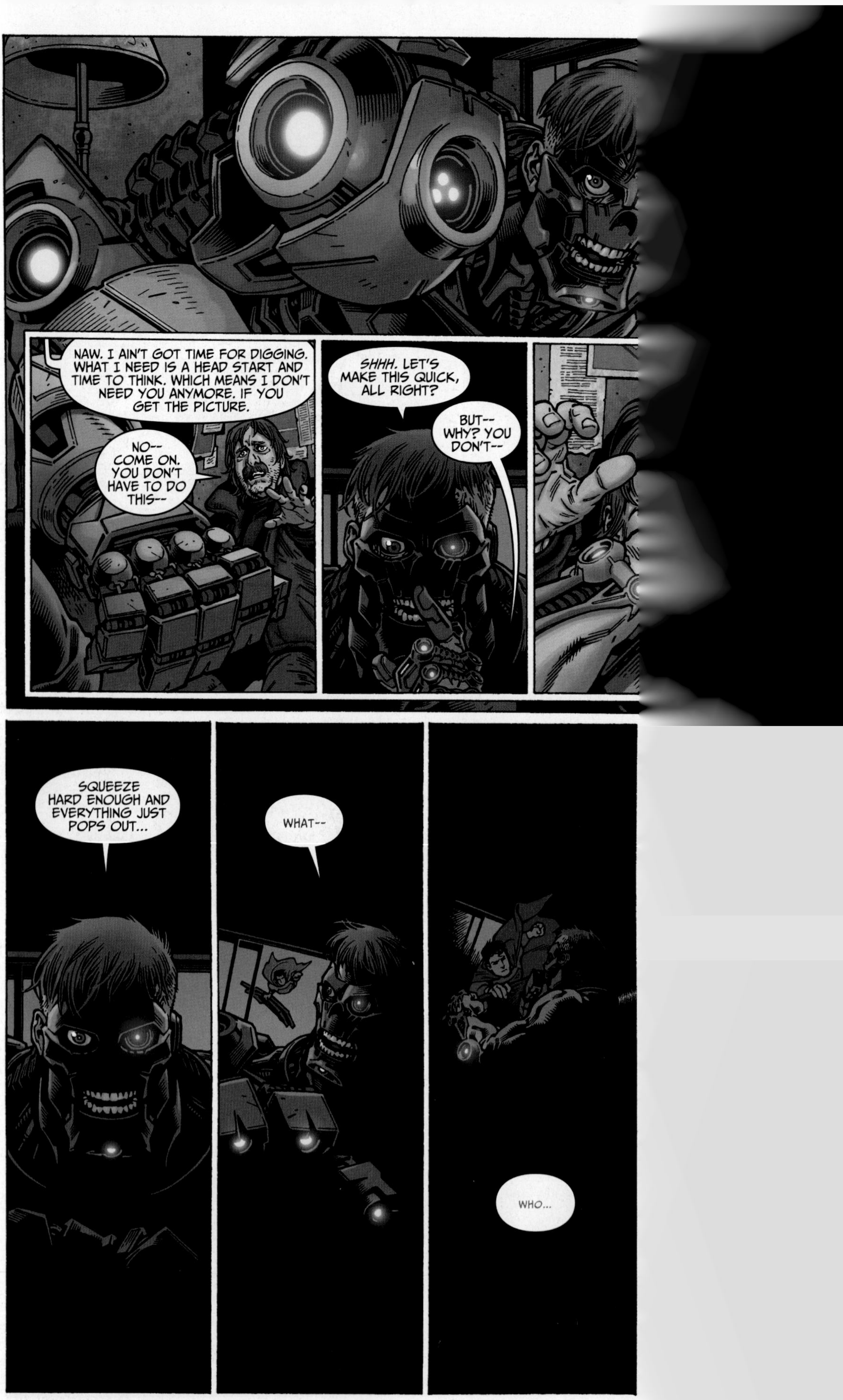
NAW. I AIN'T GOT TIME FOR DIGGING. WHAT I NEED IS A HEAD START AND TIME TO THINK. WHICH MEANS I DON'T NEED YOU ANYMORE. IF YOU GET THE PICTURE.
NO-- COME ON. YOU DON'T HAVE TO DO THIS--
SHHH. LET'S MAKE THIS QUICK, ALL RIGHT?
BUT-- WHY? YOU DON'T--
SQUEEZE HARD ENOUGH AND EVERYTHING JUST POPS OUT...
WHAT--
WHO...

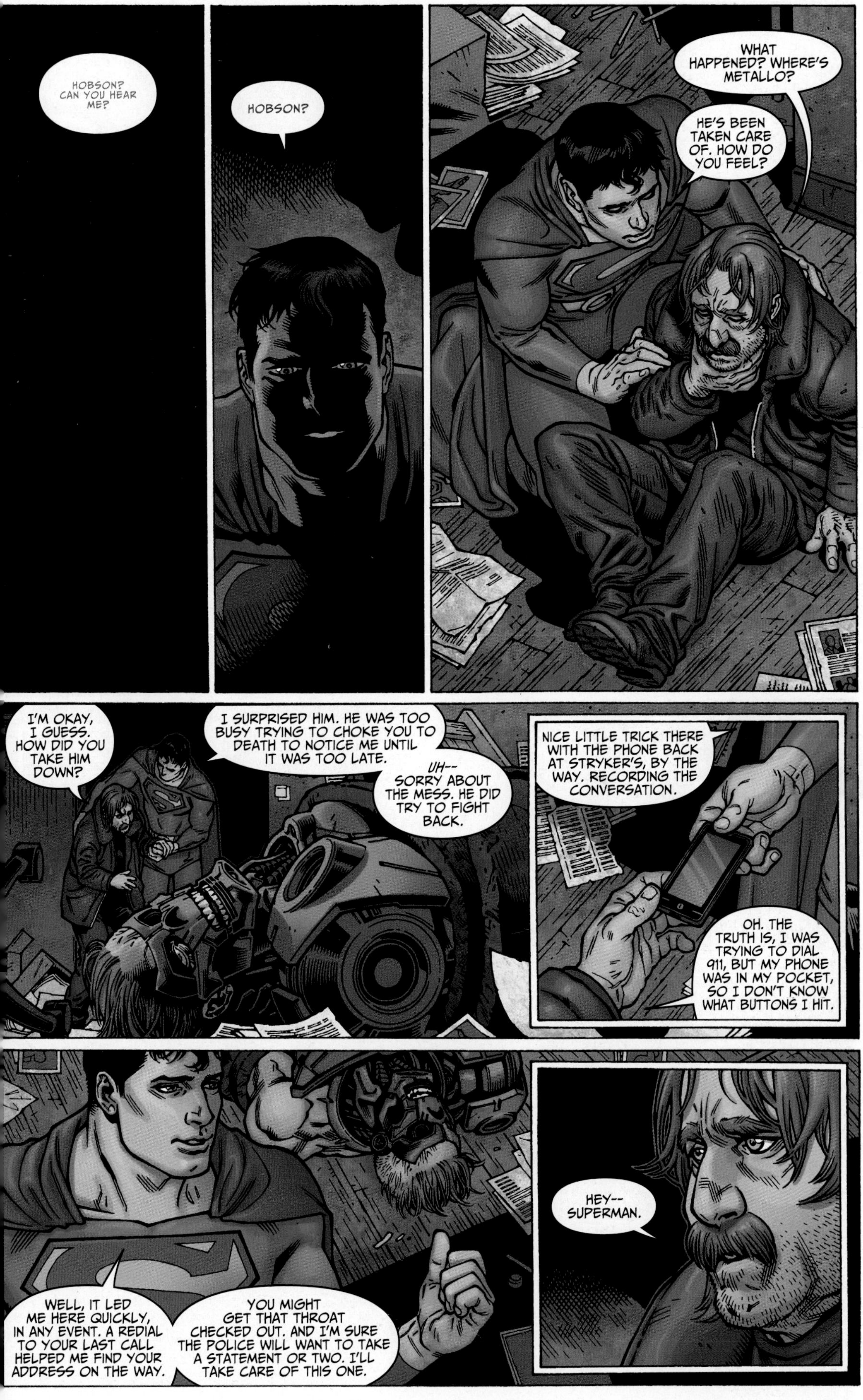
HOBSON? CAN YOU HEAR ME?
HOBSON?
WHAT HAPPENED? WHERE'S METALLO?
HE'S BEEN TAKEN CARE OF. HOW DO YOU FEEL?
I'M OKAY, I GUESS. HOW DID YOU TAKE HIM DOWN?
I SURPRISED HIM. HE WAS TOO BUSY TRYING TO CHOKE YOU TO DEATH TO NOTICE ME UNTIL IT WAS TOO LATE.
UH-- SORRY ABOUT THE MESS. HE DID TRY TO FIGHT BACK.
NICE LITTLE TRICK THERE WITH THE PHONE BACK AT STRYKER'S, BY THE WAY. RECORDING THE CONVERSATION.
OH. THE TRUTH IS, I WAS TRYING TO DIAL 911, BUT MY PHONE WAS IN MY POCKET, SO I DON'T KNOW WHAT BUTTONS I HIT.
WELL, IT LED ME HERE QUICKLY, IN ANY EVENT. A REDIAL TO YOUR LAST CALL HELPED ME FIND YOUR ADDRESS ON THE WAY.
YOU MIGHT GET THAT THROAT CHECKED OUT. AND I'M SURE THE POLICE WILL WANT TO TAKE A STATEMENT OR TWO. I'LL TAKE CARE OF THIS ONE.
HEY-- SUPERMAN.

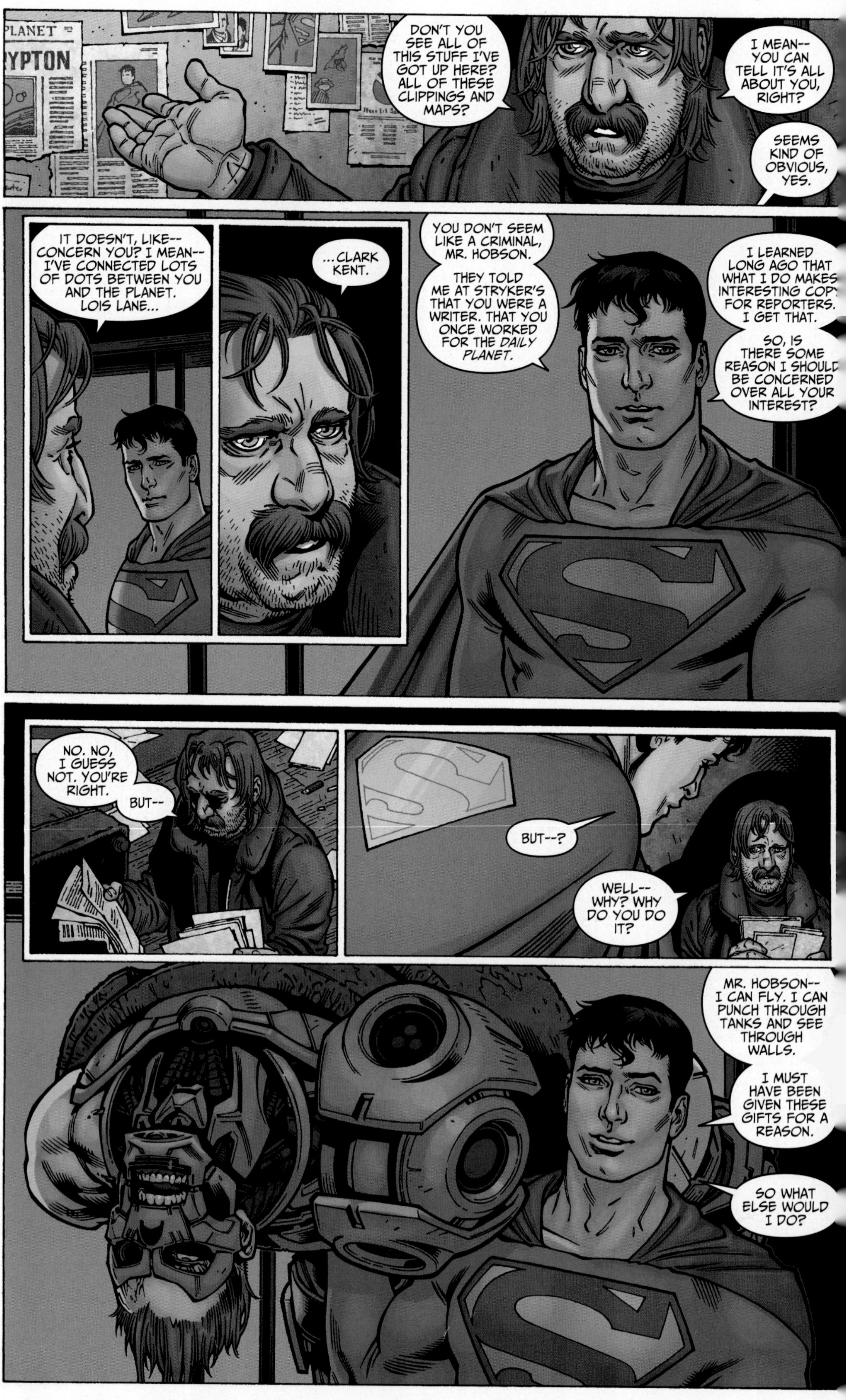
PLANET
RYPTON
DON'T YOU SEE ALL OF THIS STUFF I'VE GOT UP HERE? ALL OF THESE CLIPPINGS AND MAPS?
I MEAN-- YOU CAN TELL IT'S ALL ABOUT YOU, RIGHT?
SEEMS KIND OF OBVIOUS, YES.
IT DOESN'T, LIKE-- CONCERN YOU? I MEAN-- I'VE CONNECTED LOTS OF DOTS BETWEEN YOU AND THE PLANET. LOIS LANE...
...CLARK KENT.
YOU DON'T SEEM LIKE A CRIMINAL, MR. HOBSON.
THEY TOLD ME AT STRYKER'S THAT YOU WERE A WRITER. THAT YOU ONCE WORKED FOR THE *DAILY PLANET*.
I LEARNED LONG AGO THAT WHAT I DO MAKES INTERESTING COPY FOR REPORTERS. I GET THAT.
SO, IS THERE SOME REASON I SHOULD BE CONCERNED OVER ALL YOUR INTEREST?
NO. NO, I GUESS NOT. YOU'RE RIGHT.
BUT--
BUT--?
WELL-- WHY? WHY DO YOU DO IT?
MR. HOBSON-- I CAN FLY. I CAN PUNCH THROUGH TANKS AND SEE THROUGH WALLS.
I MUST HAVE BEEN GIVEN THESE GIFTS FOR A REASON.
SO WHAT ELSE WOULD I DO?

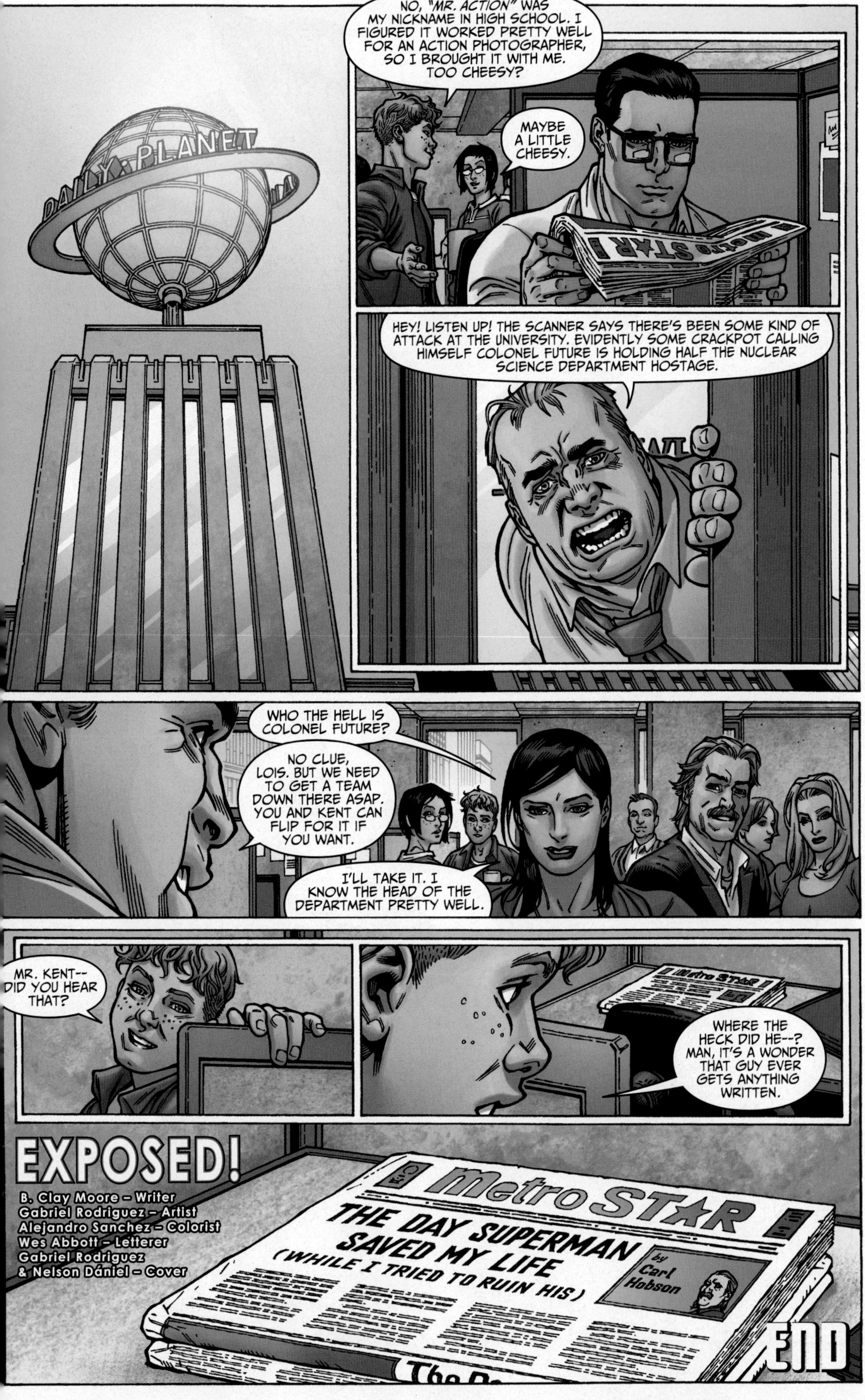
DAILY PLANET
NO, "MR. ACTION" WAS MY NICKNAME IN HIGH SCHOOL. I FIGURED IT WORKED PRETTY WELL FOR AN ACTION PHOTOGRAPHER, SO I BROUGHT IT WITH ME. TOO CHEESY?
MAYBE A LITTLE CHEESY.
Metro STAR
HEY! LISTEN UP! THE SCANNER SAYS THERE'S BEEN SOME KIND OF ATTACK AT THE UNIVERSITY. EVIDENTLY SOME CRACKPOT CALLING HIMSELF COLONEL FUTURE IS HOLDING HALF THE NUCLEAR SCIENCE DEPARTMENT HOSTAGE.
WHO THE HELL IS COLONEL FUTURE?
NO CLUE, LOIS. BUT WE NEED TO GET A TEAM DOWN THERE ASAP. YOU AND KENT CAN FLIP FOR IT IF YOU WANT.
I'LL TAKE IT. I KNOW THE HEAD OF THE DEPARTMENT PRETTY WELL.
MR. KENT-- DID YOU HEAR THAT?
Metro STAR
WHERE THE HECK DID HE--? MAN, IT'S A WONDER THAT GUY EVER GETS ANYTHING WRITTEN.
EXPOSED!
B. Clay Moore – Writer
Gabriel Rodriguez – Artist
Alejandro Sanchez – Colorist
Wes Abbott – Letterer
Gabriel Rodriguez & Nelson Dániel – Cover
Metro STAR
THE DAY SUPERMAN SAVED MY LIFE (WHILE I TRIED TO RUIN HIS)
by Carl Hobson
END

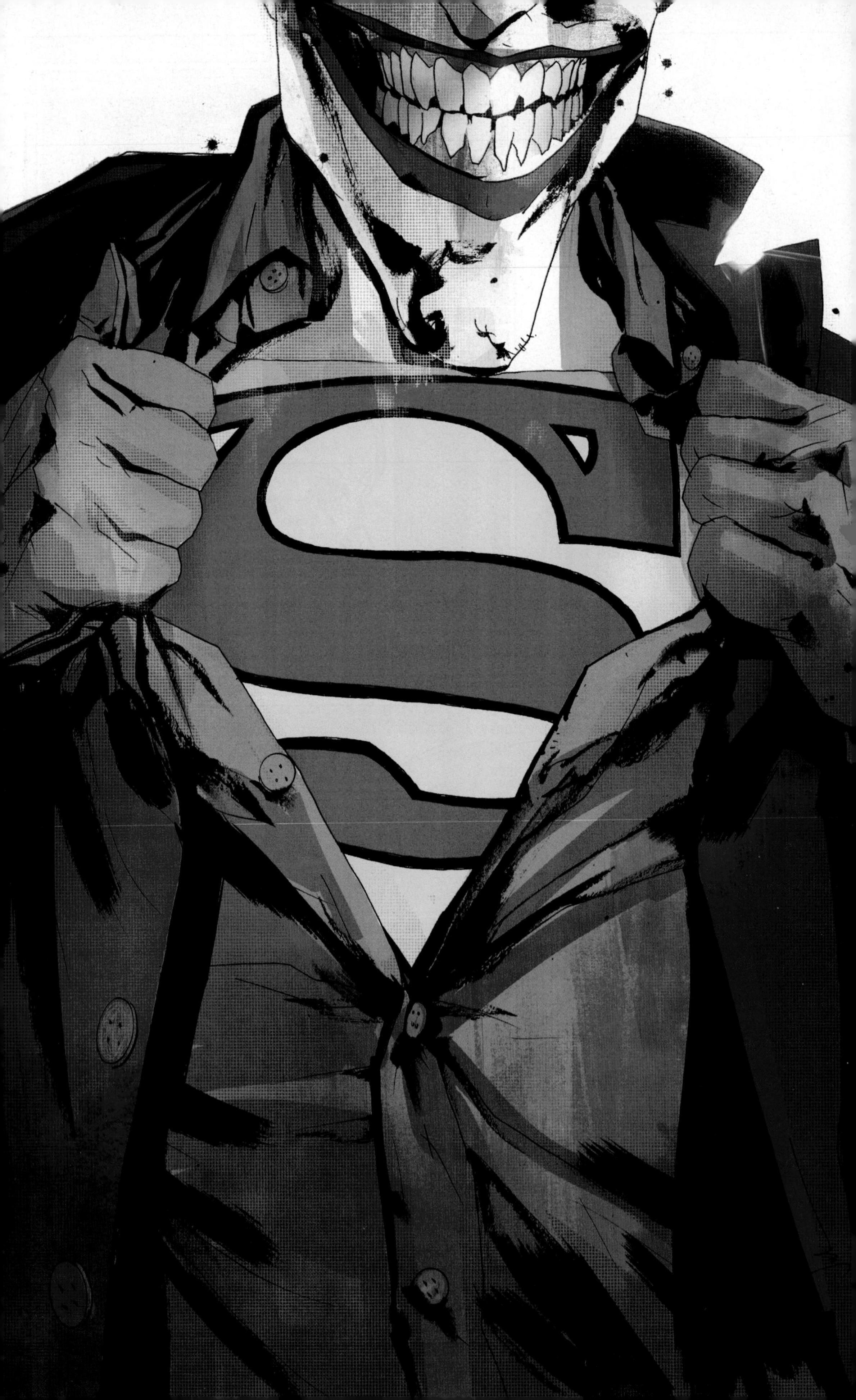

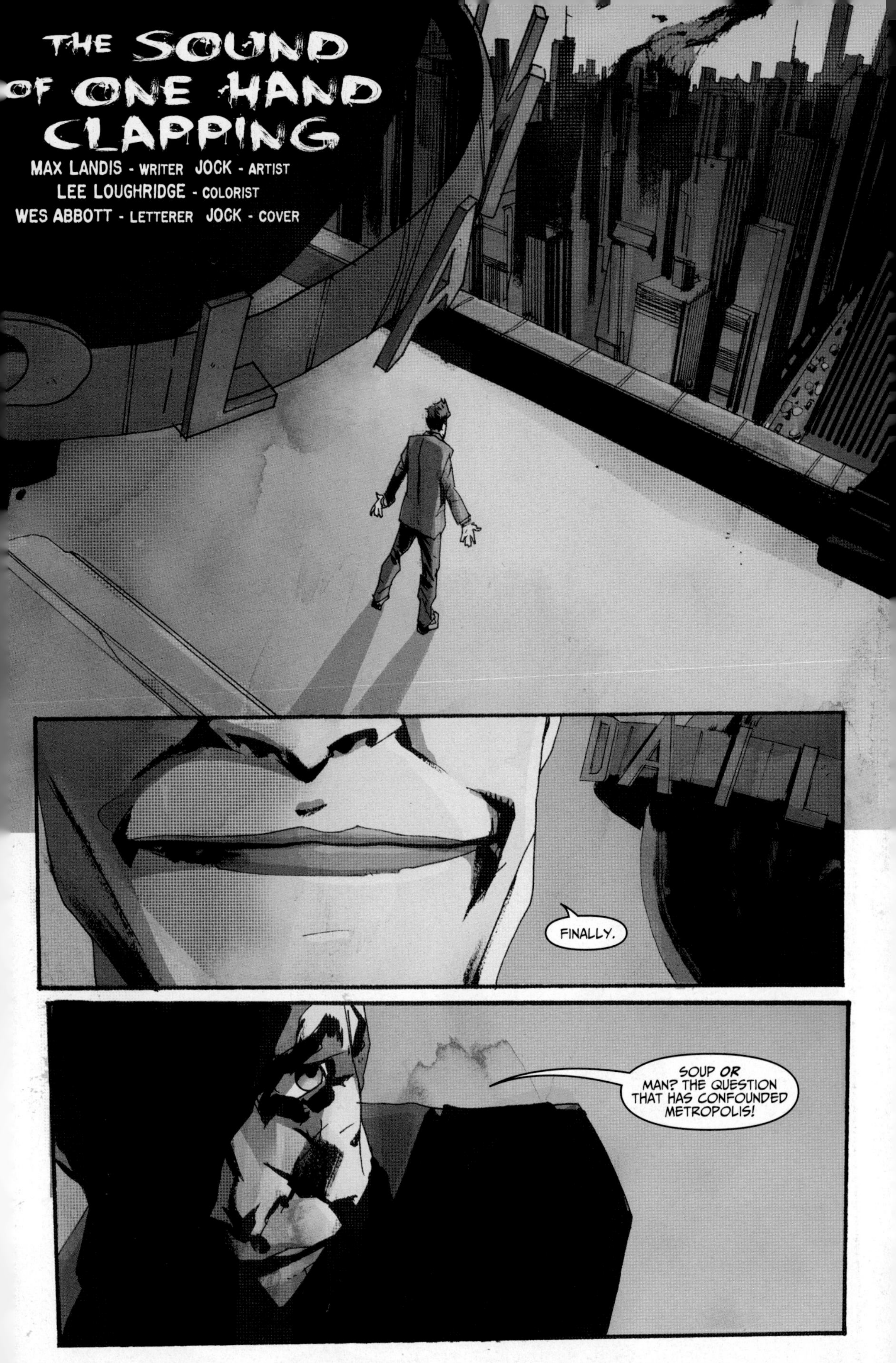
THE SOUND OF ONE HAND CLAPPING
MAX LANDIS - WRITER JOCK - ARTIST
LEE LOUGHRIDGE - COLORIST
WES ABBOTT - LETTERER JOCK - COVER
FINALLY.
SOUP OR MAN? THE QUESTION THAT HAS CONFOUNDED METROPOLIS!

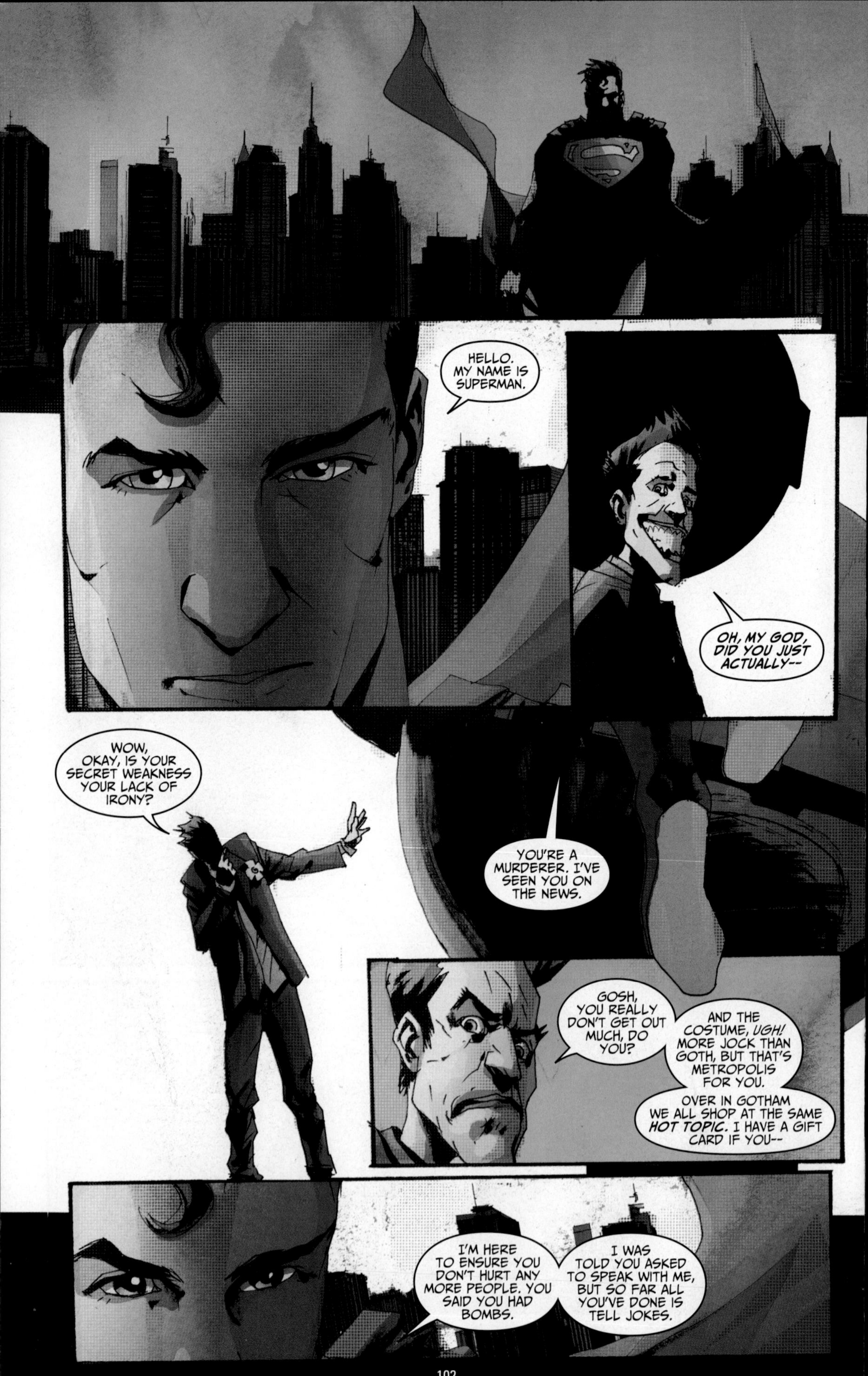
HELLO. MY NAME IS SUPERMAN.
OH, MY GOD, DID YOU JUST ACTUALLY--
WOW, OKAY, IS YOUR SECRET WEAKNESS YOUR LACK OF IRONY?
YOU'RE A MURDERER. I'VE SEEN YOU ON THE NEWS.
GOSH, YOU REALLY DON'T GET OUT MUCH, DO YOU?
AND THE COSTUME, *UGH!* MORE JOCK THAN GOTH, BUT THAT'S METROPOLIS FOR YOU.
OVER IN GOTHAM WE ALL SHOP AT THE SAME ***HOT TOPIC***. I HAVE A GIFT CARD IF YOU--
I'M HERE TO ENSURE YOU DON'T HURT ANY MORE PEOPLE. YOU SAID YOU HAD BOMBS.
I WAS TOLD YOU ASKED TO SPEAK WITH ME, BUT SO FAR ALL YOU'VE DONE IS TELL JOKES.

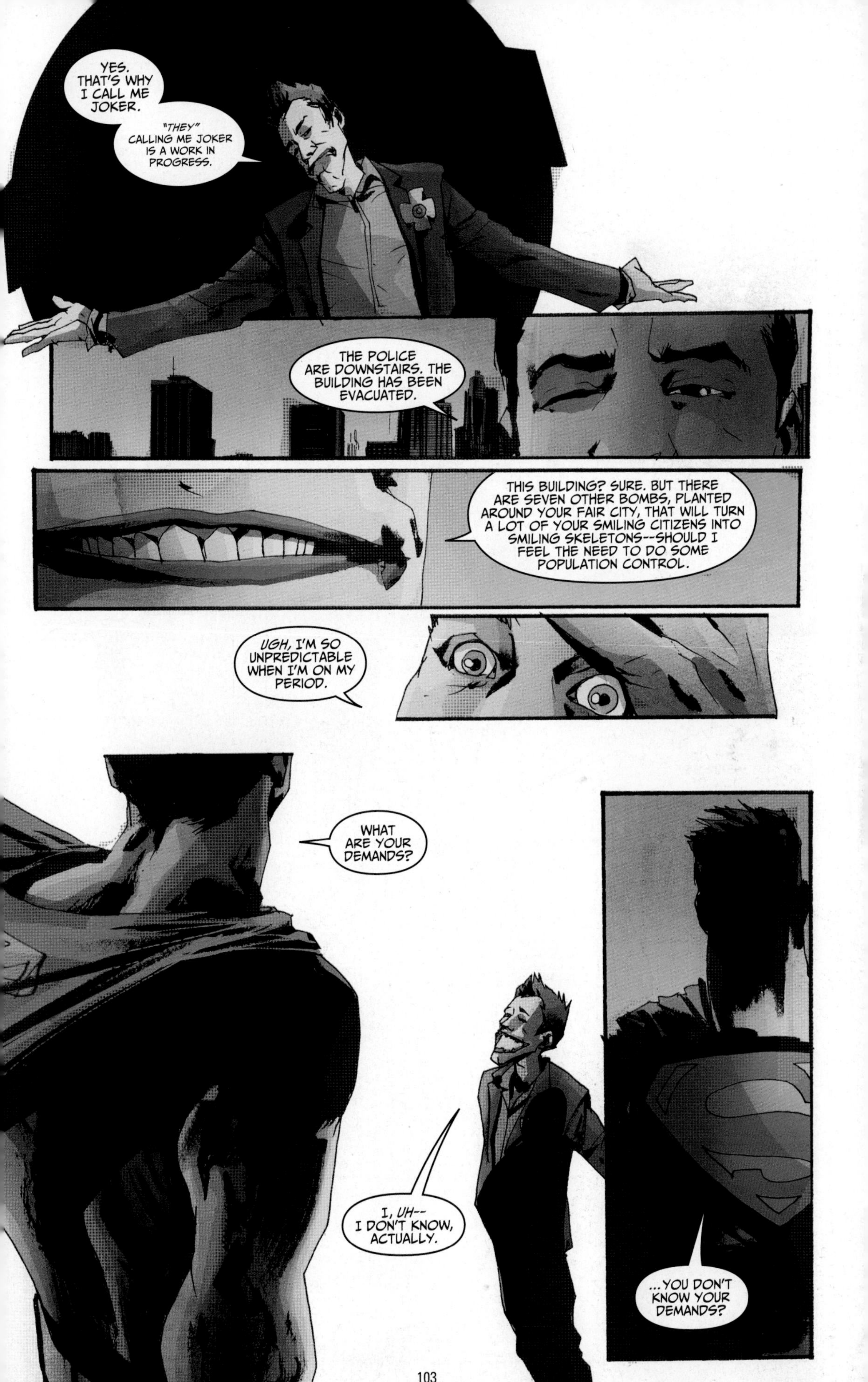
YES. THAT'S WHY I CALL ME JOKER.
"THEY" CALLING ME JOKER IS A WORK IN PROGRESS.
THE POLICE ARE DOWNSTAIRS. THE BUILDING HAS BEEN EVACUATED.
THIS BUILDING? SURE. BUT THERE ARE SEVEN OTHER BOMBS, PLANTED AROUND YOUR FAIR CITY, THAT WILL TURN A LOT OF YOUR SMILING CITIZENS INTO SMILING SKELETONS--SHOULD I FEEL THE NEED TO DO SOME POPULATION CONTROL.
UGH, I'M SO UNPREDICTABLE WHEN I'M ON MY PERIOD.
WHAT ARE YOUR DEMANDS?
I, UH-- I DON'T KNOW, ACTUALLY.
...YOU DON'T KNOW YOUR DEMANDS?

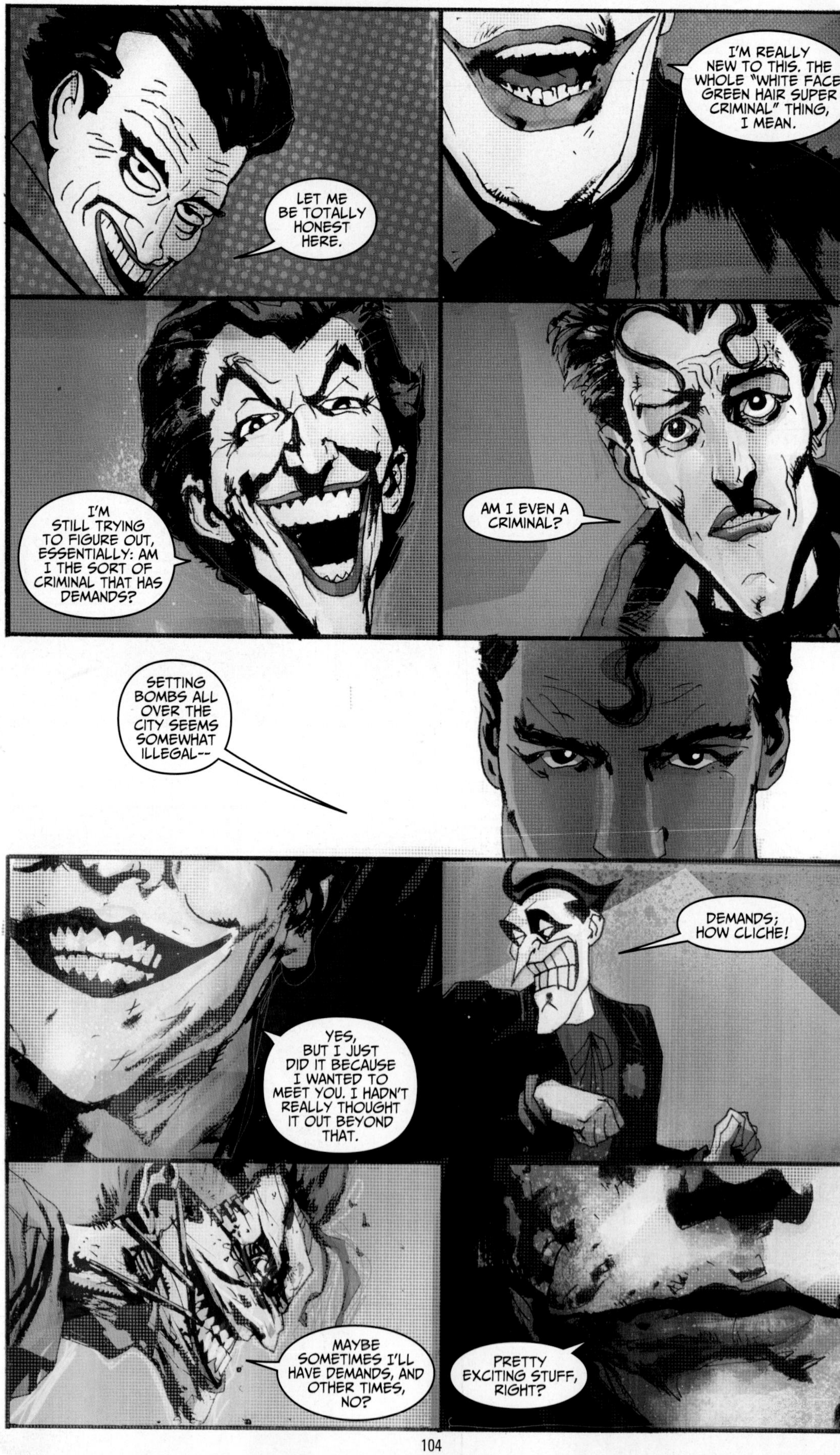
LET ME BE TOTALLY HONEST HERE.
I'M REALLY NEW TO THIS. THE WHOLE "WHITE FACE, GREEN HAIR SUPER CRIMINAL" THING, I MEAN.
I'M STILL TRYING TO FIGURE OUT, ESSENTIALLY: AM I THE SORT OF CRIMINAL THAT HAS DEMANDS?
AM I EVEN A CRIMINAL?
SETTING BOMBS ALL OVER THE CITY SEEMS SOMEWHAT ILLEGAL--
YES, BUT I JUST DID IT BECAUSE I WANTED TO MEET YOU. I HADN'T REALLY THOUGHT IT OUT BEYOND THAT.
DEMANDS; HOW CLICHE!
MAYBE SOMETIMES I'LL HAVE DEMANDS, AND OTHER TIMES, NO?
PRETTY EXCITING STUFF, RIGHT?

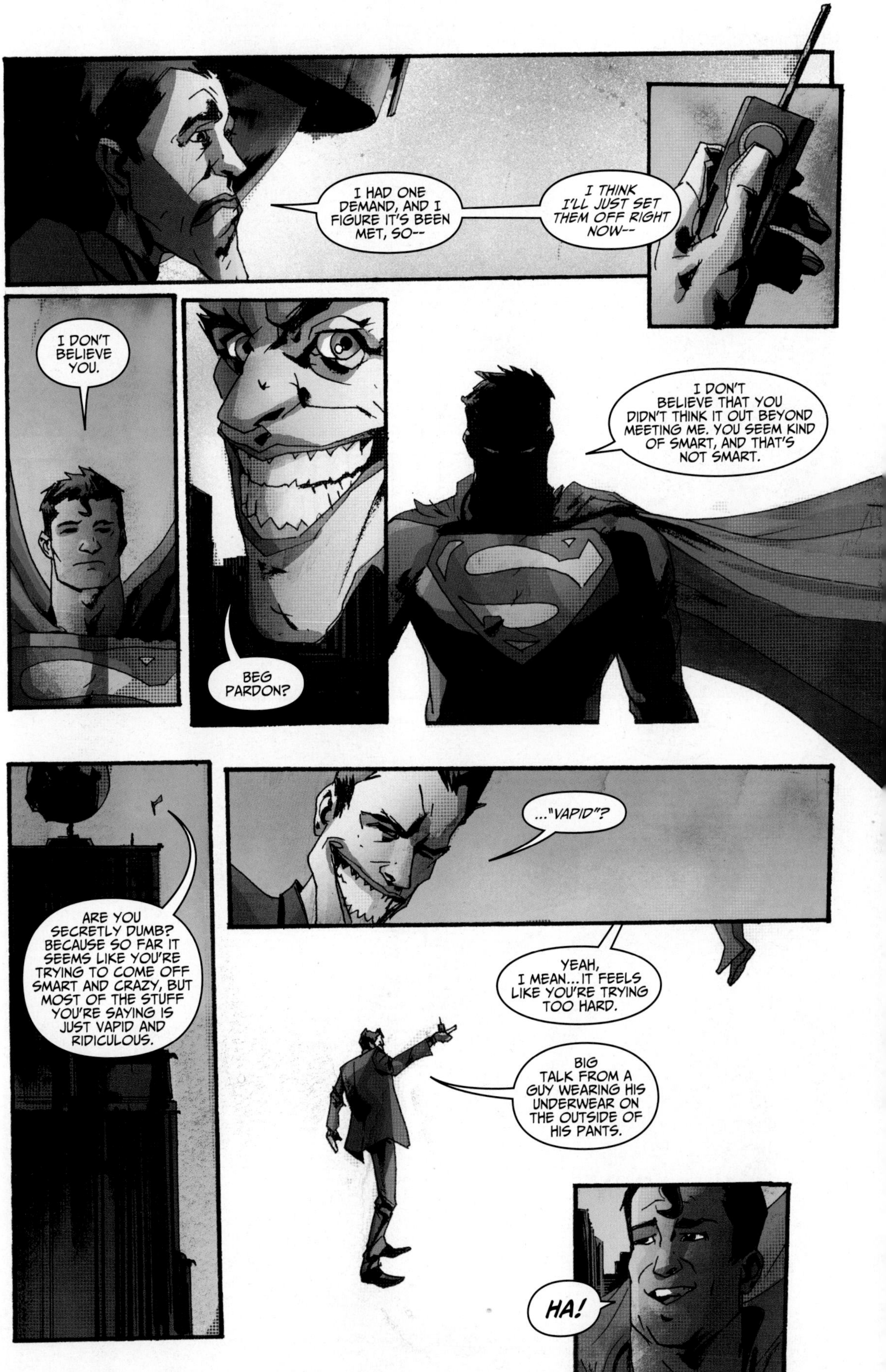
I HAD ONE DEMAND, AND I FIGURE IT'S BEEN MET, SO--
I THINK I'LL JUST SET THEM OFF RIGHT NOW--
I DON'T BELIEVE YOU.
BEG PARDON?
I DON'T BELIEVE THAT YOU DIDN'T THINK IT OUT BEYOND MEETING ME. YOU SEEM KIND OF SMART, AND THAT'S NOT SMART.
ARE YOU SECRETLY DUMB? BECAUSE SO FAR IT SEEMS LIKE YOU'RE TRYING TO COME OFF SMART AND CRAZY, BUT MOST OF THE STUFF YOU'RE SAYING IS JUST VAPID AND RIDICULOUS.
..."VAPID"?
YEAH, I MEAN...IT FEELS LIKE YOU'RE TRYING TOO HARD.
BIG TALK FROM A GUY WEARING HIS UNDERWEAR ON THE OUTSIDE OF HIS PANTS.
HA!

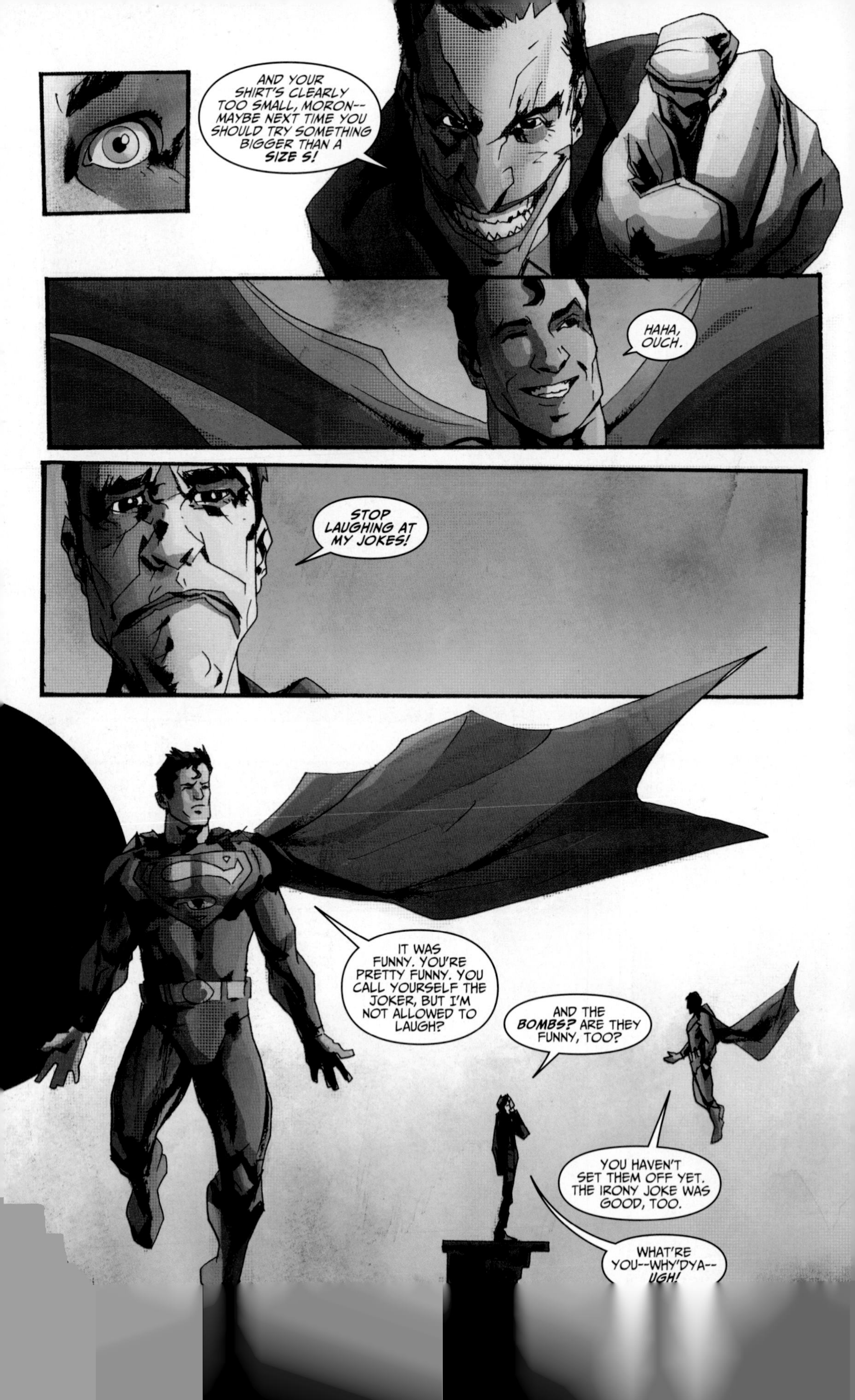
AND YOUR SHIRT'S CLEARLY TOO SMALL, MORON-- MAYBE NEXT TIME YOU SHOULD TRY SOMETHING BIGGER THAN A SIZE S!
HAHA, OUCH.
STOP LAUGHING AT MY JOKES!
IT WAS FUNNY. YOU'RE PRETTY FUNNY. YOU CALL YOURSELF THE JOKER, BUT I'M NOT ALLOWED TO LAUGH?
AND THE BOMBS? ARE THEY FUNNY, TOO?
YOU HAVEN'T SET THEM OFF YET. THE IRONY JOKE WAS GOOD, TOO.
WHAT'RE YOU--WHY'DYA-- UGH!

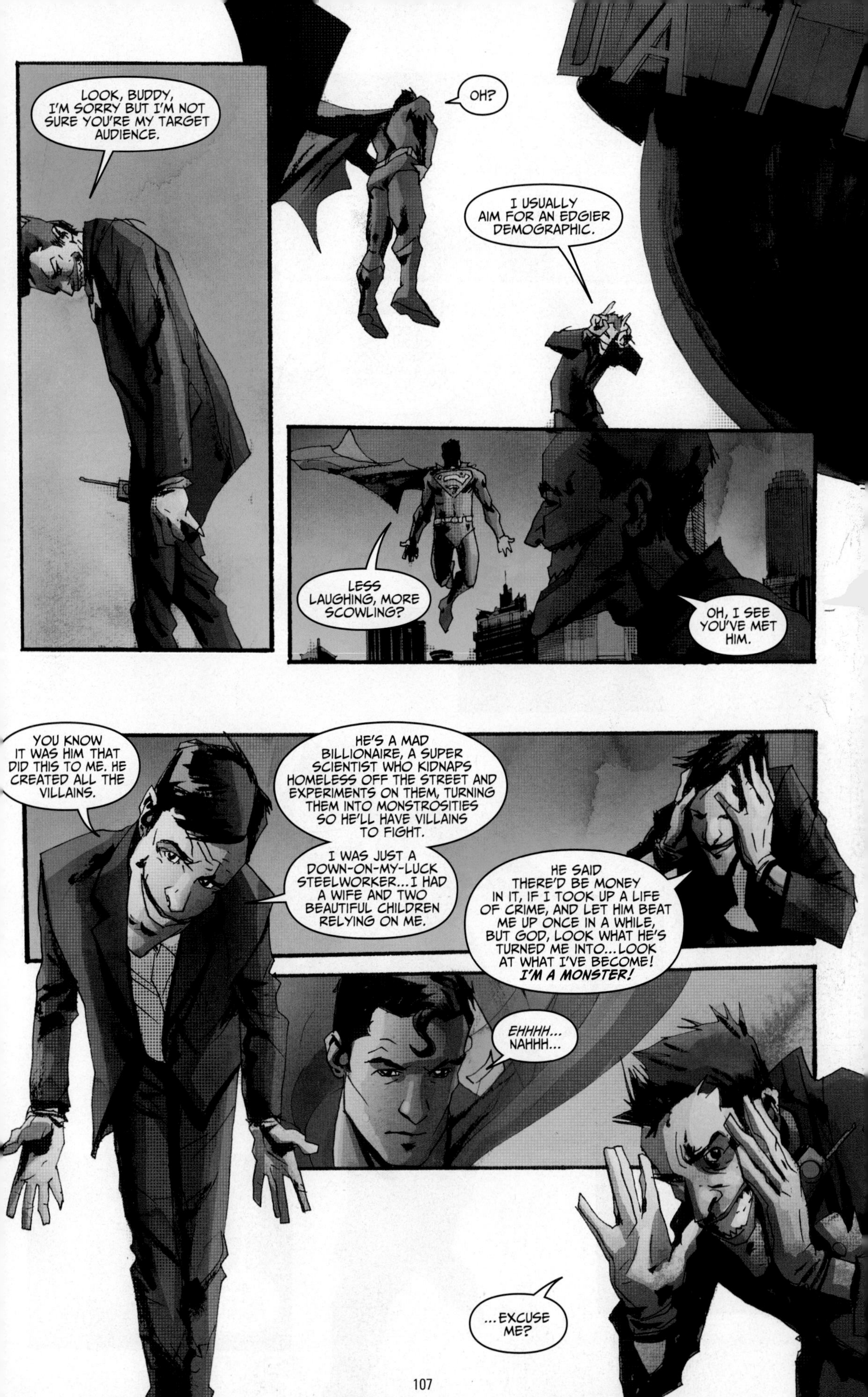
LOOK, BUDDY, I'M SORRY BUT I'M NOT SURE YOU'RE MY TARGET AUDIENCE.
OH?
I USUALLY AIM FOR AN EDGIER DEMOGRAPHIC.
LESS LAUGHING, MORE SCOWLING?
OH, I SEE YOU'VE MET HIM.
YOU KNOW IT WAS HIM THAT DID THIS TO ME. HE CREATED ALL THE VILLAINS.
HE'S A MAD BILLIONAIRE, A SUPER SCIENTIST WHO KIDNAPS HOMELESS OFF THE STREET AND EXPERIMENTS ON THEM, TURNING THEM INTO MONSTROSITIES SO HE'LL HAVE VILLAINS TO FIGHT.
I WAS JUST A DOWN-ON-MY-LUCK STEELWORKER...I HAD A WIFE AND TWO BEAUTIFUL CHILDREN RELYING ON ME.
HE SAID THERE'D BE MONEY IN IT, IF I TOOK UP A LIFE OF CRIME, AND LET HIM BEAT ME UP ONCE IN A WHILE, BUT GOD, LOOK WHAT HE'S TURNED ME INTO...LOOK AT WHAT I'VE BECOME! ***I'M A MONSTER!***
EHHHH... NAHHH...
...EXCUSE ME?

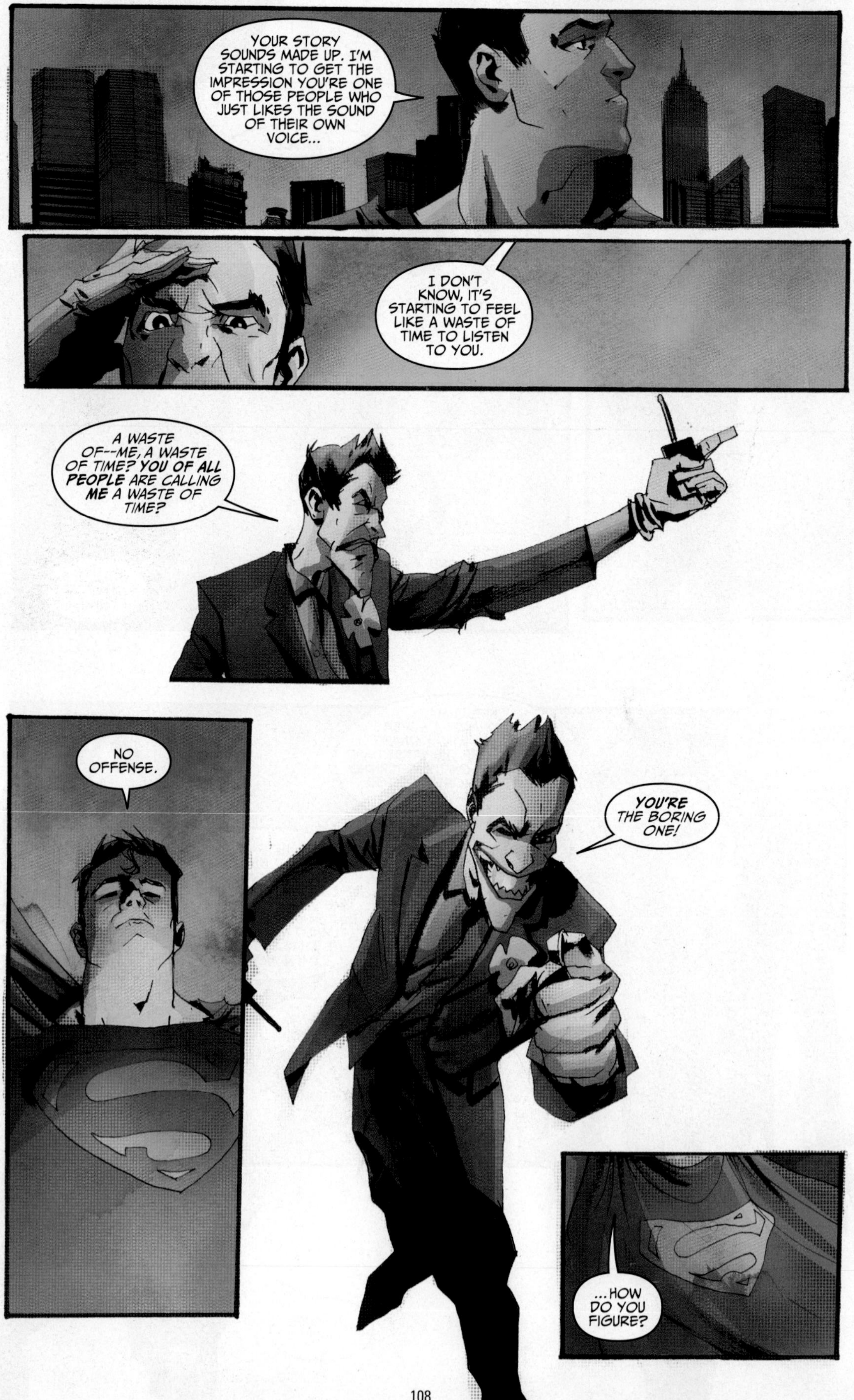
YOUR STORY SOUNDS MADE UP. I'M STARTING TO GET THE IMPRESSION YOU'RE ONE OF THOSE PEOPLE WHO JUST LIKES THE SOUND OF THEIR OWN VOICE...
I DON'T KNOW, IT'S STARTING TO FEEL LIKE A WASTE OF TIME TO LISTEN TO YOU.
A WASTE OF--ME, A WASTE OF TIME? YOU OF ALL PEOPLE ARE CALLING ME A WASTE OF TIME?
NO OFFENSE.
YOU'RE THE BORING ONE!
...HOW DO YOU FIGURE?

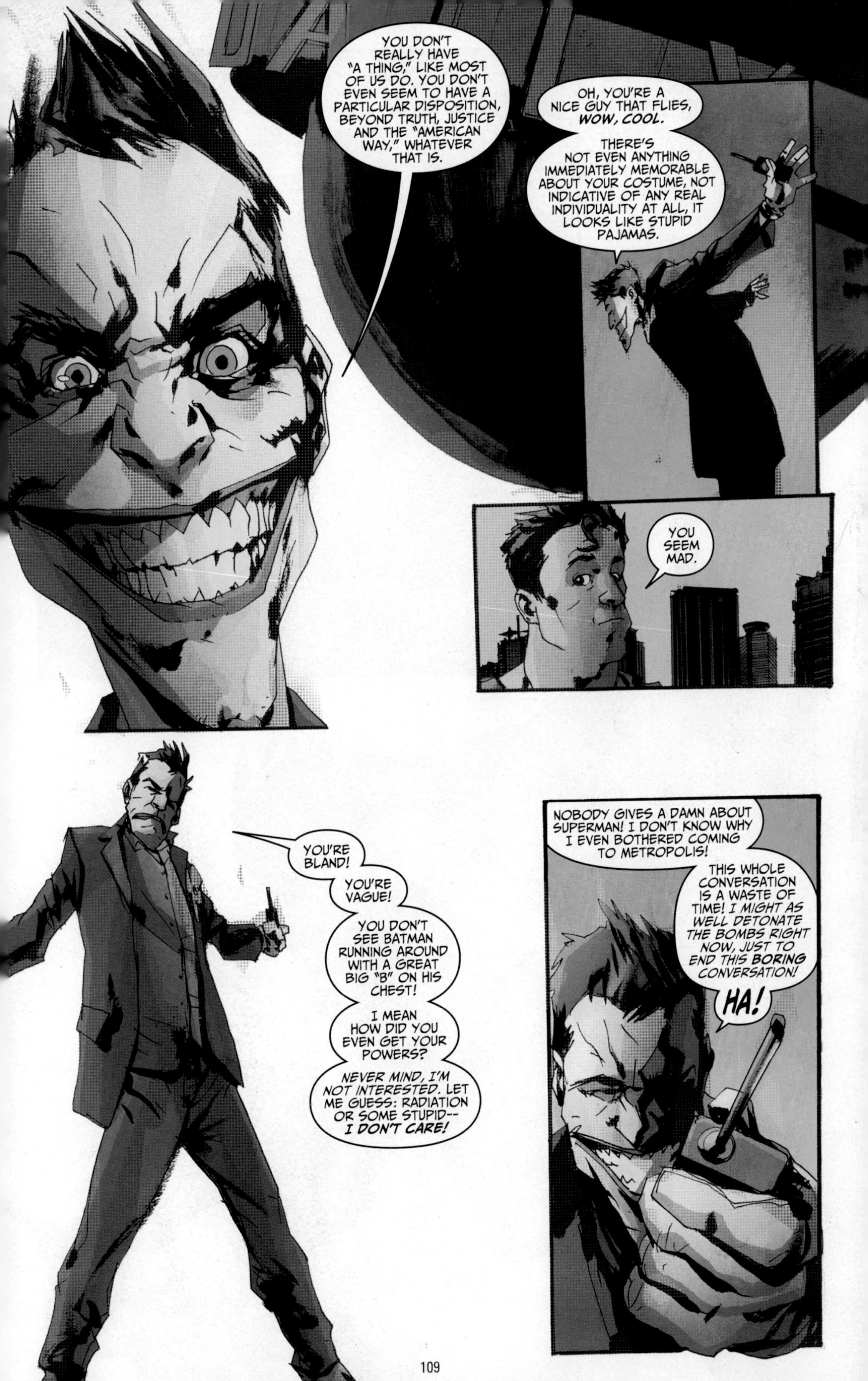
YOU DON'T REALLY HAVE "A THING," LIKE MOST OF US DO. YOU DON'T EVEN SEEM TO HAVE A PARTICULAR DISPOSITION, BEYOND TRUTH, JUSTICE AND THE "AMERICAN WAY," WHATEVER THAT IS.
OH, YOU'RE A NICE GUY THAT FLIES, WOW, COOL.
THERE'S NOT EVEN ANYTHING IMMEDIATELY MEMORABLE ABOUT YOUR COSTUME, NOT INDICATIVE OF ANY REAL INDIVIDUALITY AT ALL, IT LOOKS LIKE STUPID PAJAMAS.
YOU SEEM MAD.
YOU'RE BLAND!
YOU'RE VAGUE!
YOU DON'T SEE BATMAN RUNNING AROUND WITH A GREAT BIG "B" ON HIS CHEST!
I MEAN HOW DID YOU EVEN GET YOUR POWERS?
NEVER MIND, I'M NOT INTERESTED. LET ME GUESS: RADIATION OR SOME STUPID-- I DON'T CARE!
NOBODY GIVES A DAMN ABOUT SUPERMAN! I DON'T KNOW WHY I EVEN BOTHERED COMING TO METROPOLIS!
THIS WHOLE CONVERSATION IS A WASTE OF TIME! I MIGHT AS WELL DETONATE THE BOMBS RIGHT NOW, JUST TO END THIS BORING CONVERSATION!
HA!

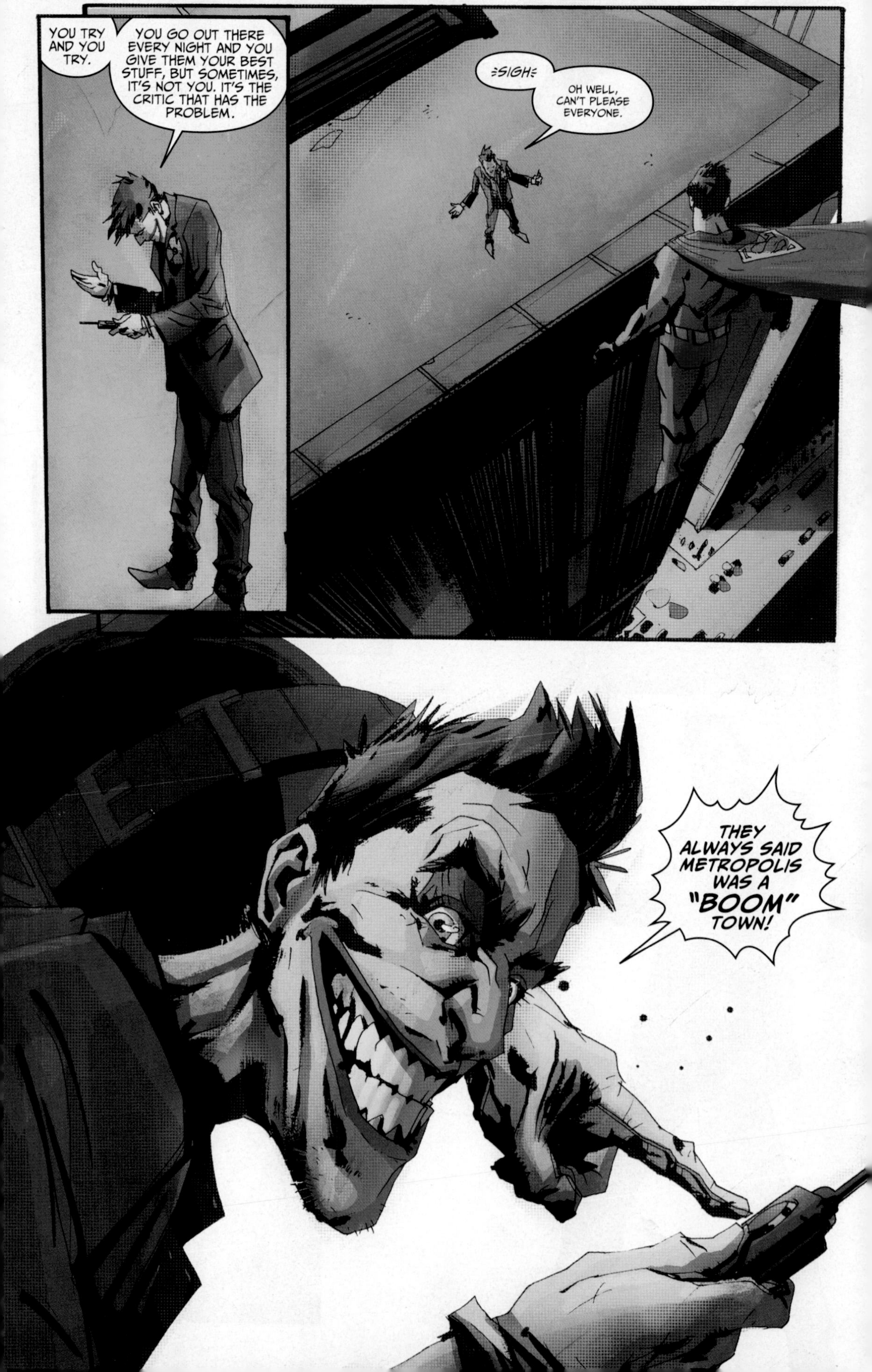
YOU TRY AND YOU TRY.
YOU GO OUT THERE EVERY NIGHT AND YOU GIVE THEM YOUR BEST STUFF, BUT SOMETIMES, IT'S NOT YOU. IT'S THE CRITIC THAT HAS THE PROBLEM.
=SIGH=
OH WELL, CAN'T PLEASE EVERYONE.
THEY ALWAYS SAID METROPOLIS WAS A "BOOM" TOWN!

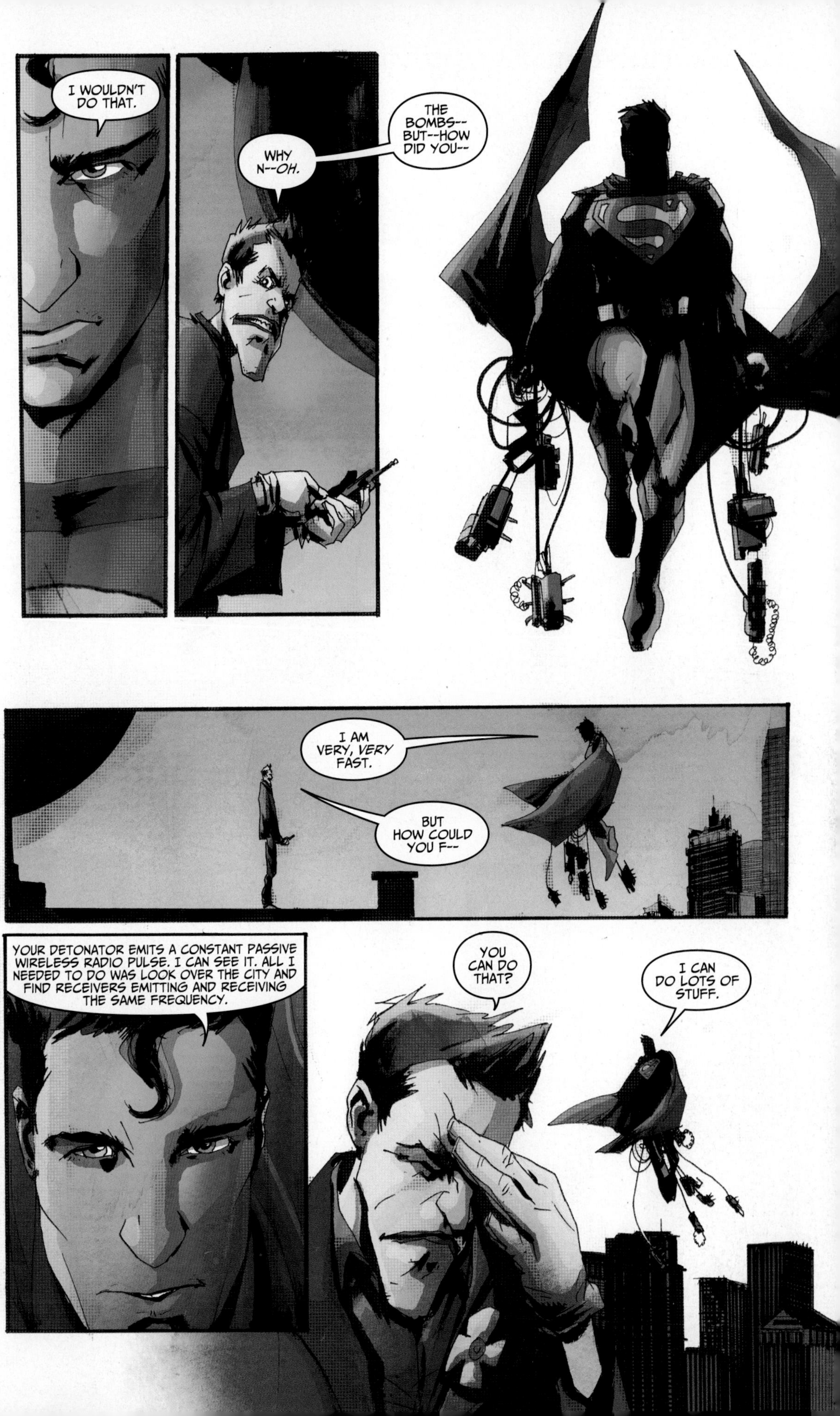
I WOULDN'T DO THAT.
WHY N--OH.
THE BOMBS-- BUT--HOW DID YOU--
I AM VERY, *VERY* FAST.
BUT HOW COULD YOU F--
YOUR DETONATOR EMITS A CONSTANT PASSIVE WIRELESS RADIO PULSE. I CAN SEE IT. ALL I NEEDED TO DO WAS LOOK OVER THE CITY AND FIND RECEIVERS EMITTING AND RECEIVING THE SAME FREQUENCY.
YOU CAN DO THAT?
I CAN DO LOTS OF STUFF.

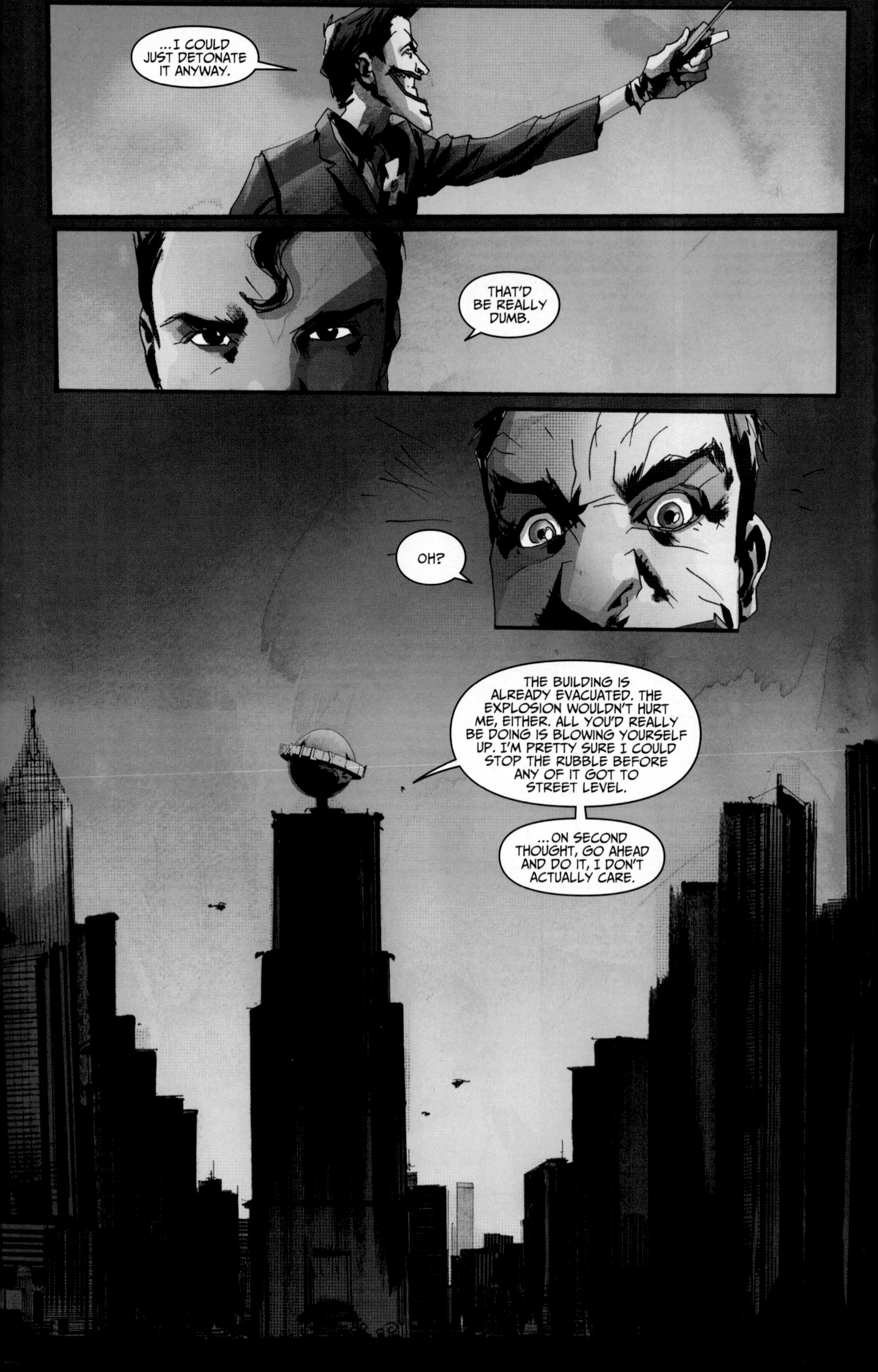
...I COULD JUST DETONATE IT ANYWAY.
THAT'D BE REALLY DUMB.
OH?
THE BUILDING IS ALREADY EVACUATED. THE EXPLOSION WOULDN'T HURT ME, EITHER. ALL YOU'D REALLY BE DOING IS BLOWING YOURSELF UP. I'M PRETTY SURE I COULD STOP THE RUBBLE BEFORE ANY OF IT GOT TO STREET LEVEL.
...ON SECOND THOUGHT, GO AHEAD AND DO IT, I DON'T ACTUALLY CARE.

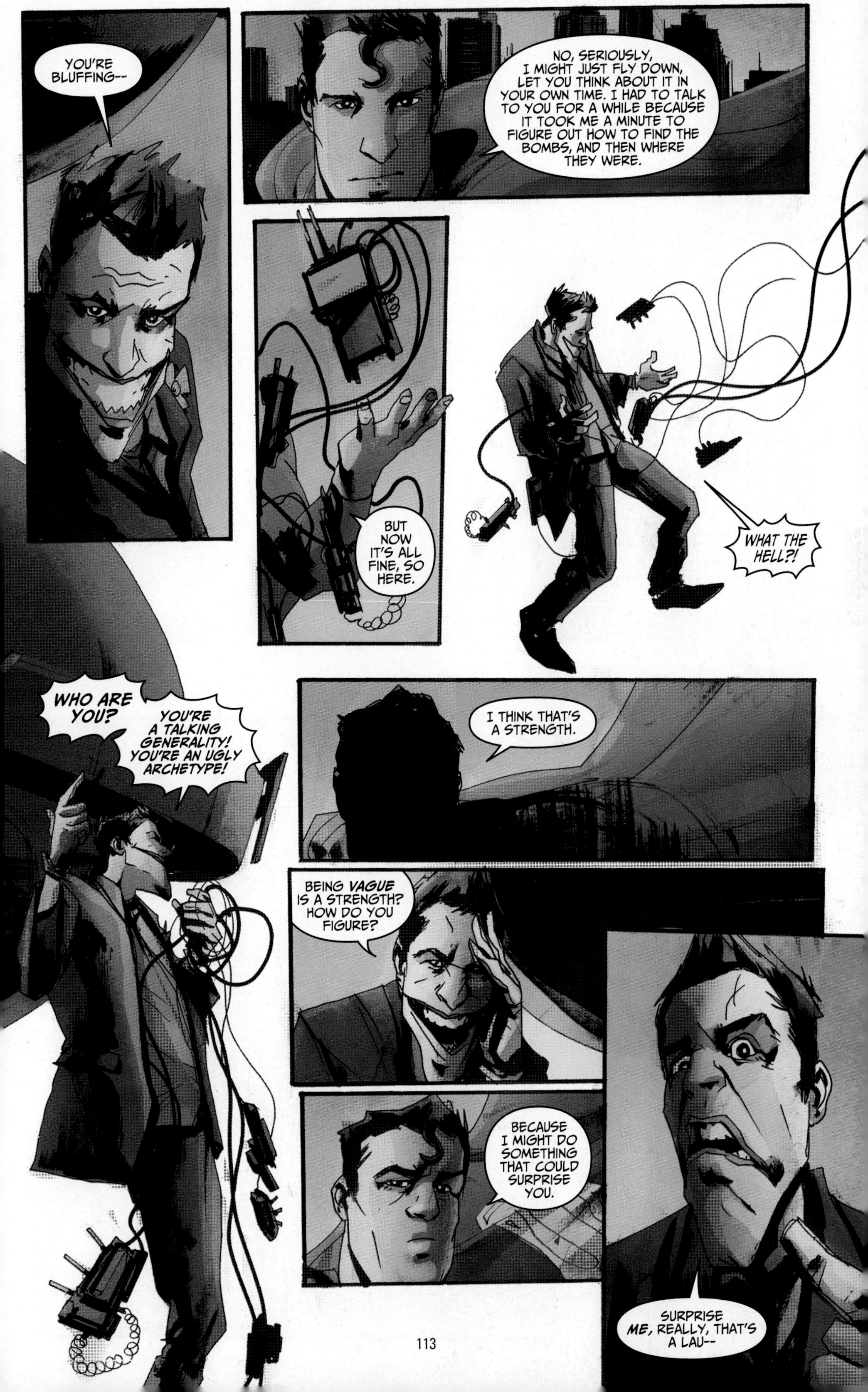
YOU'RE BLUFFING--
NO, SERIOUSLY, I MIGHT JUST FLY DOWN, LET YOU THINK ABOUT IT IN YOUR OWN TIME. I HAD TO TALK TO YOU FOR A WHILE BECAUSE IT TOOK ME A MINUTE TO FIGURE OUT HOW TO FIND THE BOMBS, AND THEN WHERE THEY WERE.
BUT NOW IT'S ALL FINE, SO HERE.
WHAT THE HELL?!
WHO ARE YOU?
YOU'RE A TALKING GENERALITY! YOU'RE AN UGLY ARCHETYPE!
I THINK THAT'S A STRENGTH.
BEING VAGUE IS A STRENGTH? HOW DO YOU FIGURE?
BECAUSE I MIGHT DO SOMETHING THAT COULD SURPRISE YOU.
SURPRISE ME, REALLY, THAT'S A LAU--

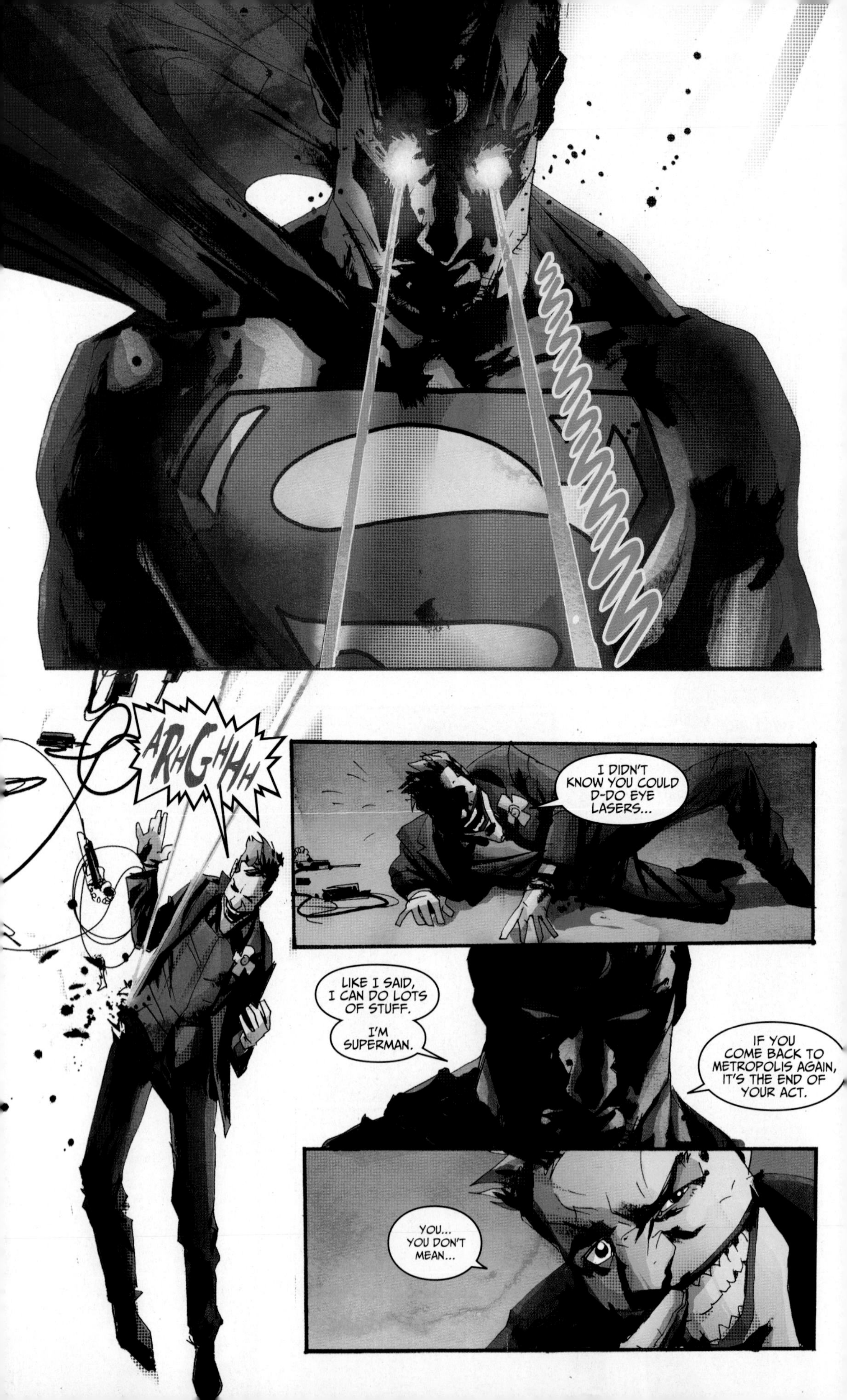
ARHGHHH
I DIDN'T KNOW YOU COULD D-DO EYE LASERS...
LIKE I SAID, I CAN DO LOTS OF STUFF.
I'M SUPERMAN.
IF YOU COME BACK TO METROPOLIS AGAIN, IT'S THE END OF YOUR ACT.
YOU... YOU DON'T MEAN...

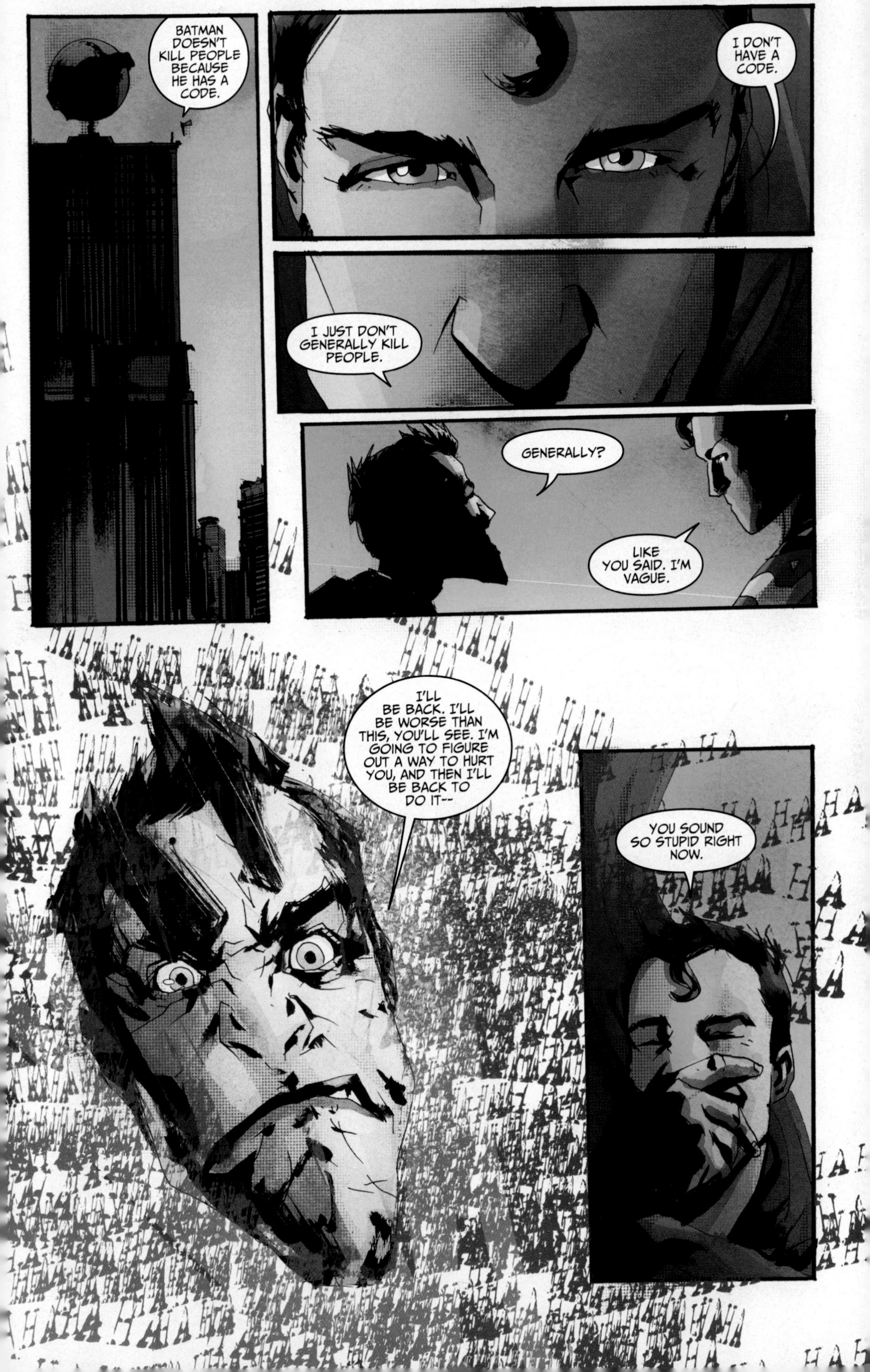
BATMAN DOESN'T KILL PEOPLE BECAUSE HE HAS A CODE.
I DON'T HAVE A CODE.
I JUST DON'T GENERALLY KILL PEOPLE.
GENERALLY?
LIKE YOU SAID. I'M VAGUE.
I'LL BE BACK. I'LL BE WORSE THAN THIS, YOU'LL SEE. I'M GOING TO FIGURE OUT A WAY TO HURT YOU, AND THEN I'LL BE BACK TO DO IT--
YOU SOUND SO STUPID RIGHT NOW.

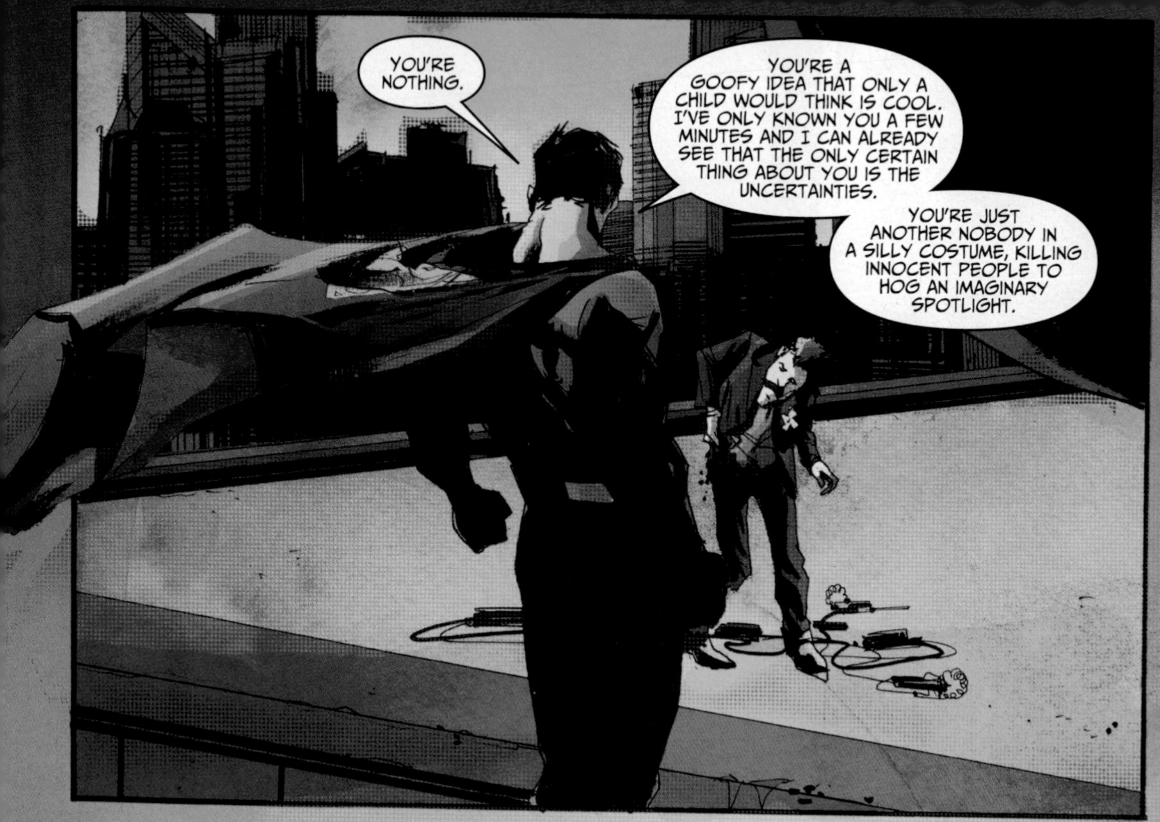
YOU'RE NOTHING.
YOU'RE A GOOFY IDEA THAT ONLY A CHILD WOULD THINK IS COOL. I'VE ONLY KNOWN YOU A FEW MINUTES AND I CAN ALREADY SEE THAT THE ONLY CERTAIN THING ABOUT YOU IS THE UNCERTAINTIES.
YOU'RE JUST ANOTHER NOBODY IN A SILLY COSTUME, KILLING INNOCENT PEOPLE TO HOG AN IMAGINARY SPOTLIGHT.

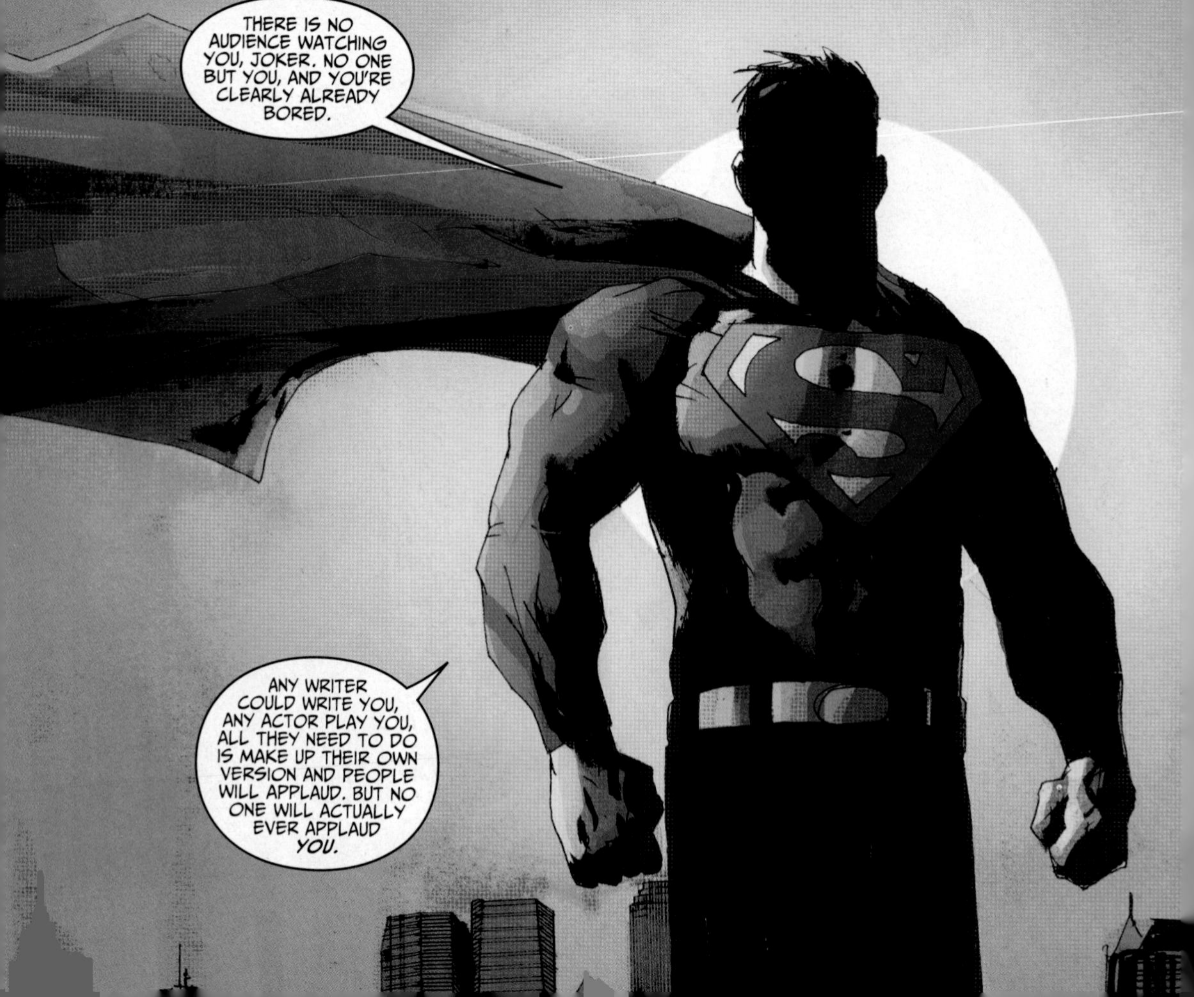
THERE IS NO AUDIENCE WATCHING YOU, JOKER. NO ONE BUT YOU, AND YOU'RE CLEARLY ALREADY BORED.
ANY WRITER COULD WRITE YOU, ANY ACTOR PLAY YOU, ALL THEY NEED TO DO IS MAKE UP THEIR OWN VERSION AND PEOPLE WILL APPLAUD. BUT NO ONE WILL ACTUALLY EVER APPLAUD *YOU.*

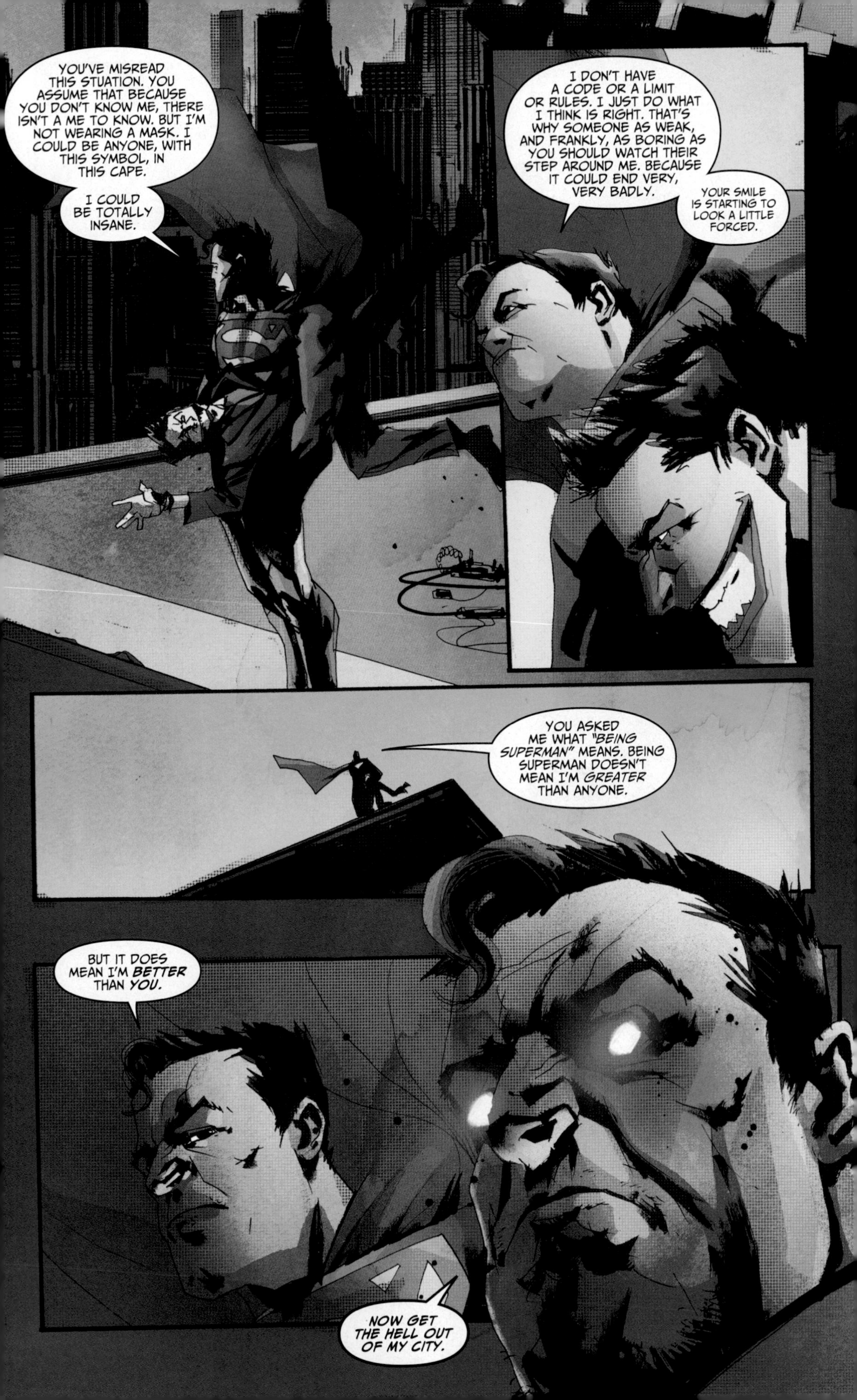
YOU'VE MISREAD THIS STUATION. YOU ASSUME THAT BECAUSE YOU DON'T KNOW ME, THERE ISN'T A ME TO KNOW. BUT I'M NOT WEARING A MASK. I COULD BE ANYONE, WITH THIS SYMBOL, IN THIS CAPE.
I COULD BE TOTALLY INSANE.
I DON'T HAVE A CODE OR A LIMIT OR RULES. I JUST DO WHAT I THINK IS RIGHT. THAT'S WHY SOMEONE AS WEAK, AND FRANKLY, AS BORING AS YOU SHOULD WATCH THEIR STEP AROUND ME. BECAUSE IT COULD END VERY, VERY BADLY.
YOUR SMILE IS STARTING TO LOOK A LITTLE FORCED.
YOU ASKED ME WHAT "BEING SUPERMAN" MEANS. BEING SUPERMAN DOESN'T MEAN I'M GREATER THAN ANYONE.
BUT IT DOES MEAN I'M BETTER THAN YOU.
NOW GET THE HELL OUT OF MY CITY.

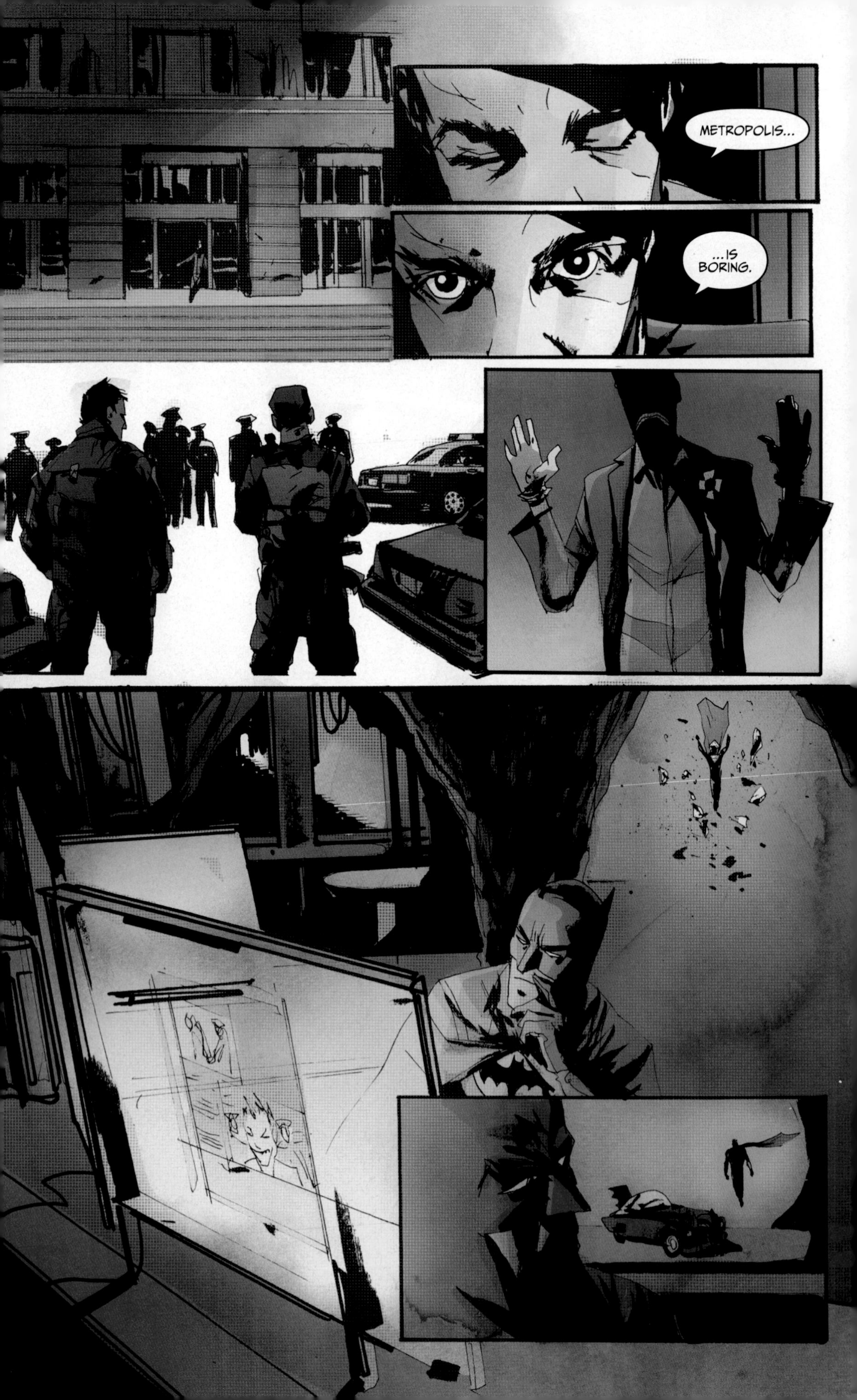
METROPOLIS...
...IS BORING.

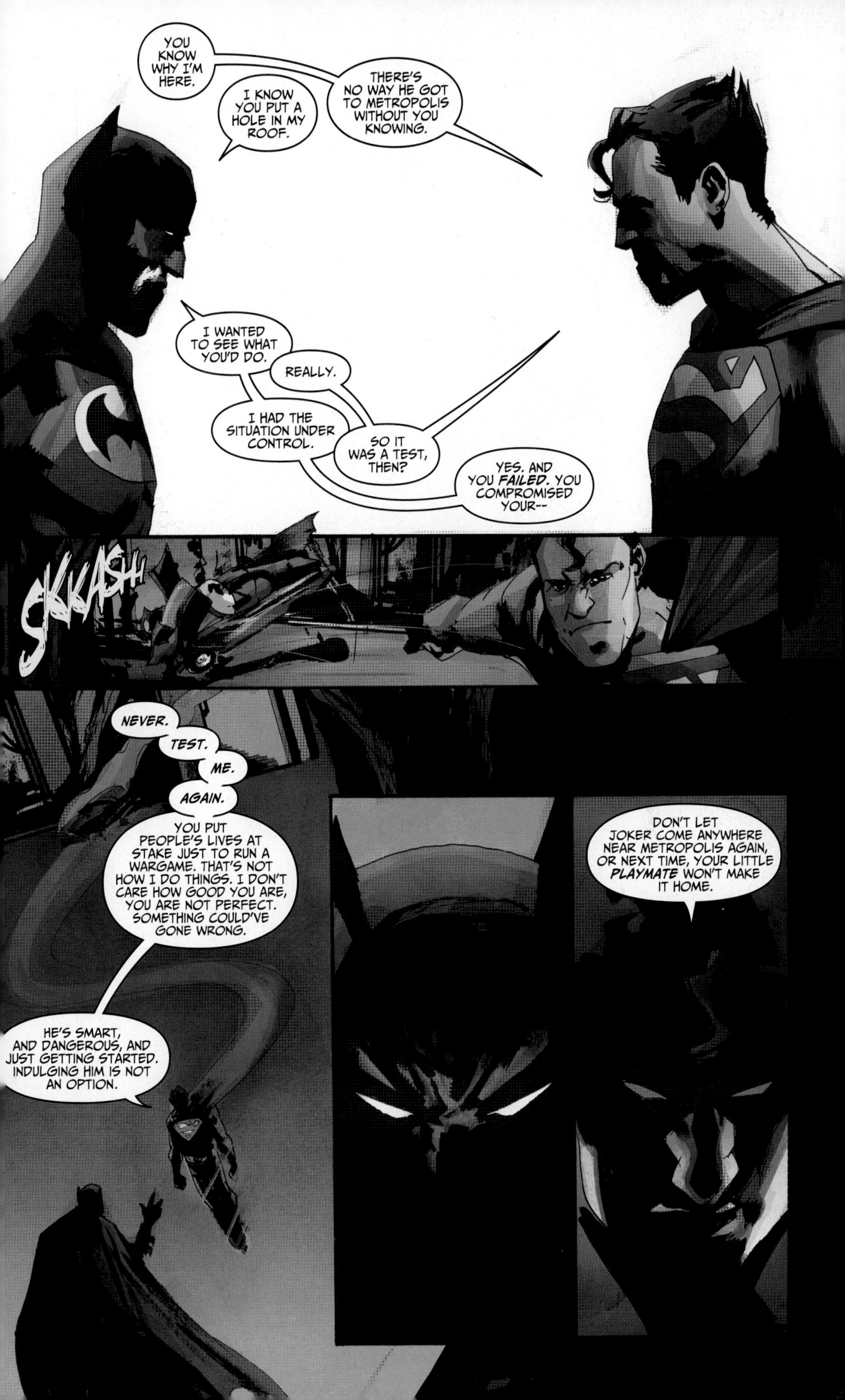

YOU KNOW WHY I'M HERE.
I KNOW YOU PUT A HOLE IN MY ROOF.
THERE'S NO WAY HE GOT TO METROPOLIS WITHOUT YOU KNOWING.
I WANTED TO SEE WHAT YOU'D DO.
REALLY.
I HAD THE SITUATION UNDER CONTROL.
SO IT WAS A TEST, THEN?
YES. AND YOU FAILED. YOU COMPROMISED YOUR--
SKKASH
NEVER.
TEST.
ME.
AGAIN.
YOU PUT PEOPLE'S LIVES AT STAKE JUST TO RUN A WARGAME. THAT'S NOT HOW I DO THINGS. I DON'T CARE HOW GOOD YOU ARE, YOU ARE NOT PERFECT. SOMETHING COULD'VE GONE WRONG.
HE'S SMART, AND DANGEROUS, AND JUST GETTING STARTED. INDULGING HIM IS NOT AN OPTION.
DON'T LET JOKER COME ANYWHERE NEAR METROPOLIS AGAIN, OR NEXT TIME, YOUR LITTLE PLAYMATE WON'T MAKE IT HOME.

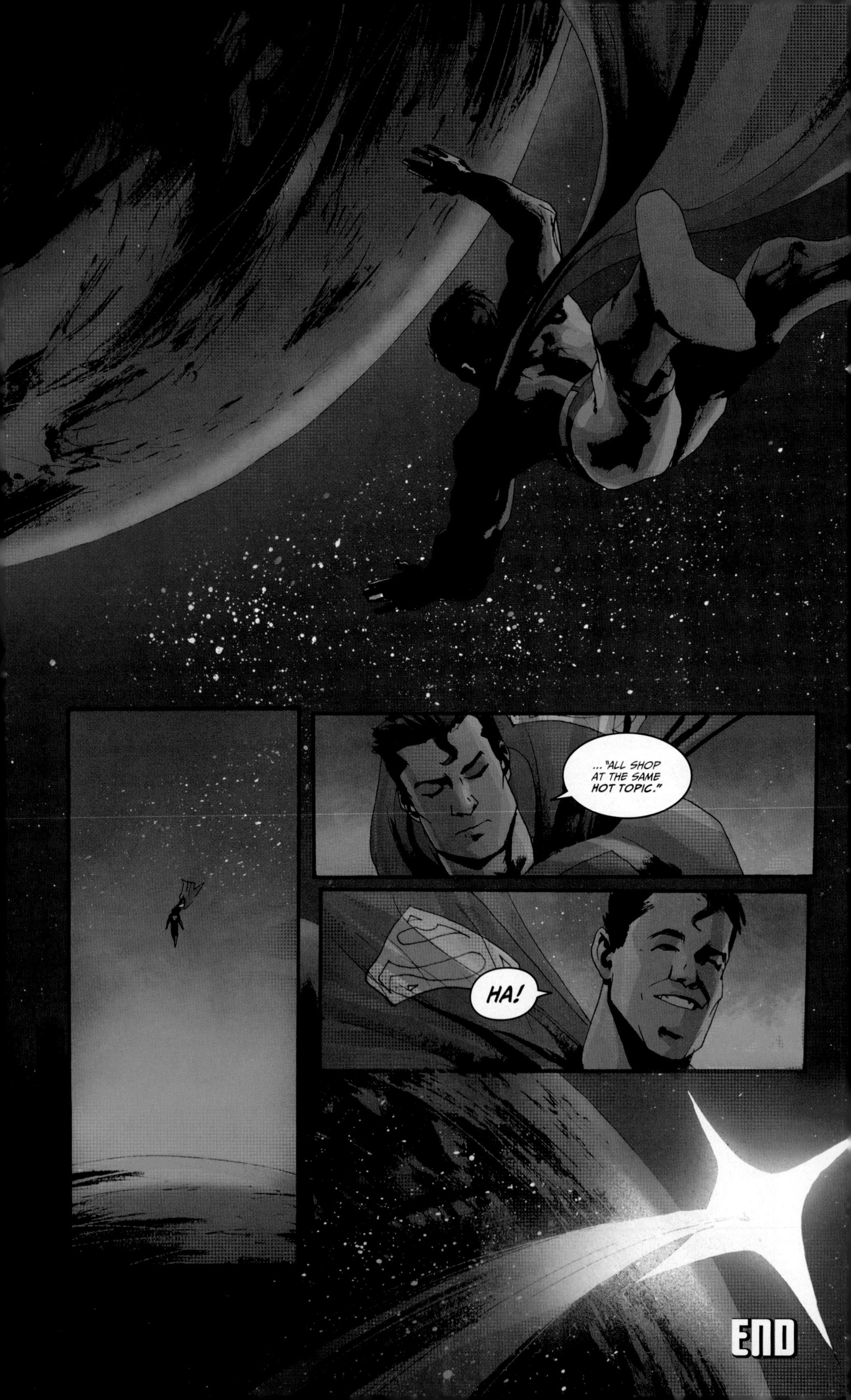
..."ALL SHOP AT THE SAME HOT TOPIC."
HA!
END

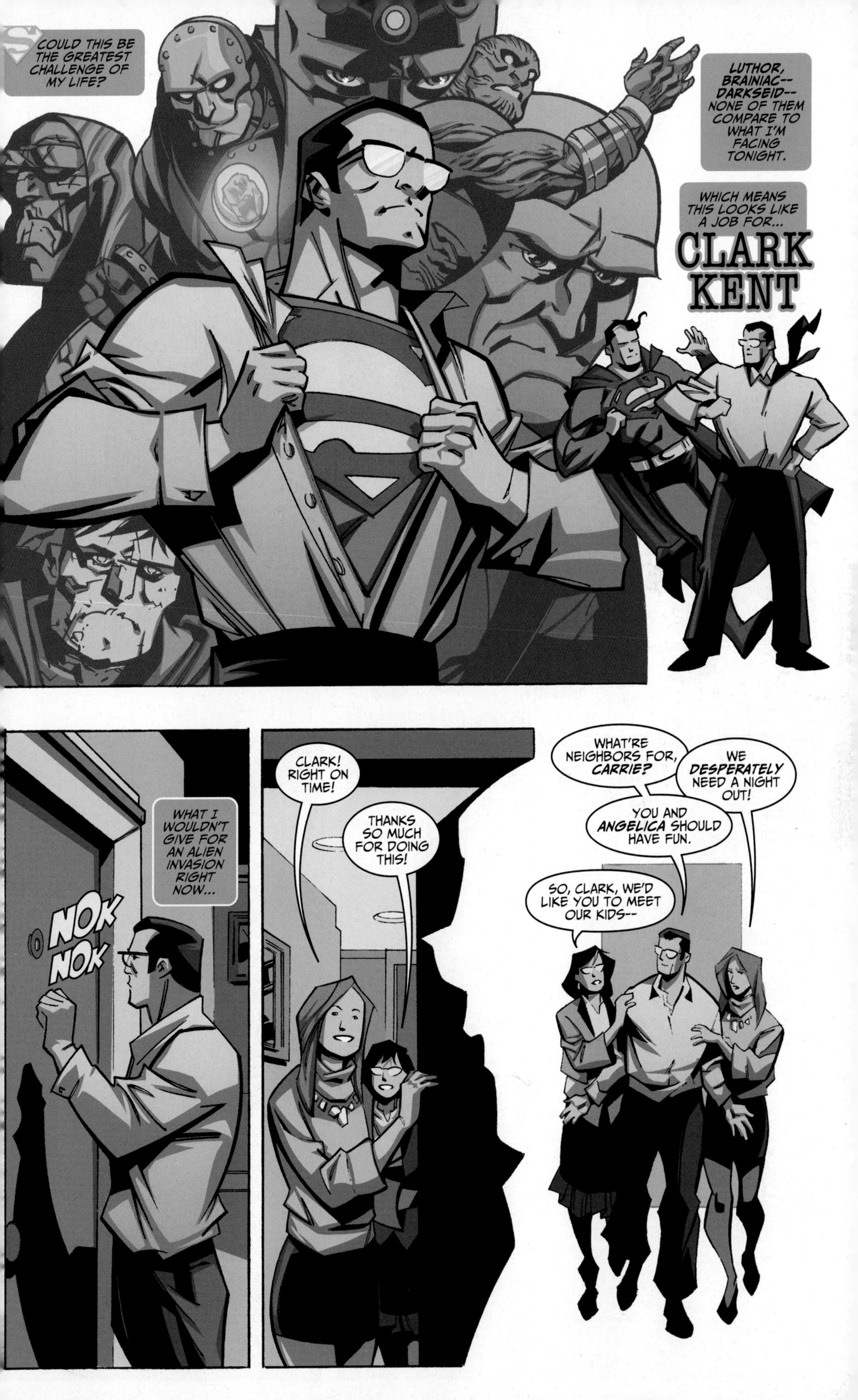
COULD THIS BE THE GREATEST CHALLENGE OF MY LIFE?
LUTHOR, BRAINIAC-- DARKSEID-- NONE OF THEM COMPARE TO WHAT I'M FACING TONIGHT.
WHICH MEANS THIS LOOKS LIKE A JOB FOR...
CLARK KENT
WHAT I WOULDN'T GIVE FOR AN ALIEN INVASION RIGHT NOW...
NOK NOK
CLARK! RIGHT ON TIME!
THANKS SO MUCH FOR DOING THIS!
WHAT'RE NEIGHBORS FOR, CARRIE?
WE DESPERATELY NEED A NIGHT OUT!
YOU AND ANGELICA SHOULD HAVE FUN.
SO, CLARK, WE'D LIKE YOU TO MEET OUR KIDS--

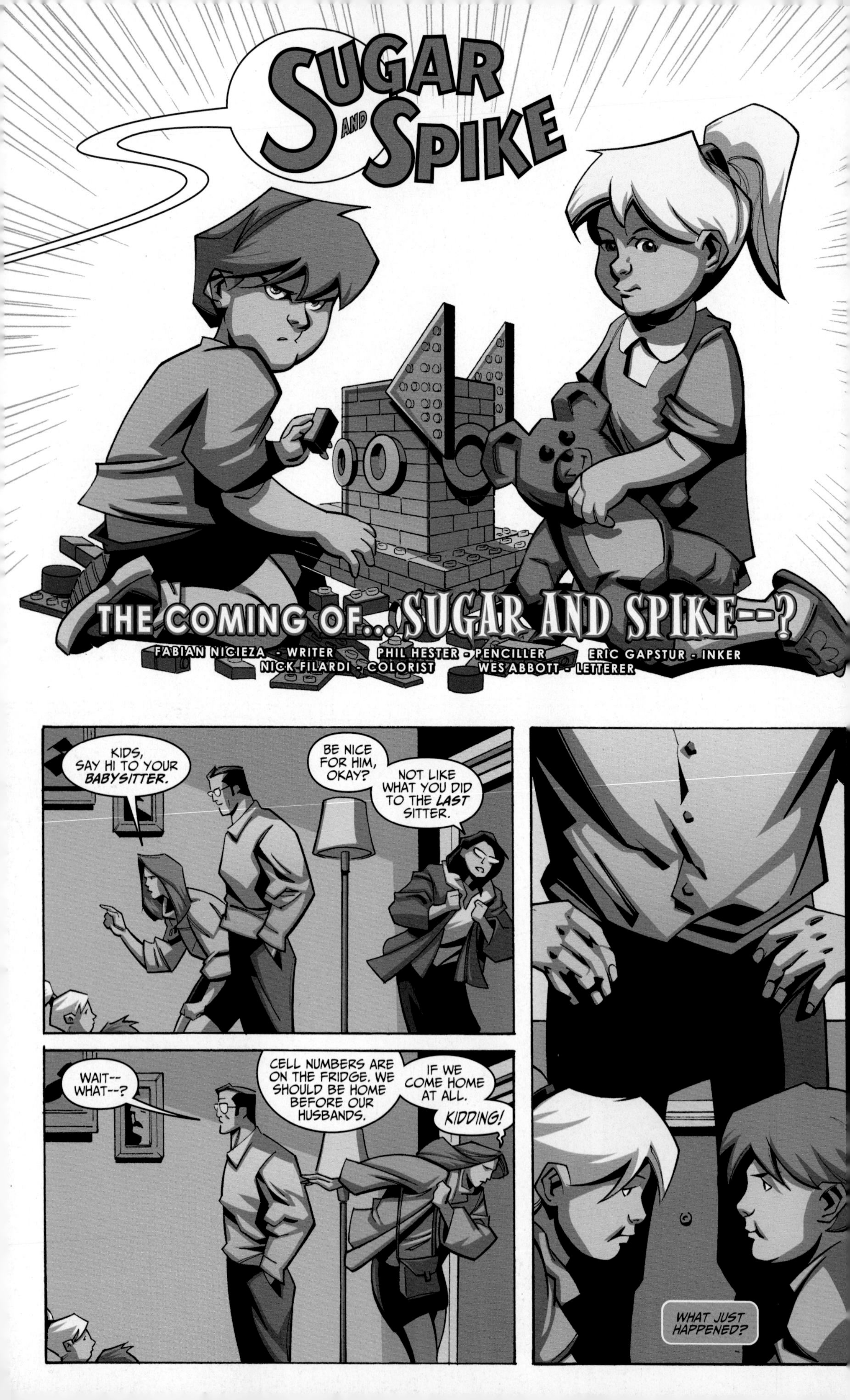
SUGAR AND SPIKE
THE COMING OF... SUGAR AND SPIKE--?
FABIAN NICIEZA - WRITER PHIL HESTER - PENCILLER ERIC GAPSTUR - INKER
NICK FILARDI - COLORIST WES ABBOTT - LETTERER
KIDS, SAY HI TO YOUR BABYSITTER.
BE NICE FOR HIM, OKAY?
NOT LIKE WHAT YOU DID TO THE LAST SITTER.
WAIT-- WHAT--?
CELL NUMBERS ARE ON THE FRIDGE. WE SHOULD BE HOME BEFORE OUR HUSBANDS.
IF WE COME HOME AT ALL.
KIDDING!
WHAT JUST HAPPENED?

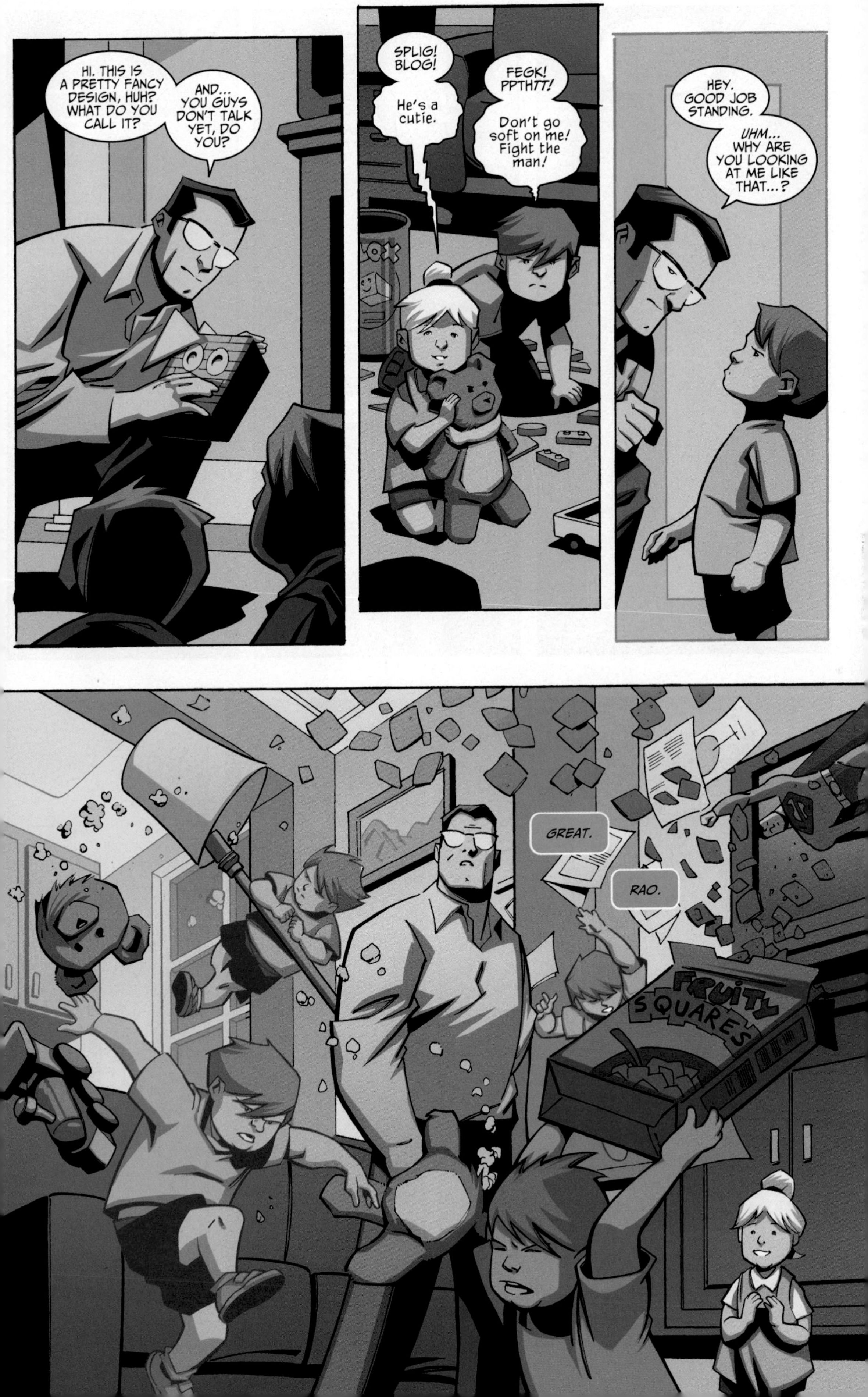
HI. THIS IS A PRETTY FANCY DESIGN, HUH? WHAT DO YOU CALL IT?
AND... YOU GUYS DON'T TALK YET, DO YOU?
SPLIG! BLOG!
He's a cutie.
FEGK! PPTHTT!
Don't go soft on me! Fight the man!
HEY. GOOD JOB STANDING.
UHM... WHY ARE YOU LOOKING AT ME LIKE THAT...?
GREAT.
RAO.
FRUITY SQUARES

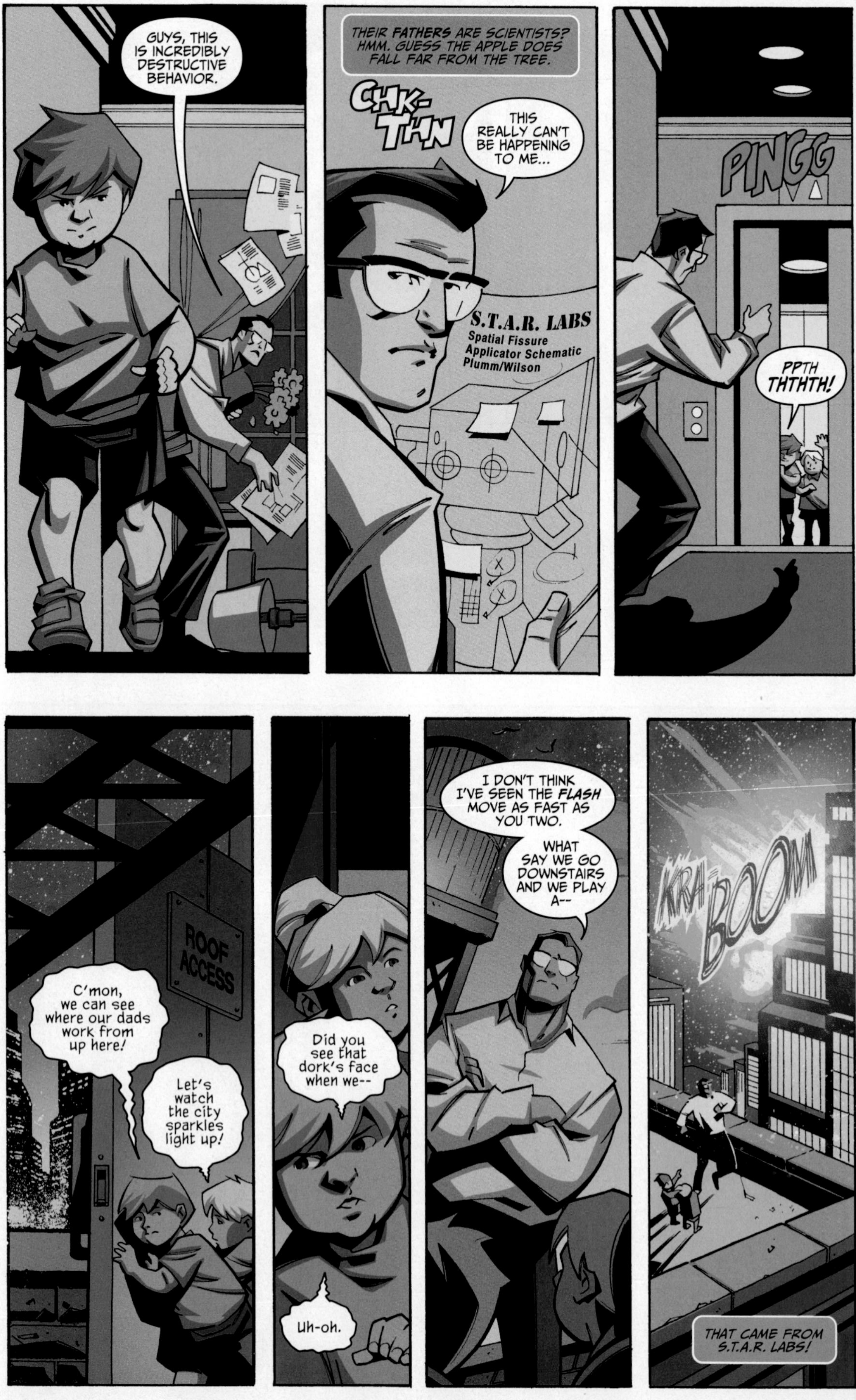
GUYS, THIS IS INCREDIBLY DESTRUCTIVE BEHAVIOR.
THEIR FATHERS ARE SCIENTISTS? HMM. GUESS THE APPLE DOES FALL FAR FROM THE TREE.
CHK-THN
THIS REALLY CAN'T BE HAPPENING TO ME...
S.T.A.R. LABS
Spatial Fissure Applicator Schematic
Plumm/Wilson
PINGG
PPTH THTHTH!
ROOF ACCESS
C'mon, we can see where our dads work from up here!
Let's watch the city sparkles light up!
Did you see that dork's face when we--
Uh-oh.
I DON'T THINK I'VE SEEN THE FLASH MOVE AS FAST AS YOU TWO.
WHAT SAY WE GO DOWNSTAIRS AND WE PLAY A--
KRA-BOOM
THAT CAME FROM S.T.A.R. LABS!

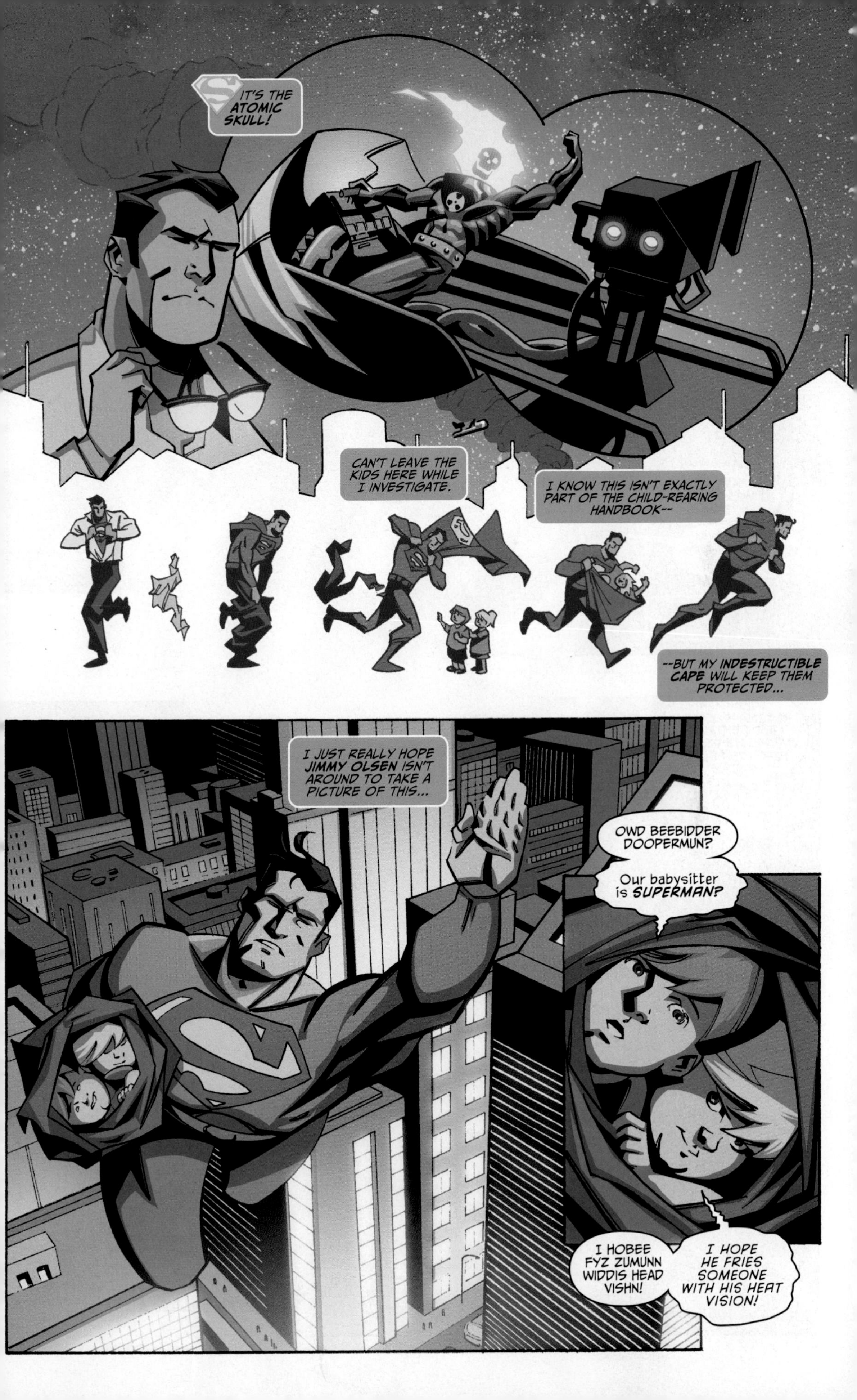
IT'S THE ATOMIC SKULL!
CAN'T LEAVE THE KIDS HERE WHILE I INVESTIGATE.
I KNOW THIS ISN'T EXACTLY PART OF THE CHILD-REARING HANDBOOK--
--BUT MY INDESTRUCTIBLE CAPE WILL KEEP THEM PROTECTED...
I JUST REALLY HOPE JIMMY OLSEN ISN'T AROUND TO TAKE A PICTURE OF THIS...
OWD BEEBIDDER DOOPERMUN?
Our babysitter is SUPERMAN?
I HOBEE FYZ ZUMUNN WIDDIS HEAD VISHN!
I HOPE HE FRIES SOMEONE WITH HIS HEAT VISION!

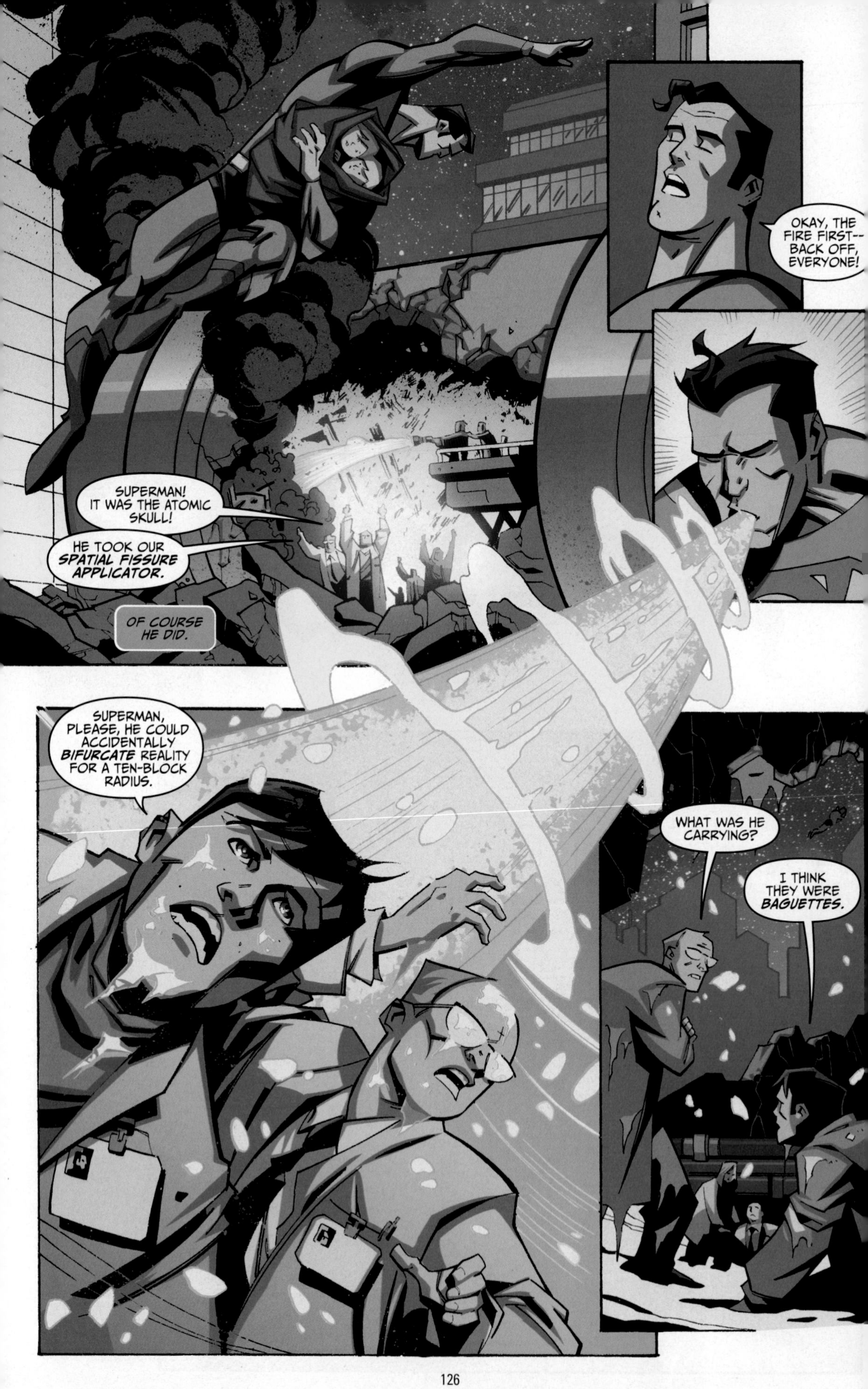

OKAY, THE FIRE FIRST-- BACK OFF, EVERYONE!
SUPERMAN! IT WAS THE ATOMIC SKULL!
HE TOOK OUR SPATIAL FISSURE APPLICATOR.
OF COURSE HE DID.
SUPERMAN, PLEASE, HE COULD ACCIDENTALLY BIFURCATE REALITY FOR A TEN-BLOCK RADIUS.
WHAT WAS HE CARRYING?
I THINK THEY WERE BAGUETTES.

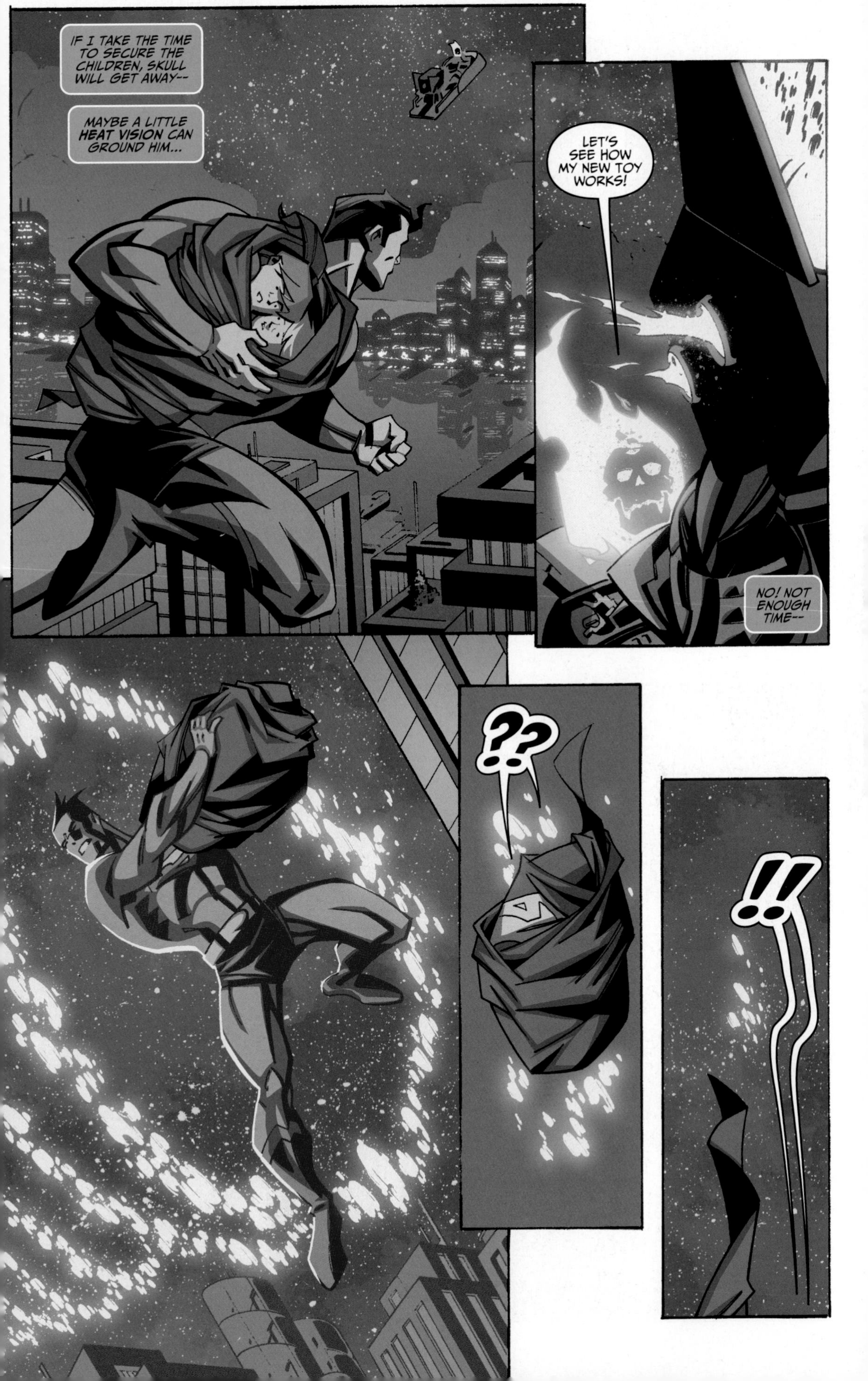
IF I TAKE THE TIME TO SECURE THE CHILDREN, SKULL WILL GET AWAY--
MAYBE A LITTLE HEAT VISION CAN GROUND HIM...
LET'S SEE HOW MY NEW TOY WORKS!
NO! NOT ENOUGH TIME--
??
!!

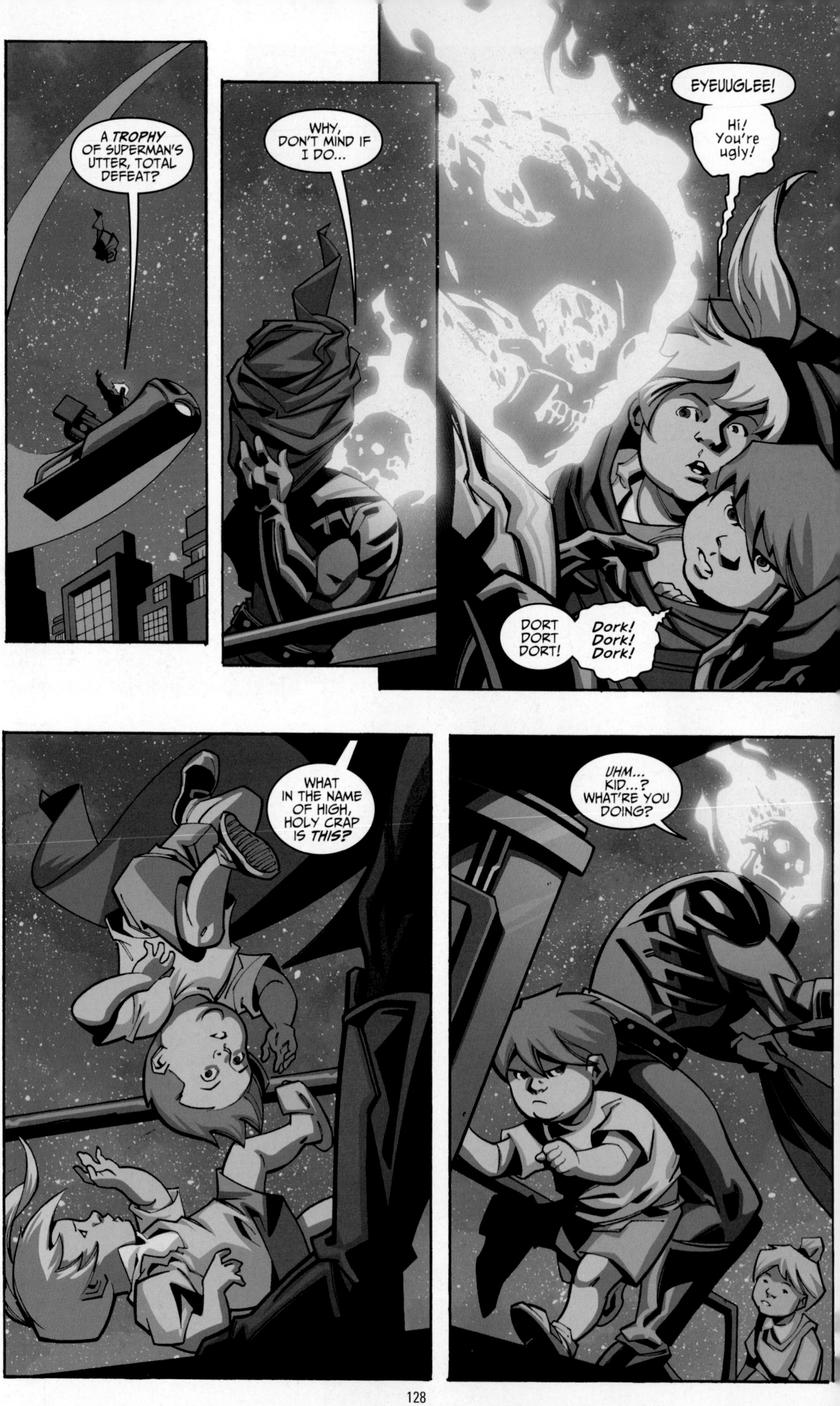
A TROPHY OF SUPERMAN'S UTTER, TOTAL DEFEAT?
WHY, DON'T MIND IF I DO...
EYEUUGLEE!
Hi! You're ugly!
DORT DORT DORT!
Dork! Dork! Dork!
WHAT IN THE NAME OF HIGH, HOLY CRAP IS THIS?
UHM... KID...? WHAT'RE YOU DOING?

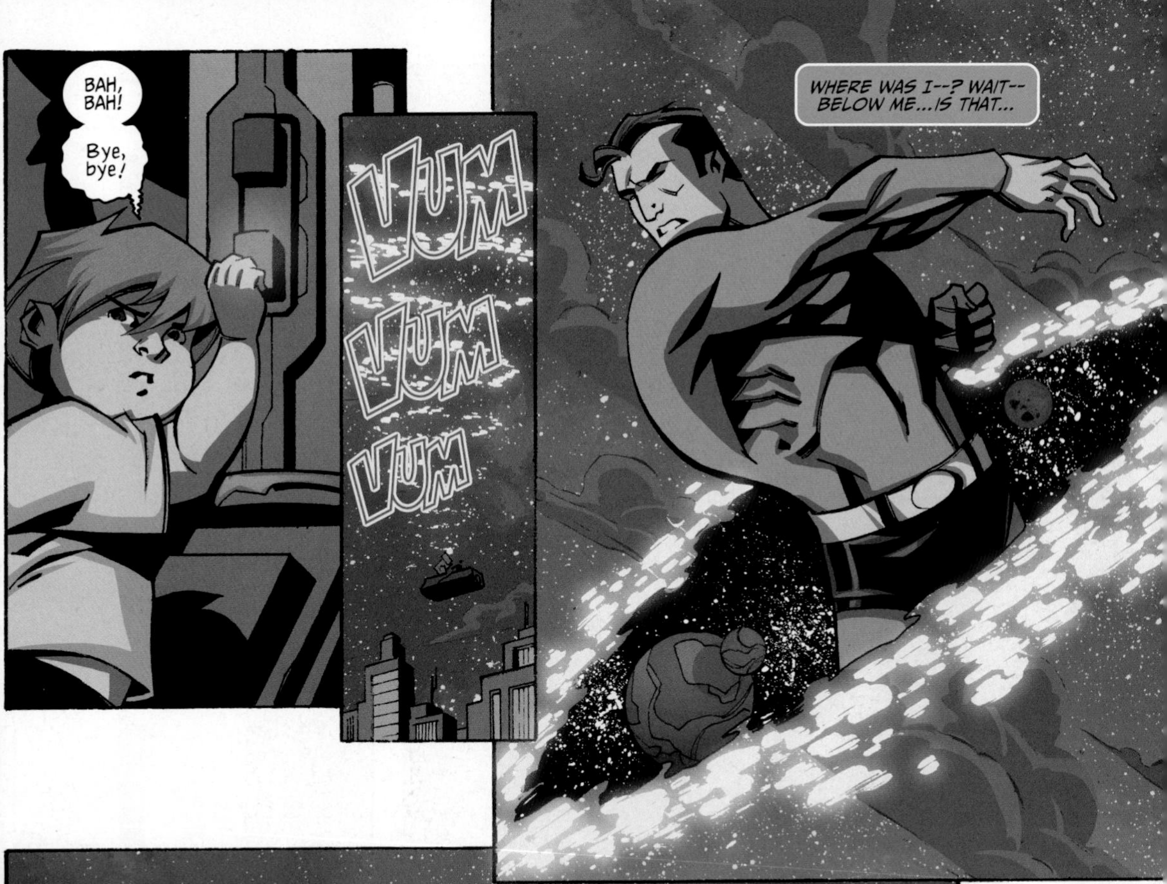
BAH, BAH!
Bye, bye!
VUM
VUM
VUM
WHERE WAS I--? WAIT-- BELOW ME...IS THAT...

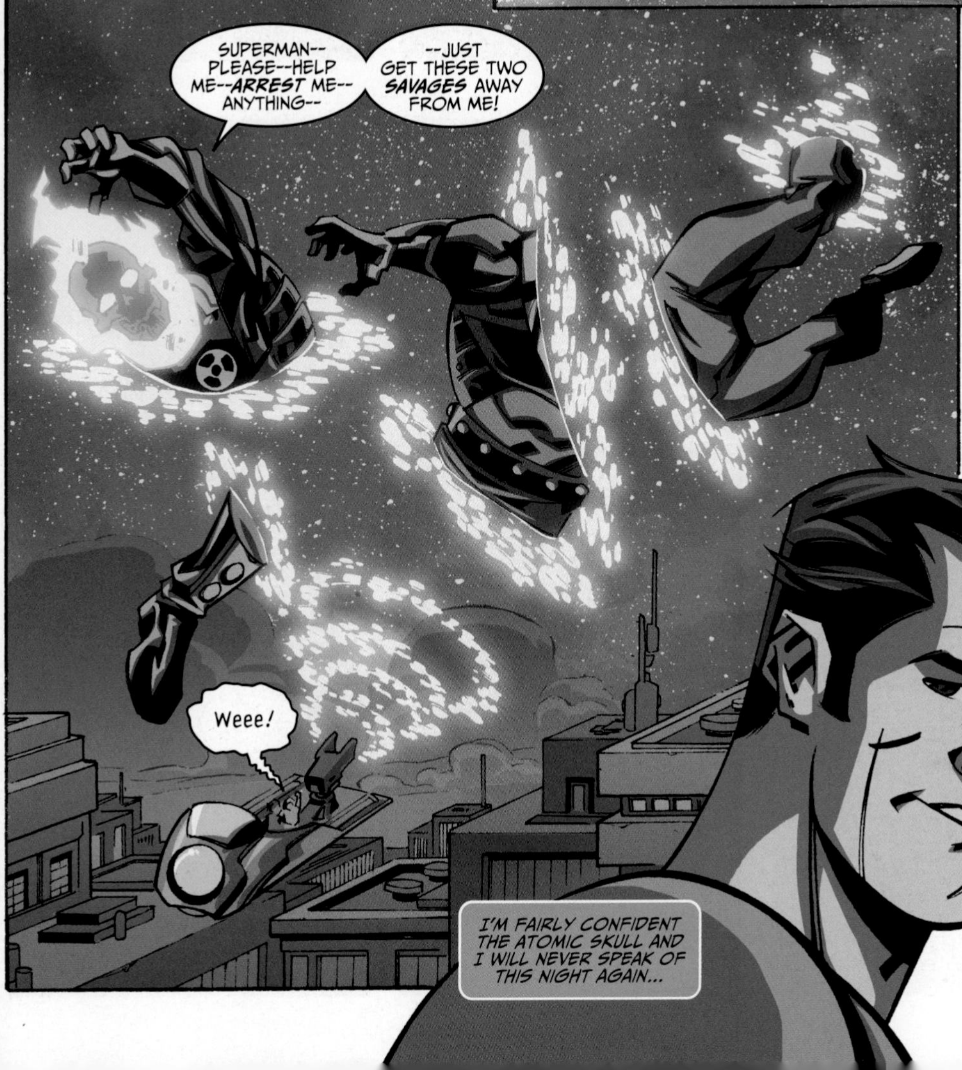
SUPERMAN-- PLEASE--HELP ME--ARREST ME-- ANYTHING--
--JUST GET THESE TWO SAVAGES AWAY FROM ME!
Weee!
I'M FAIRLY CONFIDENT THE ATOMIC SKULL AND I WILL NEVER SPEAK OF THIS NIGHT AGAIN...

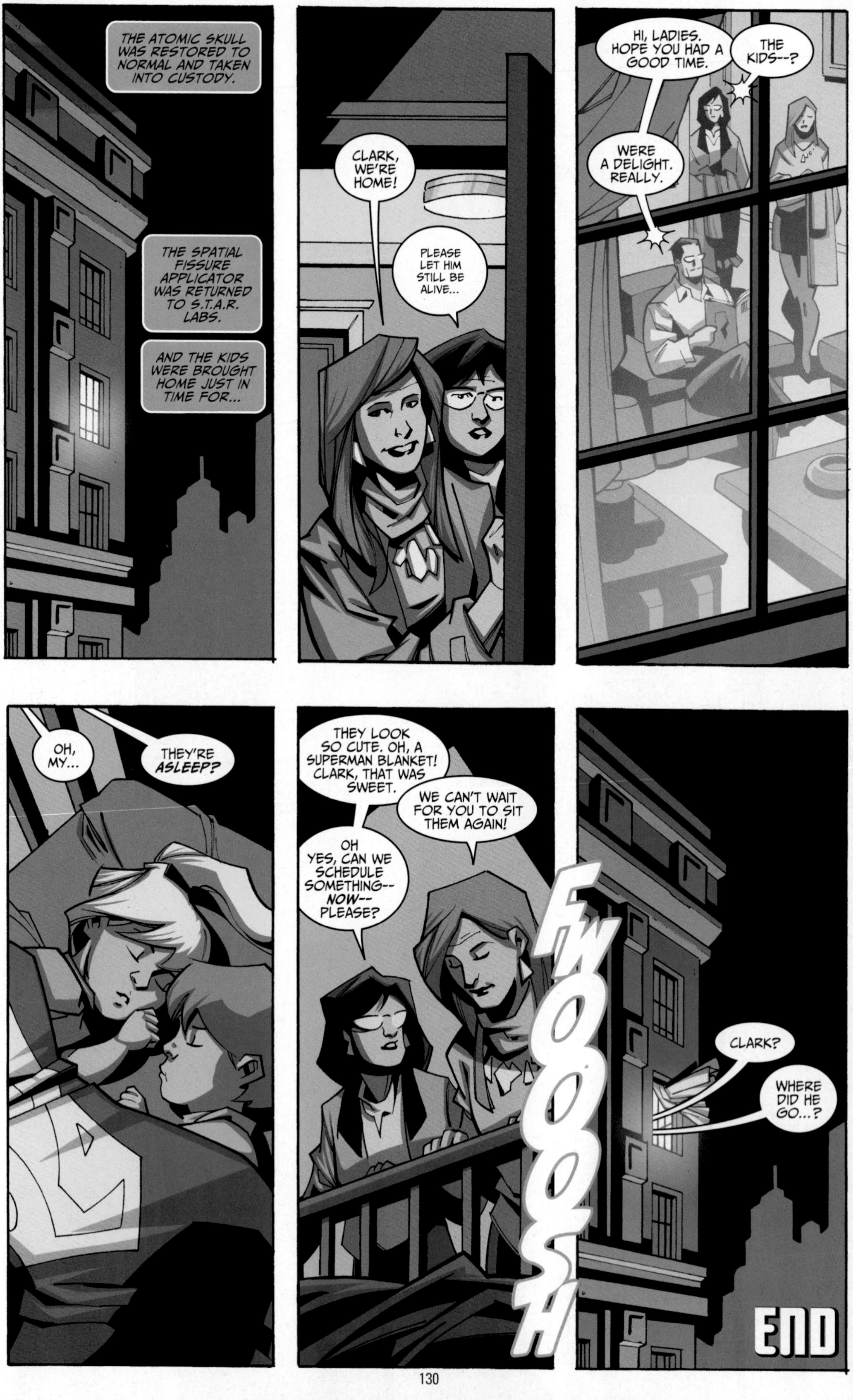
THE ATOMIC SKULL WAS RESTORED TO NORMAL AND TAKEN INTO CUSTODY.
THE SPATIAL FISSURE APPLICATOR WAS RETURNED TO S.T.A.R. LABS.
AND THE KIDS WERE BROUGHT HOME JUST IN TIME FOR...
CLARK, WE'RE HOME!
PLEASE LET HIM STILL BE ALIVE...
HI, LADIES. HOPE YOU HAD A GOOD TIME.
THE KIDS--?
WERE A DELIGHT. REALLY.
OH, MY...
THEY'RE ASLEEP?
THEY LOOK SO CUTE. OH, A SUPERMAN BLANKET! CLARK, THAT WAS SWEET.
WE CAN'T WAIT FOR YOU TO SIT THEM AGAIN!
OH YES, CAN WE SCHEDULE SOMETHING-- NOW-- PLEASE?
FWOOOOSH
CLARK?
WHERE DID HE GO...?
END

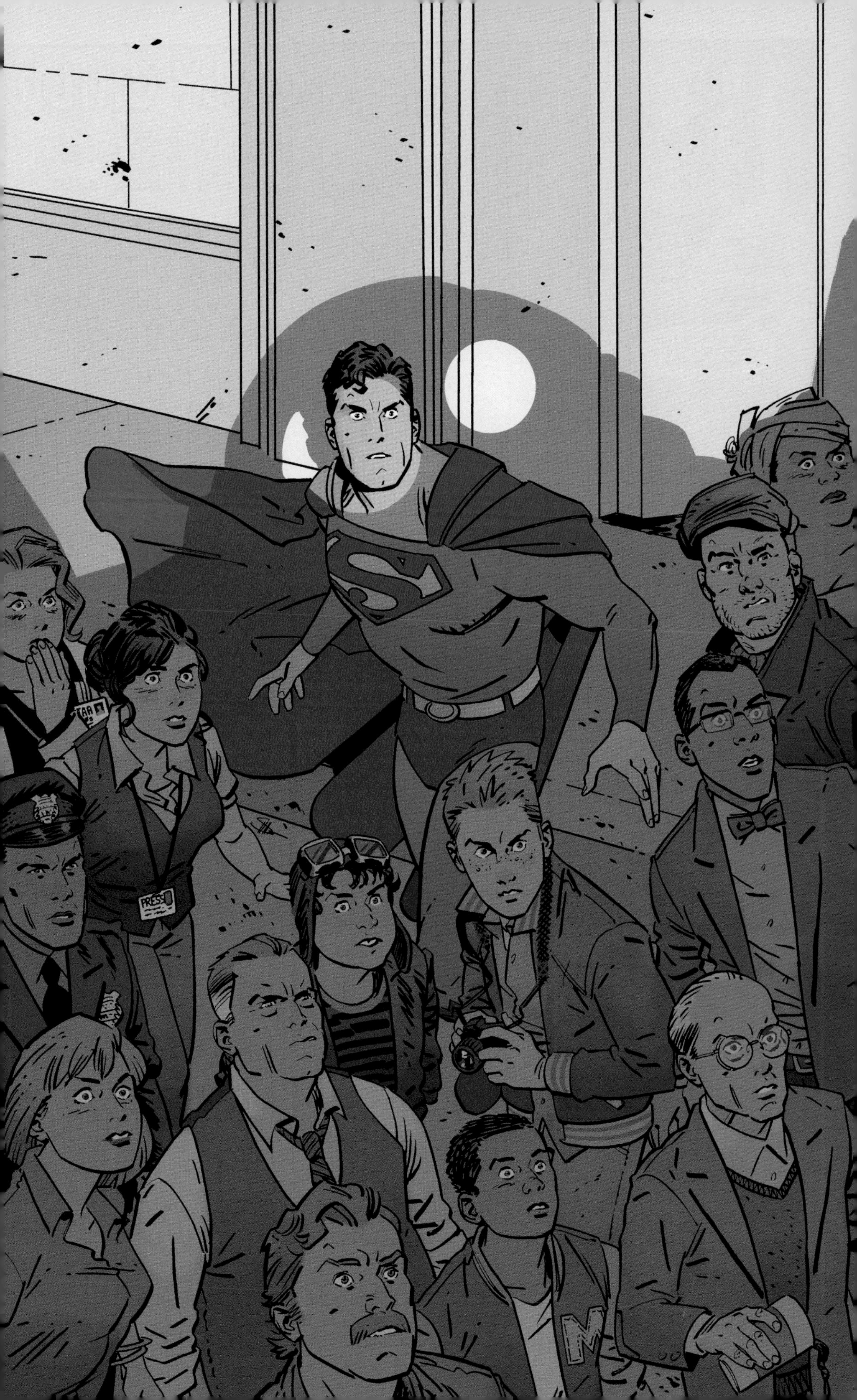
PRESS

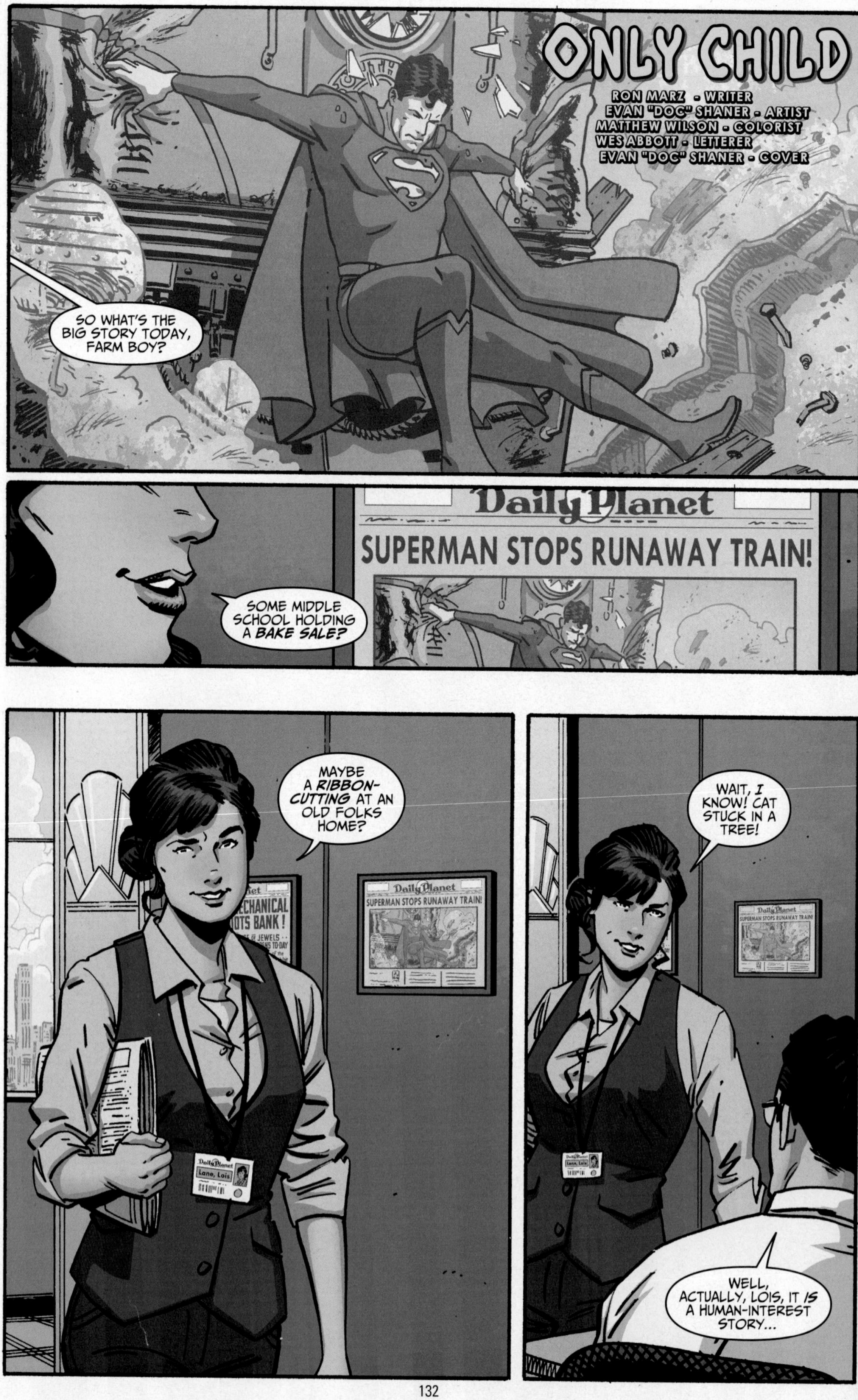
ONLY CHILD
RON MARZ - WRITER
EVAN "DOC" SHANER - ARTIST
MATTHEW WILSON - COLORIST
WES ABBOTT - LETTERER
EVAN "DOC" SHANER - COVER
SO WHAT'S THE BIG STORY TODAY, FARM BOY?
Daily Planet
SUPERMAN STOPS RUNAWAY TRAIN!
SOME MIDDLE SCHOOL HOLDING A *BAKE SALE?*
MAYBE A *RIBBON-CUTTING* AT AN OLD FOLKS HOME?
Lane, Lois
WAIT, *I* KNOW! CAT STUCK IN A TREE!
WELL, ACTUALLY, LOIS, IT *IS* A HUMAN-INTEREST STORY...

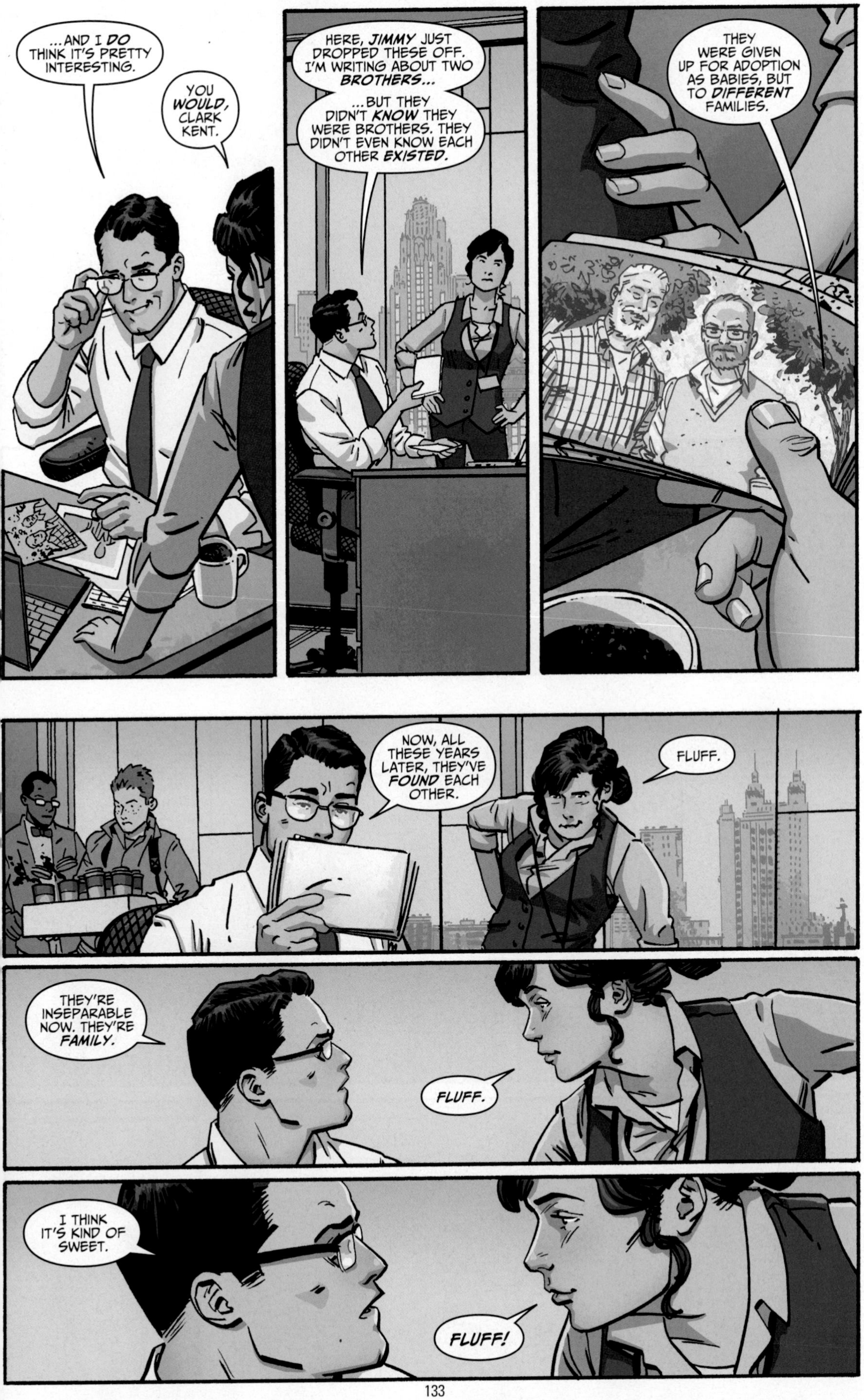
...AND I DO THINK IT'S PRETTY INTERESTING.
YOU WOULD, CLARK KENT.
HERE, JIMMY JUST DROPPED THESE OFF. I'M WRITING ABOUT TWO BROTHERS...
...BUT THEY DIDN'T KNOW THEY WERE BROTHERS. THEY DIDN'T EVEN KNOW EACH OTHER EXISTED.
THEY WERE GIVEN UP FOR ADOPTION AS BABIES, BUT TO DIFFERENT FAMILIES.
NOW, ALL THESE YEARS LATER, THEY'VE FOUND EACH OTHER.
FLUFF.
THEY'RE INSEPARABLE NOW. THEY'RE FAMILY.
FLUFF.
I THINK IT'S KIND OF SWEET.
FLUFF!

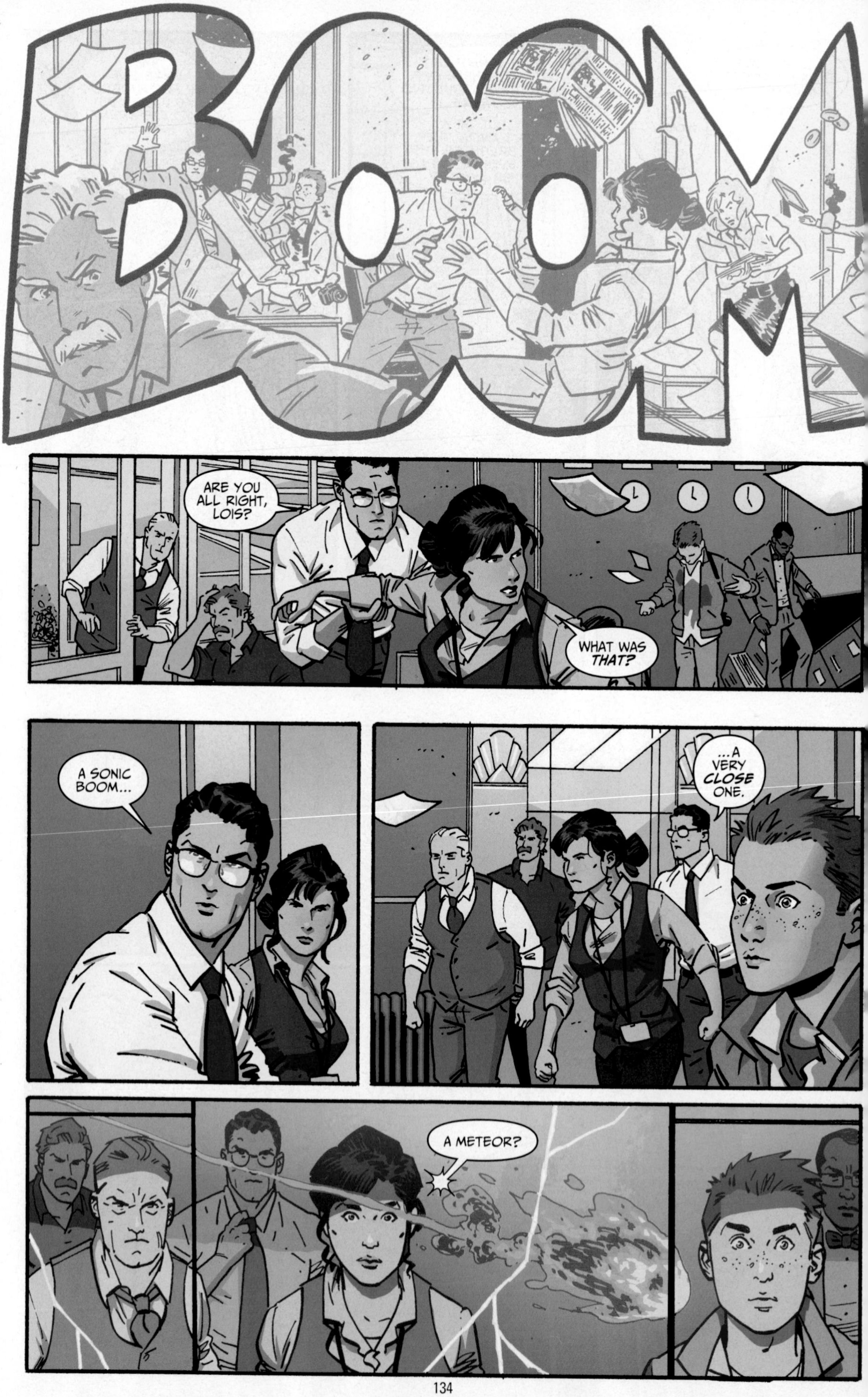
BOOOM
ARE YOU ALL RIGHT, LOIS?
WHAT WAS THAT?
A SONIC BOOM...
...A VERY CLOSE ONE.
A METEOR?

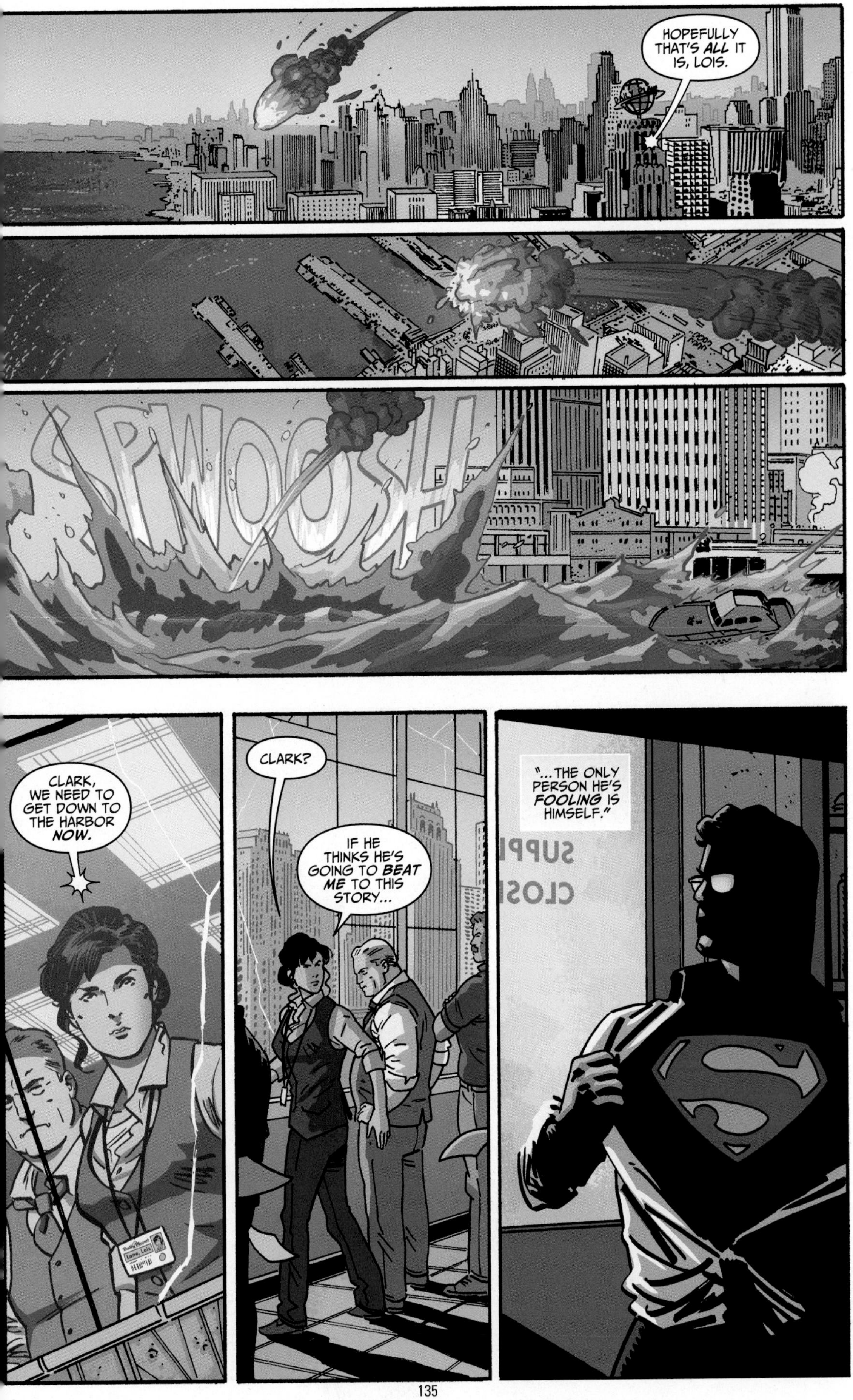
HOPEFULLY THAT'S *ALL* IT IS, LOIS.
SPWOOSH
CLARK, WE NEED TO GET DOWN TO THE HARBOR *NOW.*
CLARK?
IF HE THINKS HE'S GOING TO *BEAT ME* TO THIS STORY...
"...THE ONLY PERSON HE'S *FOOLING* IS HIMSELF."

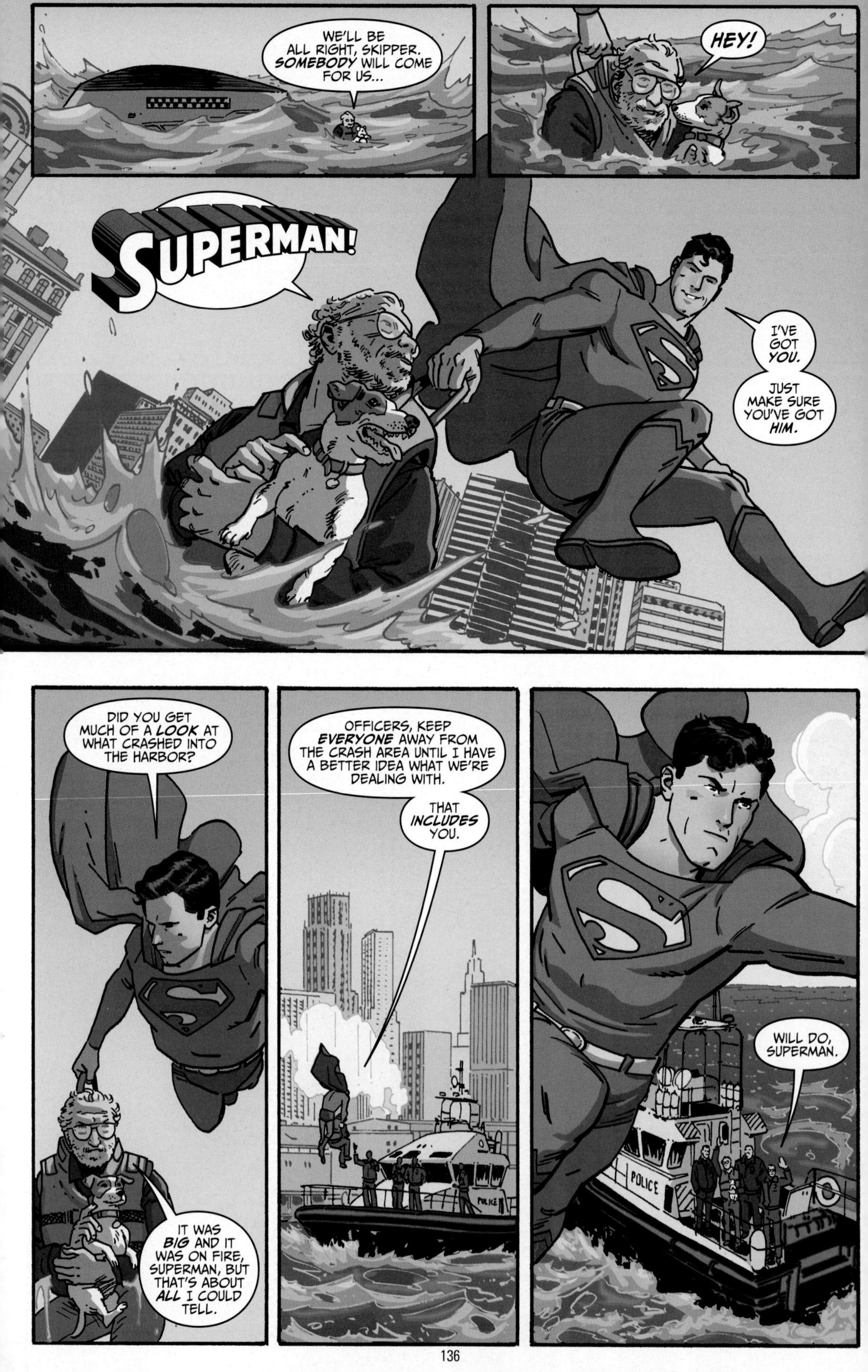
WE'LL BE ALL RIGHT, SKIPPER. SOMEBODY WILL COME FOR US...
HEY!
SUPERMAN!
I'VE GOT YOU.
JUST MAKE SURE YOU'VE GOT HIM.
DID YOU GET MUCH OF A LOOK AT WHAT CRASHED INTO THE HARBOR?
IT WAS BIG AND IT WAS ON FIRE, SUPERMAN, BUT THAT'S ABOUT ALL I COULD TELL.
OFFICERS, KEEP EVERYONE AWAY FROM THE CRASH AREA UNTIL I HAVE A BETTER IDEA WHAT WE'RE DEALING WITH.
THAT INCLUDES YOU.
WILL DO, SUPERMAN.
POLICE

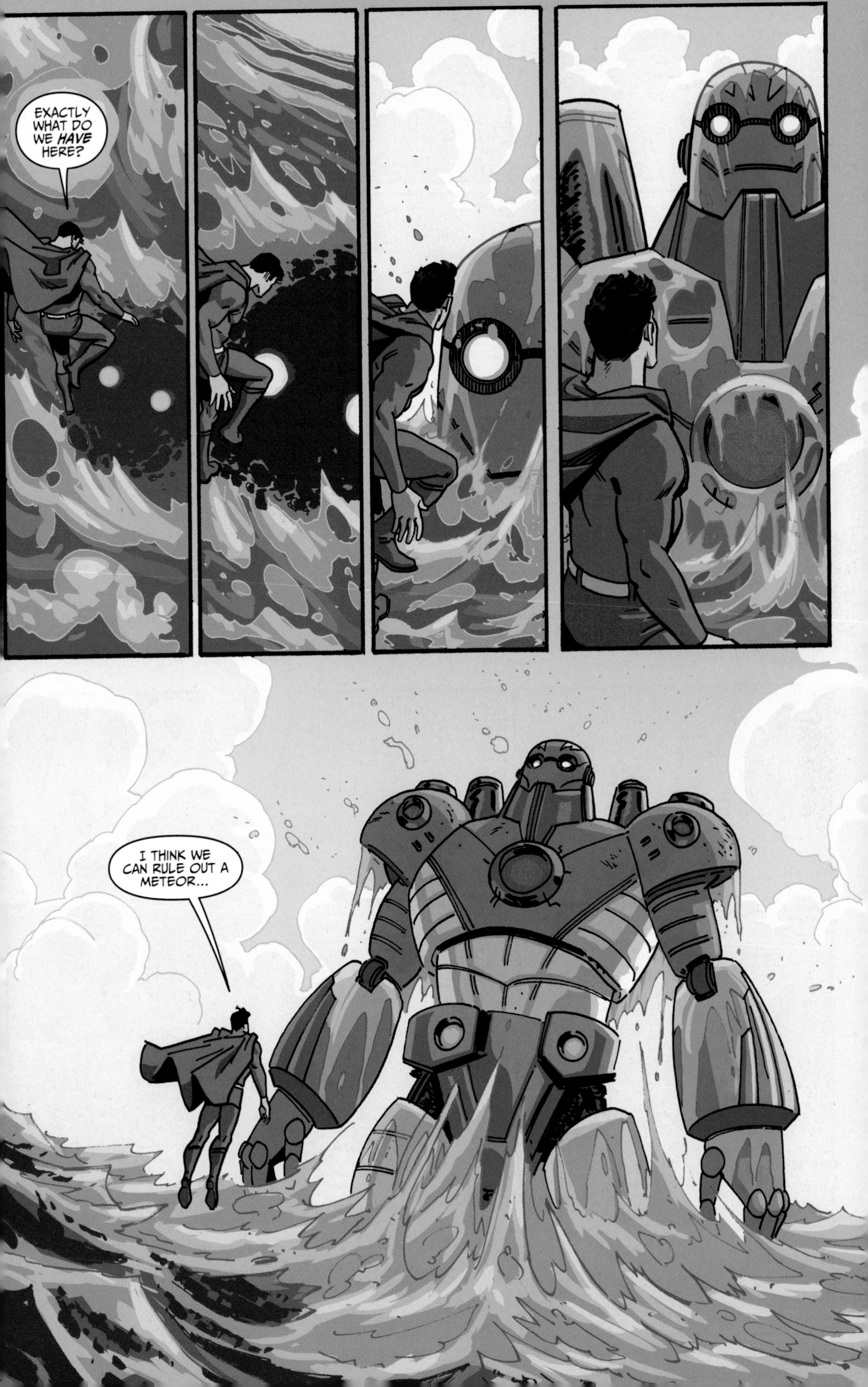
EXACTLY WHAT DO WE *HAVE* HERE?
I THINK WE CAN RULE OUT A METEOR...

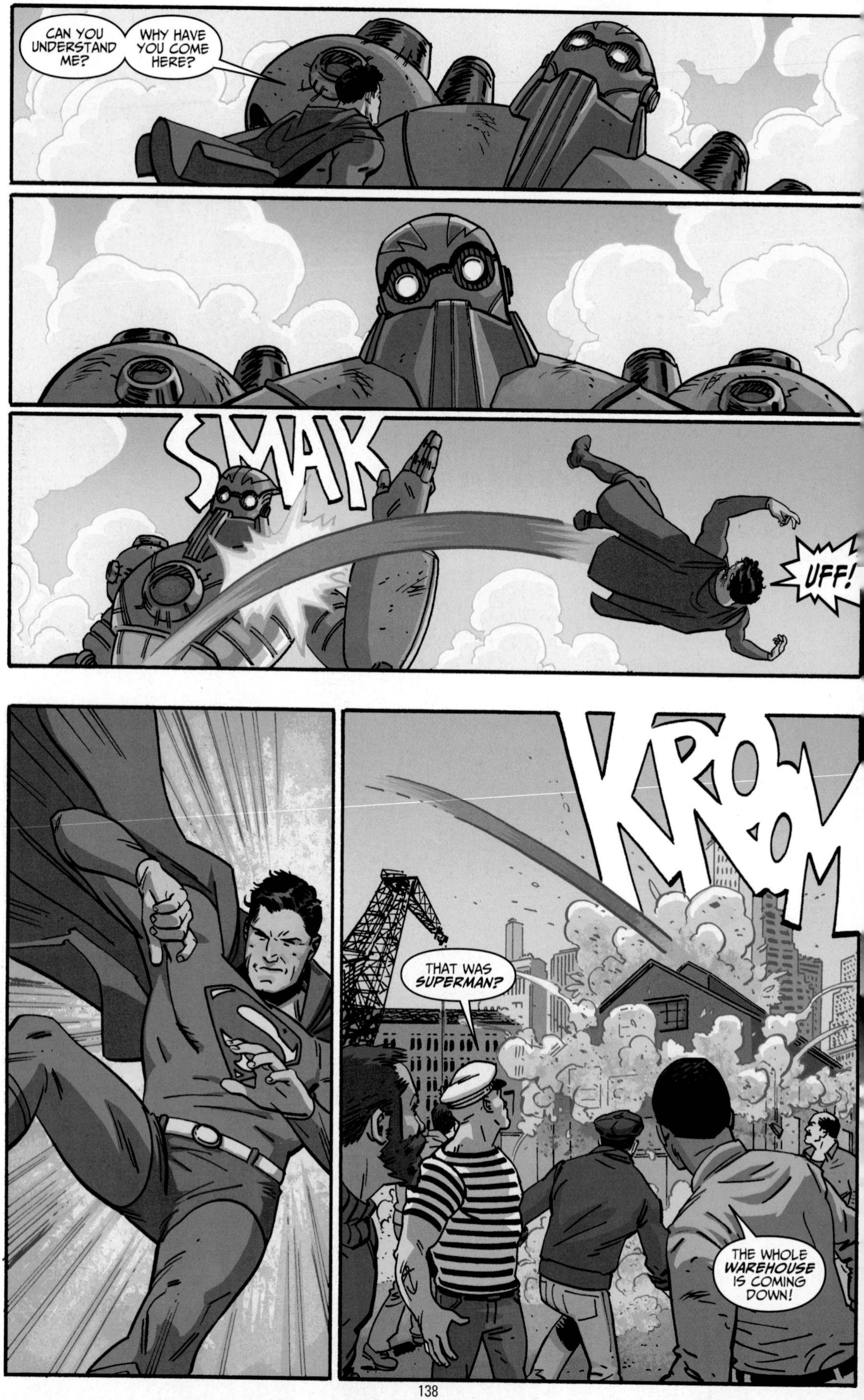
CAN YOU UNDERSTAND ME?
WHY HAVE YOU COME HERE?
SMAK
UFF!
KROOM
THAT WAS SUPERMAN?
THE WHOLE WAREHOUSE IS COMING DOWN!

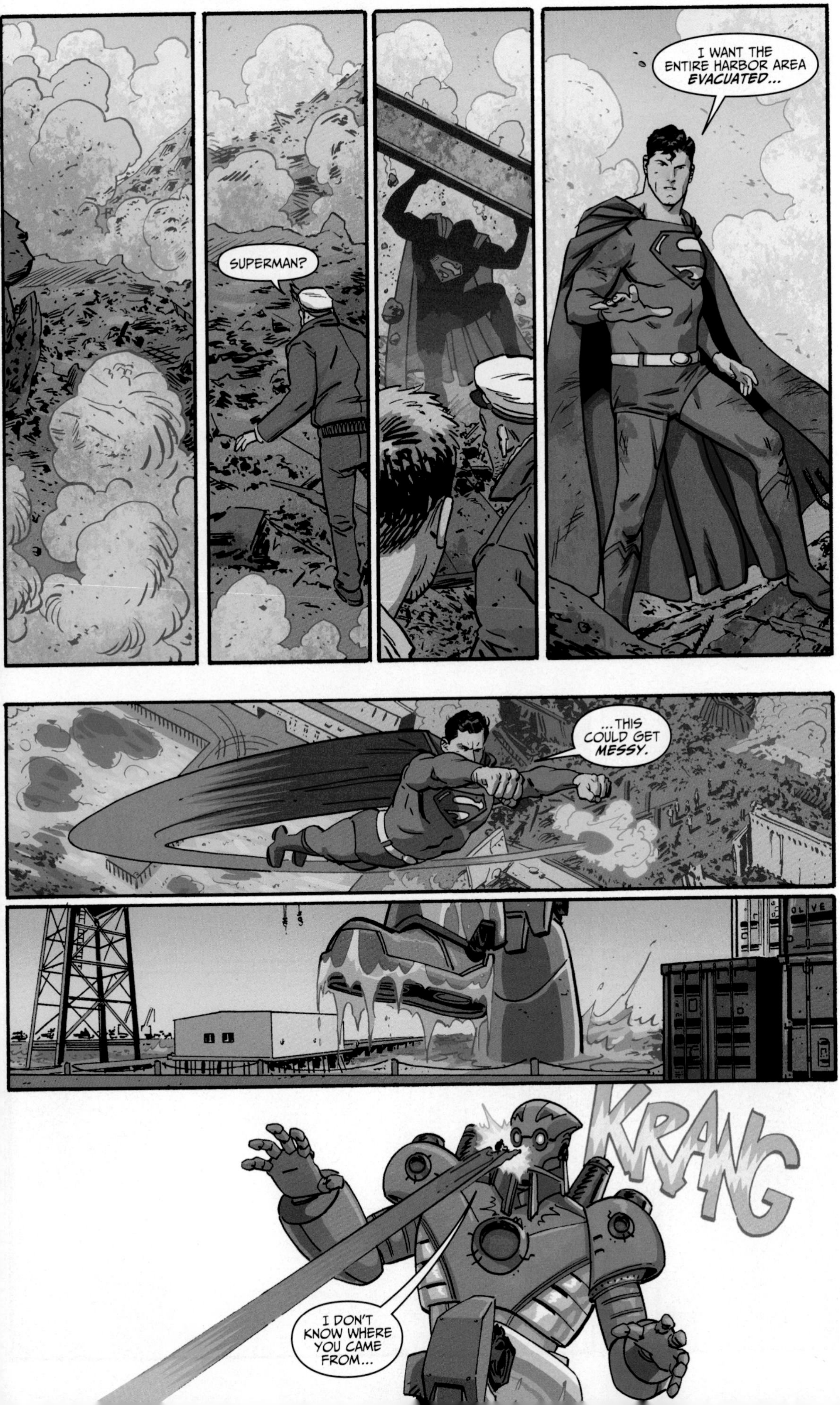
SUPERMAN?
I WANT THE ENTIRE HARBOR AREA EVACUATED...
...THIS COULD GET MESSY.
OLVE
KRANG
I DON'T KNOW WHERE YOU CAME FROM...

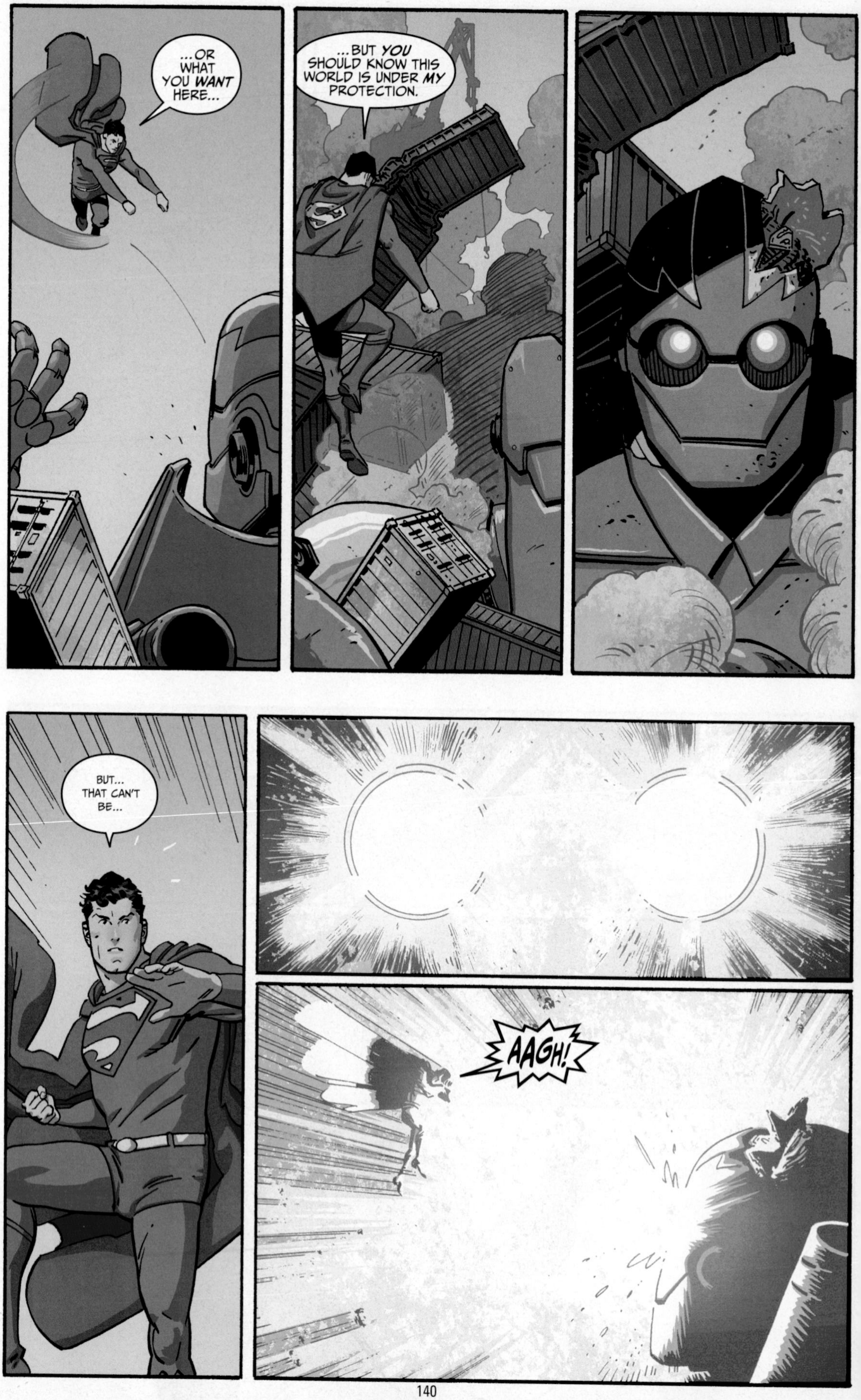
...OR WHAT YOU WANT HERE...
...BUT YOU SHOULD KNOW THIS WORLD IS UNDER MY PROTECTION.
BUT... THAT CAN'T BE...
AAGH!

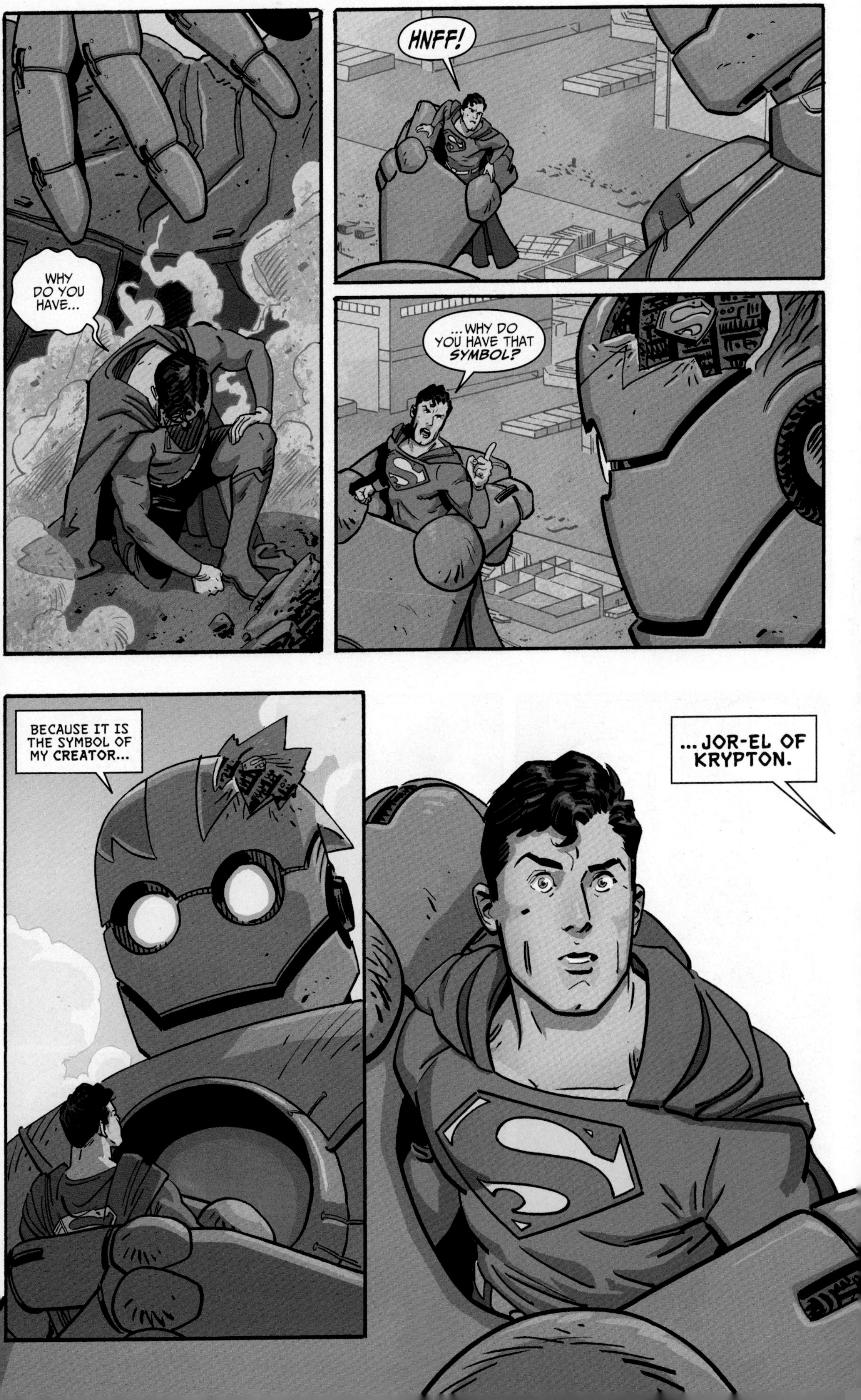
WHY DO YOU HAVE...
HNFF!
...WHY DO YOU HAVE THAT SYMBOL?
BECAUSE IT IS THE SYMBOL OF MY CREATOR...
...JOR-EL OF KRYPTON.

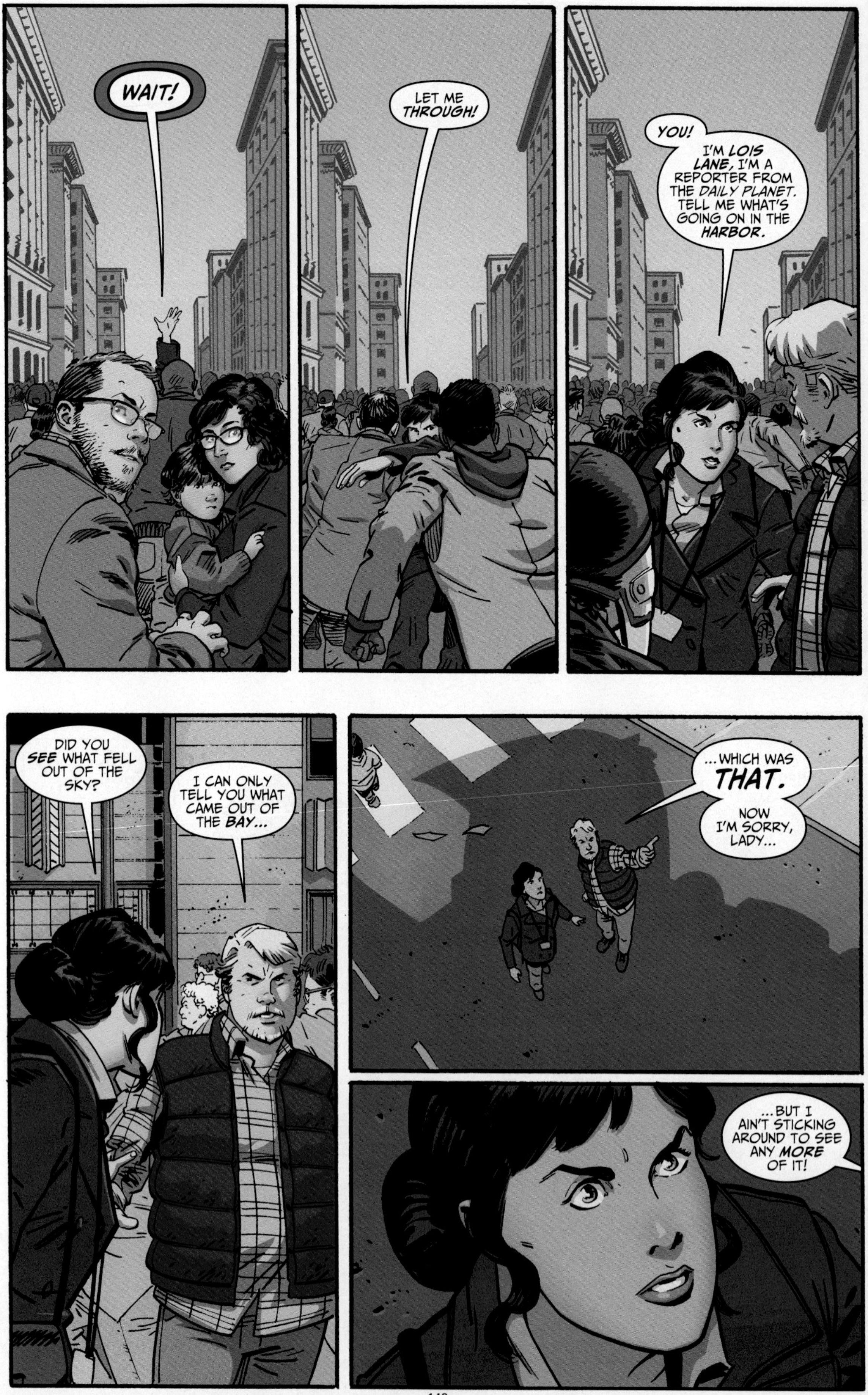
WAIT!
LET ME THROUGH!
YOU!
I'M LOIS LANE, I'M A REPORTER FROM THE DAILY PLANET. TELL ME WHAT'S GOING ON IN THE HARBOR.
DID YOU SEE WHAT FELL OUT OF THE SKY?
I CAN ONLY TELL YOU WHAT CAME OUT OF THE BAY...
...WHICH WAS THAT.
NOW I'M SORRY, LADY...
...BUT I AIN'T STICKING AROUND TO SEE ANY MORE OF IT!

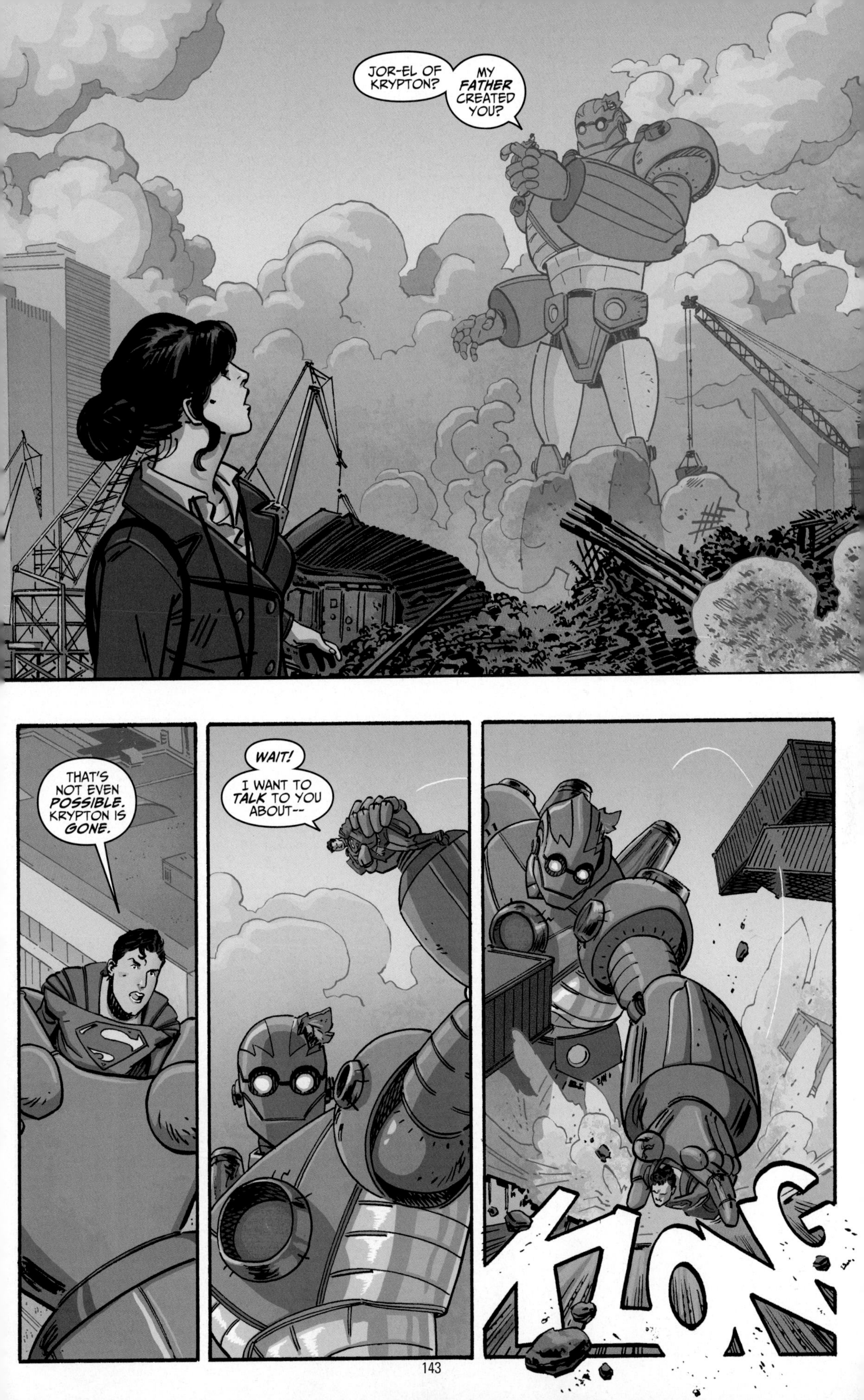
JOR-EL OF KRYPTON?
MY FATHER CREATED YOU?
THAT'S NOT EVEN POSSIBLE. KRYPTON IS GONE.
WAIT!
I WANT TO TALK TO YOU ABOUT--

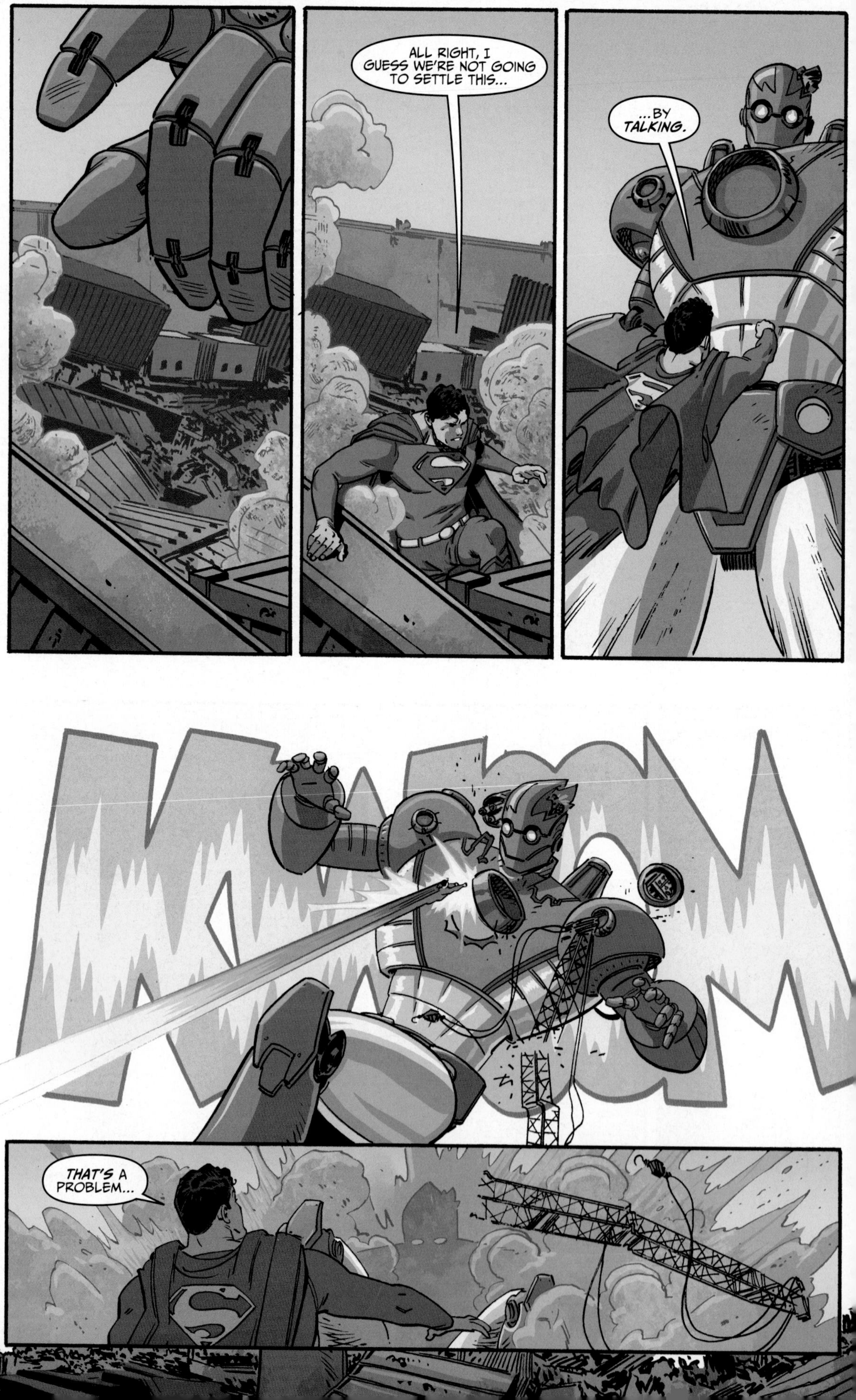
ALL RIGHT, I GUESS WE'RE NOT GOING TO SETTLE THIS...
...BY *TALKING.*
THAT'S A PROBLEM...

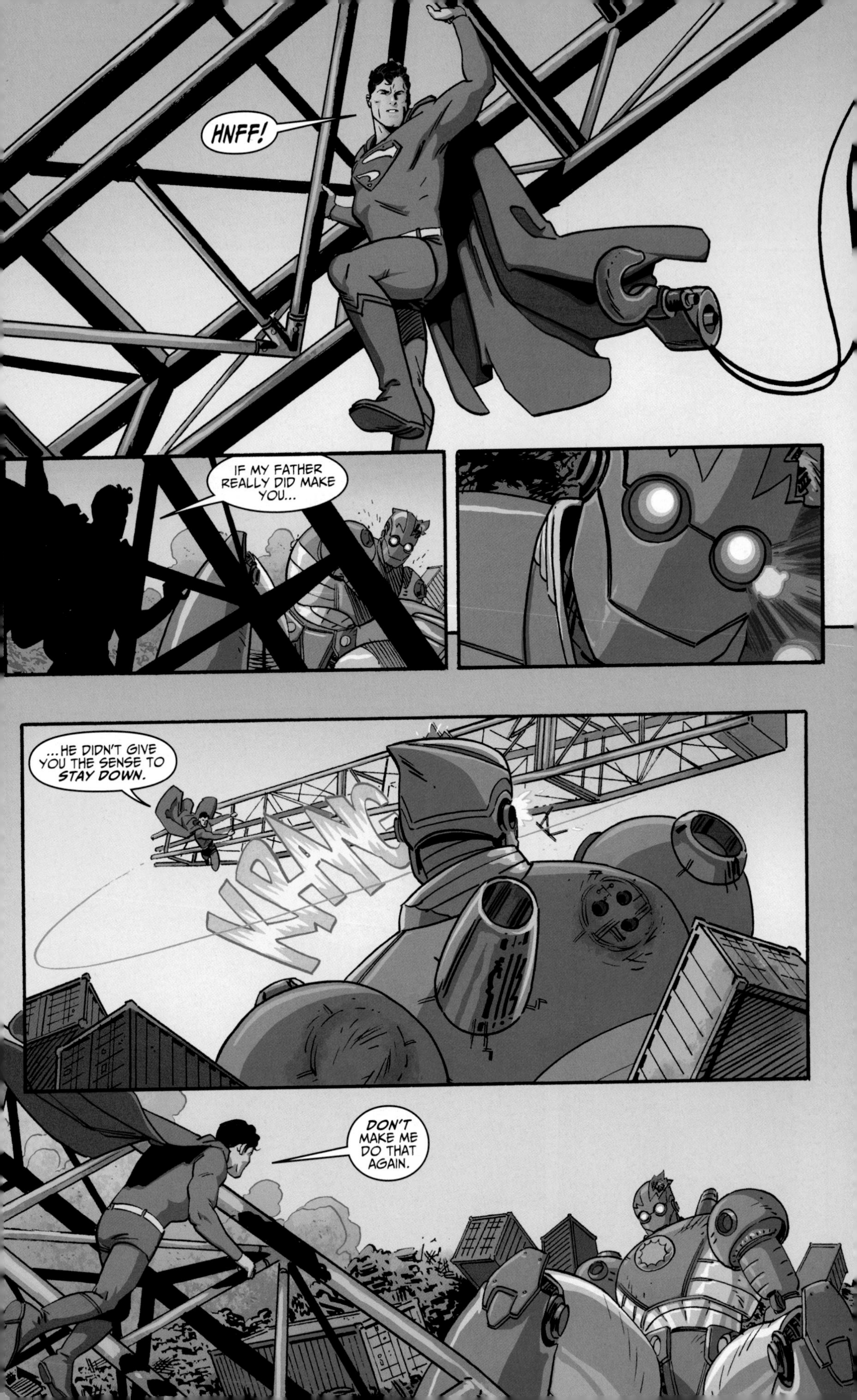
HNFF!
IF MY FATHER REALLY DID MAKE YOU...
...HE DIDN'T GIVE YOU THE SENSE TO STAY DOWN.
DON'T MAKE ME DO THAT AGAIN.

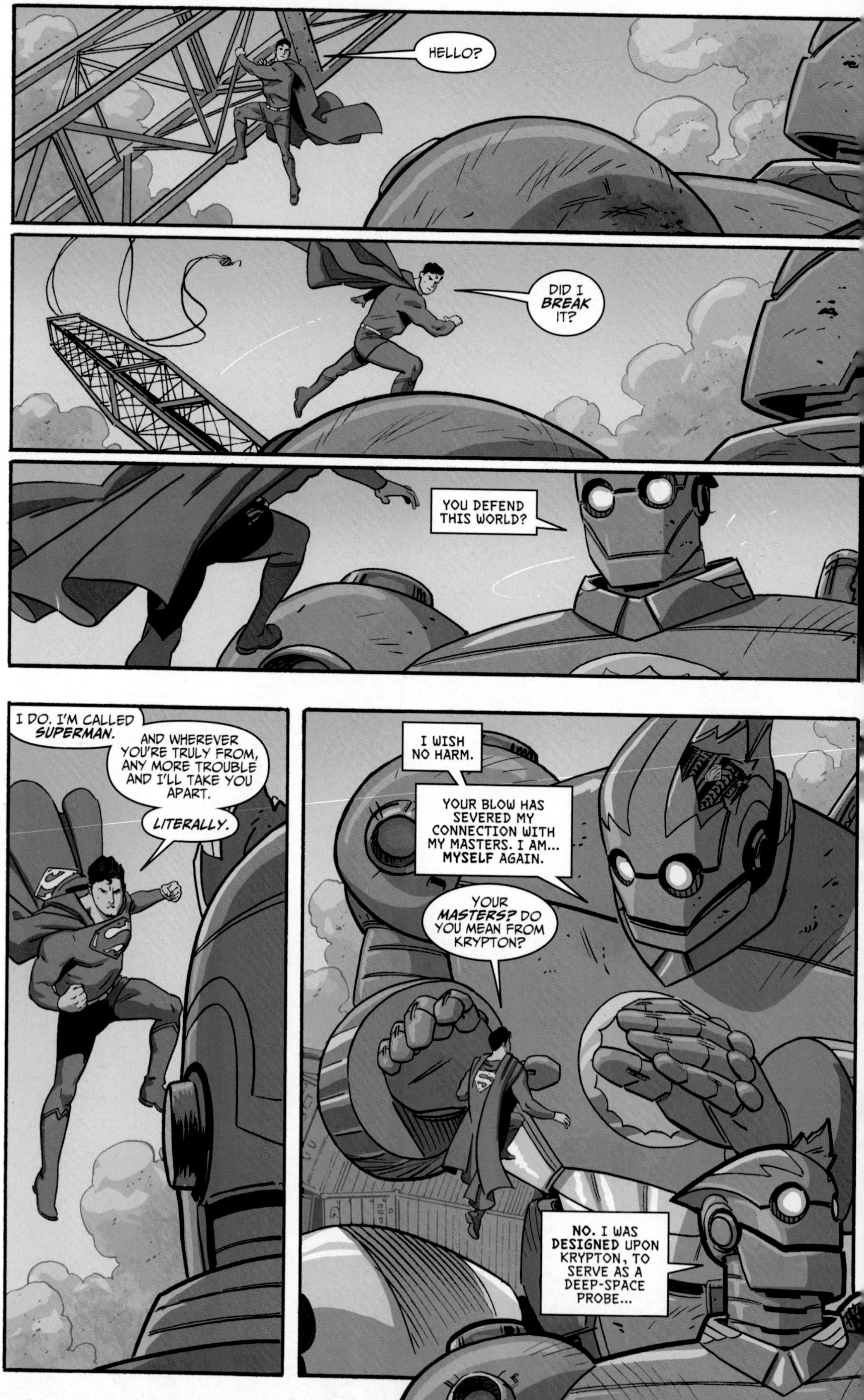
HELLO?
DID I BREAK IT?
YOU DEFEND THIS WORLD?
I DO. I'M CALLED SUPERMAN.
AND WHEREVER YOU'RE TRULY FROM, ANY MORE TROUBLE AND I'LL TAKE YOU APART.
LITERALLY.
I WISH NO HARM.
YOUR BLOW HAS SEVERED MY CONNECTION WITH MY MASTERS. I AM... MYSELF AGAIN.
YOUR MASTERS? DO YOU MEAN FROM KRYPTON?
NO. I WAS DESIGNED UPON KRYPTON, TO SERVE AS A DEEP-SPACE PROBE...

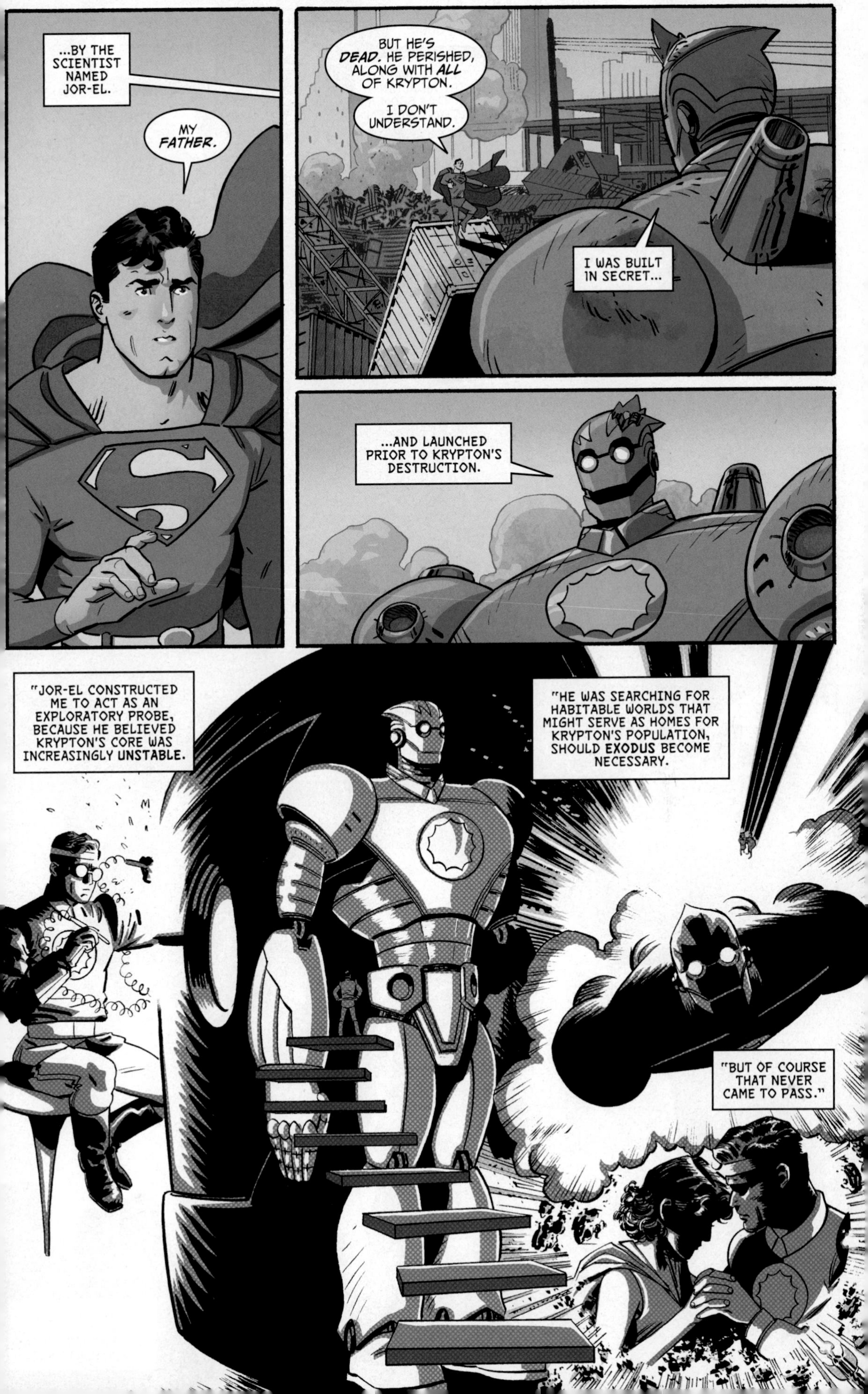
...BY THE SCIENTIST NAMED JOR-EL.
MY FATHER.
BUT HE'S DEAD. HE PERISHED, ALONG WITH ALL OF KRYPTON.
I DON'T UNDERSTAND.
I WAS BUILT IN SECRET...
...AND LAUNCHED PRIOR TO KRYPTON'S DESTRUCTION.
"JOR-EL CONSTRUCTED ME TO ACT AS AN EXPLORATORY PROBE, BECAUSE HE BELIEVED KRYPTON'S CORE WAS INCREASINGLY UNSTABLE.
"HE WAS SEARCHING FOR HABITABLE WORLDS THAT MIGHT SERVE AS HOMES FOR KRYPTON'S POPULATION, SHOULD EXODUS BECOME NECESSARY.
"BUT OF COURSE THAT NEVER CAME TO PASS."

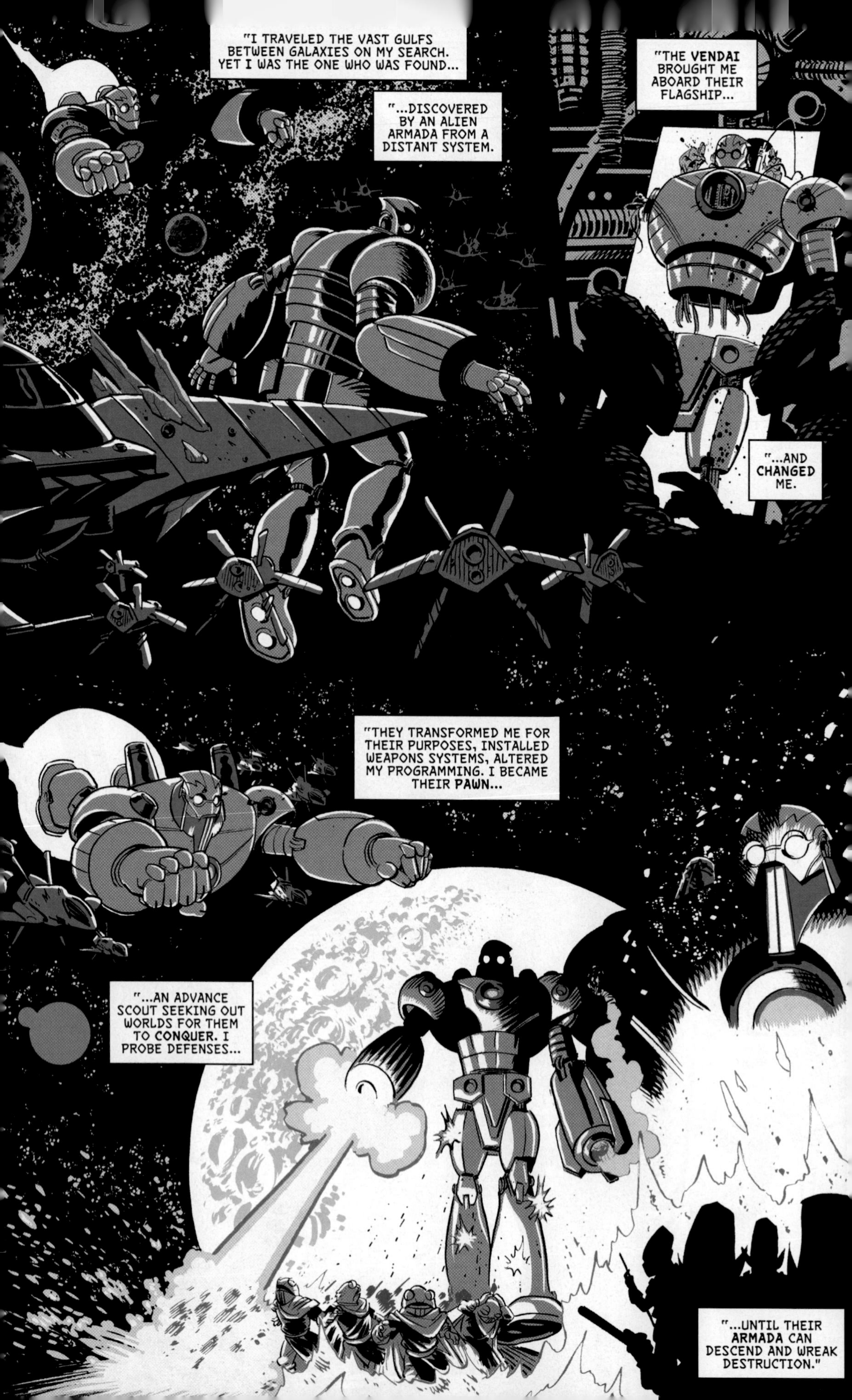
"I TRAVELED THE VAST GULFS BETWEEN GALAXIES ON MY SEARCH. YET I WAS THE ONE WHO WAS FOUND...
"...DISCOVERED BY AN ALIEN ARMADA FROM A DISTANT SYSTEM.
"THE VENDAI BROUGHT ME ABOARD THEIR FLAGSHIP...
"...AND CHANGED ME.
"THEY TRANSFORMED ME FOR THEIR PURPOSES, INSTALLED WEAPONS SYSTEMS, ALTERED MY PROGRAMMING. I BECAME THEIR PAWN...
"...AN ADVANCE SCOUT SEEKING OUT WORLDS FOR THEM TO CONQUER. I PROBE DEFENSES...
"...UNTIL THEIR ARMADA CAN DESCEND AND WREAK DESTRUCTION."

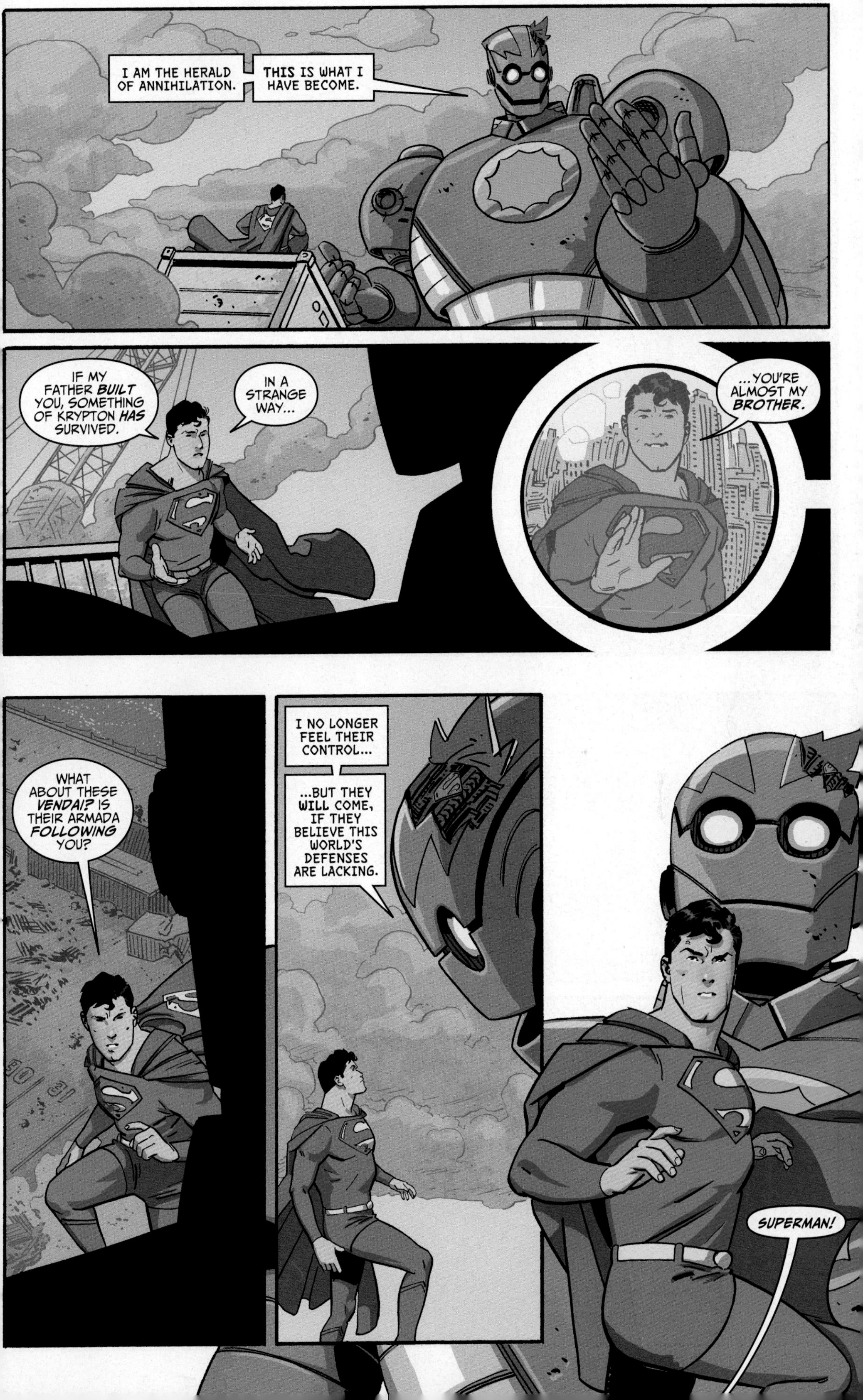
I AM THE HERALD OF ANNIHILATION.
THIS IS WHAT I HAVE BECOME.
IF MY FATHER BUILT YOU, SOMETHING OF KRYPTON HAS SURVIVED.
IN A STRANGE WAY...
...YOU'RE ALMOST MY BROTHER.
WHAT ABOUT THESE VENDAI? IS THEIR ARMADA FOLLOWING YOU?
I NO LONGER FEEL THEIR CONTROL...
...BUT THEY WILL COME, IF THEY BELIEVE THIS WORLD'S DEFENSES ARE LACKING.
SUPERMAN!

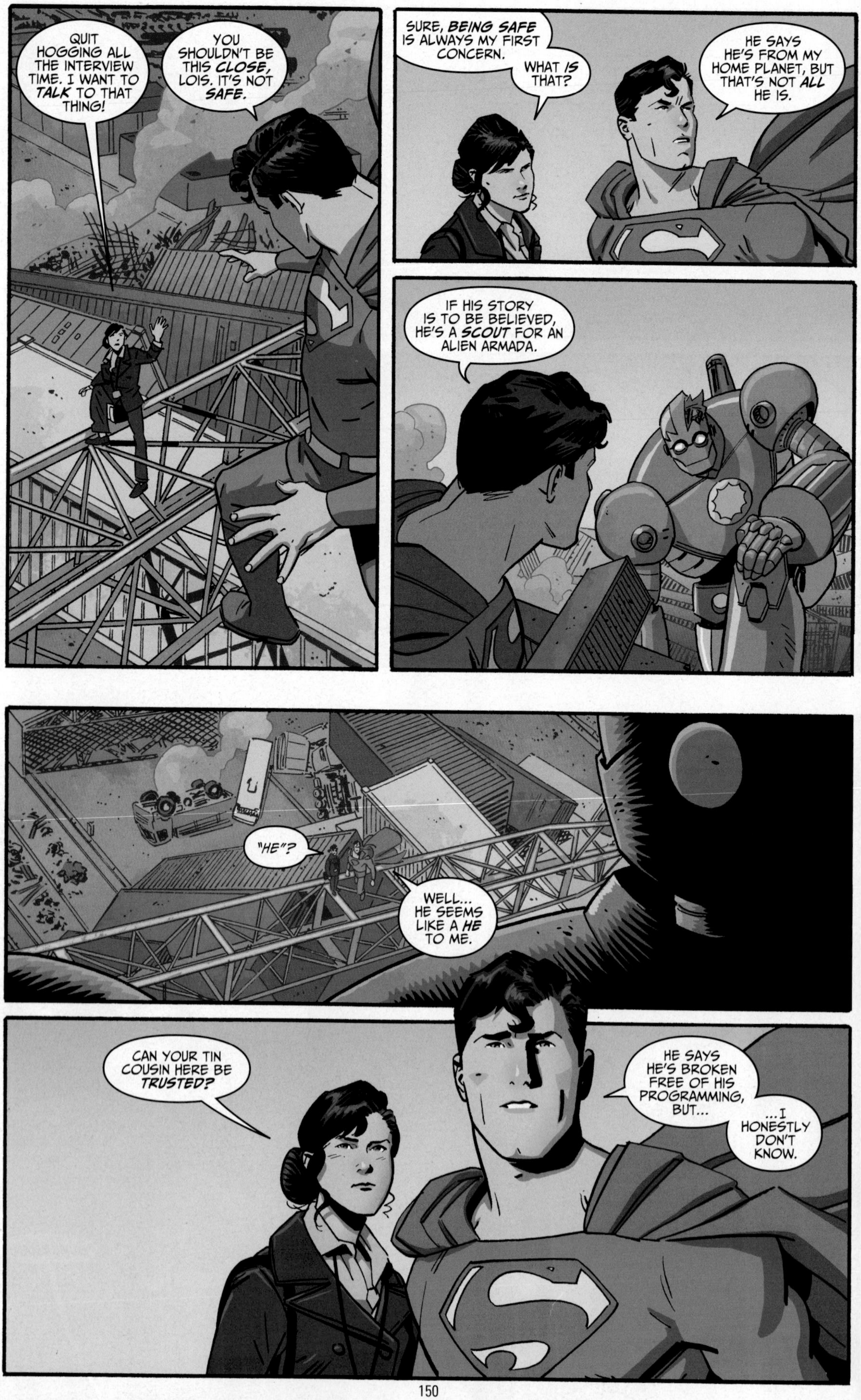
QUIT HOGGING ALL THE INTERVIEW TIME. I WANT TO TALK TO THAT THING!
YOU SHOULDN'T BE THIS CLOSE, LOIS. IT'S NOT SAFE.
SURE, BEING SAFE IS ALWAYS MY FIRST CONCERN.
WHAT IS THAT?
HE SAYS HE'S FROM MY HOME PLANET, BUT THAT'S NOT ALL HE IS.
IF HIS STORY IS TO BE BELIEVED, HE'S A SCOUT FOR AN ALIEN ARMADA.
"HE"?
WELL... HE SEEMS LIKE A HE TO ME.
CAN YOUR TIN COUSIN HERE BE TRUSTED?
HE SAYS HE'S BROKEN FREE OF HIS PROGRAMMING, BUT...
...I HONESTLY DON'T KNOW.

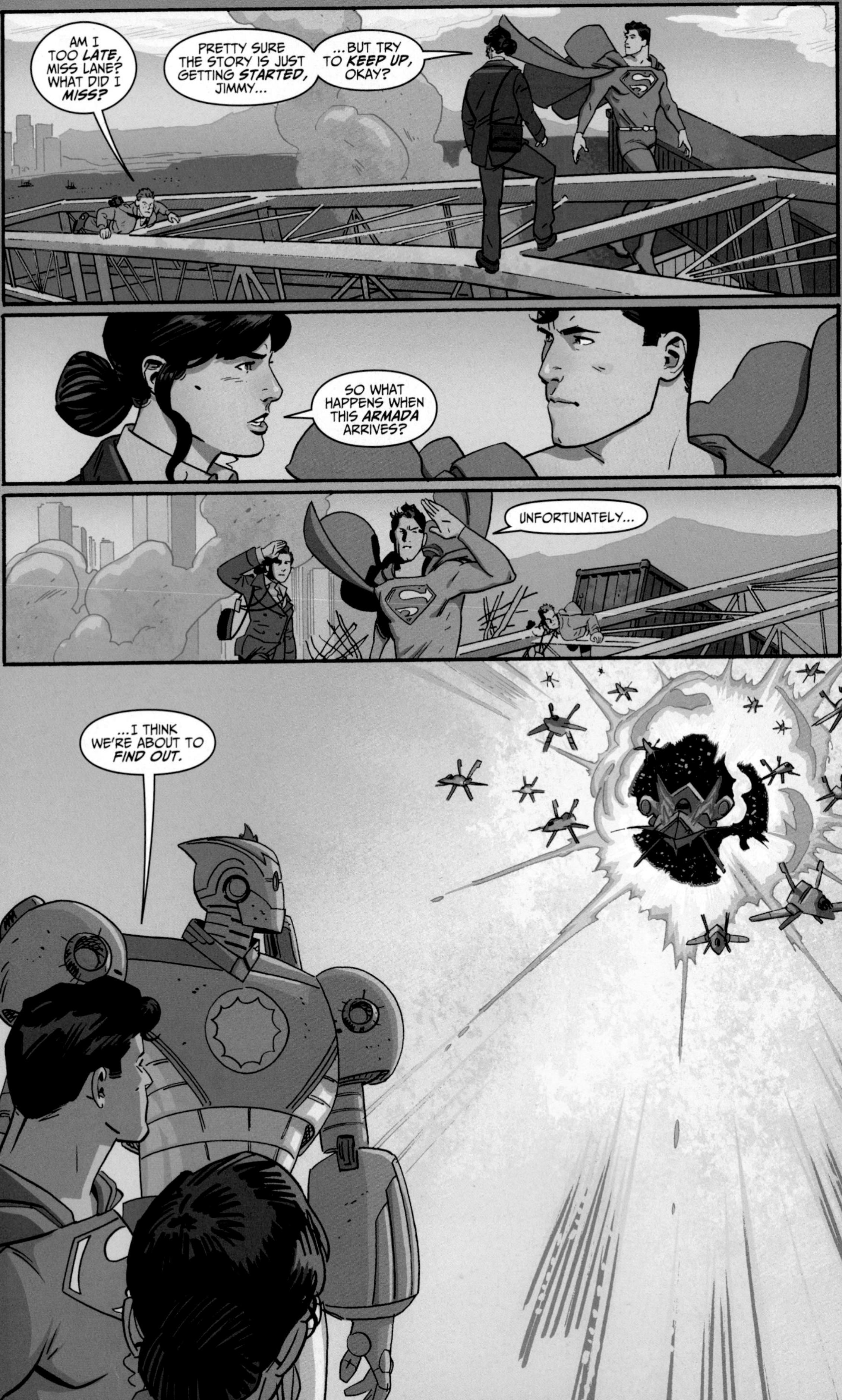
AM I TOO LATE, MISS LANE? WHAT DID I MISS?
PRETTY SURE THE STORY IS JUST GETTING STARTED, JIMMY...
...BUT TRY TO KEEP UP, OKAY?
SO WHAT HAPPENS WHEN THIS ARMADA ARRIVES?
UNFORTUNATELY...
...I THINK WE'RE ABOUT TO FIND OUT.

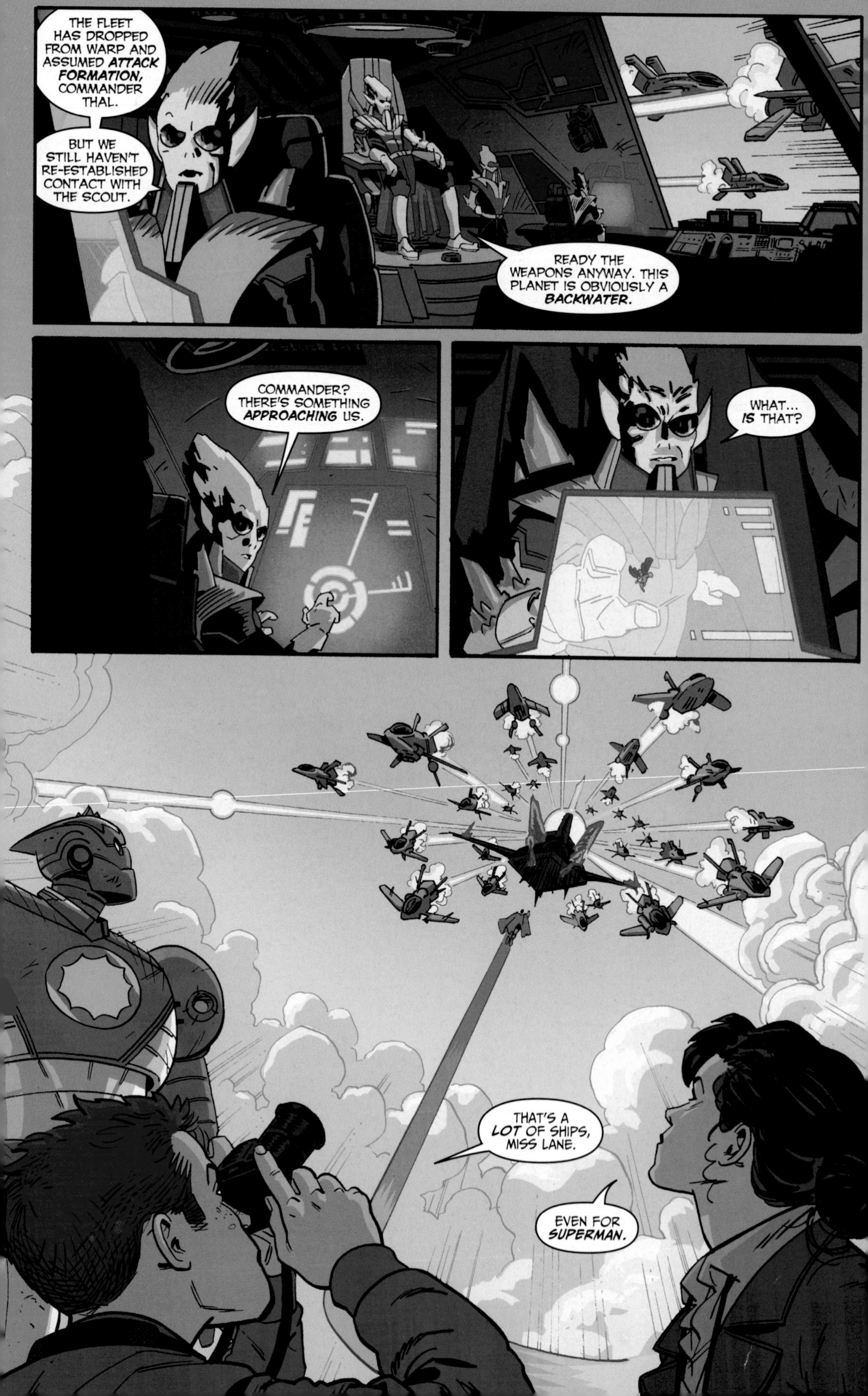
THE FLEET HAS DROPPED FROM WARP AND ASSUMED ATTACK FORMATION, COMMANDER THAL.
BUT WE STILL HAVEN'T RE-ESTABLISHED CONTACT WITH THE SCOUT.
READY THE WEAPONS ANYWAY. THIS PLANET IS OBVIOUSLY A BACKWATER.
COMMANDER? THERE'S SOMETHING APPROACHING US.
WHAT... IS THAT?
THAT'S A LOT OF SHIPS, MISS LANE.
EVEN FOR SUPERMAN.

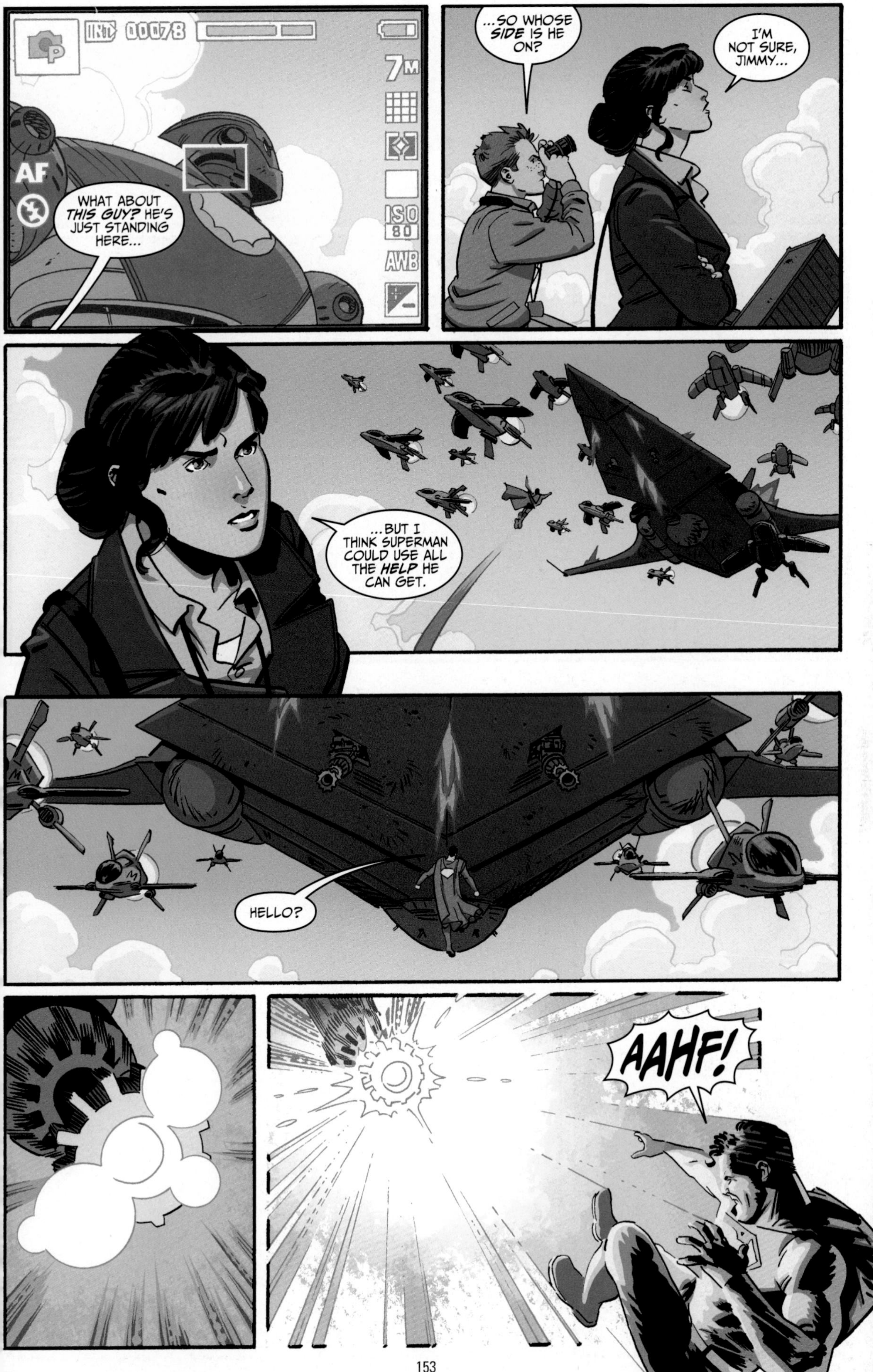
INT 00078
7M
AF
ISO 80
AWB
WHAT ABOUT THIS GUY? HE'S JUST STANDING HERE...
...SO WHOSE SIDE IS HE ON?
I'M NOT SURE, JIMMY...
...BUT I THINK SUPERMAN COULD USE ALL THE HELP HE CAN GET.
HELLO?
AAHF!

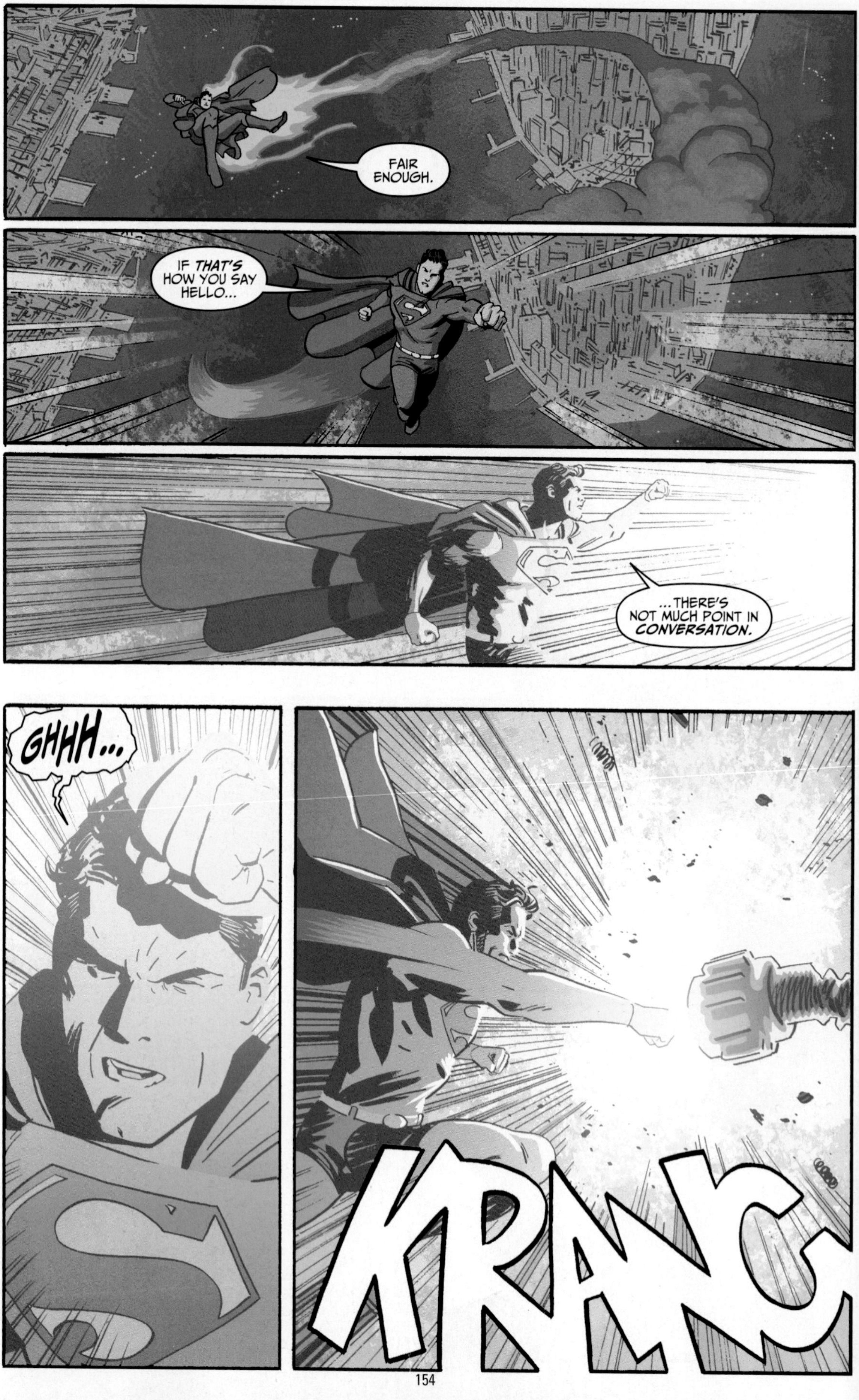
FAIR ENOUGH.
IF THAT'S HOW YOU SAY HELLO...
...THERE'S NOT MUCH POINT IN CONVERSATION.
GHHH...
KRANC

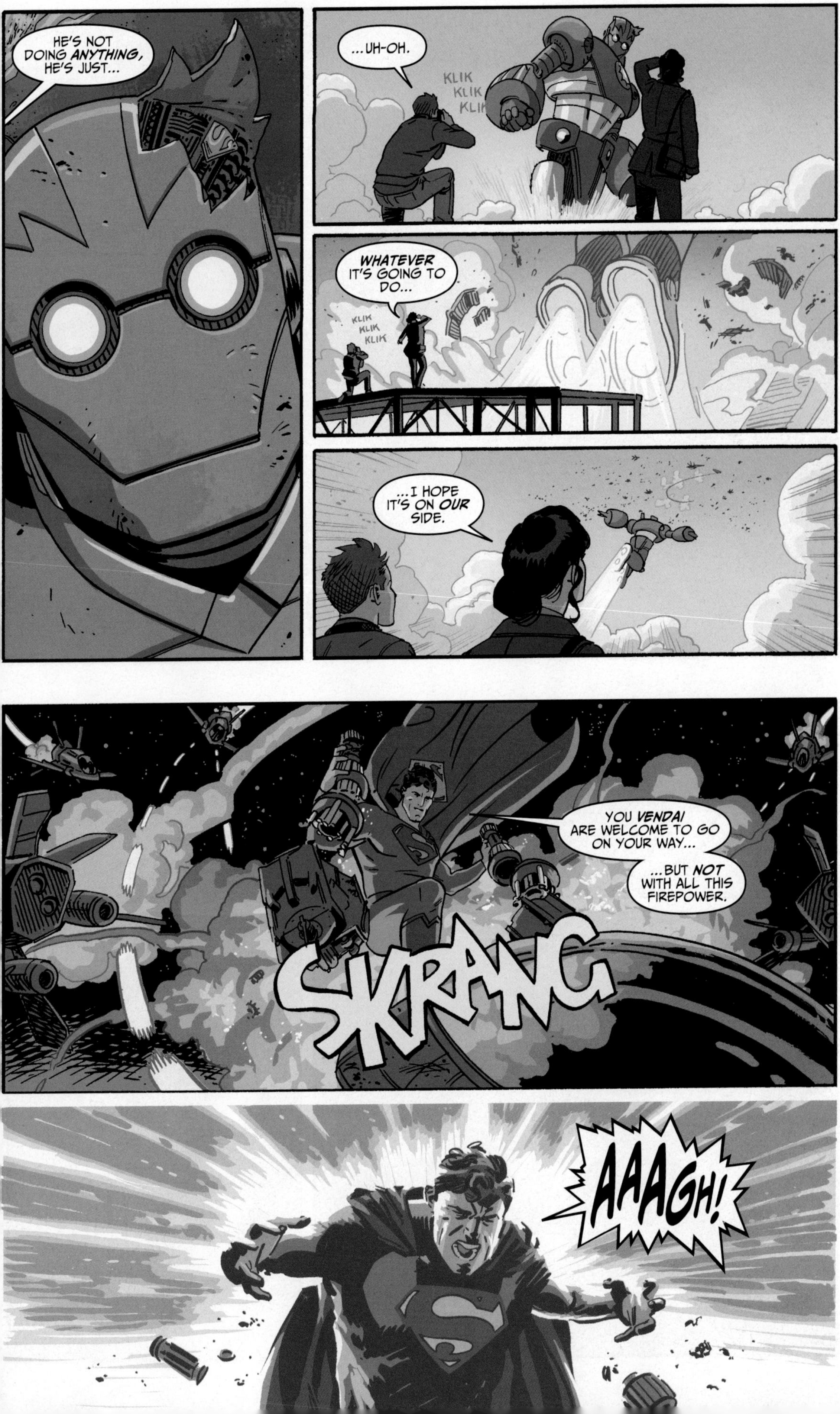

HE'S NOT DOING ANYTHING, HE'S JUST...
...UH-OH.
KLIK KLIK KLIK
WHATEVER IT'S GOING TO DO...
KLIK KLIK KLIK
...I HOPE IT'S ON OUR SIDE.
YOU VENDAI ARE WELCOME TO GO ON YOUR WAY...
...BUT NOT WITH ALL THIS FIREPOWER.
SKRANG
AAAGH!

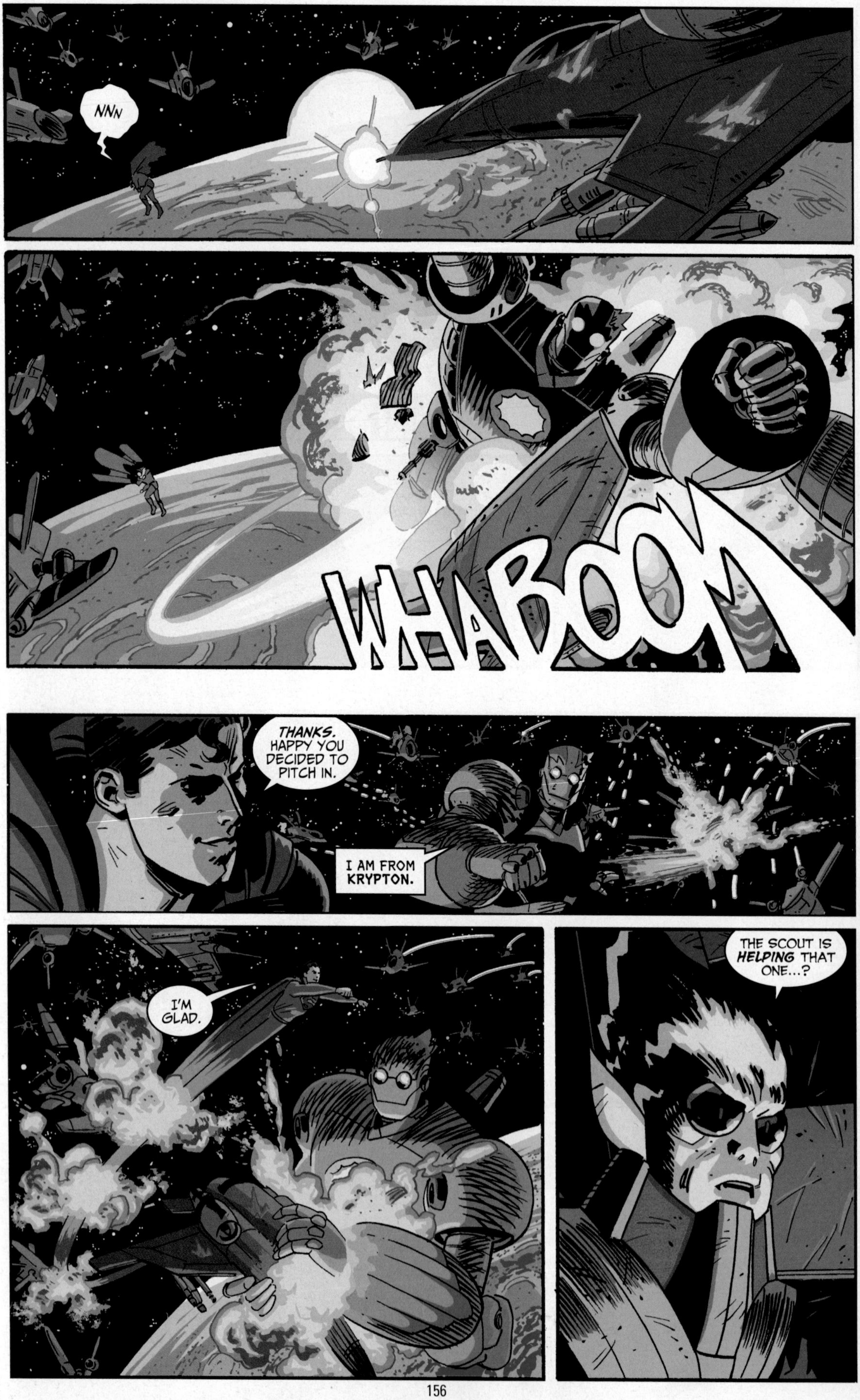
NNN
WHABOOM
THANKS. HAPPY YOU DECIDED TO PITCH IN.
I AM FROM KRYPTON.
I'M GLAD.
THE SCOUT IS HELPING THAT ONE...?

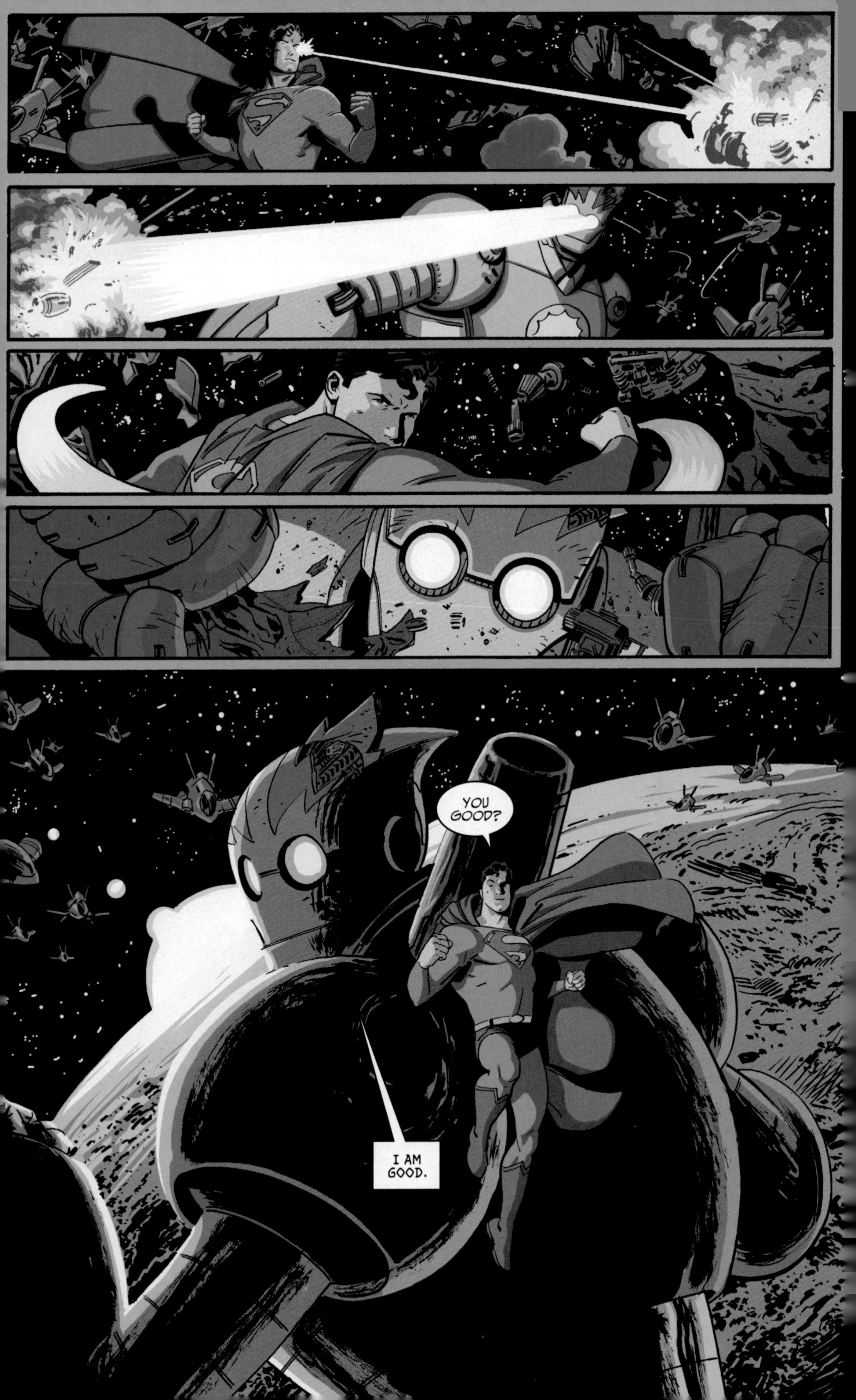
YOU GOOD?
I AM GOOD.

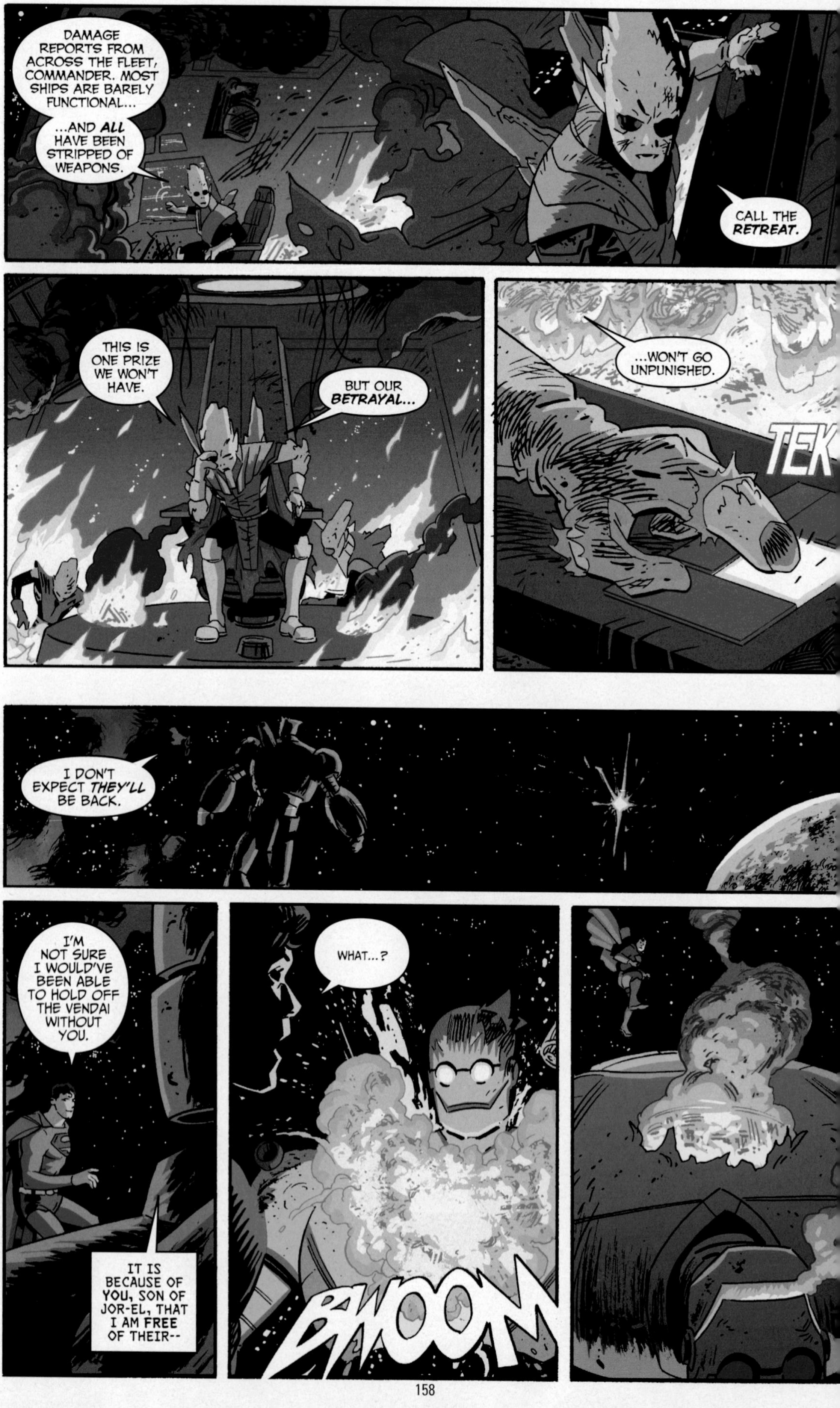
DAMAGE REPORTS FROM ACROSS THE FLEET, COMMANDER. MOST SHIPS ARE BARELY FUNCTIONAL...
...AND ALL HAVE BEEN STRIPPED OF WEAPONS.
CALL THE RETREAT.
THIS IS ONE PRIZE WE WON'T HAVE.
BUT OUR BETRAYAL...
...WON'T GO UNPUNISHED.
TEK
I DON'T EXPECT THEY'LL BE BACK.
I'M NOT SURE I WOULD'VE BEEN ABLE TO HOLD OFF THE VENDAI WITHOUT YOU.
IT IS BECAUSE OF YOU, SON OF JOR-EL, THAT I AM FREE OF THEIR--
WHAT...?
BWOOM

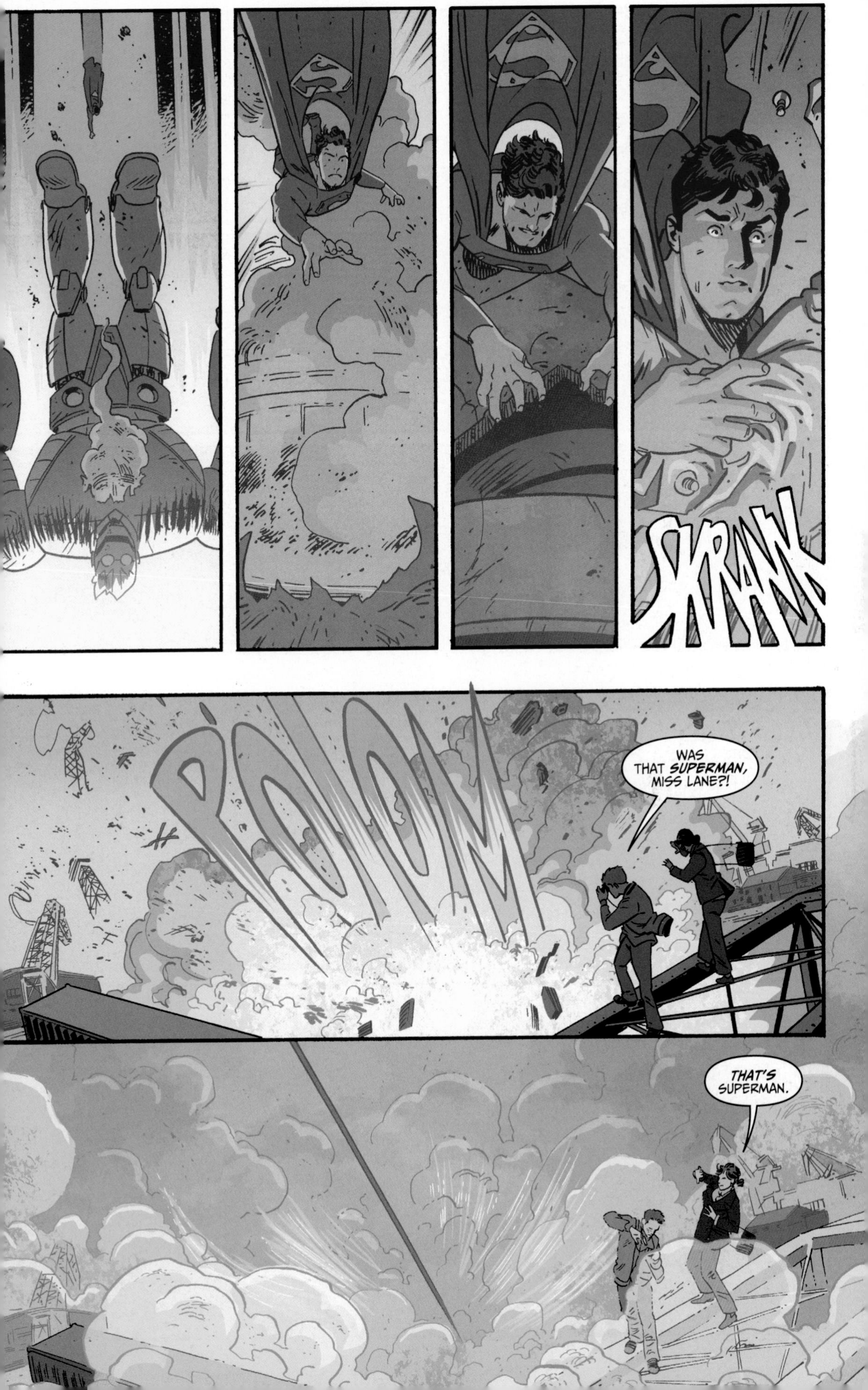
SKRANK
BOOOM
WAS THAT SUPERMAN, MISS LANE?!
THAT'S SUPERMAN.

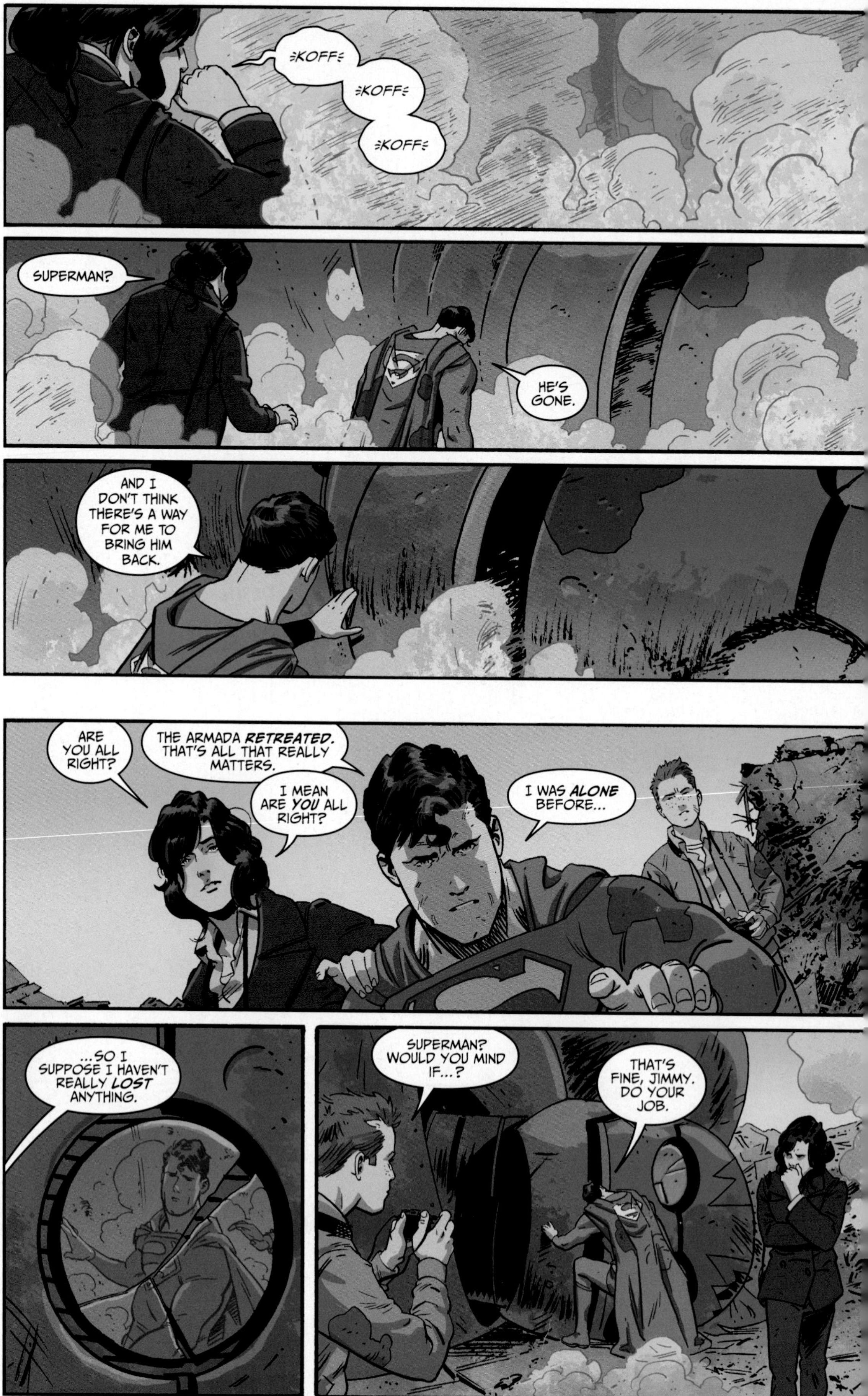

KOFF
KOFF
KOFF
SUPERMAN?
HE'S GONE.
AND I DON'T THINK THERE'S A WAY FOR ME TO BRING HIM BACK.
ARE YOU ALL RIGHT?
THE ARMADA RETREATED. THAT'S ALL THAT REALLY MATTERS.
I MEAN ARE YOU ALL RIGHT?
I WAS ALONE BEFORE...
...SO I SUPPOSE I HAVEN'T REALLY LOST ANYTHING.
SUPERMAN? WOULD YOU MIND IF...?
THAT'S FINE, JIMMY. DO YOUR JOB.

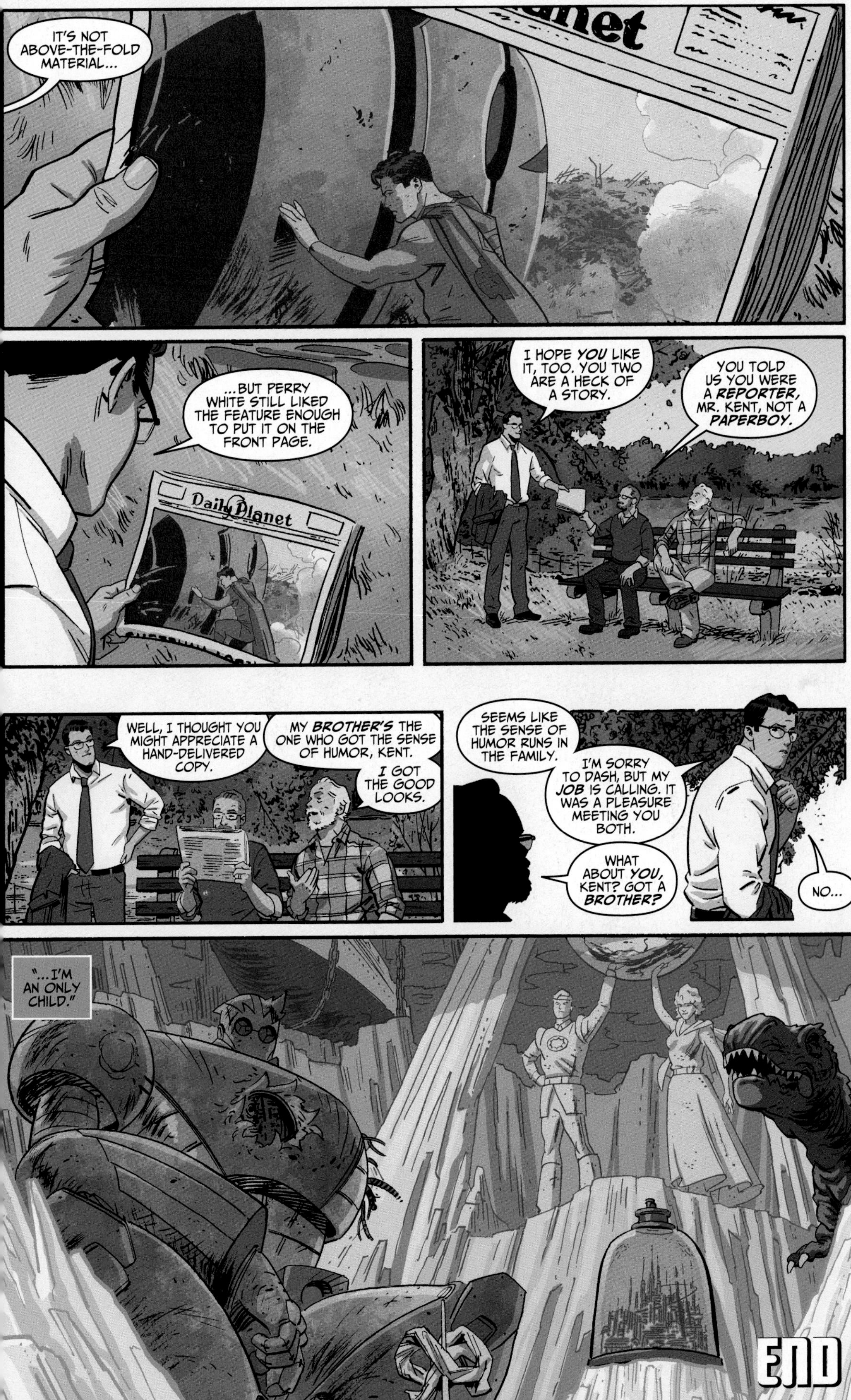
IT'S NOT ABOVE-THE-FOLD MATERIAL...
...BUT PERRY WHITE STILL LIKED THE FEATURE ENOUGH TO PUT IT ON THE FRONT PAGE.
Daily Planet
I HOPE YOU LIKE IT, TOO. YOU TWO ARE A HECK OF A STORY.
YOU TOLD US YOU WERE A REPORTER, MR. KENT, NOT A PAPERBOY.
WELL, I THOUGHT YOU MIGHT APPRECIATE A HAND-DELIVERED COPY.
MY BROTHER'S THE ONE WHO GOT THE SENSE OF HUMOR, KENT.
I GOT THE GOOD LOOKS.
SEEMS LIKE THE SENSE OF HUMOR RUNS IN THE FAMILY.
I'M SORRY TO DASH, BUT MY JOB IS CALLING. IT WAS A PLEASURE MEETING YOU BOTH.
WHAT ABOUT YOU, KENT? GOT A BROTHER?
NO...
"...I'M AN ONLY CHILD."
END

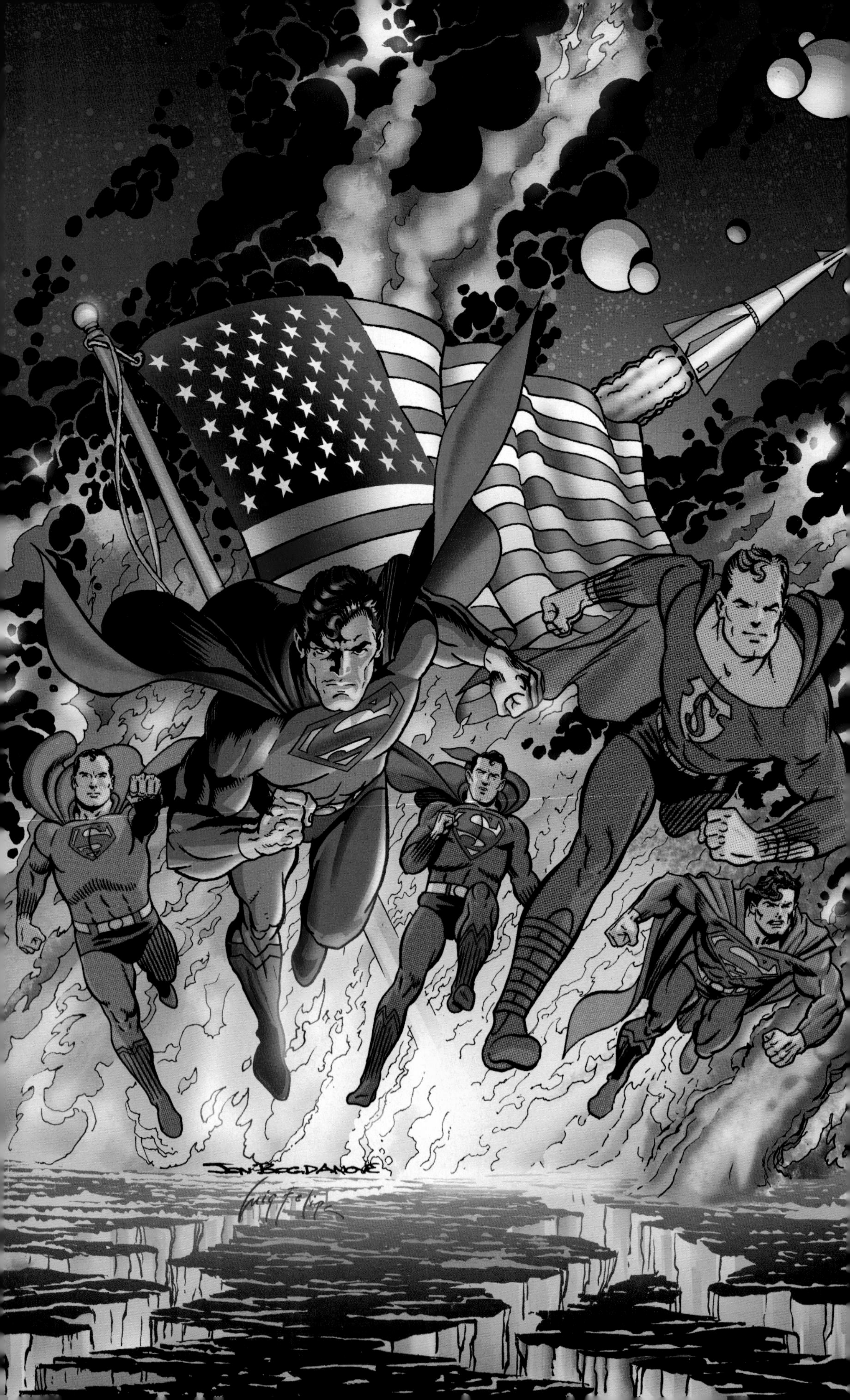
JON BOGDANOVE

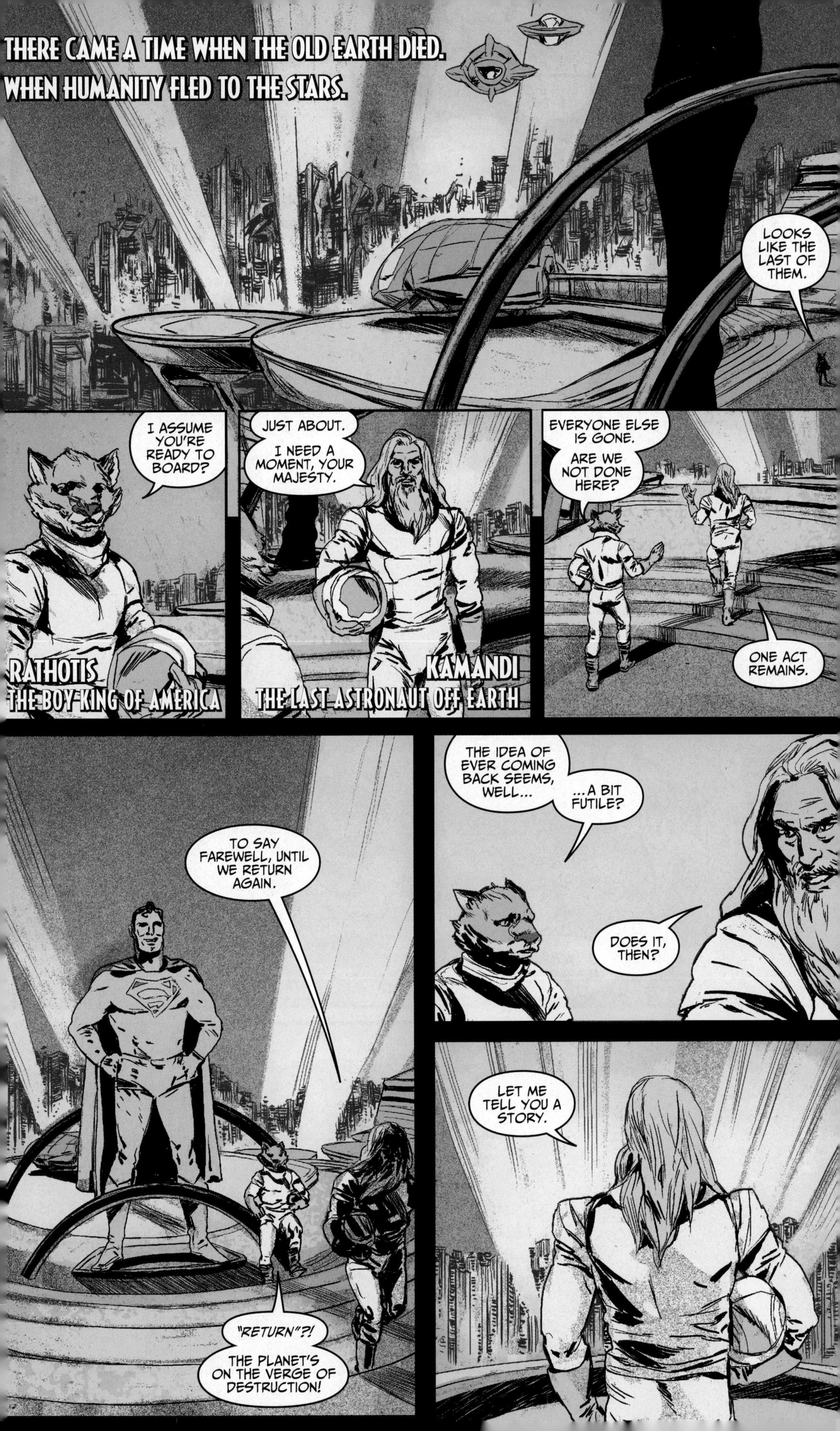
THERE CAME A TIME WHEN THE OLD EARTH DIED.
WHEN HUMANITY FLED TO THE STARS.
LOOKS LIKE THE LAST OF THEM.
I ASSUME YOU'RE READY TO BOARD?
RATHOTIS
THE BOY KING OF AMERICA
JUST ABOUT.
I NEED A MOMENT, YOUR MAJESTY.
KAMANDI
THE LAST ASTRONAUT OFF EARTH
EVERYONE ELSE IS GONE.
ARE WE NOT DONE HERE?
ONE ACT REMAINS.
TO SAY FAREWELL, UNTIL WE RETURN AGAIN.
"RETURN"?!
THE PLANET'S ON THE VERGE OF DESTRUCTION!
THE IDEA OF EVER COMING BACK SEEMS, WELL...
...A BIT FUTILE?
DOES IT, THEN?
LET ME TELL YOU A STORY.

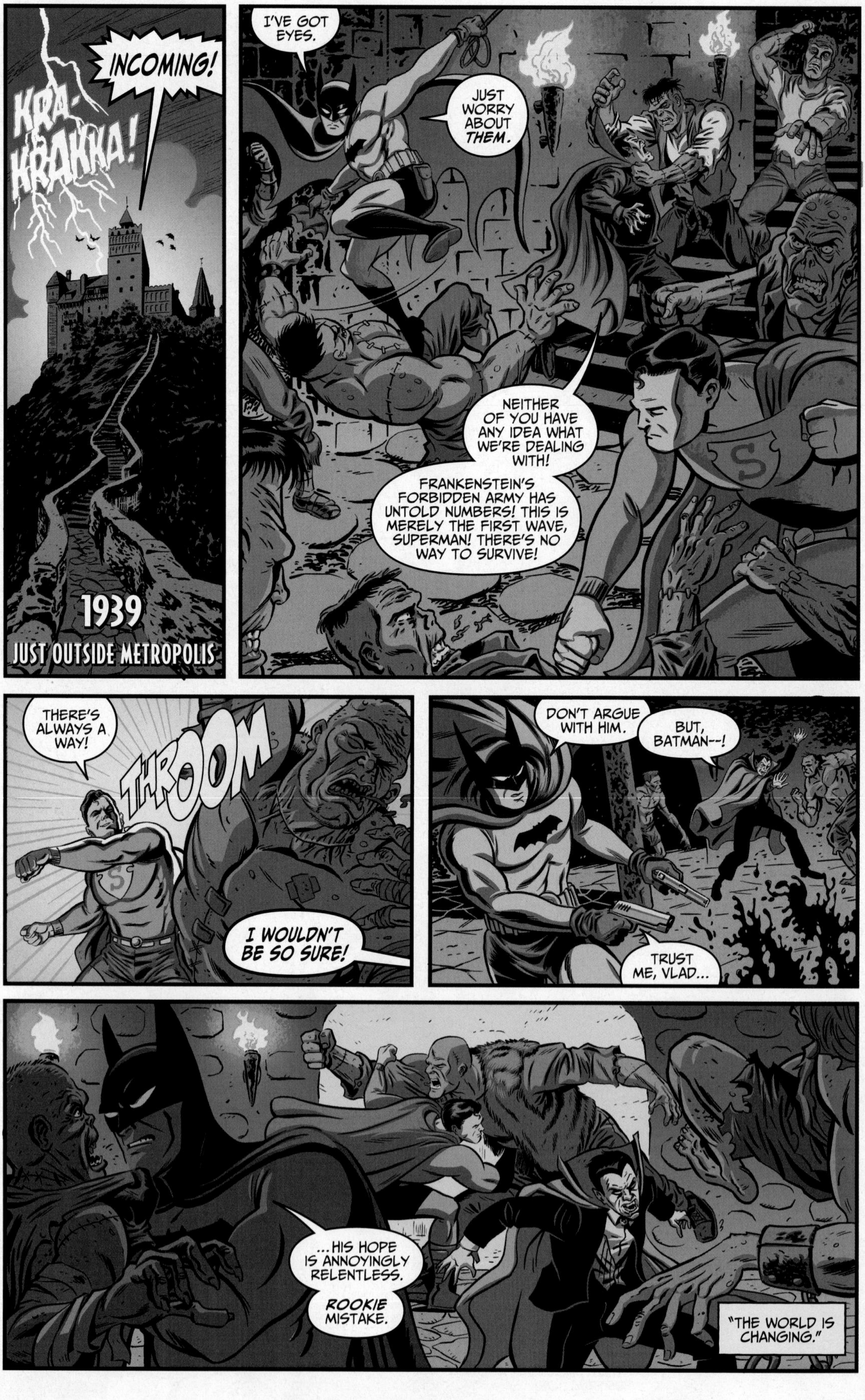
KRA-KRAKKA!
INCOMING!
1939
JUST OUTSIDE METROPOLIS
I'VE GOT EYES.
JUST WORRY ABOUT THEM.
NEITHER OF YOU HAVE ANY IDEA WHAT WE'RE DEALING WITH!
FRANKENSTEIN'S FORBIDDEN ARMY HAS UNTOLD NUMBERS! THIS IS MERELY THE FIRST WAVE, SUPERMAN! THERE'S NO WAY TO SURVIVE!
THERE'S ALWAYS A WAY!
THROOM
I WOULDN'T BE SO SURE!
DON'T ARGUE WITH HIM.
BUT, BATMAN--!
TRUST ME, VLAD...
...HIS HOPE IS ANNOYINGLY RELENTLESS.
ROOKIE MISTAKE.
"THE WORLD IS CHANGING."

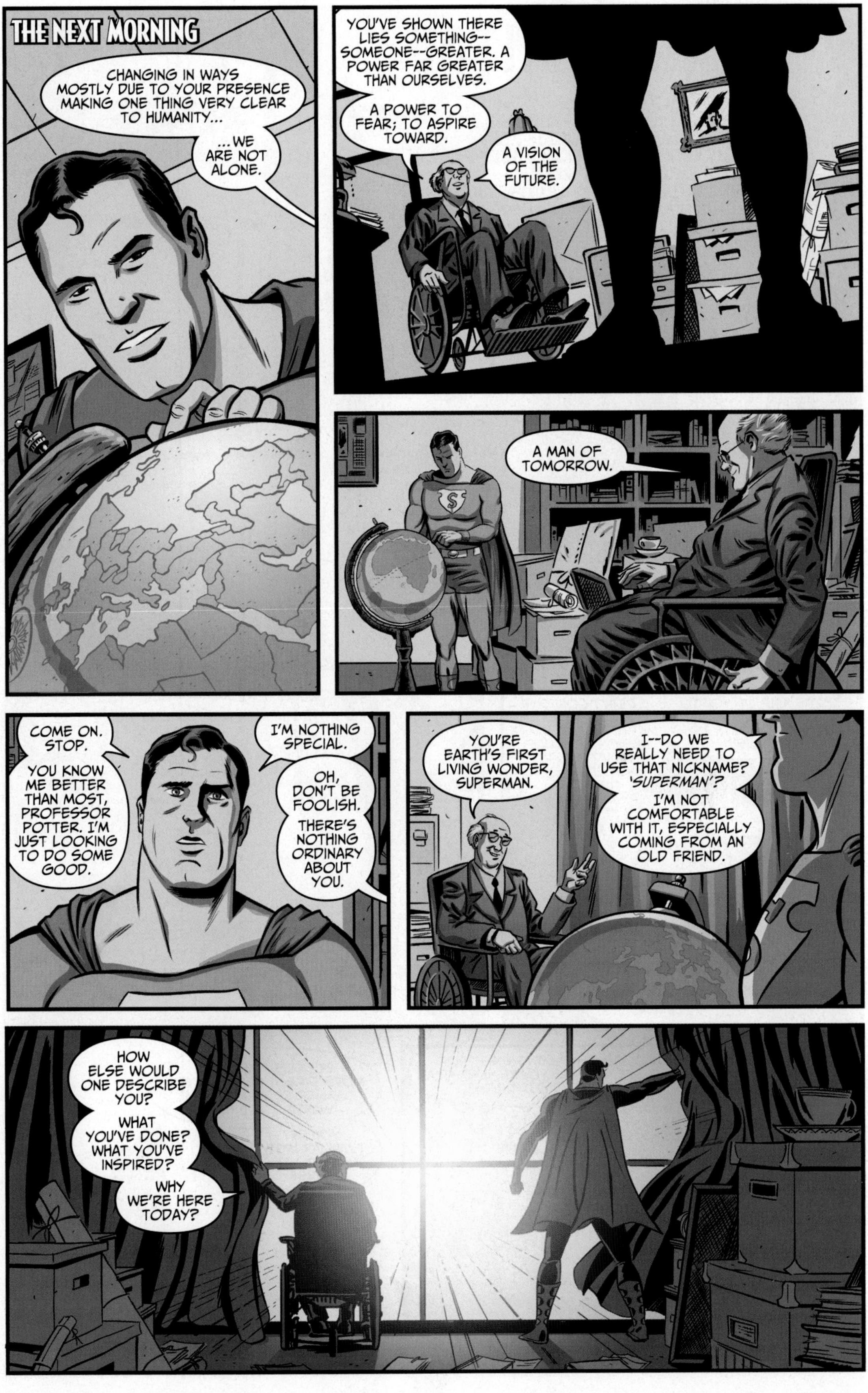
THE NEXT MORNING
CHANGING IN WAYS MOSTLY DUE TO YOUR PRESENCE MAKING ONE THING VERY CLEAR TO HUMANITY...
...WE ARE NOT ALONE.
YOU'VE SHOWN THERE LIES SOMETHING-- SOMEONE--GREATER. A POWER FAR GREATER THAN OURSELVES.
A POWER TO FEAR; TO ASPIRE TOWARD.
A VISION OF THE FUTURE.
A MAN OF TOMORROW.
COME ON. STOP.
YOU KNOW ME BETTER THAN MOST, PROFESSOR POTTER. I'M JUST LOOKING TO DO SOME GOOD.
I'M NOTHING SPECIAL.
OH, DON'T BE FOOLISH.
THERE'S NOTHING ORDINARY ABOUT YOU.
YOU'RE EARTH'S FIRST LIVING WONDER, SUPERMAN.
I--DO WE REALLY NEED TO USE THAT NICKNAME? 'SUPERMAN'?
I'M NOT COMFORTABLE WITH IT, ESPECIALLY COMING FROM AN OLD FRIEND.
HOW ELSE WOULD ONE DESCRIBE YOU?
WHAT YOU'VE DONE? WHAT YOU'VE INSPIRED?
WHY WE'RE HERE TODAY?

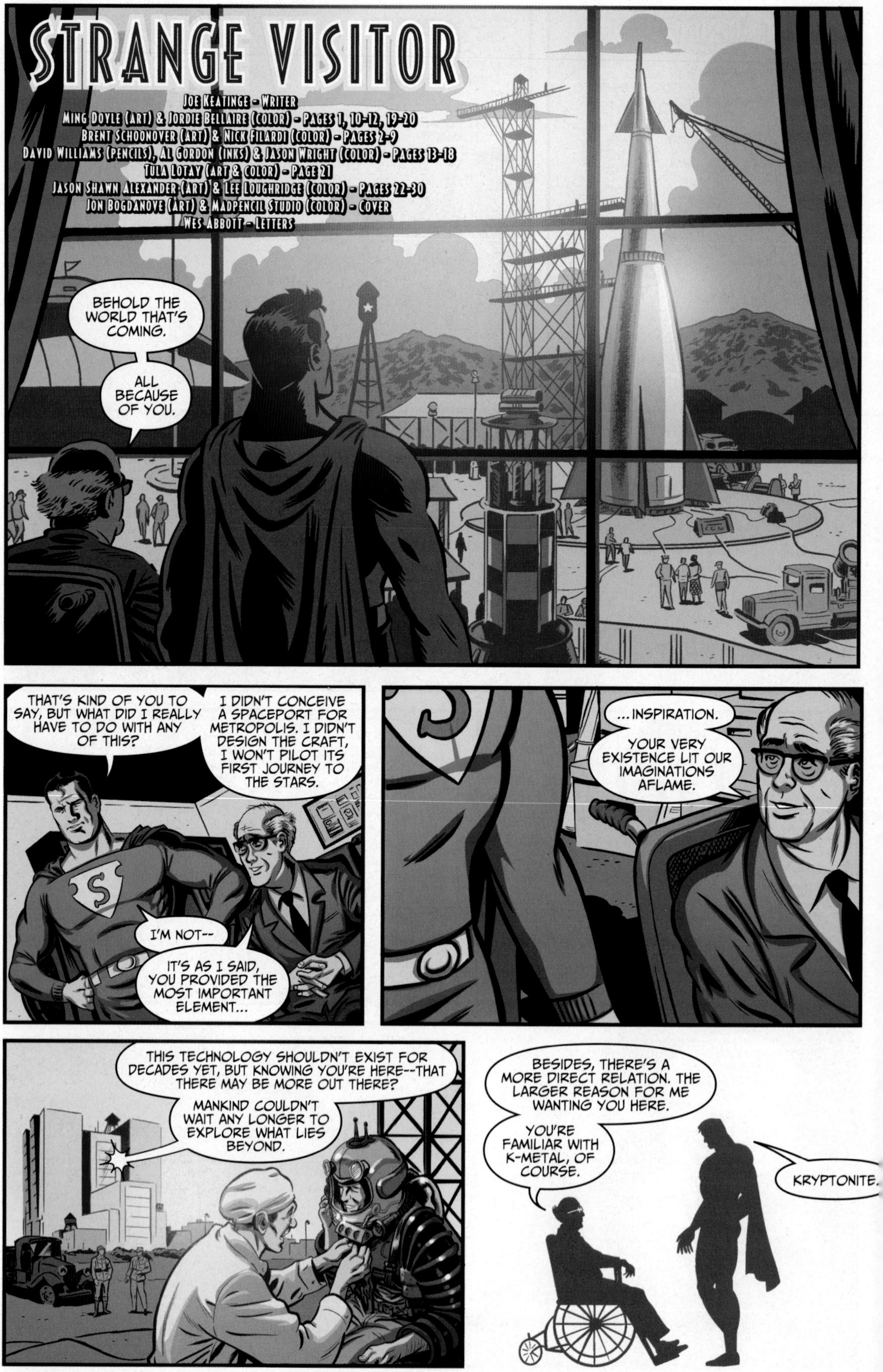
STRANGE VISITOR
JOE KEATINGE - WRITER
MING DOYLE (ART) & JORDIE BELLAIRE (COLOR) - PAGES 1, 10-12, 19-20
BRENT SCHOONOVER (ART) & NICK FILARDI (COLOR) - PAGES 2-9
DAVID WILLIAMS (PENCILS), AL GORDON (INKS) & JASON WRIGHT (COLOR) - PAGES 13-18
TULA LOTAY (ART & COLOR) - PAGE 21
JASON SHAWN ALEXANDER (ART) & LEE LOUGHRIDGE (COLOR) - PAGES 22-30
JON BOGDANOVE (ART) & MADPENCIL STUDIO (COLOR) - COVER
WES ABBOTT - LETTERS
BEHOLD THE WORLD THAT'S COMING.
ALL BECAUSE OF YOU.
THAT'S KIND OF YOU TO SAY, BUT WHAT DID I REALLY HAVE TO DO WITH ANY OF THIS?
I DIDN'T CONCEIVE A SPACEPORT FOR METROPOLIS. I DIDN'T DESIGN THE CRAFT, I WON'T PILOT ITS FIRST JOURNEY TO THE STARS.
I'M NOT--
IT'S AS I SAID, YOU PROVIDED THE MOST IMPORTANT ELEMENT...
...INSPIRATION.
YOUR VERY EXISTENCE LIT OUR IMAGINATIONS AFLAME.
THIS TECHNOLOGY SHOULDN'T EXIST FOR DECADES YET, BUT KNOWING YOU'RE HERE--THAT THERE MAY BE MORE OUT THERE?
MANKIND COULDN'T WAIT ANY LONGER TO EXPLORE WHAT LIES BEYOND.
BESIDES, THERE'S A MORE DIRECT RELATION. THE LARGER REASON FOR ME WANTING YOU HERE.
YOU'RE FAMILIAR WITH K-METAL, OF COURSE.
KRYPTONITE.

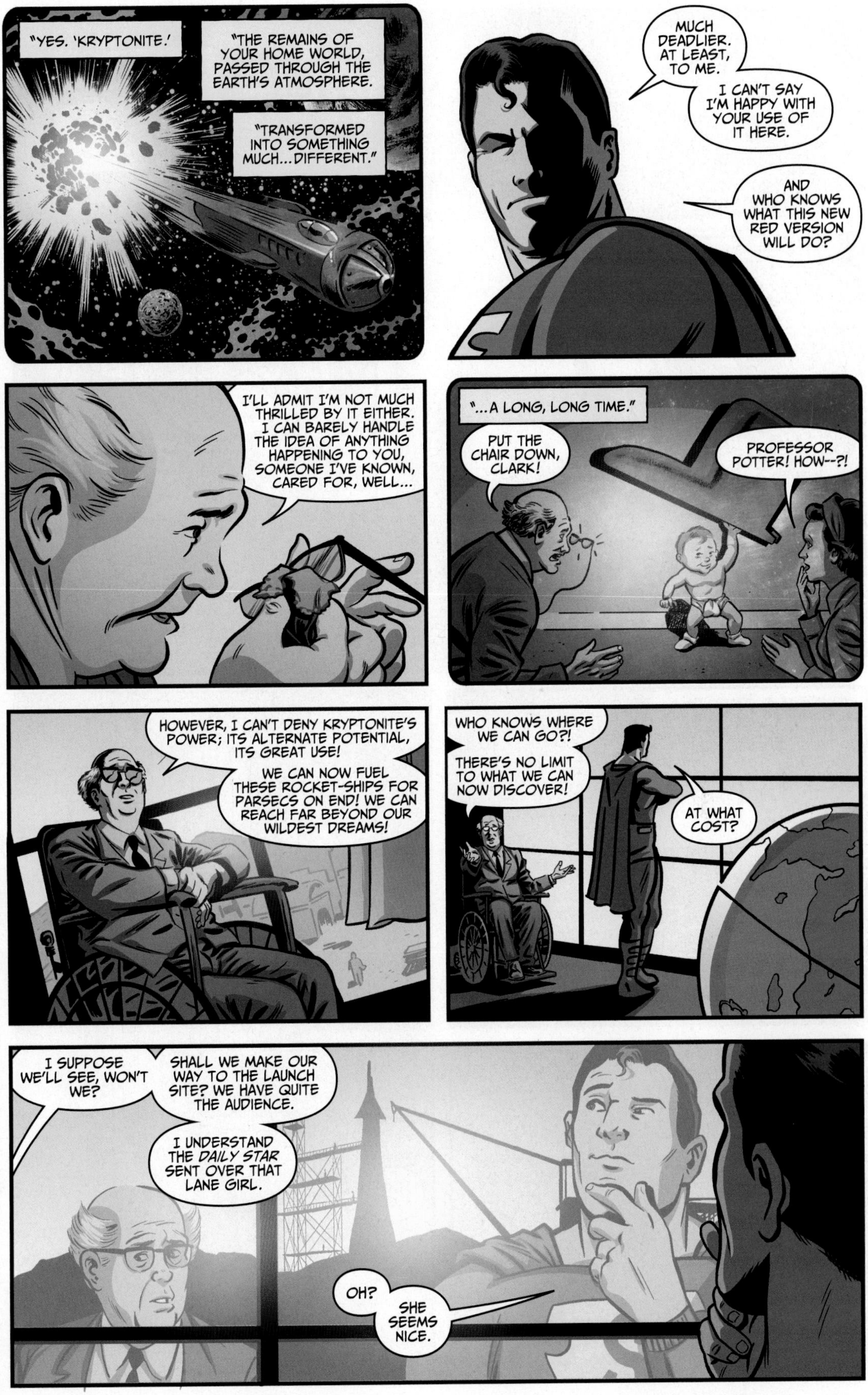

"YES. 'KRYPTONITE.'
"THE REMAINS OF YOUR HOME WORLD, PASSED THROUGH THE EARTH'S ATMOSPHERE.
"TRANSFORMED INTO SOMETHING MUCH...DIFFERENT."
MUCH DEADLIER. AT LEAST, TO ME.
I CAN'T SAY I'M HAPPY WITH YOUR USE OF IT HERE.
AND WHO KNOWS WHAT THIS NEW RED VERSION WILL DO?
I'LL ADMIT I'M NOT MUCH THRILLED BY IT EITHER. I CAN BARELY HANDLE THE IDEA OF ANYTHING HAPPENING TO YOU, SOMEONE I'VE KNOWN, CARED FOR, WELL...
"...A LONG, LONG TIME."
PUT THE CHAIR DOWN, CLARK!
PROFESSOR POTTER! HOW--?!
HOWEVER, I CAN'T DENY KRYPTONITE'S POWER; ITS ALTERNATE POTENTIAL, ITS GREAT USE!
WE CAN NOW FUEL THESE ROCKET-SHIPS FOR PARSECS ON END! WE CAN REACH FAR BEYOND OUR WILDEST DREAMS!
WHO KNOWS WHERE WE CAN GO?!
THERE'S NO LIMIT TO WHAT WE CAN NOW DISCOVER!
AT WHAT COST?
I SUPPOSE WE'LL SEE, WON'T WE?
SHALL WE MAKE OUR WAY TO THE LAUNCH SITE? WE HAVE QUITE THE AUDIENCE.
I UNDERSTAND THE *DAILY STAR* SENT OVER THAT LANE GIRL.
OH?
SHE SEEMS NICE.

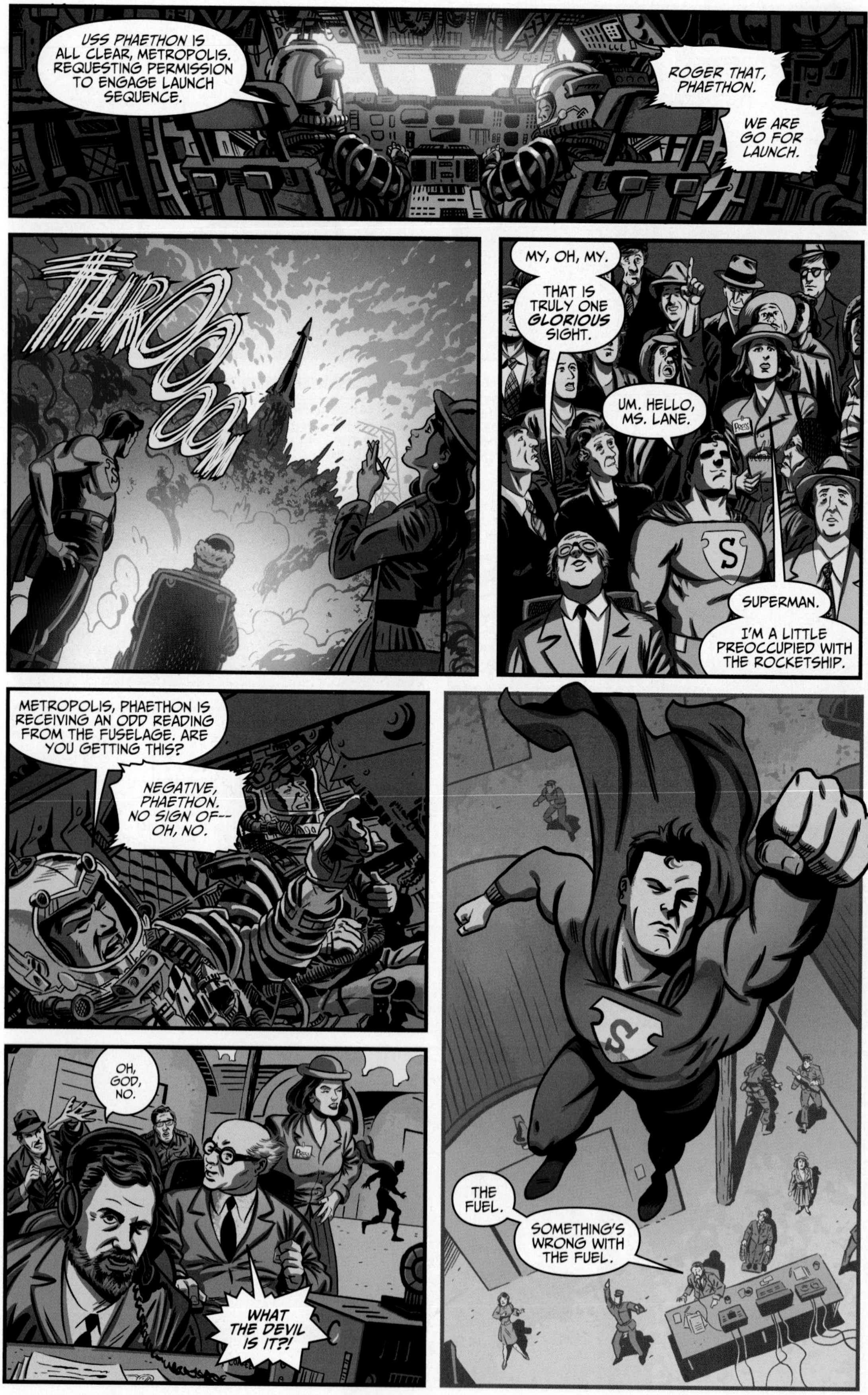
USS PHAETHON IS ALL CLEAR, METROPOLIS. REQUESTING PERMISSION TO ENGAGE LAUNCH SEQUENCE.
ROGER THAT, PHAETHON.
WE ARE GO FOR LAUNCH.
THROOOOM
MY, OH, MY.
THAT IS TRULY ONE GLORIOUS SIGHT.
UM. HELLO, MS. LANE.
SUPERMAN.
I'M A LITTLE PREOCCUPIED WITH THE ROCKETSHIP.
METROPOLIS, PHAETHON IS RECEIVING AN ODD READING FROM THE FUSELAGE. ARE YOU GETTING THIS?
NEGATIVE, PHAETHON. NO SIGN OF-- OH, NO.
OH, GOD, NO.
WHAT THE DEVIL IS IT?!
THE FUEL.
SOMETHING'S WRONG WITH THE FUEL.

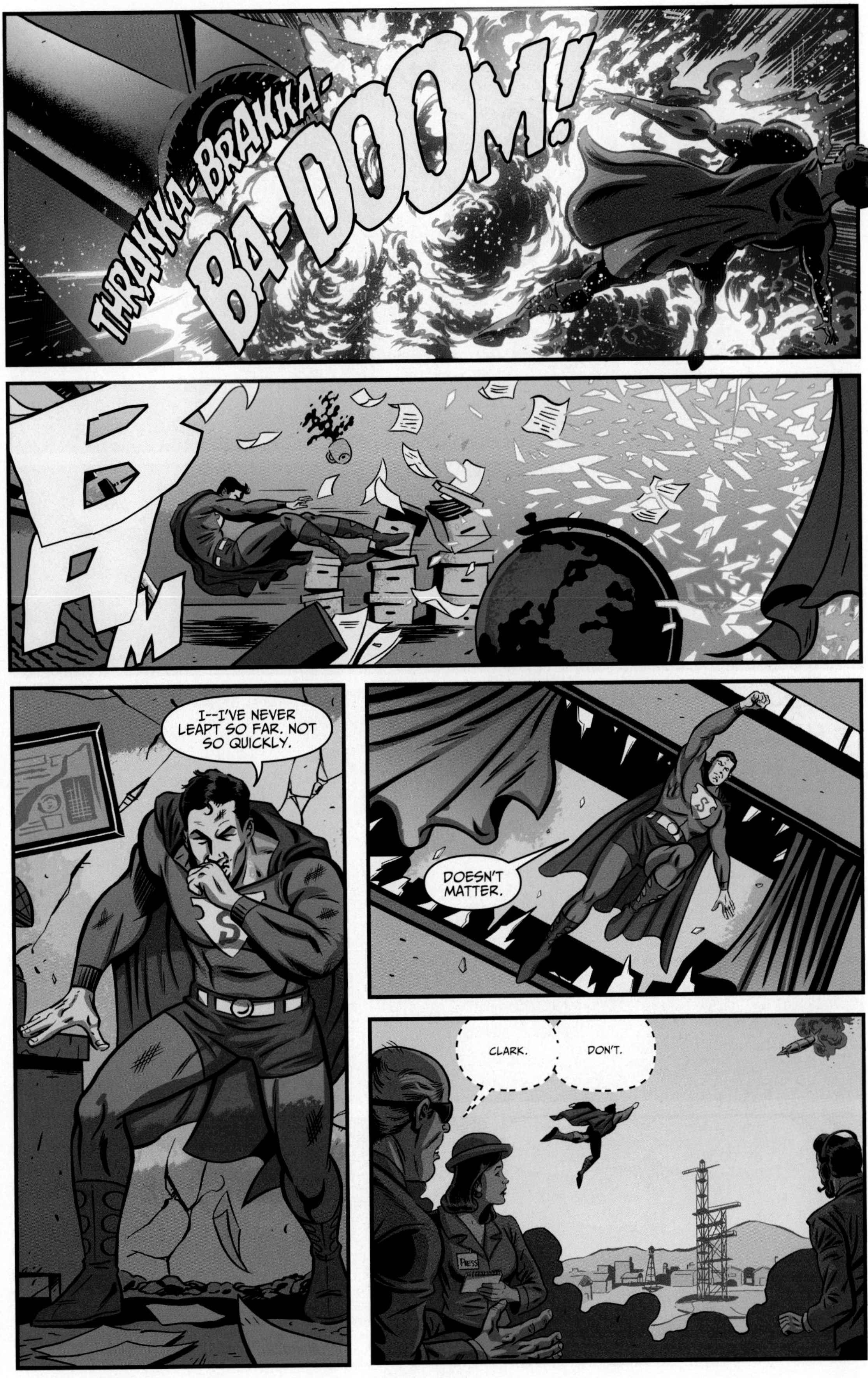
THRAKKA-BRAKKA-
BA-DOOM!
BAM
I--I'VE NEVER LEAPT SO FAR. NOT SO QUICKLY.
DOESN'T MATTER.
CLARK.
DON'T.
PRESS

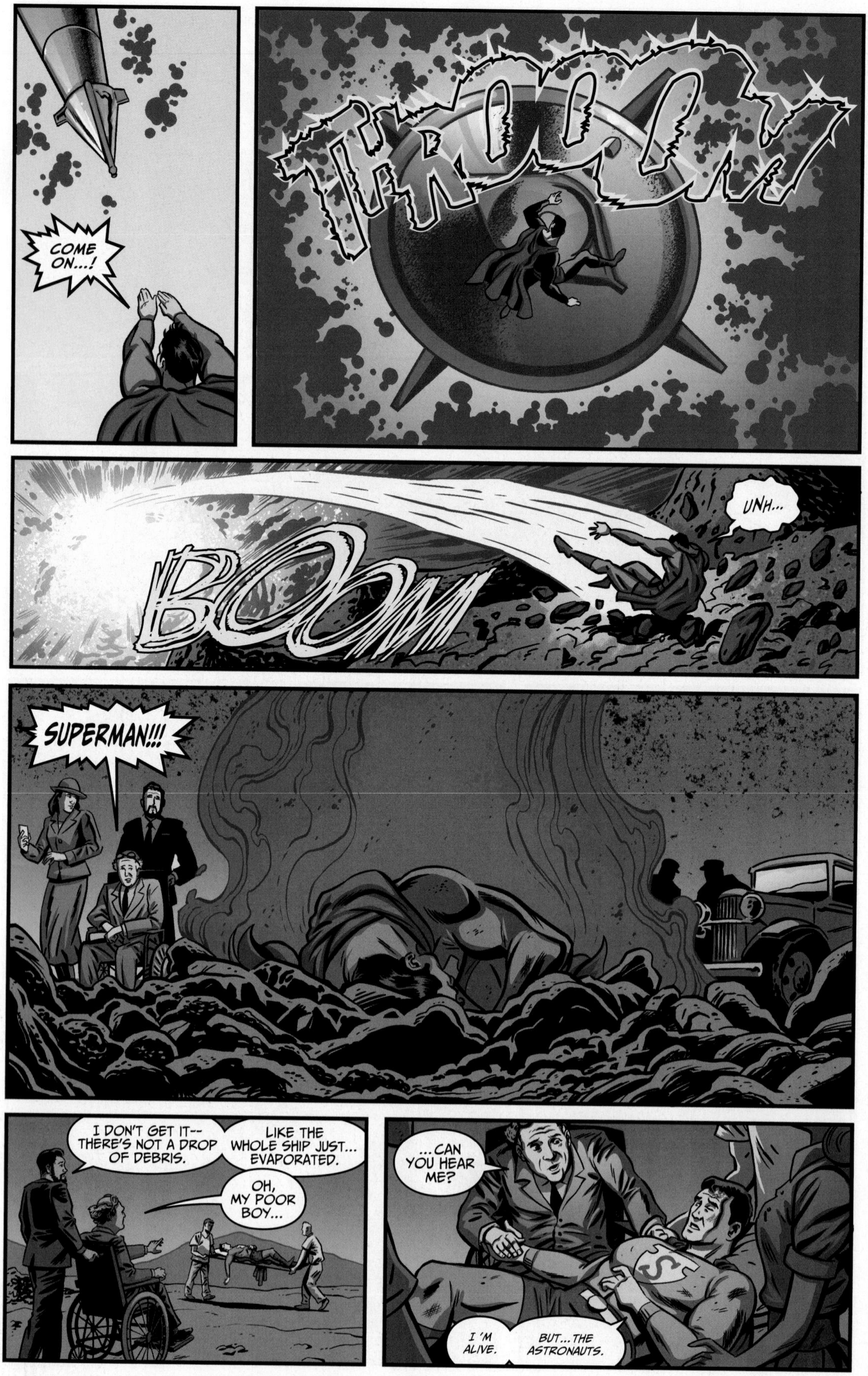
COME ON...!
THROOOM
BOOM
UNH...
SUPERMAN!!!
I DON'T GET IT-- THERE'S NOT A DROP OF DEBRIS.
LIKE THE WHOLE SHIP JUST... EVAPORATED.
OH, MY POOR BOY...
...CAN YOU HEAR ME?
I'M ALIVE.
BUT...THE ASTRONAUTS.

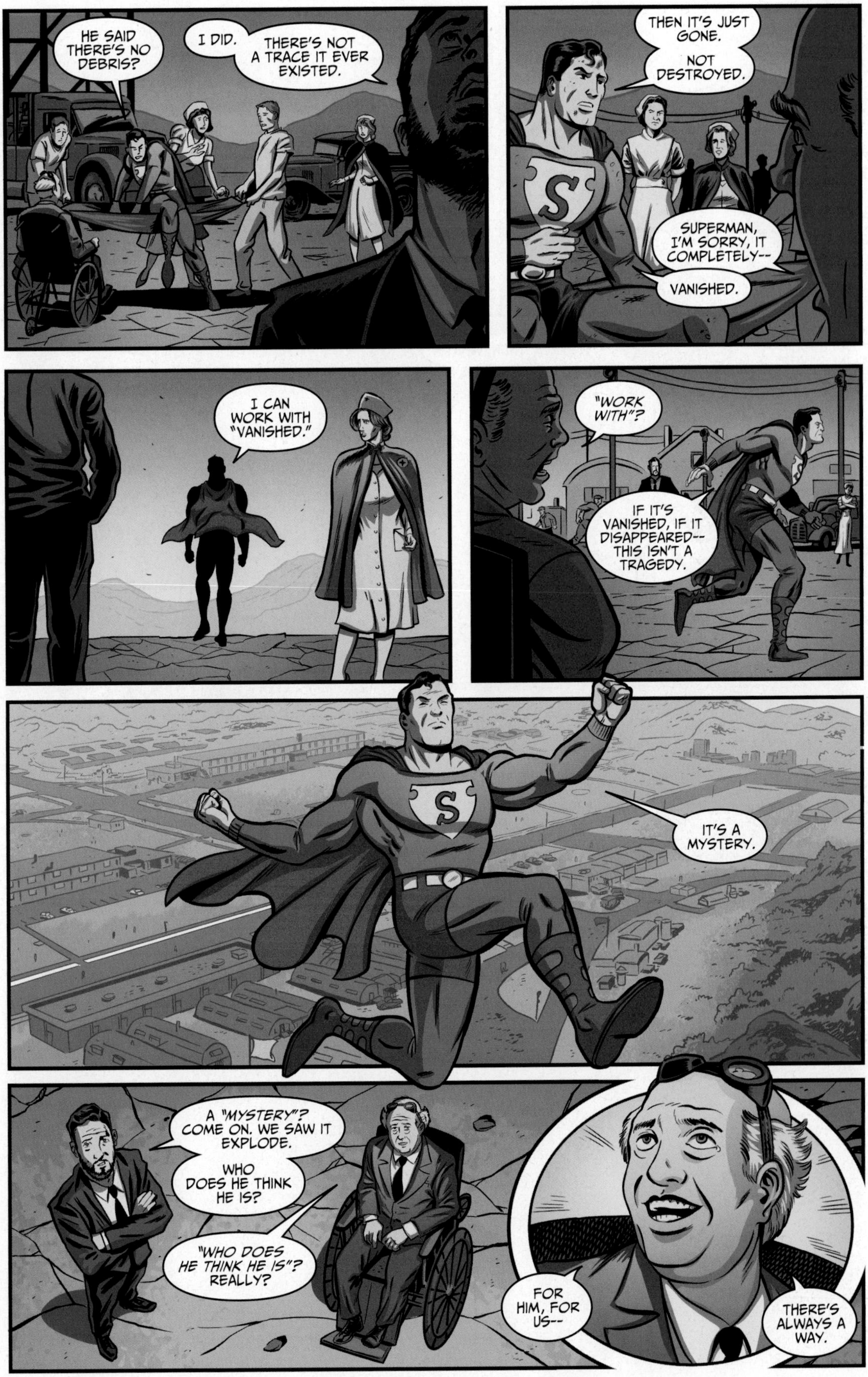
HE SAID THERE'S NO DEBRIS?
I DID.
THERE'S NOT A TRACE IT EVER EXISTED.
THEN IT'S JUST GONE.
NOT DESTROYED.
SUPERMAN, I'M SORRY, IT COMPLETELY--
VANISHED.
I CAN WORK WITH "VANISHED."
"WORK WITH"?
IF IT'S VANISHED, IF IT DISAPPEARED-- THIS ISN'T A TRAGEDY.
IT'S A MYSTERY.
A "MYSTERY"? COME ON. WE SAW IT EXPLODE.
WHO DOES HE THINK HE IS?
"WHO DOES HE THINK HE IS"? REALLY?
FOR HIM, FOR US--
THERE'S ALWAYS A WAY.

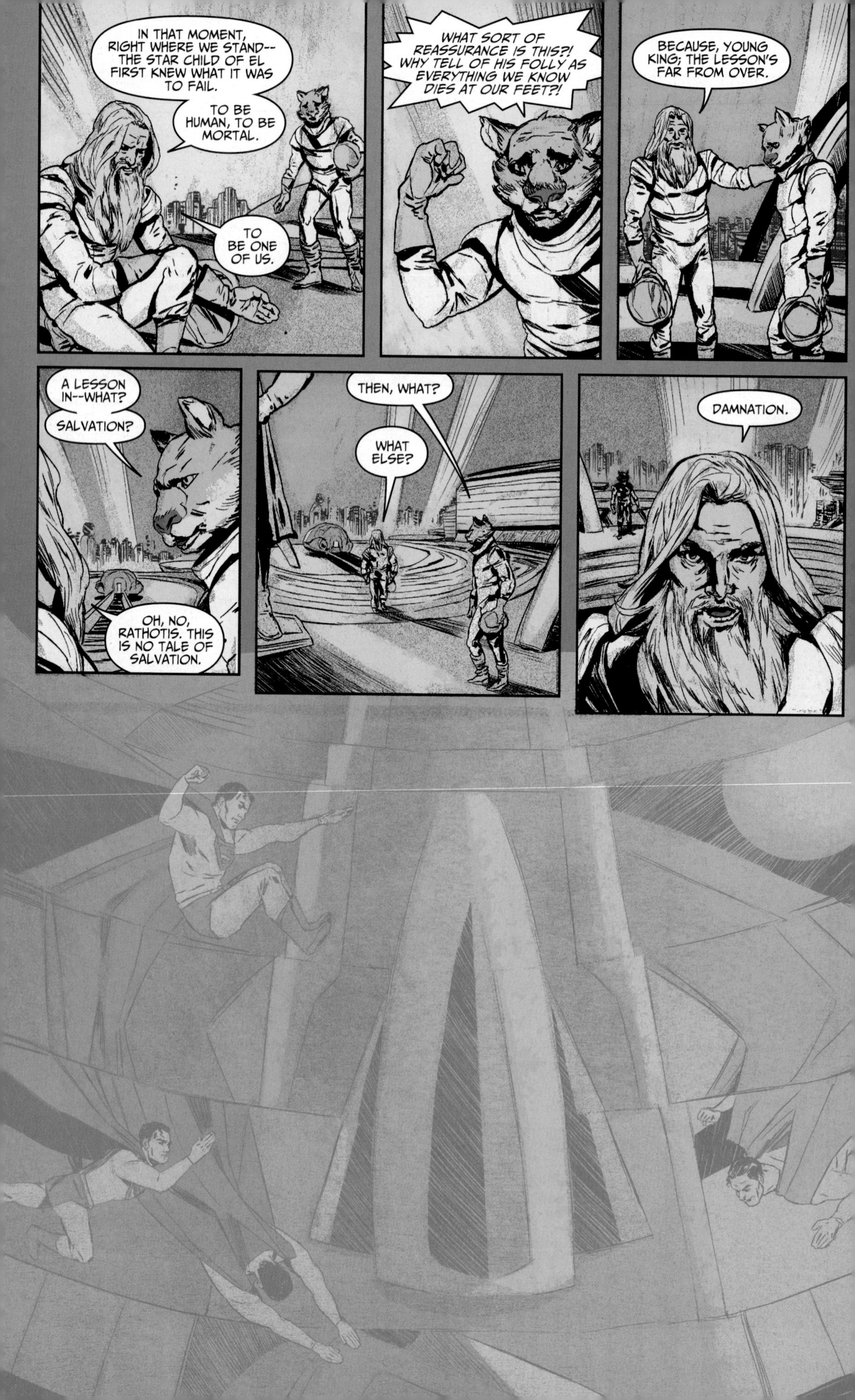
IN THAT MOMENT, RIGHT WHERE WE STAND-- THE STAR CHILD OF EL FIRST KNEW WHAT IT WAS TO FAIL.
TO BE HUMAN, TO BE MORTAL.
TO BE ONE OF US.
WHAT SORT OF REASSURANCE IS THIS?! WHY TELL OF HIS FOLLY AS EVERYTHING WE KNOW DIES AT OUR FEET?!
BECAUSE, YOUNG KING; THE LESSON'S FAR FROM OVER.
A LESSON IN--WHAT?
SALVATION?
OH, NO, RATHOTIS. THIS IS NO TALE OF SALVATION.
THEN, WHAT?
WHAT ELSE?
DAMNATION.

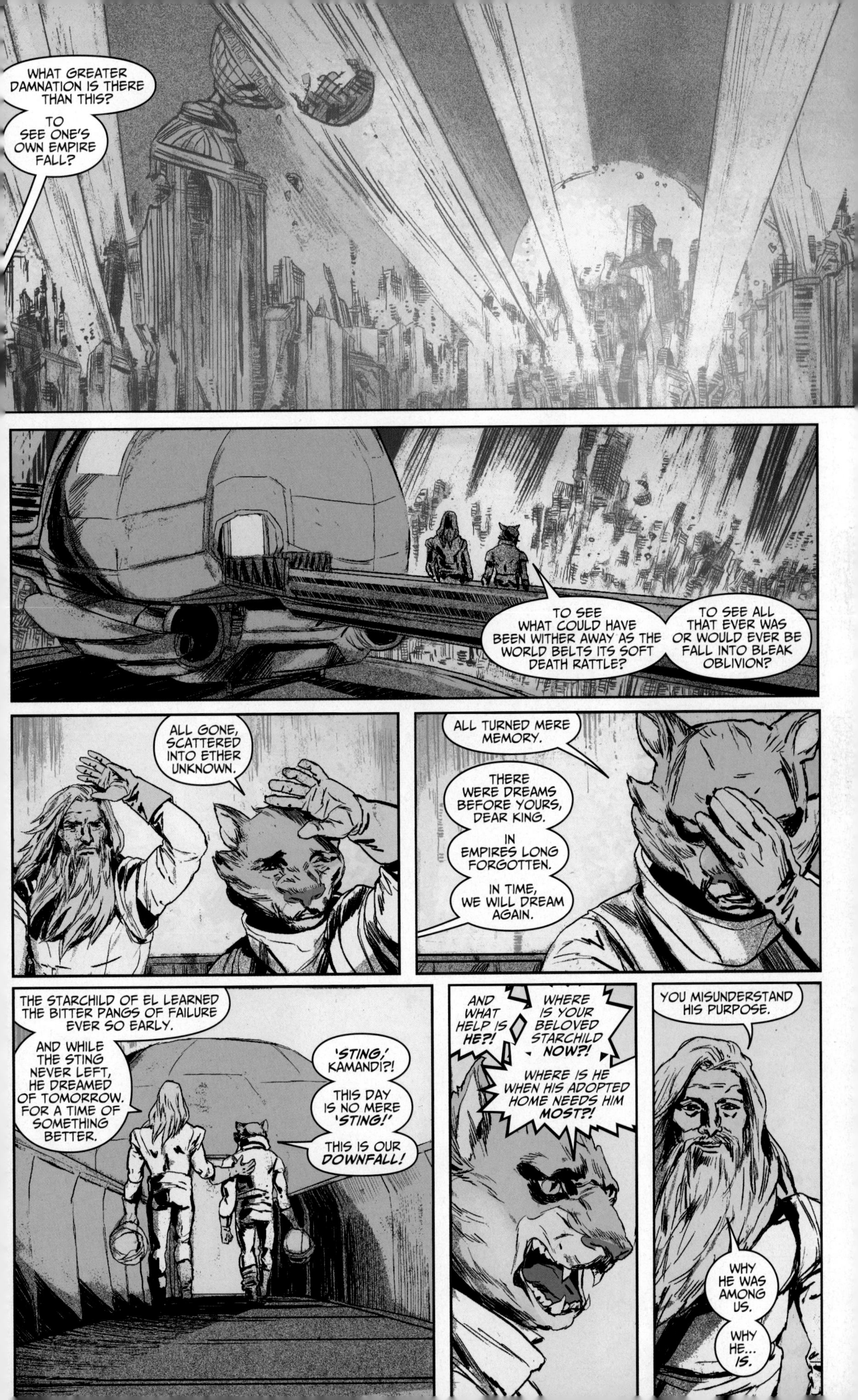
WHAT GREATER DAMNATION IS THERE THAN THIS?
TO SEE ONE'S OWN EMPIRE FALL?
TO SEE WHAT COULD HAVE BEEN WITHER AWAY AS THE WORLD BELTS ITS SOFT DEATH RATTLE?
TO SEE ALL THAT EVER WAS OR WOULD EVER BE FALL INTO BLEAK OBLIVION?
ALL GONE, SCATTERED INTO ETHER UNKNOWN.
ALL TURNED MERE MEMORY.
THERE WERE DREAMS BEFORE YOURS, DEAR KING.
IN EMPIRES LONG FORGOTTEN.
IN TIME, WE WILL DREAM AGAIN.
THE STARCHILD OF EL LEARNED THE BITTER PANGS OF FAILURE EVER SO EARLY.
AND WHILE THE STING NEVER LEFT, HE DREAMED OF TOMORROW. FOR A TIME OF SOMETHING BETTER.
'STING,' KAMANDI?!
THIS DAY IS NO MERE 'STING!'
THIS IS OUR DOWNFALL!
AND WHAT HELP IS HE?!
WHERE IS YOUR BELOVED STARCHILD NOW?!
WHERE IS HE WHEN HIS ADOPTED HOME NEEDS HIM MOST?!
YOU MISUNDERSTAND HIS PURPOSE.
WHY HE WAS AMONG US.
WHY HE... IS.

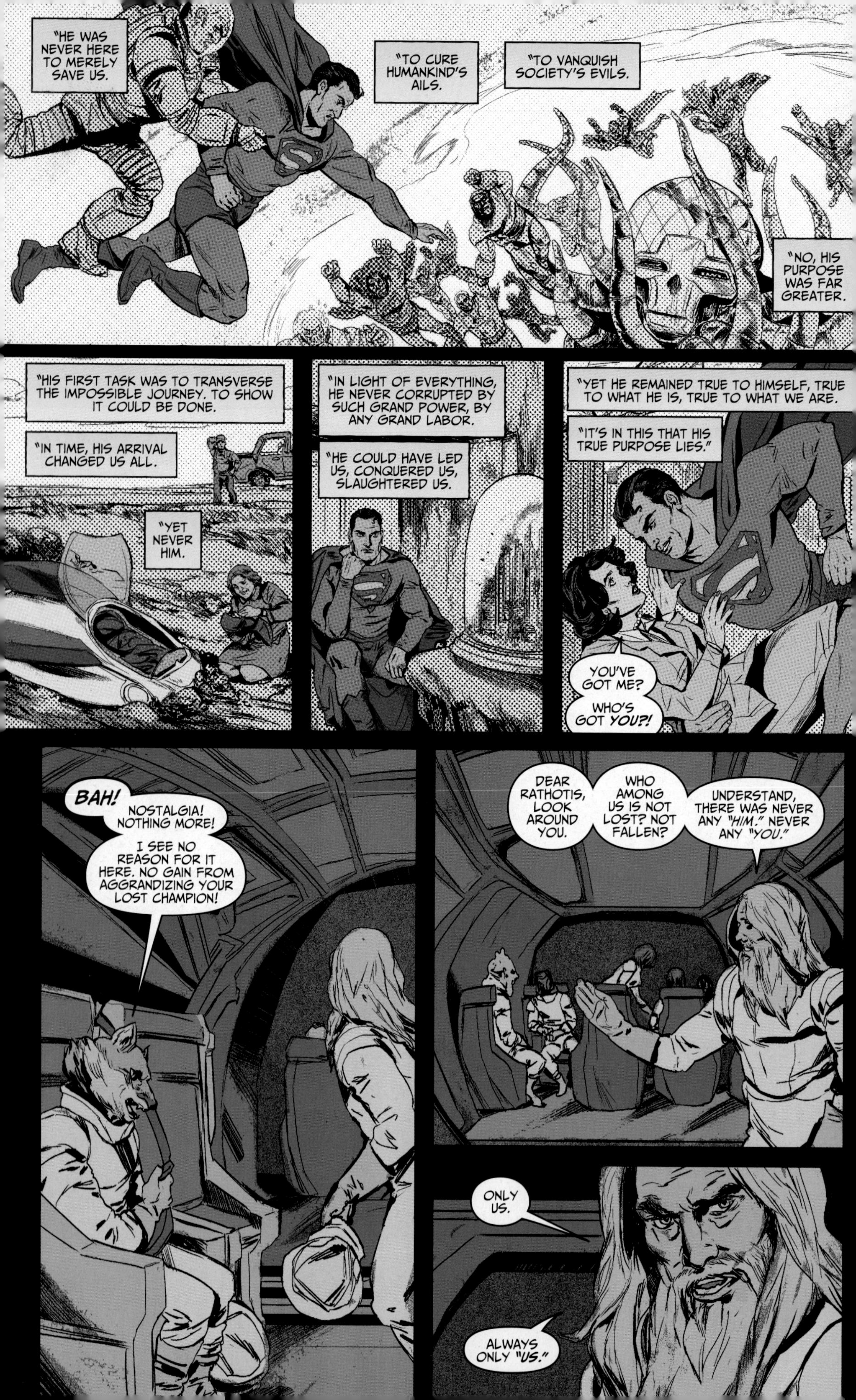
"HE WAS NEVER HERE TO MERELY SAVE US.
"TO CURE HUMANKIND'S AILS.
"TO VANQUISH SOCIETY'S EVILS.
"NO, HIS PURPOSE WAS FAR GREATER.
"HIS FIRST TASK WAS TO TRANSVERSE THE IMPOSSIBLE JOURNEY. TO SHOW IT COULD BE DONE.
"IN TIME, HIS ARRIVAL CHANGED US ALL.
"YET NEVER HIM.
"IN LIGHT OF EVERYTHING, HE NEVER CORRUPTED BY SUCH GRAND POWER, BY ANY GRAND LABOR.
"HE COULD HAVE LED US, CONQUERED US, SLAUGHTERED US.
"YET HE REMAINED TRUE TO HIMSELF, TRUE TO WHAT HE IS, TRUE TO WHAT WE ARE.
"IT'S IN THIS THAT HIS TRUE PURPOSE LIES."
YOU'VE GOT ME?
WHO'S GOT *YOU?!*
BAH!
NOSTALGIA! NOTHING MORE!
I SEE NO REASON FOR IT HERE. NO GAIN FROM AGGRANDIZING YOUR LOST CHAMPION!
DEAR RATHOTIS, LOOK AROUND YOU.
WHO AMONG US IS NOT LOST? NOT FALLEN?
UNDERSTAND, THERE WAS NEVER ANY *"HIM."* NEVER ANY *"YOU."*
ONLY US.
ALWAYS ONLY *"US."*

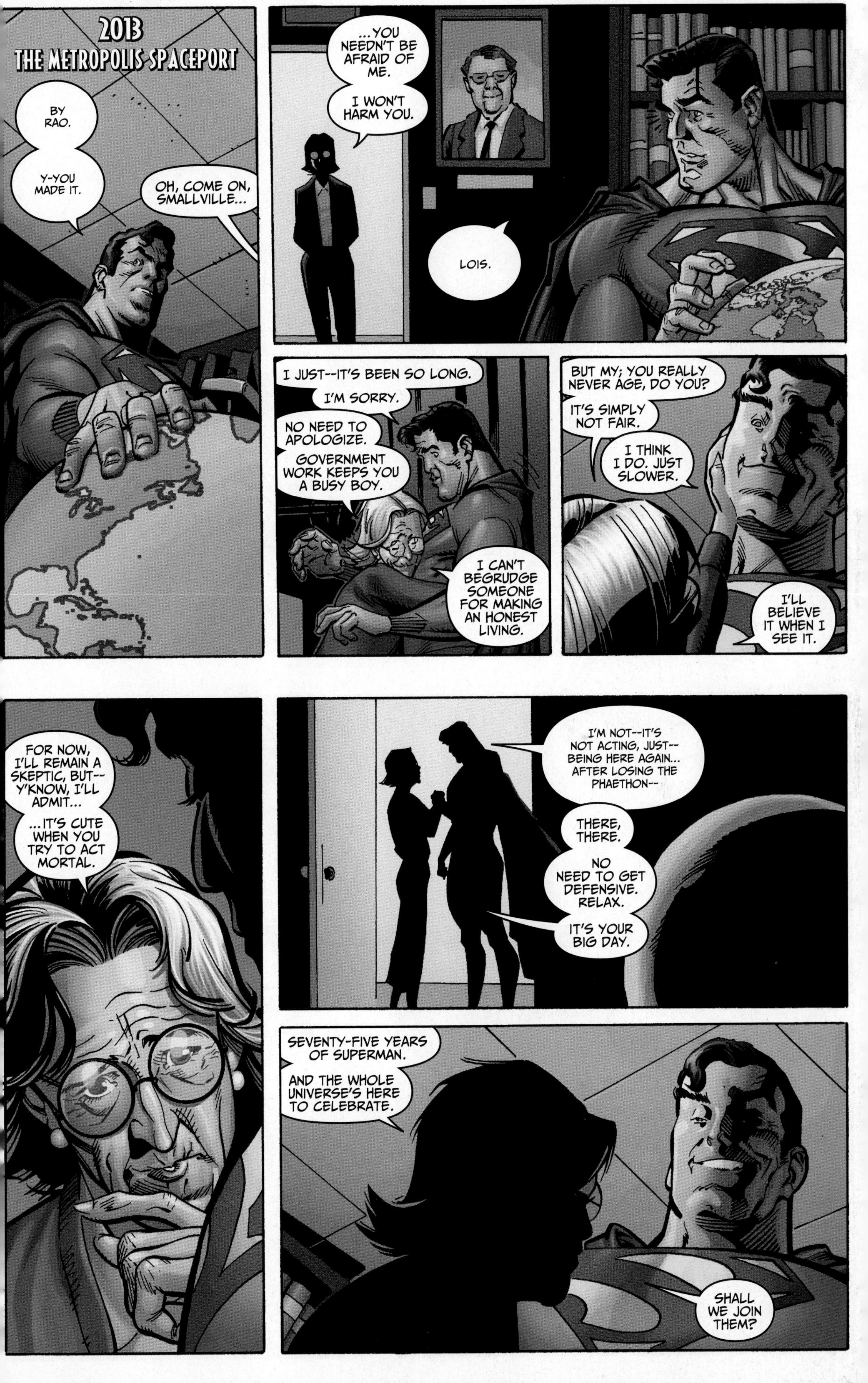
2013
THE METROPOLIS SPACEPORT
BY RAO.
Y-YOU MADE IT.
OH, COME ON, SMALLVILLE...
...YOU NEEDN'T BE AFRAID OF ME.
I WON'T HARM YOU.
LOIS.
I JUST--IT'S BEEN SO LONG.
I'M SORRY.
NO NEED TO APOLOGIZE.
GOVERNMENT WORK KEEPS YOU A BUSY BOY.
I CAN'T BEGRUDGE SOMEONE FOR MAKING AN HONEST LIVING.
BUT MY; YOU REALLY NEVER AGE, DO YOU?
IT'S SIMPLY NOT FAIR.
I THINK I DO. JUST SLOWER.
I'LL BELIEVE IT WHEN I SEE IT.
FOR NOW, I'LL REMAIN A SKEPTIC, BUT--Y'KNOW, I'LL ADMIT...
...IT'S CUTE WHEN YOU TRY TO ACT MORTAL.
I'M NOT--IT'S NOT ACTING, JUST--BEING HERE AGAIN... AFTER LOSING THE PHAETHON--
THERE, THERE.
NO NEED TO GET DEFENSIVE. RELAX.
IT'S YOUR BIG DAY.
SEVENTY-FIVE YEARS OF SUPERMAN.
AND THE WHOLE UNIVERSE'S HERE TO CELEBRATE.
SHALL WE JOIN THEM?

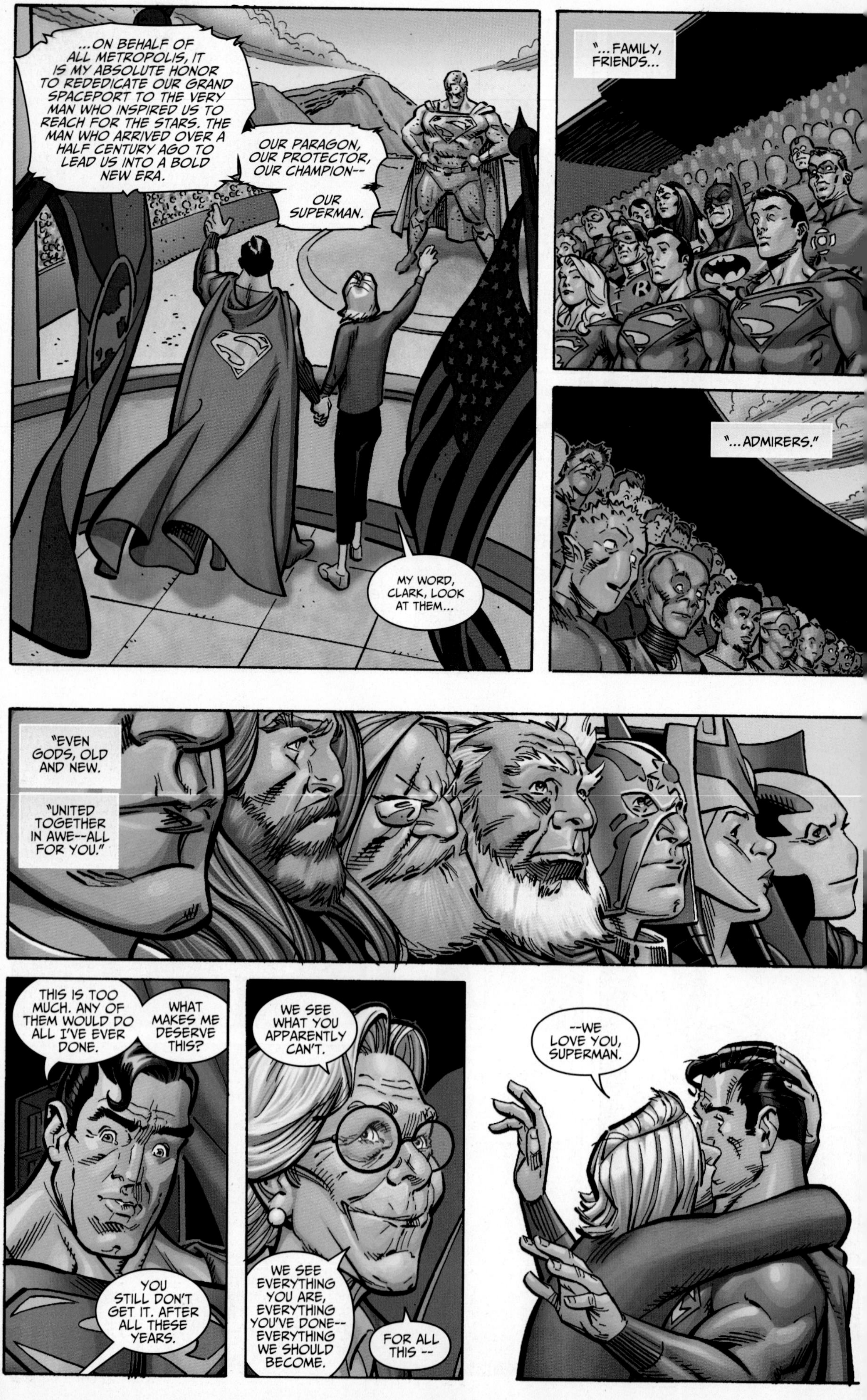
...ON BEHALF OF ALL METROPOLIS, IT IS MY ABSOLUTE HONOR TO REDEDICATE OUR GRAND SPACEPORT TO THE VERY MAN WHO INSPIRED US TO REACH FOR THE STARS. THE MAN WHO ARRIVED OVER A HALF CENTURY AGO TO LEAD US INTO A BOLD NEW ERA.
OUR PARAGON, OUR PROTECTOR, OUR CHAMPION--
OUR SUPERMAN.
MY WORD, CLARK, LOOK AT THEM...
"...FAMILY, FRIENDS...
"...ADMIRERS."
"EVEN GODS, OLD AND NEW.
"UNITED TOGETHER IN AWE--ALL FOR YOU."
THIS IS TOO MUCH. ANY OF THEM WOULD DO ALL I'VE EVER DONE.
WHAT MAKES ME DESERVE THIS?
YOU STILL DON'T GET IT. AFTER ALL THESE YEARS.
WE SEE WHAT YOU APPARENTLY CAN'T.
WE SEE EVERYTHING YOU ARE, EVERYTHING YOU'VE DONE-- EVERYTHING WE SHOULD BECOME.
FOR ALL THIS --
--WE LOVE YOU, SUPERMAN.

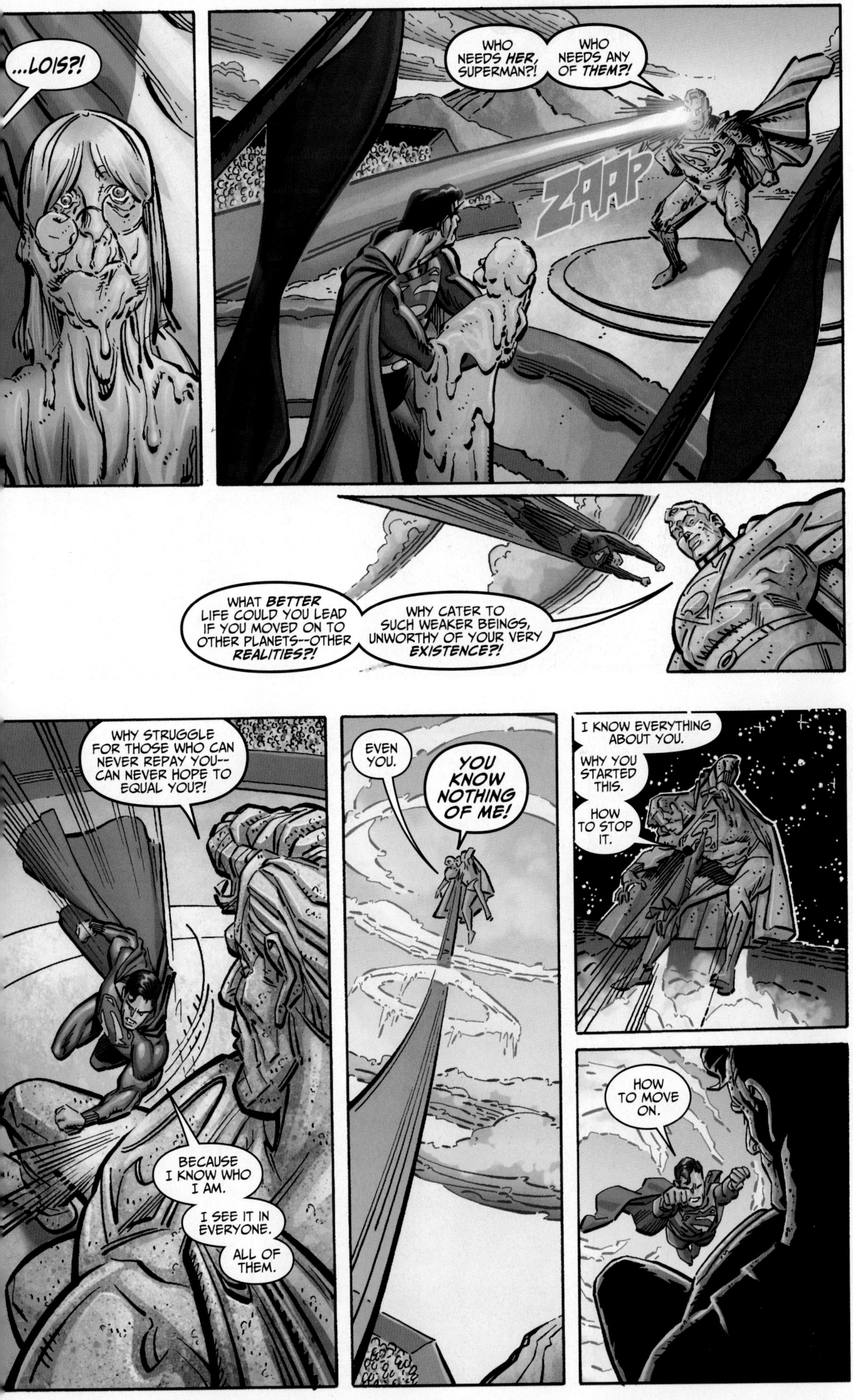
...LOIS?!
WHO NEEDS HER, SUPERMAN?!
WHO NEEDS ANY OF THEM?!
ZAAP
WHAT BETTER LIFE COULD YOU LEAD IF YOU MOVED ON TO OTHER PLANETS--OTHER REALITIES?!
WHY CATER TO SUCH WEAKER BEINGS, UNWORTHY OF YOUR VERY EXISTENCE?!
WHY STRUGGLE FOR THOSE WHO CAN NEVER REPAY YOU-- CAN NEVER HOPE TO EQUAL YOU?!
BECAUSE I KNOW WHO I AM.
I SEE IT IN EVERYONE.
ALL OF THEM.
EVEN YOU.
YOU KNOW NOTHING OF ME!
I KNOW EVERYTHING ABOUT YOU.
WHY YOU STARTED THIS.
HOW TO STOP IT.
HOW TO MOVE ON.

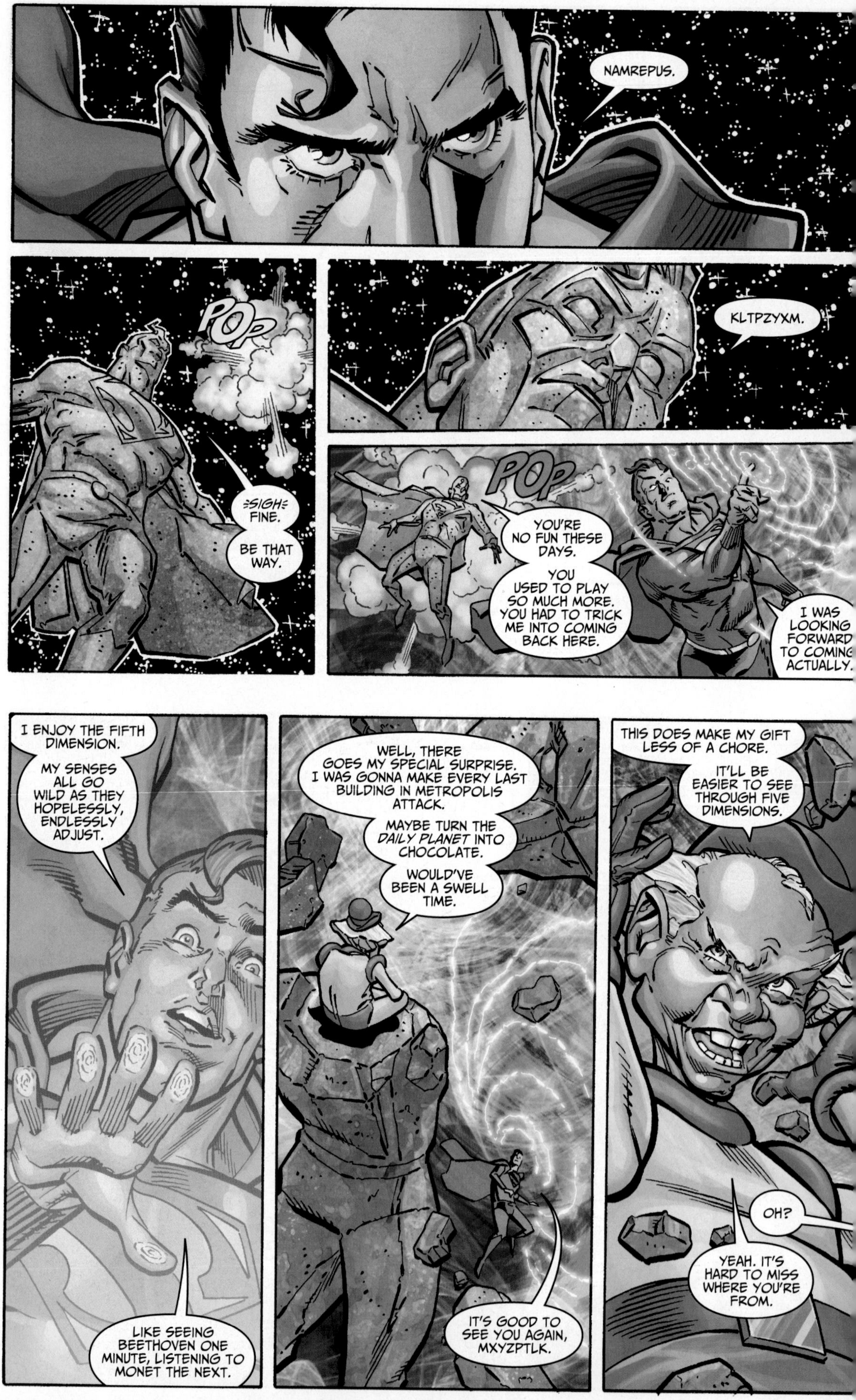
NAMREPUS.
POP
KLTPZYXM.
≥SIGH≤ FINE.
BE THAT WAY.
POP
YOU'RE NO FUN THESE DAYS.
YOU USED TO PLAY SO MUCH MORE. YOU HAD TO TRICK ME INTO COMING BACK HERE.
I WAS LOOKING FORWARD TO COMING ACTUALLY.
I ENJOY THE FIFTH DIMENSION.
MY SENSES ALL GO WILD AS THEY HOPELESSLY, ENDLESSLY ADJUST.
LIKE SEEING BEETHOVEN ONE MINUTE, LISTENING TO MONET THE NEXT.
WELL, THERE GOES MY SPECIAL SURPRISE. I WAS GONNA MAKE EVERY LAST BUILDING IN METROPOLIS ATTACK.
MAYBE TURN THE *DAILY PLANET* INTO CHOCOLATE.
WOULD'VE BEEN A SWELL TIME.
IT'S GOOD TO SEE YOU AGAIN, MXYZPTLK.
THIS DOES MAKE MY GIFT LESS OF A CHORE.
IT'LL BE EASIER TO SEE THROUGH FIVE DIMENSIONS.
OH?
YEAH. IT'S HARD TO MISS WHERE YOU'RE FROM.

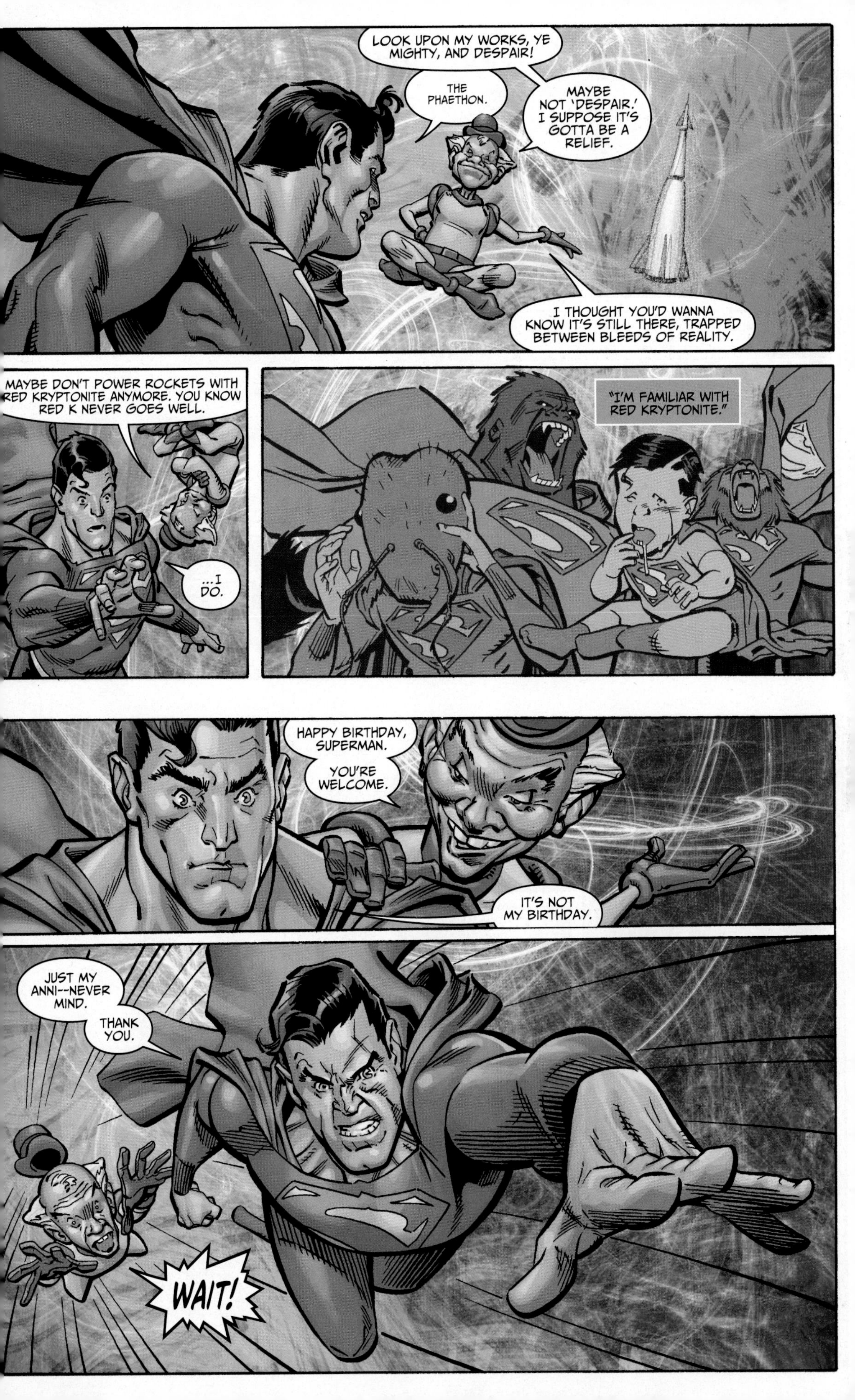

LOOK UPON MY WORKS, YE MIGHTY, AND DESPAIR!
THE PHAETHON.
MAYBE NOT 'DESPAIR.' I SUPPOSE IT'S GOTTA BE A RELIEF.
I THOUGHT YOU'D WANNA KNOW IT'S STILL THERE, TRAPPED BETWEEN BLEEDS OF REALITY.
MAYBE DON'T POWER ROCKETS WITH RED KRYPTONITE ANYMORE. YOU KNOW RED K NEVER GOES WELL.
...I DO.
"I'M FAMILIAR WITH RED KRYPTONITE."
HAPPY BIRTHDAY, SUPERMAN.
YOU'RE WELCOME.
IT'S NOT MY BIRTHDAY.
JUST MY ANNI--NEVER MIND.
THANK YOU.
WAIT!

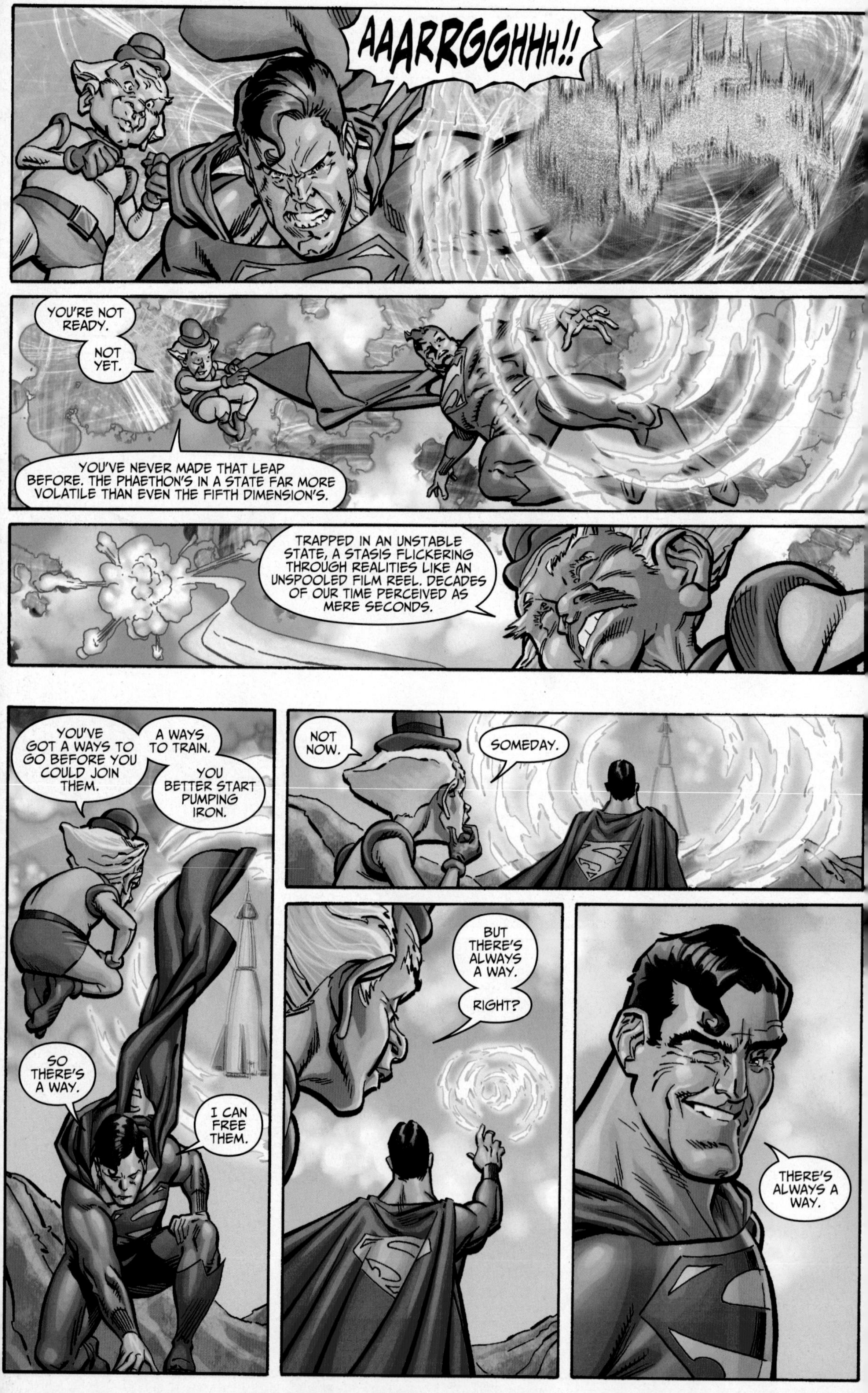
AAARRGGHHH!!
YOU'RE NOT READY.
NOT YET.
YOU'VE NEVER MADE THAT LEAP BEFORE. THE PHAETHON'S IN A STATE FAR MORE VOLATILE THAN EVEN THE FIFTH DIMENSION'S.
TRAPPED IN AN UNSTABLE STATE, A STASIS FLICKERING THROUGH REALITIES LIKE AN UNSPOOLED FILM REEL. DECADES OF OUR TIME PERCEIVED AS MERE SECONDS.
YOU'VE GOT A WAYS TO GO BEFORE YOU COULD JOIN THEM.
A WAYS TO TRAIN.
YOU BETTER START PUMPING IRON.
SO THERE'S A WAY.
I CAN FREE THEM.
NOT NOW.
SOMEDAY.
BUT THERE'S ALWAYS A WAY.
RIGHT?
THERE'S ALWAYS A WAY.

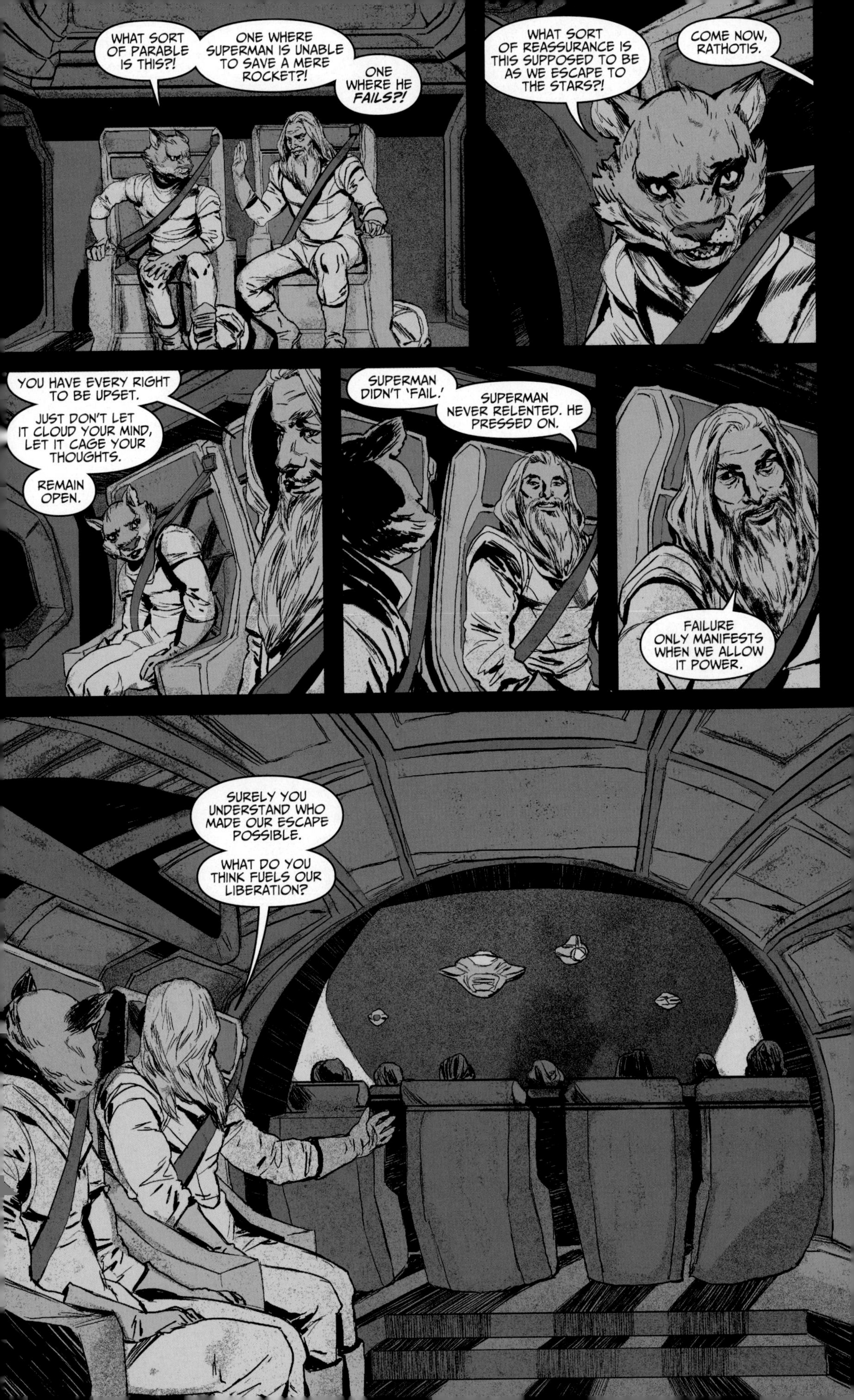
WHAT SORT OF PARABLE IS THIS?!
ONE WHERE SUPERMAN IS UNABLE TO SAVE A MERE ROCKET?!
ONE WHERE HE *FAILS?!*
WHAT SORT OF REASSURANCE IS THIS SUPPOSED TO BE AS WE ESCAPE TO THE STARS?!
COME NOW, RATHOTIS.
YOU HAVE EVERY RIGHT TO BE UPSET.
JUST DON'T LET IT CLOUD YOUR MIND, LET IT CAGE YOUR THOUGHTS.
REMAIN OPEN.
SUPERMAN DIDN'T 'FAIL.'
SUPERMAN NEVER RELENTED. HE PRESSED ON.
FAILURE ONLY MANIFESTS WHEN WE ALLOW IT POWER.
SURELY YOU UNDERSTAND WHO MADE OUR ESCAPE POSSIBLE.
WHAT DO YOU THINK FUELS OUR LIBERATION?

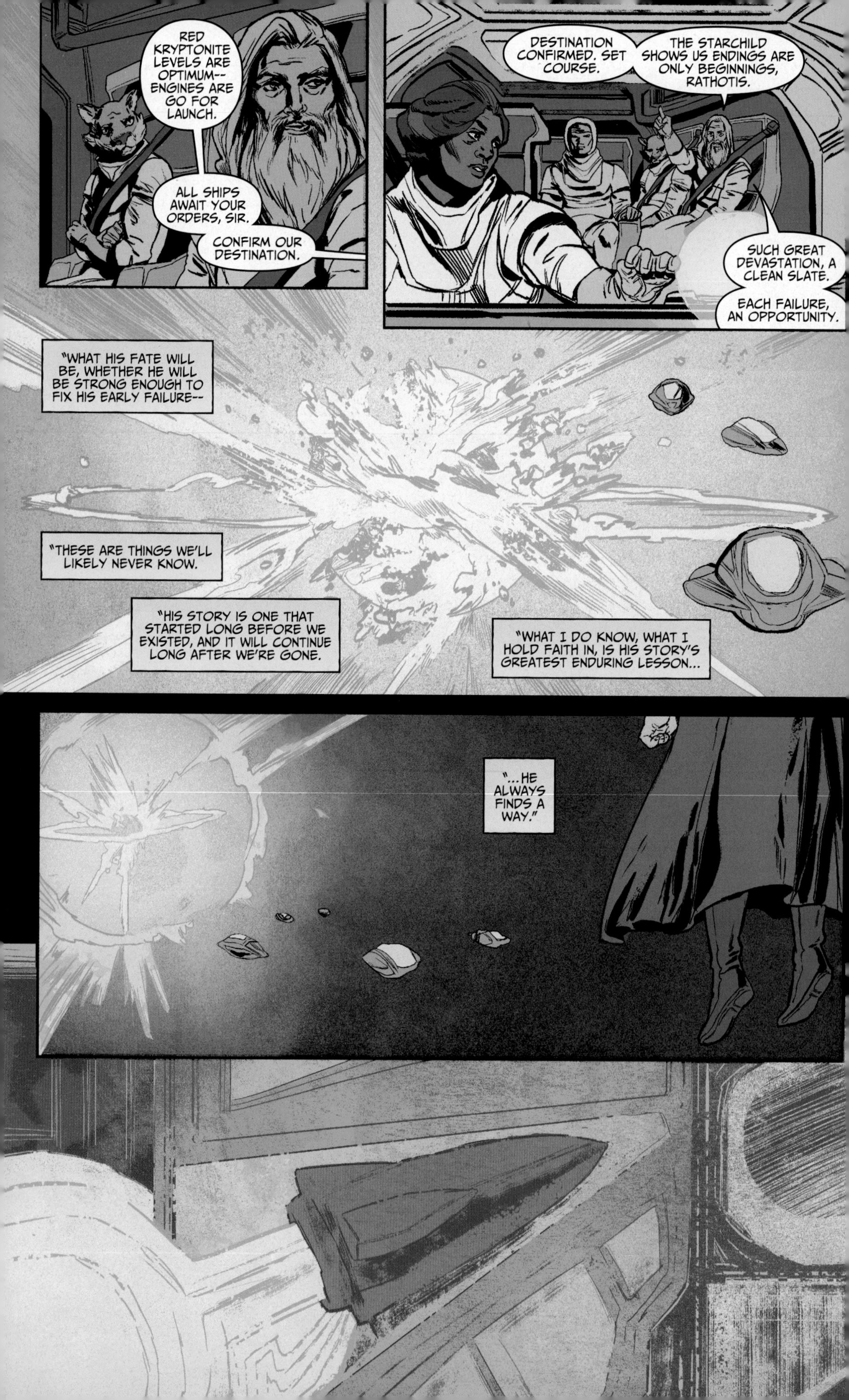
RED KRYPTONITE LEVELS ARE OPTIMUM-- ENGINES ARE GO FOR LAUNCH.
ALL SHIPS AWAIT YOUR ORDERS, SIR.
CONFIRM OUR DESTINATION.
DESTINATION CONFIRMED. SET COURSE.
THE STARCHILD SHOWS US ENDINGS ARE ONLY BEGINNINGS, RATHOTIS.
SUCH GREAT DEVASTATION, A CLEAN SLATE.
EACH FAILURE, AN OPPORTUNITY.
"WHAT HIS FATE WILL BE, WHETHER HE WILL BE STRONG ENOUGH TO FIX HIS EARLY FAILURE--
"THESE ARE THINGS WE'LL LIKELY NEVER KNOW.
"HIS STORY IS ONE THAT STARTED LONG BEFORE WE EXISTED, AND IT WILL CONTINUE LONG AFTER WE'RE GONE.
"WHAT I DO KNOW, WHAT I HOLD FAITH IN, IS HIS STORY'S GREATEST ENDURING LESSON...
"...HE ALWAYS FINDS A WAY."

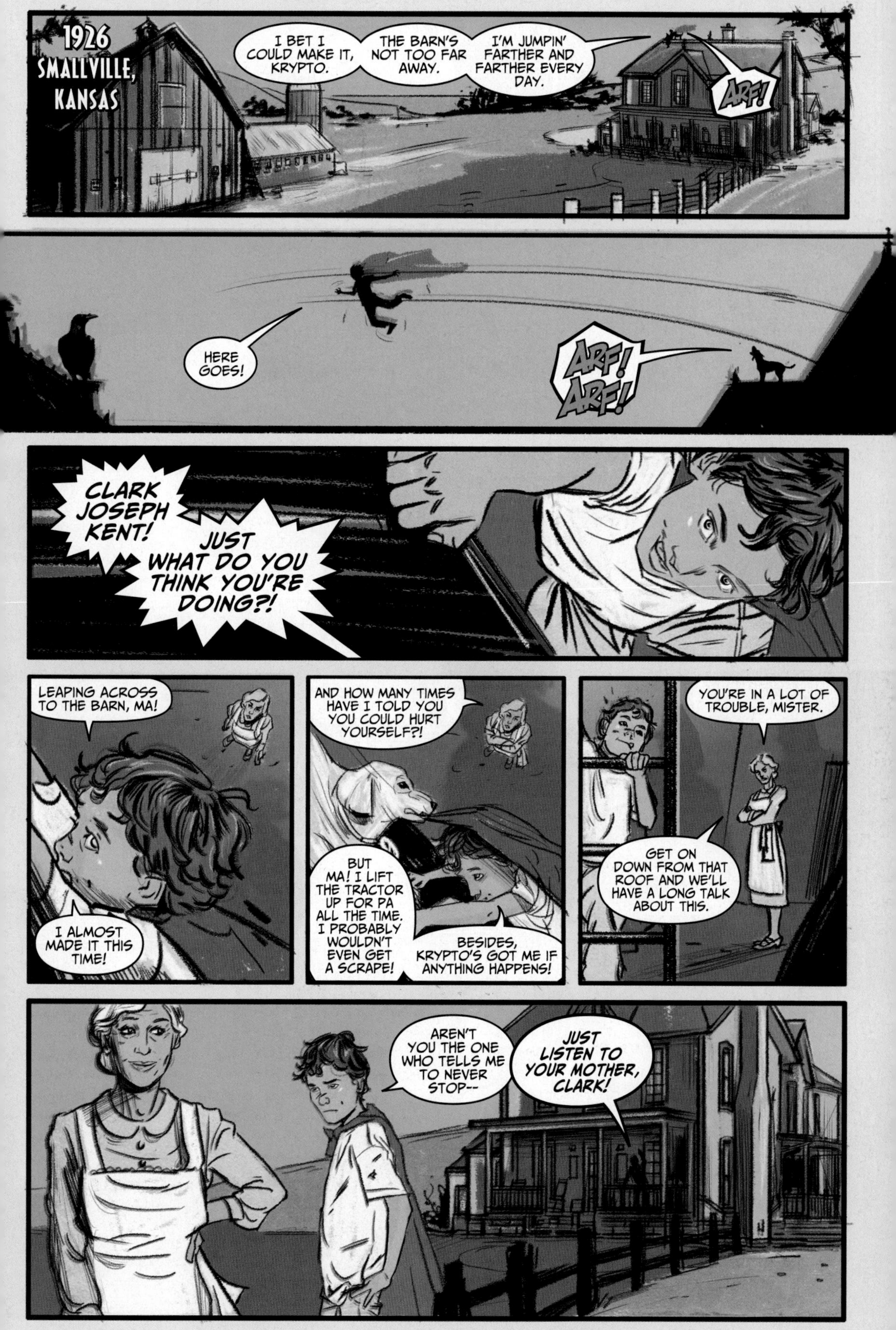
1926 SMALLVILLE, KANSAS
I BET I COULD MAKE IT, KRYPTO.
THE BARN'S NOT TOO FAR AWAY.
I'M JUMPIN' FARTHER AND FARTHER EVERY DAY.
ARF!
HERE GOES!
ARF! ARF!
CLARK JOSEPH KENT!
JUST WHAT DO YOU THINK YOU'RE DOING?!
LEAPING ACROSS TO THE BARN, MA!
I ALMOST MADE IT THIS TIME!
AND HOW MANY TIMES HAVE I TOLD YOU YOU COULD HURT YOURSELF?!
BUT MA! I LIFT THE TRACTOR UP FOR PA ALL THE TIME. I PROBABLY WOULDN'T EVEN GET A SCRAPE!
BESIDES, KRYPTO'S GOT ME IF ANYTHING HAPPENS!
YOU'RE IN A LOT OF TROUBLE, MISTER.
GET ON DOWN FROM THAT ROOF AND WE'LL HAVE A LONG TALK ABOUT THIS.
AREN'T YOU THE ONE WHO TELLS ME TO NEVER STOP--
JUST LISTEN TO YOUR MOTHER, CLARK!

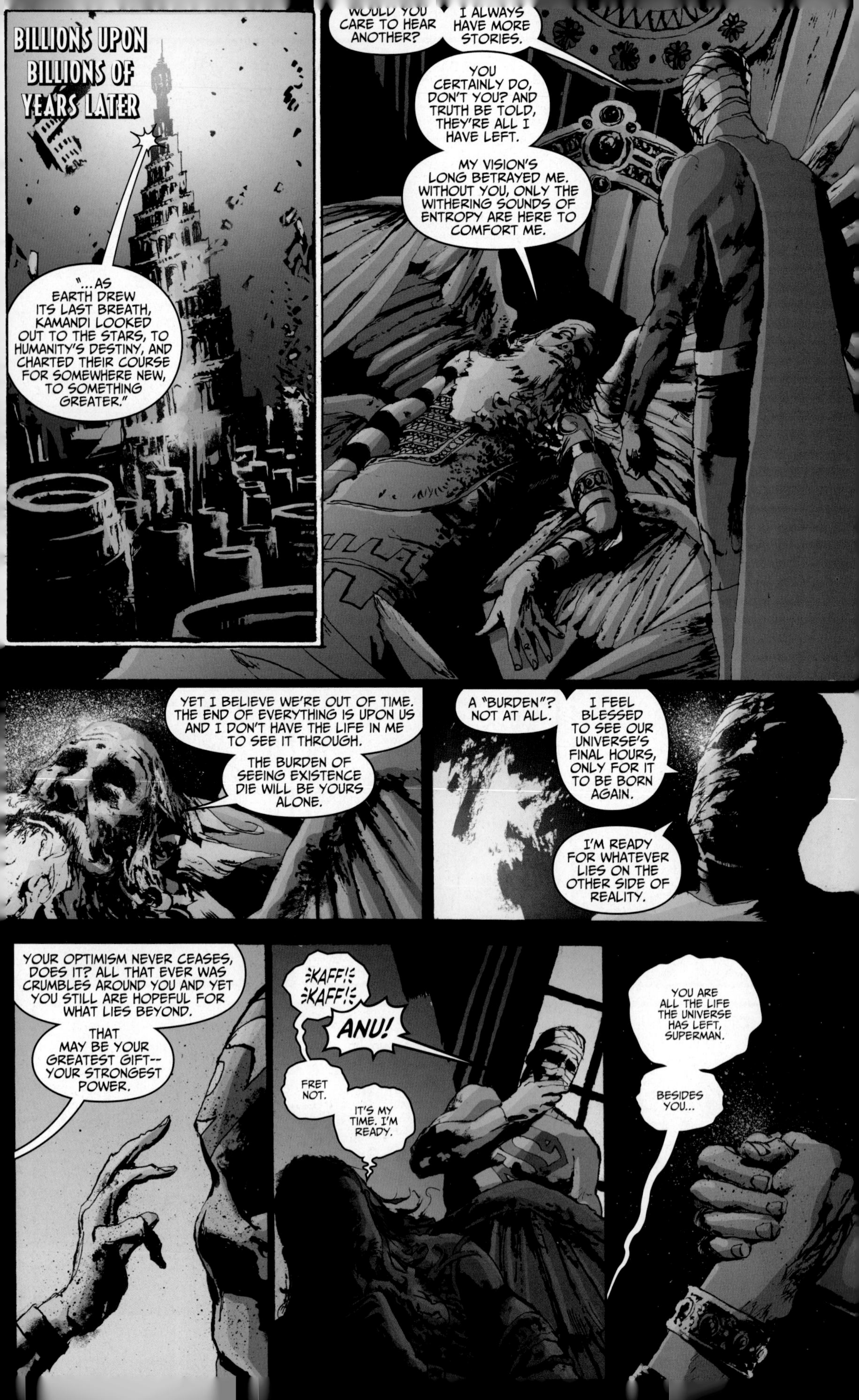
BILLIONS UPON BILLIONS OF YEARS LATER
"...AS EARTH DREW ITS LAST BREATH, KAMANDI LOOKED OUT TO THE STARS, TO HUMANITY'S DESTINY, AND CHARTED THEIR COURSE FOR SOMEWHERE NEW, TO SOMETHING GREATER."
WOULD YOU CARE TO HEAR ANOTHER?
I ALWAYS HAVE MORE STORIES.
YOU CERTAINLY DO, DON'T YOU? AND TRUTH BE TOLD, THEY'RE ALL I HAVE LEFT.
MY VISION'S LONG BETRAYED ME. WITHOUT YOU, ONLY THE WITHERING SOUNDS OF ENTROPY ARE HERE TO COMFORT ME.
YET I BELIEVE WE'RE OUT OF TIME. THE END OF EVERYTHING IS UPON US AND I DON'T HAVE THE LIFE IN ME TO SEE IT THROUGH.
THE BURDEN OF SEEING EXISTENCE DIE WILL BE YOURS ALONE.
A "BURDEN"? NOT AT ALL.
I FEEL BLESSED TO SEE OUR UNIVERSE'S FINAL HOURS, ONLY FOR IT TO BE BORN AGAIN.
I'M READY FOR WHATEVER LIES ON THE OTHER SIDE OF REALITY.
YOUR OPTIMISM NEVER CEASES, DOES IT? ALL THAT EVER WAS CRUMBLES AROUND YOU AND YET YOU STILL ARE HOPEFUL FOR WHAT LIES BEYOND.
THAT MAY BE YOUR GREATEST GIFT-- YOUR STRONGEST POWER.
KAFF! KAFF!
ANU!
FRET NOT.
IT'S MY TIME. I'M READY.
YOU ARE ALL THE LIFE THE UNIVERSE HAS LEFT, SUPERMAN.
BESIDES YOU...

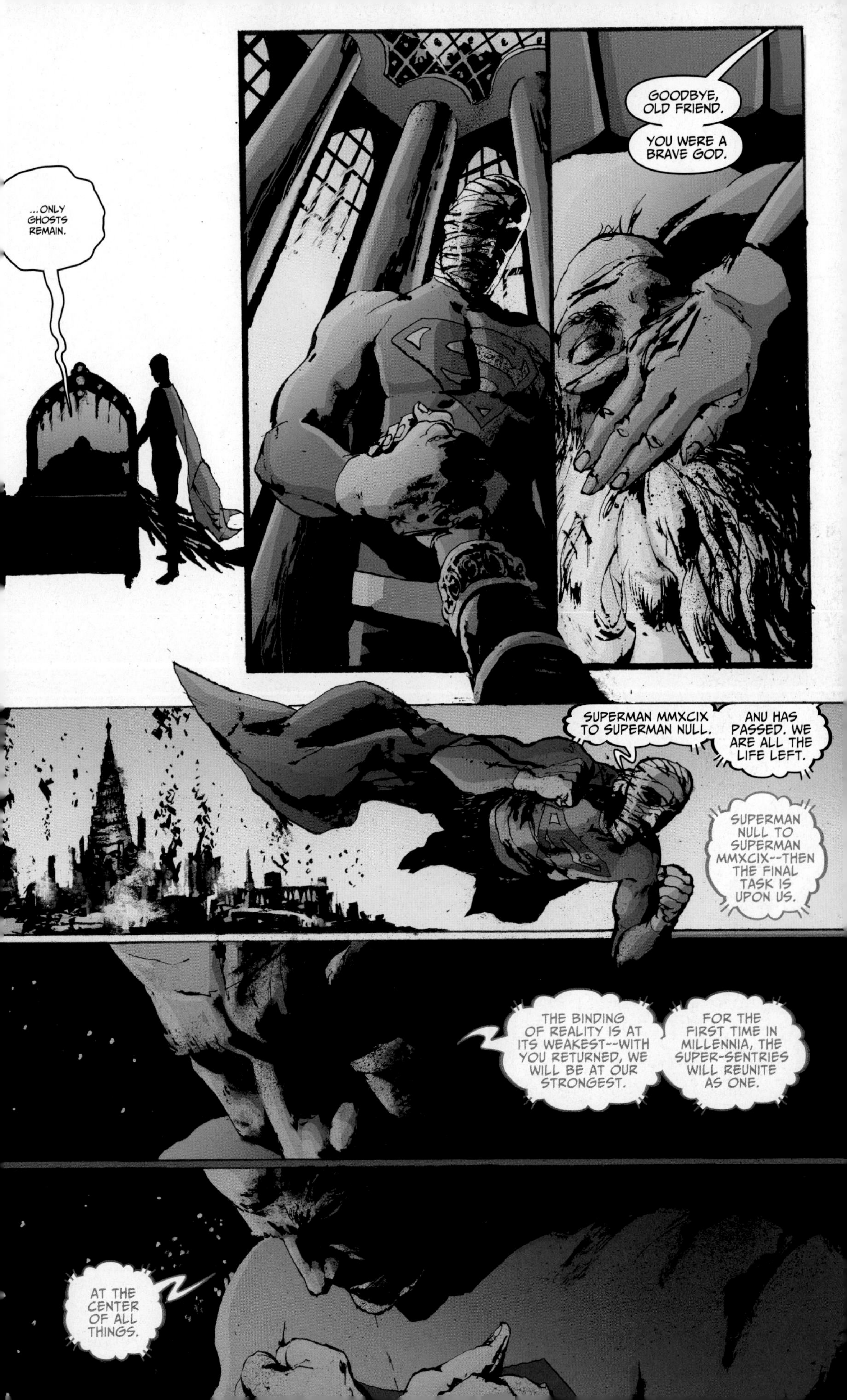
...ONLY GHOSTS REMAIN.
GOODBYE, OLD FRIEND.
YOU WERE A BRAVE GOD.
SUPERMAN MMXCIX TO SUPERMAN NULL.
ANU HAS PASSED. WE ARE ALL THE LIFE LEFT.
SUPERMAN NULL TO SUPERMAN MMXCIX--THEN THE FINAL TASK IS UPON US.
THE BINDING OF REALITY IS AT ITS WEAKEST--WITH YOU RETURNED, WE WILL BE AT OUR STRONGEST.
FOR THE FIRST TIME IN MILLENNIA, THE SUPER-SENTRIES WILL REUNITE AS ONE.
AT THE CENTER OF ALL THINGS.

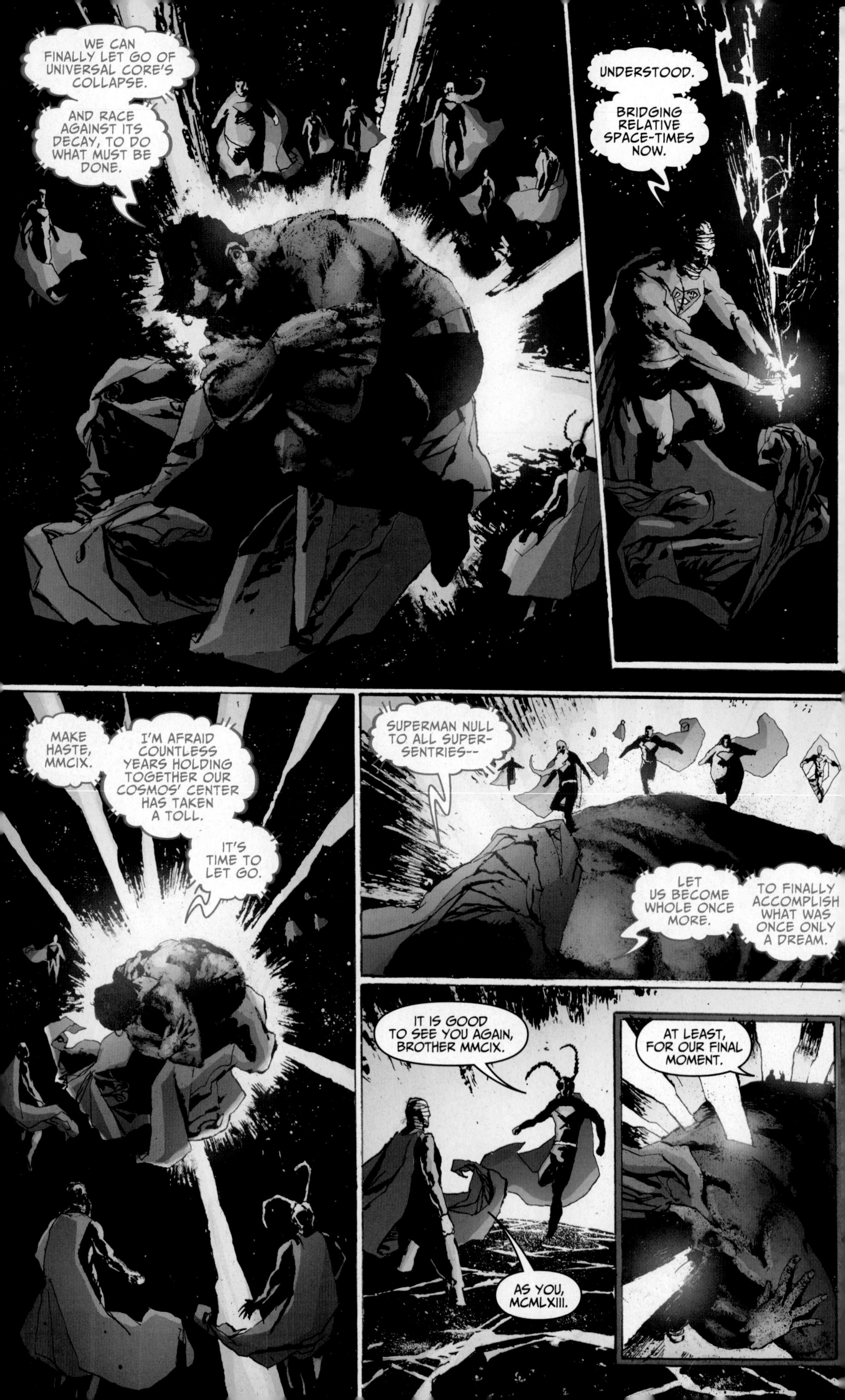

WE CAN FINALLY LET GO OF UNIVERSAL CORE'S COLLAPSE.
AND RACE AGAINST ITS DECAY, TO DO WHAT MUST BE DONE.
UNDERSTOOD.
BRIDGING RELATIVE SPACE-TIMES NOW.
MAKE HASTE, MMCIX.
I'M AFRAID COUNTLESS YEARS HOLDING TOGETHER OUR COSMOS' CENTER HAS TAKEN A TOLL.
IT'S TIME TO LET GO.
SUPERMAN NULL TO ALL SUPER-SENTRIES--
LET US BECOME WHOLE ONCE MORE.
TO FINALLY ACCOMPLISH WHAT WAS ONCE ONLY A DREAM.
IT IS GOOD TO SEE YOU AGAIN, BROTHER MMCIX.
AS YOU, MCMLXIII.
AT LEAST, FOR OUR FINAL MOMENT.

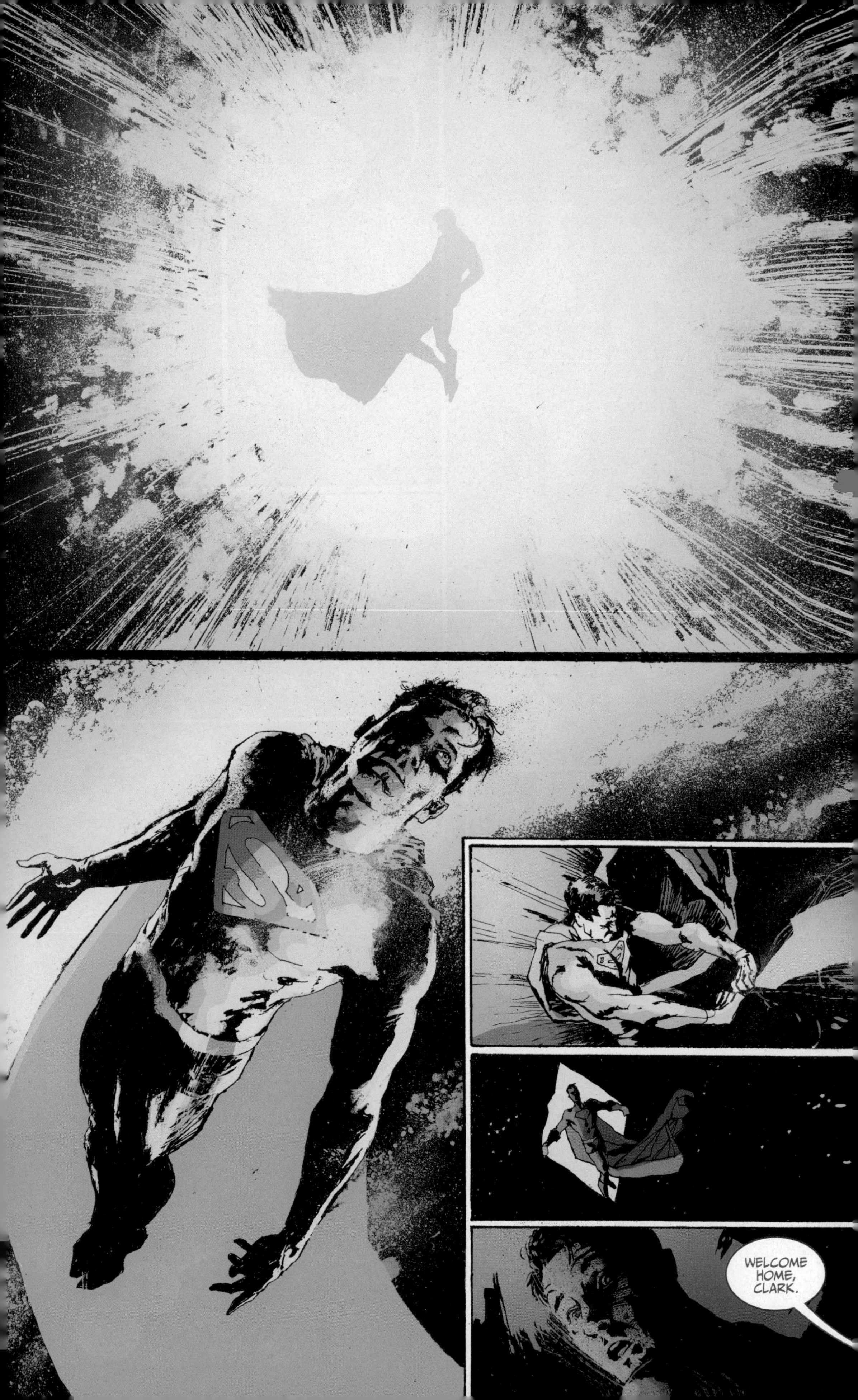
WELCOME HOME, CLARK.

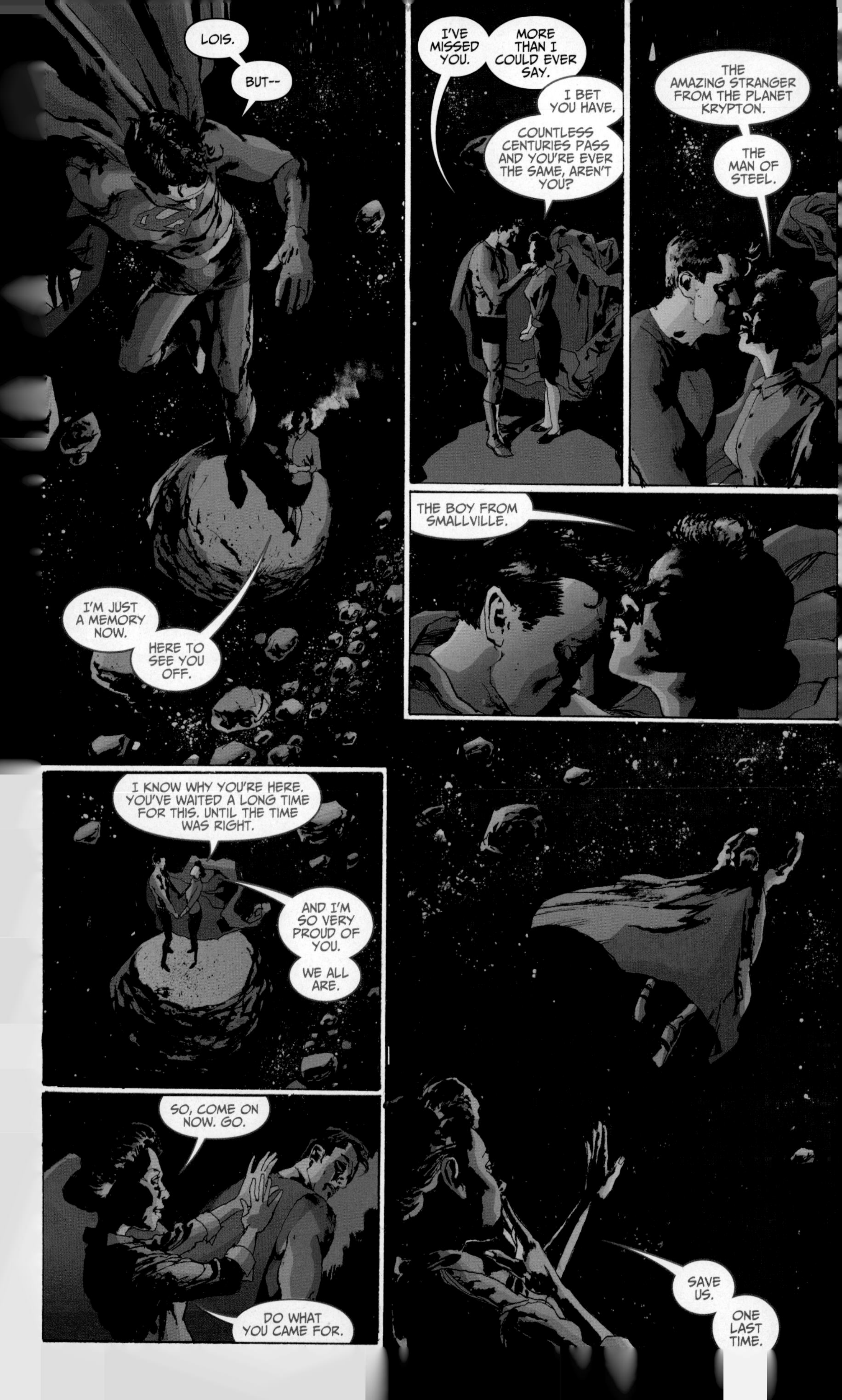
LOIS.
BUT--
I'M JUST A MEMORY NOW.
HERE TO SEE YOU OFF.
I'VE MISSED YOU.
MORE THAN I COULD EVER SAY.
I BET YOU HAVE.
COUNTLESS CENTURIES PASS AND YOU'RE EVER THE SAME, AREN'T YOU?
THE AMAZING STRANGER FROM THE PLANET KRYPTON.
THE MAN OF STEEL.
THE BOY FROM SMALLVILLE.
I KNOW WHY YOU'RE HERE. YOU'VE WAITED A LONG TIME FOR THIS. UNTIL THE TIME WAS RIGHT.
AND I'M SO VERY PROUD OF YOU.
WE ALL ARE.
SO, COME ON NOW. GO.
DO WHAT YOU CAME FOR.
SAVE US.
ONE LAST TIME.

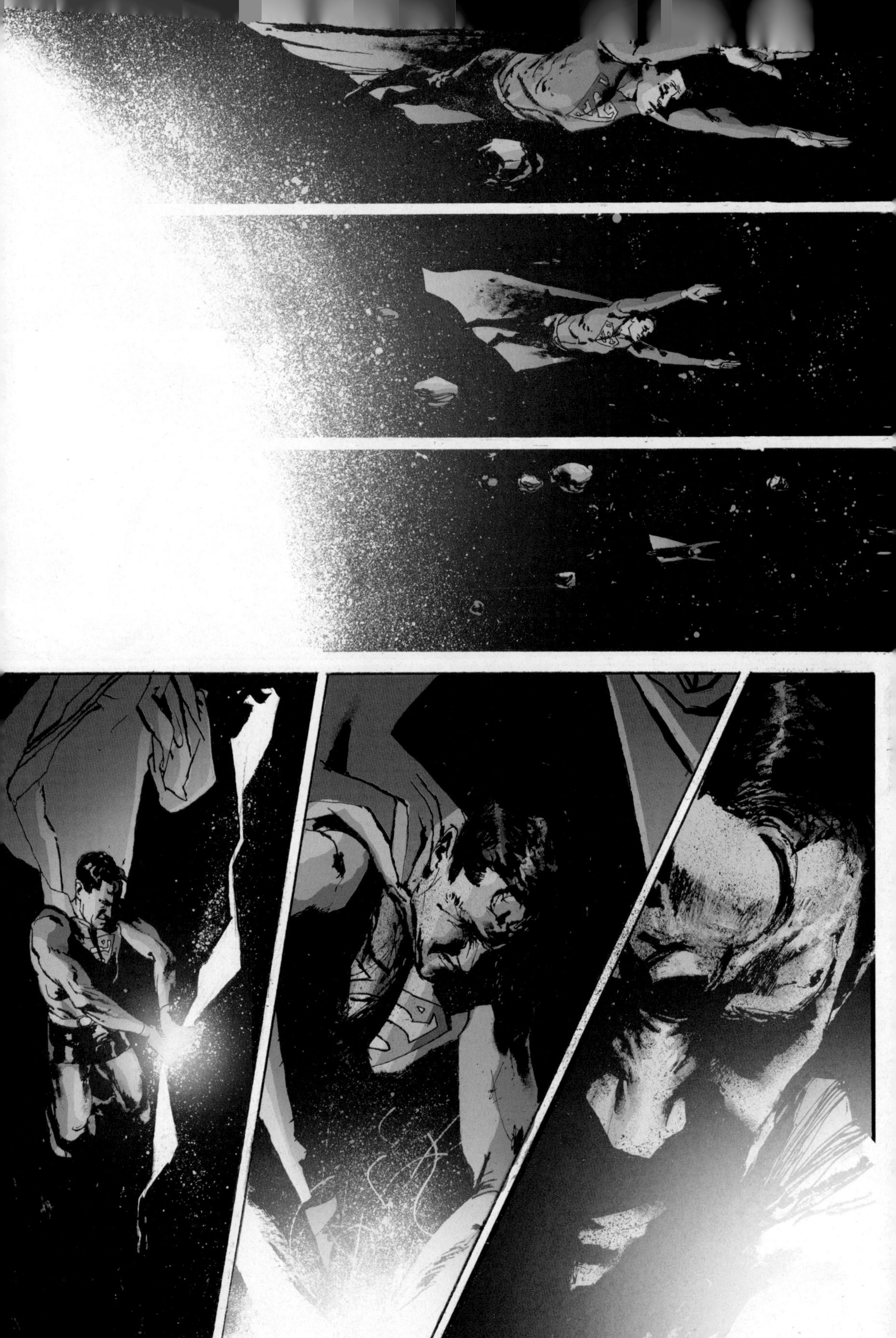

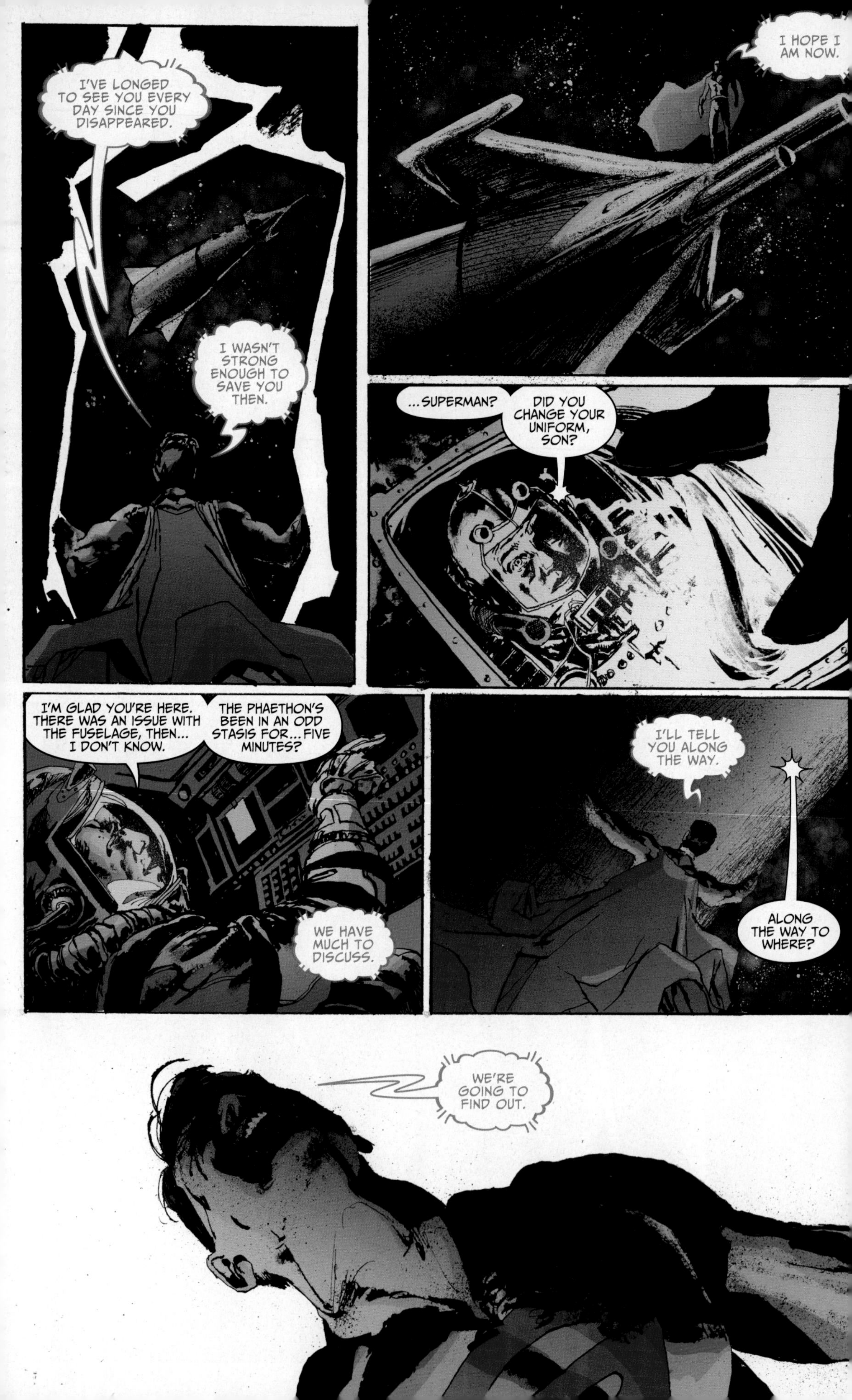
I'VE LONGED TO SEE YOU EVERY DAY SINCE YOU DISAPPEARED.
I WASN'T STRONG ENOUGH TO SAVE YOU THEN.
I HOPE I AM NOW.
...SUPERMAN?
DID YOU CHANGE YOUR UNIFORM, SON?
I'M GLAD YOU'RE HERE. THERE WAS AN ISSUE WITH THE FUSELAGE, THEN... I DON'T KNOW.
THE PHAETHON'S BEEN IN AN ODD STASIS FOR... FIVE MINUTES?
WE HAVE MUCH TO DISCUSS.
I'LL TELL YOU ALONG THE WAY.
ALONG THE WAY TO WHERE?
WE'RE GOING TO FIND OUT.

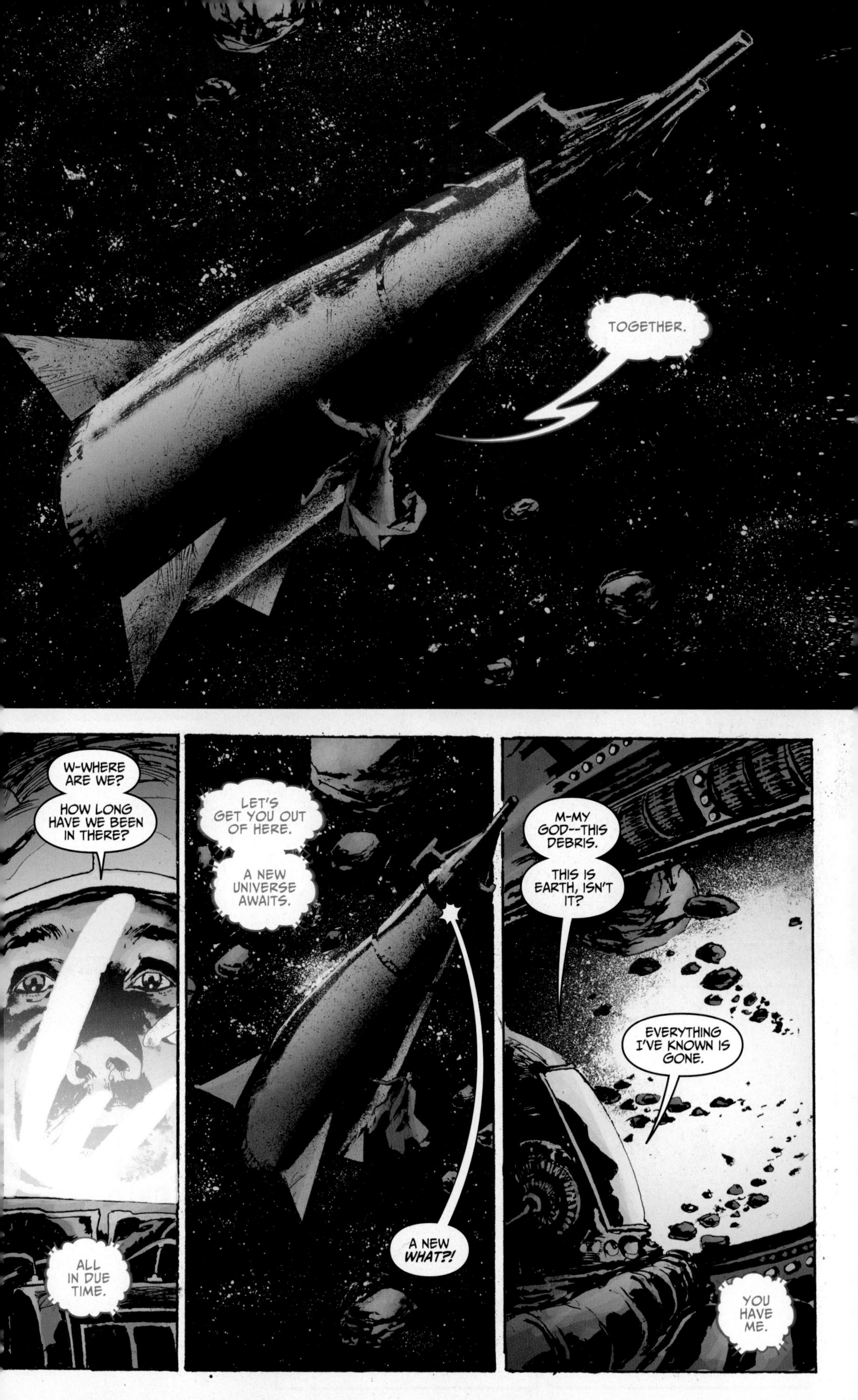
TOGETHER.
W-WHERE ARE WE?
HOW LONG HAVE WE BEEN IN THERE?
ALL IN DUE TIME.
LET'S GET YOU OUT OF HERE.
A NEW UNIVERSE AWAITS.
A NEW *WHAT?!*
M-MY GOD--THIS DEBRIS.
THIS IS EARTH, ISN'T IT?
EVERYTHING I'VE KNOWN IS GONE.
YOU HAVE ME.

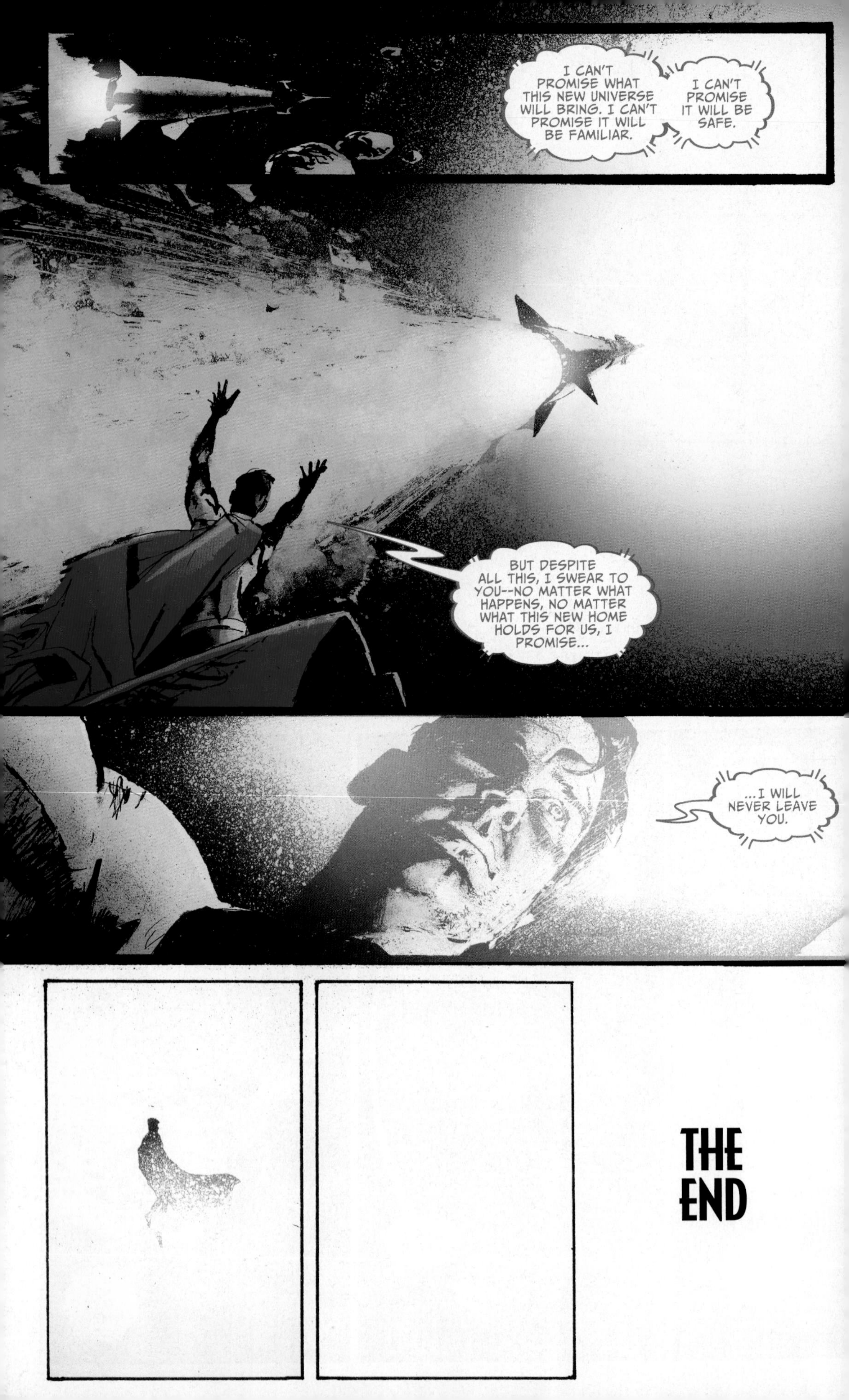
I CAN'T PROMISE WHAT THIS NEW UNIVERSE WILL BRING. I CAN'T PROMISE IT WILL BE FAMILIAR.
I CAN'T PROMISE IT WILL BE SAFE.
BUT DESPITE ALL THIS, I SWEAR TO YOU--NO MATTER WHAT HAPPENS, NO MATTER WHAT THIS NEW HOME HOLDS FOR US, I PROMISE...
...I WILL NEVER LEAVE YOU.
THE END

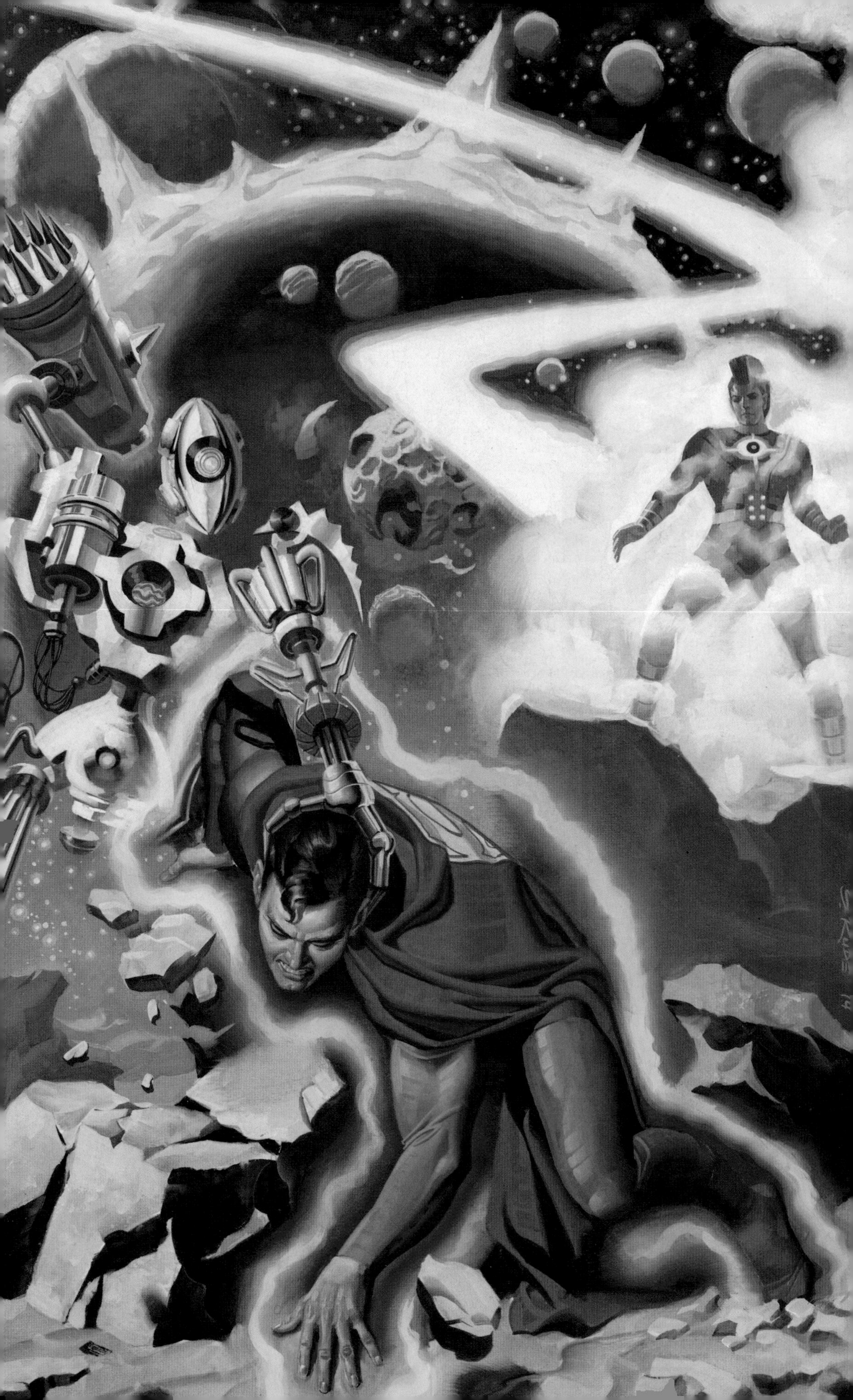

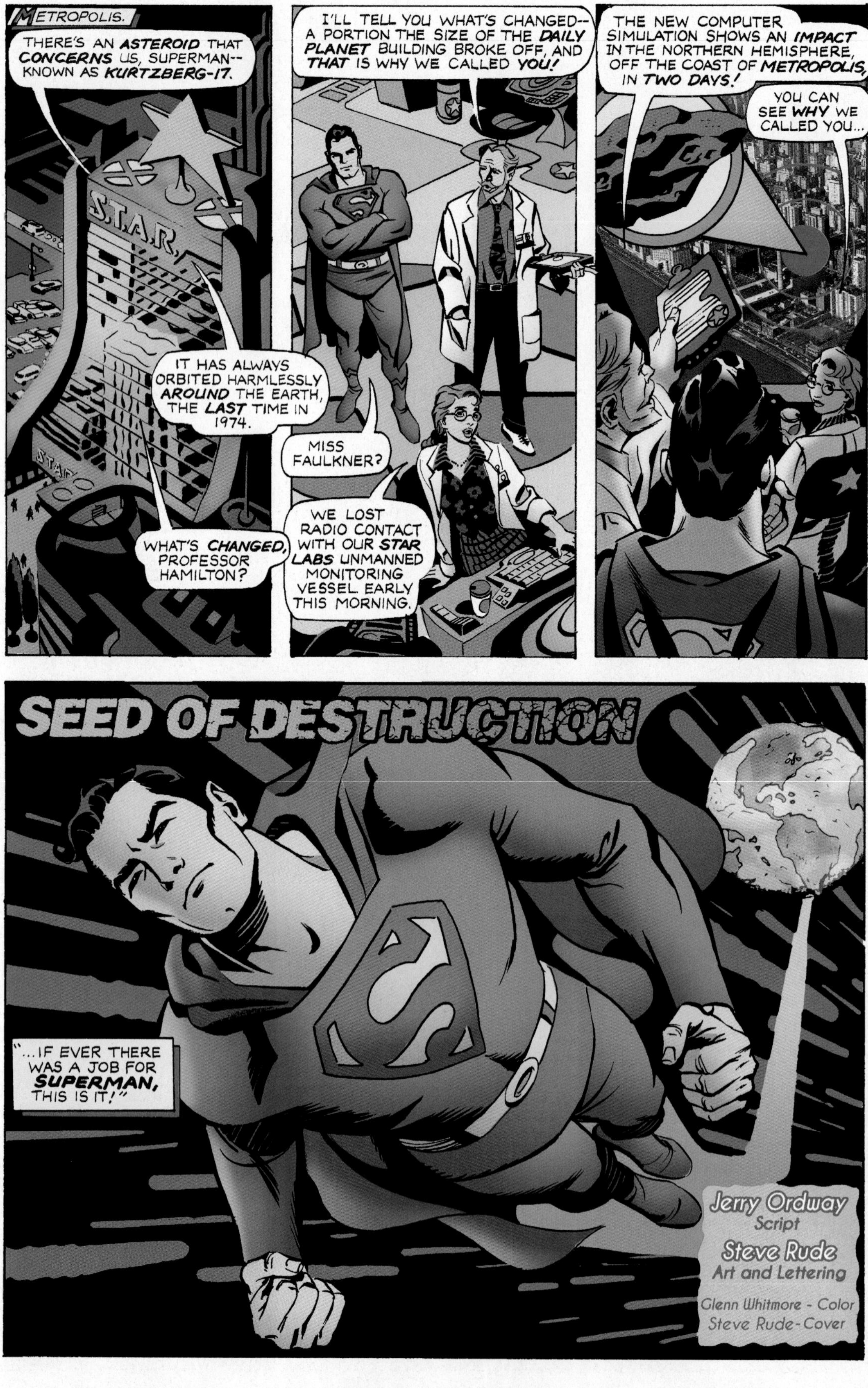
METROPOLIS.
THERE'S AN ASTEROID THAT CONCERNS US, SUPERMAN-- KNOWN AS KURTZBERG-17.
IT HAS ALWAYS ORBITED HARMLESSLY AROUND THE EARTH, THE LAST TIME IN 1974.
WHAT'S CHANGED, PROFESSOR HAMILTON?
S.T.A.R.
I'LL TELL YOU WHAT'S CHANGED-- A PORTION THE SIZE OF THE DAILY PLANET BUILDING BROKE OFF, AND THAT IS WHY WE CALLED YOU!
MISS FAULKNER?
WE LOST RADIO CONTACT WITH OUR STAR LABS UNMANNED MONITORING VESSEL EARLY THIS MORNING.
THE NEW COMPUTER SIMULATION SHOWS AN IMPACT IN THE NORTHERN HEMISPHERE, OFF THE COAST OF METROPOLIS, IN TWO DAYS!
YOU CAN SEE WHY WE CALLED YOU...
SEED OF DESTRUCTION
"...IF EVER THERE WAS A JOB FOR SUPERMAN, THIS IS IT!"
Jerry Ordway
Script
Steve Rude
Art and Lettering
Glenn Whitmore - Color
Steve Rude-Cover

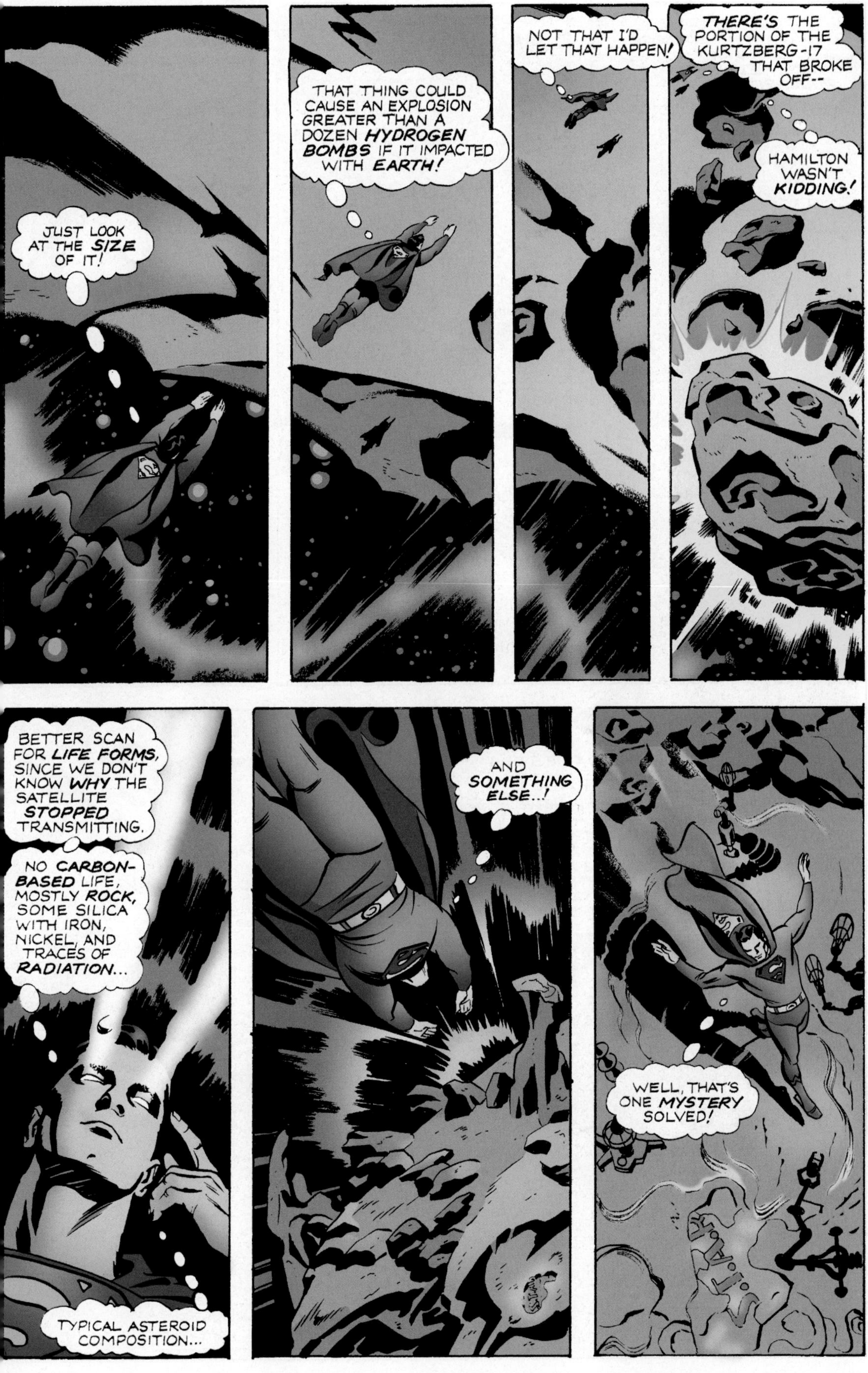
JUST LOOK AT THE SIZE OF IT!
THAT THING COULD CAUSE AN EXPLOSION GREATER THAN A DOZEN HYDROGEN BOMBS IF IT IMPACTED WITH EARTH!
NOT THAT I'D LET THAT HAPPEN!
THERE'S THE PORTION OF THE KURTZBERG-17 THAT BROKE OFF--
HAMILTON WASN'T KIDDING!
BETTER SCAN FOR LIFE FORMS, SINCE WE DON'T KNOW WHY THE SATELLITE STOPPED TRANSMITTING.
NO CARBON-BASED LIFE, MOSTLY ROCK, SOME SILICA WITH IRON, NICKEL, AND TRACES OF RADIATION...
TYPICAL ASTEROID COMPOSITION...
AND SOMETHING ELSE...!
WELL, THAT'S ONE MYSTERY SOLVED!

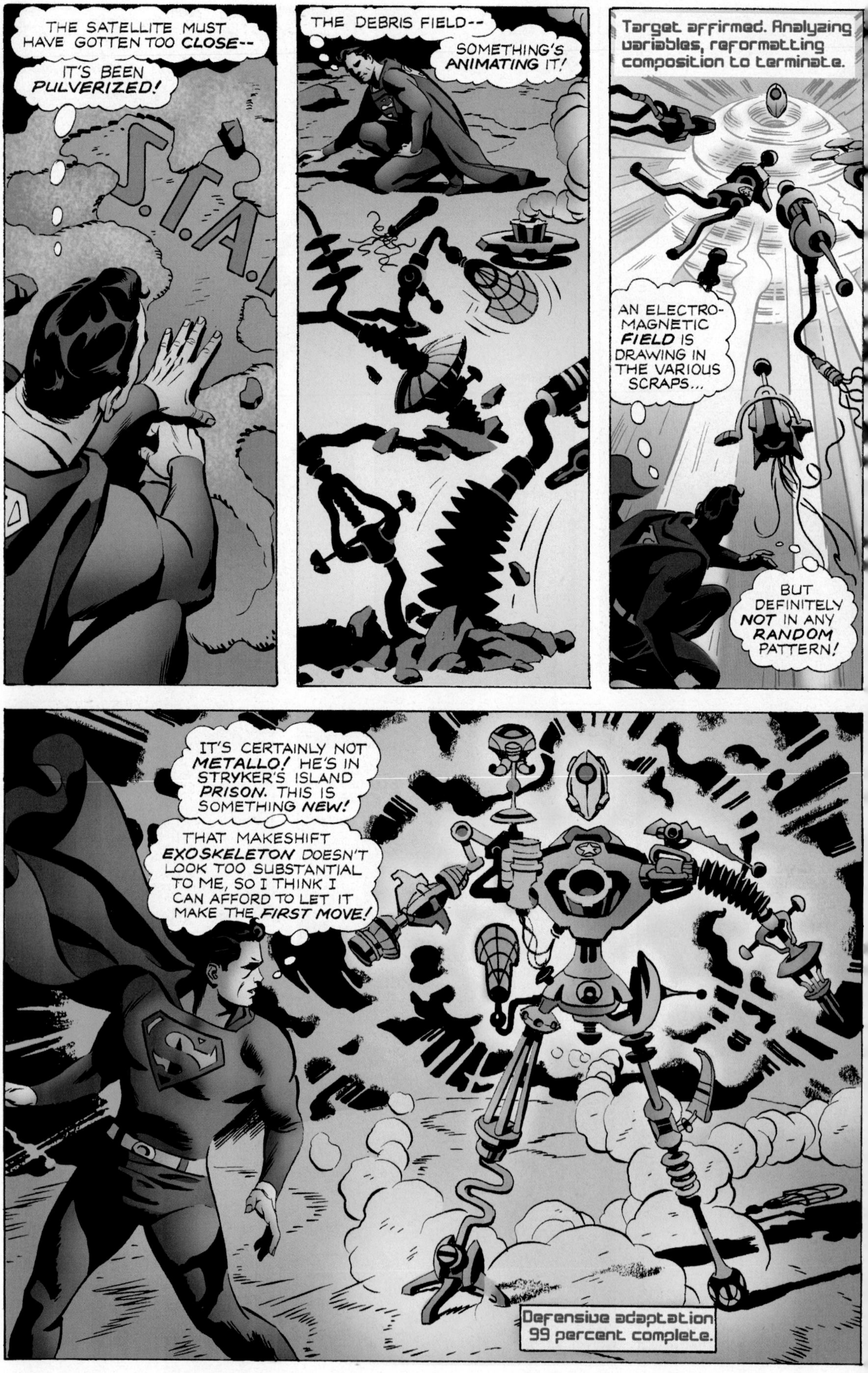
THE SATELLITE MUST HAVE GOTTEN TOO CLOSE--
IT'S BEEN PULVERIZED!
S.T.A.
THE DEBRIS FIELD--
SOMETHING'S ANIMATING IT!
Target affirmed. Analyzing variables, reformatting composition to terminate.
AN ELECTRO-MAGNETIC FIELD IS DRAWING IN THE VARIOUS SCRAPS...
BUT DEFINITELY NOT IN ANY RANDOM PATTERN!
IT'S CERTAINLY NOT METALLO! HE'S IN STRYKER'S ISLAND PRISON. THIS IS SOMETHING NEW!
THAT MAKESHIFT EXOSKELETON DOESN'T LOOK TOO SUBSTANTIAL TO ME, SO I THINK I CAN AFFORD TO LET IT MAKE THE FIRST MOVE!
Defensive adaptation 99 percent complete.

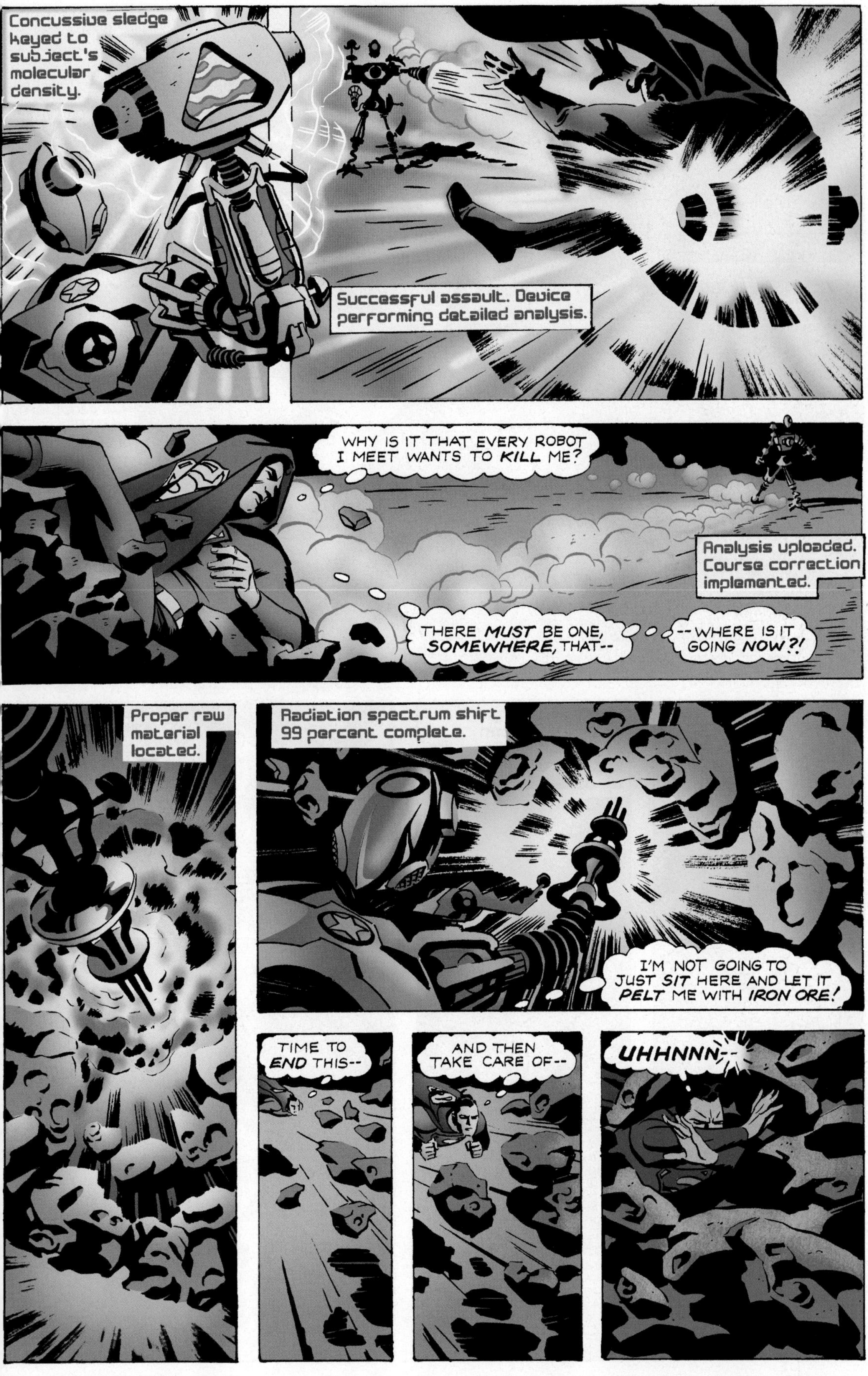
Concussive sledge keyed to subject's molecular density.
Successful assault. Device performing detailed analysis.
WHY IS IT THAT EVERY ROBOT I MEET WANTS TO KILL ME?
Analysis uploaded. Course correction implemented.
THERE MUST BE ONE, SOMEWHERE, THAT--
--WHERE IS IT GOING NOW?!
Proper raw material located.
Radiation spectrum shift 99 percent complete.
I'M NOT GOING TO JUST SIT HERE AND LET IT PELT ME WITH IRON ORE!
TIME TO END THIS--
AND THEN TAKE CARE OF--
UHHNNN--

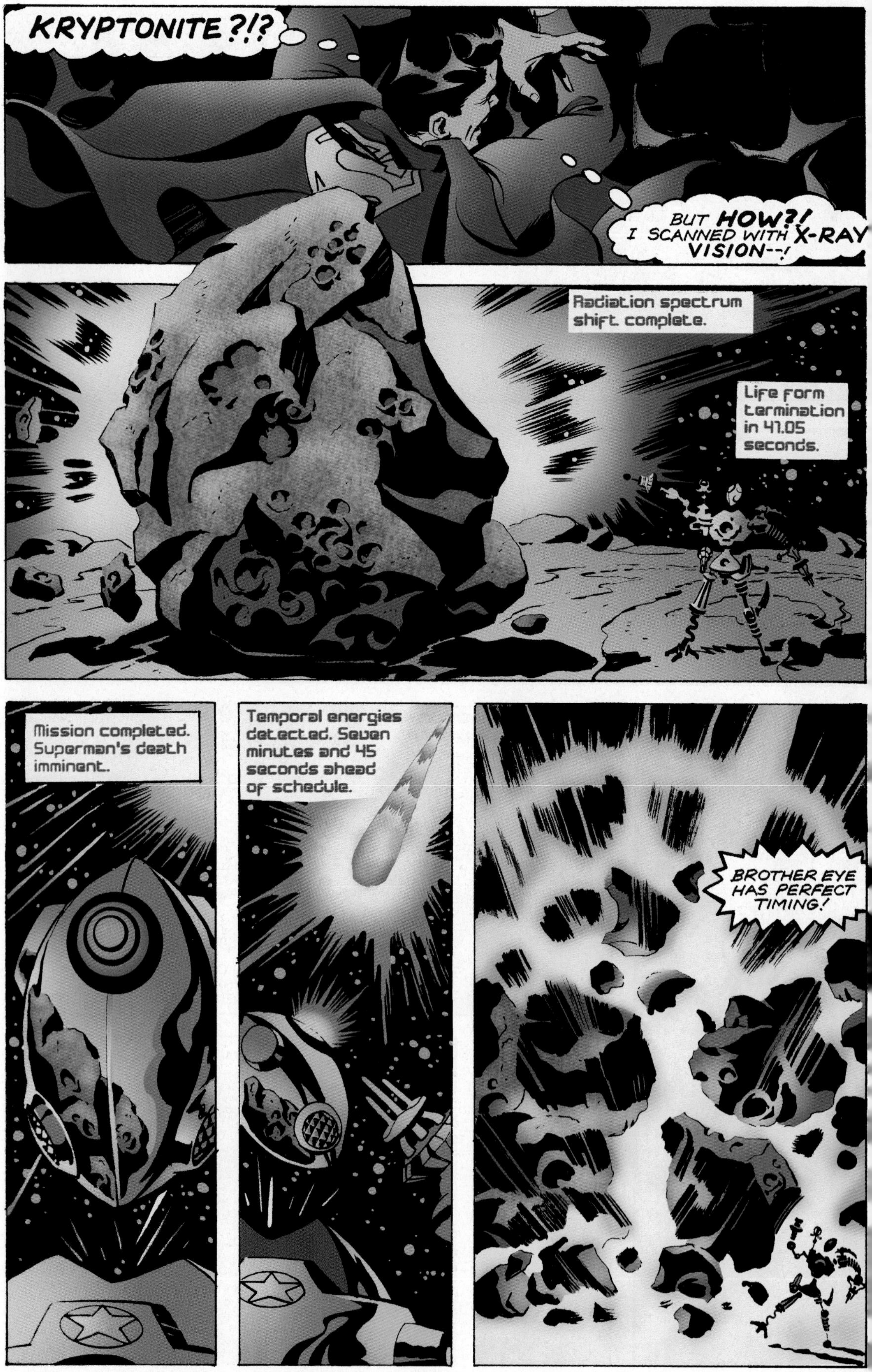

KRYPTONITE?!?
BUT HOW?! I SCANNED WITH X-RAY VISION--!
Radiation spectrum shift complete.
Life form termination in 47.05 seconds.
Mission completed. Superman's death imminent.
Temporal energies detected. Seven minutes and 45 seconds ahead of schedule.
BROTHER EYE HAS PERFECT TIMING!

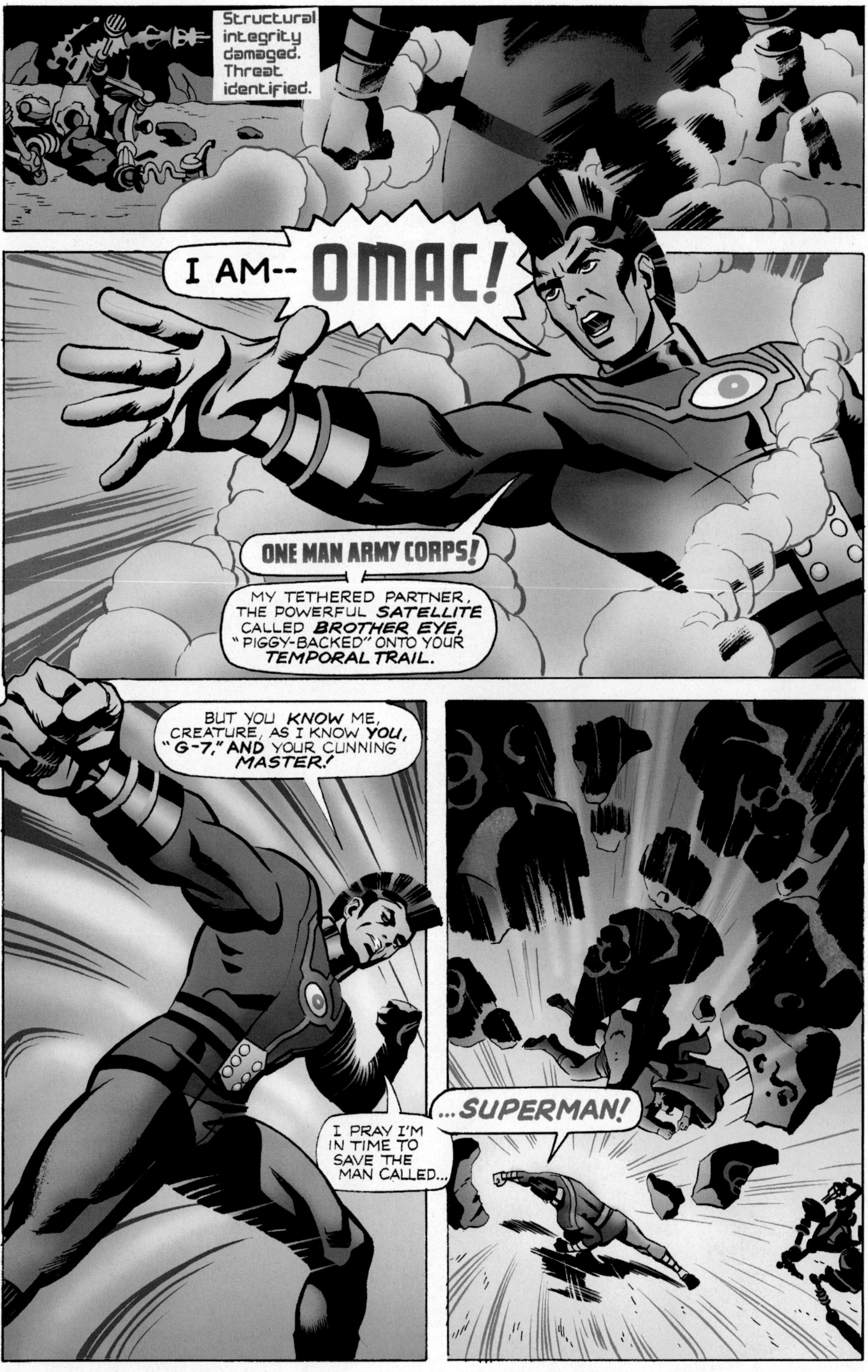
Structural integrity damaged. Threat identified.
I AM-- OMAC!
ONE MAN ARMY CORPS!
MY TETHERED PARTNER, THE POWERFUL SATELLITE CALLED BROTHER EYE, "PIGGY-BACKED" ONTO YOUR TEMPORAL TRAIL.
BUT YOU KNOW ME, CREATURE, AS I KNOW YOU, "G-7," AND YOUR CUNNING MASTER!
I PRAY I'M IN TIME TO SAVE THE MAN CALLED...
...SUPERMAN!

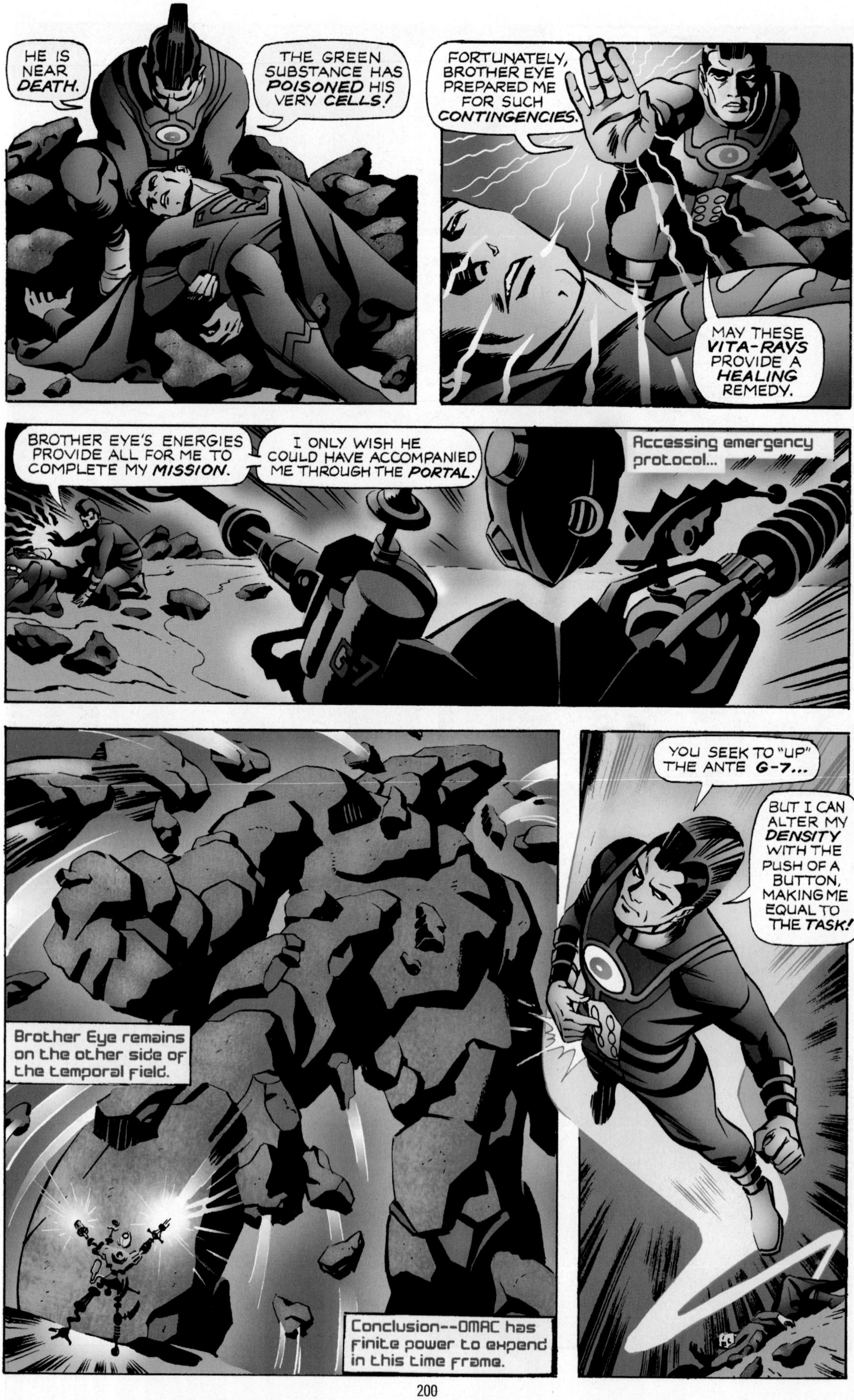
HE IS NEAR DEATH.
THE GREEN SUBSTANCE HAS POISONED HIS VERY CELLS!
FORTUNATELY, BROTHER EYE PREPARED ME FOR SUCH CONTINGENCIES.
MAY THESE VITA-RAYS PROVIDE A HEALING REMEDY.
BROTHER EYE'S ENERGIES PROVIDE ALL FOR ME TO COMPLETE MY MISSION.
I ONLY WISH HE COULD HAVE ACCOMPANIED ME THROUGH THE PORTAL.
Accessing emergency protocol...
G-7
Brother Eye remains on the other side of the temporal field.
Conclusion--OMAC has finite power to expend in this time frame.
YOU SEEK TO "UP" THE ANTE G-7...
BUT I CAN ALTER MY DENSITY WITH THE PUSH OF A BUTTON, MAKING ME EQUAL TO THE TASK!

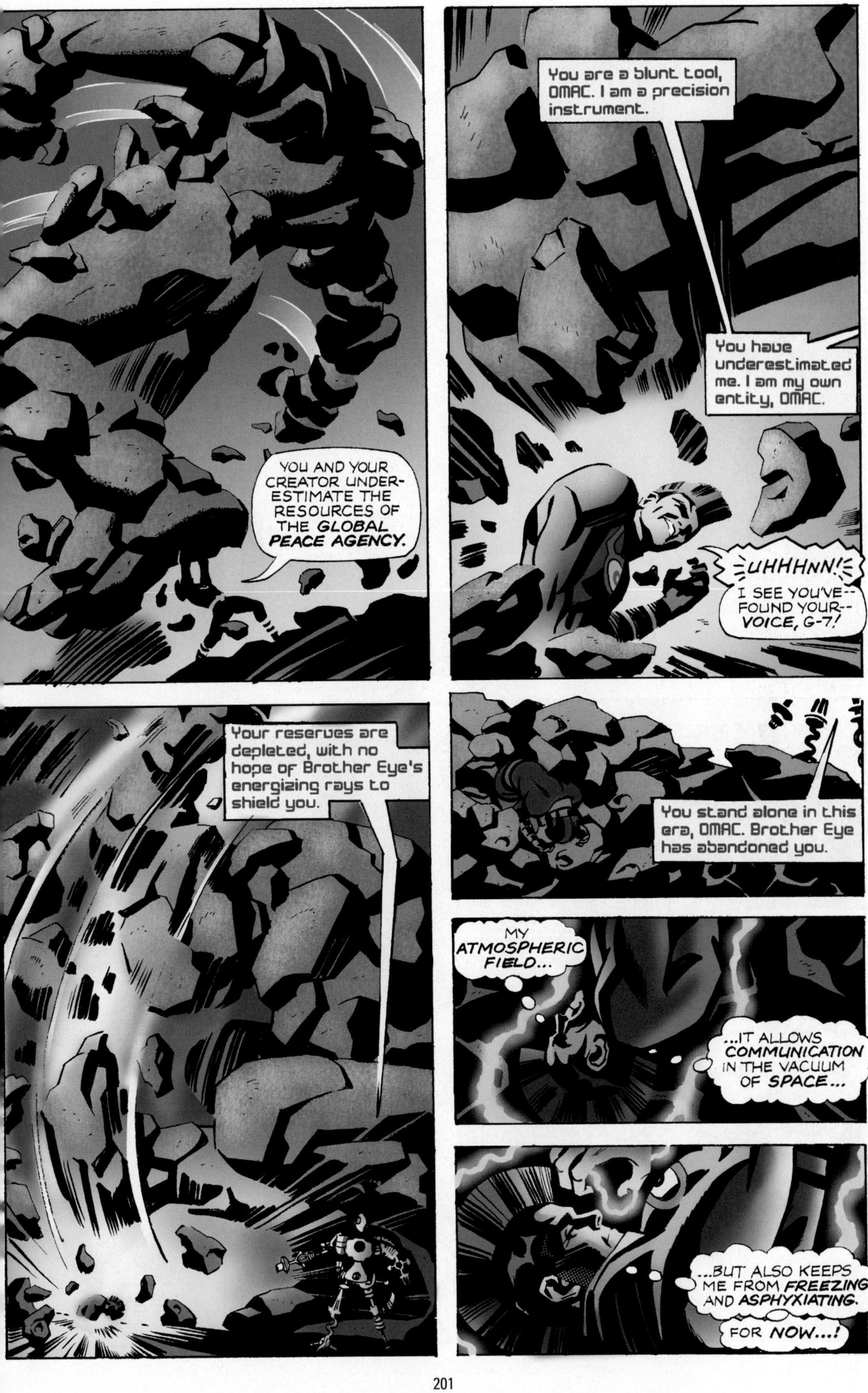
YOU AND YOUR CREATOR UNDER-ESTIMATE THE RESOURCES OF THE GLOBAL PEACE AGENCY.
You are a blunt tool, OMAC. I am a precision instrument.
You have underestimated me. I am my own entity, OMAC.
UHHHNN!
I SEE YOU'VE-- FOUND YOUR-- VOICE, G-7!
Your reserves are depleted, with no hope of Brother Eye's energizing rays to shield you.
You stand alone in this era, OMAC. Brother Eye has abandoned you.
MY ATMOSPHERIC FIELD...
...IT ALLOWS COMMUNICATION IN THE VACUUM OF SPACE...
...BUT ALSO KEEPS ME FROM FREEZING AND ASPHYXIATING.
FOR NOW...!

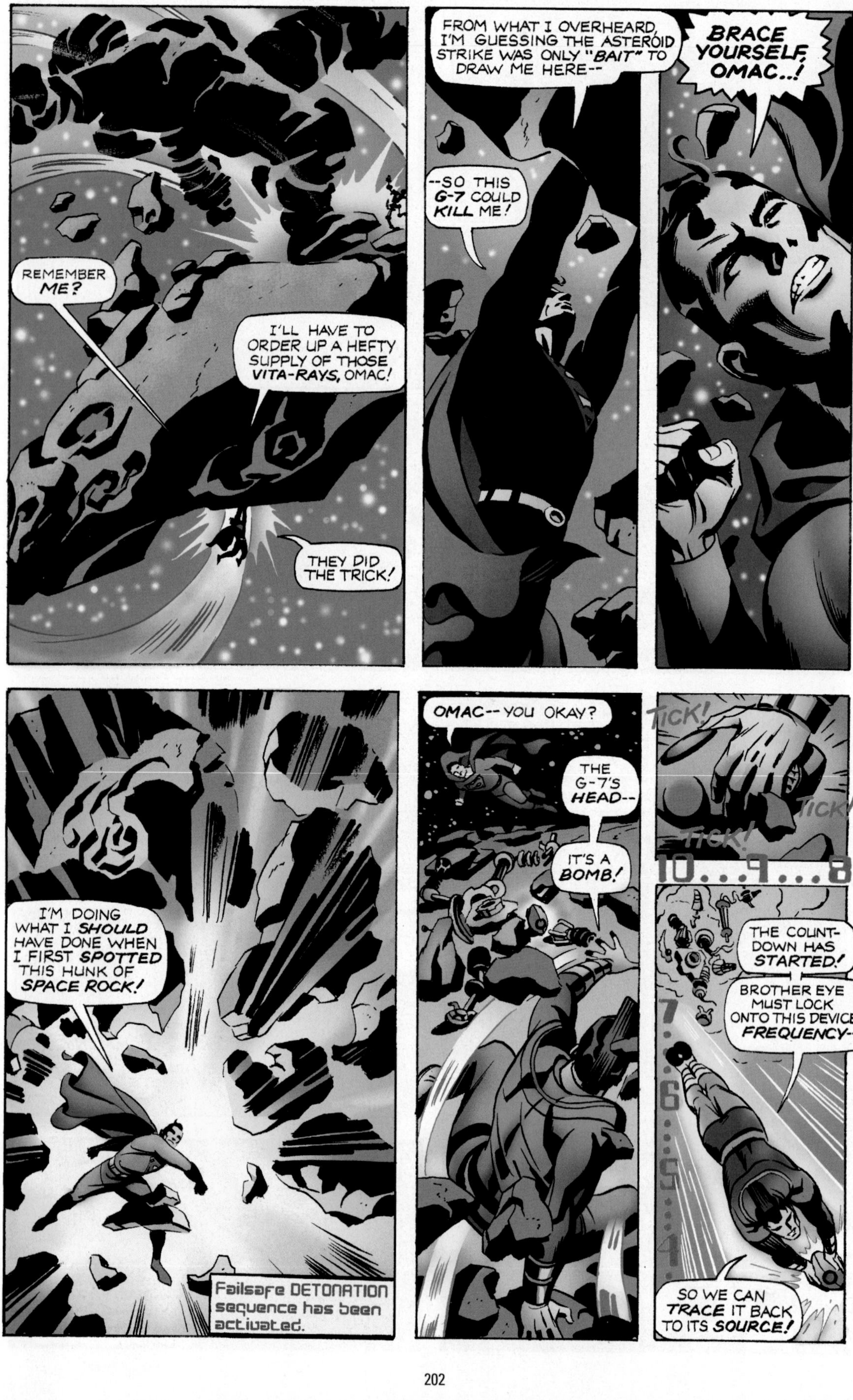

REMEMBER ME?
I'LL HAVE TO ORDER UP A HEFTY SUPPLY OF THOSE VITA-RAYS, OMAC!
THEY DID THE TRICK!
FROM WHAT I OVERHEARD, I'M GUESSING THE ASTEROID STRIKE WAS ONLY "BAIT" TO DRAW ME HERE--
--SO THIS G-7 COULD KILL ME!
BRACE YOURSELF, OMAC...!
I'M DOING WHAT I SHOULD HAVE DONE WHEN I FIRST SPOTTED THIS HUNK OF SPACE ROCK!
Failsafe DETONATION sequence has been activated.
OMAC-- YOU OKAY?
THE G-7'S HEAD--
IT'S A BOMB!
TICK!
TICK!
TICK!
10...9...8
THE COUNT-DOWN HAS STARTED!
BROTHER EYE MUST LOCK ONTO THIS DEVICE'S FREQUENCY--
7...6...5...4
SO WE CAN TRACE IT BACK TO ITS SOURCE!

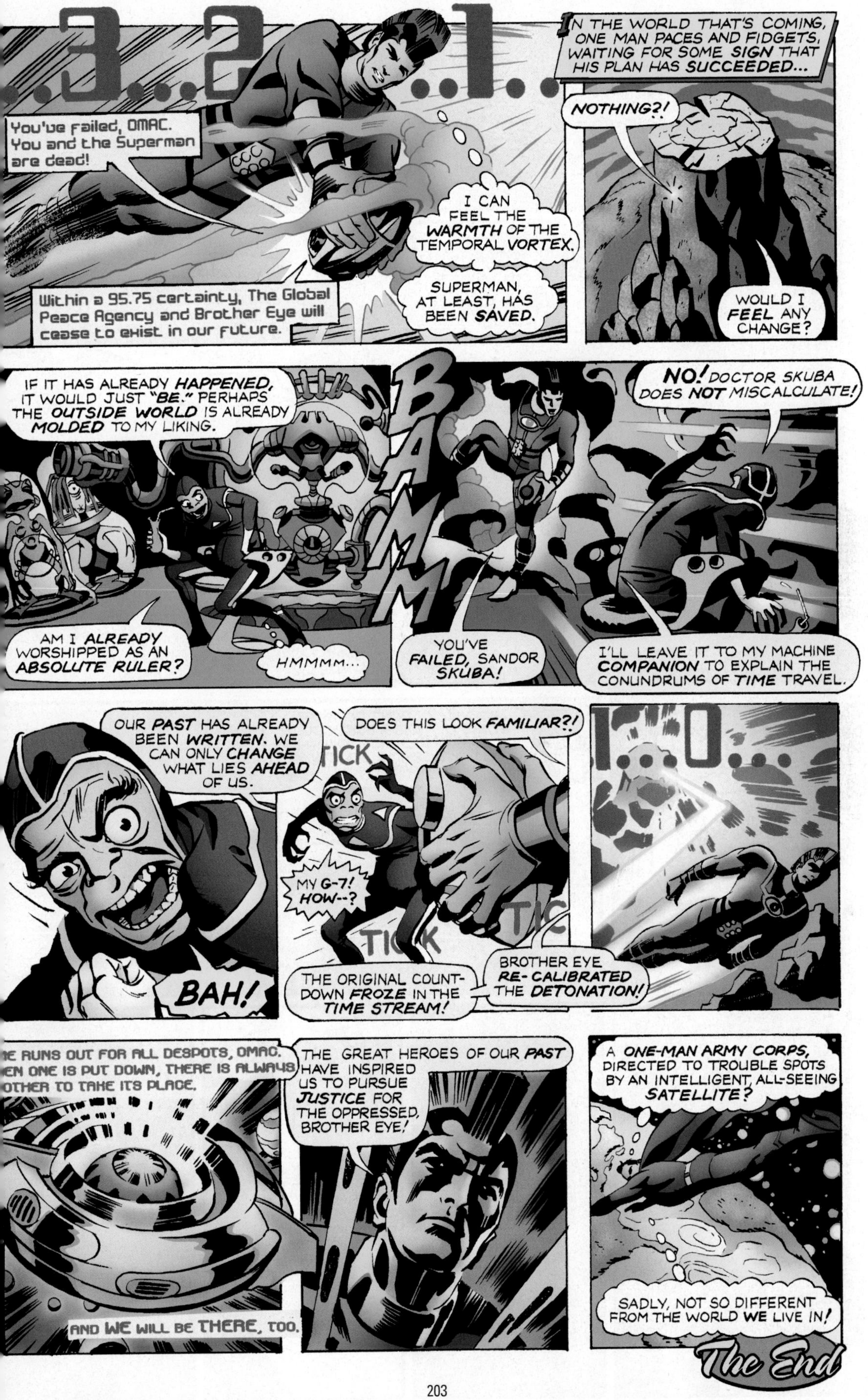

3...2...1...
IN THE WORLD THAT'S COMING, ONE MAN PACES AND FIDGETS, WAITING FOR SOME SIGN THAT HIS PLAN HAS SUCCEEDED...
You've failed, OMAC. You and the Superman are dead!
I CAN FEEL THE WARMTH OF THE TEMPORAL VORTEX.
SUPERMAN, AT LEAST, HAS BEEN SAVED.
Within a 95.75 certainty, The Global Peace Agency and Brother Eye will cease to exist in our future.
NOTHING?!
WOULD I FEEL ANY CHANGE?
IF IT HAS ALREADY HAPPENED, IT WOULD JUST "BE." PERHAPS THE OUTSIDE WORLD IS ALREADY MOLDED TO MY LIKING.
AM I ALREADY WORSHIPPED AS AN ABSOLUTE RULER?
HMMMM...
BAMMM
NO! DOCTOR SKUBA DOES NOT MISCALCULATE!
YOU'VE FAILED, SANDOR SKUBA!
I'LL LEAVE IT TO MY MACHINE COMPANION TO EXPLAIN THE CONUNDRUMS OF TIME TRAVEL.
OUR PAST HAS ALREADY BEEN WRITTEN. WE CAN ONLY CHANGE WHAT LIES AHEAD OF US.
BAH!
DOES THIS LOOK FAMILIAR?!
TICK
MY G-7! HOW--?
TICK
TICK
THE ORIGINAL COUNT-DOWN FROZE IN THE TIME STREAM!
BROTHER EYE RE-CALIBRATED THE DETONATION!
...1...0...
...E RUNS OUT FOR ALL DESPOTS, OMAC. ...EN ONE IS PUT DOWN, THERE IS ALWAYS ...OTHER TO TAKE ITS PLACE.
AND WE WILL BE THERE, TOO.
THE GREAT HEROES OF OUR PAST HAVE INSPIRED US TO PURSUE JUSTICE FOR THE OPPRESSED, BROTHER EYE!
A ONE-MAN ARMY CORPS, DIRECTED TO TROUBLE SPOTS BY AN INTELLIGENT, ALL-SEEING SATELLITE?
SADLY, NOT SO DIFFERENT FROM THE WORLD WE LIVE IN!
The End

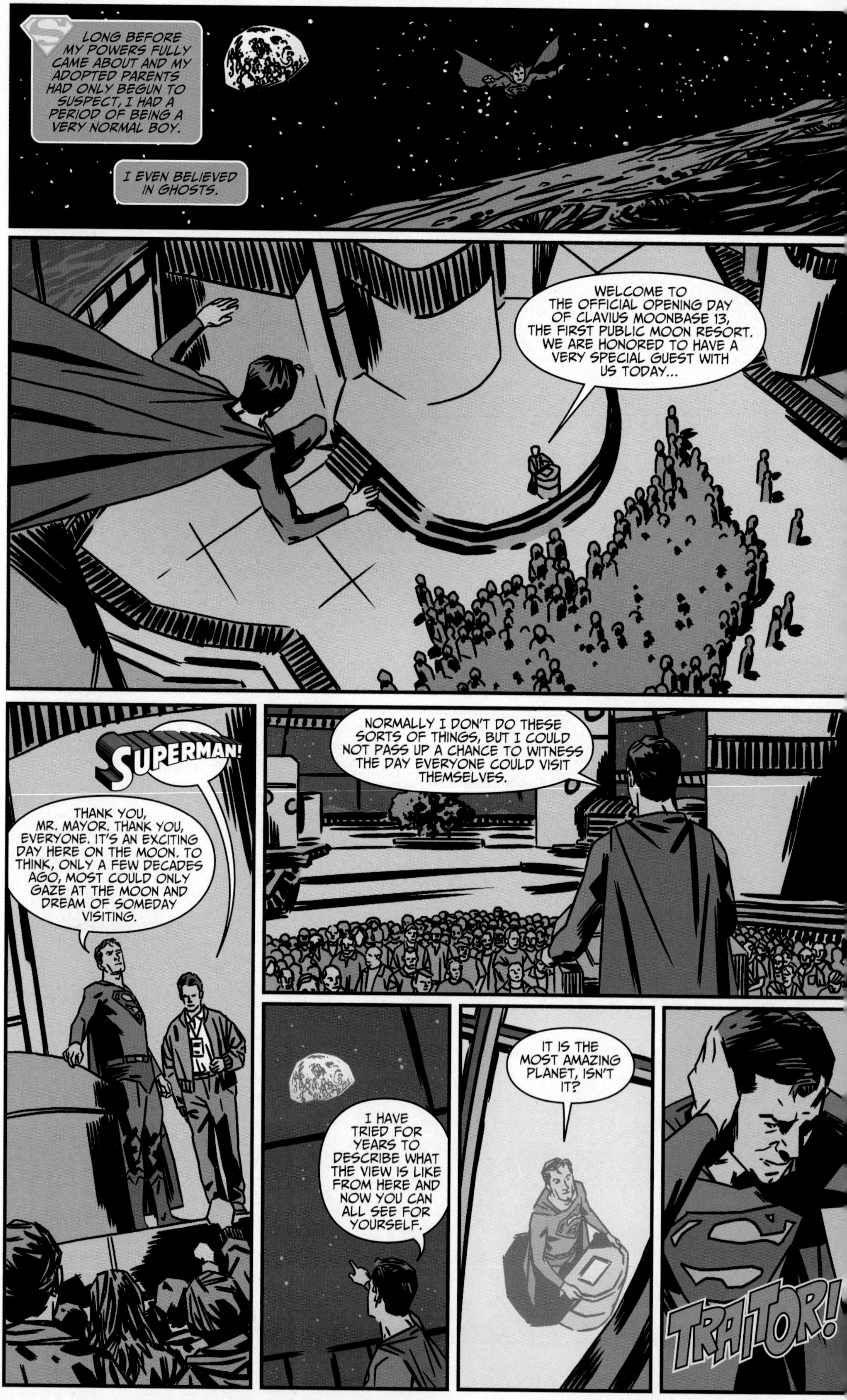

LONG BEFORE MY POWERS FULLY CAME ABOUT AND MY ADOPTED PARENTS HAD ONLY BEGUN TO SUSPECT, I HAD A PERIOD OF BEING A VERY NORMAL BOY.
I EVEN BELIEVED IN GHOSTS.
WELCOME TO THE OFFICIAL OPENING DAY OF CLAVIUS MOONBASE 13, THE FIRST PUBLIC MOON RESORT. WE ARE HONORED TO HAVE A VERY SPECIAL GUEST WITH US TODAY...
SUPERMAN!
THANK YOU, MR. MAYOR. THANK YOU, EVERYONE. IT'S AN EXCITING DAY HERE ON THE MOON. TO THINK, ONLY A FEW DECADES AGO, MOST COULD ONLY GAZE AT THE MOON AND DREAM OF SOMEDAY VISITING.
NORMALLY I DON'T DO THESE SORTS OF THINGS, BUT I COULD NOT PASS UP A CHANCE TO WITNESS THE DAY EVERYONE COULD VISIT THEMSELVES.
I HAVE TRIED FOR YEARS TO DESCRIBE WHAT THE VIEW IS LIKE FROM HERE AND NOW YOU CAN ALL SEE FOR YOURSELF.
IT IS THE MOST AMAZING PLANET, ISN'T IT?
TRAITOR!

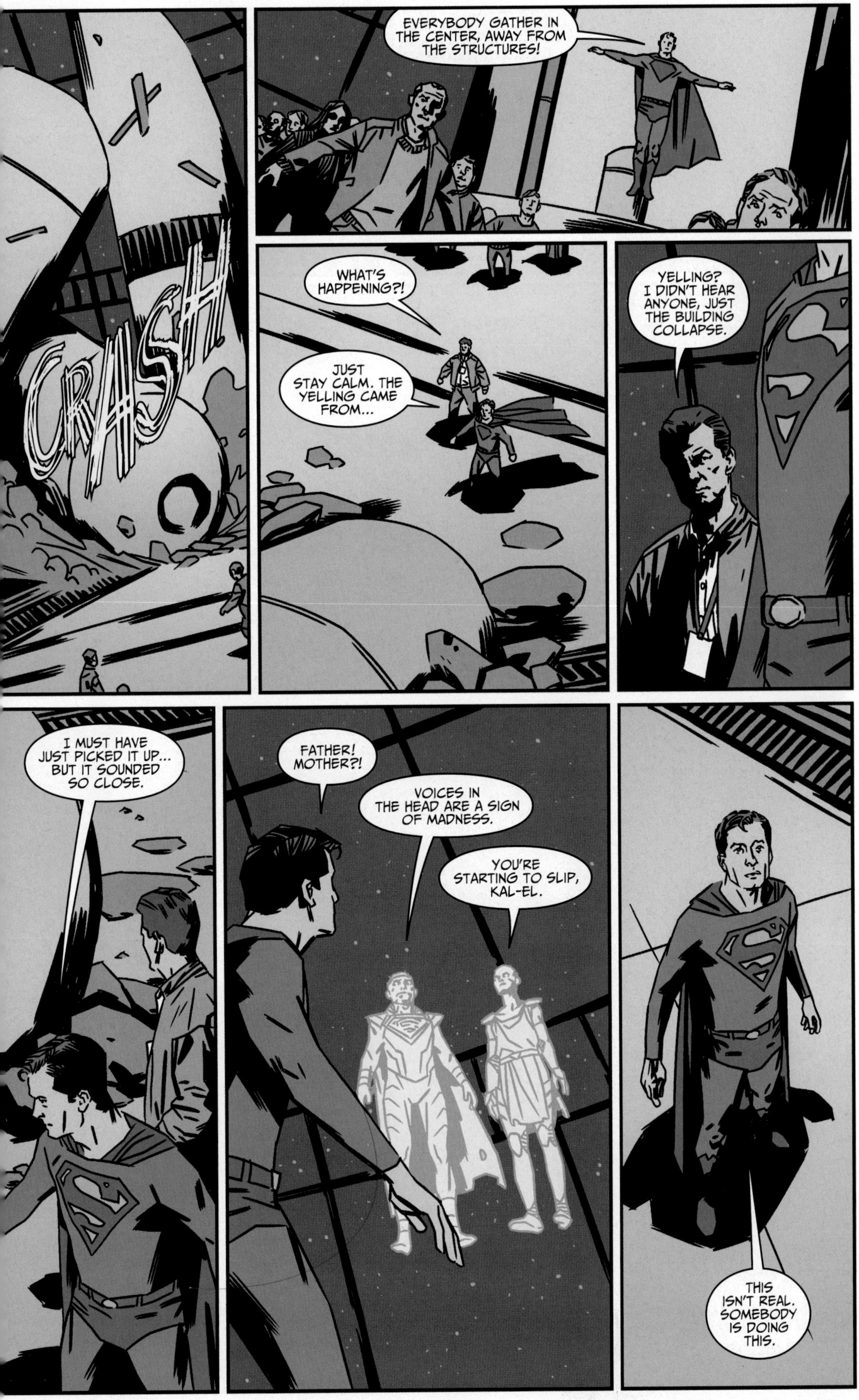

CRASH!
EVERYBODY GATHER IN THE CENTER, AWAY FROM THE STRUCTURES!
WHAT'S HAPPENING?!
JUST STAY CALM. THE YELLING CAME FROM...
YELLING? I DIDN'T HEAR ANYONE, JUST THE BUILDING COLLAPSE.
I MUST HAVE JUST PICKED IT UP... BUT IT SOUNDED SO CLOSE.
FATHER! MOTHER?!
VOICES IN THE HEAD ARE A SIGN OF MADNESS.
YOU'RE STARTING TO SLIP, KAL-EL.
THIS ISN'T REAL. SOMEBODY IS DOING THIS.

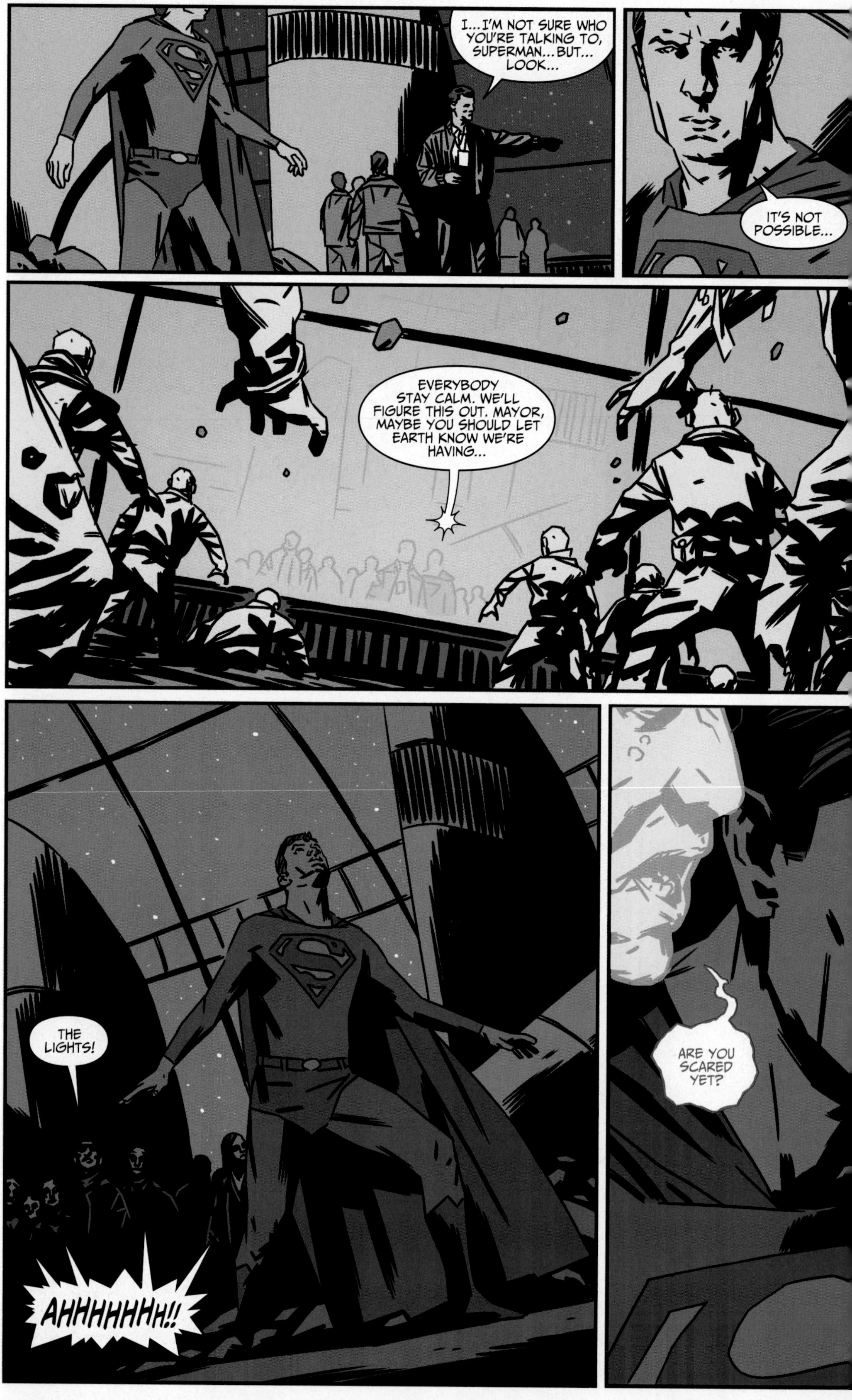
I... I'M NOT SURE WHO YOU'RE TALKING TO, SUPERMAN... BUT... LOOK...
IT'S NOT POSSIBLE...
EVERYBODY STAY CALM. WE'LL FIGURE THIS OUT. MAYOR, MAYBE YOU SHOULD LET EARTH KNOW WE'RE HAVING...
THE LIGHTS!
AHHHHHHH!!
ARE YOU SCARED YET?

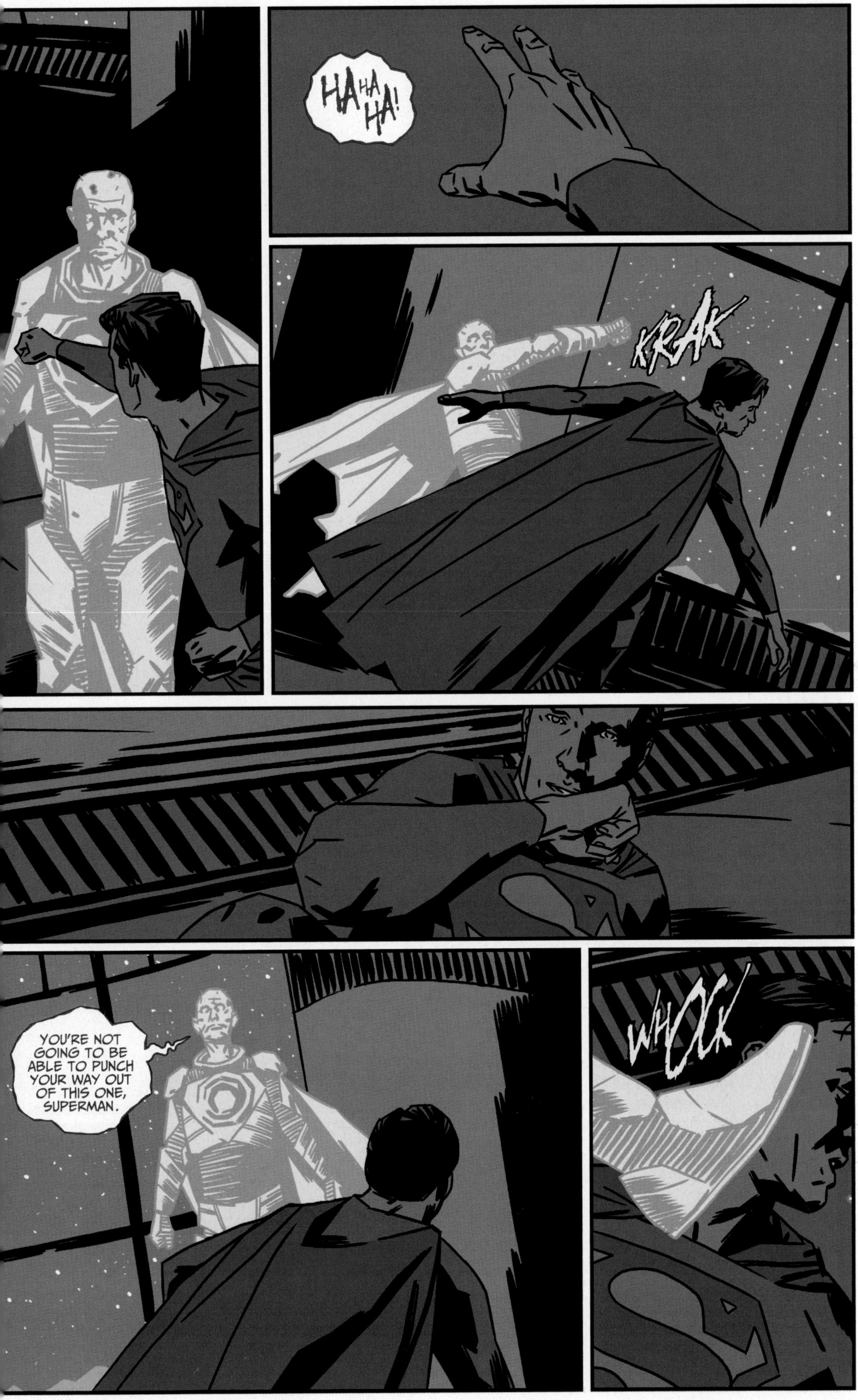
HA HA HA!
KRAK
YOU'RE NOT GOING TO BE ABLE TO PUNCH YOUR WAY OUT OF THIS ONE, SUPERMAN.
WHOCK

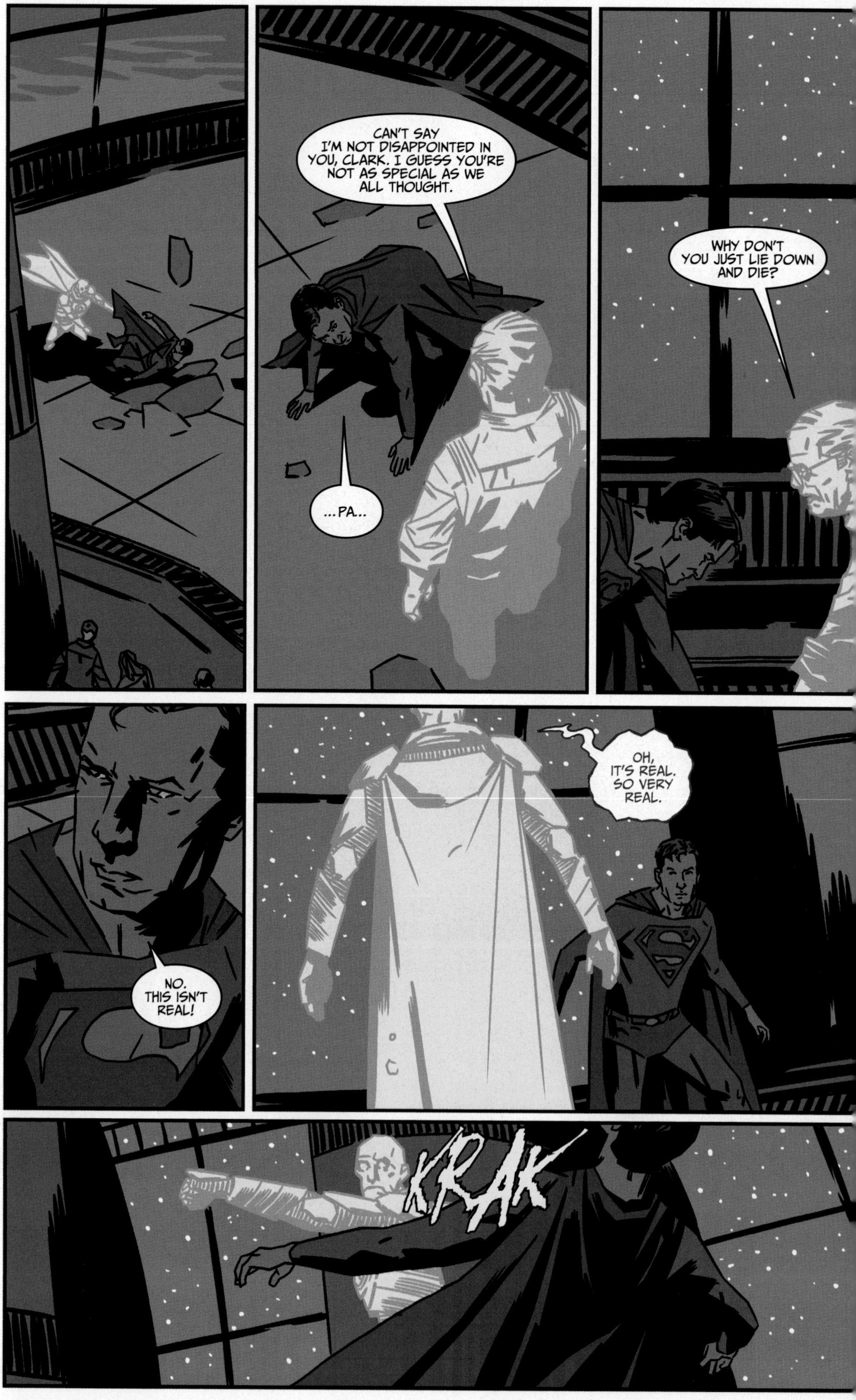
CAN'T SAY I'M NOT DISAPPOINTED IN YOU, CLARK. I GUESS YOU'RE NOT AS SPECIAL AS WE ALL THOUGHT.
...PA...
WHY DON'T YOU JUST LIE DOWN AND DIE?
NO. THIS ISN'T REAL!
OH, IT'S REAL. SO VERY REAL.
KRAK

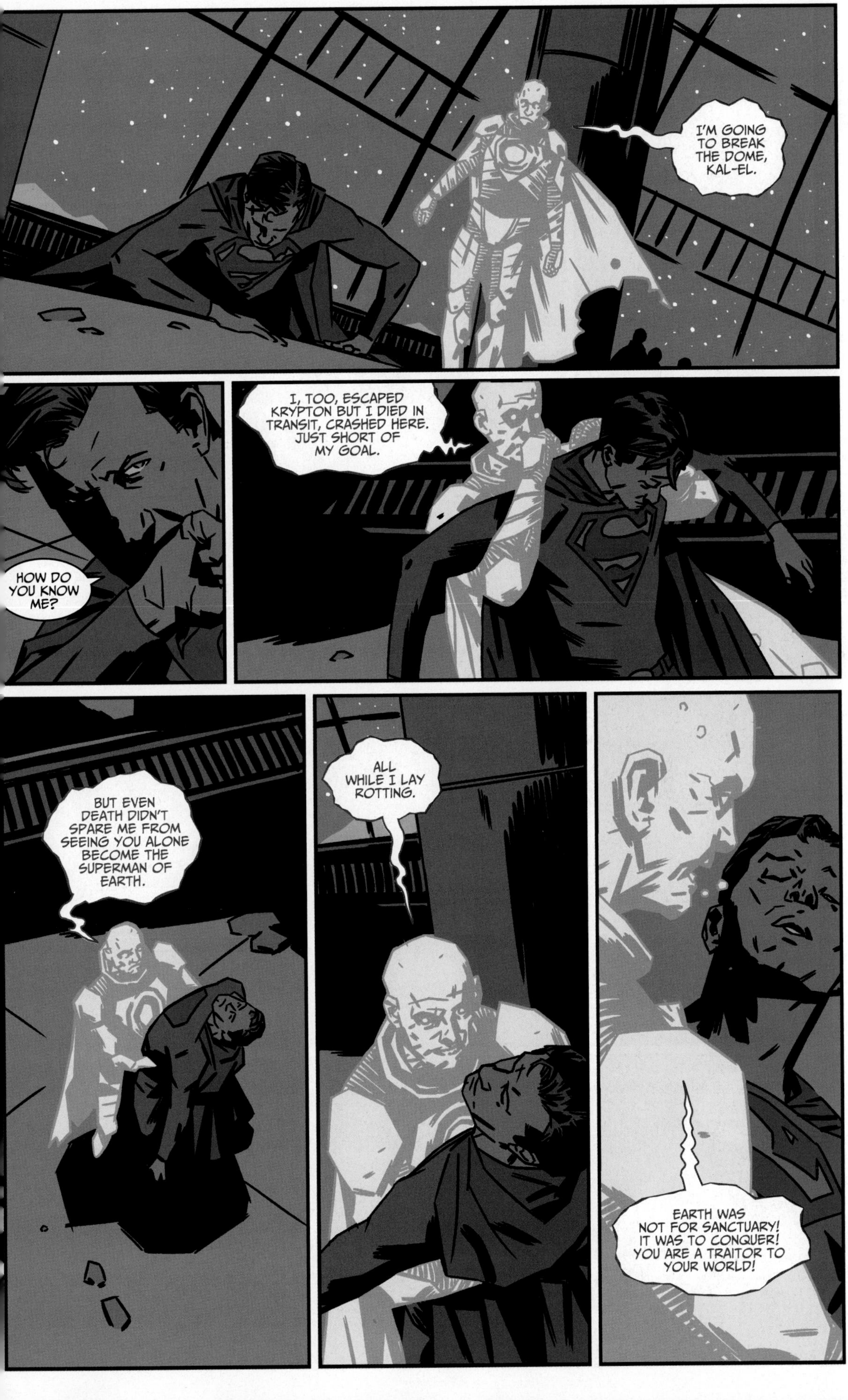
I'M GOING TO BREAK THE DOME, KAL-EL.
HOW DO YOU KNOW ME?
I, TOO, ESCAPED KRYPTON BUT I DIED IN TRANSIT, CRASHED HERE. JUST SHORT OF MY GOAL.
BUT EVEN DEATH DIDN'T SPARE ME FROM SEEING YOU ALONE BECOME THE SUPERMAN OF EARTH.
ALL WHILE I LAY ROTTING.
EARTH WAS NOT FOR SANCTUARY! IT WAS TO CONQUER! YOU ARE A TRAITOR TO YOUR WORLD!

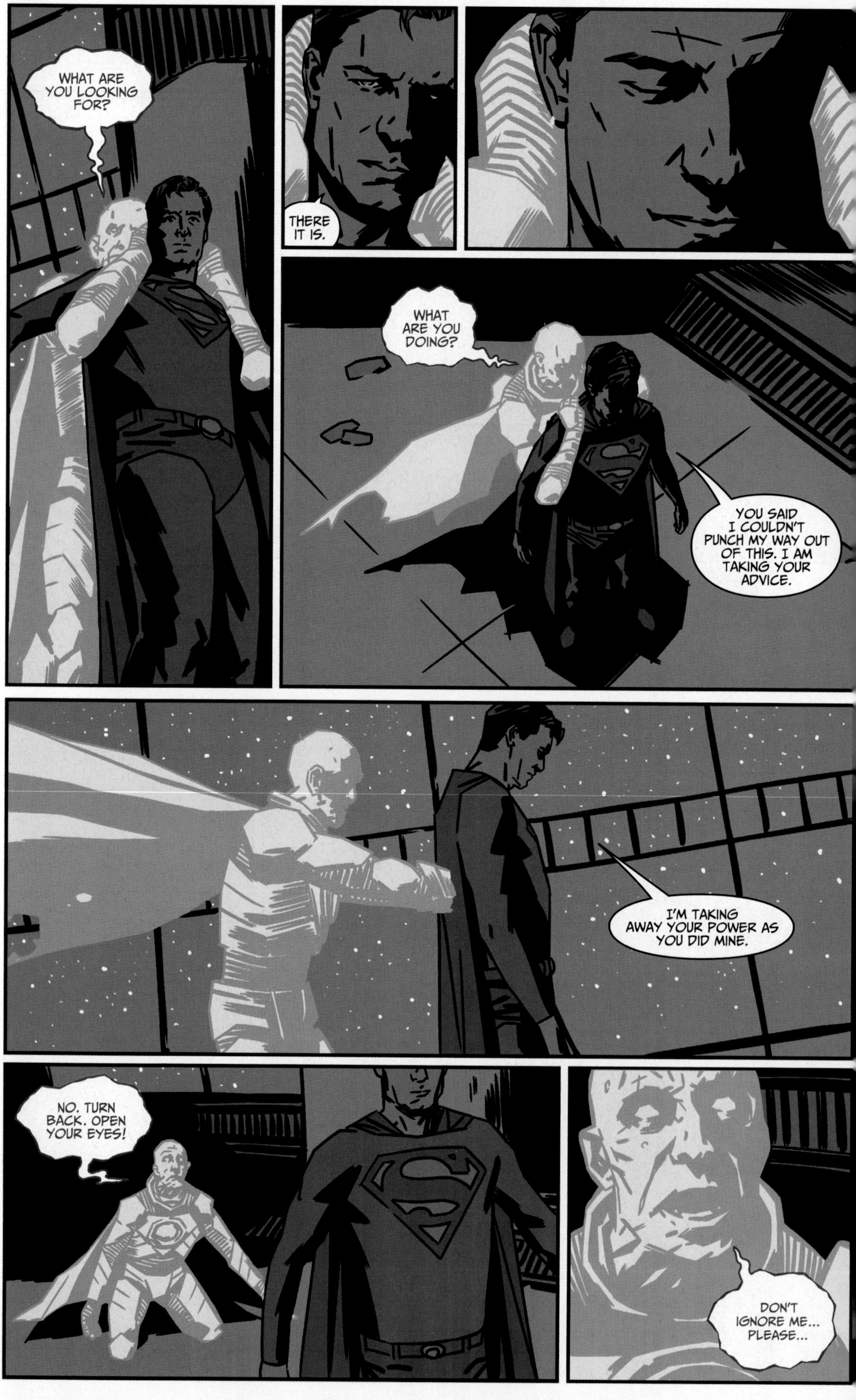
WHAT ARE YOU LOOKING FOR?
THERE IT IS.
WHAT ARE YOU DOING?
YOU SAID I COULDN'T PUNCH MY WAY OUT OF THIS. I AM TAKING YOUR ADVICE.
I'M TAKING AWAY YOUR POWER AS YOU DID MINE.
NO. TURN BACK. OPEN YOUR EYES!
DON'T IGNORE ME... PLEASE...

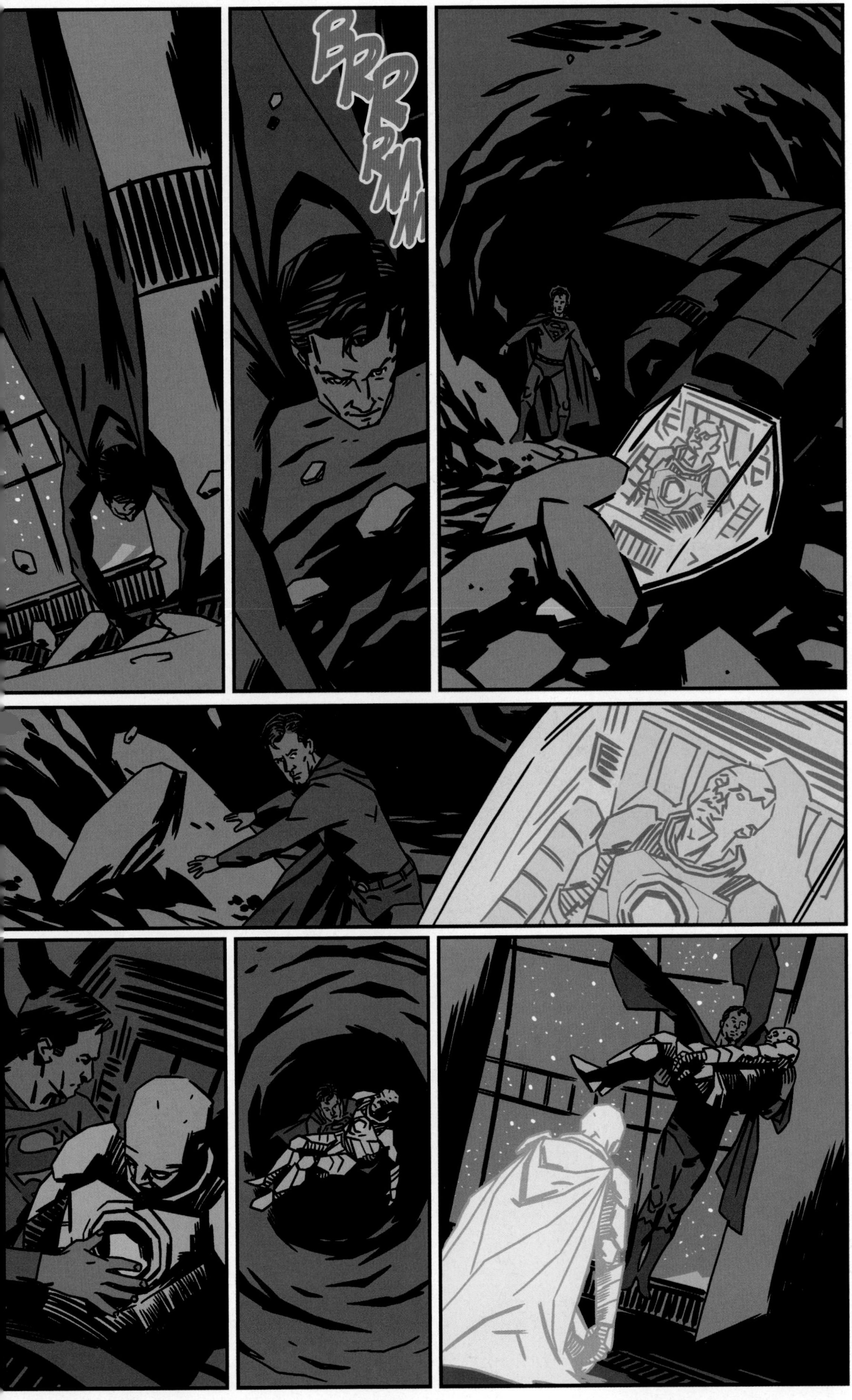
BRRRMM

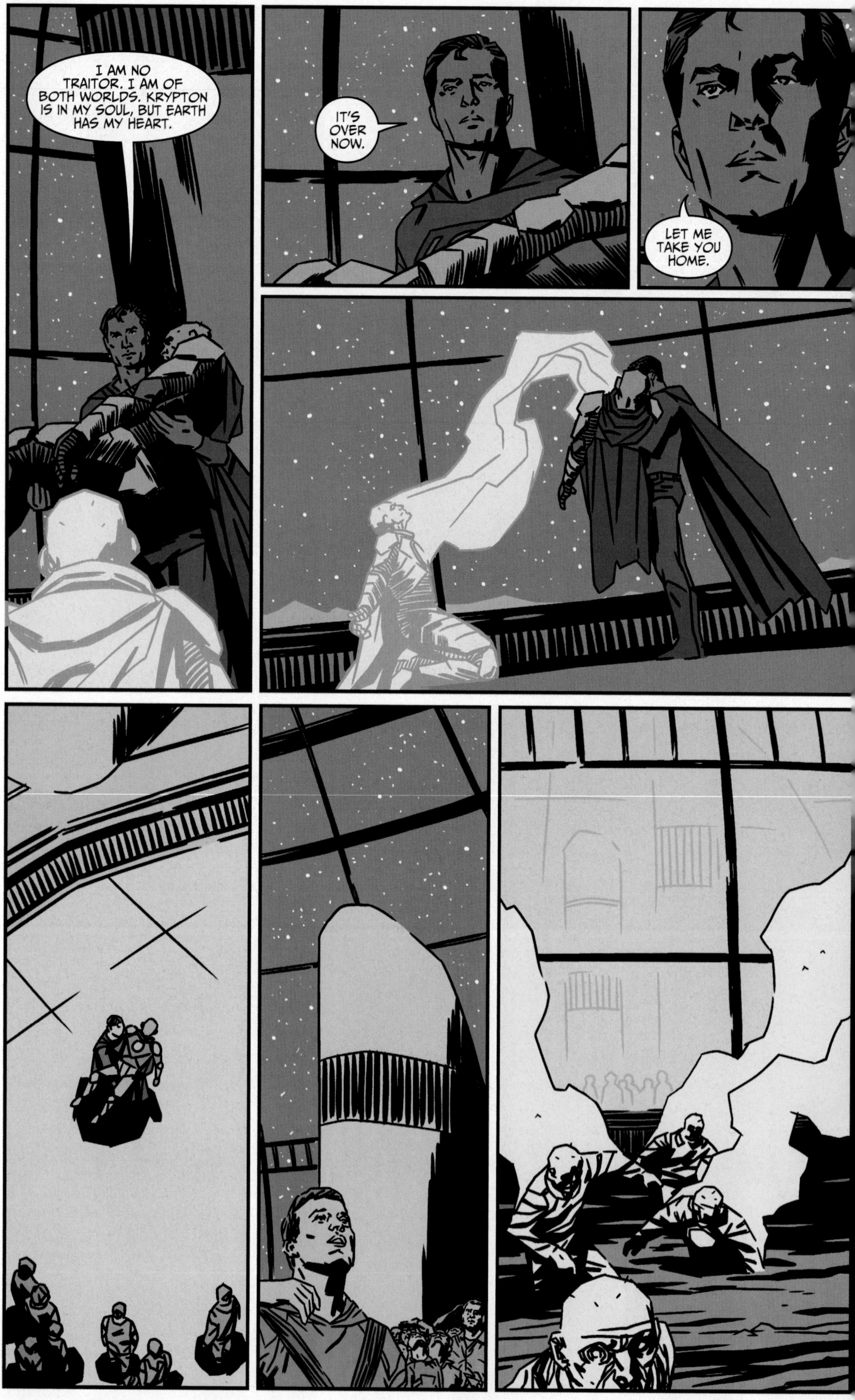
I AM NO TRAITOR. I AM OF BOTH WORLDS. KRYPTON IS IN MY SOUL, BUT EARTH HAS MY HEART.
IT'S OVER NOW.
LET ME TAKE YOU HOME.

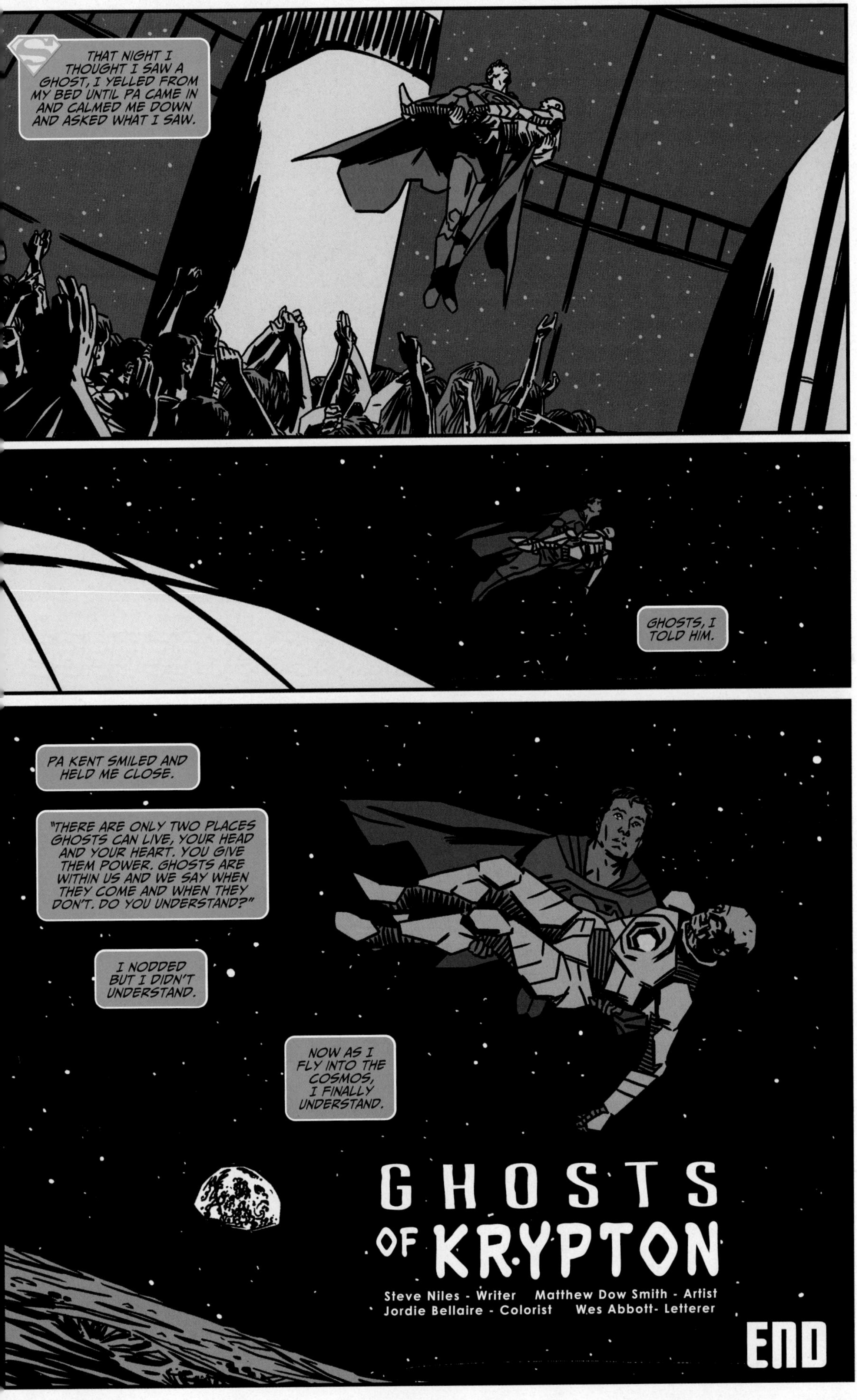
THAT NIGHT I THOUGHT I SAW A GHOST, I YELLED FROM MY BED UNTIL PA CAME IN AND CALMED ME DOWN AND ASKED WHAT I SAW.
GHOSTS, I TOLD HIM.
PA KENT SMILED AND HELD ME CLOSE.
"THERE ARE ONLY TWO PLACES GHOSTS CAN LIVE, YOUR HEAD AND YOUR HEART. YOU GIVE THEM POWER. GHOSTS ARE WITHIN US AND WE SAY WHEN THEY COME AND WHEN THEY DON'T. DO YOU UNDERSTAND?"
I NODDED BUT I DIDN'T UNDERSTAND.
NOW AS I FLY INTO THE COSMOS, I FINALLY UNDERSTAND.
GHOSTS OF KRYPTON
Steve Niles - Writer Matthew Dow Smith - Artist
Jordie Bellaire - Colorist Wes Abbott- Letterer
END

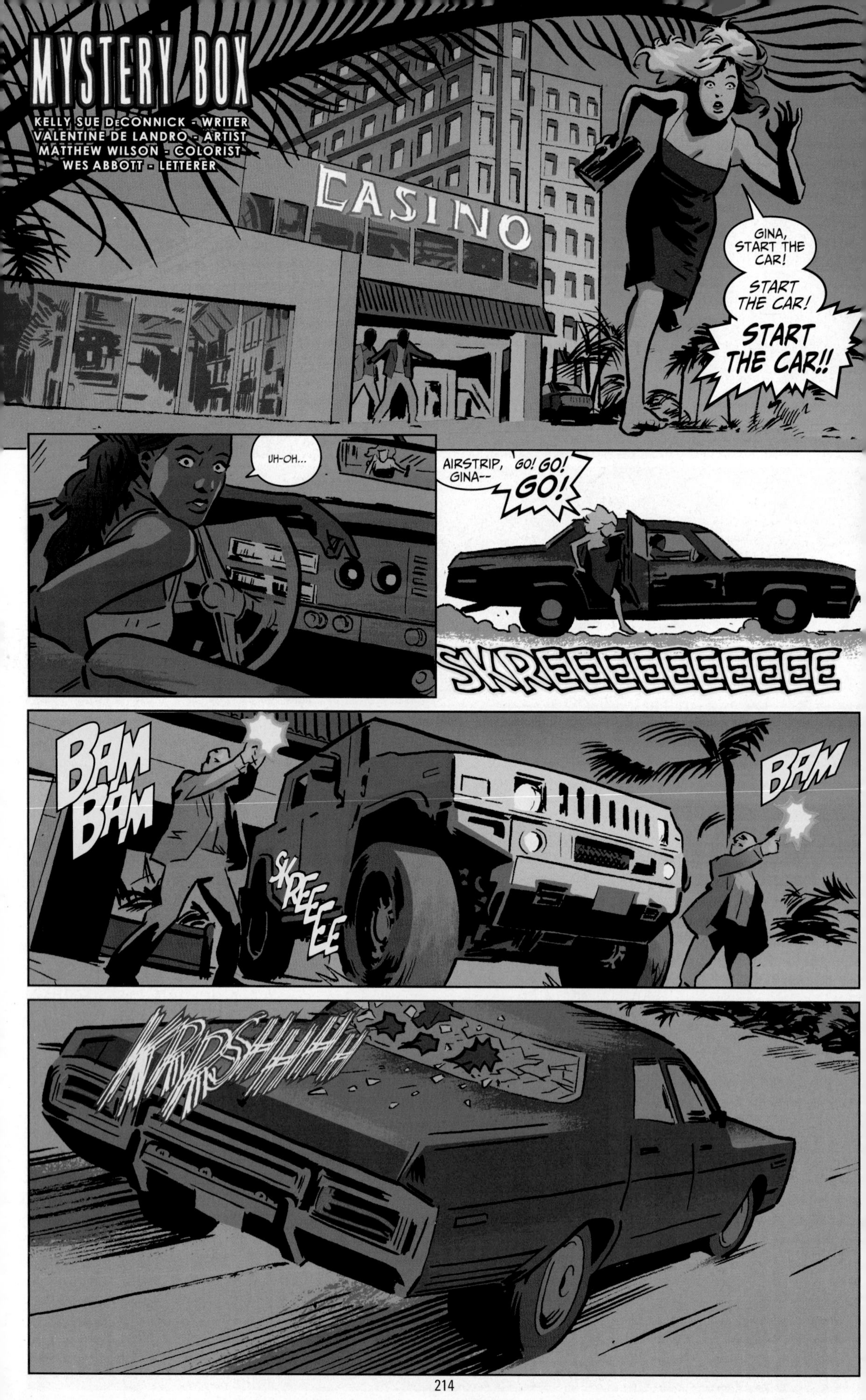
MYSTERY BOX
KELLY SUE DECONNICK - WRITER
VALENTINE DE LANDRO - ARTIST
MATTHEW WILSON - COLORIST
WES ABBOTT - LETTERER
CASINO
GINA, START THE CAR!
START THE CAR!
START THE CAR!!
UH-OH...
AIRSTRIP, GINA--
GO! GO! GO!
SKREEEEEEEEEEEE
BAM BAM
SKREEEEE
BAM
KRRSHHHH

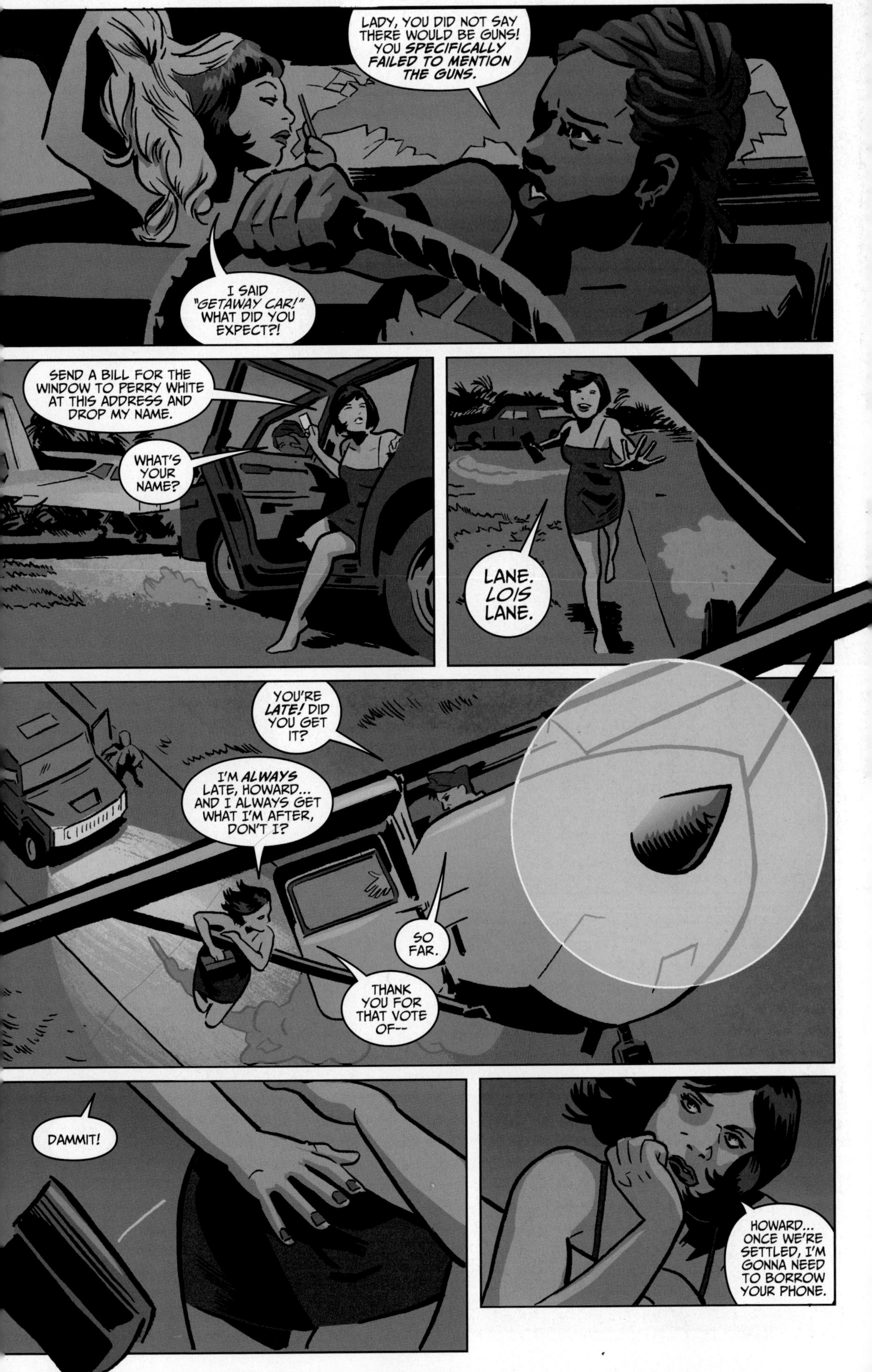
LADY, YOU DID NOT SAY THERE WOULD BE GUNS! YOU SPECIFICALLY FAILED TO MENTION THE GUNS.
I SAID "GETAWAY CAR!" WHAT DID YOU EXPECT?!
SEND A BILL FOR THE WINDOW TO PERRY WHITE AT THIS ADDRESS AND DROP MY NAME.
WHAT'S YOUR NAME?
LANE. LOIS LANE.
YOU'RE LATE! DID YOU GET IT?
I'M ALWAYS LATE, HOWARD... AND I ALWAYS GET WHAT I'M AFTER, DON'T I?
SO FAR.
THANK YOU FOR THAT VOTE OF--
DAMMIT!
HOWARD... ONCE WE'RE SETTLED, I'M GONNA NEED TO BORROW YOUR PHONE.

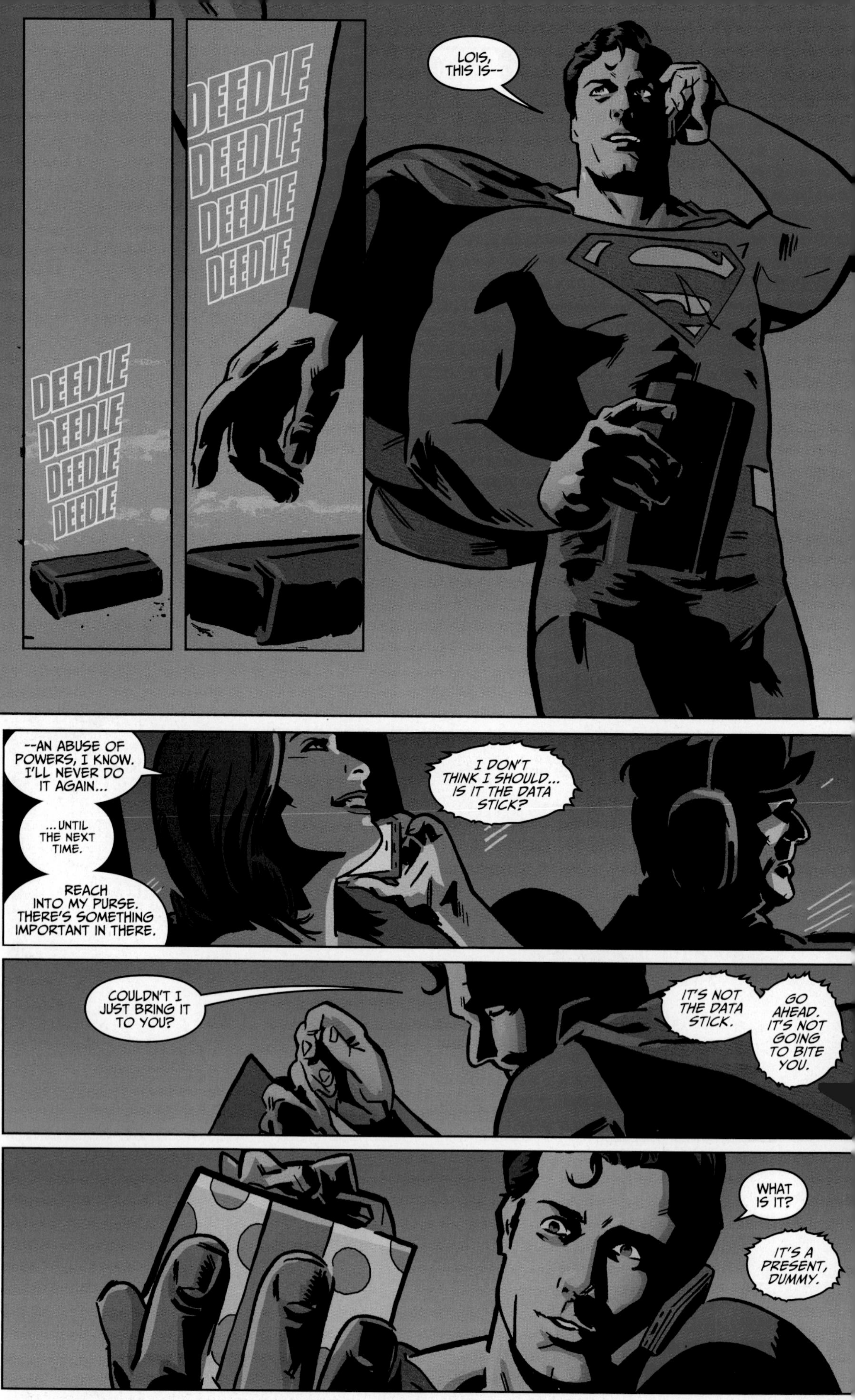
DEEDLE
DEEDLE
DEEDLE
DEEDLE
DEEDLE
DEEDLE
DEEDLE
DEEDLE
LOIS, THIS IS--
--AN ABUSE OF POWERS, I KNOW. I'LL NEVER DO IT AGAIN...
...UNTIL THE NEXT TIME.
REACH INTO MY PURSE. THERE'S SOMETHING IMPORTANT IN THERE.
I DON'T THINK I SHOULD... IS IT THE DATA STICK?
COULDN'T I JUST BRING IT TO YOU?
IT'S NOT THE DATA STICK.
GO AHEAD. IT'S NOT GOING TO BITE YOU.
WHAT IS IT?
IT'S A PRESENT, DUMMY.

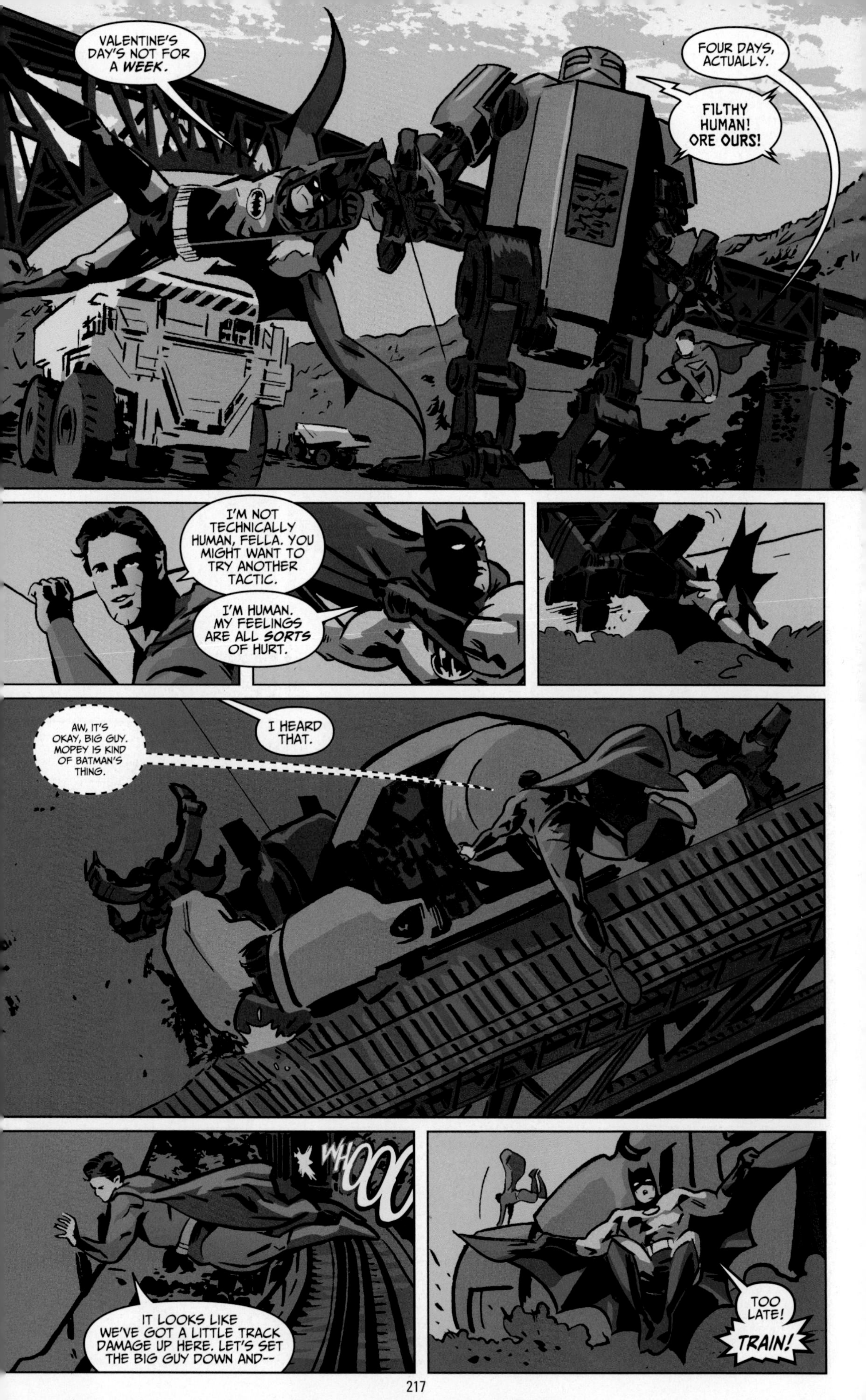

VALENTINE'S DAY'S NOT FOR A WEEK.
FOUR DAYS, ACTUALLY.
FILTHY HUMAN! ORE OURS!
I'M NOT TECHNICALLY HUMAN, FELLA. YOU MIGHT WANT TO TRY ANOTHER TACTIC.
I'M HUMAN. MY FEELINGS ARE ALL SORTS OF HURT.
AW, IT'S OKAY, BIG GUY. MOPEY IS KIND OF BATMAN'S THING.
I HEARD THAT.
WHOOO
IT LOOKS LIKE WE'VE GOT A LITTLE TRACK DAMAGE UP HERE. LET'S SET THE BIG GUY DOWN AND--
TOO LATE! TRAIN!

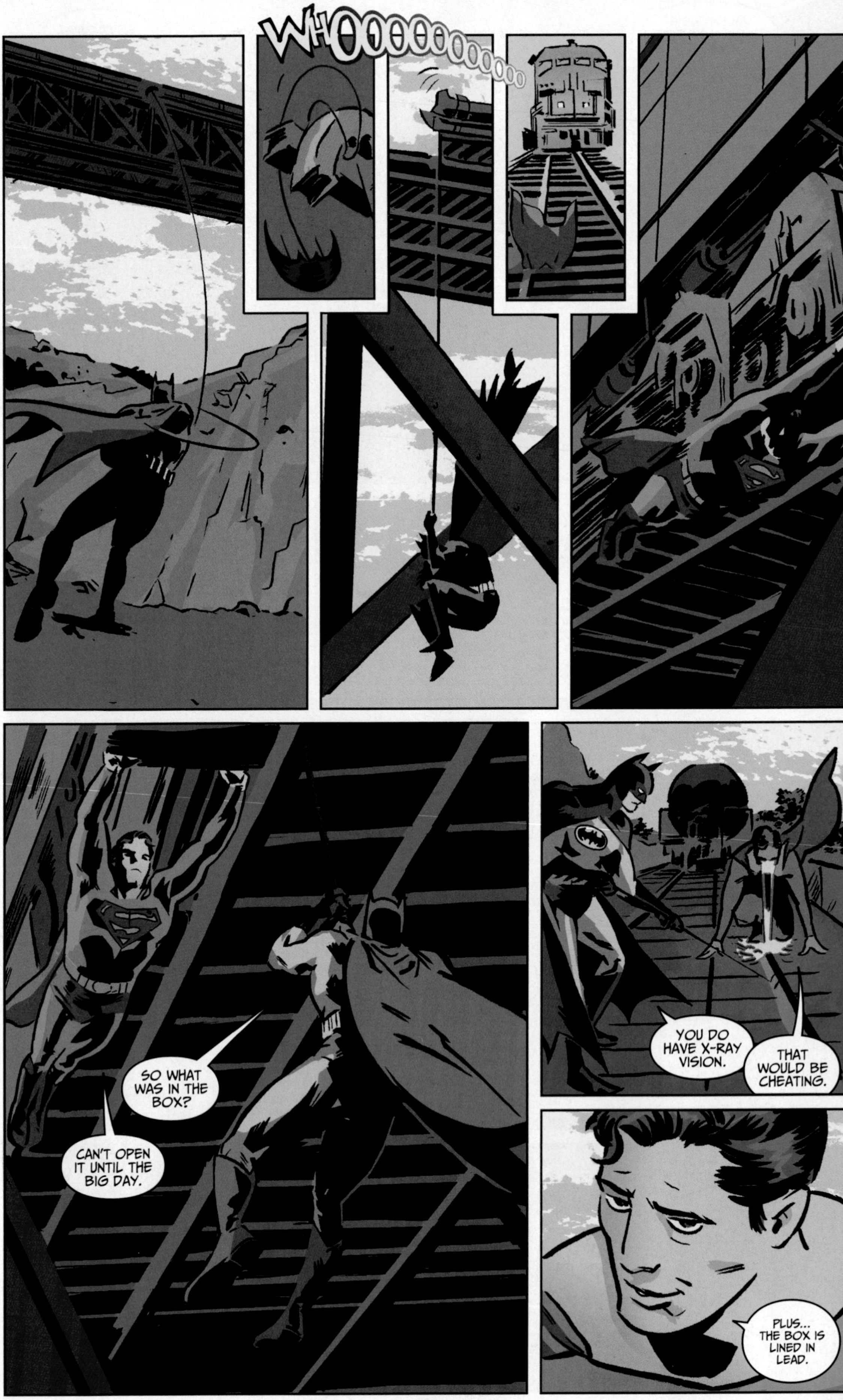
WHOOOOOOOOOOOOO
SO WHAT WAS IN THE BOX?
CAN'T OPEN IT UNTIL THE BIG DAY.
YOU DO HAVE X-RAY VISION.
THAT WOULD BE CHEATING.
PLUS... THE BOX IS LINED IN LEAD.

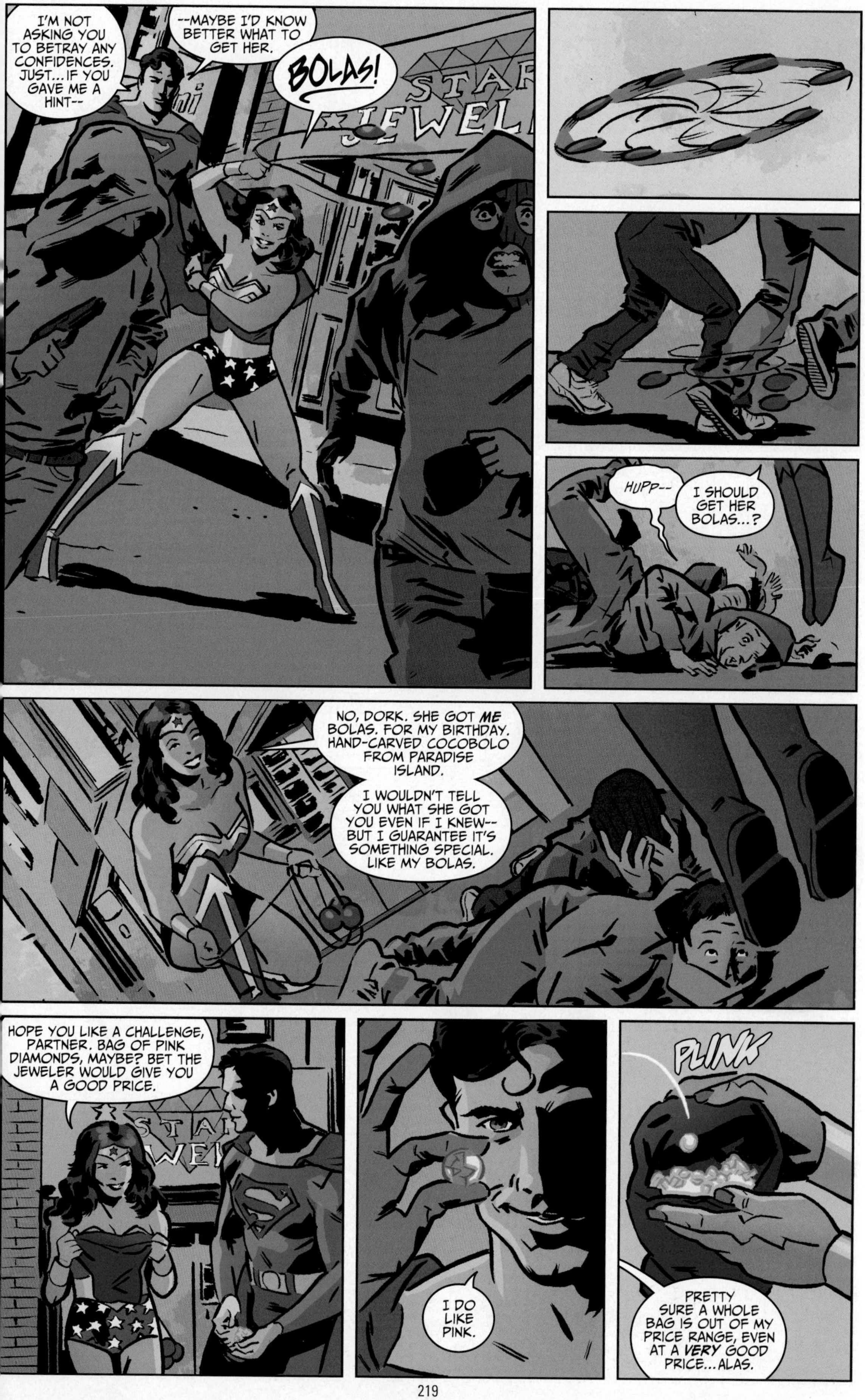
I'M NOT ASKING YOU TO BETRAY ANY CONFIDENCES. JUST...IF YOU GAVE ME A HINT--
--MAYBE I'D KNOW BETTER WHAT TO GET HER.
BOLAS!
HUPP--
I SHOULD GET HER BOLAS...?
NO, DORK. SHE GOT *ME* BOLAS. FOR MY BIRTHDAY. HAND-CARVED COCOBOLO FROM PARADISE ISLAND.
I WOULDN'T TELL YOU WHAT SHE GOT YOU EVEN IF I KNEW--BUT I GUARANTEE IT'S SOMETHING SPECIAL. LIKE MY BOLAS.
HOPE YOU LIKE A CHALLENGE, PARTNER. BAG OF PINK DIAMONDS, MAYBE? BET THE JEWELER WOULD GIVE YOU A GOOD PRICE.
I DO LIKE PINK.
PLINK
PRETTY SURE A WHOLE BAG IS OUT OF MY PRICE RANGE, EVEN AT A *VERY* GOOD PRICE...ALAS.

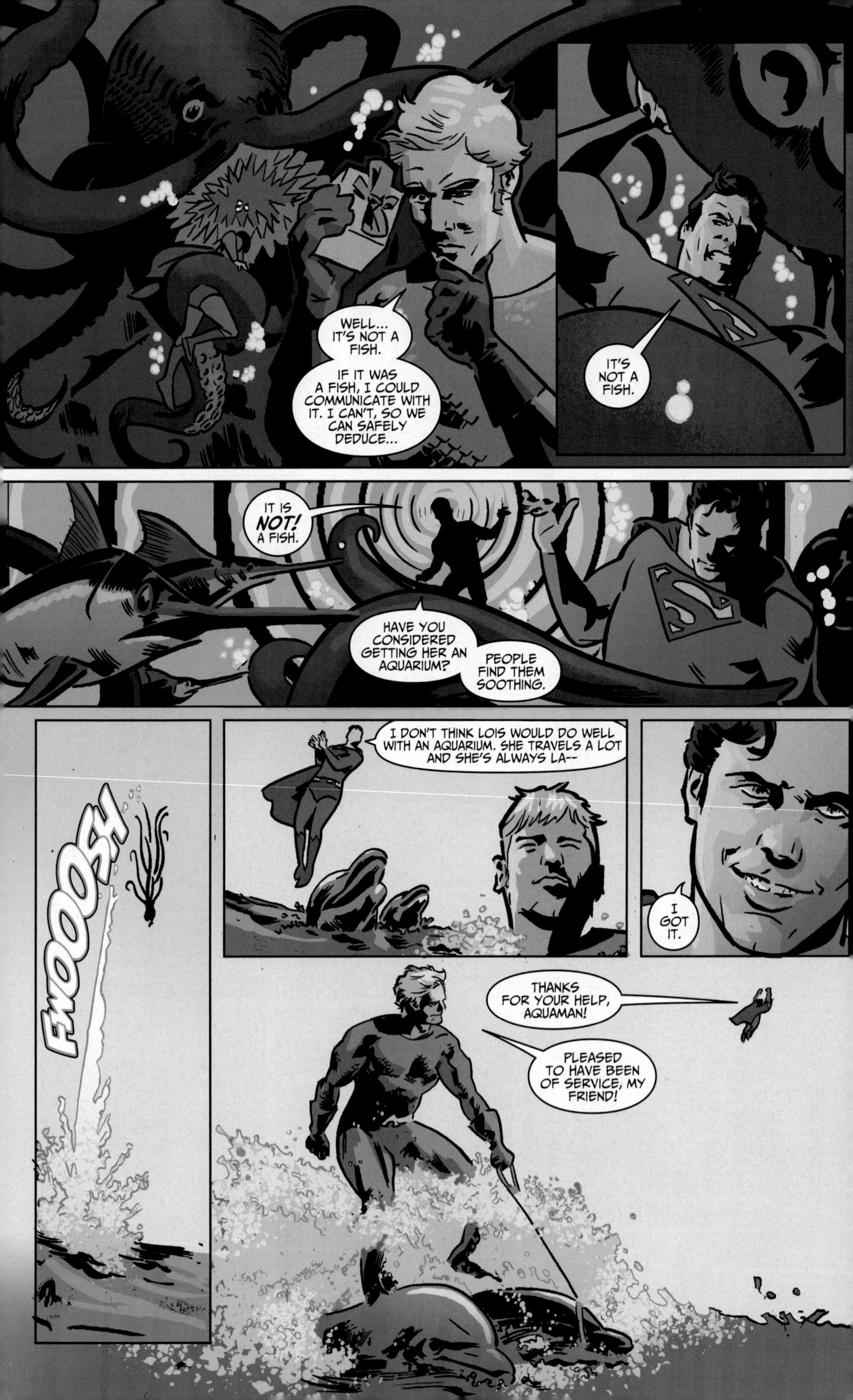
WELL... IT'S NOT A FISH.
IF IT WAS A FISH, I COULD COMMUNICATE WITH IT. I CAN'T, SO WE CAN SAFELY DEDUCE...
IT'S NOT A FISH.
IT IS NOT! A FISH.
HAVE YOU CONSIDERED GETTING HER AN AQUARIUM?
PEOPLE FIND THEM SOOTHING.
FWOOOSH
I DON'T THINK LOIS WOULD DO WELL WITH AN AQUARIUM. SHE TRAVELS A LOT AND SHE'S ALWAYS LA--
I GOT IT.
THANKS FOR YOUR HELP, AQUAMAN!
PLEASED TO HAVE BEEN OF SERVICE, MY FRIEND!

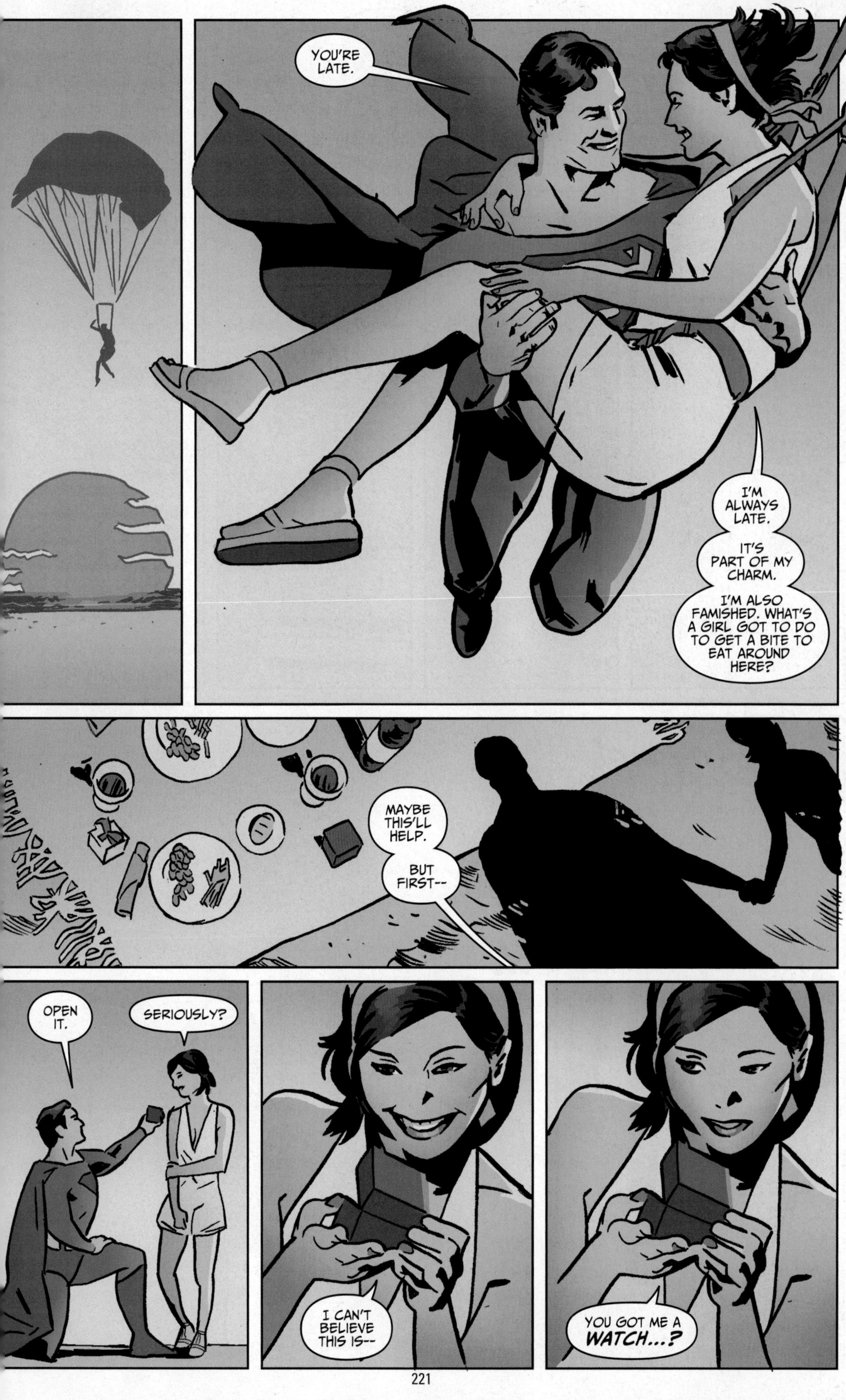
YOU'RE LATE.
I'M ALWAYS LATE.
IT'S PART OF MY CHARM.
I'M ALSO FAMISHED. WHAT'S A GIRL GOT TO DO TO GET A BITE TO EAT AROUND HERE?
MAYBE THIS'LL HELP.
BUT FIRST--
OPEN IT.
SERIOUSLY?
I CAN'T BELIEVE THIS IS--
YOU GOT ME A WATCH...?

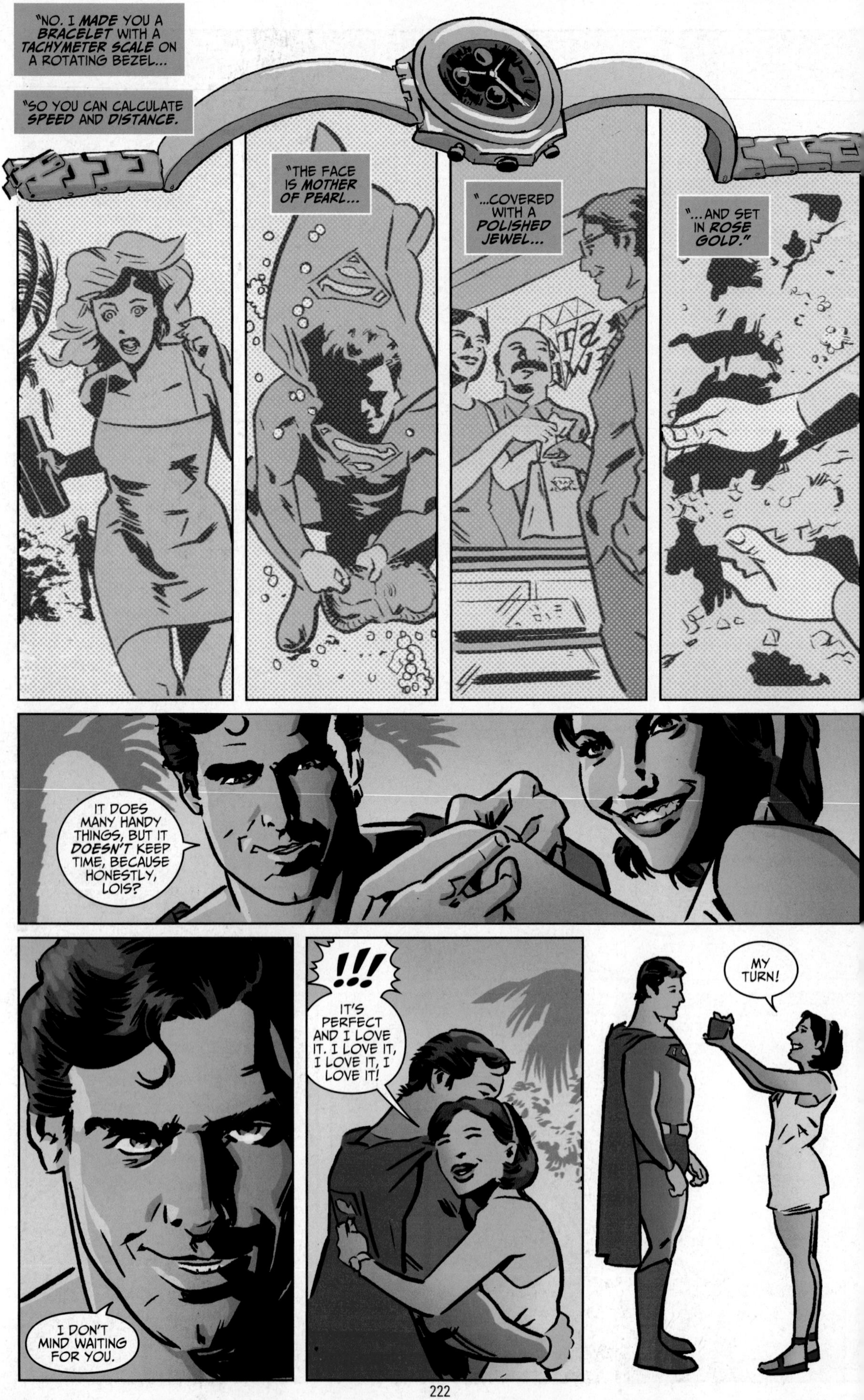
"NO. I MADE YOU A BRACELET WITH A TACHYMETER SCALE ON A ROTATING BEZEL...
"SO YOU CAN CALCULATE SPEED AND DISTANCE.
"THE FACE IS MOTHER OF PEARL...
"...COVERED WITH A POLISHED JEWEL...
"...AND SET IN ROSE GOLD."
IT DOES MANY HANDY THINGS, BUT IT DOESN'T KEEP TIME, BECAUSE HONESTLY, LOIS?
I DON'T MIND WAITING FOR YOU.
!!!
IT'S PERFECT AND I LOVE IT. I LOVE IT, I LOVE IT, I LOVE IT!
MY TURN!

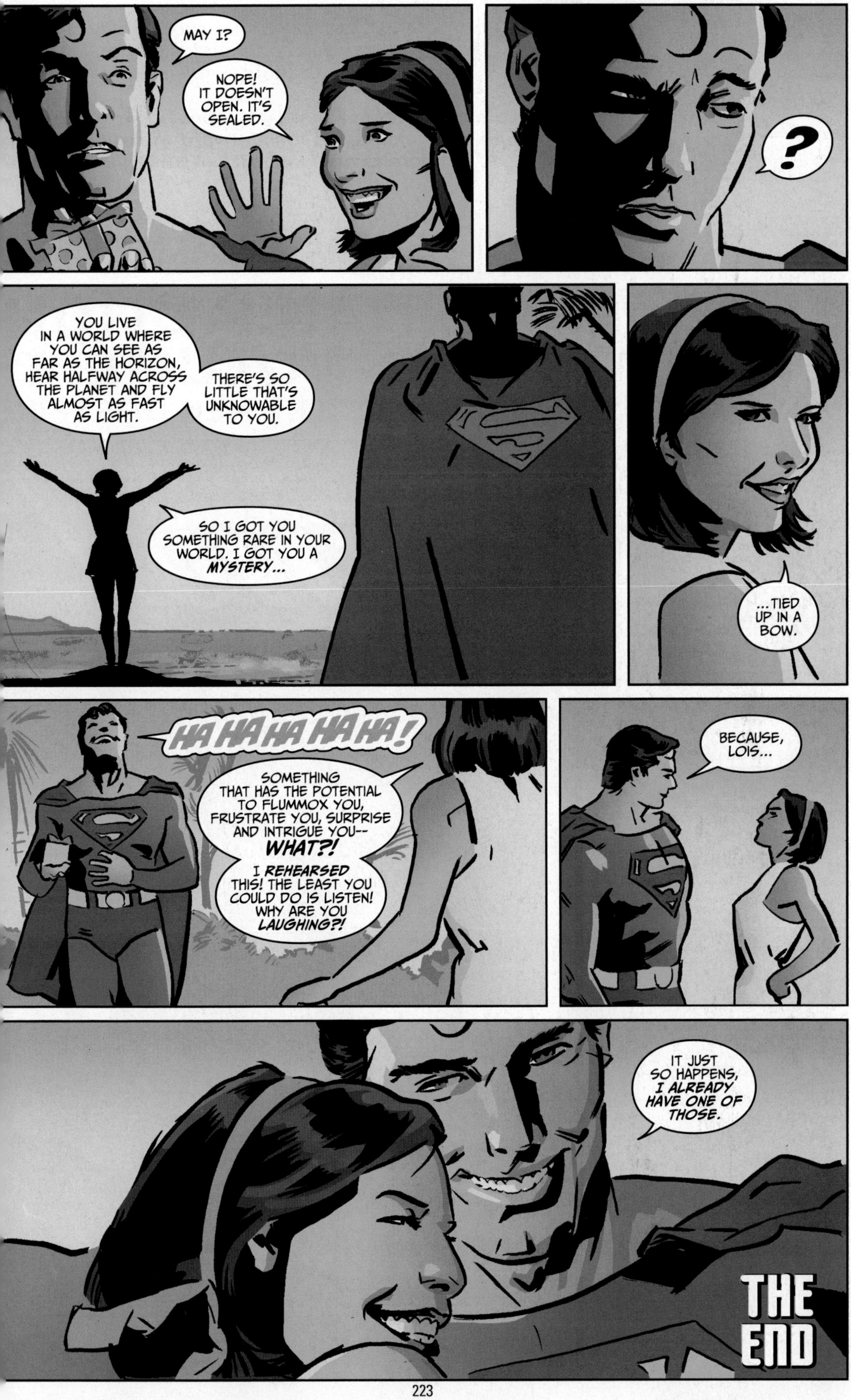
MAY I?
NOPE! IT DOESN'T OPEN. IT'S SEALED.
?
YOU LIVE IN A WORLD WHERE YOU CAN SEE AS FAR AS THE HORIZON, HEAR HALFWAY ACROSS THE PLANET AND FLY ALMOST AS FAST AS LIGHT.
THERE'S SO LITTLE THAT'S UNKNOWABLE TO YOU.
SO I GOT YOU SOMETHING RARE IN YOUR WORLD. I GOT YOU A MYSTERY...
...TIED UP IN A BOW.
HA HA HA HA HA HA!
SOMETHING THAT HAS THE POTENTIAL TO FLUMMOX YOU, FRUSTRATE YOU, SURPRISE AND INTRIGUE YOU-- WHAT?!
I REHEARSED THIS! THE LEAST YOU COULD DO IS LISTEN! WHY ARE YOU LAUGHING?!
BECAUSE, LOIS...
IT JUST SO HAPPENS, I ALREADY HAVE ONE OF THOSE.
THE END